The Development of Islam in West Africa

Mervyn Hiskett

The Development of Islam in West Africa

Longman

London and New York

Longman Group Limited
London and New York

Longman Group Limited
Longman House,
Burnt Mill, Harlow,
Essex, U.K.

Published in the United States of America
by Longman Inc., New York

Associated companies, branches and
representatives in Africa and throughout
the world

First published in 1984

Printed in Hong Kong by
Wah Cheong Printing Press Ltd.
ISBN 0 582 64692 8 (cased)
0 582 64694 4 (paper)

The cover photograph shows Kano
Central Mosque, Nigeria. Photograph by
Bob Croxford (ZEFA).

British Library Cataloguing in Publication data

Hiskett, Mervyn
The development of Islam in West Africa.
1. Islam—Africa, West—History
I. Title
297'.0966 BP64.A4W4

ISBN 0-582-64692-8
ISBN 0-582-64694-4 Pbk

Library of Congress Cataloging in Publication Data

Hiskett, M.
The development of Islam in West Africa.

(Longman studies in African History)
Bibliography: p.
Includes index.
1. Islam—Africa, West—History. I. Title.
II. Series.
BP64.A4W354 297'.0966 82-6545
ISBN 0-582-64692-8 AACR2
ISBN 0-582-64694-4 (pbk.)

Contents

Preface

The task I originally set out to accomplish when I began writing this book was to trace the development of Islam, with particular reference to its theological and intellectual aspects, in the west and central Sudan. The 'west and central Sudan' is a tidy geographical concept, bounded by the Sahel in the north, the Atlantic in the west, Lake Chad in the east and the southern savanna in the south. Moreover, it was the location of several medieval Muslim empires and more recent *jihāds*. West Africa, in contrast, lacks this geographical tidiness. It raises problems of how far to the north, south and east 'West' Africa extends and while it contains significant Muslim populations, large areas of it are non-Muslim. It soon became apparent, none the less, that it was necessary to pay some attention not only to the Sahara in the north but also to the south, beyond the southern edge of the savanna. In consequence, I broadened the title of the book to refer to West Africa as a whole, although the emphasis still remains on the west and central Sudan.

Annotation

Although this work is intended primarily for students it is also for the general reader. Therefore, the problem arises of how much annotation is necessary. The fact that my publisher required from me a book of not more than approximately 350 pages certainly had a bearing on my decision. Apart from that it is obvious that if every statement and opinion in the book were to be supported by reference to the primary or secondary source that gives rise to it, the result would be, on every page, a voluminous skirt of footnotes beneath a slender waist of text. I therefore decided to annotate only when the reader might be seriously inconvenienced by the lack of such assistance and to rely on the Bibliography as the main indicator of my sources.

There is also the particular question of external, medieval Arabic sources. For the most part these are now easily accessible in Cuoq's usually reliable French translations (the no doubt equally admirable English *Corpus of early Arabic sources for West African history*, translated by J.F.P. Hopkins and annotated by N. Levtzion and J.F.P. Hopkins which has been notified, was still not available at the time this manuscript went to press). Realism suggests that only a tiny proportion of those who read this book will wish to trace the passages and references in question back to the original Arabic. However, those who do, can accomplish this by referring to Cuoq's index, which will put them in touch with the French translation, and from this they can use Cuoq's ample references to proceed from there to the Arabic. This being so, to repeat references that Cuoq has already given seems to involve an unnecessary and avoidable expense, but in those few cases where the passage or reference in question does not appear in

Cuoq, I have given other suitable references.

Another point to be noted in connection with the external sources is that all authors who wrote in classical Arabic are referred to as 'Arabic', regardless of their bloodline, place of birth, etc. In fact, of course, some of them were Berbers, Persians or Turks by origin. It is also convenient to point out here that the adjectives Sūdānī and 'Sudanic' are used, in the case of the first, in reference to people and society and in the case of the second, in reference to places and institutions, in preference to 'Sudanese', which is now too closely associated with the Nilotic Sudan.

Arabic and vernacular words, names etc.

The transcription of Arabic and vernacular names in a West African context presents certain problems. They are that one has to deal with Arabic names from classical sources alongside West African names of Arabic origin that have been naturalised into West African languages. Thus, while one might find ᶜAbdullāhi b. Muḥammad, as opposed to ᶜAbd Allāh b. Muḥammad acceptable, what is one to do about 'Audu', 'Braima' and similar forms? To change them all back into their classical spellings is to introduce such a degree of unfamiliarity as to perplex the reader entirely. In fact, this has been tried on occasions and seems to me to have been unsuccessful. The standard rule in cases where classical Arabic and colloquial Arabic names are mixed together – to treat everything before AD 1900 as classical and everything after that date as colloquial – is also not helpful when the result diverges so much from local usage. Thus I decided that the sensible procedure was to exercise empirical judgement as to which form is likely to be the most familiar to the reader in each individual case. For example the Shehu is more commonly referred to by the Hausa Usumanu ɗan Fodio or Usman ɗan Fodio than by the Arabic ᶜUthmān b. Fūdī. On the other hand his younger brother, the learned author of *Tazyīn al-waraqāt*, *Ḍiyā' al-ḥukkām* and many other works, is usually known as ᶜAbd Allāh b. Muḥammad, perhaps reflecting the fact that he was pre-eminently the scholar of the Fulani reform movement. As for Muḥammad Bello or Muhammadu Bello, one might as well toss a coin – except that 'Muḥammad' seems to call for 'Balū' and that is ridiculous. The result of such considerations has been a decision to use 'Usumanu ɗan Fodio' but 'ᶜAbd Allāh b. Muḥammad' and there are other deliberate inconsistencies of this nature.

In the case of adjectives of Arabic origin, and proper names derived from them, I have normally adopted such Arabic forms as Mālikī or Qādirīs in preference to the anglicised forms except when an anglicised form is well-established, as for example 'Fatimid' and 'Fatimids'.

Another problem associated with the occurrence of foreign words in an English text is that of plurals. The form ᶜ*ulamā'* is so frequently used in works on Islamic subjects that it would be odd to use ᶜ*ālims*. However, if one writes ᶜ*ulamā'*, why should one then write '*sharīfs* instead of *shurafā'*? Of course, there is a case here, too, for sensible flexibility but I have used Arabic and Hausa plurals as far as possible. The only reason I have not done so in the case of other West African vernacular words is that I do not always know what their plurals are. To find out in the case of so many words of so many – and sometimes so uncertain – linguistic origins would be a task the magnitude of which would be out of all proportion to the importance of the point involved.

A similar stylistic dilemma occurs in the case of proper names of tribes and peoples. Here it seems to me that the English plural is stylistically more acceptable than a form that may or may not be a local plural or collective. Thus 'Yorubas' is preferred to 'Yoruba', 'Kwararafas' to 'Kwararafa' and so on. However, there are a few exceptions. For instance 'Fulani' is so commonly used as a plural that 'Fulanis' seems odd and I have therefore avoided it.

Dating

As a general rule, I give the date according to the *Hijra*, followed by the date AD – thus 1227/1812, being AH 1227/AD 1812. Occasionally, however, when referring to events that happened in an entirely non-Islamic context, I give only the date AD. Moreover, as is customary in works on Islamic subjects, I give only AD dates for AD 1900 and after.

To give both the date AH and AD is not always entirely straightforward. Occasionally a *Hijra* century spans two centuries AD by more than just a few years. Thus, where some degree of precision is desirable, I write 'the 12–13/18 century' since the period in question may extend between 1199/1784 and 1214/1799. Sometimes, too, it seems more helpful to write, for instance, 'the last half of the 18 century AD (AH 1164–1214)'.

I have used C.S.P. Freeman-Grenville's tables for all conversions. But any errors are to be attributed to me.

Maps and diagrams

All the maps in this book are sketch maps. The diagrams at Appendix I consist of directional lines indicating that certain main centres of the west and central Sudan were linked to each other and to centres in neighbouring areas at certain periods. They are not intended to trace the exact course of particular routes and all the intermediate points through which they passed; nor do they show all subsidiary routes.

I am greatly indebted to a number of friends and colleagues who read my typescript, or parts of it, and who made innumerable valuable corrections and suggestions. Those who made major contributions in this way are: Dr Hassan Ibrahim Gwarzo, my colleague for many years at the School for Arabic Studies, Kano and now the Grand Alkali of Kano State, whose PhD thesis on al-Maghīlī has been a great help to me; Dr Abdulgadir Dangambo, who kindly gave me permission to quote extensively from his PhD thesis while it was still in preparation and who gave me much encouragement and support during the three years that we worked together at the School for Oriental and African Studies while I was writing this book; Professor Peter Holt, who was kind enough to read the first chapter and thus help me with certain aspects of Islamic history that are outside my normal field of research and teaching; Dr Harry Norris, whose own books I have relied on constantly, who read and commented on several chapters and generously gave me access to as yet unpublished information; Dr Humphrey Fisher, who helped me in several ways while extremely busy with his own work; Richard Tames, who read through the whole manuscript and made extremely valuable suggestions concerning the type of language and presentation most likely to be helpful to students whose mother tongue is not English. John E. Lavers of Bayero University, Kano, also read the whole work and made most valuable comments upon it and I am grateful to him for correspondence upon certain matters that has been most useful to me; my friend and former colleague in Nigeria, Professor D.J.M. Muffett, whose works on the occupation of Hausaland and the life of Sir George Goldie I admire so much, also read several chapters and put me right on a number of points concerning the occupation and subsequent administration of Northern Nigeria; Professor John R. Willis was kind enough to make a typescript of his fine *Studies in West African Islamic history*, vol. 1, 'The cultivators of Islam', available to me many months before its publication, and the annotations to this book, and its Bibliography, indicate the extent of my indebtedness to him. I have also profited from discussing with him a number of problems, one or two of which we have continued to disagree on in some measure; none the less, my understanding of them all was enriched by the opportunity to discover his scholarly and thoughtful views.

I am also indebted to Jenny Lee, of Longman, and to several of her colleagues, who helped me in the preparation of this book by placing the publisher's many essential facilities at my disposal; and by seeing the book through the press.

I am grateful to all these friends and scholars, and to others too numerous to list here, who have helped me along the way. None the less, all imperfections and errors in this book are mine and I take full responsibility for them.

Kano
February 1982

MERVYN HISKETT

Abbreviations

Books and Journals

ALS	*African language studies*
BSOAS	*Bulletin of the School of Oriental and African Studies*
CHA	*The Cambridge History of Africa*, general editors, J.D. Fage and Roland Oliver
HWA	*History of West Africa*, editors, J.F. Ajayi and Michael Crowder
IJAHS	*The international journal of African historical studies*
JAH	*Journal of African History*
JAL	*Journal of African Law*
JHSN	*Journal of the Historical Society of Nigeria*
JICH	*The Journal of Imperial and Commonwealth History*
MES	*Middle Eastern Studies*
RBCAD	*Research Bulletin of the Centre of Arabic documentation*

Unpublished Hausa manuscripts

*ABM**	*Alamomin bayyanar Mahadi*, attributed to Usumanu ɗan Fodio, CSNL
KG	*Kashf al-ghumma*, M. Hiskett, private collection
*KLH**	*Kasidatu bi lisanin Hausa*, of Malam Muhammadu Na Maigangi, CSNL
M	*Ma'ama'are* of Shehu Usumanu ɗan Fodio, rendered into Hausa by Malam Isa ɗan Shehu, M. Hiskett, private collection; uncritical roman edition, Zaria, nd.
MB	*Mai Basmallah* of Malam Inuwa, Limamin Zawiya, M. Hiskett, private collection
*WG**	*Waƙar gargadi* of Shehu Usumanu ɗan Fodio, CSNL
*WW**	*Waƙar wa'azi* of ᶜAbd Allāh b. Muḥammad, CSNL
WY	*Waƙar yabon Sir Ahmadu Bello*, M. Hiskett, private collection
WZA	*Waƙar zuwan Annasarawa*, M. Hiskett, private collection.

Public collections of manuscripts and archives

CSNL	Centre for the Study of Nigerian Languages, Bayero University, Kano
IAS	Institute of African Studies, University of Ghana, Lagon, Accra

* The Hausa texts and English translations of starred manuscripts are now available in Abdulgadir Dangambo, PhD thesis, London, 1980.

List of Maps and Diagrams

Maps

Diagrams

CHAPTER ONE

The Sahara, North Africa and Egypt in relation to the west and central Sudan

A BRIEF GEOGRAPHICAL INTRODUCTION: THE LAND AND PEOPLE OF THE WEST AND CENTRAL SUDAN

The main concern of this book, especially during the earlier centuries, is with the area commonly referred to as 'the west and central Sudan'. It is that belt of West Africa that extends, roughly, from 10° to 20° north latitude, 17° west to 15° east longitude. It can be described in vegetational terms as extending from the desert scrub in the north to the southern edge of the savanna in the south. From west to east it extends across this scrub and savanna belt, from the Atlantic coast to the eastern shore of Lake Chad. However, these boundaries are only approximate and the account will, from time to time, reach farther north, into the true desert; and farther south, into the lowland rain forests. It will also, occasionally, reach beyond Lake Chad, into the lands that are usually thought of as the eastern Sudan, and in one chapter, at least, it will turn its attention mainly to Europe.

The people of the west and central Sudan vary from the predominantly light-skinned Berbers and Toureg nomads and pasturalists of the northern area – the desert and the scrub savanna – to the dark-skinned Negroes of the southern savanna and the forest who are, in the main, town-and-village dwellers, cultivators and farmers. However, once again, this is an approximate division only. There has been much racial mixing in the west and central Sudan and it is now impossible to draw firm dividing lines between the various racial groups and blood-lines of the area.

Neighbours of the west and central Sudan

In this chapter, however, the story begins not in the west and central Sudan itself but in the lands that lie to the north and east of it, namely the Sahara, North Africa and Egypt. Although they are not part of the west and central Sudan, these lands, because they are so near to it, have constantly influenced its history, especially since the dawn of Islam. For this reason it is necessary to understand the broad outlines of their histories during and immediately before their Islamic periods.

The Sahara

Islam came to the west and central Sudan, not directly from Arabia where the Prophet Muḥammad first preached it in AD 610, but little by little from North Africa and Egypt, across the Sahara and then down into the savanna. That this could happen was largely due to the relatively recent introduction of the camel, for without that essential beast of burden the great Saharan caravan routes could not have developed and the desert would have remained a more formidable obstacle to human intercourse than in fact it did.

The early population of the Sahara was made up of black African farmers. This is clear from implements and utensils that have been excavated around its northern oases, and also from stone arrow heads, for the nomadic inhabitants of the Sahara have never used the bow and arrow, as far as is known, whereas it is a common weapon among the black people of the savanna. So, too, the stone pestles and mortars for pounding corn must have belonged to agriculturalists whose staple food is grain, not to nomads who live on milk and dates.

It is uncertain when the camel first appeared in the Sahara but it was probably during the 2 century AD and by the end of the Byzantine period in North Africa it was well established there. With its arrival the whole pattern of desert life and economy began to change. The Berbers had been present in the northern Sahara since the first millenium BC, if not earlier. The old, static economy of the Negroes gradually gave way to the shifting, pastoral economy that the Berbers now adopted, as the camel gave them greater range and mobility. Moreover, under the control of the new camel masters, the desert routes, which had already been opened up to a limited extent by ox and horse transport, were extended and multiplied (see Appendix A, Diagram 1). Also, as the nomads, more aggressive than the settled peoples, pushed farther south into the Sahara, they pushed the Negroes before them into the grasslands of the Sudanic savanna. The disturbances and the movements of peoples along the southern border of the Sahara and the savanna that this caused were important in the early history of many Sūdānī peoples and they are reflected in their folklore and legends of origin. It may be that this very early pressure from people who originally inhabited the lands that border the Mediterranean upon the Negroes of the Sudan, ought to be regarded as the beginning of that spread of Mediterranean influences that the French historian, Fernand Braudel, has seen in later North African penetrations southward, across the Sahara and beyond.[1]

Some centuries before Islam arrived in the Sahara, the desert and the northern termini of its trade routes were already in the hands of the Berbers. However, substantial communities of the earlier Negro population still flourished, with their most northerly bastion the powerful Soninke kingdom of Ghana. Tension between the Berber nomads and these Negroes had become part of the pattern of Saharan life; so too had some measure of cooperation between them in servicing the routes and the trade that passed up and down them. The prosperity of both these peoples came increasingly to depend upon this trade. Thus the two societies, the nomads and the farmers, now largely town-dwelling as the trading economy gradually replaced the old agricultural economy, competed for political and economic advantage in a relationship where material interests rather than religion were probably the motivating forces. This situation has been explained in terms of tension between 'white' nomads and 'black' peasants. Such an explanation should be treated cautiously. The conflicting economic interests of the two sides – the nomads' need for vast, empty tracts of grazing ground and their habit of living by raiding, as against the needs of the town-dwellers for clean water sources, agricultural land and secure trade routes – are enough in themselves to explain periodic confrontations. To bring skin colour into it assumes attitudes that are not proved to have been general or even widespread at that time and in that place.

Certainly black men and women and white men and women may sometimes have felt themselves to be different from one another and may have been hostile to each other in consequence. However, there were clearly other occasions when it was to their advantage to cooperate together and it is known that they did so. Thus it is going too far to suggest that skin colour was a constant factor in every conflict that took place between Saharan nomads on the one hand and peasants and town-dwellers on the other.

It was into this situation of conflicting interests and brief, shifting alliances that Islam intruded when it flowed, at first uncertainly, then with a sudden fierce momentum, out of North Africa into the caravan cities and oases of the northern desert.

ISLAM IN NORTH AFRICA

In the 1/7 century, when the Muslims, starting from Egypt, penetrated into North Africa, that rich and fertile land was under the control of the Byzantine empire, that is the eastern half of the old Roman empire, that had survived after the western half had been destroyed by barbarian invasions. However, the Byzantines' control was incomplete, they only held the towns. The villages, the countryside and the mountains belonged to the native Berbers. These Berbers followed a way of life that was partly pastoral and partly agricultural. Their political system was patriarchal – government was in the hands of 'patriarchs' or family elders, not chiefs or kings – and democratic, based on small, decentralised tribal and clan groups – groups that governed themselves and were not subject to any central ruler or government. They had little in common with, and no love for their town-dwelling masters, now somewhat isolated from their imperial centre in Constantinople by the Muslim conquest of Egypt in 20/641, at least as regards the overland route. Although the Byzantine empire proved able to defend its heartland for several centuries to come before it eventually succumbed to the Muslims, it did not at this moment have the will or the means to hold its outposts. Moreover, the Byzantines in North Africa had suffered a series of crippling heresies in the Christian church which reflected not only religious but also political discontents, while the Byzantine governor of North Africa had recently revolted against his emperor, Constans II. These disturbances had left them weak and disunited. They were thus in no fit state to beat off the onslaught of the Arab Muslims, fired as they were by their new and fervent ideology with its own set of religious and political ideas.

The Muslim conquest and its aftermath

This onslaught began in 26/647, when the Caliph ᶜUthmān b. ᶜAffān (24–36/644–56) authorised ᶜAbd Allāh b. Saᶜd to lead an expedition from Egypt into Ifrīqiya, the Arab name for what is, approximately, present Tunisia. This he did and he defeated the Byzantines at the battle of Sbeitla. However, it appears that the Muslims had intended this attack as no more than a plundering raid for after Sbeitla they withdrew with their booty. It was not until 43/663–4 that the real Muslim conqueror of North Africa, ᶜUqba b. Nāfiᶜ al-Fihrī, arrived and founded Qayrawān, a fortress city at the edge of the desert, garrisoned by Arab tribesmen, From here he waged *jihād*, Islamic holy war, against the Byzantines and the Berbers until he was slain in 63/682–3, in battle against Kusayla, a proud Berber chief who had sworn to kill the Muslim conqueror.

Ḥassān b. al-Nuᶜmān arrived to take his place but he was immediately challenged by the still-hostile Berbers under their prophetess, al-Kāhina, 'the Soothsayer'. This brave and remarkable woman fought the Muslims fiercely. In the end she was killed near the well, Bīr al-Kāhina, that bears her name. After this, Ḥassān b. al-Nuᶜmān turned to driving the remaining Byzantines out of Carthage and other coastal towns where they had sought refuge.

Al-Kāhina slain, Berber resistance suddenly ebbed and under Ḥassān's successor, Mūsā b. Nuṣayr, the Berbers began to come over to Islam. Perhaps they were attracted by the austere simplicity of that faith, so well suited to their own hardy way of life and so different from the ornate splendour of Byzantine Christianity. Some, too, may have felt that the defeat and death of al-Kāhina reflected the failure of their traditional religion and made further resistance to Islam pointless. Whatever the reason, a development now took place that was certainly neither desired nor anticipated by the Arab conquerors.

No sooner had the Berbers accepted Islam than that Islamic sect known as the Khārijiyya appeared in North Africa. It was radical in that it wanted to go back to the roots of Islam, puritanical in that it sought absolute purity in belief and practice, and egalitarian in that it insisted all Muslims were equal in every way. It challenged the elitism or claim to superiority of the Arabs, and the privileges they enjoyed. The Berbers took to it enthusiastically, and in 122/740 they turned in revolt against the Arab conquerors. Their revolt was largely successful and only in Qayrawān and a few other fortified cities did the Arabs manage to hold out against this Berber tide. By *c.* 132/750 the Berbers had regained a measure of freedom, although they still remained in theory subjects of the central caliphate in Baghdad. However, their resentment at Arab domination had done nothing to diminish their reverence for the Arabian Prophet, or their respect for members of his family. Now, certain *shurafā'* (Arabic sing. *sharīf*), persons claiming descent from the Prophet's family, set up local dynasties and political groups that were acceptable to the Berbers. Best known among them were the Idrisids, who established their rule in Morocco *c.* 171/788. Other important dynasties that were set up shortly after the Khārijī revolt were the Aghlabids in Ifrīqiya and the Rustamids, in Tāhert. This latter dynasty was itself Khārijī and under these dynasties North Africa enjoyed a century of stable government.

Fatimids, Zirids and the Banū Hilāl

Late in the 3/9 century – the exact date is not known – there arrived in Ifrīqiya a certain Abū ᶜAbd Allāh al-Shīᶜī. He, as his name indicates, was a Shiᶜite, a member of an Islamic sect that regarded the succession to the caliphate (the office of *khalīfa*, caliph, the supreme ruler of the whole Islamic community) as belonging exclusively to the descendants of the Prophet's son-in-law, ᶜAlī b. Abī Ṭālib. This sect also looked for a mahdi, an Islamic Deliverer who shall come at the End of Time, from ᶜAlī's line. Al-Shīᶜī won certain Berber groups to his side and then launched a revolt that overthrew the Aghlabids and enabled the Shiᶜite family of the Fatimids (who claimed descent from Fāṭima, daughter of the Prophet and wife of ᶜAlī b. Abī Ṭālib) to establish themselves in Tunis in 297/910. From here they challenged the reigning caliph in Baghdad for

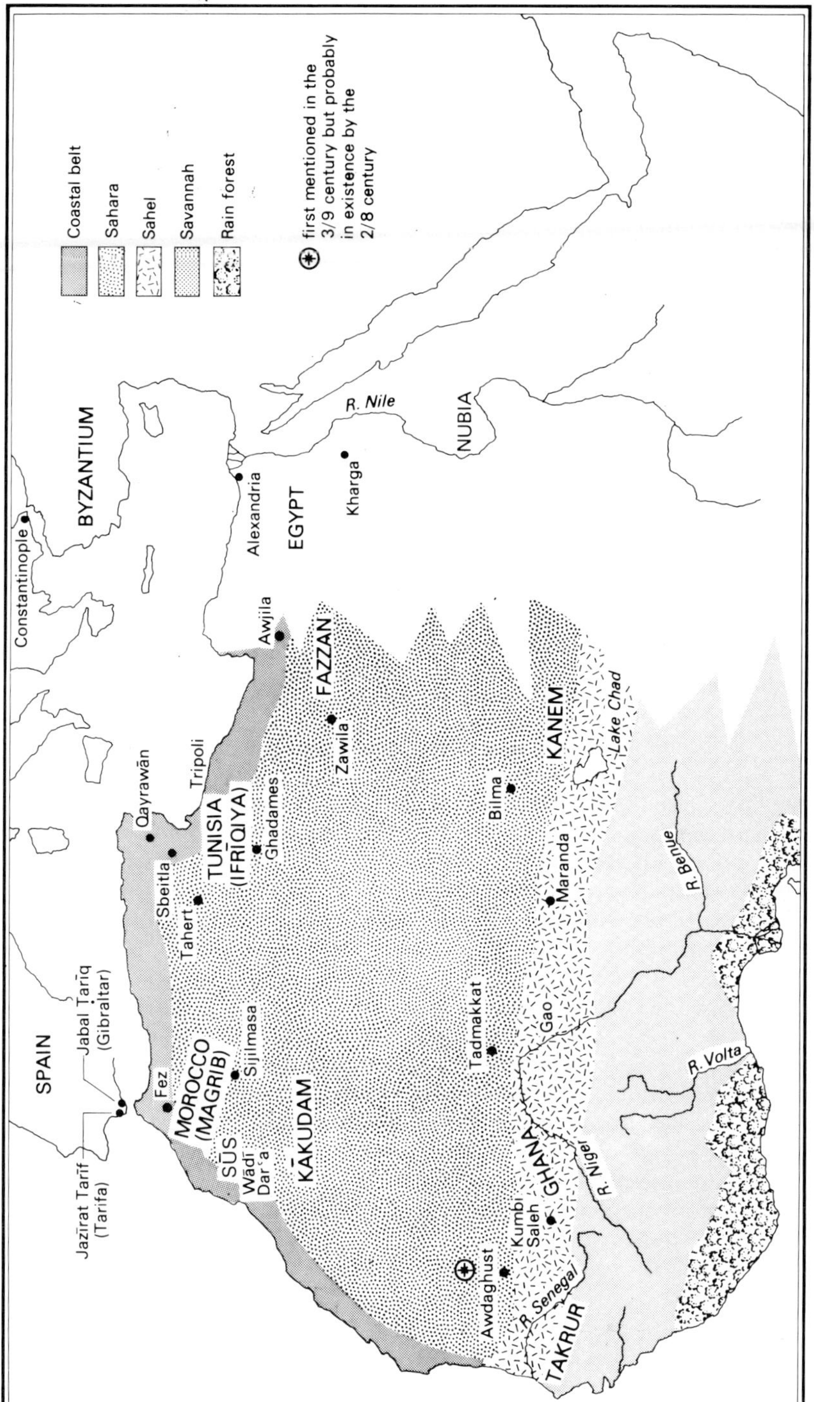

Map 1 North Africa, Egypt, the Sahara and the west and central Sudan during the 2/8 century.

headship of the whole Islamic world.

The Fatimids also defeated the last uprising of the Khārijīs and politically, this marked the end of the Khārijiyya in North Africa. However, a kingdom of the Ibāḍīs (members of the Ibāḍiyya, a sub-sect of the Khārijiyya called after its founder, Ibn Ibāḍ) continued in the Fazzan until 571/1175–6. The Khārijīs were not 'driven out into the desert', as some have supposed, to become merely the folk heroes of later Western African myths of origin; they, and especially the Ibāḍiyya, continued to be commercially influential in the caravan cities of the Sahara and the Sahel for several generations to come.

The Fatimids were supported by the Zirids, members of a Berber clan. When, some six years later, they moved their capital from Ifrīqiya to Egypt, they left the Zirids in charge of the North African half of their empire. *C.* 440/1047 the Zirids turned on their patrons, renounced Shiᶜism and returned to Sunnī Islam, that is the Islam of the Muslim majority that considers itself to represent orthodoxy. Their aim was probably to win the support of the *ᶜulama'* (Arabic sing. *ᶜālim*), Muslim scholars of Qayrawān. This city had now become a centre of Islamic learning devoted to the Mālikī *madhhab* (plur. *madhāhib*), legal system, and of Sunnī Islam and its *ᶜulama'* were bitterly opposed to Shiᶜism. The story goes that the Fatimids, incensed by this treachery, incited the Banū Hilāl and Banū Sulaym, unruly tribes of Arab bedouins at that time disturbing Upper Egypt, to invade North Africa. The bedouins complied and by 443/1052 Banū Hilāl had reached Ifrīqiya and defeated the Zirids. They then spread throughout North Africa like a 'plague of locusts', to quote the 8/14-century Arab historian, Ibn Khaldūn. (d. 808/1406).

That is the story but the reality may have been different. It seems unlikely that the Fatimids were solely responsible for launching the Banū Hilāl and Banū Sulaym on their turbulent way. The tribes were probably attracted already by the rich grazing lands of North Africa and their invasion fits into a wider pattern of population movements in Africa and the Middle East at that time. Also, the destruction they are alleged to have wrought has almost certainly been exaggerated (Ibn Khaldūn was a Berber and a town-dwelling Muslim intellectual who disliked bedouins!). The invaders probably numbered no more than about 150,000 souls. That they caused some destruction is certainly true but the worst damage that they did was probably to destroy the ancient irrigation system in some areas. The claim that they devastated great tracts of the North African countryside, as Ibn Khaldūn and others have suggested, seems far-fetched. What they certainly did do, however, was bring about an acceleration in the switch from a Berber culture to an Arab culture in North Africa. Before their arrival Arabic had been widely used as the literary, religious, legal and administrative language, mainly by the educated classes. Now, through intermarriage and other social and economic contacts, it began to spread among the nomadic Berbers as a spoken language but it never drove out the Berber tongue entirely. However, it did change the linguistic character of North Africa and thus its culture.

The Almoravids

Long before Islam – it is impossible to say how long – tribes of nomadic Sanhaja Berbers (the word 'Sanhaja' is an arabised form of the Berber word *iznāgen*, 'speakers of the Znaga tongue') had roamed the Saharan country of Kākudam.

This semi-mythical land of the Arabic geographers was, in all probability, in or near the Sāqiyat al-Ḥamrā, south of Sūs, in the extreme north of the present-day Republic of Mauritania. In the accounts of some of the geographers, the Sanhaja lived near the 'Gleaming Mountain' and the 'City of Brass', the home of the djinns and of Solomon's magic. They were separated from an unknown land beyond by only the 'Sea of Sand . . . a land which is very soft to tread in and in which man and camel can sink'.[2] However, the Sanhaja themselves were far from mythical; they played their part in organising the trans-Saharan caravan trade; they were also among those who interacted with the Negroes, at one time cooperating with them to the common advantage, at other times competing with them and tending to push them farther south, towards the sub-Saharan savanna.

When the Muslim Arabs arrived they nicknamed these Sanhaja *al-Mulaththamūn*, 'the Veiled Ones', because of their habit of wearing a *lithām*, a mouth veil. The Mulaththamūn, like other Saharan Berbers, seem to have been but lightly touched by Islam before the 5/11 century. *C.* 437/1045 one of their chiefs set out on Pilgrimage to the Holy Places of Islam. The closer acquaintance with the Faith he thus acquired left him discontented with its imperfections among his own people. On his way home he stopped at Qayrawān, by now a university city devoted to the study and teaching of Malikism – the school of Islamic law, or *madhhab*, taught by the Imām Mālik of Medina (d.*c.* 179/795). Here he sought a teacher willing to go back with him into the desert to teach the restless Sanhaja the true Islam and was put in touch with a certain ᶜAbd Allāh b. Yāsīn, himself a Muslim Berber trained in Qayrawān.

Ibn Yāsīn proved to be not only a teacher who took his task seriously – he subjected his Sanhaja pupils to a severe discipline of reform and punishment – but also an able and inspiring military leader. He was soon leading the Sanhaja in *jihād* against their traditional enemies, the Zanata Berbers, at that time established in the Darᶜa oasis and in the caravan cities of Sijilmasa and Awdaghust. He seems to have had two main objectives: a religious one, to root out what he considered to be religious error among the Berbers and impose strict Malikism according to the rule of Qayrawān; and an economic one, to seize control of the northern termini of the Saharan caravan routes from the Zanata, who controlled them. He and his followers came to be known in Arabic as *al-Murābiṭūn* (sing. *al-murābiṭ*), later latinised into Almoravids. They were so called because of Ibn Yāsīn's association with the North African *rubuṭ* (sing. *ribāṭ*), border fortresses, built by the Arab conquerors in the first instance, from which to wage *jihād* against the Byzantines and Berbers. The *rubuṭ*, in the manner of Qayrawān, later developed into centres of Islamic learning and propaganda. Indeed, by Ibn Yāsīn's day the word *murābiṭ*, originally 'frontier warrior', may have come to mean simply 'Muslim militant' or 'reformer'.

Ibn Yāsīn was killed in 451/1059, fighting against the Barghawāta, a group of Berbers with their own version of Islam, which differed from that of the Sunnīs. He was succeeded by Abū Bakr b. ᶜUmar al- Lamtūnī, a chief of the Lamtuna Berbers, also Mulaththamūn. Abū Bakr gradually subdued southern and central Morocco. In 452/1070 he founded the town of Marrākush, but then dissension among the Saharan Berbers caused him to return to the desert. This happened in or about 496/1102–3. He left Morocco in the hands of his cousin, the able and ambitious Yūsuf b. Tāshfīn, who observed allegiance in name only to Abū Bakr and soon struck out on his own. He subdued most of North Africa and even set up an Almoravid state in al-Andalus, that is Muslim Spain.

The Muslim conquest of Spain had begun in 91/710, when Ṭarīf, a client of Mūsā b. Nuṣayr, landed on the peninsular at the point now known as 'Tarifa', from its original Arabic name Jazīrat Ṭarīf, the 'Isle of Ṭarīf'. He was followed by a Berber general of Mūsā b. Nuṣayr, Ṭāriq b. Ziyād who, with a force of Berbers, landed on the huge rock at the south-eastern point of the Spanish peninsular now known as Gibraltar, from its original Arabic name Jabal Ṭāriq, the 'Rock of Ṭāriq'. Ṭāriq went on to defeat the Visigoth rulers of Spain and by 94/713 Spain had become a province of the caliphate in Damascus. In 132/750, when the ᶜAbbasids seized the caliphate from the Umayyads, one member of the Umayyad family, ᶜAbd al-Raḥmān, escaped the massacre that followed and made his way to Spain, al-Andalus as it had now come to be known to the Arabs. Here he set up the Umayyad emirate and declared himself independent of the ᶜAbbasid caliphate in 156–7/773. His dynasty lasted until 422–3/1031, when it disappeared and was replaced by a number of petty dynasties, constantly at war with one another. It was the ruler of one of these dynasties – the ᶜAbbadids of Seville – who called in the Almoravids to aid him against the Spanish Christians and his Muslim enemies which thus gave them a foothold that led to the Almoravid conquest of al-Andalus.

Meanwhile, back in the desert south of Morocco, Abū Bakr and his Sanhaja launched a *jihād* against the non-Muslim Sūdānīs. Thus the Almoravid movement was split into two wings – the northern wing under Yūsuf b. Tāshfīn, the conqueror of al-Andalus; and the southern, desert wing under Abū Bakr. The full story of these southern Almoravids will be told in Chapter 2.

The Almohads

Muḥammad b. ᶜAbd Allāh b. Tūmart was a Berber from Sūs, in southern Morocco, where he returned after travelling widely in search of ᶜ*ilm*, Islamic religious knowledge. What he learnt on his travels, and what he found on his return to Marrākush – music, wine shops and loose living – outraged him. It also convinced him that the Almoravids had betrayed the high ideals of their own movement. At first he tried to reform them, but finding that impossible, he became their outright enemy. He and his followers became known as *al-Muwaḥḥidūn* (an Arabic word derived from *waḥḥada*, 'to assert the unity [of God]'), latinised to Almohads. They were so named because of their insistence on the unity of God and His immaterialness.

By 555/1160, the Almohads had ousted the Almoravids and had become masters of both the Maghrib, the western half of North Africa, and Ifrīqiya, the eastern half. To this they later added the Almorivad possessions in Spain.

Like the Almoravids, the Almohads were firm supporters of the Mālikī *madhhab*. However, they differed from them in several important aspects of theology. First, the Almoravids had insisted on a strictly literal interpretation of the Koran and in consequence tended to describe God in material terms – that is as if He had a body like a human being and the characteristics and qualities of humans. The Almohads argued that God was immaterial and not to be described in such terms. They also taught that He was present not only in Heaven but also throughout the whole creation, for this was the meaning of His unity. Moreover, they accepted the idea of the Mahdī, the Islamic Deliverer, who was to come and reform the world at the 'End of Time'. This they may have inherited from the Fatimids, although their notion of the Mahdī was different from that of the Fatimids in several important respects. Clearly, their ideas were more mystical than those of the Almoravids; that is to say, they believed there were things in religion that could not be understood by the human mind but simply had to be accepted as divine mysteries. This may have had something to do with the appearance in North Africa during the Almohad period of individual Sufis, Muslim mystics. Among these Sufis were such greatly respected and beloved personalities as Abū Madyan (d. 594/1197–8) and Abu 'l-Ḥasan al-Shādhilī (d. 656/1258). Before long, disciples began to gather round these Sufis, to form *ṭuruq* (Arabic sing. *ṭarīqa*), 'paths', that followed their teachings. The Almoravids had viewed such tendencies with disapproval and had even publicly burned the works of the great Sufi teacher, al-Ghazālī, but the Almohads tolerated Sufism and extended their patronage to Sufi leaders.

At its height the Almohad period became what has been called the 'Golden Age' of Islamic civilisation in North Africa, but no golden age lasts for ever. By 674/1275 the Almohad empire had collapsed as a result of internal divisions and military defeat. Its place was taken by three successor dynasties that divided the Almohad empire up between them: the Hafsids in Ifrīqiya, the Marinids in Morocco and the Wadids in Tlemcen.

The Almohads' successors

The history of these three dynasties and those that followed them is long and complex and is not part of the concern of this book. All three, however, continued the intellectual and theological tradition established by the Almohads. Under the Marinids, especially, Sufism underwent further important developments. It was during the Marinid period, in Morocco (*c.* 673/1274–5 to 869/1465) that the *ṭuruq* began to emerge not just as simple Sufi 'paths' but as formal organisations or orders. Each had its own degrees of rank and set of doctrines, based on the teachings of the founder which were then put into the form of books and passed on to future generations. This was the work of learned Sufis and resulted in the establishing in North Africa of such well-known Sufi orders as the Qādiriyya, founded in the 6/12 century in Baghdad by ᶜAbd al-Qādir al-Jīlānī (sometimes Jaylānī or Kaylānī), and the Shādhiliyya, founded by Abu 'l-Ḥasan al-Shādhilī, mentioned above. However, alongside this learned Sufism was another, that of the non-literate or only partially literate masses. For them Sufism was a felt, emotional experience that had nothing to do with books or learning. It expressed itself in veneration for the *awliyā'* (sing. *walī*), 'Sufi holy man', and their tombs, in the use of Koranic charms and in an enthusiastic belief in miracles. This religion of the ordinary people was taken up by the *murābiṭūn*, 'frontier warriors', who, after the age of Almoravid military expansion had passed, became wandering preachers, dedicated to spreading Islam among the people. The two traditions – that of the Sufi *awliyā'* and the wandering *murābiṭūn* – came together during the Marinid period and gave rise to what many European historians describe as 'maraboutism', from the French form *marabout*, which in turn comes from the Arabic *murābiṭ*. It denotes this popular Sufism as distinct from the intellectual and bookish Sufism of the scholars.

Another characteristic of both the Maghrib and Ifrīqiya in the post-Almohad period was the increasing European, Christian intrusion into these areas. Encouraged by the Christian reconquest of al-Andalus, which reached a climax in 897/1492 with the fall of Granada, the last Muslim kingdom in Spain, the Spanish and the Portuguese became more and more daring in their attacks on Muslim North Africa. The failure of the post-Almohad dynasties to check them caused the people to turn for leadership to the Sufi orders described above. So the *ṭuruq* became not only religious orders but also political organisations that spearheaded *jihād* against the Christians and consequently, they acquired a powerful influence over North African political life in general.

The Marinids were replaced *c.* 869/1465 by a dynasty of Zanata Berbers known as the Wattasids. They too were unable to halt the Christians, in this case the Portuguese. Certain *shurafā'* of the Banū Saᶜd, claiming descent from the Prophet, rose against the Wattasids at the same time as declaring *jihād* against the Christians, and because of their noble descent they were able to gain maraboutic and popular support. By 960/1553 they had ousted the Wattasids and established a Sharifian Saᶜdid empire over all of Morocco.

Mawlay Aḥmad al-Manṣūr

The greatest of the Sharifian Saᶜdid sultans was Mawlay Aḥmad al-Manṣūr (986–1012/1578–1603), whose title *al-Manṣūr* means 'The Victor [through the help of God]'. He was also popularly regarded as the victor of the battle of al-Qaṣr al-Kabīr (986/1578), in which the Portuguese were defeated. In fact, this victory belonged to his brother, who did not survive the battle. However, it brought al-Manṣūr great prestige and he began to assert his claim to be the leader of *jihād* against the infidels and also the caliph of Islam, at least in North Africa, the Sahara and the west and central Sudan. He also had ambitions in the western world and at one point hoped to win certain Spanish territories in association with Elizabeth I of England, the arch enemy of Spain.

One consequence of these ambitious claims was to bring him into confrontation with the Ottoman Turks, now becoming influential in North Africa, where they, too, were seeking to stem the Christian advance. Another consequence was to cause him to look enviously towards the western Sudan for this country, with its valuable sources of gold and salt, promised the wealth he needed to finance his schemes of caliphal power and victory. The Songhay empire, the history of which is told in Chapter 2, had had long and friendly relations with Morocco and also controlled the salt mines of Taghaza, in the Sahara, and the routes that led to the gold-bearing areas of the western Sudan. First, al-Manṣūr demanded a contribution from the *askiya* (ruler) of Songhay, to help the *jihād*. The *askiya* responded generously, but not generously enough. Then the sultan tried to persuade the ᶜ*ulamā'* of Timbuktu that they owed allegiance to him, as caliph, not to the *askiya*. This and other devices failed to gain him power over Songhay and the access to the wealth of the Sudan that he desired. Finally, in 999/1591, he despatched a military expedition under the Pasha Jawdhar. Jawdhar reached the Niger and conquered Gao, the Songhay capital. The results of that conquest for the development of Islam in the west and central Sudan will be described in chapters 2 and 7. It is worth noting at this point that the great French historian, Fernand Braudel, has seen this Moroccan pressure to the south, into and beyond the Sahara, as part of the general extension of Mediterranean influence and culture to what he considers to be its southern boundary, the loop of the Niger.[3] In fact, the links between the west and central Sudan and the world of the Mediterranean were much more numerous and more important than merely the military conquest of Songhay by a Moroccan army, as will be argued in several places below.

In Morocco the Sharifian Saᶜdids were replaced *c.* 1065/1654 by the ᶜAlawids, who also claimed descent from the Prophet. They came to power during a period of anarchy that followed the collapse of Sharifian Saᶜdid authority. It was during this same period of anarchy that the Sharifian Saᶜdid administration Mawlay Aḥmad al-Manṣūr had set up in Songhay finally broke away from its allegiance to Morocco and became virtually independent. The ᶜAlawid dynasty survived until the French Protectorate was set up in AD 1912 but under that Protectorate the ᶜAlawids continued to be the nominal rulers of Morocco. Elsewhere in North Africa the Ottoman Turks gradually extended their control. However, in due course, local dynasties emerged from the Ottoman military and administrative institutions and became effectively independent of the central Ottoman government. This situation continued until the pattern of North African government was changed by the European occupations of the 19 and 20 centuries AD.

ISLAM IN EGYPT

Like North Africa, Egypt was a rich Byzantine province when it caught the envious eyes of the Muslim Arabs. During the year 20–1/641 the Muslim general ᶜAmr b. al-ᶜĀṣ, encouraged by the conquest of Palestine and eager for further glory, invaded Egypt and took Alexandria, the capital of the Byzantine province. Egypt thus became a province of the Muslim Arab empire and for approximately the next two centuries it was ruled by governors appointed by the central caliphate.

Egyptian dynasties

By *c.* 235–6/850 a weakened ᶜAbbasid caliphate was no longer able to exercise effective control over its provinces. Profiting from this, Aḥmad b. Tūlūn, the Turkish governor of Egypt, took power in 254/868 and established the first independent Muslim dynasty in that country. It was short lived. In 323/935, after an interval of thirty years during which Egypt reverted to direct rule from Baghdad, a new dynasty, the Ikhshidids came to power and nominally they were still governors responsible to the ᶜAbbasids in Baghdad. By 302/914, however, the Fatimids of North Africa had taken Alexandria in the course of their plan to establish a Shiᶜite empire, and by 358/969 they had seized the country from the Ikhshidids and Egypt became the centre of their empire.

The Fatimids ruled Egypt for 200 years during which time they built Cairo (Arabic: al-Qāhira), founded the great university mosque of al-Azhar and contributed much to the development of architecture, learning and civilised life in Egypt. They also did their best to impose Shiᶜite beliefs on the Egyptian people but in this they failed. When, in 567–8/1171, Ṣalāḥ al-Dīn Ayyūb, famous in the history of the Crusades as Saladin and at that time a military governor of the Fatimids, withdrew his recognition from the dying Fatimid caliph, al-ᶜĀdid, and became the real ruler of Egypt, there was little to show that those beliefs had taken hold. The Muslim population of Egypt readily returned to the Sunnī Islam of their new rulers, the Ayyubids.

The Ayyubid period coincided with the height of the Christian Crusades. Saladin was the great champion of Islam against the Crusaders, but his sphere of activity, and that of his successors, lay mainly in the Middle East. In 568/1172–3 a party of Ayyubids, sent in the first instance by Ṣalāḥ al-Dīn Ayyūb or Tāj al-Dīn Ayyūb, but subsequently probably acting independently, took Tripoli in North Africa. In 571/1175–6 they went on to invade Zawila, in the Fazzan, but there is no evidence that they penetrated farther south to Kanem/Borno or westward, into the western Sudan. However, it is possible that they did so.

The Ayyubid dynasty lasted for less than a century and in 648/1250 power passed into the hands of the Mamlūks, originally the slave-soldiers of the Ayyubids. There were two lines of Mamlūks, the Baḥrī or Turkish Mamlūks, and after them the Burjī or Circassian Mamlūks. The greatest of the Baḥrī sultans were Baybars (658–76/1260–77) and Qalā'ūn (678–89/1279–90). It was in 724/1324, during the reign of Qalā'ūn's son, al-Nāṣir b. Qalā'ūn, that Mansa Mūsā, the king of the powerful Sudanic kingdom of Mali, passed through Cairo on his way to perform Pilgrimage in Mecca.

The Turkish, Baḥrī Mamlūks were replaced by the Burjī, Circassian Mamlūks, the first of whose sultans, Barqūq, seized power in 784/1382. These Burjīs ruled until 922/1516. In 922/1517 they were defeated by a Turkish dynasty, the Ottomans, at the Battle of Raydāniyya, near Cairo. The Ottomans, however, did not drive the Mamlūks out, but the last of the Burjī sultans was executed. The old Mamlūk system of administration was left largely intact under an Ottoman viceroy and, bit by bit, the Mamlūks regained control of the government.

It continued so until, at the end of the 18 century AD, the French, under Bonaparte, briefly occupied Egypt. However, under pressure from the British fleet and an expeditionary force, the French were unable to hold their conquest, and, in 1215–16/1801, they withdrew. By this time the Ottoman empire was weakened by internal revolt and the interference of the European powers. In 1219–20/1805 an Ottoman commander, Muḥammad ᶜAlī, established himself in Cairo and became virtually independent of his Ottoman overlords in Istanboul. Egypt continued to be governed by him and his successors, the Khedives, but by the end of the 19 century AD the Khedives had become figureheads and the British were the real masters of Egypt.

The Nubian Christian kingdoms

The Nubian kingdoms lay astride the Nile, south of Aswan. At the time of the Muslim conquest of Egypt they were still Christian, linked to the Monophysite Church in Alexandria and to the Christian kingdom of Ethiopia. They remained so for approximately three more centuries. Geographically and culturally they formed a barrier to the expansion of Islam from the Nile valley into the countries on their western borders, and the presence of these stable kingdoms contributed to the security of the area. It is possible, too, that some Christian influences spread west from these kingdoms into the central Sudan.

Islamic influences had begun to reach Nubia even before the Fatimid period. Those largely responsible for introducing them were Arab Muslim traders engaged, no doubt, in the slave trade. Nubian slaves were greatly valued in the western Islamic world and the gold mines of Wādī al-ᶜAllāqī attracted traders too. As a result of contacts with these Muslim traders some Nubians were influenced by Islam and began to adopt an Arab way of life.

C. 394–5/1004 a mixed tribe of Nubians and Arabs who had rendered political services to the Fatimid caliph al-Ḥākim, was given the title of *Kanz al-Dawla*, 'Treasure of the Dynasty'. They thus became known as the Banū Kanz and then established themselves as rulers of a powerful kingdom in the Aswan area. From that time on, sometimes in alliance with the rulers of Egypt, sometimes in revolt against them, the Banū Kanz pushed the frontiers of Islam farther south into Nubia.

It was during the early Mamlūk period that Nubia was finally won for Islam, at least in a military sense. In 674–5/1276 the Mamlūk sultan Baybars sent an expedition deep into Nubia which decisively defeated the Nubian army and in consequence al-Marīs, the northern part of the Nubian kingdom of al-Maqurra, became a Mamlūk possession. By 714–15/1315 a Muslim Nubian prince had been appointed by the Mamlūks to govern Nubia. In 716–17/1317 the cathedral of Dongola was turned into a mosque. Christianity in Nubia was not entirely driven out, but it did suffer a setback and this affected the position of Christians in Egypt. Moreover, the change-over to Muslim rule led to the influx into Nubia of nomadic Arab tribes, in much the same way that the Banū Hilāl and Banū Sulaym had moved into North Africa. From Nubia these Arab nomads spread into the Sudan, reaching as far west as present-day Wadai and the Lake Chad region. One result of this was to render the area between Lake Chad and the Nile Valley somewhat insecure and for this reason contacts between the Sudan and the Nile Valley along the short southerly route through the savanna rather than the desert farther north failed to develop until much later. When, from the 11/17 century on, settled kingdoms began to emerge in Wadai, Darfur and Funj, such a route was opened up.

Egyptian contacts with the west and central Sudan

During the Byzantine period Egypt and North Africa were united in that both were provinces of the Byzantine empire, but during the Muslim period there was little to encourage contacts between the two countries. First, Egypt was a province of the central caliphate until 358/969 while the North African dynasties for the most part claimed to be independent of it. Second, when Egypt did become an independent state, its dynasties, with the exception of the Fatimids, were Turkish or Circassian and had nothing in common with the predominantly Berber dynasties of North Africa. Thus the Egyptians were separated from the west and central Sudan in the north by North Africa and on their western border by the Christian kingdom of Nubia. It is true that a very early caravan route is said by the early 3/9-century Arabic geographer, Ibn al-Faqīh, to have run from the Sudanic kingdom of Ghana, via Gao on the Niger Bend, diagonally across the Sahara, to enter Egypt probably by way of the oasis of Kharga (see Appendix A, Diagram 1).[4] Perhaps this route was in use during the Byzantine period, but the 4/10-century Arabic geographer, Ibn Ḥawqal, states that it was abandoned in the middle of the 3/9 century because it became too insecure. It is impossible to say how busy this route may have been in its heyday as so far no firm evidence has come to light to show that Islamic influences from Egypt entered the Sudan along this early route. However, the Egyptian geographer, al-Muhallabī, who flourished *c.* 370/980, states that in his day Gao was a Muslim city with a Muslim ruler, a mosque and one other place of prayer. This was at least one hundred years after the diagonal route had fallen into disuse. However, the fact that this city was influenced by Islam at so early a date, and that the influence was somewhat developed, may have had something to do with its position on this ancient road to Egypt.

Under the Fatimids North Africa and Egypt were briefly united. The defection of the Zirids, the Hilalian invasion and the rise of the Almoravids quickly disrupted this union. In the central Sudan, Egyptian influence did not, as far as is known, extend beyond the Fazzan up to the end of the 6/12 century. It is true there is a tradition that Mai Dunama b. Ḥumay, of Kanem, performed Pilgrimage on at least two occasions between 490/1097 and 545/1150. If so, he certainly passed through Egypt, but the tradition is based on a very late source and may not be reliable. There is also some evidence that, by the end of the 6/12 century, Kanem was exercising something of its own influence over the affairs of the Fazzan, thus Egyptians and Sūdānīs from the interior could certainly have met in the Fazzan. However, if such contacts occurred, there is no way of telling how extensive they may have been. Sūdānī slaves were certainly exported to Egypt from the Maghrib but this was an indirect trade, conducted through North African middlemen. There is no direct evidence that significant numbers of Egyptians penetrated into Kanem/Borno or farther west towards the Niger Bend between *c.* 235/850, when the old route between Gao and Egypt was abandoned, and the mid-8/14 century, by which time an Egyptian presence in the western Sudan had become considerable. All the same, some Egyptian advances into the central Sudan, and even beyond, into the western Sudan, must have begun to develop by, at the latest, the beginning of the 8/14 century. Otherwise the situation in the middle of that century, to which I have just referred, could never have come about. There are at least some indications as to when this may have started to happen. By the middle of the 7/13 century a *riwāq*, hostel, had been established in Cairo for students from Kanem. This shows that, by this time, there must have been some coming and going between Kanem and Egypt. Between then and the middle of the following century, Egyptian trade began to flow along newly-opened east to west routes into the western Sudan, by-passing North Africa. Then, by 753–4/1352–3, the picture suddenly becomes clear and detailed. At that time the Arabic-speaking traveller, Ibn Baṭṭūṭa, visited the western Sudan. He makes it obvious that, by then, there was a vigorous exchange of trade and people between Egypt and the western Saharan caravan town of Walata, a key point on the road to Egypt. By the same date the Saharan copper-producing centre of Takedda traded almost entirely with Egypt and offered a good market for Egyptian textiles. The new routes all converged on the Niger Bend from where secondary routes led to the Sudanic towns farther south. They thus gave the Egyptians direct access to the interior Sudanic markets. In this connection it is interesting to note that the slave trade that now developed as part of a more general trading pattern, was by no means one-way. Not only did Egyptians buy slaves for export out of the Sudan, they also imported Ethiopian and Turkish slaves into the Sudanic empire of Mali for the use of the wealthy citizens of that thriving commercial state.

Important in opening Egyptian eyes to the opportunities that direct trade with the western Sudan offered was the Pilgrimage of the king of Mali, Mansa Mūsā, in 724/1324. Mansa Mūsā travelled from Mali via Walata, Tuwāt and probably along the coast of Tripoli, to Cairo, on his way to Mecca. He was accompanied, so it is recorded, by a caravan of 60,000 followers and 80 camels carrying gold. In addition, there were 500 slaves also laden with the precious metal and his arrival in Cairo created great excitement. It is said that the sudden huge influx of gold disrupted the Egyptian economy. More than a century and a half later, in 902/1496–7, Askiya Muḥammad of Songhay, the successor empire to Mali, also passed by way of Cairo on Pilgrimage but by this time the links between the western Sudan and Egypt were many and firmly established.

Three developments were probably responsible for bringing about these increased contacts between Egypt and the west and central Sudan. One was the fact that at this time the Nubian gold mines at Wadī al-ᶜAllāqī, upon which the Egyptians had previously relied, began to run out. Thus they turned to the western Sudan for their supply of gold. This opened their eyes to the wider commercial possibilities of the Sudan, and encouraged them to take a direct part in the Sudanic trade. A second was the emergence of Egypt as the cultural and political centre of the western Islamic world during the Mamlūk period. This caused the Muslims of the Sudan to be attracted to Egypt, whereas previously their interest had centred mainly on North Africa. A third was the spread of Islam in the Sudan itself. As more and more people were converted to Islam, so the Pilgrim traffic increased and this passed through Egypt where the pilgrims often stopped to study and to trade. In these ways, relations between the two Muslim communities – that of Egypt and that of the Sudan – were built up, until they reached the thriving state described by Ibn Baṭṭūṭa in the 8/14 century.

There were two major routes that, in the first instance, made these new links possible. There was a single route out of Egypt, via Awjila, in the Libyan desert. Beyond Awjila the route divided, one road going to Tripoli, the other to the Fazzan. This road to the Fazzan then divided again, one branch leading to Bilma, the other to Ghat. From Ghat the route went on to Tadmakkat and the Niger region. Later, a route opened up from Ghat to Agades, and from there into the savanna beyond the southern Saharan border. Yet another route developed at a much later date, via Darfur and Wadai, to Chad. However, as was said above, this was not until the growth of the kingdoms of Wadai and Darfur had brought about stability in these regions (see Appendix A, Diagram II).

The intellectual contacts that the trade along these routes generated not only brought Sūdānī Muslims to Egypt to study under Egyptian ᶜ*ulamā*', they also encouraged these ᶜ*ulamā*' to visit the west and central Sudan where there were rich rewards to be gained for service in the courts of the Sūdānī rulers. Some settled there permanently and during the 9/15 century there were Egyptian ᶜ*ulamā*' as deep in the Sudan as Kano. In Timbuktu, by 956/1550, Egyptian influences were fully evident in the teaching mosque of Sankore. Indeed, it seems that during the 9/15 century Egypt rather than North Africa became the source of intellectual authority for many Sūdānī Muslims. Representative of that authority was the Egyptian ᶜ*ālim* Jalāl al-Dīn al-Suyūṭī

(d. 911/1505). Askiya Muḥammad of Songhay, ᶜAlī Gaji of Borno, Ibrāhīm Sura of Katsina, in Hausaland, and Muḥammad Saṭṭafan of the kingdom of Agades all sought his help on matters relating to the government of their states and the conduct of a Muslim society. The importance of al-Suyūṭī's ideas for the development of West African Islam will become apparent as this book proceeds.

Egyptian Islam in the Mamlūk and Ottoman periods

The new Egyptian influences that now began to reach the west and central Sudan were, of course, largely Islamic and were in addition to those already reaching there from North Africa. Did they differ from those North African Islamic influences in any significant ways?

The answer is that they did, in several important respects. North Africa was solidly Mālikī while Mamlūk and Ottoman Egypt was pluralistic. It accommodated all four *madhāhib*, the Mālikī, the Shafiᶜī, the Ḥanafī and the Ḥanbalī. Sūdānī Muslims did not waver in their attachment to Malikism, even after Egyptian influences had made their mark upon them. None the less, contact with Egypt meant that the Sūdānī ᶜ*ulamā*' were able to extend their intellectual horizons beyond the rather restricted limits of North African scholarship. They thus gained a better understanding of the Islamic world and acquired concepts of Islamic universalism – they came to think of Islam as a world religion and of all Muslims as members of a worldwide community.

North African attitudes continued to be influenced by the puritancial reforming zeal of the Almoravids and Almohads, even after these dynasties had passed away but in Egypt attitudes were less rigorous during the Mamlūk and Ottoman periods. The Egyptian ᶜ*ulamā*' of that time were more accustomed than their North African colleagues to tolerating differences of opinion, so long as these remained within the Sunna, the 'Tradition' of the Prophet. They were also less insistent on the duty of perpetual *jihād* of the sword. Most of them looked tolerantly on the 'mixed' Islam of the Sūdānīs, that is on forms of Islam that compromised with traditional customs and beliefs and fell short of applying the full Sharīᶜa, the Islamic legal code. This lenient attitude was apparent in the teaching of the Egyptian scholar al-Suyūṭī, mentioned below. It is to be contrasted with that of Muḥammad b. ᶜAbd al-Karīm al-Maghīlī, his North African contemporary, who also made his mark on Sudanic Islam. Probably the tough attitudes of al-Maghīlī proved most popular in the end. None the less, the ideas and attitudes of the Egyptian al-Suyūṭī and of the many-sided culture he represented, had considerable effect upon the Sūdānī ᶜ*ulamā*'.

Both North Africa and Egypt were centres of Sufism. North Africa was mainly Qādirī and Shādhilī, that is, it was the Qādiriyya order and the Shādhiliyya order that largely filled the Sufi scene but Egypt was more catholic. By the end of the 12/18 century at least nineteen major Sufi orders flourished in and around Cairo. It was in the Azhar and the *zawāyā* (sing. *zāwiya*), the Sufi hostels of Mamlūk and Ottoman Egypt, that Sūdānī Muslims came into contact with their teachings. They took these back home with them, where they then began to influence the ideas of Sufis already established in the Sudan.

The Mamlūk and Ottoman period in Egypt also witnessed the development of the two-tier system of Islamic education. That system was based on the *katātīb* (sing. *kuttāb*), the primary schools that taught literacy in the Arabic script and the memorisation and recitation of the Koran. Above the *katātīb* were the *madāris* (sing. *madrasa*), schools of higher Islamic education, of which the Azhar was the finest example. This system was not unique to Egypt and it existed elsewhere in the Islamic world. However, the Mamlūks were often patrons of learning and builders of schools, and the system of education in Egypt was among the most highly developed in Islam. It certainly influenced the growth of a similar system in the west and central Sudan, from the great Sankore teaching mosque in Timbuktu where the organisation of the Azhar was deliberately imitated, down to the innumerable *makarantan allo* (*katātīb*) and *makarantan ilimi* (*madāris*) of Hausaland.

This extensive educational development in Egypt was accompanied by a corresponding degree of intellectual activity. An enormous volume of Arabic literature in prose and verse, covering every aspect of Islam, had been produced in Egypt by 1214/1799. It was freely available to Sūdānī Muslims and they studied it eagerly, especially the work of the Egyptian poets, whose ideas, poetic forms and techniques played a part in the growth of the verse literatures in the local languages of the Sudan, for example that of the Hausas.

Not only was written Egyptian literature important in shaping Sudanic Islam. Egypt, above all Cairo, was also a centre from which Islamic folklore and popular stories were disseminated through the activities of professional story-tellers. Thus such well-known Islamic folklore cycles as the *Sīrat ᶜAntar*, the 'Life of ᶜAntar', the *Sīrat Abī Zayd*, the 'Life of Abū Zayd', the *Sīrat Sayf b. Dhī Yazan*, the 'Life of Sayf b. Dhī Yazan', and the well-known *Alf Layla*, the 'Arabian Nights', were told and retold in the Cairo market-places. They were picked up by Sūdānī pilgrims and students and thus found their way, in many different forms, not only into the folklore and vernacular literature of the Sudan but also into its genealogies and myths of origin.

In conclusion contacts with Egypt meant that, from the 6/13 century on, Sūdānī Muslims were drawn into an intellectual world of activity and vigour.[5] It was one that represented many different strands of Islamic thought. There was the tolerance of al-Suyūṭī and his opposition to attempts at reform by *jihād*. There was the great variety of mystical ideas spread by the Sufi *ṭuruq*. Later, by 1215/1800 there was the influence of the Wahhābīs. They were fierce radicals who sought to return to the simple Islam of the Prophet's day and wanted to do away with all changes and additions that had been introduced since his time. Contacts that the Sūdānīs had with all these different views and attitudes did much to shape Islam in the west and central Sudan.

NOTES

1 See note 3, below.
2 Norris, 1972, p. 77.
3 Braudel, I, p. 167ff.
4 This, and other references to medieval Arabic sources mentioned in this chapter will be found in Cuoq, 1975, and can be easily traced by referring to Cuoq's index.
5 This view conflicts with that of the late H. Heyworth-Dunne, who wrote that 'The eighteenth century gives us an Egypt predominantly Islamic in culture and at the tail end of a period where Islamic thought had gradually become stagnant . . .' (1968, p. 1). It also conflicts with Ivan Hrbek (*CHA*, 3, p. 93), who takes the view that Islamic learning in Egypt was in decline during the period when Sūdānī Muslims came into

contact with it and who speaks of 'a rather fossilised kind of learning'. It is not possible to discuss this matter fully here. But it is obvious that descriptions such as 'stagnant' and 'fossilised' are subjective and may relate more to the critic's own intellectual values than to those of the society he describes. Heyworth-Dunne's own excellent study of Egyptian intellectual achievement, quoted from above, surely contradicts his opening statement. Hrbek's view, more sweeping than Heyworth-Dunne's and apparently including everything from the 7/13 century on, seems to ignore the vast literature on *taṣawwuf*, Sufi mysticism, which, far from being fossilised, was in many respects highly innovative. It seems, too, to ignore the immensely rich Islamic folklore of Egypt, as well as its written and oral verse.

CHAPTER TWO

Islam in the states and cities of the Sahara and the western Sudan

The rise of the Almoravids, and their excursion into the desert under Abū Bakr, mentioned briefly in chapter I, was a dramatic incident that brought Islam fully into the light of West African history. However the Almoravids did not introduce Islam. At the moment when Abū Bakr turned his wild Sanhaja loose against the non-Muslim Sūdānīs, Islam had been slowly penetrating into the Sudan for at least 200 years.

Islam in the western Sudan before the rise of the Almoravids

A clue as to when this infiltration of Islam may first have started is given by the 2/8-century Arabic writer and astronomer, al-Fazārī, who knew of the Sudanic state of Ghana as a source of gold.[1] Since al-Fazārī was probably writing between 132/750 and 182/799, this indicates that Muslim merchants were among those who were in touch with the Sudanic interior by the beginning of the 2/8 century, or shortly after. Of course, they may have been in touch much earlier, almost as soon as they became established in North Africa but al-Fazārī is the earliest Arabic author to refer to the Sudanic gold. Another clue is given by the Arabic geographer, Ibn al-Faqīh (fl. 290/903), who tells of the diagonal trans-Saharan route from Ghana to Egypt via Gao, the caravan town in the Niger Bend mentioned in chapter I (see Appendix A, Diagram I). As was said there, this route was abandoned in the 3/9 century but it must obviously have been in use for some time before this happened, perhaps even before the Muslim conquest of Egypt. In this case, some Islamic influences could have been coming into the western Sudan from as early as the 1/7 century. It must be stressed that there is no proof that this was so, but it is certainly a possibility. The information of the 4/10-century Arabic geographer, al-Muhallabī (d. 380/990), referred to in chapter I, that Gao had a Muslim king and a mosque in his day, lends support to this possibility, for such a state of affairs was not brought about overnight. The report of the 5/11-century Arabic author, al-Bakrī (fl. 460/1068) is a further indication of the continuing presence of Islam in Gao for he states that there was a Muslim quarter in the city and that the king was a Muslim. Moreover, his description indicates that it was the Sunnī form of Islam and not Ibāḍī that was followed there.

Another very early contact – the earliest for which there is a definite written record – is said to have taken place in the 2/8 century. The 3/9-century Arabic writer, Ibn ᶜAbd al-Ḥakam (187–257/803–871) states that, *c.* 116/734, an expedition set out from southern Morocco into the Sudan, where it won a great victory and took much gold. It seems that in the course of this expedition the raiders captured two Zanata girls whom they brought home with them. Ibn ᶜAbd al-Ḥakam also adds the improbable information that Zanata women had only a single breast! This is surely just a soldier's tale, believed, perhaps, by town and city dwellers for whom the desert was still the habitat of djinns and strange, half-human creatures. It was hardly to be taken seriously by the merchants and camel-masters who travelled the Saharan routes. Perhaps it was to the reports of this expedition that the astronomer, al-Fazārī, owed his information.

Ibn al-Ṣaghīr, an Arabic geographer who flourished *c.* 290/902–3, tells that the North African town of Tāhert was a centre for the gold trade in his time; and that a route led from there into the Sudan. Tāhert was also a centre of Ibāḍīs, members of the sub-sect of the Khārijiyya. Thus this route into the Sudan must have been one that carried not only merchandise but Ibāḍī Muslim ideas as well.

Half a century later, another Arabic author, al-Mas^cūdī (d. *c* 355/965), records that Muslim merchants from the southern Moroccan town of Sijilmasa, also an Ibāḍī centre, were in touch with a gold mining centre on the river Senegal. The most likely location for this centre is certainly Bambuk; thus there must, by this time, have been a well-established route from North Africa across the western Sahara deep into the western Sudan, and it seems clear that it was Ibāḍī Muslims who were then in control of the gold trade with the interior. By 390/999, the ruler of the Saharan city of Awdaghust is known to have been a Muslim, closely associated with the Sudanic empire of Ghana, which was by this time a thriving commercial centre.

However during the 4/10 century it was above all the Saharan city of Tadmakkat, situated in the Adrar-n-Ifoghas, that was the source of Islamic influences reaching the Sudan. Tadmakkat was an ancient market and for this reason it acquired its Arabic nickname *al-sūq*, 'the market'. Its origins are unknown but it may have been a staging-point on a chariot route linking North Africa with the Niger during the pre-Christian era. Certainly, as from the 4/10 century, it functioned as the meeting place for routes that were established between North Africa and the Sudan. It may even be that Islamic influences went out from there into the Sudan almost as soon as Islam took root in North Africa – simultaneously perhaps with those that may have flowed in along the old route between Egypt and Gao. Once again, however, this cannot at present be proved.

The earliest mention of Tadmakkat in an Arabic source is that of the Arabic geographer Ibn Ḥawqal, who was writing *c.* 363/973.[2] He describes the city as being in the possession of Berbers although at an earlier date it may have been in the hands of Saharan Negroes. It is mentioned again by al-Bakrī, writing *c.* 460/1068. He describes it as having commercial relations with Qayrawān, Ghadames and Tripoli in the north, and with Gao and Ghana in the south.

According to the Ibāḍī Arabic writer Ibn Ḥammād (d. 628/1230) Tadmakkat was visited by at least one well-known Ibāḍī merchant *c.* 270/884. It is unlikely that he was the one and only member of his sect who made his way there. Two 6/12-century Ibāḍī writers, Abū Zakarīyā' al-Warjlānī writing *c.* 500/1106 and Abu'l-Rabī^c al-Wisyānī, writing between 544/1150 and 595/1199, make it clear that Tadmakkat became a major centre for Ibāḍī merchants during the period *c.* 338/950 to 389/999 and continued to be so throughout the 5/11 century. It is true that each of these three Ibāḍī writers lived a century and a half or more after the events that they describe – and Ibāḍī historians were apt to claim more for their sect as the early spreader of Islam among the Sūdānīs than was really justified. However, in the case of these three writers, it seems they were simply recording traditions that had been preserved in their families over several generations and that there was no particular propaganda motive behind what they wrote. It is therefore reasonable to accept their word that Ibāḍīs were present in Tadmakkat from *c.* 270/884. Since they were traders, involved in the gold trade, they may have moved up and down the Saharan caravan routes, to and from the western Sudanic markets. If so, they surely spread their ideas among the Sūdānīs with whom their trading activities brought them into contact.

During this early period Tadmakkat was ruled by the Banū Tānamāk, a tribe of the Sanhaja Berbers, but there were many influential Zanata Berbers resident there too. Although the Ibāḍī presence was strong in Tadmakkat, it does not follow that the whole community was Muslim. There may still have been a strong Berber animist element there, but there is little doubt that Tadmakkat served not only as a trading centre but also as a centre from which very early notions of Islam spread outwards into the Sahel and the western Sudan, as early, perhaps, as the end of the 3/9 century.

According to the 6/12-century Arabic author al-Zuhrī (fl. *c.* 527/1133) the conversion of Tadmakkat from Ibāḍī to Sunnī Islam came about as a result of the conquest by the Sudanic empire of Ghana, acting in alliance with the Almoravids, in 476/1083–84. The Ghanaians, with the Almoravids' help, then wiped out the Ibāḍiyya in the town and it became a centre of Sunnī, Mālikī Islam until its ᶜ*ulamā*' were driven out by the Songhay king, Sonni ᶜAlī, *c.* 874/1470.

In the rest of the western Sudan the Ibāḍī sect now dwindled although traces of it remained at least into the 8/14 century.

To sum up what has been said so far: the evidence for the presence and spread of Islam in the western Sudan during this early period – that is from 26/647 or perhaps even 20–21/641, until 469/1076 which, as will be seen below, was a turning-point after which the position becomes clearer – is fragmentary and sometimes confusing and no certain statements can be made on the strength of it. However, the total effect of all the comments and observations by the Arabic authors who wrote about the Sudan during this period is to leave one convinced that Islam did begin to make an impact there almost as soon as the Muslims conquered Egypt, let alone North Africa. To assess accurately the extent of that influence, or the depth to which it penetrated, is not possible. What can be said, however, is that both the Sunnī and the Ibāḍī forms of Islam were represented.

The medieval state of Ghana

Ghana, the first-known political state of the western Sudan, is believed, on good archaeological evidence, to have been sited originally at Kumbi Saleh, west of the great bend of the Niger and south-east of Awdaghust. The kingdom is said to have been founded by a dynasty known as the Kaya Maga, in the 4 century AD, or perhaps earlier. Some have supposed the Kaya Maga to have been North African Berbers, but the name is not Berber and seems more likely to be Mande. Also, the word 'Kumbi' is Mande and means 'burial ground'. It has therefore been suggested that the place was chosen as the site of the first settlement because it was the resting place of the royal ancestors. However evidence as to the identity of this early dynasty that is supposed to have founded Ghana and the date at which it was founded, is so scanty and uncertain that little trust can be placed in it. It is unlikely that the real origins of the state of Ghana can now ever be known for certain.

'Ghana' seems originally to have been the title of the ruler, but the Arabic historians adopted it to identify the state over which he ruled. The word has continued to be used in this sense ever since.

It seems likely that, by *c.* 133/750, the founding dynasty – whatever that may have been – had been replaced by a Negro Soninke dynasty.

The first to mention Ghana was the 2/8-century Arabic astronomer al-Fazārī, mentioned before. He knew that it was a source of gold and for this reason one can assume that by the 2/8 century it was being visited by Muslim traders. In the 3/9 century it was sufficiently well known to appear on the map of the Arabic geographer, al-Khwarizmī (d. *c.* 220/835 or 231–2/846). In the 4/10 century Ibn Ḥawqal mentioned it again. By this time it had clearly become a powerful and wealthy state.

Ghana in or about 460/1067 is vividly described by the 5/11-century Arabic writer, al-Bakrī. By this time it was an empire in the sense that it exercised political and military control over a wide expanse of territory from the edge of the Sahara, south into the Niger region, and west to the river Senegal. It also controlled the trade in salt and gold between the Maghrib and the western Sudan. Al-Bakrī tells of a city, built largely of stone and wood, not mud, divided into two quarters, a Muslim quarter and a quarter inhabited by the still polytheist Soninke. While culturally and religiously distinct, the Muslims were none the less deeply involved in the life of the state and they served it as government officials, scribes and in other roles where their literacy was useful to the Ghanaian rulers. A number of them even became ministers of state in the Ghana government and served alongside their non-Muslim colleagues. No doubt others made their main contribution in divination, dream interpretation, faith-healing, and prayer; for these were among the skills that caused non-Muslim rulers to employ Muslims in those far-off days. Their presence in Ghana was surely connected with the trading contacts with Tāhert and Tadmakkat, described above. Probably, most of them were engaged in trade as well as in their other employments. The Ghanaian rulers tolerated Islam and welcomed the services of these Muslims, but they remained polytheists and their court reflected this in its African ceremonies and way of life. However, the Muslims, although they constantly attended court, were not expected to conform to its rituals of dusting, prostration – bowing down before the king –, and so on. For them certain polite conventions were accepted, that paid respect to the ruler's authority but which were not offensive to their Islamic faith. For their part, these foreign Muslims made no attempt to force conversion on the polytheists, they accepted them as they found them and lived among them apparently without serious thought of *jihād*.

This thriving and tolerant society depended for its prosperity on control of the trade mentioned above. However this caused it to clash more and more frequently with the Berbers of the Saharan city of Awdaghust, its rival in the profitable Saharan commerce. Some scholars have seen this commercial rivalry as part of the wider tension between nomadic Berbers and settled Negroes that was mentioned in chapter I. Apart from the objections to that theory raised in that chapter, it is open to the additional objection that the Berbers of Awdaghust were themselves by this time no longer simple nomads but largely town-dwelling traders. Moreover, the greed for profit is, in itself, an adequate explanation to account for the rivalry between the two groups.

By *c.* 390/999, the Berber threat to Ghana's commercial interest had become such that the Soninke reacted by seizing control of the approach routes to Awdaghust, thus cutting the city off from the trade. At this time it was in the hands of the Zanata Berbers who were apparently unable to prevent this interference and, according to al-Bakrī, even accepted Ghanaian rule. By about 469/1076, the Zanata Berbers had been replaced in Awdaghust by the militant Sanhaja Almoravids. As was described in chapter I, while the northern wing of these Almoravids went off to carve out an empire in Spain, the southern, desert wing, under Abū Bakr, turned in *jihād* against certain non-Muslim Sūdānīs. This probably took place in 469/1076.

Until recently it has been believed by most historians of West Africa, though certainly not by all, that these desert Almoravid jihadists conquered Ghana and took over control of its territories. Ghana is then thought to have become an Almoravid kingdom and to have continued thus until it was conquered in its turn by the non-Muslim Susu. This belief rests on a rather uncertain reference in the work of al-Zuhrī, mentioned above, and on statements by much later Arabic authors, particularly the 8/14-century Ibn Khaldūn. It also receives support from the fact that some of the later kings of Ghana appear to have been Lamtuna Berbers, that is Almoravid Sanhaja. However, recent research into the writings of a large number of other Arabic authors, some much nearer to the 5/11 century than Ibn Khaldūn, casts doubt on whether such a conquest really ever took place at all.[3] These authors have quite a lot to say about Ghana but they do not mention any conquest by the Almoravids or by anybody else; on the contrary, several of them speak of Ghana as if it continued to be a sovereign state of the Soninke long after the 5/11 century. Thus the whole story of the conquest becomes rather doubtful. Certainly the Almoravids did wage *jihād* against some non-Muslim Sūdānīs, but there is no real evidence that the Ghanaians were among them. They may have been but there are however several other candidates, especially the Susu. They are known to have remained ardent polytheists despite the Islamic influences that surrounded them. It seems more likely that the Soninke of Ghana were on good terms with the desert Almoravids, that they became their allies not their enemies, and were peacefully persuaded by them to adopt Sunnī Islam as the official religion in the Ghana empire. Some of these desert Almoravids subsequently returned to North Africa, attracted by the expansion of the northern Almoravids. Others remained in the Sudan and integrated with the Soninke of Ghana. This may account for the possibility that some of the later kings of Ghana were Lamtuna Berbers and also for the increasingly Almoravid way of life that seems to have grown up there.

In due course several smaller Soninke states emerged out of what had been the original empire of Ghana and some of these, too, were strongly coloured by the Almoravid way of life. One of the most important was that of Diafunu, the Zāfūn of the Arabic writers. Before 540/1145, in which year the Almoravids in

North Africa were finally defeated by the Almohads, the king of the Diafunu had been firmly won over to Sunnī Islam and the Almoravid way of life. He wore the *lithām*, the Almoravid mouth-veil and had also visited the Almoravid court in Marrākush where he obviously enjoyed close and friendly relations with the North African Almoravids. The kingdom of Diafunu was of brief duration, but it is an interesting early example of the way in which Islam, essentially a foreign religion and culture in the western Sudan, was taken over by Sūdānī people and made their own.

Early in the 7/13 century the Susu, a group of the Soninke who had not been converted to Islam, took over by conquest the territories that belonged to Ghana, under their leader Sumanguru. The result was that the Muslims – Arabs, Berbers and Soninke – fled from the area and set up a new city at Walata. They took their trade with them and Walata now began to replace Ghana as the hub of commerce in the Sahel, largely under Muslim Berber control.

Meanwhile, a new Sudanic empire was about to emerge. A Mandingo chief, Sunjata Kaita, from Mali, a former dependency of Ghana, turned on the Susu, drove them out of Ghana and made its territories part of his own state. He did not destroy what remained of Ghana, however, and it continued to exist with some measure of self-government within the framework of the Mali empire.

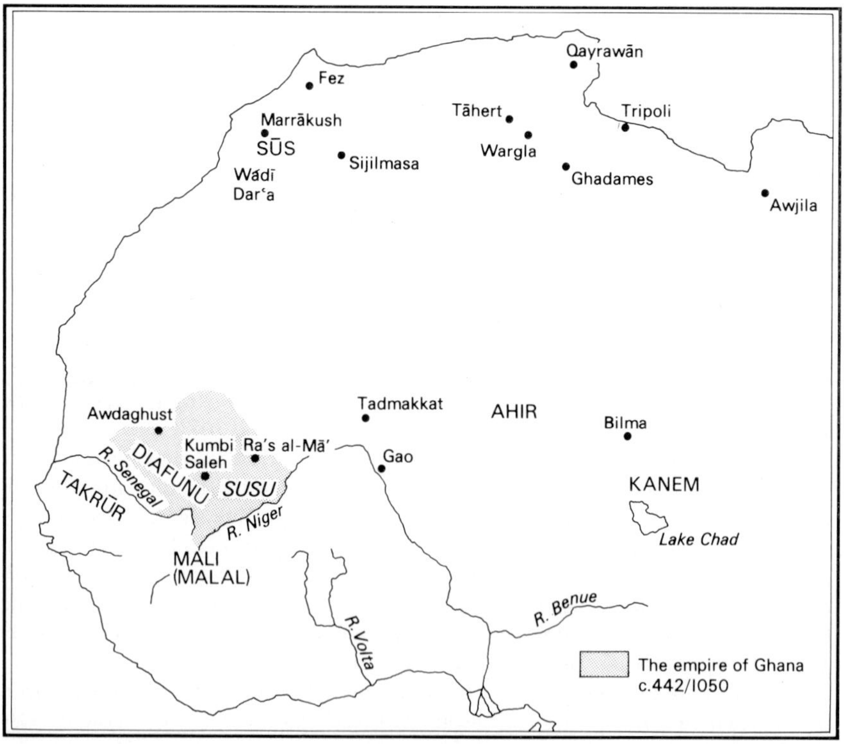

Map 2 The empire of Ghana c. *442/1050.*

The stages of Islam's advance in the empire of Ghana

The truth about when Islam first came to Ghana, and what form it took there, is hard to come by. What evidence there is, is patchy and often contradictory. The most one can do is to take the fragments and interpret them within a framework of reasonable guesses based on what is known of the general history of North Africa, the Sahara and the west and central Sudan from the 1/7 century to 469/1076. By that date it is known that an Islamic presence was definitely established in Ghana.

The sources from which these fragments of information come are the writings of Arabic authors from the 2/8 century on. A number of them were mentioned earlier in this chapter, but they should not be regarded as absolute authorities. They were the journalists and travel-writers of their day and they recorded information and opinions that they picked up from travellers and traders. Such reports were not always necessarily either accurate or complete and there is no reason to be surprised when they turn out to be contradictory.

In considering Islam and Ghana, the first fact that comes to mind is that Ghana was the centre of the gold trade. It was therefore certainly in touch with such Ibāḍī centres as Tāhert and Tadmakkat. As was said above, Tadmakkat, which was especially closely associated with Ghana, was probably a centre for Ibāḍī traders by *c.* 272/885. It is therefore also probable that Ibāḍī ideas reached Ghana from Tadmakkat and began to circulate in the Ghanaian empire, within the lifetime of the following generation – say by *c.* 302/915.

Ghana, however, was in touch with other North African and Saharan centres that were not Ibāḍī. Thus there is every reason to suppose that the Sunnī, Mālikī form of Islam, as it was being argued out by the earnest and learned *ʿulamāʾ* of Qayrawān, reached Ghana, if not at the same time as the Ibāḍiyya, at least as soon as the zealous Ibn Yāsīn began to preach it to his wayward Sanhaja. This is, of course, supposition. What can be said with confidence is that a Sunnī *shaykh* had converted the king of Malal, Mali, to Islam before 460/1067, because the well-informed 5/11-century writer, al-Bakrī, says so. Mali was then part of the empire of Ghana. It would be remarkable if the *shaykh* converted no more than just the king so it is a reasonable conclusion that both the Ibāḍiyya and the Mālikī *madhhab* were in the air of the Ghana empire before 460/1067, although it is not possible to say precisely how long before.

Al-Bakrī's description of Ghana *c.* 460/1067 has been summarised above. It is true that at that date the king and his court still worshipped fetishes (Arabic *dakākīr*). However, if al-Bakrī's description was correct, there must have been a good many Ghanaians who had converted to Islam as a result of contacts with their Muslim visitors, or who had at least come to interest themselves in Islamic ideas. To imagine otherwise would be contrary to normal trends of human behaviour.

To return to al-Zuhrī, who is one of the main sources for information on Ghana, and perhaps the most puzzling. He states that the Ghanaians had remained steadfast in their ancestral religion until the year 469/1076 (in one manuscript 496/1102–03 but that is almost certainly a scribe's error). In that very year, under the influence of the Almoravids, they changed to Islam. Then, seven years later, they called on the Almoravids to help them overcome the Ibāḍīs of Tadmakkat. His evidence thus seems to contradict the suggestion made above, that Islam must have been accepted by at least some Ghanaians before 460/1067. On the other hand, it is very hard to believe that all the Ghanaians suddenly stepped out of fetish worship into Islam as one man. The probable explanation is that al-Zuhrī was referring to the king and his court and, like most people of his day, he simply assumed that the population as a whole followed the example of the ruler. It is, of course, easy to believe that the king and his court converted and then, in their new-found enthusiasm, decided to impose Mālikī Islam upon the Ibāḍīs of Tadmakkat.

While nothing of this can be proved beyond final doubt, the most reasonable interpretation of all the available evidence is that the Ibāḍiyya was almost certainly known in Ghana by *c.* 302/915. Mālikī Islam cannot have been far behind and it must have reached a province of the empire before 460/1067. Some form of fetish worship was still the official cult at that time, but there must have been individual Ghanaians who were Ibāḍī Muslims and others who were Sunnī, Mālikī Muslims. Then, in 469/1076, the king and his court converted to Sunnī, Mālikī Islam and from that point on, the empire of Ghana was largely, though perhaps not entirely, won over to that form of Islamic belief and practice. Whether it then continued to be ruled by Soninkes or whether, at some time, Lamtuna Sanhaja took over from them, it is not possible to say.

How important were the Almoravids in the conversion of Ghana? Certainly the movement as a whole was important in speeding up the process and al-Zuhrī gives them the credit for the conversion of 469/1076. However, it is possible to over-estimate the particular role played by the southern, desert Almoravids and some of the evidence of the Arabic authors suggests that these southern Almoravids had largely run out of steam by the time they reached the desert. It would be hasty to assume that they were still operating at the same level of zeal and efficiency as the northern Almoravids, who drove their conquering spearheads through North Africa and deep into the body of Spain. Would the final conversion of Ghana have taken place even if Abū Bakr and his men had never moved out of Marrākush? The answer should probably be 'Yes', for the weight of circumstances leans in that direction.

Neither the Ibāḍīs nor the Almoravids had the last word in making good Muslims out of the Ghanaians. The anonymous 6/12-century Arabic author of the *Kitāb al-istibsār*, the 'Book of Scrutiny into Hidden Things', reports that by 587/1191, doctrines that seem to have been those of the Almohads, the successors to the Almoravids in North Africa, had reached Ghana and Gao, in the Niger Bend.[4] The theological implications of this information are indeed considerable for the Almohads believed in the Mahdī, who was to prove so important in the future history of Islam in West Africa. Also, unlike the Almoravids, they encouraged Sufism. The great Sufi *shaykh*, Abū Madyan, did not die until 594/1197–8. Surely, then, both Mahdism and Sufism must have been among the Almohad ideas that reached Ghana and the Niger Bend in 587/1191.

There is a sequel to this account of how Islam came to Ghana. The zeal of the newly converted Ghanaians for Mālikī Islam, and their attempt to crush the Ibāḍiyya in Tadmakkat, did not quite mark the end of that tenacious creed. *C.* 650/1252–3, a certain al-Darjīnī, an Ibāḍī *shaykh* from the Maghrib, wrote his *Kitāb ṭabaqāt al-mashāyikh*, the 'Book of Ranks of the Shaykhs'. It was a collection of biographies of learned Ibāḍī scholars and in it he tells how his great grandfather, Shaykh ᶜAlī b. Yakhlaf, visited the empire of Ghana and converted the king of Malal, Mali, to the Ibāḍiyya. He goes on to say that his great grandfather was, in fact, the *shaykh* mentioned by al-Bakrī as having brought Islam to Malal and that al-Bakrī had omitted to mention who he was. He clearly tries to give the impression that al-Bakrī deliberately claimed for the Sunnīs an honour that rightly belonged to the Ibāḍīs! He closes this pious but untruthful little story by bewailing the fact that, although the king of Malal had been converted to Ibāḍī Islam, he and his people subsequently switched to Sunnī Islam.

His story is untruthful because his great grandfather, ᶜAlī b. Yakhlaf, cannot have been alive much earlier than *c.* 545/1150. That was long after al-Bakrī's *shaykh* had carried out his conversion, which certainly took place before 460/1067. This is not to deny that Shaykh ᶜAlī b. Yakhlaf went on a mission journey to Mali and converted its king to the Ibāḍiyya. No doubt he did, but it was a late conversion to this now fading version of Islam, which must have taken place despite the prevailing Malikism of that time. Al-Darjīnī, the ardent champion of the Ibāḍiyya, who was so grieved that Ibadism gave way to Sunnī Islam would have been happy if he could have known that the traveller, Ibn Baṭṭūṭa, in the course of his journey through the western Sudan in 753–4/1352–3, was to find a small group of Ibāḍīs still surviving in what was by that time the empire of Mali.

Some scholars regard the Almoravid movement, especially that of the southern, desert Almoravids who are supposed to have conquered Ghana, as a precedent that inspired later jihadists. They believe it set off a distinct *jihād* tradition that was kept alive by later Muslim reformers and that it was a constant force in Sudanic politics from then on. Perhaps this was so for the memory of the conquering Almoravid Sanhaja has certainly been perpetuated in the folklore of the Saharan Touregs. All the same, it is possible to argue against it on the following grounds: first, there is little in the folklore or written literature of other major Muslim groups such as the Hausas to suggest that active memories of the Almoravids survived over the centuries or that they were in the foreground of the minds of 12/18- and 13/19-century Muslim reformers. Second, the notion of *jihād* needs no precedent; it must inevitably arise from the application of Koranic teaching in certain political and ideological situations. Third, particular *jihāds* sprang out of a multitude of particular political, ideological, social and economic circumstances that hardly existed in the Almoravids' day. Fourth, later *jihāds* were brought about, in part at any rate, by the individual experiences, attitudes and psychologies of men unborn when the Almoravids first burst out of Kākudam. The later jihadists did not need the Almoravids' example. The challenges of their own times were sufficient to set them on their way.

Takrūr

Takrūr was an early Sudanic state located astride the middle Senegal valley and was formed by the interaction of the Negro Serer and Wolof with Saharan Berbers. The route from Sijilmasa to Bambuk, mentioned by al-Masᶜūdī before 355/965, must have passed by way of Takrūr (see Appendix A, Diagram I). One may therefore suppose that Islamic ideas flowed in almost as fast as the gold flowed out. However, al-Bakrī states that Takrūr was won over to Islam by its king, War Jabi (d. 432/1040–1), a generation before the Almoravids embarked on their conquest. War Jabi's son, Labi, then entered into an alliance with the Almoravids and helped them in their *jihād*.

Contrary to what has often been supposed, Islam, even if in a somewhat impure form, has continued to be the religion and culture of the majority of the people of Takrūr, rulers and commoners alike, ever since that time.

As Ghana declined, Takrūr took over much of its western territory, gained control of part of the western Saharan trade and became a flourishing market. With the rise of Mali, Takrūr was gradually dominated by that empire but as Mali declined, Takrūr broke up into kingdoms ruled by kings of the Wolof and Denianke, a Fulani dynasty.

Takrūr gave rise to a well-known name, 'Takrūrī'. This was used by Arabic geographers and historians to describe, first, the people of Takrūr and later, used loosely and very inaccurately, to describe all Sūdānī Muslims, even occasionally those as far east as Borno! This is probably to be accounted for by the fact that West African pilgrims who arrived in Cairo, Mecca and Medina, tended to be referred to by the local peoples as 'Takrūrī' and so the term came to be generally used in this wide sense. In due course it may have given rise to a corrupt form, 'Tukolor'. The people of Takrūr and their descendants did not employ this name to refer to themselves, they called themselves 'Hal Pulor', speakers of Pulor, that is Fulfulde. Others, however, persisted in using it of them and eventually, it came to mean those people of various tribal groups – Fulani, Wolof, Serer – who lived in the Senegambia and were united by being the Muslim subjects of the Wolof or Denianke kings. It is with this meaning that the word 'Tukolor' is used in this book.

The rise of the empire of Mali

Mali, or Malal as it was sometimes called, was the name given to a Mandingo or Malinke kingdom of the Niger Bend. It was ruled originally by the Kaita dynasty. Its early history is obscure, but it is clear that it was at one time part of the empire of Ghana, though independently governed by its own kings. It was one of those kings who was converted to Sunnī Islam by the *shaykh* mentioned by al-Bakrī, certainly before 460/1067. Later, it was won over for the Ibāḍiyya by ᶜAlī b. Yakhlaf but later still Sunnī Islam once again triumped. All the same, Islam whether Ibāḍī or Sunnī, seems to have exerted only a superficial influence over the ruling Kaita dynasty before the second half of the 7/13 century.

Probably shortly after 596/1200, Sunjata Kaita, sometimes known as Mari Jata and nominally a Muslim, emerged as the great hero of the Mandingo people. As was mentioned above, he drove out the Susu and conquered Ghana. His fight against the Susu chief, Sumanguru, is still remembered by the *griots*, the professional reciter-musicians of the Mandingoes. The story is told in the great epic poem of the Mandingo people. This passage from one version of it tells how Sunjata, who clearly possessed magical powers, struck down Sumanguru with a chicken spur.

> . . .
> Susu Sumanguru took his horse back some distance,
> . . .

He charged on horseback with his three-pronged spear;
He raised it aloft and struck Sunjata with it;
The three-pronged spear shattered and fell to the ground.
. . .
He struck Sunjata with his long sword;
The long sword broke into three pieces and fell to the ground.
He retired again.
Then he returned with his iron rod.
He raised it aloft and was about to strike Sunjata with the iron rod,
But his arm remained aloft, immovable.
He said to Sunjata, 'Go ahead.'
Sunjata came and struck Sumanguru with his three-pronged spear;
The three-pronged spear was shattered.
. . .
He produced the chicken spur at that point
And shot Sumanguru with it;
He fell.[5]

Of course, it need not be assumed that Sunjata really did kill Sumanguru with a chicken spur. That is probably just a symbol meant to indicate that it was by magic that the great chief overcame his rival and, perhaps, to express scorn for that rival.

By defeating Sumanguru, Sunjata freed his people from the domination of the Susu. At the same time he founded the empire of Mali, in which he united all the branches of the Mandingoes. He also founded a new capital, Niani, on the Niger, east of Jariba, the earlier centre of the kings of Mali.

Despite a nominal allegiance to Islam, Sunjata was a hero of traditional African polytheism and he is celebrated as such in the epic poems of the Mandingo people, such as that quoted from above. He was succeeded by his son, Mansa Ulli. Mansa Ulli was sufficiently committed to Islam to perform Pilgrimage, passing through Egypt during the reign of the Mamlūk sultan, Baybars (658/1260–676/1277). He was thus one of the first Sūdānī Muslims to set up the links with Egypt described in chapter I. He also established his own position as a legitimate ruler in the eyes of Muslims inside and outside the Sudan. During his reign the empire of Mali expanded widely over the Sahel and he probably brought Walata, Timbuktu and Gao within his sphere of control. At the same time important trading and cultural links were set up with the Maghrib.

Towards the end of the 7/13 century a freed slave, Sakura, seized the throne and under his rule the empire expanded yet farther. He, too, made the Pilgrimage but died at Tajura, near Tripoli, on the return journey. The greatest of the kings of Mali was certainly Mansa Mūsā, who reigned from *c.* 712/1312 to 738/1337 and presided over what has been called the 'Golden Age' of Mali. So great was his fame that his portrait figures on an early European map of West Africa, the Catalan map of AD 1375. Here he sits in majesty, apparently presiding over the whole Sahara. It was certainly his Pilgrimage in 724/1324, described in chapter I, that brought him this renown. Tales of his visit spread from Cairo all over the Middle East and from there into Europe, turning him into a legendary figure. The wider importance of Mansa Mūsā's reign, reaching far beyond the borders of the Sudan, is made clear by Fernand Braudel, who comments, 'Thus [Sudanic] gold played its part in the history of the Mediterranean as a whole, entering general circulation from the fourteenth century, perhaps after the spectacular pilgrimage to Mecca of Mansa Musa, King of Mali, in 1324'.[6] There is also ample evidence that the empire of Mali, in its turn, came closely into touch with both North Africa and Egypt after this date. Thus it seems equally true to observe that the 8/14 century was a time when the association, which had been formed much earlier, between the west and central Sudan and the world of the Mediterranean took a large step forward in what was destined to become a continuing development.

Under Mansa Mūsā, Mali reached the height of its power. At its fullest extent the empire united the conquered non-Mandingo Sahel with the native Mandingo country to the south. Beyond the Sudan, it acquired great prestige for not only were the new links with Egypt extended and consolidated but the longer established associations with North Africa were also developed by trade, especially in gold, and by diplomatic relations.

Mansa Mūsā's reign was also the turning point of the Mali empire. Under his successors there followed a period of decline, brought about by two flaws in the empire's structure. One being the uncertainty over the succession. Ever since the day of the usurper Sakura, this had been largely determined by court intrigue, which in the end gave rise to civil war. The second cause of weakness was the fact that the northern half of the empire was non-Mandingo and was therefore obedient to the Mali rulers only as long as they were strong enough to enforce that obedience. When they ceased to be able to do so, both the Touregs and the Mossi began to harass Mali. During the 9/15 century Mali was in decline and by the early 11/17 century the decline was complete.

Islam in the empire of Mali

With the rise of the empire of Mali new Islamic influences began to be felt in the western Sudan and royal Pilgrimage was established as both a religious and a political institution. It not only served to associate Islam with Sudanic kingship; it also drew the Sudan more closely into the world of international politics, diplomacy and trade. Trade was especially important in the development of Sudanic Islam at this time. As the traders of the Mali empire moved to and fro along the caravan routes that linked the Sudanic and Saharan markets, their constant contacts with Saharan Muslims made them among the first Sūdānīs to be converted to Islam (see Appendix A, Diagram II). Indeed, it has been suggested that some Sūdānīs may have adopted Islam largely in order to ease the way for more profitable trading relations with the Saharans. It is a common human characteristic that people who think alike and follow the same way of life are inclined to assist each others' trading activities more readily. Moreover, where credit is based very largely on personal reputations and contracts have to be fulfilled to unknown or distant persons, men are more likely to trust those who share their own religion. This was especially so in the case of Muslims. The Sharīᶜa includes strict regulations for the conduct of trade. As the trade expanded, so conversion to Islam grew and with Islam came literacy in Arabic and notions of a codified – that is a written – system of law; also ideas of a written constitution and the written chronicling of history, Islamic knowledge of the stars and planets and so on. The usefulness of these techniques soon became apparent to the rulers, not only in Mali but also in other Sudanic kingdoms. These rulers began to incorporate them into their own administration and to employ foreign Muslim experts as advisers and teachers. In this way Islam began to play an increasingly important part in the development of Sudanic states.

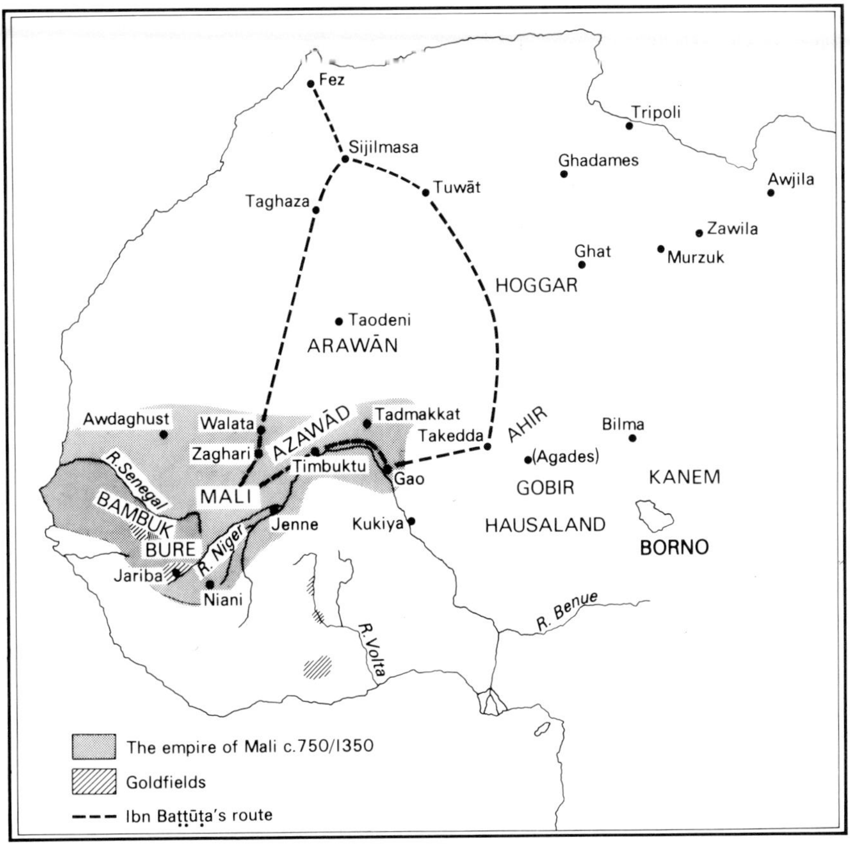

Map 3 The empire of Mali c. *750/1350.*

Islam's victory was by no means complete. It is true that the rulers of Mali were Muslims, solid enough in their faith to perform Pilgrimage, while some of their subjects, too, were good Muslims who brought up their children strictly and made them learn the Koran. The traveller Ibn Baṭṭūṭa testified to this and he was pleased to note that if these children failed to memorise the Koran, they were put in chains until such time as they learnt their lessons properly.[7] However other Malians were clearly still polytheists. Islam's literacy, its impressive rituals and its annual festivals were all acceptable to these people. They brought additional prestige and spectacle to the conduct of state affairs. But the polytheists were not ready to abandon their ancestral cult and go over to Islam entirely. Had the ruler attempted to enforce this, it would almost certainly have torn the kingdom apart in bitter strife. Thus, in Mali, a compromise arose. On the surface much Islamic ceremonial was observed, the rulers often attended Friday prayer and they celebrated the Islamic festivals. On the other hand, as Ibn Baṭṭūṭa tells, notions of traditional African divine kingship survived which were even encouraged by court ritual, where Muslims as well as polytheists had to take part. In contrast to what had been the case in Ghana, Muslims in Mali were not excused from conforming to these non-Islamic customs. Moreover, it was still native African customary law, not the Islamic Sharīᶜa, that governed the country. In social life Islamic dress and other outward forms were frequently adopted. Islamic morals, on the other hand, were often ignored, even sometimes by the ᶜ*ulamā*'. In the end, the empire of Mali made an institution out of mixed Islam. Dr P.F. de Moreas Farias describes the situation deftly when writing of Ghana and her successor states: 'the orbit of the king's power also went round two focii: trade and Islam, on the one hand, and the land and Animism on the other'.[8] This certainly applied in the case of Mali and then became the normal pattern for other kingdoms in the west and central Sudan, for the next four hundred years.

As was mentioned above, although Mali was substantially Sunnī during the 8/14 century, Ibn Baṭṭūṭa did find a small group of Ibāḍīs living in the town of Zaghari, ten days journey from Walata (see Map 3). It was composed of members of the Saghanughu clan, and Ibn Baṭṭūṭa describes them as 'whites'. This may not mean that they were in fact white-skinned, it may simply mean that, as Ibāḍīs, they claimed descent from North African Berbers, possibly even from Shaykh ᶜAlī b. Yakhlaf, the great grandfather of al-Darjīnī.

The founding of the Songhay state

The original home of the Songhay people was Dendi, on the eastern arm of the Niger. The kingdom may have been founded during or even before the 1/7 century by Sorka fishermen who were probably mixed with Berbers. It was ruled from Kukiya, south of Gao, on the east bank of the Niger. According to tradition the first prince of the dynasty bore the title 'Za Aliamen'. Some traditions attempt to associate this name with an Arabic phrase *jā' min al-yaman*, 'He came from the Yemen', or from other Arabic phrases such as *Dha 'l-yaman*, 'One who comes from the Yemen'. All of these are very unlikely, however, and the name is most probably from the Songhay language. None the less, the dynasty did claim Yemenite origin. Such claims are very common in the Muslim Sudan and they probably arose from the need of newly converted royal dynasties to find themselves a place in the classical Arabic genealogy. This would invest the dynasty with Islamic legitimacy. These claims should not be regarded as historically accurate, but they are certainly important as indications of the date when these local dynasties adopted Islam.

C. 399–400/1009 the Za dynasty is traditionally supposed to have moved from Kukiya to Gao, an important trading station on the Niger and the meeting-point of the salt route from the west and the trans-Saharan route from the north-east. It is on his arrival in Gao that Za Kosoi, the ruler of the day, is said to have adopted Islam but, according to al-Muhallabī (d. 380/990), Gao was not just a town but also the centre of a small Islamic kingdom of the Niger Bend in his day. It therefore seems likely that the Za dynasty, which perhaps replaced earlier local Muslim rulers in Gao, converted to Islam before

399–400/1009. The move to Gao may have arisen out of a decision to adopt a Muslim city as the capital of their kingdom. This incident is a good example of the way in which trade and Islam often combined to bring about the development of major, settled Sudanic states.

By 494/1100 it seems likely that Gao had become an Islamic centre of cultural as well as political and commercial importance. A tombstone found there records the death in that year of a certain royal personage and it bears the following inscription, in Kufic Arabic writing, *al-malik al-nāṣir li-dīn Allāh al-mutawakkil ᶜalā Allāh*, 'the king, the helper of God's religion, the reliant upon God'. The inscription goes on to name him as Abū ᶜAbd Allāh Muḥammad b. ᶜAbd Allāh b. Zāghī. Although this person's name does not appear in any of the lists of the kings of Songhay given in other sources, it seems probable that he was in fact the ruler of that state at the turn of the 5/11 to the 5–6/12 century. What is more significant is the fact that this tombstone, in its Kufic Arabic inscription and in the marble out of which it is made, closely resembles tombstones found at Almeria, a part of Spain subject to the Almoravids at that time. The assumption therefore must be that it was imported from Spain. If tombstones were imported from Muslim Spain to the Niger Bend, it is safe to conclude that there were other cultural as well as commercial links between the two areas. All of this must have contributed to strengthening Islam in Gao. Other Arabic inscriptions found in Gao and relating to royal persons, date from 502/1108–9; 503/1109–10; 511/1117–18 and 514/1120–1. Yet other inscribed tombstones have been found elsewhere in the Niger Bend, bearing dates ranging from the 5/12 century to the 9/14 century.[9]

The Sonni dynasty

During the 7/13 century, Songhay was annexed to Mali and two Songhay princes were taken as hostages. Ten years later, *c.* 673/1275, one of them, ᶜAlī Kolon, escaped and set himself up independently as Sonni, that is 'king' of Songhay. He thereby founded the dynasty of the Sonnis. In 869/1464–5, the most famous – or notorious – of all the Sonni line succeeded to the throne. His name was Sonni ᶜAlī. He greatly extended the Songhay state and delivered it finally from Mali overlordship. In 873/1468 he took the city of Timbuktu, then in the hands of the Touregs. Five years later he conquered Jenne. In 898/1492 his spectacular reign came to an end when, it was said, he was drowned crossing a river. However, his death may have been contrived by his enemies.

Sonni ᶜAlī was nominally a Muslim. However he has gone down in history – a history largely written by Sunnī ᶜ*ulamā*' – as a wicked and impious man who mocked Islam and whose true loyalty was to the ancestral cult. The truth may be more complex. It seems that Sonni ᶜAlī, like his Malian predecessors, was really a practitioner of that compromising mixed Islam that sought to avoid an open breach with the ancestral cult. Whatever his own beliefs may have been, he recognised his political dependence upon this cult. However it is no doubt true that he did have an affection for the ways of his ancestors and was personally reluctant to break with them. Also, he was much given to traditional African magic. In this situation Sonni ᶜAlī was faced with a new development that must have created difficulties for him. The Sanhaja ᶜ*ulamā*' of Timbuktu and Walata – the descendants of the Almoravids and their Ghanaian allies – had long been strengthening their influence in these two centres. As their commercial prosperity and power increased, they became aware of their own strength and were thus tempted to interfere in the politics of the Songhay state. They were also reluctant to submit to the authority of a ruler whose Islam was suspect. Moreover, their close and growing links with Islamic North Africa and their ever-widening command of Islamic literacy served to stiffen their opposition to the mixed Islam with which they were surrounded. Perhaps these links also helped to sow in their minds the conviction that political power belonged by right to them and not to a mere illiterate magician. This situation, like others before and after it, has been seen in terms of 'white' Sanhaja Islam in confrontation with 'black' Sūdānī Islam – yet another phase of the ancient struggle for power between whites and blacks that began in the Sahara. There is little to justify such a view. Concubinage, that is sexual intercourse with slave-girls, and marriage with local women must by this time have produced a society of mixed colour that virtually eliminated the colour division between the town-dwelling Sanhaja and the Songhays. Even when this was not so, there is no evidence that men in the 9/15-century Songhay empire were sensitive about the colour of their skins. A difference of opinion about the proper way to observe Islam, combined with a clash of political interests, is, therefore, fully sufficient to explain the way in which the situation developed.

Clearly, these ᶜ*ulamā*' presented a challenge to Sonni ᶜAlī's authority, the more so since they had close links with, and supported the Touregs, who were his enemies. He attempted to solve the problem by persecuting them, especially those in Timbuktu and Walata. On the other hand he began to favour the ᶜ*ulamā*' of Jenne and elsewhere, who turned out to be more willing to accept his authority. He earned himself an evil name among the Timbuktu ᶜ*ulamā*', and has gone down in history as a 'Khārijī', a term of abuse that reflects the very early Islamic quarrels in North Africa and the Saharan caravan towns. 'Khārijī' means a 'warmonger' or a tyrant which no doubt he partly deserved. He may well have had certain Khārijī ideas and attitudes, but what little is known of him suggests that he was not a sufficiently serious Muslim to hold to the Ibāḍīyya, or indeed any other Muslim sectarian belief, with conviction. However as is the case with all rulers, his policies were necessarily determined by the nature of the problems that faced him, and by the political circumstances of his day.

On Sonni ᶜAlī's death civil war broke out. It was resolved by the victory of Muḥammad Ture, one of his generals and a Muslim.

The Askiya dynasty

In 898/1493 Muḥammad Ture took the title of 'Askiya', by which the dynasty he founded came to be known. His reign marked the high point of political and cultural development so far attained in the western Sudan. He led the Songhay empire into a more strict Islamic stance than that adopted by Sonni ᶜAlī. In particular, he achieved an understanding with the Sanhaja ᶜ*ulamā*' that ensured their cooperation, even though they remained somewhat distant from the Songhay court. He then created a standing army, divided the empire into provinces and created a number of administrative posts. Among these were the city mayors of Timbuktu and Jenne, the Timbuktu-Koi and the Jenne-Koi. In 902/1496, or 903/1497, he set out on Pilgrimage. In Cairo he met the Cairene scholar al-Suyūṭī. Through his help he was invested as *khalīfa*, caliph, in the

Sudan, by the last ᶜAbbasid caliph, al-Mutawakkil. Al-Mutawakkil was then living in Cairo under the protection of the Mamlūk sultan. He may also have received similar recognition from the Sharīf of Mecca. He thus used Islam to build up his own constitutional position and to bring the Songhay empire more firmly into the network of diplomatic and cultural relations that made up the world of western Islam. In contrasting his era with that of his predecessor, Sonni ᶜAlī, Professor Levtzion puts it succinctly when he says, 'the pilgrim-king' replaced the 'magician-king'.[10] With his authority firmly established, Askiya Muḥammad returned to Songhay and resumed the task of government. He then proved himself a great conqueror. He extended the boundaries of the Songhay empire westward to the lower Senegal, eastward to Ahir, and south to Segu. He led what he chose to call a *jihād* against the polytheists of Mossi, although he failed to completely subdue these bitter enemies of settled states. He also incorporated what was left of Mali into his own empire.

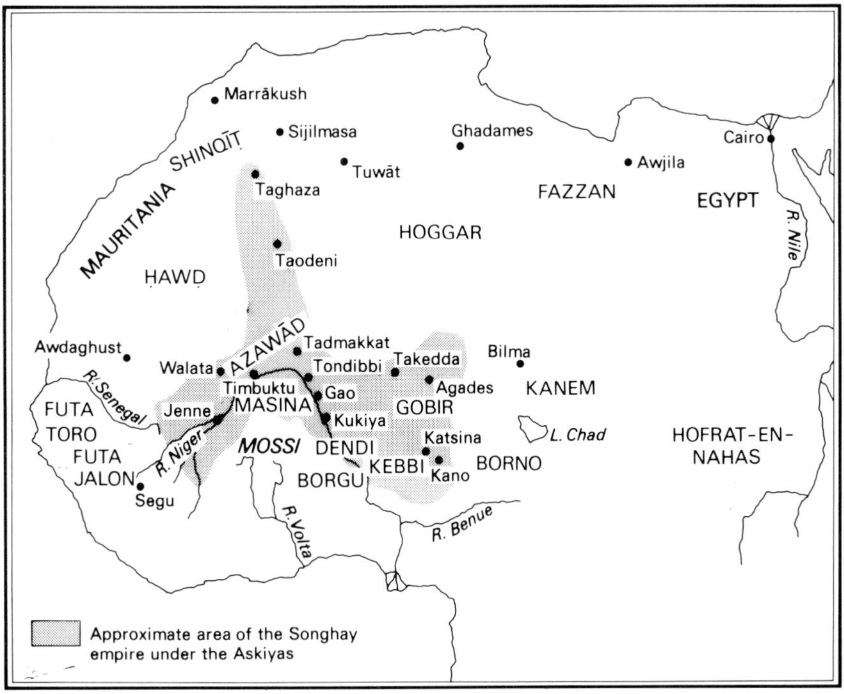

Map 4 The Songhay empire under the askiyas (10/16 century).

It is claimed for him on the authority of the early 10/16-century traveller and author, Leo Africanus, that, in alliance with Kanta of Kebbi, he conquered the Hausa states. Recent research has thrown serious doubt on this as there is no other evidence that such conquests ever took place. There is no mention of the fact in the 'Kano Chronicle', nor notice of it in Hausa tradition. Therefore as Humphrey Fisher has shown, there must now be some uncertainty as to whether what Leo originally wrote was accurately reported by G.B. Ramusio. He was the Italian who translated Leo's work from the Arabic in which it was first written but has since been lost.[11] It now seems that the sultanate of Agades marked the farthest extent of the Songhay conquests in the east and that they were never pushed effectively south of that point, into Hausaland. Leo may have been mistaken, or Ramusio may have misinterpreted him. If not, then the so-called Songhay conquest of the Hausa kingdoms can have been little more than a raid, of no long-term significance.

Islam under the *askiyas*

Askiya Muḥammad is especially remembered for his initiative in consulting two outstanding Muslim intellectuals of his day as to how he ought to govern his empire in the way of Islam. These scholars were the North African ᶜ*ālim* Muḥammad b. ᶜAbd al-Karīm al-Maghīlī and the Egyptian ᶜ*ālim* Jalāl al-Dīn al-Suyūṭī.

Al-Maghīlī was a Muslim lawyer of Tuwāt, in North Africa. After a violent career there, in which he became involved in the persecuting of Jews, he moved to the Sudan. Here he visited Ahir, Takedda, Katsina, Kano and finally Gao, the Songhay capital. In all these centres he gave courses in Koran studies and Islamic law.

He has been credited with introducing Sufism into the Sudan. He may have contributed something to this, but it was certainly not his primary contribution to Sudanic Islam. That he was the first to introduce the idea of the Mahdī to the western Sudan is also doubtful. This idea must have been known along the caravan routes since Almohad times as it was a central point in Almohad doctrine. What al-Maghīlī may have done is to introduce the later idea of the *mujaddid*, the 'Renewer', whom God will send once in every century to prepare the way for the Mahdī. He certainly brought it into prominence by giving it his considerable authority. He wrote:

> And accordingly it is related that at the beginning of every century God will send a learned man to the people to renew their faith, and the characteristics of this learned man in every century must be that he commands what is right and forbids what is disapproved of, and reforms the affairs of the people and judges justly between them . . . in contrast to the characteristics of other learned men of his age.[12]

Indeed, as Dr Hassan Gwarzo has pointed out in his excellent study of him there is reason to think that al-Maghīlī believed he was himself the Mujaddid of his century.

Of more immediate relevance to the situation in Songhay was his ruling on the legal status of Sonni ᶜAlī and, by implication, that of Askiya Muḥammad. He wrote:

> There is no doubt that they [Sonni ᶜAlī and his people] are the greatest of tyrants and wrongdoers.
>
> The Holy War of the *amīr* [commander] Askia against them and his taking of the sultanate from their hands is the most meritorious Holy War, and the most important . . .[13]

In reference to those mixers who claimed Islam but continued to practise polytheism, he said:

> As for these people whose characteristics you describe, they are polytheists without doubt . . . and there is no doubt that the Holy War against them is better and more meritorious than Holy War against unbelievers who do not say, There is no god but God; Muḥammad is His Apostle . . .[14]

Al-Maghīlī thus damned the memory of the wretched Sonni ᶜAlī, legitimatised Askiya Muḥammad's seizure of power and gave his approval to *jihād* as the proper course of action in the face of mixed Islam. After leaving the Sudan he returned to Tuwāt, where he died in 909/1504.

Jalāl al-Dīn al-Suyūṭī (d. 911/1505) was an Egyptian *ᶜālim* of Cairo and was probably the foremost Muslim literary figure of his day. He produced over five hundred works, although some of them were quite minor. He was certainly a pious and sincere Muslim, but less of a fire-eater than his contemporary, al-Maghīlī. He was a realist, concerned to help the Sūdānī Muslims who consulted him to create a stable and workable Islamic society in the Sudan. There is no evidence that he ever visited the Sudan, but he met Askiya Muḥammad in Cairo. Earlier, *c.* 889/1484, he had met ᶜAlī Gaji, of Borno, and had obtained investiture for him as caliph. He also corresponded with Askiya Muḥammad, with his contemporaries Ibrāhīm Sura of Katsina and Sultan Muḥammad Ṣaṭṭifan of Agades, as well as with other Sūdānī *ᶜulamā'*. He advised on how best the Sharīᶜa should be interpreted to meet the special needs of the Sahara and the Sahel, where the interests of nomads and the settled population often clashed. He showed how the Mamlūk system of land ownership could be useful in Agades. His opinions were usually remarkable for their common sense. When consulted on the thorny question of *jihād* of the sword, and when it was or was not justifiable to have resort to it, he replied, with admirable directness, that it was always more meritorious to keep the peace. However he also preached Mahdism. Indeed, it seems that, like al-Maghīlī, he too considered himself to be the Mujaddid of the Age. Moreover, he made prophecies as to when the Mahdī would appear that proved useful to future reformers.

These two men, al-Maghīlī and al-Suyūṭī, have been seen by some as personifying the two opposing forces in West African Islam. These forces were militancy and its opposite, quietism, the acceptance of the situation as it is or trying to change it by only peaceful means. It is certainly true that al-Maghīlī was intellectually fiery and physically violent, while al-Suyūṭī seems to have been a more bland and less aggressive person. To see them as symbols of perpetually opposing forces is neat, but perhaps misleading. Many moderates quoted al-Maghīlī when it suited their purpose. Jihadists like the Shehu Usumanu ɗan Fodio frequently quoted al-Suyūṭī. Moreover, both men preached Mahdism, and that was essentially a militant reforming ideology. It would be difficult to decide whether the firebrand al-Maghīlī or the amiable easy-going al-Suyūṭī did more in the end to popularise Mahdism in the west and central Sudan, and thus to encourage *jihād*. However, it remains true that al-Suyūṭī was personally opposed to violence, whatever the outcome of his Mahdist ideas may have turned out to be in practice.

It can be assumed that Askiya Muḥammad listened with respect and attention to the views of these two scholars, but he did little to implement their advice. One of his wars was styled a *jihād*, and this was a useful justification. In reality, however, it was as much a war of imperial conquest as of religion. Al-

Maghīlī's endorsement of his overthrow of the Sonni dynasty helped to establish his legal right to rule, as did his Pilgrimage. These two facts also made him acceptable to the Sanhaja ᶜ*ulamā*ʾ of Timbuktu and Walata. In return for their support he allowed the ᶜ*ulamā*ʾ considerable freedom to run their affairs in these two cities. He even conceded them some say in the affairs of the Songhay empire, especially as regards the administration of the Sharīᶜa in its towns and cities. Such cooperative attitudes towards the ᶜ*ulamā*ʾ were continued by his successors.

On the other hand, and despite the urging of al-Maghīlī, Askiya Muḥammad and the *askiyas* who followed him remained firmly within the limits set by Sudanic mixed Islam. The administrative structure of their empire was based on traditional African political concepts, not on Islamic constitutionalism. The Sharīᶜa had little jurisdiction outside the cities. Court ritual still reflected the notion of divine kingship. The observance of Islamic morality was still largely confined to the circle of the ᶜ*ulamā*ʾ and was virtually unknown among commoners. The *askiyas* made no serious attempt to push conformity to Islamic observance in their empire beyond this point. They were practical statesmen who recognised the usefulness of Islam and its growing political power. They were neither Almoravids nor true jihadists, and they did not adopt the blue-prints either of al-Maghīlī or al-Suyūṭī. They found it expedient to treat both these worthies with great respect, and in this way they smoothed the ruffled feathers of ᶜ*ulamā*ʾ.

Some important consequences resulted from the *askiyas*ʾ adoption of Islam, incomplete though it was. Songhay won substantial international recognition throughout the western Islamic world, and it forged close links with the Sharifian Saᶜdids of Morocco. This led to great cultural gains, although, politically, the Sharifian connection turned out to be disastrous as will be seen below. The *askiyas* patronage of the ᶜ*ulamā*ʾ of Timbuktu greatly enhanced the fame and influence of that city, which became a great intellectual centre as well as a great market. In consequence Islamic education made substantial advances not only in Songhay but also throughout the west and central Sudan. The security of the empire, to which the *askiyas* paid great attention, helped trade and the Saharan caravan routes were probably never busier than in the days of the early *askiyas*. As will be seen in chapter 4 not only Muslim merchants from North Africa and Egypt, but also certain Christian, Italian-speaking merchants, travelled to and fro along them. All this, the political stability, commercial prosperity and a vigorous intellectual life, had long-term advantages for the spread of Islam in the west and central Sudan.

The decline of Songhay and the Moroccan conquest

In 934/1528 Askiya Muḥammad, now ageing, blind and feeble, was deposed by his son, Mūsā. This started off a series of intrigues among ambitious rival princes, and Askiya Muḥammad's considerable harem had procured him many sons. After a short reign Mūsā was assassinated and over the fifty years following Askiya Muḥammad's deposition, eight *askiyas* succeeded. Several of them were able men who continued the founder's policies with success, but rivalries over the succession and consequent outbreaks of civil strife weakened the empire. None the less, it remained the strongest state in the western Sudan until it was overthrown by the Moroccans in 999/1591.

Despite the close cultural and diplomatic relations between Songhay and the Sharifian Saᶜdids of Morocco, there had long been friction between them over ownership of the salt mines of Taghaza. These mines were no more than a month's journey from the southern Moroccan border, but they were under Songhay control. This annoyed the powerful Moroccan sultan, Mawlay Aḥmad al-Manṣūr. Shortly after the battle of al-Qaṣr al-Kabīr (986/1578), which brought Mawlay Aḥmad such great prestige, the reigning *askiya*, Dāwūd, conceded him the lease of the salt mines for a year. This did not satisfy the sultan, who promptly made an attempt to seize them by force. This the *askiyas* cleverly defeated by simply withdrawing the labour of the Songhay slaves, who alone knew how to work the mines. Mawlay Aḥmad however, was not deterred by this set-back. As was explained in chapter 1 he was greedy for the gold of the Sudan to finance his ambitious schemes. He claimed to be the *khalīfa* caliph, the supreme temporal and religious head of Islam. He argued – and there is no need to doubt his sincerity – that the wealth of the Islamic Sudan ought to be used for the benefit of all Muslims; to repel the Christian aggressors who were driving the Muslims out of Spain and now attacking the Maghrib. He first tried to extend his control over Songhay by courting the Songhay ᶜ*ulamā*', on the ground that they owed allegiance to him, as caliph, and not to the *askiyas*. When this failed he dispatched the Pasha Jawdhar with an army largely composed of European musketeers who had taken service with the Moroccans. In 999/1591 Jawdhar reached Songhay. The Askiya Iṣḥāq, distracted by internal rivalries and grossly underestimating the threat posed by the Moroccans, made inadequate preparations to defend his empire. Although his army greatly outnumbered the Moroccans, it was no match for the fire-power of the musketeers. The Songhay army was defeated at Tondibi and the Moroccans occupied Timbuktu. A surviving member of the *askiya* dynasty took refuge in Dendi and for some time continued to offer resistance to the Moroccan occupation. The Moroccans, for their part, maintained a puppet *askiya* responsible for local administration but the Songhay empire was for all practical purposes at an end. It had become a Moroccan province.

Al-Manṣūr's Sudanic adventure has been widely condemned. It was even opposed by many of his own ᶜ*ulamā*', who thought it morally wrong to attack a friendly Muslim state. Some have even argued that, while it brought al-Manṣūr immediate advantages, it nevertheless started off the decline of his own Sharifian state. This is hard to accept. The causes of the Sharifian decline were at work before al-Manṣūr invaded Songhay. They would have continued to operate even if he had not done so. The fact is that his ruthless action in the face of the moral opposition of many of his ᶜ*ulamā*' paid off handsomely. He gained enormous wealth in gold, as a consequence of which Moroccan gold coins became highly valued on the European money markets. He became known as al-Dhahabī, 'The Golden', and the gold greatly enhanced the splendour of the Sharifian empire. Morally his action has to be judged in the light of the circumstances of his day. The Christian pressure against North Africa was a real threat to Islam and the Ottoman Turks were unable to contain it. It seemed that al-Manṣūr alone was able to do so after the victory over the Portuguese at al-Qaṣr al-Kabīr. However for this he needed money and in the context of the international power politics of his day, his seizure of this Sudanic source of wealth was probably inevitable. For the Songhay empire it was a political disaster that quite simply destroyed it. It had serious economic and intellectual consequences, too, but these were less catastrophic and should not be exaggerated.

Walata

When the Susu chief Sumanguru attacked Ghana early in the 7/13 century, the Muslims who fled from him took refuge in a village called Biru, south-east of Awdaghust, in the country of Shinqīṭ. Here they founded a commercial centre that acquired the Berber name Walata. In due course it replaced both Awdaghust and Ghana as the main centre for the caravan trade. It became an important town inhabited mainly by Masufa Berber Muslims, although there were some Sūdānī Muslims as well. It was visited by Ibn Baṭṭūṭa in 753/1352. He describes it as a very hot place, two months journey from Sijilmasa. He stayed there fifty days and was not impressed by the city or by its inhabitants. He did observe that the women were 'of surpassing beauty' and that there was plenty of mutton to be had![15] His account also makes it clear that the city had close commercial and cultural relations with both the Maghrib, to which it was linked via Taghaza and Sijilmasa, and Egypt, via the eastern Hoggar route. During the 8/14 century Walata was part of the Malian empire but with the decline of Mali the Touregs took over. During the first half of the 9/15 century Timbuktu largely superceded Walata and Toureg traders and scholars, migrating from Walata to Timbuktu, helped to establish the community of the Sanhaja *ᶜulamā'* in that city. Sonni ᶜAlī's persecution of the Timbuktu Sanhaja drove many of them back to Walata and under the *askiyas* Walata shared with Timbuktu in a period of prosperity.

The importance of Walata lies in the fact that it was an early centre of Berber Islam, that is, it belonged to the Almoravid Sanhaja tradition. It had close links with both North Africa and Egypt and from it Islam spread eastward and southward along the trade routes, and into the savanna and the central Sudan.

Timbuktu

Timbuktu began as a late 5/11-century Toureg encampment, serving the caravan trade. From this small beginning it grew into a great city that gradually assumed a position of commercial and intellectual dominance in the western Sudan. It was mentioned by Ibn Baṭṭūṭa in 754/1353, at which time it was part of the empire of Mali. He describes it as inhabited mainly by Masufa Berbers, wearers of the mouth veil, which suggests it was by then already dominated by the Sanhaja rather than by Sūdānī Muslims.

The position of Timbuktu, on the north bank of the Niger river at the apex of the Bend, gave it a commanding position over the land routes out of the Bend and also over the important water route to the south. It was largely for this reason that it began to overtake Walata as an increasingly prosperous commercial centre. As the Berber scholars of Walata joined those of Timbuktu, there grew up there a Sanhaja, that is a Berber, Znaga-speaking Muslim community centred around the Sankore mosque. This mosque had been founded in the city late in the 8/14 century (AH 799 = AD 1396). Under the guidance of the Sanhaja community it developed into an important centre of Islamic learning that has sometimes been referred to as a university. The medieval usage of that term, meaning a collection of scholars and students living in a single community for the common purpose of religious teaching and learning, correctly describes Timbuktu at that time. From it Islamic scholarship spread far out into the Sahara and the western Sudan.

The earliest intellectual influences that made their mark on the scholarly community of Timbuktu came from Marinid Morocco, including, no doubt, many Sufi ideas and teachings. Later, during the 10/16 century, Egyptian influences took over and scholarship in Timbuktu centred more and more around Sankore. Indeed, it seems likely that this institution was deliberately organised after the model of the Azhar in Cairo. The Egyptian connection was important in enabling the Sūdānī *ᶜulamā'* to break away from the rather narrow North African Malikism and familiarise themselves with the wider theological and intellectual attitudes of Egyptian Islam. At its height the scholars of Sankore were known far beyond the limits of the Sudan. Timbuktu *ijāzāt* (sing. *ijāza*), that is academic pedigrees linking the student to his teachers, were highly regarded in North Africa and Egypt as well as in the Sudan.

The Moroccan invasion damaged the intellectual life of Timbuktu and temporarily disrupted its trade. However, as will be explained in a subsequent chapter, others picked up the tradition of learning where the *ᶜulamā'* of Timbuktu were, for the time being, forced to leave it. In Timbuktu itself at least some degree of recovery subsequently took place.

Takedda

This town of Masufa Berbers was a copper-mining centre south-east of Tadmakkat, five kilometres from the present Tegidda-n-tesemt. It was visited by Ibn Baṭṭūta in 754/1353. He describes the life of its inhabitants as follows:

> The inhabitants of Takedda have no occupation except trade. They travel to Egypt every year, and import quantities of all the fine fabrics to be had there and of other Egyptian wares. They live in luxury and ease, and vie with one another in regard to the number of their slaves and serving-women. . . . The copper mine is in the outskirts of Takedda. They dig the ore out of the ground, bring it to the town, and cast it in their houses. This work is done by their male and female slaves. When they obtain the red copper, they make it into bars a span and a half in length, some thin and others thick. The thick bars are sold at the rate of four hundred for a *mithqāl* of gold, and the thin at the rate of six or seven hundred to the *mithqāl*. . . . The copper is exported from Tekedda to the town of Kūbar (Gobir), in the region of the heathens, to Zaghay (Wadai?) and to the country of Bornu, which is forty days journey from Takedda.[16]

It is clear from this account that the inhabitants of Takedda lived by exporting copper to Hausaland, Kanem and elsewhere; and that they used their profits to import luxury goods from Egypt. In Ibn Baṭṭūṭa's time the town was clearly prosperous. Also from that time until it began to decline during the 9/15 century, it was a centre of learning as well as trade. Al-Maghīlī stayed there and taught for a time. Moreover the *ᶜulamā'* of Takedda are said to have been especially influenced by the ideas of al-Suyūṭī, with which they were familiar because of their close ties with Egypt. Its copper trade with the Hausa-speaking kingdoms to the south, especially Gobir, must have contributed to spreading Islamic ideas into that region.

It is uncertain why Takedda declined; perhaps its copper workings became exhausted or it simply gave way in importance to the neighbouring sultanate of Agades. Today nothing remains of Takedda but its ruins.

Agades

Agades is situated south of the Ahir massif, an area that was a centre for the Touregs as early as the 5/11 century. There was a sultanate of Ahir in existence in the 8/14 century, probably in Assodé. However, it is said that the sultans were not Touregs but Negroes, appointed to ensure impartiality towards the various Toureg tribes in the area. Another reason for the setting up of the sultanate was to protect the new caravan route that had been opened to carry the growing traffic to Egypt that developed in this century. The town of Agades is said to have been founded *c.* 815/1413. From *c.* 865/1460 it came to function increasingly as the capital of this sultanate. It was populated by Touregs, intermarrying with people who, probably, had originally been Hausa-speaking and who had been the former masters of the area. Later, however, under Songhay influence, many of them became Songhay speakers. As will be seen in chapter 4 some of the early Hausa-speakers may have been associated with the emergence of Gobir as one of the Hausa states.

Agades quickly became a meeting-point for the caravan trade between Hausaland and Borno, and a meeting-place for caravans plying the routes that linked Gao, Tripoli and Egypt. Thus it must have been in increasingly close contact with Egypt from 815/1413 on, and so became a centre for ideas as well as trade. Muḥammad Ṣaṭṭafan, sultan of Agades from 892/1487 to *c.* 900/1494, was one of those Sūdānī rulers with whom al-Suyūṭī corresponded. Al-Maghīlī visited Ahir, and therefore almost certainly Agades, in the late 9 or early 10 century AH, 15 century AD. Like neighbouring Takedda, Agades was not only a caravan market but also a centre for Islamic scholarship. As Takedda declined, Agades grew in importance, as regards both trade and intellectual activity. In particular, it became the gateway for the entry of Sufi mysticism from Egypt into the western Sudan, especially Hausaland. The importance of the Sufi development that took place in Agades will be discussed below, in chapters 8 and 13.

NOTES

1 The passage from al-Fazāri referred to here, and passages from other medieval Arabic writers referred to in this chapter, will be found in Cuoq, 1975, unless otherwise indicated. Since they can be easily traced in Cuoq, it has not seemed necessary to annotate each one individually.

2 Cuoq omits this passage from Ibn Ḥawqal. See Norris, 1975, p.12; also Lewicki, 1969, p.44.

3 I am indebted to Dr Humphrey Fisher for the opportunity to peruse the draft article 'The Almoravid conquest of Ghana in 1076. Part I: the external Arabic sources', at present being prepared by him together with David Conrad and Lamin Sanneh. It is to their conclusions that I refer.

4 Fisher, draft article.

5 Innes, 1974, pp.229–31.

6 Braudel, I, p.467.

7 H.A.R. Gibb, *Ibn Battúta*, 1963, p.330.
8 P.F. de Moreas Farias, 1974, p. 483.
9 A.D.H. Bivar, article *Encyclopaedia of Islam* new edition.
10 CHA, 1977, 3, p.428.
11 Humphrey J. Fisher, 'Leo Africanus and the Songhay conquest of Hausaland', forthcoming in *IJAHS*.
12 *BSOAS*, XXV, 3, 1962, p.584.
13 ibid, p.585.
14 ibid, p.584.
15 Gibb, p.320.
16 Gibb, p.335–6. In the opinion of some scholars the name Wadai did not come into use until early in the 11/17 century and is said to have been derived from the family name of 'Abd al-Karīm, who overthrew the Tunjur dynasty and founded the Islamic Sultanate at that time. However, Ibn Baṭṭūṭa's mention of Zaghay seems to me suggestive of the contrary; and I am in any case uneasy about the feasibility of the derivation of this name from Arabic Wadāʿī, or something of the sort. It seems to me inherently unlikely that the names of whole areas, as opposed simply to towns, can be created out of thin air at the whim of individual conquerors in this way. However, since there is obviously some doubt about the matter, I have placed Wadai in brackets on map 5.

CHAPTER THREE

Teachers and messengers of Islam

The last chapter discussed the ways in which the empires and cities of the medieval Sahara and Sudan contributed to the spread of Islam. However it was their people who in the end determined the way in which events developed.

These people were of several different racial origins. There were those of Berber stock, who had inhabited the Sahara from ancient times, there were Africans from the Atlantic coast, the Sahel and the savanna, and there were nomadic Arabs who had drifted into the Sahara from the Nile valley and North Africa over the course of many centuries. Finally, there were groups formed by intermarriage between the above, especially between Arabs and Berbers.

As a result of their contact with Islam, literate clerical and religious classes grew up within all these different Saharan, Sahelian and savanna groups, some of whom had strong trading interests as well. Their part in the spreading of Islam was especially important. The purpose of this chapter is to describe the contribution they made.

To some extent, certainly, it is artificial to split them up into tribal or other groups. They were all Muslims, sharing a common culture. For this reason their social institutions and their ways of life were very similar as were the ways in which they operated to spread Islam. However they themselves regarded themselves as distinct groups. This is shown by the pride and tenacity with which they preserved their several traditions of origin. Even if their contributions to Islam did not differ in essentials, they certainly did in emphases. Therefore, while it is well to remember what united them, it is sensible to treat them one by one.

The post-Almoravid Sanhaja

After their assumption of power in Ghana – whether by conquest or by other means – and the death of Abū Bakr, the southern Almoravids gradually lost their military and political superiority over the non-Muslim Negroes. However they did not lose their Islamic ardour. As they abandoned the sword, they began to take up the scholar's pen and to mount the preacher's pulpit, in order to spread their powerful but simple ideas as to how Islam ought to be practised. These second and third generation Almoravids, who were widely known by their Berber name, Sanhaja, now became wandering preachers, moving up and down the caravan routes from Sijilmasa to Ghana and fanning out into the western Sahara. From Shinqīṭ, from Sijilmasa and from Walata, they spread their teaching to the Niger region and from there into the grasslands of the western and central Sudan even as far west as the coastal kingdoms of the Senegambia. As has been shown in chapter 2, their migration from Walata to Timbuktu contributed much to the intellectual supremacy of that city, which they dominated from *c*. 905/1500. Sanhaja scholars were also influential in Tadmakkat and in Takedda from *c*. 699/1300 on. It was they who welcomed al-Maghīlī to the latter city and embraced his ideas. On the decline of Takedda, many of them moved to Agades. From here some moved out into more remote desert centres from which they worked as mystics and teachers. During the 9/15 century they took the Qādirī *wird*, ritual, from North African sources and were among the first to diffuse the teachings of that *ṭarīqa* in the Sahara and the central Sudan.

During their wanderings in the Sahara, the Sanhaja became associated, through marriage and in other ways, with the Ḥassāniyya Arabs. These were a nomadic Muslim Arab people who pastured their flocks in the western Sahara. In consequence, the Sanhaja gradually lost their separate identity and became drawn into the wider group of the Ineslemen/Zwāya described below. None the less, there were still people claiming the title 'Sanhaja' in Ahir during the 13/19 century. In the period after the fall of Songhay, however, the Sanhaja, as a distinct class, were increasingly replaced by other groups who possessed greater cohesion.

The Dyula/Wangarawa

The Dyulas are people of Mande origin, originally associated with the Mali empire. They include several broad occupational categories such as traders, farmers, warriors and rulers of clans. The Dyula traders probably acquired Islam earlier than the non-trading classes and then spread it along the caravan routes and in the cities in the course of their work. However they were not only traders. Many became Muslim literates and turned to the profession of Islamic scholarship, that is, they became travelling, Mande-speaking *ᶜulamā'*. Most continued to trade as well as following their clerical profession.

Among the best-known of the Dyula group is the Saghanughu clan. This Mande clan had a very early association with Islam. There is reason to believe that its members were associated with the Ibāḍiyya sect even before the days of the Almoravid conquests. Later, as a result of those conquests, they embraced the Mālikī *madhhab* and became the main carriers of the Sunna, the 'Way', or 'Tradition' of the Prophet, into the Volta region. Saghanughu names among the Malian *ᶜulamā'* of the 9/15 and 10/16 centuries onwards show clearly that the Saghanughu occupied important positions as teachers and leaders of Islamic thought. They are still important at the present day.

The Dyulas did not stop in Mali and the Volta lands, however. These energetic and enterprising Muslims undertook what has been called a 'commercial diaspora', a spreading out from the home country, to set up settlements in other lands, far and wide. The Dyula diaspora took place mainly eastward, into the central Sudan, and southward, into the savanna fringe lands. As it got under way the Dyulas began to acquire an alternative name – Wangarawa. The origin of this word is something of a puzzle. In the form Wangara or Ungara it seems to have applied in the first instance to the people of Galam, Bambuk and Bure, in the area between the upper Senegal and Niger rivers and it is used by the medieval Arabic geographers as a blanket term for gold traders. The form Wangarawa appears to have acquired the Hausa plural suffix *-awa*, normally applied to nouns of origin and profession. It may be that this apparently Hausa form came into general use from the 8/14 century on, when Dyula/Wangarawa began to reach Kano and other parts of Hausaland. Waves of these Dyula/Wangarawa may have reached Kano as early as *c.* 786/1385 while others reached Katsina between 856/1452 and 867/1463. Yet others arrived in Kano *c.* 895/1490 led, so tradition says, by a certain Shaykh ᶜAbd al-Raḥmān Zagaiti. According to one account, Dyula/Wangarawa associated with this semi-legendary personality reached Gobir and Kebbi as well as Kano and Katsina. By this time most of the Dyula/Wangarawa were no longer citizens of Mali but of the Songhay empire and many even became Songhay speakers. This second, Songhay phase of their expansion lasted until *c.* 999/1590–1, that is until the fall of the Songhay empire. This and the commercial difficulties it created, moved them on again, south-east, into Borgu. Here some Mande influence had already been established even before 906/1500. They moved on into the Hausa states and in Borgu especially, they became the main link in the trade from Borno and Hausaland to the Volta region, the 'Gonja' of Hausa folkloric tradition. Gradually, the Wangarawa became absorbed into the peoples among whom they settled but even to this day the descendants of the early Wangarawa in Kano have preserved the memory of their own distinct identity.

Obviously, the Dyula/Wangarawa contributed greatly to the economic development of the west and central Sudan. Intellectually, they made two main contributions. First, they helped to spread the Mālikī *madhhab* but in this they were not unique. For, apart from the early Saghanughu connection with the Ibāḍiyya, all the Saharan and Sūdānī learned classes were Mālikī. No other legal rite established a significant presence in West Africa after the Ibāḍiyya faded, but the Dyula/Wangarawa part in introducing the Mālikī *madhhab* was certainly one of the most important. Second, they spread a very early form of Sufi mysticism that may have been Qādirī. More probably, however, it was a form of Sufism current in North Africa in the 7/13 century, before the *ṭuruq* had fully emerged. In particular the Saghanughu, with their pre-Almoravid Islamic tradition, seem to have been the main exponents of this early Sufism. It was characterised by the belief that man could achieve *fanā'*, 'absorption', directly in God through the Angels. Later on, as will be seen below, most Sufis abandoned this idea and taught that *fanā'* was only possible in and through the Prophet Muḥammad, as *al-Insān al-kāmil*, the 'Perfect Man' or *Afḍal al-khalq*, the 'Most Excellent of Creation'.

Often associated with the Dyula/Wangarawa is a group known as the Jakhanke. In their role as spreaders and teachers of Islam they are indeed similar. However, the most recent and best-informed authority on them, Dr Lamin Sanneh, believes that they have never been primarily traders but rather migrating farmers. He holds, moreover, that they were originally Sarakole, not Mande-speakers.[1] His view has been challenged,[2] but none the less, it seems to be based on full and firm evidence. The Shaykh ᶜAbd al-Raḥmān Zagaiti, mentioned above as the leader of the Wangarawa who came to Kano probably *c.* 895/1490, appears to have been a Jakhanke. Perhaps he was the leader of a party of Jakhanke who arrived at about the same time as the Wangarawa, so that Kano people gave them all the same name. Or perhaps the party was in reality a mixed one, of Wangarawa, Jakhanke and perhaps others as well. What is certain is that tradition insists he came and brought Islamic learning with him.

The Ineslemen/Zwāya

Ineslemen is a Berber word derived from one of the forms arising from the Arabic root S.L.M., which gives the word 'Islam'. It describes the Muslim lettered class among Berber-speaking Touregs and distinguishes them from other Toureg classes, such as the Imajaghen, the warrior class. There are a number of groups that call themselves Ineslemen: for instance the Kel Aghlal, the Ishsherifen, the Kel Takarannet, the Ifoghas and the Kel-Es-Suq.

The word Zwāya comes from the Ḥassāniyya Arabic dialect and is derived from the classical Arabic *zāwiya*, a Sufi seminary. Its meaning is almost identical with Ineslemen, in that it describes the religious class among the speakers of Ḥassāniyya Arabic. The speakers of Ḥassāniyya were predominantly members of the Banū Maᶜqil, of Yemenite origin, who for centuries had mixed with the Sanhaja and dominated them. They had moved south from the Darᶜa and Sūs and controlled such towns as Wādān and Tīshīt. They spread into the Ḥawḍ around Walata and the area of the modern Mauritanian and Mali border. Some intermarried with the Touregs although the two peoples tended to remain distinct and generally hostile to each other. Among those who call themselves Zwāya are the Banū Daymān, the Idaw al-Ḥajj, the Kunta, the Shamasīd Ahl Barikallah and the Kel Intasar. The word Zwāya is surely associated with the early spread of Sufism in the Sahara, although there is no evidence that Sufism is stronger among those who call themselves Zwāya than it is among those who call themselves Ineslemen.

It is not possible to deal with the history of all the Ineslemen/Zwāya groups here. The following are considered in some detail because they are typical of their class; and because their contribution to the spread of Islam was especially important.

The Kel-Es-Suq:

Some Kel-Es-Suq claim descent from Maghribī *shurafā'*, others from Lamtuna Sanhaja and yet others from Companions of a certain ᶜUqba b. ᶜĀmir, the Yemenite, not ᶜUqba b. Nāfiᶜ, the conqueror of North Africa.

Up to *c*. 874/1470, they were centred in the Saharan city of Tadmakkat and were the religious class of the Touregs there. Contrary to what has sometimes been supposed, that they belonged to no Sufi *ṭarīqa*, they are now known to have adopted the Qādiriyya from North Africa while in Tadmakkat. They also became specialists in Mālikī law, Arabic rhetoric and calligraphy. *C*. 874/1470 they dispersed out of Tadmakkat, probably as a result of Sonni ᶜAlī's hostility, and migrated across the Sahara and the Sahel. Sahel means 'coast' in Arabic; it refers to the strip of country, stretching right across the Sudan, where the true desert merges into the grassy savanna. By *c*. 1008/1600 they had set up centres of Toureg scholarship in the Azawād, in the south-western Sahara. There were also Kel-Es-Suq in Agades by 885/1480 and it may have been from these Kel-Es-Suq that the Qādiriyya first reached Kano, in Hausaland.

Two aspects of Kel-Es-Suq Islam are especially important. First, they refused to participate in *jihād* of the sword. *C*. 898/1493, a Kel-Es-Suq scholar called Muḥammad b. Muḥammad b. ᶜAlī enquired of the Egyptian *ᶜālim*, al-Suyūṭī, about the status of him who dies as a martyr in Holy War. It was then that the master replied, 'He who does not fight is more exalted'.[3] Resting on this dictum the Kel-Es-Suq argued that fighting was the job of Imajaghen, the

Toureg warrior class, whom they despised, or of *amīrs*. This is not to say that these 9/15-century Saharan Muslims had adopted pacifism as an ideology, as it is understood by present-day pacifists. To imagine this would involve a serious distortion of the reality. It means simply that with their knowledge of Islamic law and Islamic mysticism, they achieved their greatest influence within Saharan society by acting as mediators. They settled the constant quarrels over land, grazing and water that cropped up among the Saharan people, 'by the Book' and not by the sword. Their knowledge of the Law enabled them to assess these tangled problems and their mysticism gave them insight into how God would have them resolved. Their role was certainly a humane and civilizing one and its function was to distinguish them occupationally from the warrior class, not to strike a moral attitude. The Kel-Es-Suq, like other Muslim religious classes, could fight well enough when they had to, and they sometimes did.

The Kel-Es-Suq pursued their mediation both in nomadic and in settled situations, such as those of Tadmakkat and the Agades sultanate. They thus did valuable work in applying the Sharīᶜa to a variety of different Saharan problems.

The second aspect of the work of the Kel-Es-Suq concerns the development of Sufism. *C.* 949/1542, a certain Sīdī Maḥmūd al-Baghdādī arrived in Agades from Egypt. He was a Sufi mystic who was associated both with the Persian *ṭarīqa* known as the Suhrawardiyya and with the new Khalwatiyya, that was strong in Egypt and the Ottoman empire at that time.[4] Both these *ṭuruq* were highly mystical and laid great stress on miracle-working. Sīdī Maḥmūd al-Baghdādī's teachings were accepted by certain Ineslemen of the Kel-Es-Suq, as well as by other Ineslemen. They thus opened up a second channel of Sufi influence in the western Sudan, that from Egypt, that was independent of the older Qādirī link with North Africa. More will be said about the importance of Sīdī Maḥmūd al-Baghdādī and his ideas in chapter 13.

The Kel Intasar and the Ineslemen/Zwāya revival:

The Kel Intasar are another important Saharan religious group. As their name implies, they claim descent from the *Anṣār*, the Medinan 'Helpers' of the Prophet Muḥammad. They are part Toureg and part Ḥassāniyya Arab, from Mauritania in the western Sahara. Many of them speak the Ḥassāniyya Arabic dialect as well as a Berber tongue. They thus often refer to themselves as Zwāya.

The Kel Intasar have close links, through marriage and genealogy, with the Kel-Es-Suq. They were active in the Niger Bend by *c.* 750/1350, and probably earlier. Like the Kel-Es-Suq, they were originally pacifist mediators and were forbidden by their constitution to carry arms.

During the first half of the 11/17 century, however, an Islamic revivalist movement took place in the Arawān. It was led by two scholars, Muḥammad Quṭb al-Anṣārī of the Kel Intasar (d. *c.* 1060/1650) and Aḥmad b. Addah al-Sūqī, of the Kel-Es-Suq. This revival was probably started off by the opening up of salt-mining at Taodeni. This replaced the salt industry at Taghaza, closed down in the second half of the 10/16 century, partly because the mines were almost exhausted and partly because of Moroccan interference. The new industry gave rise to a general increase in activity in the area, that attracted scholars. The enterprise of these two *shaykhs* and their followers caused them to clash with the Kunta, also active in the Arawān. This coincided with a more general rise in Ineslemen/Zwāya militancy that seems to have come about as a result of resentment against the Imajaghen. Some Ineslemen/Zwāya at this time also began to entertain ideas of Tuareg empire, based on Islamic egalitarianism and opposed both to the Imajaghen and to the Agades sultanate. This militancy resulted in a so-called *jihād* against the Sultan of Agades between 1049–61/1640–50, led by Ḥadāḥadā, an Ineslemen of obscure origin. It had no decisive result. From this time on there was a distinct shift by the Ineslemen/Zwāya groups away from their earlier pacific role, towards more vigorous, activist and aggressive attitudes associated with Islamic reform and even *jihād*.

It is important to note that there were groups of Ineslemen/Zwāya settled in the area of Gobir and Zamfara at least by 1163/1750, if not earlier. They surely contributed to the reforming zeal of the Muslim Fulani in that area, to whom they were linked by marriage and common interest.

It is also important that Mahdist ideas had become widely accepted among the Ineslemen/Zwāya during the 12/18 century. These ideas that the world of time is about to end and that before that divine event the Mahdī, the Islamic Deliverer, will appear to impose true Islam and reign in justice over all mankind, must have coloured the views of Islamic reformers as they gradually built up their presence in Hausaland.

The Kunta:

The Kunta are a family group of Saharan Arabs who married on the male, but not normally the female, side, with the Sanhaja. They usually term themselves Zwāya. As merchants and scholars, they were wealthy and pious. From the 9/15 century on, their devotion to Islam, to say nothing of their search for honest profit, carried them from the shores of the Atlantic to the Niger Bend and on as far east as Borno.

It is said that their ancestors first left Ifrīqiya, the eastern half of North Africa, as a result of the troubles there of the Fatimid period and that they eventually settled in Tuwāt. This is said to have happened *c.* 789/1387, although the family's traditions concerning the chronology of their movements at this early period are somewhat confused. Whenever it took place, the move was the first episode in the family's southward penetration into the Sahara.

C. 802/1400 a certain Sīdī ᶜAlī al-Kuntī emerged as a *quṭb*, 'Axis' or 'Pole' of the Q̱ādiriyya order of Sufis. He also began what then became the standard practice among the Kuntī *shaykhs*. This was the undertaking of *siyāḥa*, extended touring in the Sahara for the purpose of preaching and trade. Sīdī ᶜAlī's son, Sīdī Muḥammad al-Kuntī also a Q̱ādirī *quṭb*, led the family out of Tuwāt on the next stage of their migration into the Sahara in about 853/1450. This Sīdī Muḥammad lived at a time when there was considerable rivalry between the Berber Lamtuna and the Ḥassāniyya Arabs for supremacy in the western Sahara. At one point this broke out into open warfare and Sīdī Muḥammad allied himself with the Ḥassanids in an attack on the Lamtuna. As a result of this the Ḥassanids became dominant. With their support Sīdī Muḥammad then laid the foundations for Kunta pre-eminence in the western Sahara, although he also earned the enmity of the Lamtuna.

Sīdī Muḥammad's son was Sīdī Aḥmad al-Bakkā'ī, Aḥmad the Weeper', so named because of his God-fearing habit of weeping for the sins of men. Sīdī

Aḥmad is said to have reached the highest level of Sufi knowledge, and he claimed to be *al-Quṭb al-Kāmil*, 'the Perfect Axis'. He settled in Walata during the second half of the 9/15 century. Here he trained Sufi disciples, and undertook long preaching expeditions into the desert where he converted many desert-dwellers to Islam. He quickly gained the reputation of a great *walī*, a Sufi holy man with the power to work miracles. One story tells how the people of Walata were terrorised by lions and other wild animals that roamed the surrounding countryside. Sīdī Aḥmad was able to go unharmed among them and by his prayers he persuaded them to leave the neighbourhood of Walata. Thus people were able to walk abroad again without fear. So impressed were they with the *walī*'s miracles that they persuaded him, much against his will for he loved the desert, to settle in their city. He died there in 920/1514–15. That is the story. It must be added that the country around Walata is not at the present day the habitat either of lions or of other wild creatures that are likely to be dangerous to man. However there is good reason to believe that, during the 9/15 and 10/16 centuries, wild beasts were both more numerous and more ready to attack humans than they usually are today in Europe and North Africa. The advance of man's civilization has now reduced their numbers and rendered them more timid. The same may be true of the Sahara and it is therefore not impossible that Sīdī Aḥmad may have possessed some unusual powers that enabled him to control these creatures. Perhaps the same sort of powers that the Christian saint of the 12–13 century AD, Saint Francis of Assissi, is reputed to have possessed.

Many individuals and groups, over many generations, contributed to establishing the Qādiriyya *ṭarīqa* in the Sahara and spreading it from there into the Sudan. It would be easy to attribute too much to any single individual, but Sīdī Aḥmad al-Bakkā'ī's contribution was one of the most important.

Sīdī Aḥmad had a number of sons but a quarrel broke out between two of them which is said to have caused the Kunta to split into two groups. These became known as 'Kunta of the west' in and around the Ḥawḍ, in what is today southern Mauritania and the 'Kunta of the east', in and around the Azawād, that area of the Sahara immediately south-west of Tadmakkat. The Kunta of the east emerged not only as pious Sufis but also as a trading family. Their caravans toured the Sahara and the Niger Bend as well as the Sudanic centres of Katsina, Gobir, Dendi, and as far east as Borno. Stories abound of the miracles performed by Kunti *shaykhs* in the course of these trading journeys. These stories certainly helped their business ventures and they prospered greatly. In 1133/1720–1 they founded the trading town of Mabrūk, in the Azawād. From here they sent out teachers to spread the Qādiriyya among the Touregs and other Saharan groups. These activities reached a peak under the leadership of Sīdī al-Mukhtār al-Kabīr al-Kuntī.

Sīdī al-Mukhtār al-Kabīr was born in 1142/1729. He was greatly gifted intellectually and grew up to be an outstanding scholar and mystic. When only 25 years old, he was given the title *Shaykh al-ṭarīqat al-qādiriyya*, Shaykh of the Qādirī order'. The holder of this office had to possess Sufi learning, extreme piety and the power to perform *karāma*, miracles. Indeed, he needed to be in all ways an exemplary *walī*, a person raised to a state of *qurba*, special nearness to God. Sīdī al-Mukhtār had these qualities. His fame and influence extended from southern Morocco, across the Sahel, and east into Borno. No doubt it also reached Hausaland, where it must have mingled with other more direct Sufi influences to help formulate the attitudes of the Muslim reformers there.

Sīdī al-Mukhtār al-Kabīr lived at a time when Sufism had reached a point of great complexity. It had developed an elaborate theory of *wilāya*, the state of being a *walī*; of the nature of *qurba*, 'nearness' the essential quality of the *walī*; of *baraka*, the spiritual power that a *walī* can pass on to those associated with him; of *kashf*, the power to draw aside the veils that hide *al-ḥaqā'iq*, the Divine Truths; and of the way of the *sālik*, the 'traveller' along the mystic path. Moreover, by his day the Sufi hierarchy had become elaborate. *Awliyā'* were divided into grades: *al-Aqṭāb* (sing. *quṭb*), the 'Poles' or 'Axes'; *al-Awtād*, the 'Supports'; *al-Abdāl*, the 'Substitutes'; *al-Nuqabā'*, those learned in the divine secrets; *al-Nujabā'*, those gifted with *kashf*. Above them all was the *Quṭb*, the Axis, or sometimes *Ghawth*, 'Succour' of the age, with special powers to intercede with God on behalf of his followers. These mysteries Shaykh Sīdī al-Mukhtār understood and he explained them in his writings and his teaching. He thus helped to lay the foundations for that blossoming of Sufi learning that was such a feature of the Islamic literature of the western Sudan, especially that of the Muslim Hausas, from 1214/1800 on.[5]

Shaykh al-Mukhtār al-Kabir died in 1226/1811, a few years before his contemporary, Shehu Usumanu ɗan Fodio, with whom he was at one time briefly associated.

The Kunta were often in conflict with other Saharan groups, especially the Kel Intasar. Their quarrelling sometimes broke down into open warfare. Yet, like the Kel-Es-Suq, they were usually pacifist and were opposed to *jihād* as a means of conversion. No doubt this had something to do with their trading interests for war and trade do not usually go well together. Also, like other Ineslemen/Zwāya, their reputation as scholars and mystics made them especially acceptable as mediators. There is no doubt that, whenever possible, they preferred to be peace-makers rather than warriors.

The main contribution of the Kunta to the spread of Islam lay in their spreading of more advanced and systematised Sufi ideas; and in developing the structure of rank within the Qādiriyya *ṭarīqa*. They also drew a number of minor Qādirī groups together within their organisation, thus giving greater unity to the *ṭariqa*. However theirs was an elitist form of Sufism – the Sufism of learned *shaykhs*, not of the common people. This elitism persisted in the Qādiriyya. It helped to provoke the rise of the populist Tijāniyya *ṭarīqa* from *c.* 1247/1831, for this new *ṭarīqa* was to some extent a reaction against Qādirī exclusiveness.

The Muslim Fulani

The Fulani are a nomadic, cattle-raising people of Negro origin, springing from the Halpular of the middle Senegal valley. Their language, Fulfulde, is related to that of the Wolofs. At some time before 390/1000, they were caught up in the formation of the Sudanic state of Takrūr, but the spread of the towns and cities pushed some of them out and they began to migrate into the savanna. On the way they came into contact with Berber pastoralists, moving south from the Sahara, and they intermarried with them. It may be that some of them thus acquired a lighter skin colour than that of the more settled groups to which they are related. This is by no means certain, for there is no biological evidence that racial mixing invariably produces generalised and uniform modifications in skin colour. It obviouslyaffects skin colour to some extent but the pattern seems to be a random one. Some offspring of mixed unions have light pigmentation, while others have a darker colouring. It would be hasty to assume that those Fulani who are light in colour owe this to intermarriage with Berbers, or with any other group for that matter.

During the 8/14 century one wave of these migrants formed the Fulani communities of Masina; another reached Futa Jalon, in the Mali empire. Early in the 10/16 century a Fulani kingdom had been founded in Futa Toro, which lies astride the river Senegal.

The Fulani had originally followed an African polytheist religion. Some still do but individuals adopted Islam at an unknown date, probably as a result of their contacts with the Mali empire. A group of these Muslim Fulani then emerged, known as Torodbe, in Hausa Toronkawa. They became a literate, clerical Muslim class, still partly nomadic but no longer cattle-rearing and devoted to the profession of Islamic scholarship.

One authority, Professor John Willis, has argued, in an extremely interesting and scholarly article, that these Torodbe/Toronkawa were originally a 'mass of rootless people who perceived in Islam a source of cultural identity. Bound in a new persuasion – linked by a common oppression – they shook the sense of ethnic difference and sought to stimulate a countertrend of a levelling nature'.[6] He then goes on to argue that they were originally slaves, or at least clients, of the true nomadic, cattle-rearing Fulani and that they were not necessarily of the same blood origin as the cattle-rearers. They adopted Islam in order to differentiate themselves from their polytheist masters. Professor Willis believes that their servile origin is attested by their folklore and that of others associated with them. He attaches significance to the fact that they are known to have been beggars at one point in their history and believes that other submerged groups then joined them, making up the Torodbe/Toronkawa. This then became the name for a class distinguished not by blood but by the profession of Islam. He argues, further, that it was specifically the Torodbe/Toronkawa and not just Muslim Fulani, who were responsible for the Islamic reform movement and *jihāds* that took place from *c.* 1101/1690 in the Senegambia to the 13/19 century in Hausaland and the Niger Bend. Moreover this ought to be recognised by referring to 'Torodbe/Toronkawa' and not just to 'Muslim Fulani' when discussing the leadership of the *jihāds*.

This theory is often persuasive but it is possible to object to it on several grounds. First, it is by no means clear who were the original masters of the allegedly servile Torodbe/Toronkawa or how they came to be freed from these masters. It is not clear who they were or where they came from before they became enslaved except, perhaps, that they were individuals from a number of different bloodlines who only had in common the fact that they were enslaved by certain masters. This is not impossible but it cannot, in my opinion, be accepted without firmer evidence.

Second, the Torodbe/Toronkawa certainly behave as if they are Fulani and have been so for many, many generations. Indeed, until *c.* 1266/1850 most of them spoke Fulfulde as their mother tongue. They also adhered closely to Fulani culture patterns.[7]

A further objection has to do with the link Professor Willis proposes between the fact that they once begged and their allegedly servile origin. It is common throughout much of the Islamic world for Koran-school students, and other pious persons, to beg. Despite certain Prophetic traditions condemning begging, it is not, in practice, usually considered by other Muslims to be shameful and it is certainly not the mark of a slave. Thus, in my opinion, folkloric stories concerning an early period when the Torodbe/Toronkawa were beggars have no significance, one way or the other, when considering the question of their origin. These stories are just as likely to have arisen to support their reputation for piety. As for those stories that mock them as slaves and beggars, these bear the marks of a non-Muslim origin and therefore prove nothing except the hostility of adherents of the traditional cult toward Muslims.

Undoubtedly the Torodbe/Toronkawa were prominent in the reform movement and *jihāds* mentioned above, but so too were Muslim Fulani from other groups, as well as certain non-Fulani people. Thus it still seems preferable to go on speaking of 'the Muslim Fulani' rather than to refer to all of the reformers and jihadists from the Senegambia, through Hausaland, to Masina and Segu, as Torodbe/Toronkawa.

However, there are two points concerning which I believe Professor Willis to be right in this well-argued and important thesis. The first is when he points to the way in which the Torodbe/Toronkawa formed a point of attraction for other groups that chose to enter Islam. There is ample evidence in the Senegambia, of Wolofs and certain Mande-speakers joining the ranks of the Torodbe/Toronkawa; although the extent to which they then became absorbed within them or retained their own identity is perhaps more open to question. A similar process of attraction certainly occurred in the Hausa states, where the Torodbe/Toronkawa were a focus around whom reform-minded *ʿulamāʾ* of several different bloodlines gathered.

The second point about which he is surely right is when he stresses the fact that it was their acquiring of literacy that gave the Torodbe/Toronkawa a special status. The crucial nature of literacy in determining the development of Islam in the west and central Sudan is also the central argument of this book. I differ from Professor Willis on this point only in that I believe it to have a much wider reference than to the Torodbe/Toronkawa alone.

One party of Toronkawa, migrating eastward, had reached Birni Konni, in Hausaland, by *c.* 854/1450. Other Muslim Fulani reached Kano in this century. Yet others found their way to Borno and on to the area of what later became the kingdom of Baghirmi, before 906/1500. Meanwhile, in Senegambia, some Muslim Fulani remained behind, living among the Wolof, Serer and others in the area. They were strengthened by waves of Fulani immigrants from the Niger Bend, who joined them from time to time. It was they who in due course, launched the *jihāds* in Senegambia that will be described in chapter 6.

About 1111/1700, certain Toronkawa – the Fodiawa family – moved south from Birni Konni. By *c.* 1167/1754 they had become established in the Haɓe kingdom of Gobir. (Haɓe is the name used to refer to the dynasties of Hausaland from their foundation at an undetermined date, up to their overthrow by Muslim Fulani jihadists early in the 13/19 century). They had as their neighbours certain nomadic Fulani clans, not Toronkawa, who were less deeply influenced by Islam than themselves. Among these clans were the Sullebawa, the Kasarawa and the Alibawa. The Toronkawa maintained close links with these nomadic cattle-rearers and intermarried with them. They themselves did not rear cattle, they lived by the profession of Islamic scholarship, as scribes, teachers, manuscript copiers and by other literate occupations. Occasionally, too, they practised simple crafts, but more as symbols of pious poverty than as a real means of earning a living. They also owned slaves, who kept house for them and may have farmed their land. Thus freed of menial tasks the Toronkawa ᶜ*ulamā'* played a foremost part in the Islamic system of education that developed in Hausaland. Like the Ineslemen/Zwāya, they were ardent Qādirīs who had strong links with the Sufis of Agades. They embraced the doctrines of the Expected Mahdī with enthusiasm and viewed the imperfect mixed Islam of the Haɓe courts with distaste and contempt. With such characteristics and attitudes they stood poised, with the help of certain allies, to launch an Islamic reform movement in Hausaland. By 1187/1774, under the leadership of the Shehu Usumanu ɗan Fodio, that movement was well under way.

The *Shurafā'*

The *shurafā'*, often referred to in books on West African history by the English plural 'Sharifs', differ from the clerical classes described above in that, whereas the latter were wholly or partly indigenous Saharans or West Africans, the former were, in theory at least, of pure Arab origin. The word *sharīf*, an Arabic word meaning 'noble', was used from an early date to describe those who were descended from the Prophet's tribe, Quraysh.

Shurafā' were important in North African history from 184/800 when, after the Khārijī revolt, they established dynasties in the Maghrib and Ifrīqiya. The Fatimids, too, claimed Sharifian descent. Even the invading Banū Hilāl acquired a folkloric link to the *shurafā'*, through their legendary hero and leader, Abū Zayd, who was said to have been a Quraishite. However the most spectacular Sharifian interlude in the history of North Africa was the rise and fall of that dynasty known as the 'Sharīfs in Morocco, from 960/1553 to 1065/1654. This dynasty was sometimes called the Saᶜdids, a term originally used by their enemies as an insult and to deny their claim to Sharifian descent. This family claimed Quraishite origin through the line of the Prophet's daughter, Fāṭima, and his son-in-law, ᶜAlī b. Abī Ṭālib. It came to power through an alliance with Moroccan Sufis, especially those of the Shādhiliyya and the Jazūlī branch of the Qādiriyya. It was to this dynasty that the alleged victor of al-Qaṣr al-Kabīr and conqueror of Songhay, Mawlay Aḥmad al-Manṣūr belonged.

Individual *shurafā'*, or persons claiming to be *shurafā'*, from North Africa, quickly established themselves in the Sahara and the west and central Sudan once Islam began to penetrate there. The North African ᶜ*ālim*, al-Maghīlī, was regarded as a *sharīf*, as were the followers that he left behind in Kano. *Shurafā'* are said to have been present in Gobir, before the *jihād* in Hausaland that began in 1219/1804 (see chapter 8).

It was perhaps in the central Sudan, rather than in the west, that *shurafā'* made their greatest contribution to the spread of Islam. The Fazzan, half-way between Tripoli and Chad, was governed from *c.* 916/1511 until *c.* 1227/1812–13 by another Sharifian dynasty known as the Awlād Muḥammad.

The cities of Murzuk and Zawila, in the Fazzan, were centres where *shurafā'* gathered. Inevitably, Sharifian influences played a considerable part in the development of Islam in Kanem and Borno.

Shurafā' were greatly venerated wherever they went in the Islamic world; nowhere was this more so than in West Africa. Whereas the clerical classes in general acquired their status and reputation through scholarship, the *shurafā'* were felt to possess inherited piety and holiness. They thus became regarded, above all other Muslims, as guardians of the Sunna. It was also believed that their noble descent conferred on them powers of healing, of telling the future, of interpreting dreams and of especially effective prayers (Ar. *duʿā'*), asking God's help for those on behalf of whom they prayed. It was by using these gifts that the *shurafā'* mainly lived, although many of them also engaged in commerce.

While many *shurafā'* were learned, their contribution to the spread of Islam in West Africa was for the most part at the popular level. It was the *shurafā'* who were the most successful manufacturers of Islamic charms, and the most successful practitioners of Islamic divination and medicine. The Islam of the illiterate and semi-literate masses in West Africa was largely formed by contact with the *shurafā'*.

Islamic education in the west and central Sudan

The activities of the several literate religious groups described above could not have been carried on without some framework of organisation within which to work. That framework was the traditional Islamic system of education as it evolved in the special circumstances of the west and central Sudan. These were the vast and often empty areas of desert and savanna where many of the people were nomadic and settled communities widely scattered.

As the towns and cities of the Sahara, the Sahel and the savanna were won over to Islam, so there developed within them elementary schools and institutions of higher learning that followed a certain pattern. Sūdānī Muslims had become familiar with this pattern from their contacts with the surrounding Islamic world of North Africa and Egypt and from experience farther afield on Pilgrimage. It was broadly the same over most of the Islamic world, although of course it varied in detail from place to place. It was a feature of Marinid Morocco, of Mamlūk and Ottoman Egypt and of the two Holy Places of Pilgrimage, Mecca and Medina. The basis of the system was the Koran school, *kuttāb* (plur. *katātīb*) in classical Arabic, *makarantan allo* in Hausa. Here, children learned the Arabic alphabet and then how to recite the Koran. This did not take them very far but it fulfilled the requirements of the great mass of Muslims in the Middle Ages, indeed up to quite recent times, in that it gave them basic literacy. It is worth observing, at this point, that the level of literacy among the masses of the people of the Islamic world during the Middle Ages, and perhaps even up to the establishment of state primary education in European countries, was probably higher than in Christendom.

Above the *katātīb* were the *madāris*, in Hausa *makarantan ilimi*. These were much more advanced institutions where Muslims who intended to take up the professions open to the *ʿulamā* – as scribes, theologians, Muslim magistrates, and so on – did their training. Such disciplines as *tafsīr*, Koran exegesis, that is the interpretation of the Koran; *ḥadīth*, 'Prophetic tradition'; *fiqh*, Islamic law and many more made up higher Islamic learning. Some of these *madāris* were small schools where one *shaykh* taught a few students. Others were much bigger institutions, where many *shaykhs* taught and where students came from far and wide to sit at their feet. The centres of learning that grew up in Timbuktu, for example Sankore, were *madāris*. Similar *madāris*, though not always so large and well-known, developed wherever there were permanently settled Muslim communities of any size. For instance, it is known that there was a well-established *madrasa* in Katsina *c.* 1060/1650. What went on there is described by Shaykh Muḥammad b. al-Ṣabbāgh (d. 1065/1655), who studied and probably taught in it. First he describes learning as a garden and scholars as those who pick its fruits. Then he says,

> Then I have sat as one replete,
> With every science, I have tasted it to the full,
> the Law, Koran exegesis and prophetic tradition,
> Grammar, syntax. . . .
> Philogy [the study of the development of language] and logic. . . .
> The study of grammatical particles and of the
> Names of God. . . .
> Knowledge of Koran recitation,
> . . . .
> The science of rhyme and metre.[8]

Such were the levels of scholarly endeavour to which the ᶜ*ulamā*' of Hausaland had advanced by Ibn al-Ṣabbāgh's day.

However the special conditions of the west and central Sudan – its vast spaces, the fact that many ᶜ*ulamā*' combined trade with learning, the fact that it took many years of a man's life to complete the Pilgrimage and return home – led to the creation of a peripatetic, that is a 'walking' or travelling system of education alongside the settled institutions. As the scholars moved to and fro along the caravan routes for trade or Pilgrimage, so they stopped from time to time and set up schools. Sometimes they would make use of an existing school but at other times they would set up temporary establishments for a year or two, before they moved on. Students, too, were peripatetic. A *shaykh* would acquire a name as an expert in the Law even in just one of its standard texts, such as the *Mukhtaṣar* of al-Khalīl; or perhaps in the classic volume of *ḥadīth* known as the *Ṣaḥīḥ* of al-Bukhārī. Students would travel to him and remain to hear his lectures and explanations until they had mastered the text.

The method of teaching and learning in these institutions was broadly the same throughout the west and central Sudan. The *shaykh*, or *malam*, would usually sit cross-legged on a low couch composed of piled carpets and sheepskins; by his side would be the books and manuscripts he needed immediately for the lesson; above him, in the wall, was a large niche or recess that accommodated the rest of his library; in front of him, on the floor, was a shallow tray of clean sand in which he traced numbers and letters with his finger, much as a modern teacher uses a blackboard. In the cool seasons there was usually also a charcoal brazier burning beside him and near to him there was often a spittoon, a brass bowl or calabash, into which he spat the kolanut that Sūdānīs habitually chew. The students would sit in front of him, in rows, on mats and skins. They too would have their books and manuscripts for the lesson;

and also quill pens and inkpots filled with locally made vegetable ink. With these pens they made notes in the margins of their manuscripts. It is common to find the margins of West African Arabic manuscripts covered in Arabic writing in a different hand from that of the scribe. This usually means that the manuscript has been annotated by a student in a *makarantan ilimi*, from the commentary on the text given by the teacher.

One common teaching technique involved the reading of passages of the Arabic text by the *shaykh*, followed by his explanation and commentary upon it, sometimes in classical Arabic, but often in Hausa, Fulfulde or another West African language. Such commentaries in vernacular languages were normally given in the same form and even in the same words over many generations. They tended to be full of learned Arabic loan-words, Islamic technical terms and Arabic stylistic features and this was probably one important way by which Arabic loans passed into these vernacular languages.

Another common teaching procedure involved the reading of certain passages that puzzled them by individual students. The *shaykh*, having listened to the reading, would then explain the passage while the student made his notes.

There were no set fees for attendance at the *makarantan ilimi* or *madāris*. Each student gave the *shaykh* whatever he could afford, sometimes in cash but often in kind. At the end of his course of study he usually received an *ijāza*, 'academic pedigree' from his *shaykh*, in which the *shaykh* affirmed that the student had received from him the same teaching that he had received from his own teachers. The following *ijāza* was issued for studies in Mālikī law in AD 1955 to a certain al-Ḥājj Yaq^{c}ūb of Wenchi, in Ghana. It was given to him by his *shaykh*, al-Ḥājj Muḥammad al-Bakrī b. Hārūn al-Qāḍī Tarwārī, who received it from al-Zāhid al-Ḥājj Ṣāliḥ, who in turn received it from his father, Muḥammad b. ^{c}Uthmān Tarwārī, who received it from the Imām Sa^{c}īd b. ^{c}Uthmān and so on, through twenty-five generations of Saghanughu *shaykhs* to the Imām Ṣaḥnūn and finally to the Imām Mālik himself, the last name in this impressive chain. The twentieth name in this document is that of the 7/13-century North African scholar, the Imām Aḥmad b. ^{c}Alī al-Būnī, the author of the well-known *Shams al-ma^{c}ārif*, the 'Sun of the Sciences'. One would not go so far as to insist that this *ijāza* and others like it are historically fully accurate beyond the first few generations; but they do furnish a magnificent testimony to the ancient tradition of learning among the Saghanughu people; and it is easy to understand what authority these academic pedigrees carry and what respect they command.

When a student had finished his studies under one *shaykh*, he would move on to another. Many, whether they were teachers or students, were bound ultimately for the Holy Places while others followed roads that began and ended in the Sudan. This peripatetic system linked the more permanent institutions together and supplemented them. It created a wide network of intellectual endeavour that bound Muslims together and constantly pushed the frontiers of Islam farther and farther afield. For wherever it went, it carried the lure and the power of literacy with it; and it drew men into the circle of learning and of faith. In the following passage Shaykh ^{c}Abd Allāh b. Muḥammad describes how he and his brother, the young Shehu Usumanu ɗan Fodio, travelled to study under the learned ^{c}Uthmān Biddūrī:

> The *shaykh* [Usumanu ɗan Fodio] read the Koran with his father, and learnt *al-ᶜIshrīniyāt* and similar works from his *shaykh*, known as Biddu al-Kabawī. . . . He read *al-Mukhtaṣar* with our paternal and maternal uncle ᶜUthmān, known as Biddūrī b. al-Amīn b. ᶜUthmān b. Ḥamm b. ᶜAlī, etc. This *shaykh* of his was learned and pious. . . . He it was whom our *shaykh* ᶜUthmān imitated in states [probably Sufi practices] and deeds. He accompanied him for nearly two years, moulding himself according to his pattern in piety. . . [Our maternal uncle, Muḥammad Thanbu] . . . was learned, having successfully memorised most of what he had read, and it was he who read to them the commentary of al-Karāshī. If [Shehu Usuman] made a mistake, or let anything slip, this maternal uncle of ours would correct it for him without looking in a book, for he knew the commentary of al-Karāshī by heart. Then he went to the country of the two Holy Places, performed the Pilgrimage, and remained there for over ten years. He then returned and reached the town of Agades, and there he died. . . . Then the *shaykh* ᶜUthmān [Usumanu ɗan Fodio] went to seek knowledge to our *shaykh* Jibrīl [the Ineslemen scholar, Jibrīl b. ᶜUmar mentioned above], and he accompanied him for almost a year, learning from him until he came with him to the town of Agades. Then the *shaykh* Jibrīl returned him to his father and went on Pilgrimage. . . .[9]

Elsewhere, Shaykh ᶜAbd Allāh b. Muḥammad says,

> And many schools, I languished with desire to be present at them.
> In them is attainment of the needs of one who is made desirous [of learning].[10]

It was such a system as this that supported the activities of the learned classes described above.

NOTES

1 *JAH* XVII, 1, 1976.
2 Paul E. Lovejoy, *JAH* XIX, 2, 1978.
3 Quoted in Norris, 1975, p.27.
4 I am indebted to Dr H.T. Norris for this, as yet unpublished, information, concerning Sīdī Maḥmūd's link with the Persian Suhrawardiyya.
5 I am especially indebted to Dr A.A. Batran's chapter entitled 'The Kunta, Sīdī al-Kuntī, and the Office of Shaykh al-Ṭarīq al-Qādiriyya', in Willis, editor, 1979 for this summary of Sīdī al-Mukhtār's teaching.
6 *JAH*, XIX, 2, 1978; see also his chapter in Willis, ed. 1979.
7 See for instance Hiskett, Ibadan, 1963, p.5, for a Fulani view of origin.
8 Hiskett, *Hausa Islamic verse*, 1975, p.14.
9 Hiskett, *BSOAS*, XIX, 3, 1957, p.563.
10 Hiskett, Ibadan, 1963, p.91.

CHAPTER FOUR

Kanem and Borno from *c*.184/800 to 1219/1804

Early Kanem and Borno

From very early times there had been a trade-route linking Tripoli, in North Africa, with Lake Chad, via Zawila in the Fazzan and the Kawar oasis. Another route, from east to west, which forked at Awjila, joined this north-south route and linked it with Egypt. Trade along these routes was probably interrupted by the Muslim conquest of North Africa in the 1/7 century but it quickly picked up again, and the routes seem to have been fully in use by the 2/8 century. It was surely along them that information on Kanem first found its way to the Islamic world beyond the Sudan.

Little is known about the origins of the kingdom of Kanem. It probably consisted of a number of separate statelets which were later welded into a larger unit, possibly by a semi-nomadic people called the Zaghawa who lived north-east of Lake Chad. They are first mentioned, very briefly, by Wahb b. Munabbi[1], an early 2/8-century Arabic writer. Therefore we may assume that the Zaghawa were known to the camel drivers who used the Tripoli-Zawila-Kawar route by this century (see Appendix A, diagram I). The Zaghawa are mentioned again, specifically as the inhabitants of Kanem, by the Arabic geographer al-Yaqᶜūbī who was writing in 259/872. Other Arabic writers then took up the tale and from their accounts it becomes clear that in the 4/10 century the kingdom of Kanem was still non-Islamic. It was based on a form of divine kingship, in which the king, who was known as the *mai*, was worshipped in the belief that life and death, sickness and health, all depended on him.

By this time Kanem was certainly in touch with Zawila which, from *c.* 132/750, was under Ibāḍī control. By 306/918 the whole Fazzan was united into a single Ibāḍī state that continued until 571/1175–6, although there is some evidence that the ruling dynasty, the Banū Khaṭṭāb, abandoned Ibadism for Sunnī Islam in its last years of rule. Despite this, Islamic influences of an Ibāḍī nature must have filtered through to Kanem but they were not sufficient to make any significant impact on the traditional system of divine kingship.

The Saifawa in Kanem

In the late 5/11 century – 467/1075 and 477–8/1085 have been proposed as possible dates – a Muslim, Umme or Ḥummay, seized power in Kanem. He established the Muslim dynasty of the Saifawa. This name arises from the dynasty's claim to be linked to the pre-Islamic Yemenite hero, Sayf b. Dhī Yazan, regarded by Muslims as having prepared the way for Islam. It is very unlikely that this genealogical claim reflects historical reality. Linguistic evidence gives no support to the notion of a Middle Eastern origin for any language group established in Kanem and Borno, except of course the Shuwa

Arabs; and they were in no way connected with the early Kanem dynasty. The most likely significance of this legend of origin is that the family of Ḥummay had recently converted to Islam, probably as a result of contacts made with Muslims in Zawila and elsewhere along the caravan routes. Desiring an aristocratic Islamic pedigree to support their political ambitions, they chose one from the well-known Islamic folk tales about Sayf b. Dhī Yazan who was a heroic warrior against the infidel tyrants of his day. Such genealogies going back to Sayf and to Yemen were frequently adopted all over West Africa when a family or group went over to Islam. There can be no certainty as to their exact source but there was an historical Sayf, mentioned by the 3/10-century Arabic historian, al-Ṭabarī. There was also another, more legendary Sayf, who figures in the *Sīra*, the 'Biography' of the Prophet Muḥammad, of which there are numerous versions. Either of these sources – or oral tales based upon them – could have supplied the newly converted Muslims with the genealogies they needed.

In addition to this Yemenite origin, the Saifawa also claimed to be descended from the Prophet's tribe, Quraysh, thus they claimed to be *shurafā'*.

With the establishment of Islam in the state of Kanem the southern, Kanembu people began to emerge as the dominant group. It is uncertain what then happened to the Zaghawa. Some think they simply merged with the Kanembu while others believe they were all pushed out to the east where they survive to the present day. A recent view, put forward by Dr Humphrey Fisher, is that some Zaghawa accepted Islam and became absorbed into the new Islamic state of Kanem, while others resisted and were driven out east, taking their old system of divine kingship with them.[2] That system did not disappear entirely from the Islamic state of Kanem and traces of it remained even into the 13/19 century, in for example the custom of secluding the *mai* from the gaze of his subjects.

The first Saifawid dynasty may have established diplomatic links with the surrounding Islamic world by the end of the 5/11 century or the beginning of the 6/12 century. It is reported, admittedly by a source dating from the 10/16 century, that Mai Dunama b. Ḥummay performed Pilgrimage at least twice. If these journeys really did take place, they must certainly have helped to establish relations with Egypt and the *mai* of Kanem to become accepted as a legitimate Muslim ruler. They must also have opened the door to the introduction of Islamic constitutional forms into the government of Kanem.

The Saifawid empire reached its height in the first half of the 7/13 century, under Mai Dunama Dibalami (*c.* 607/1210–646/1248), a successor of Dunama b. Ḥummay who is mentioned above. He conquered extensive territories to the north of Kanem, including the Fazzan, which he occupied. By this time, too, it seems likely that cultural influences from Borno had reached westward, at least as far as Kano. It may be as a result of this early contact with an Islamic neighbour that the first Arabic words – basic Islamic terms like *ṣalāt* (Hausa *salla*) 'prayer', *al-qur'ān* (Hausa *Alkur'an*) 'the Koran' and so on were adopted as loan-words into Hausa. At the same time that this imperial expansion was taking place within the Sudan, diplomatic and trading relations were set up with the Hafsid state in Tunisia. This also helped to promote Islamic influences in the Kanem empire.

Recent, more critical research into the often confusing and sometimes contradictory reports of the Arabic writers and Borno chroniclers has given rise to a somewhat different interpretation. Dr Dierk Lange, in an important article,[3] has suggested that the Zaghawa kings, whom he refers to as the 'Banū Dūkū', were in touch with the surrounding Islamic world perhaps as early as the second half of the 1/7 century – that is from the first appearance of Islam in North Africa and Egypt – as a result of their involvement in the slave trade. However, being the representatives of a powerful non-Islamic African religion, they strongly resisted the spread of Islam in Kanem. None the less, *c.* 459/1067, the Zaghawa ruler of the day did convert to Islam, perhaps in response to a popular movement outside his court. Thus he, and not Ḥummay, became the first Muslim king. Despite this conversion, or perhaps because of it, Zaghawa authority was weakened and, some years later, probably *c.* 467/1075 this led to a change of dynasty. It was at this point that Ḥummay displaced the now Muslim Banū Dūkū dynasty and replaced it with that of the Saifawa. Contrary to what Borno tradition seems to suggest, this did not bring about drastic changes within Kanem; for about the next century and a half the Saifawa continued to govern in much the same way as the Banū Dūkū making little attempt to promote Islam. Moreover, the economy of the country, and thus the power of its kings, continued to depend largely on the availability of slaves for the trade. These were obtained from within the kingdom by simply enslaving the kings' own subjects, as had been the practice in the days of the Banū Dūkū. However, as Islam advanced among the people, it became more and more difficult to obtain slaves in this way. The Sharīᶜa forbids the enslaving of free Muslims and such a practice was objectionable to the ᶜ*ulamā*', whose influence, Dr Lange believes, was greatly increased as Islam became more widely adopted. By the reign of Dunama Dibalami, which Dr Lange places *c.* 607/1210–646/1248, Islam had become well established among all classes of the population in Kanem; and Dunama Dibalami, in response to this, switched to much more positively Islamic policies. Clearly such a situation was no longer favourable to the old practice of gathering slaves from within the kingdom and Dunama Dibalami's drive for imperial expansion must be seen as, in some measure, an attempt to obtain sufficient slaves from outside the kingdom by war against neighbouring non-Muslim peoples.

Dr Lange's thesis is an interesting one and some of his arguments are persuasive: in particular, that which draws attention to the probability of earlier contacts with Islam on the part of the Kanemite rulers than have so far been proposed and that which questions whether the coming of Islam was the abrupt turn-around that Borno tradition deptics (he himself suggests a more gradual process). However, there are grounds for objecting to some of his other arguments and conclusions.

First, it is difficult to believe that the Banū Dūkū really did maintain the economic basis of their state by enslaving their own subjects, even when these subjects were still non-Muslims. The raiding of a ruler's own subjects for slaves, except on a very small scale for punitive purposes, would have been contrary to what was surely the accepted custom all over West Africa – that a ruler held office by virtue of his ability to protect his subjects. It would also have been extremely stupid, for to diminish the number of his own subjects would be to reduce his own power. If the Banū Dūkū did live by slave-raiding they must have raided the subjects of other rulers, not their own; or they raided in fringe areas that they may have dominated but which were not properly part of their kingdom.

Second, Dr Lange surely overemphasises the role of the slave-trade in bringing about the extension of Dunama Dibalami's empire. There is little doubt that slave-trading was economically important, but it was surely not the most important interest of the state. As one scholar has observed, 'War is an extension of politics and diplomacy and slaves are an incidental, if valuable, by-product'.[4] It really does seem unlikely that Mai Dunama Dibalami embarked on his imperial conquests solely, or even mainly, to acquire an area in which he could harvest slaves. The power politics of the time and place, of which unfortunately, we know almost nothing, were surely what induced him to take this course.

Even if we admit the unlikely proposition that the early rulers of Kanem were accustomed to raid their own subjects for slaves, another objection seems to me to arise from the role Dr Lange proposes for the *ᶜulamā'* as guardians of the strict Sharīᶜa. He suggests their power was such that they were able to cause the *mai* to abandon established patterns of slave-raiding and embark on the conquest of an empire to recoup his consequent losses. Without in any way underestimating the influence of the *ᶜulamā'* at certain times and in certain places, it seems to me doubtful whether in 7/13-century Kanem they can have acquired that degree of political power and solidarity. Furthermore, if slave-raiding in traditional areas was still profitable, would any but those *ᶜulamā'* of the most delicate conscience have opposed it? It would not have been difficult for those who wished to question the genuineness of Islam in these newly converted peasants and nomads, to do so, and thus justify enslaving them. Objections on the part of the more scrupulous which may well have been raised, are none the less unlikely to have been effective in reversing the trend of established economic and political policies. The picture of the Kanemite *ᶜulamā'*, united in moral opposition to the traditional practice of enslaving peasants and nomads who had recently chosen to claim Islamic immunity, is uplifting but unfortunately, not convincing.

Whatever the reasons for Mai Dunama Dibalami's policy, the heyday of the first Saifawid empire in Kanem lasted only until the beginning of the 8/14 century. Even before then internal quarrels had begun to break out and the Saifawid hold over the Fazzan became weaker. A period of anarchy seems to have developed but there is little real evidence that the Fazzan broke away from the Saifawid empire, as has sometimes been suggested. The So, a non-Kanuri people living south of Lake Chad, and who had never been fully subjugated by Kanem, intensified their resistance to Saifawid attempts to control them. The Bulala, a rival branch of the ruling family, embarked on a revolt that lasted almost twenty years. These disturbances may have been reactions on the part of the resolute supporters of the traditional religion, against the Islamic policies of the later Saifawa. Apart from these internal disputes, Arabs from the east, perhaps descendants of the 5/11-century Banū Hilāl, raided Kanem and carried off the people into slavery. By the end of the 8/14 century these mounting troubles forced the reigning *mai*, ᶜUmar b. Idrīs, to abandon Kanem and flee into neighbouring Borno. It has been suggested that this move from Kanem to Borno was a much more gradual affair that began as early as the end of the 7/13 century, but whatever the time span, this flight gave rise to a new Saifawid state in Borno. At about this time, also, a new group of people, the Kanuris, began to emerge as dominant in Borno affairs. They seem to have evolved out of the mixing of Kanemite Kanembus and other tribal groups and henceforth were to play an important part in the affairs of the state of Borno.

The Saifawa in Borno

At first the Saifawa in Borno continued to be troubled by the same kind of problems that had afflicted them in Kanem. It was not until the reign of Mai ᶜAlī Gaji b. Dunama, that began *c.* 874–5/1470 or perhaps 881/1476, that stability was achieved. Mai ᶜAlī destroyed his dynastic rivals and established a new, permanent walled capital at Gazargamu. He thus ensured security within metropolitan Borno and created the conditions that enabled his successors to embark on imperial expansion.

The 10/16 century marked the rise of a new Saifawid empire, this time centred in Borno. Kanem was reoccupied but the *mais* showed no desire to leave Gazargamu and return there, to their ancestral seat at Njimi. By the beginning of the century Borno was conducting a flourishing trade with Egypt and diplomatic relations were established with the Ottoman province of Tripoli (see Appendix A, Diagram II and III). These were strengthened by the dispatch of a mission there in 959–60/1552, to conclude a treaty of friendship and commerce.

This developing link with Tripoli was brought about, in part, by the importance of that town to the *mais* as a source of European goods. They proved willing to trade with whoever actually controlled it, be it the Spaniards, the Knights of Saint John or the Ottoman Turks. This link may also have been brought about by rivalry between Borno and the state of Kebbi, farther west, over control of the Hausa states; and possibly over control of the southern termini of the trade routes leading to North Africa. Amongst other things, the *mais* sought arms from Tripoli to aid them in this struggle.

The best-known of all the Borno *mais*, Mai Idrīs Aloma, came to the throne in 977/1569–70. This *mai*, a contemporary of the Sharifian Saᶜdid, Mawlay Aḥmad al-Manṣūr of Morocco, had inherited the title *khalīfa* from his predecessors. However, he entertained wider ambitions than they had, for it seems he wished to be recognised as caliph not only in Borno but also by all the Muslims of the Sudan. It was this *mai* who established direct links with Istanboul. These first came about as a result of the encroachments into Borno territory by a Turkish official in the Fazzan. By this time the Fazzan had passed largely into Ottoman control, in practice if not formally; and Mai Idrīs Aloma dispatched a mission to Istanboul in 981–2/1574 to protest about the encroachment. After some years of deliberation the Ottoman government eventually instructed its officials in the Fazzan to safeguard the property and subjects of Mai Idrīs and not to harass them.

Under the banner of *jihād* Mai Idrīs waged wars of expansion and he conquered the non-Muslim So and Tubu. He also besieged the Hausa city of Kano, but failed to take it. For these wars he sought arms and other military aid from the Ottomans but these were not forthcoming. This was probably due to political and military problems within the Ottoman empire rather than to unfriendliness on the part of the Ottoman authorities. Whatever the reason, Mai Idrīs now turned to the Sharifian Saᶜdids of Morocco instead. An exchange of correspondence took place between them and the haughty Mawlay Aḥmad al-Manṣūr played with the idea of giving aid. He made it clear that he expected the Borno *mai* to acknowledge him as *khalīfa* of all the Muslims, including those of Borno; and that he was to obey his instructions as to when and against whom *jihād* should be fought. Despite the probably false Moroccan claim that Mai Idrīs did in fact make *bayʿa*[9], homage, to al-Manṣūr, the Borno ruler found these conditions unacceptable. Relations between the two states lapsed but these contacts, with the Sharifian Saʿdids as well as those with the Ottoman Turks, meant that influences from two advanced Islamic societies entered Borno. They had a marked effect on the way of life there, especially those influences from Ottoman Turkey, and from Borno they spread west, into Hausaland.

It seems clear that Mai Idrīs Aloma used the principle of *jihād* to justify wars of imperial conquest. However, this is not to say that he was insincere, for there is no doubt that his conquests did bring many non-Islamic peoples under Islamic government and this was a first step towards their conversion. Moreover, within Borno itself he pursued a strongly Islamic policy. He introduced many reforms designed to strengthen Islamic observance and also initiated a programme of mosque building. There is no doubt that his reign witnessed the marked advance of Islam in Borno and surrounding territories.

The 10/16 century was not only a time of imperial expansion in Borno; it was also one of great commercial activity. The Borno armies had a great need for horses and these were obtained from North Africa, in exchange for slaves. Other forms of trade also increased at the same time. One result of this activity was that the caravan routes linking Borno with both North Africa and Egypt carried a very heavy merchant traffic during this century. The kingdom of Borno and neighbouring areas became, above all other areas of the west and central Sudan, familiar to traders and travellers generally from the outside world. Borno, in the 10/16 century, was certainly in no way either unfamiliar or inaccessible from the point of view of men from the Mediterranean countries or the Middle East. It was, on the contrary, almost as well known then as it later became, following the period of European exploration of West Africa in the 18 and 19 centuries AD. Purely in terms of the location of places and the direction of routes, the later European explorers had very little to add to the information about Borno left behind by 10/16-century travellers.

During the 11/17 century Borno continued to dominate an empire; although it had to resist increasing pressure from the Touregs in the north and the Kwararafas in the south. Nevertheless, the 11/17 century was probably the period of Borno's greatest power and extent, especially under Mai ʿAlī b. ʿUmar (*c.* 1047/1637–1087/1676). At this time neighbouring states voluntarily placed themselves under the protection of the *mai* or caliph, by which title he was now generally recognised. However, by the following century Borno began to decline as an imperial power; but as a centre of Islamic, especially Ottoman Islamic culture and ideas, it remained important right up to the outbreak of the *jihād* in Hausaland in 1219/1804.

To the east of Kanem/Borno lay Baghirmi and Wadai. Nomadic Fulani had reached the area of Baghirmi, before the establishment of a centralised state there, early in the 10/16 century. At that time an Islamic government was set up probably as a result of influences from Borno. In Wadai a Muslim revolutionary, a certain ᶜAbd al-Karīm, overthrew the faintly Muslim Tunjur dynasty early in the 11/17 century and set up a fully Islamic sultanate. This sultanate became a great problem to Borno during the 13/19 century.

Islamic intellectual development in Kanem/Borno

There can be little doubt that the first Islamic ideas to enter Kanem were Ibāḍī ones. The trade links between the Fazzan and the early statelets of the Zaghawa were so close that it is hard to believe the people of Kanem can have remained entirely unaware of the nature of the enormous religious and political changes that had affected the Fazzan, to say nothing of North Africa and Egypt beyond it, since the 1/7 century. They must surely have acquired some knowledge of what their Muslim Berber trading partners believed; and how they worshipped. Indeed, according to one story current in the second half of the 9/15 century, a governor of Jabal Nefusa in the 3/9 century had been able to speak the language of Kanem. If this is really true – and the lateness of the source must throw some doubt on this – it can be assumed that there was considerable freedom of communication between the Zaghawa and the Fazzanis. Under such circumstances Ibāḍī Islam must surely have been in the air of Kanem long before the first king converted.

It is not known for certain what form of Islam Ḥummay, or perhaps the last of the Zaghawa, adopted. However, even if the Banū Khaṭṭāb in the Fazzan did abandon Ibāḍī Islam for Sunnī Islam in their last years of rule, it seems likely none the less, that it was the Ibāḍī form that must first have reached Kanem.

Borno tradition, which is of course a Sunnī tradition, attributes the introduction of Islam to a certain Sunnī *ᶜālim*, Muḥammad al-Mānī, who visited the Saifawid court early in the 5/11 century and claimed to be a *sharīf*. However the authority for his presence is very late – not earlier than the 10/16 century – and no great reliance can be placed on it.[5] Even if Muḥammad al-Mānī did teach in Kanem at this early date, his teachings must surely have had to compete with those of the Ibāḍīs.

Muḥammad al-Mānī is not the only *ᶜālim* to have gone down in tradition as the first to preach Islam in Kanem. An earlier, and therefore perhaps more reliable source – the Arab writer of the first half of the 8/14 century, al-ᶜUmarī (d. 749/1349) – attributes this distinction to a certain al-Hādī al-ᶜUthmānī, who claimed to be descended from the third caliph of Islam, ᶜUthmān b. ᶜAffān. It is al-Hādī al-ᶜUthmānī who is supposed to have brought about the conversion of the first Kanemite ruler to Islam. Al-Hādī al-ᶜUthmānī also appears to have been a Sunnī and probably a Mālikī *ᶜālim*. Whenever he may have arrived, it seems clear that the court of Kanem was Sunnī and Mālikī by al-ᶜUmarī's day, otherwise that scholar would surely have commented upon the fact.

Whatever the form of Islam first practised in Kanem, there must have been a good deal of mixing with the ancestral cult. This is made clear by the story of the *Mune*. This object was a fetish and Mai Dunama Dibalami finally broke it open in the 7/13 century – or so the story goes. It seems most likely that it was a Koran enclosed in leather casing. It is not an unlikely story, for an incident is recorded in Kano in the late 10/16 or early 11/17 century, when a similar fetish called *Dirki* was opened and found to contained a Koran. Such fetishes are striking evidence of the way in which African animists and polytheists and sometimes Muslims regarded the Muslim books, whether Korans or other scriptures, as supernatural objects.

The 'Borno *maḥrams*',[6] state documents conferring certain privileges and exemptions, suggest that government may already have been influenced by Islam even in the 7/13 century. They mention such Islamic titles as *Qāḍī*, *Wazīr*, *Imām*, but they are late sources claiming to describe a much earlier period and cannot therefore be considered wholly reliable.

By the reign of Mai ᶜAlī Gaji, at the end of the 9/15 century, the record has greater authority. By this time the *ᶜulamā'* were clearly enjoying privileged positions in government and Mai ᶜAlī Gaji now began to use the title *Khalīfa*; a clear indication that Islamic constitutional theory had been adopted by the ruling class. The title was used by the *mais* from then on and, as was pointed out above, Mai Idrīs Aloma tried to invoke it to establish his authority well beyond the confines of Borno.

By the 9/15 century an Islamic system of education was well established in Borno and scholarly communities grew up from Mai ᶜAlī Gaji's reign onwards. These developed into *madāris*, centres of higher Islamic education; a well-known one was that of Shaykh Aḥmad Fāṭimī, in the 9/15 century and another was that at Kalumbardo.

This centre at Kalumbardo was situated 50 miles north-east of the capital, Birni Gazargamu, and developed early in the 11/17 century or perhaps at the end of the previous century. It was at its height during the reign of the Caliph/Mai ᶜAlī b. ᶜUmar. The most famous of the scholars of Kalumbardo during its early period were the Toureg *ᶜālim*, Shaykh al-Wālī b. al-Jarmī al-Tarqī and Shaykh Wal Dede al-Fallātī, a Fulani of the Toronkawa who came from the same lineage as the 13/19-century reformer of Hausaland, Shehu Usumanu ɗan Fodio. The centre of Kalumbardo had strong links with Ahir; and Shaykh Wal Dede is known to have studied at both Timbuktu and Agades. Both *shaykhs* were Qādirīs and Kalumbardo was certainly a centre for the spread of the Qādiriyya in Borno during this century. Shaykh al-Wālī b. al-Jarmī al-Tarqī was unfortunate enough to make an enemy of the reigning *mai*, although whether this was Mai ᶜUmar b. Idrīs (d. *c.* 1047/1637) or his brother and predecessor, Mai Ibrāhīm b. Idrīs, is uncertain. However Shaykh al-Wālī b. al-Jarmī was killed and Shaykh Wal Dede fled to Baghirmi: the scholarly community of Kalumbardo then broke up. This first period of Kalumbardo's activity probably lasted from *c.* 1024/1615 to 1046/1636. The settlement was later revived by Mai ᶜAlī b. ᶜUmar, under the leadership of Shaykh ᶜAbd Allāh al-Barnāwī, who flourished *c.* 1075/1664–5. It was said of Mai ᶜAlī b. ᶜUmar, who performed Pilgrimage five times, that the journey to Mecca was for him but a night's ride; it was also said of him that he could bring books from the Azhar at need. These traditions reflect the high level of Islamic intellectual activity during his reign and Borno's close links with centres of scholarship in the surrounding Islamic world; to all of which Kalumbardo certainly made a considerable contribution. Shaykh ᶜAbd Allāh al-Barnāwī had studied under the Toureg scholar, Aḥmad al-Ṣadīq b. Abī Muḥammad Uways, and had links with the Qādirī community to the east in the Nile valley. He was active in converting the animists of Borno to Islam and is known to have practised *khalwa*, the religious exercises by which the Sufis try to achieve *fanā'*, absorption in the divine essence. In 1088/1678 he was killed by his Toureg enemies and the settlement of Kalumbardo again broke up; the scholars scattered and some of them went as far south as Nupeland.

Although Kalumbardo declined, other *madāris* had been set up by the 12/18 century in Machina and the capital, Birni Gazargamu. The scholars and students of these establishments were helped and supported by the court and Borno became a centre of learning that attracted many Muslims from other parts of the Sudan. Moreover, the Borno schools had links with the Azhar, in Egypt; and they attracted the services of both Ottoman Turkish scholars and scholars from Moorish Spain. These Spanish scholars were especially well known for Koran studies and for teaching the Law. Indeed, Borno has retained its reputation for excellence in Koran studies up to recent times. A Hausa poet, writing *c.* AD 1950, said,

> Borno . . . city of the Shehu, place of the Koran,
> Ancient city of the Faith,
> No matter how times change,
> They will not stray from the Truth.[7]

The development of Sufism in Borno is dealt with in detail in chapter 13. Here, it is sufficient to say that Sufi ideas reached Borno at least as early as the 9/15 century and by the 11/17 century the Qādiriyya was well established in Kalumbardo. Elsewhere in Borno the practice of belonging to a specific *ṭarīqa* was slower to develop than in neighbouring Hausaland, although it is not possible on the evidence at present available to say why this should have been so.

Islam was accepted and observed among the common people of Borno more thoroughly than elsewhere in the sub-Saharan areas; for even Muhammadu Bello, who was no friend of Borno, confirms this in his *Infāq al-maysūr*.[8] There was still some misbelief among them however, and non-Islamic customary practices certainly persisted up to 1215/1800. This gave rise to a reform movement among certain *ʿulamāʾ* in Borno, especially the Muslim Fulani living there but the movement was not regarded favourably by the *mais*. They thought of themselves as the guardians of Islam and resented the reformers' interference. Finally, the reformers launched a *jihād* against the *mais* similar to that which took place in Hausaland; but, as will be explained in chapter 10, it turned out to be much less successful.

NOTES

1 Cuoq, p.41; see Cuoq for other Arabic writers mentioned in this chapter unless otherwise indicated.
2 *CHA*, 3, p.289.
3 *JAH*, XIX, 4, 1978, p.495–513.
4 John E. Lavers, in the course of correspondence on the subject of slavery in the west and central Sudan.
5 Lange, ibid., p.495–6.
6 Palmer, 1936.
7 Hausa text, *Wakokin Mu'azu Hadeja*, Zaria, 1964.
8 E.J. Arnett, 1922, p.6.

CHAPTER FIVE

Hausaland *c.*184/800 to 1219/1804

Hausaland is situated due west of Borno, with which it has a common border, and due south of Ahir. The most southerly state of Hausaland is Zaria, also known as Zegzeg or Zazzau although at certain periods the political, cultural and commercial influence of the Hausa states may have extended as far south as the north bank of the river Benue, or even perhaps beyond. The common language of Hausaland is Hausa, although Fulfulde (the language of the Fulani) and certain other languages are spoken there by minority groups. There are several dialects of Hausa. The most important are 'western' Hausa, of which the speech of Sokoto is typical; and 'eastern' Hausa, of which the speech of Kano is typical. The states or kingdoms that made up Hausaland before the Fulani *jihād* in the early 13/19 century are often referred to as the 'Haɓe' states. *Haɓe* is a Fulfulde word meaning 'strangers'. It was used by the 13/19-century Fulani to describe the pre-*jihād* Hausa rulers whom they ousted. The Hausa nation has been built up, over many generations, of peoples of many different bloodlines who have migrated into Hausaland and joined the original stock. What unites them is a common language and, to an ever increasing extent over the course of their history, common adherence to Islam.

The early Hausa kingdoms

The earliest pattern of society in Hausaland, as it appears in Hausa legends of origin, was one of small hamlet settlements based on kinship; without any form of government beyond the authority of the head of the family, or perhaps clan. The people lived by hunting, gathering and some agriculture. There may even have been distinct groups of hunters and farmers who exchanged their produce with one another,

> Hunting was his craft, evening and morning,
> Travelling day after day,he came to a flowing river,
> Fruitfulness and meat, there was no limit to it,
> When he had traversed the bush he came to a land of scattered farmsteads,
> Their craft was farming, they never caught so much as a hedgehog.
> . . . .
> When he had settled, all the farmsteads heard the news,
> Meat they were seeking, they came one by one,
> When they came to barter for meat, they used to say they came
> to the hut of Haɗe and Ja, beneath the tamarind tree.[1]

It may well be that this traditional account does, in fact, describe the essentials of how the settlement of Hadejia, and others like it, first began. Whether the people so described were Hausa-speakers at that time, or speakers of some other language, can now no longer be determined.

More centralised political groupings – that is groups with a chief or king at their head – probably began to develop with the arrival in Hausaland of newcomers. These newcomers are generally believed to have come from the north and to have established themselves among the original inhabitants; then they built settlements around which kingdoms grew up. Many different Hausa traditions tell of this. Here is a passage from one of them,

> Bagauda made the first clearing in the Kano bush,
> It was then uninhabited jungle,
> . . .
> Now Gwade [came] together with Yakasa, Sheshe
> And Guguwa, the mighty men of the Maguzawa [the non-Muslim Hausas],
> It is said of them that they were farmer
> Chieftains, coming to explore the bush.
> . . .
> There was no chief, no protecting town wall [in Kano at that time],
> The elders said: Let a chieftaincy be established.
> They appointed Bagauda, the Protector.
> Bagauda reigned for fifty years.
> . . .
> Nawatau reigned for seventy years,
> In the very month that he cleared a site to build a town wall, it was built![2]

The account from which this passage is taken omits an interesting and colourful episode that occurs in another version, namely the well-known Kano Chronicle. This tells how the newcomers to Kano clashed with the local headman, Barbushe, who appears to have been both a political and military leader and oracle-priest. In his second role, however, he may have been assisted by a guardian of the sacred grove known as Mai Tchunburburai. Eventually, the newcomers came to terms with Barbushe and his god, Tchunburburai, so that they could settle in the land. Afterwards however, slowly and with great cunning, they overcame the original inhabitants and made themselves masters.

Another story tells how a certain Bayajidda, the grandfather of Bagauda, arrived in the town of Daura by way of Borno, to find the people living in fear of a huge snake that lived in their well and prevented them drawing water. Bayajidda slew the snake, married the queen of Daura and their sons founded the seven Haɓe dynasties of Hausa tradition.[3]

The stories are good ones, with a lot of dramatic colour and detail. They offered people in earlier times a satisfactory account of their own history. They deserve to be treated with respect, as pieces of traditional literature. However today's historians must also treat them with caution; and with an understanding of how they probably arose. 'Bayajidda' may be a Hausa form of the classical Arabic Abū Zayd. Abū Zayd was, of course, the legendary leader of the Banū Hilāl and a noble *sharīf*. This is hardly to be taken as evidence that these newcomers into Hausaland were members of the Banū Hilāl who figure in North African history, although some historians have suggested this. The invasion of North Africa by the Banū Hilāl quickly gave rise to a collection of folkloric stories that spread widely all over the western Islamic world. These stories crop up in all sorts of forms in the folk tales of the Hausas and of other African Muslim peoples, as well as in the folk tales of North Africa and Egypt. Perhaps, therefore, several centuries after the Hilalian invasion of North Africa took place, certain *ᶜulamā'* – perhaps North Africans, perhaps Egyptians, perhaps Berbers, or perhaps Hausa Muslims who had travelled abroad – heard local stories of strangers who had entered Hausaland long ago. These *ᶜulamā'* then adapted versions of the Abū Zayd legend, already familiar to them, as neat, Islamic explanations for this piece of local history. Their audiences would certainly have taken up the stories with delight; and it is easy to imagine that this is how the Bayajidda story, and indeed the Bagauda story, in their several versions, came to be adopted by the Hausas.

Another theory as to the identity of these strangers who are said to have entered Hausaland so long ago rests on the fact that a certain Abū Yazīd – which may equally well be the original Arabic name from which Bayajidda arose – was the leader of the last of the North African Khārijīs. He fought the Fatimids and was defeated by them in 336/947. His followers fled into the desert and it is suggested that some of them may have got as far as Borno, from where they may then have drifted west into Hausaland. The leader of such a group, who may have assumed the name of Abū Yazīd was, it is proposed, the legendary Bayajidda.[4] It is certainly not impossible that there were individual refugees from North Africa among those who at one time or another reached Hausaland; but the evidence for believing that those referred to in this story were really followers of the 4/10-century Abū Yazīd is very slender. It is rather unlikely that the fighting between the Fatimids and Khārijīs was on such a scale that fugitives were driven out of North Africa – a vast area and at that time still with sufficient sparsely populated areas outside its heavily populated towns to shelter considerable numbers of refugees – in sufficient numbers to make any noticeable impact on societies farther south that they may have joined. Moreover, if such Khārijī refugees were driven out into the desert, they would surely have become scattered there and absorbed among the northern desert peoples long before they had drifted as far south as Hausaland. In any case, as has already been explained above, most of the Khārijīs were not driven out into the desert, let alone did they wander down to Borno and Hausaland. They formed prosperous Ibāḍī trading communities along the border between North Africa and the Sahara; and there they lived in considerable comfort for several generations. Therefore it is an unlikely story that Bayajidda was, in reality, a Khārijī refugee from the Fatimids. What is possible however, is that the tale of Abū Yazīd, who was known as 'the man on the donkey', spread among Muslims in Hausaland and they then applied it to some local incident for which it provided a convenient explanation. The fact is we simply do not know when these movements of people really occurred, nor where the strangers came from. The most probable explanation is that the stories dramatise a long and continuous process, perhaps even going back to pre-historic times, in which various groups of people drifted into the Sahel and on into the savanna. They gradually became absorbed into the original populations of the areas in which they settled and did not, as some historians would have it, bring about an abrupt, once-for-all change in the character of the people of Hausaland. It is also reasonably certain that they did not create the Hausa language. Linguistic evidence shows beyond doubt that Hausa belongs to what is now known as the Plateau-Sahel sub-group of the wider Chadic language family and this is an African family. The way in which languages that belong to it have developed, and how they are distributed, suggests that speakers of these languages must have inhabited the Chad area and Hausaland from very early times, probably long before Islam came to North Africa. The newcomers may have modified the original languages of the peoples they joined, including Hausa, by adding new words and new ideas to them; but they certainly did not create new languages and new peoples overnight.

It was not the newcomers alone who created the seven Hausa, or Haɓe kingdoms that eventually emerged. They played an important part, but so too did the everyday activities of the original people. These hunters and farmers searched for good places to settle; for mineral resources, especially iron, to forge tools and weapons; for good hunting grounds; for permanent water sources and so on.

Trade may also have contributed to the formation of the Hausa kingdoms; for where markets were situated there was a tendency for an increasing number of people to settle. Sooner or later chiefs emerged among them, around whom centralised organisations grew up to form kingdoms. Each kingdom then established its control over tracts of the surrounding countryside. This it exploited for purposes of agriculture, for trade, for the mining of metals, especially iron, for hunting and perhaps, too, for slave-raiding. However, the importance of this activity in very early times – that is before the 9/15 century – should not be over-emphasised; we simply do not know what the level and intensity of slave-raiding may then have been. This surrounding area of countryside the chief and his people would come to regard as their own and they would fight to keep intruders out. It seems likely, for instance, that the early history of *ƙasar Kano*, the 'land' of Kano, was one of struggle between several settlements for domination; and that present-day *Birnin Kano*, Kano 'walled city', did not emerge as the capital of *ƙasar Kano* until approximately the 9/15 century. Much the same seems to have been true of Katsina, where *ƙasar Katsina* existed long before the present *Birnin Katsina*, Katsina walled city, developed. The eventual emergence of these walled cities was probably due, in part at least, to the growing involvement of the original settlements in the trans-Saharan trade (see Appendix A, diagrams II and III). The settlements served as the southern termini of that trade, expanded and grew rich upon it and in each case a walled city grew up. This became the seat of the ruling dynasty and the capital of a prosperous and powerful kingdom.

It seems, too, that some early kingdoms may have adopted a policy of enforced movements of populations. In the course of these movements relatively large bodies of captives were moved from their original homeland in a war zone and resettled in new towns, set up in the bush country around the growing capital city. How this happened in the case of Kano will be described later on in this chapter.

A rather different interpretation of the early history of the Hausas has been advanced by J.E.G. Sutton, in a most interesting and well-argued article.[5]

Sutton believes, largely on linguistic evidence, that as the Hausa language is a member of the Chadic group, they originated not to the north of present Hausaland, as has usually been supposed, but to the east, probably along the western shore of Lake Chad. He then argues that they pushed gradually west, imposing their language and their culture on the earlier inhabitants of what is now the Hausa-speaking area, who were speakers of languages belonging to the Benue-Congo family. He points to the survival of pockets of such Benue-Congo languages within the present predominantly Hausa-speaking area, notably Ningi and the Jos Plateau, as evidence for this process. At the same time as he demonstrates the linguistic evidence, Sutton points to certain ecological evidence; he argues that it has been largely due to the east-to-west spread of Hausa agriculture that Hausaland has been turned from woodland to grassland and arable countryside. He also points out that the well-known 'Hausa Bakwai', the Seven Hausa states that are traditionally supposed to have been the earliest states of Hausaland, are all located in eastern, not western Hausaland.

Sutton's arguments are convincing and, in my opinion, he is most probably correct in his theory, first, that a people out of whom the Hausas arose came into their present location from the east, not the north; and, second, that they were speakers of a Chadic language who took over from earlier Benue-Congo speakers. Indeed, this in no way conflicts with the account of Hausa history given above. I disagree with him, however, concerning the time-scale he proposes for this process. Sutton believes that it happened within the last thousand years – that is to say, the east-to-west movement of the Chadic speakers began in the 4/10 century. This seems to me to be far too short a time span. The extent to which the present Hausa language has taken over from the earlier Benue-Congo languages – despite pockets like Ningi and Jos – and the extent to which it has diverged, especially grammatically, from other Chadic languages still spoken farther to the east of the present Hausa speech area, seem to me to indicate a considerably longer time span than a mere thousand years. However I think it would be rash to attempt a guess at what the true chronology of the Chadic speakers' east-to-west migration may have been. The way in which languages develop and how they diverge from other languages to which they are related, is an immensely complex matter involving problems of both interference and isolation. In the case of the Hausas, we have almost no information at all.

It is interesting to speculate on the relation of the Bayajidda/Bagauda folklore cycle to the process Sutton proposes. It can be argued that, making allowances for the later Islamic colouring given to the stories by Muslim literates, Bayajidda and his people were the original Chadic-speaking immigrants from the east; and that the inhabitants of Daura, Barbushe's Kano and so on, were the Benue-Congo speakers whom they overran. I am inclined to doubt this, on the basis that, while I agree that the Chadic speakers came from the east, tradition insists that the Bayajidda/Bagauda people came from the north, or at any rate the north-east. The more likely argument therefore seems to me to be that the Chadic speakers were already established in present Hausaland long before the 4/10 century and that the Bayajidda/Bagauda stories are, as was said above, dramatisations of a long process of population movements. These population movements took place over an unknown time span, by several different groups of peoples whose origins can now no longer be determined; but some of these people, at least, may indeed have come from the north or from the north-east.

One should be careful, however, not to assume that the early Chadic speakers were similar let alone identical in culture with the present Hausas. The community now known as the Hausas has been made up of people from many different blood-lines brought together by conquest, by slavery, by trade and by many other factors. It is, moreover, doubtful when the term 'Hausa' first became used to describe them. Several explanations of the meaning of the word have been offered. The most satisfactory, in my view, is that it means simply 'language' and, as often happens among African people, the word for 'language' became extended to refer to the people who spoke that language. Its use in this sense may have begun no earlier than the 8/14 century or the early 9/15 century, when certain developments in the economy of Hausaland, which are discussed below, brought about changes in the structure of society. By this time, of course, the majority of the Benue-Congo speakers, as well as many other groups, had all become speakers of the 'Hausa' language that had developed out of Chadic. Thus the early Chadic speakers, whenever they may have arrived in what is now known as Hausaland, are no doubt to be numbered among the remote ancestors of those whom we now describe as Hausas. However they were by no means necessarily the same people, either by blood, by culture, by religion, in their economy, in their political institutions or in their way of life.

The seven Hausa states, the 'Hausa Bakwai', believed to have developed out of the Bayajidda/Bagauda incidents are Daura, Gobir, Katsina, Kano, Zaria, Rano and Biram. Only four however, Kano, Katsina, Zaria and Gobir, have been substantial in recorded history. To these should be added the eastern Hausa kingdom of Shira, situated in the south-western corner of what is now Katagum emirate and which was probably founded in the 4/10 century. Although Shira is not counted among the 'Hausa Bakwai' it was none the less important because it came to act as a buffer state between Kano and Bornu.

Tradition says it was Yaji ɗan Tsamiya (750/1349–85), the eleventh chief of Kano after Bagauda, who introduced Islam. This date coincides with the arrival in Kano of the Wangarawa, the Muslim merchant/missionaries described in chapter 3. They, too, probably brought with them a set of Arabic terms, an Arabic Islamic lexicon, relating to ritual, theology and the Law. This would have been adopted into the Hausa language in the form of loan words, thus adding to the layer acquired by contact with Borno. From this time on, as the Hausas' contacts with Islam increased, more and more Arabic loans were taken into Hausa and given Hausa forms. So too were pious Muslim names. Thus newly converted Hausas adopted names like ᶜAbd Allāh, the 'Servant of God', which in due course became Audu; Khalīl, a shortened form of Khalīl Allāh, the 'Friend of God', an Arabic epithet of the Prophet Abraham, which became Halilu; Abū Bakr, the 'Father of Bakr, the name of the first caliph of Islam, which became Bubakari, and so on. The study of Arabic loanwords in Hausa, and other West African languages like Fulfulde and Kanuri, is a fascinating one, which tells much about the stages by which Islam developed among West African peoples.

It was about a century later – the mid 9/15 century – that the first Muslim chief of neighbouring Katsina, Muḥammad Korau, took over the reins of government. He is said to have been a Wangara, or at any rate closely associated with the Wangarawa. At the same time Muḥammad Rabbo is said to have become the first Muslim chief of Zazzau (Zaria), farther to the south. This is likely to have come about as a result of the opening-up of trade links between Hausaland and the Volta region, which was one of the Sudanic gold-bearing regions. It was almost certainly the gold trade that first linked Hausaland, and also Borno, with the Volta country (see Appendix A, diagram III). Zaria lay on the route between the more northerly Hausa cities of Kano and Katsina and the Volta. Thus the beginning of Islam in Zaria was probably connected with the passage of Wangarawa gold merchants – and possibly Hausa and Borno Muslim merchants as well – through Zaria, on their way to and from Hausaland. The Kano Chronicle mentions kola-nuts as being part of the tribute paid by Nupe to the ruler of Zaria early in the 9/15 century. One could be forgiven for assuming that these, too, originated from the kola-bearing regions south-west of the Volta river, the 'Gonja' of later Hausa tradition and folklore. In fact, however, they were almost certainly the *cola acuminata* from the eastern forests of Yorubaland and Nupeland, not the choicer *cola nitida* from the forests of what is now southern Ghana. The state of Gonja was not founded until the 10/16 century and, as will be explained in chapter 7, the kola trade from there to Hausaland did not develop until the late 12/18 century. It is of course possible however, that small quantities of *cola nitida* did find a way through earlier than this, as a subsidiary to the trade in gold.

This necessarily very brief account of the early rise of Muslim Zaria is based on the tradition that has, until quite recently, been widely accepted. However, Professor Murray Last has arrived at somewhat different conclusions, that add up to an alternative account. He believes that the state that first arose in what is the present Zaria province was a federation called Kankuma or Kangoma, somewhat south of present Zaria town, with its centre at Turunku; and that its economy was largely based on the trade in metals, especially gold and iron. Then, in the 10/16 century, the Kangoma state of Turunku became internationally known as 'Zegzeg', a word he believes to have been derived from Arabic *zanj*, which the Arabic-speaking traders used to describe Africans. During the 10/16 century foreign traders settled in the town of Zaria, north of Turunku, on the edge of the Kangoma state. In consequence, the centre of trade in the area now shifted to Zaria and, in the early 11/17 century, it developed into a political state that largely took over from the old Kangoma state. He also believes that, as a result of its growing commercial importance, 10/16-century Zaria became Hausa-speaking and Hausa in culture, in contrast to Kangoma, which had been populated by speakers of one of the Benue-Congo languages (which he describes as 'Plateau'). Thus, according to this theory, Zaria before the 10/16 century was simply a small Muslim settlement in the midst of surrounding, non-Muslim Kangoma; and it did not develop into a major Muslim kingdom until the early 11/17 century. Professor Last also believes that the ruler of Zaria, Muḥammad Rabbo, who is held to have officially established Islam there, reigned in the middle of the 11/17 century, and not in the 9/15 century, as traditionally reported.[6]

Professor Last's theory is of great interest. However, as he himself recognises, it is unlikely that it will be finally accepted or rejected until enough archaeological research has been done to confirm or disprove the literary evidence upon which it is at present largely based.

To return to the Wangarawa, a second wave of these people is said to have reached Kano during the 9/15 century, led by that ᶜAbd al-Raḥmān Zagaiti referred to in chapter 3. However as Professor Hunwick has pointed out, tradition compresses 'a long process [of Wangarawa immigration] into a single immigration under the charismatic leader ᶜAbd al-Raḥmān Zagaiti'.[7] It seems likely that Wangarawa immigration into Hausaland was a continuous process that began in the 8/14 century and continued, on and off, from then on.

There is more than one view as to the starting point of these Wangarawa. Some think they came directly from Mali while others regard the forest area south-west of the river Volta as their most likely starting point. It has been suggested that the later waves came from Takedda, when that commercial centre began to decline in the 9/15 century. Yet another theory is that by the 9/15 century some, at least, of the Wangarawa were citizens of Songhay, not of Mali. Certainly, this seems most likely. Whatever their starting point, one thing is reasonably sure; they were drawn to the Hausa cities because these cities were now caught up in the web of trade that stretched from North Africa and Egypt across the Sahara and into the Sudan. What they sought was surely gold; some of which was no doubt brought in from the Volta area and the Senegambia; while some was also produced in Hausaland from mining in Zamfara and perhaps from washings from the small gold deposits in Kangoma, south of Zaria. The Wangarawa probably also sought ivory, the product of elephant-hunting in and around Hausaland, especially in the Benue valley.

By *c.* 802/1400, Kano and the other Hausa kingdoms had become powerful, while the Saifawa had suffered the collapse of their authority in Kanem and the flight to Borno. Thus these Hausa kingdoms were freed from whatever overlordship the Kanemite state may previously have imposed upon them, and became independent.

How and when the fourth major Hausa kingdom, Gobir, emerged is a question to which there is no certain answer. One theory is that it was created by a family, or clan, that was driven out of Ahir by the Touregs, probably about 906/1500; it then imposed its authority upon the people of Gobir, to whose country its members came. Another theory has it that the kingdom originated from the mass emigration out of Ahir of the whole Gobir people, who then settled in their new home north of Kebbi and Zamfara. If this second theory is correct – and it is inconsistent with the theory of an east-to-west movement of the Hausas, described above – then the flight out of Ahir must surely have taken place before the 8/14 century; for Gobir was almost certainly the 'Kubar' mentioned by Ibn Baṭṭūṭa in 754/1353. He describes it as 'in the region of the heathen'.[8] Unfortunately, he does not make it altogether clear whether this expression refers to the mountainous country of Ahir to the north-east of Takedda, which was his point of reference; or to the savanna country due south of it. However, it is implicit in his account as a whole that the country of the heathen is the country of the Blacks, south of the Saharan network of trade routes along which he travelled. That the Gobirawa – or most of them – had been driven out of Ahir before the 9/15 or 10/16 century is also supported by the fact that the 5/11-century Arabic geographer, al-Bakrī, writing about Ahir *c.* 460/1068, spells it 'Ayir'. This is the Toureg form of the name, whereas the

Hausas call the area 'Absen' or sometimes 'Asben'. This indicates that the area was in the hands of Berber-speaking peoples, not Hausa-speaking Gobirawa in al-Bakrī's day, otherwise it would surely have been known by its Hausa name. For all of these reasons it is therefore generally accepted that Gobir, in Ibn Baṭṭūṭa's day, was situated just north of Kebbi and Zamfara, in the savanna.

There is, however, another account that seems to contradict that of Ibn Baṭṭūṭa. It is the one given by that sometimes rather questionable authority, Leo Africanus, alias Ḥasan b. Muḥammad. He states that, in the early 10/16 century, Gobir was still located 300 miles east of Gao, in a mountainous country; and that it was conquered by Askiya Muḥammad of Songhay, who killed its king.[9] Since there is no mountainous country in the savanna south of Takedda, it seems obvious that Leo must have believed Gobir to be in Ahir. As was pointed out in chapter 2, there are reasons for doubting the accuracy of Leo's account, at least in parts, while Ibn Baṭṭūṭa, on the other hand, can usually be shown to be very reliable. However it is not necessary, in this instance, to disregard Leo entirely. There is a strong tradition among the people of Gobir, that they were driven from their original home in Ahir by the aggression of the Songhay during Askiya Muḥammad's time; while others believe they were driven out by the Touregs. The most likely explanation for these apparently conflicting accounts would seem to be that a kingdom, or perhaps just a clan group known as Gobir, existed south of Takedda in 754/1353. Then, about 906/1500, a particular family, or perhaps a larger group, was forced out of Ahir by pressure from both expansionist Songhay and the turbulent Touregs. They moved down to Gobir and there succeeded in imposing their rule on the indigenous inhabitants of that area. This explanation allows all three sources, Ibn Baṭṭūṭa, Leo Africanus and the Gobir traditionalists, to be truthful. Even so, one cannot be certain that that really was what actually happened.

As for Islam, the date at which it first came to Gobir is also uncertain. Among the Gobirawa themselves it is believed that their rulers accepted Islam from Songhay between 898/1493 and 934/1528 at the time of Askiya Muḥammad. When Ibn Baṭṭūṭa mentions Gobir, he does so in order to observe that it was one of the places to which large quantities of copper bars were exported from Takedda. At this time, 754/1353, Takedda was already a centre of Islamic learning for the Ineslemen. It is therefore reasonable to assume that Takedda exported not only copper bars but Islamic ideas as well; and that these, in some form or other, must have reached the people of Gobir. It is also, perhaps, reasonable to suppose that if the Gobirawa were sufficiently advanced economically to organise the complex system required to carry on the copper trade, they were also sufficiently advanced culturally to receive these ideas in a constructive manner. It may also be supposed that some Muslims from Takedda may have found their way down to Gobir, where they settled and married local women. In other words, there is a strong probability that Muslims of a sort were present in Gobir in 754/1353. If, subsequently, 10/16 -century immigrants arrived, having taken their Islam from Songhay, they can only have contributed to the process of consolidating conversion. It is unlikely that they began it.

It is worth mentioning that the Gobirawa, like the Yorubas, have at least one legend of origin that claims Lamurudu, alias Nimrūd or Nimrod, the non-

Muslim tyrant of the Arabic *Qiṣaṣ al-anbiyā'*, 'Stories of the Muslim Prophets', as their ancestor. This story of Lamurudu, and how it arose, is discussed in greater detail below, when the history of the Yorubas is considered. It is sufficient to say here that it should not be taken literally. It is a story through which Muslim *ᶜulamā'* sought to explain the history of an African people with whom they came into contact through trade or for other reasons, who were not Muslims at the time these contacts took place. The most likely persons to have created this legend are Muslim merchants from the Muslim centre of Takedda, who first made contact with the Gobirawa before Islam became firmly established among them.

The Hausa diaspora

It was suggested above that the increasing involvement of Hausa settlements such as Kano and Katsina in the Saharan trading system was one factor that led to their emergence as the capitals of kingdoms. It also had the effect of stimulating *fatauci*, the Hausa middle- and long-distance carrying trade, that was carried on mainly in the savanna country south of the Sahara and eastward, towards Borno. It cannot be said for certain when this sub-Saharan *fatauci* first began, but by 596/1200 or shortly after the Hausas were already involved in military and political relations with the peoples to the south of Hausaland, among whom may have been the Kwararafas. It is therefore probable that trading contacts began at an even earlier date, but this cannot at present be proved. What can be said with confidence is that, on the evidence of the 'Kano Chronicle' the Hausas developed a sub-Saharan trade network that, by *c*. 825/1421–2, had reached Nupe in the south-west and the Benue valley to the south. By 856/1452 trade routes were opened to Borno in the east and to the west as far as the middle Volta Basin.

Like traders all over West Africa, the Hausa traders were the first of their people to go over to Islam. Their travels brought them into frequent contact with city centres where Islam flourished; and membership of the Muslim fraternity helped them to contact suppliers and customers. As they traded they acted as Muslim missionaries, perhaps not deliberately, but by their example.

The Moroccan conquest of Songhay was at one time thought to have brought about a sudden disastrous collapse of the trade centred on that state. This view has now been shown to be exaggerated. However, the conquest and its aftermath did accelerate a process already under way, in that it helped to speed up a shift in the Saharan trade from west to east. As Songhay's commercial importance ebbed, that of Hausaland and Borno flowed. Well before the end of the 11–12/17 century, the Saharan routes into Hausaland and Borno were probably carrying a heavier traffic than those entering the Sudan farther west (see Appendix A, diagram III). This does not mean that the Hausas took over the conduct of the trade across the Sahara for they never replaced the Saharans as camel-masters and caravan-guides. They simply received increasing quantities of Saharan imports into their cities. They then set up trading organisations at the southern end of the Saharan system to distribute these imports, as well as various Sudanic products, to the east, west and south of the Sahel and Sudan. This sub-Saharan trade was not carried principally by camel, but by donkey, oxen and human portage. The Hausas became skilled, too, in handling the canoe-borne trade across the Niger. Out of *fatauci* there grew up the profession of the *madugu*, the Hausa Muslim caravan-leader. He conducted the savanna trade much as Touregs and other Saharans conducted the trade across the desert.

The ivory trade was a factor that may have drawn the Hausas away from their homeland into areas populated by non-Hausa-speaking peoples mainly to the south of Hausaland. As Dr Mahdi Adamu has shown, by the second half of the 19 century AD, Hausa elephant hunters were making an important contribution to the spread of Hausa culture in Bauchi and the Benue valley.[10] It is likely that this process started at least as early as the 10/16 century, since there was certainly a demand for ivory from North African and certain European merchants from other Mediterranean areas living in Kano at that time, which the Hausas must have tried to satisfy (see the inset to Map 5).

This spread of the Hausas out of their homeland, to trade and often to settle in the neighbouring countries has been called a 'diaspora', a dispersion of people out of their original homeland. It took them, in the end, as far west as the Ashanti empire; as far east as Lake Chad; and as far south as the edge of the forest that lies behind the Atlantic coastline.

The settlements they founded often attracted other Muslims who were not Hausa-speakers. These people also settled and in time became Hausa-speaking. For example, Yorubas from the Lagos area and people from the country north of Ashanti settled in large numbers in the *zongos* (Hausa *zango*, a traders' camp or quarter) originally founded by Hausas in the southern Gold Coast. So numerous were these non-Hausas who joined the original Hausa settlers that some scholars have questioned whether it is correct to speak of a 'Hausa' diaspora at all. The objection is a useful one, in that it draws attention to this important qualification to the notion of a purely Hausa dispersion. However, all diaspora have surely recruited persons of other nations, tribes and bloodlines who have attached themselves to the original wanderers and settlers. In the case of the Hausa diaspora, the general use of Hausa as a trade language does seem to justify the term.

Islam in the Haɓe kingdoms

Their prosperity and their trade brought more and more Hausas into contact with Islam. However, despite the pious devotion of a growing body of Muslim *ᶜulamāʾ* in the Hausa towns and countryside, and the remarkable advance in literacy in Arabic that took place during the 10/16 and 11/17 centuries, it was still a mixed form of Islam that grew up in the courts of the Haɓe chiefs. For instance, the 'Kano Chronicle' records that, between 792/1390 and 812/1410, Kanajeji's counsellors were troubled by Kano's defeat in war. So they urged him,

> Whatever you wish for in this world, do as our forefathers did of old.

The humbled chief, who had failed to bring victory, replied,

> Show me and I will do even as they did.[11]

Muhamman Rumfa of Kano (867–904/1463–99) was host to al-Maghīlī and carefully observed the Islamic festivals. He was so given to following the ways of the Muslim Arabs resident in Kano that he was known as 'the Arab *sarki*, (chief)'. He is even regarded in Hausa tradition as a Muslim reformer and many Hausas believe that literacy in Arabic among their people first developed in his court. Yet he had a thousand wives, seized all first-born virgins for his harem and persisted in other non-Islamic practices. Mohamman Zaki (990–1027/1582–1618), Muslim though he was, allowed fetish worship in Kano. As for observance of the Islamic Sharīʿa in the Haɓe kingdoms, the author of the 'Hausa Chronicle', another source for the history of the Haɓe kingdoms, comments sharply,

> At this time [before the Fulani *jihād*] all the Hausa kings gave judgement arbitrarily, without laws; learned Mallams were attached to them but they did what the kings ordered them.[12]

Certainly, the 'Hausa Chronicle' is a late source, but the author's remark sums up neatly the evidence of the more reliable 'Kano Chronicle'.

What were the reasons for this persistence in polytheist ways (for the pre-Islamic Hausas do appear to have been polytheists, not animists) long after the Islamic way had been made clear? They are not far to seek. Kanajeji was in no position to contradict his counsellors as he had just lost a war. How could he then argue against their opinion that the old gods were angry? Mohamman Zaki's followers said to him, 'If you leave the Katsinawa alone, they will become masters of all Kano and you will have nothing to rule but a little.'[13] Under such a threat, it is easy to understand that he needed all the help he could get. So, rather than alienate the polytheists, he allowed them their fetishes. Consider Mohamman Rumfa, that most Muslim of the pre-*jihād* chiefs of Kano. It is hardly likely that he, mighty as he may have been, kept all those wives and virgins solely for the pleasures of his bed! He probably acquired them through marriages of alliance necessary to secure the support of his powerful and probably still polytheist vassals. The 'seizing' of first-born virgins, so objectionable to the Muslim moralist, may have been a customary practice necessary to demonstrate to the people his continuing manliness. Perhaps too it bestowed honour and royal favour on the girl's family. There is no reason to suppose that it was resented by Mohamman Rumfa's polytheist subjects. Perhaps the custom was associated with fertility rites in the ancestral cult and if so, the chief would have invited disaster had he abandoned it.

Some have explained the growth of states characterised by mixed Islam as the result of the slow, progressive influence of Islam on the native polytheism of the traditional oracle-priests. Thus the original polytheist constitutional system and way of life was gradually modified in favour of Islamic ways, Islamic beliefs and Islamic constitutional forms. Other factors – trade, migrations and so on – are seen as making their contribution to the total process of gradual, social, cultural and political change out of which new states resulted. The interpretation so far put forward in this chapter has been based largely on this view.

There is another view, known as 'contrapuntal paramountcy', that explains the process rather differently.[14] Contrapuntal paramountcy means simply that two opposing systems, in this case the one Islamic, the other polytheist, share power in a state of more or less even balance. According to this theory, the Muslims are seen either as strangers who arrive abruptly and seize power in their own right; or as local groups that seize it with the help of, or in alliance with Muslim strangers. Initially, the Muslims attempt to set up constitutions broadly along Islamic lines, in which the chief rules under the authority and according to the forms of the Sharīᶜa. The polytheist interest however, identified in most cases with divine kingship, or with the authority of an oracle-priest, proves too strong to be pushed aside entirely. Some give-and-take then becomes necessary, in which the Muslim chief cannot, even if he wants to, impose the full rigour of Islam. On the other hand, the polytheist leaders can no longer coax the people back into exclusive observance of the old ways for Islam has by now proved to have certain attractions. According to this view, mixed Islam is more a matter of political necessity than of what people do, or do not, believe. It is a matter of balancing two sets of interests against one another – a 'seesaw' process of constant checks and balances rather than of a slow but powerful force, moving majestically towards an inevitable climax. The contrapuntal theory is an elegant one. It fits well with the evidence of such sources as the 'Kano Chronicle'. It explains what may have been the true significance of the coming of the Wangarawa. They were perhaps, not only traders and Muslim missionaries but also persons with political interests, who allied themselves with local Muslim factions. Even so, there seem to be aspects of the truth in both theories.

The ᶜ*ulamā*' of the Haɓe period and their widening influence

At first the Muslim literates were, by and large, content with mixed Islam. In return for the patronage of the Haɓe chiefs, they refrained from challenging it too harshly. During the 10/16 century the local population of ᶜ*ulamā*' in Hausaland constantly increased and ᶜ*ulamā*' from the Sahara and beyond frequently visited the area. They followed up the work done by al-Maghīlī who, it will be remembered, had visited Kano at the end of the 9 or early 10 century AH (the late 15 century AD). Among these foreign ᶜ*ulamā*' were Shaykh Aida Aḥmad of Tazakht, who settled in Katsina and died there *c.* 936/1529; and Shaykh Makhlūf al-Balbālī (d. *c.* 940/1533), who visited Kano and Katsina. Possibly as a result of the latter's initiative an important *madrasa* later developed in Katsina. It may have been in the late 10/15 or early 10–11/16 century that the custom of writing the Hausa language using a modified form of the Arabic script called *ajami* first began to develop in Kano and Katsina, encouraged by the Arabic literacy taught by these foreign ᶜ*ulamā*'. Most of the letters of the *ajami* alphabet have Hausa names that appear to be very old words not likely to have come from the language as it has been spoken in the recent past. This suggests that the use of the *ajami* script was familiar to the Hausa malams long before the time of the Fulani reform movement. If, as was once thought, the Fulani reformers had been the first to introduce the script, its letters would surely have been given Fulfulde names. It must be stressed that no examples of written Hausa, either in the Arabic script or in any other form of writing, have been found which date back to this early period. The earliest known example of the writing of Hausa in *ajami* falls between *c.* 1176/1762 and 1244/1828, but there is a strong tradition among the Hausas that their language was being written in *ajami* in the court of Mohamman Rumfa (867/1462–904/1499).

There was more to this period in the history of Hausaland than just the adoption of writing, important as that was; it seems that the period witnessed in Kano, and perhaps in Katsina too, the beginnings of a powerful upsurge of Islamic intellectual activity. This upsurge has been compared with the

European Renaissance, the 'rebirth' or 'revival' of learning and culture that began in Europe in the 13 century AD and reached its height in the 16 century AD. The parallel is useful but not exact, for Islamic learning was not 'revived' in Hausaland, it now appeared for the first time. Moreover, and more important for avoiding the confusion that may come from loose comparisons, the European Renaissance depended largely on the revival of the pre-Christian, pagan culture of Greece and Rome, whereas this Islamic movement in Hausaland arose directly out of Islamic monotheism; it firmly and deliberately rejected all that had to do with the pre-Islamic past. Where it could not reject it, it sought to change it into an acceptably Islamic form. But both movements were an explosion of intellectual energy and both had important consequences for the development of the societies in which they occurred. The Islamic intellectual movement in Hausaland was in part the consequence of developing Islamic literacy described above; it was in part, too, the outcome of increased contacts with the surrounding Islamic countries of North Africa and Egypt, as well as the wider contacts of Pilgrimage. This intellectual movement showed itself in the production of an indigenous Arabic literature, that is a literature written in classical Arabic by Hausa scholars working in Hausaland. It did not depend on the imported literature produced in North Africa and the Middle East, upon which the Sūdānī ᶜ*ulamā*' had at first had to rely.

Another outcome of this intellectual movement was almost certainly the growth of the various legends of origin relating to the Hausas and their neighbours, which clearly derive in the first instance from Islamic written sources; the Bayajidda/Bagauda legend; the Kisra legend of the Borgu people and the Kwararafas; the Braima/Lamurudu legend of the Yorubas and so on. The Bayajidda/Bagauda legend was discussed above and the others will be discussed in greater detail below. What they all have in common, however, is that they were the productions of Muslim literates, whether merchants or scholars, participating in this Islamic intellectual activity; and attempting to describe Sudanic history within the broader Islamic historical tradition. Such an attempt, which first, locked African history into the framework of a universal time-scale, second, linked it to world geography and, third, subjected it to moral judgement by an external, monotheistic standard of values, represents a marked shift away from the past. Indigenous African historical tradition was often timeless, or at any rate only marginally concerned with relating events to the passage of time; it was also often preoccupied with particular localities and lacked a world perspective; and its judgements were those of traditional ethical systems that were certainly not those of Islam.

It is not possible to say precisely when this intellectual movement began, nor when it reached its fullest development. It seems probable, however, that it was in the second half of the 9/15 century that it got under way, especially in the court of Muhamman Rumfa; and that it continued throughout that century and the following ones, until it was overtaken by the Islamic reform movement of the 12/18 century and the events that resulted from that.

During the 11/17 century the *madrasa* in Katsina that was mentioned above became associated with the Katsina scholar, Malam Muḥammad b. al-Ṣabbāgh (fl. *c.* 1060/1650), known in Hausa as Ɗan Marina. He was the author of the poem about the Garden of Learning, quoted from in chapter 3. Ɗan Marina gathered round him a scholarly community that was well versed in all branches of Islamic learning. He himself even tried a little fortune-telling, but the pious man quickly 'abandoned it for fear of the wickedness in it'! However, there is no evidence that he, who feared to risk his soul by fortune-telling, ever thought to secure its salvation by leading Holy War. Mixed Islam is always a provocation to Muslim idealists, for, understandably, they cannot see it as a tolerant system of 'live-and-let-live' but only as disobedience to God's command. This disobedience is seen to spoil the full perfection of human life on earth that true Islam brings and sooner or later there has to be a reaction. By *c.* 1111/1700 some members of the scholarly community in Hausaland, and indeed in Borno, were restless and there is evidence of growing tension between them and the traditional rulers. They were men with a vision and of profound intellectual pride in the classical glories of Islamic culture. Some, too, had known the glowing personal experience of Pilgrimage to the heart of Islam; they had returned filled with the ambition to recreate that perfect Islam they had known there, in their birth-places. Such men were the products of many generations of Islamic education, a literate elite filled with ethical, social and political notions that were increasingly opposed to the attitudes and values of those who governed them. What is more, they were apt to wonder what right these chiefs had to rule them at all. Was it, perhaps, they and not the Haɓe chiefs whom God really intended to govern? Little by little their protest grew sharper and their discontent more bitter. During the 12/18 century many no longer bothered to conceal their hostility and contempt for the Haɓe administrations. The last half of this century witnessed a strong surge of reformist sentiment that demanded change, and at its forefront were the Muslim Fulani.

In the towns, by the middle of the 10/16 century, Islam was certainly well established among the *ᶜulamā'* and the trading classes. The ruling class, in general, made at least certain outward concessions to it, while particular royal individuals such as Mohamman Rumfa, seem to have been sincere Muslims. Moreover, the townspeople, subject to the example of the town-dwelling *ᶜulamā'*, were, no doubt, familiar with many aspects of the Islamic way of life, even if they were not very conscientious in their own observances of it. In the countryside, however, it seems likely that Islam had no more than a superficial influence over the lives of the peasants and nomads. Indeed, it is probable that it had done little more than colour their folklore with tales of impressive Muslim strangers – heroic warrior leaders or saintly holy men – and with the notion of a perpetual struggle between the power of Islam and the forces of animism expressed in stories about such symbolic figures as the Islamic sacrificial ram and Dodo, the ferocious goblin of the ancestral cult. However, as from the middle of the 12/18 century, there had been an increasing movement towards positive conversion to Islam among all classes of common and non-literate people, in town and countryside alike. This was brought about largely by the efforts of the reforming *ᶜulamā'* discussed above.

Such conversions were not always necessarily due to simple theological persuasion; no doubt some were due to social, political or economic convenience. It was easier to trade and to travel as a Muslim than as a polytheist; the Muslim chief was disposed to give greater privileges to Muslims than to non-Muslims; it was more convenient to wear Islamic dress and conform to Islamic custom than to remain the odd man out when so many others were converting –

these and many similar motives must have played their part in setting the trend towards adopting Islam. This is not to suggest that such conversions were insincere; there is not necessarily any conflict between sincerity and expediency. A man can accept an idea sincerely simply because it is so convenient and removes his doubts and troubles or he can be genuinely persuaded by the constant example of his friends. Moreover, as has been said already in this book, Islam is not only a system of belief; it is also a way of life, a total social, economic and political system. It is therefore to be expected that social, economic and political forces, as well as intellectual and spiritual forces, will play their part in bringing about conversion.

Not all the *ᶜulamā'* were militant reformers, however; some were non-militant and, like certain Saharan Ineslemen and Zwāya, advocated *tajdīd*, peaceful reform. This very often meant no more than preserving things as they were and one such community of quietist *ᶜulamā'* with an established reputation for scholarship and teaching as well as for not wishing to disturb the existing state of affairs, existed at Yandoto, on the border between Katsina and Zamfara. Many of these Yandoto *ᶜulamā'* were of Wangarawa origin, a fact that may account for their quietiest attitudes; for those associated with a trading tradition as well as with religion, are not usually given to active militancy.

There was clearly considerable intellectual debate among these quietist *ᶜulamā'* and the reformers. It was conducted through *wa'azi*, the verse of preaching and warning and through the more scholarly medium of theological treatises in learned classical Arabic, also sometimes in verse,

> O you who have come to guide us aright,
> We have heard what you have said. Listen to what we say.
> You gave advice to the best of your ability,
> But would that you had freed us from blame!
> And you spoke – Glory be to God, it was evil-speaking –
> Indeed, devils, if they come to our gathering,
> Spread evil talk, exceeding all bounds!
> We have not mixed freely with women
> [by allowing them to listen to our preaching],
> how should that be!
> . . . But I do not agree that
> Their being left to go free in ignorance is good,
> . . .
> We found the people of this country drowning in ignorance;
> Shall we prevent them from understanding religion?[15]

So the argument went on, learned, courteous and barbed, never to be resolved by agreement; and only to be interrupted by *jihād*.

Some aspects of economic and social conditions in the Haɓe kingdoms and in the west and central Sudan generally up to *c.* 1214/1800

Evidence relating to economic and social conditions in Hausaland from early times down to 1214/1800 is not abundant. What there is comes mainly from the Kano Chronicle; from works in Arabic, Fulfulde and Hausa by the Muslim

Fulani authors; from the accounts of travellers from Europe and the Middle East who visited the countries on the borders of the west and central Sudan and later penetrated in increasing numbers into the area; and from oral tradition, especially the remembered praise-songs to Haɓe chiefs and courtiers.

From hunting/gathering to an early export/import economy

The Kano chronicler's account up to the 8/14 century must be regarded as largely legendary. No doubt it represents accurately enough the early hunter-gatherer economy of the Kano area, which was probably that of Hausaland as a whole; also the conflict between the traditional religion of the indigenous inhabitants and the new cult, whatever it may have been, of the first incoming strangers. However, until the results of recent archaeological research on the early settlements around Kano are published, it seems risky to place more reliance on it than that. It does seem that Kano city, as it is at present known, may in those early days not have been the same all-important centre, dominating the surrounding countryside, that it later certainly became. Other centres, which have now declined or disappeared altogether may also have been of considerable importance in those distant times. The picture that emerges from the Kano Chronicle is one of warring groups, probably clans, fighting for territory against the background of the political struggle within Kano settlement between the non-Muslim supporters of the traditional cult and Muslim strangers backed by certain local allies. What the life of the people may have been like under such conditions must remain a matter for speculation; but most of them probably got on with their farming, hunting, iron-mining and iron-working and other crafts, largely unaffected by these goings-on, unless they were unlucky enough to become caught up in the violence that resulted. If the traditions of the present-day Hausa people can be relied upon as a guide to the way of life in those very early times, it seems that they participated in frequent festivals when sacrifices were made to the traditional gods. A great deal of dancing and merry-making went on and the oracle-priest foretold the future and gave instructions for the conduct of the community's affairs. In the absence of adequate chronicles for the early history of the other societies of Hausaland, it is not possible to say whether the situation elsewhere was the same as it was in Kano. However, the probability is that it was, especially in Katsina.

Although the Kano Chronicle is the main source for the early history of Hausaland, one important piece of information that may be applied to at least some other parts of Hausaland as early as the 8/14 century does emerge from another source. As was mentioned before, the Arab author and traveller of that century, Ibn Baṭṭūṭa, makes it clear that the kingdom of Gobir was, in his day, an importer of the copper that originated in Takedda. It is unlikely that copper was used in Gobir alone; it is more probable that the metal was distributed from there to metal-working centres in Hausaland, perhaps as far south as Ife and Igbo-Ukwu where bronze-casting was in progress as early as the 6/12 century. In this case, how was the copper paid for? The answer must surely be in the local produce of the savanna and the forest. This would have been exported through Gobir – and perhaps through other outlets, although Ibn Baṭṭūṭa mentions only Gobir – to Takedda, where some of it was no doubt used, while the rest passed into the Saharan network. If this is a true picture – and it must be stressed that it depends to some extent on guesswork – then certain centres in Hausaland, for instance Kangoma which lay on the route from Gobir to the south, may even have been linked to Takedda as early as the 6/12 century and must surely have had an export/import economy of a sort by the 8/14 century. That presupposes a prosperous way of life for those who were engaged in it. It also presupposes a higher level of material culture in such centres than that normally associated with the hunting/subsistence farming economy, seemingly characteristic of most of Hausaland before the 8/14 century.

That such an export/import economy, however rudimentary, did in fact exist in 8/14 century Hausaland seems to be indicated by the testimony of the following century. In 754/1353 Ibn Baṭṭūṭa knew of the kingdom of Gobir, although it was not sufficiently important to cause him to visit it. However he mentions none of the Hausa cities that subsequently became so important and the conclusion must therefore be that Hausaland at this time can only have been linked by a strand or two to the main caravan thoroughfares of the Sahara. But by the end of the following century, that is about one hundred and fifty years later, Shaykh ᶜAbd al-Karīm al-Maghīlī had arrived in Kano and he was quickly followed by other visitors from North Africa and Egypt. The significance of these visits for Islam has been discussed above. Economically, its importance is that, by the late 9/15 century, the Saharan caravan routes and their savanna feeder-routes, especially those on the eastern side, must have been sufficiently numerous and well-travelled to enable these *ᶜulamā'* to visit Hausaland with relative ease and frequency. This must have been a gradual process, in which the easterly trade routes out of Hausaland to Ahir, that then joined the major routes to Ghat, Ghadames, the Fazzan and Borno, were opened up and used sufficiently regularly to encourage scholars as well as merchant-adventurers to use them. Indeed, it is known that a route from Hausaland to Borno was open by 856/1452. Such a development would never have come about unless the Hausas had already been involved in an export/import exchange that made it worthwhile. Caravan routes were not carved out of the sand and the scrub for the convenience of scholars alone (Appendix A, compare Diagrams I, II and III).

Such an opening-up of trade routes to and from Hausaland must have meant a further increase in material prosperity for at least some of the inhabitants of the Hausa towns and cities. It also surely had much to do with setting in motion the strong current of Islamic intellectual activity that began to flow at this time, which was discussed above.

The society that now arose was no longer that of the early hunters, farmers and iron-workers of the Bayajidda/Bagauda era. They were dwellers in settlements, not cities. With a few exceptions such as, perhaps, Gobir and Kangoma, they depended for what trade they did conduct on an internal exchange system. However the new society had become city-centred and it was also more and more oriented toward the wider Saharan trading system. Moreover, culturally and politically as well as economically, it was drawn ever closer to the Mediterranean and Middle Eastern world. There is no doubt that a profound change had taken place in Hausa society and that an historical milestone had been passed.

As far as is known from the accounts of the Arabic authors, this economic activity in Hausaland was carried on against a background of remarkable price and exchange stability in the west and central Sudan as a whole. It is known that in the 8/14 century one gold *mithqāl* was worth approximately 1,150 cowries in Mali but the cowrie value of the *mithqāl* during the 9/15 century is not known with certainty. It is possible that it remained virtually stationary, around 1,150 cowries, but it may have dropped to something between 1,725 and 2,000 cowries. Even so, this was a gentle decline in the *mithqāl*'s value that is unlikely to have disturbed the general economy. Prices for horses and slaves, which are the main articles of trade for which the sources give details, obviously varied considerably according to the quality of individual specimens and the state of the market. However, average prices seem to have remained fairly stable from the time of al-Bakrī, in the 5/11 century, through to the 9/15 century.

During the 8/14 century the Saharans were importers of grain from the 'Negro lands' and it is reasonable to assume that these included Hausaland. On the other hand, meat, especially mutton, seems to have been cheap and plentiful in at least some parts of the Sahara. Probably therefore, most of the meat produced in the savanna was consumed there, although some hides and skins were almost certainly exported to North Africa to help supply the increasing European demand for those products. Some of what was not exported into the Saharan system is likely to have passed into the *fatauci* network, in the form of hand manufactured leather goods at the making of which the Hausa craftsmen excelled.

Hausaland in relation to the economy of the west and central Sudan in the 10/16 century. By the 10/16 century the situation in Hausaland can be filled out in much greater detail. Trade with the outside world through the Mediterranean trading system which, as was said above, became evident in Mali early in the 8/14 century, had developed considerably by *c.* 957/1550. It had spread over Hausaland as well as Borno, involved a variety of commodities and was conducted by merchants of several different nationalities. For instance, it is known that Italian-speaking merchants from Ragusa (now Dubrovnik), a port on the east coast of the Adriatic sea in present-day Yugoslavia but at that time a tribute-paying vassal of the Ottoman Turkish empire, reached Kano, probably by way of Tripoli, during the century.[16] Ragusa was a commercial centre of great importance during the 10/16 century; although it was situated on the shore of the Adriatic, it was, none the less, closely linked to the trading system of the Mediterranean world. Indeed, it was the main rival of such Italian trading cities of the Mediterranean as Genoa, Leghorn and Naples. It must have been largely through Ragusa that the produce of the west and central Sudan – gold, ivory, spices, leather goods and so on – reached Europe. The Ragusans, being Christian subjects of the Ottoman Turkish empire, enjoyed trading privileges within that empire not extended to other Christians. These privileges were also probably respected by the Muslim kingdoms of Hausaland and by the caliphate of Borno. For although none of them were subject to the Ottomans, they normally maintained friendly relations with them. Not only did the Ragusans penetrate as far inland as Kano, and perhaps even deeper to the south as far as the Benue river, it even seems there was a substantial community of them permanently resident in Kano City at a date before 981/1573, when Giovanni Lorenzo Anania, the Neapolitan author who recorded the information supplied to him by these Ragusan merchants, published his first edition. They can only have been there as agents of the trans-Saharan trade who found it profitable to operate from within the Sudan. It would not have been worth their while to make the long and difficult journey to Kano unless the trade they engaged in from there was considerable. Among the articles in which they traded were gold, ivory and the spice known in Europe as 'grains of Paradise' (*Amomum Meleguetta*), the Hausa *citta*. Thus Hausaland became linked to the trade in pepper and similar spices that was the source of such great wealth for the merchant-cities of the Mediterranean in the 10/16 century. It is worth noting, however, that the authority for this information, namely Giovanni Lorenzo Anania, does not include slaves among the commodities for export in which these foreign merchants traded, although he does say that they kept domestic slaves. Christian merchants, such as the Ragusans presumably were, might not have been allowed to purchase slaves in an Islamic state. Indeed, it is surprising to find that Christian merchants were permitted to reside permanently in the interior of an Islamic country at all in those times. Normally, they were confined to the coastal areas such as North Africa and the Senegambian kingdoms of the Atlantic coast in the case of those who engaged in the West African trade. However, the Ragusans, although Christians for the most part, were subjects of the Ottoman Turkish empire and this may have gained them a privileged position. No restrictions would have applied to North African Muslim merchants and they could certainly have traded in slaves as well as in other commodities. Anania mentions North Africans as well as Ragusans among those who resided in Kano: thus the omission of any reference to slaves for export is significant and should be borne in mind.

Since the trans-Saharan trade and the prosperity of Hausaland were closely connected, it may safely be assumed that the internal trade of the country, the Hausa *fatauci* or middle-distance carrying trade, and *kasuwanci*, the local trade of the *kasuwa*, the Hausa market-place, also expanded in response to this stimulus. Indeed, there is evidence in Anania's account to suggest that this is exactly what did take place. Not only was the country north of present Zaria – Kano, Katsina, Zamfara, Kebbi and so on – well known to that author's informants, it also appears that they were familiar with the southern *fatauci* country from the place-names that he lists. Such places as: Nin, thought to be Ningi, on the north-eastern edge of the Jos Plateau; Calon, thought to be the Kalam of the Kano Chronicle, a 10/16 century Kwararafa kingdom in what is now Gombe emirate; Aqua, the most likely location for which seems to be present-day Akwanga, due south of the Jos Plateau; Cardi, which Professor Last believes to be Hausa 'Kurdi', an alternative name for the Kangoma state referred to above in this chapter; and Doma, immediately south of Cardi, on the route to the Benue. These places stretched south from Zaria, or Kangoma which may in the 10/16 century have been the more important commercial and political centre, to the Benue. It even seems possible that another place mentioned by Anania, namely Magredi, may have been a place called Magidi, south east of Doma, on the north bank of the Benue river, near to the present Makurdi.[17] It is not difficult to understand how this can have come about; the North Africans and Ragusans in Kano were interested in procuring ivory. The Niger/Benue Confluence was, no doubt, an important elephant hunting-ground in the 10/16 century, as it certainly was later, in the 13/19 century. It is therefore to be expected that they would have taken an interest in, and may even have explored, the routes by which the ivory reached them (see Appendix A, Diagram III and the inset to Map 5).

The expansion in both the external and the internal trade must have brought great prosperity to the merchant classes and to the aristocracy. It may, too, have profited the peasant-producers to some extent, especially those who supplied food to Kano and other large cities. No doubt elephant hunters prospered as well, for the Hausas have traditionally been skilled in the craft of elephant hunting and have developed specialised weapons for the conduct of it. However, it is probably safe to assume that it was, in most cases, the middlemen rather than the primary producers who profited the most.

Scraps of information given by such authors as Anania and Leo Africanus, together with our knowledge of the Mediterranean trade generally during the 10/16 century, suggest that, in return for these products of the Sudan, they certainly exported out across the Sahara into the Mediterranean markets. The Ragusans and their merchant colleagues from the Mediterranean shores offered bales of the coarse cloth known as kersey, the silks, satins and velvets for the manufacture of which the Italian cities were famous; also glass trinkets, mirrors, hardware and manufactured copper articles as well, probably, as various specie, that is minted coins, especially silver coins, which have long been highly prized in Hausaland for dowries and for feminine adornment. In Borno, according to Anania, there was also a busy trade in horses, imported by Arab merchants presumably from Egypt and North Africa. He also says that the Ragusans in Kano kept large stables of horses but these were, apparently, for their own use, and it cannot be assumed that Kano also participated in the trade in imported bloodstock. There is, of course, no doubt that large numbers of horses were in use in Kano during the 10/16 and 11/17 centuries. However, they may have been locally bred animals, not first-generation imported stock.

Kano may not have been the only Sudanic city that the Ragusans visited, although there is so far no evidence that they settled permanently elsewhere in substantial numbers. It is known, however, that one of these intrepid merchant-adventurers, a certain Vincenzo Matteo who was an informant of Anania, travelled widely in the west and central Sudan over a period of seven years residence there. Moreover, such names as the Fazzan, Borno, Agades, Timbuktu, Katsina, Kebbi, Gobir, Zamfara, Zegzeg and even perhaps Doma and other centres in the area of the river Benue, were familiar among merchant circles in such Mediterranean or Adriatic ports as Naples and Ragusa, as well of course, as in North African and Egyptian merchant circles. It appears from this that an expanding pattern of trade in the 10/16 century was not unique to Kano but was a general feature of the whole west and central Sudan. Indeed, the impression created by Anania's account is that there was a regular caravan circuit of the Sudanic cities. This was followed at fairly frequent intervals not only by Muslim merchants from North Africa and Egypt but also, apparently, by the Italian-speaking Christian Ragusans, and probably other Italian-speaking merchants as well. Anania makes it clear that the journey across the Sahara to the Sudan was still a very dangerous one and that many travellers lost their lives in sandstorms or as a result of the drying up of water-holes. However, once they reached the Sudan, it seems that communications between the Sudanic cities were not unduly difficult during the 10/16 century.

We also know that during this century there were substantial imports of Arabic books into Kano. These were hand-written manuscripts that were very expensive luxury items in those days and they are, therefore, another testimony to the growing wealth of that city. The Kano chronicler reports that during the reign of Abubakar Kado (973/1565–980/1573) malams, that is the local *ᶜulamā'*, became numerous in Kano. This was, no doubt, a consequence of the increased opportunities to acquire learning that the greater availability of books brought about. It may also be assumed that, if first copies were imported from North Africa and Egypt, the craft of the copyist who then reproduced the books locally, must have expanded greatly in the town and city centres of Hausaland. This would have brought much profit to literates and therefore encouraged the growth of the malam class. The employment of domestic and palace slaves, especially eunuchs also probably increased, and this is another indication of the growing wealth of the propertied classes.

Such developments all contributed to the continuation of the Islamic intellectual activity that began in the 9/15 century. The material prosperity of the 10/16 century and the wider contacts with the surrounding Muslim world that commercial expansion occasioned, not only ensured that this activity was sustained, it made sure that its momentum was increased and its scope widened as the century wore on.

However the 10/16 century was not solely a time of increasing material prosperity and intellectual activity, it also saw its share of natural disaster and man-made turbulence. Towards the end of the century, or perhaps early in the 11/17 century, there was a severe famine in the land that lasted for eleven years. There were also constant wars between the Kanawa and the Katsinawa that must have brought hardship and danger to the peasants and nomads who were caught up in the paths of the armies. The Kano chronicler reports that, as a result of one campaign the Kanawa fought with the Katsinawa between 973/1565 and 980/1573, 'devastation went on and the country was denuded of people'. Perhaps they fled or perhaps they were enslaved. If the latter, it was the Katsinawa who enslaved the people of Kano. Then, at the end of the century, the Kwararafas attacked Kano and 'ate up the whole country and Kano became very weak'. In addition to these wars, Kano was at war with Borno from time to time during the century. Finally, the 10/16 century appears to have been one not only of economic growth but also of some social change and considerable warlike activity.

Why should this have been so? To some extent the increase in trade is in itself enough to explain both the social changes and the increase in military activity. A rapid expansion of wealth and consequently of expectation frequently gives rise to social and economic unrest and military rivalry.

It is possible, too, that a sharp increase in the export of slaves from the west and central Sudan during the 10/16 century was a principle cause of the economic and military turbulence there. Increased slave-hunting would sooner or later have led to conflict over hunting grounds; increased slave exports might have meant fewer slaves for home use and therefore higher prices, thus widening social and economic differences between the slave-owning class and the rest which would in turn cause social tension. However, such a possibility should be viewed with caution. As was emphasised above, Anania specifically omits any mention of slaves as an export from Kano, although he does mention

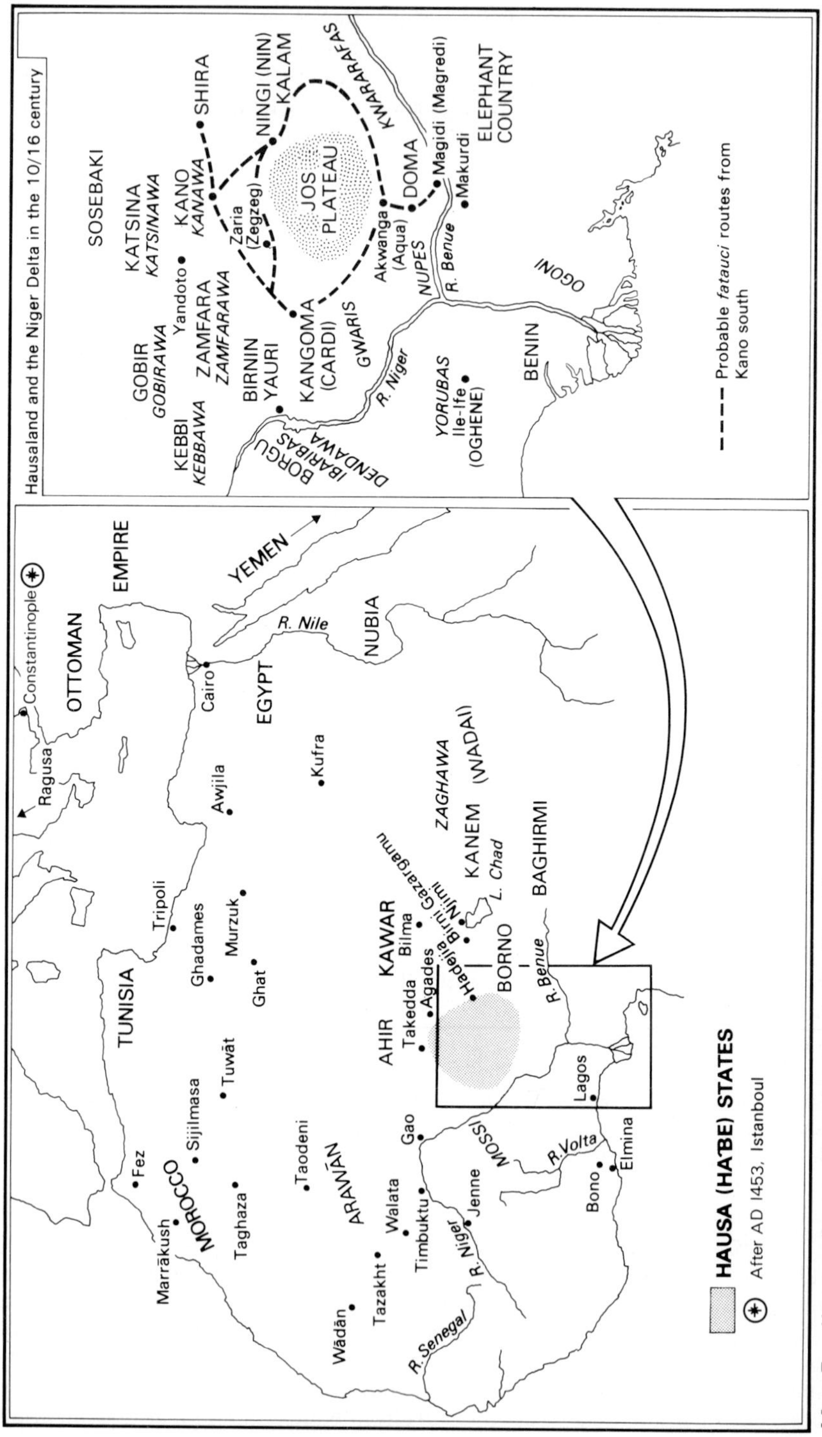

Map 5 Kanem, Borno Hausaland and the Niger from c. 802/1400 to 1008/1600.

that they were exported in considerable numbers from Borno in exchange for horses. This evidence cannot be ignored; it does not allow one to assume that there was an export trade in slaves from Kano similar to that from Borno, although some have apparently made that assumption. On the other hand, one naturally wonders what happened to all those people of whom the Kano countryside was 'denuded' between the years 973/1565 and 980/1573. Did they simply disappear into the bush? Did they pass into domestic slavery in Katsina? Were they exported from Katsina to North Africa? On the whole, the evidence suggests that the export of slaves from the west and central Sudan in the 10/16 century – or at any rate from Hausaland and Borno – was subject to wide fluctuations. Sometimes, after a campaign, there would be a glut of slaves in a particular place that exceeded domestic demand and these would be dumped on the export market, but a neighbouring trade centre might have no slaves for export. If such a picture is correct – and it depends to some extent on guesswork – then the enslavement of large numbers of people for export may have been a factor leading to turbulence from time to time and in particular places, but it cannot have been a constant factor.

It seems there may also have been considerable currency instability in some parts of the west and central Sudan during the 10/16 century, when the value of the cowrie apparently rose from its 8/14-century level of 1,150 to the *mithqāl* to only 400 to the *mithqāl*. It is true that there is some doubt as to whether this information, which comes from Leo Africanus, does represent the real state of affairs. It has been suggested, for instance, that in Leo's day a smaller *mithqāl* may have been in use than the one that was circulating in earlier centuries.[18] This is possible but unlikely, for by the end of the 10/16 century the *mithqāl* had recovered and was worth 3,000 cowries, a value more consistent with its pre-10/16-century level. This would surely not have happened if the older, heavier *mithqāl* had been replaced by a lighter coin. A more probable explanation is that the rise in the value of the cowrie at this time reflects the disturbance to the Mediterranean gold market that occurred in the 16 century AD. This was a result of the greatly increased flow of gold from the newly discovered sources of supply in the Americas; also, perhaps, the disruption caused by wars between the Christian powers of the Mediterranean area and the Ottoman Turks. Indeed, the drop in the value of gold at this time was not confined to the west and central Sudan, it occurred over most of western Europe and some authorities have suggested that it was, for all practical purposes, worldwide. Be that as it may, if such an abrupt drop in the value of gold did occur in Hausaland, it may well have contributed to disturbed conditions there. It is clear that the Hausa cities were involved in the gold trade and their economies must have depended on it to some extent.

However, owing to the growth in knowledge of the history of the countries surrounding the west and central Sudan, it is possible to suggest wider, more general causes that may explain why the 10/16 century in Hausaland was one of explosive commercial activity and considerable violence.

Fernand Braudel has argued that the 10/16 century witnessed a sharp growth in the population of the Mediterranean area, as well as a considerable increase in its trade, especially its seaborne trade. As for population, he observes that, by 957/1550 'There were too many people for comfort'.[19] He includes in this judgement the Islamic territories of North Africa and the

Ottoman empire. He goes on to point out that some authorities consider that the population of the Ottoman empire increased from 12 or 13 million in *c.* 926/1520–936/1530 to, possibly, 30 or 35 million by *c.* 1008/1600, a figure he considers 'by no means impossible'.[20] The west and central Sudan was not part of the Ottoman empire but it was closely linked to it through trade and culture; there is no reason to suppose that the causes of a population explosion in that empire can have left the Sudan entirely unaffected. Indeed, Braudel makes it clear that he believes the increase in population during the 10/16 century to have been worldwide.

Is it therefore the case that the conditions in Hausaland that are so persistently reflected in the Kano Chronicle – rapid commercial expansion, a great increase in wealth among certain classes, turbulence and constant wars, due perhaps to an increasing number of people competing for limited natural resources – are all part of a wider picture characteristic not only of the world of the west and central Sudan but also of the Mediterranean world to which it was so closely linked? It must be stressed that such a suggestion is only speculation, not fact. All the same, the 10/16 century in Hausaland provides a number of clues that leave one with the strong impression that that area in particular and the west and central Sudan in general, were indeed caught up in the greater human phenomen of a trade and population explosion that may have been worldwide.

Hausaland through the 11/17 and 12/18 centuries

Of the 11/17 and 12/18 centuries in Hausaland there is less that can be said. These centuries, too, fall before the period of extensive European penetration into the Sudan, and, except for the second half of the 12/18 century, before the period described by the Muslim Fulani authors. Moreover, the Kano Chronicle, so explicit for the 10/16 century, now becomes largely confined to accounts of dynastic struggles within Kano and of local incidents that throw little light upon what may have been going on in Hausaland as a whole. The wars between Kano and Katsina continued until *c.* 1060/1650, when peace was at last made between the two states; the Kwararafas, engaged in what must by now be seen as a long-term push out of the Benue area against the centralised, territorial states to the north, ravaged the countryside from time to time and occasionally threatened the walled city of Kano itself. Indeed, it has been suggested that the reason why Kano and Katsina made peace may have been that both were equally threatened by the Kwararafas. They may, therefore, have felt it more urgent to defend themselves against these external enemies than to pursue their long-standing rivalry for dominance within Hausaland. The threat from the militant Kwararafas was not limited to Hausaland, however, it extended also to Borno; yet by *c.* 1082/1671 it faded. After a fierce attack on Kano and Katsina in that year, the Kwararafas withdrew and there is no further record of their invasion. The reason for this sudden withdrawal is uncertain but it may have had something to do with divisions and rivalries within the Kwararafas' own kingdom.

Possibly as a reaction to the threat from the Kwararafas, Kano expanded southward during the 11/17 century into the Bauchi highlands, and south-east toward the bend of the river Gongola. It thus set up a buffer zone between Hausaland and the Kwararafas. Moreover, it seems likely that Kano was also concerned with the security of the *fatauci* trade routes that passed through these areas on the way to the Benue.

If Professor Last is right, the Muslim centre of Zaria in the south of Hausaland which had grown to commercial importance in the preceding century, became militarily powerful under a Muslim dynasty early in the 11/17 century and largely displaced the older state of Kangoma.

On the borders of Hausaland, the 11/17 century was marked by the slow decline of Kebbi from the position of military and commercial dominance, that it had enjoyed earlier, while the sultanate of Agades increased in power and influence at Kebbi's expense.

Politically and militarily the 12/18 century in Hausaland was characterised by the expansion of Gobir, especially its rivalry with Zamfara which it had come largely to dominate by early in the second half of the century. Meanwhile, an uneasy balance of power was maintained between Kano and Katsina. On its east, Kano was engaged in war with Borno which, however, proved indecisive; to the north it had to face attacks from both the Touregs and the confederation of the Sosebaki. This alliance of towns that had once been tributary to Kano but had then broken away, now challenged the power of their former overlord. Indeed, it has been suggested that during this century the Kano 'empire' had become so extensive that it faced a problem of control it did not have the military or organisational resources to cope with. As a result it began to fall apart. South of Kano, Zaria seems to have continued to grow in military power in this century and, perhaps profiting from the stalemate between Kano and Katsina, expanded into the orchard bush country of the Gwaris, to the south.

As for commerce, the Kano Chronicle reports that guns from Nupe were imported into Kano during the reign of Kumbari (1143/1731–1156/1743). In fact, these guns were probably muskets acquired in the first place at the coast. This piece of information suggests that by this reign, Kano, at least, was linked not only to the Saharan trade area but also to the Atlantic slave-trade which was at its height at this time. The normal article for which muskets were exchanged was slaves.

It is also clear from the Kano Chronicle that there was a colony of foreign merchants, probably mainly Arabic-speaking North Africans and Egyptians, resident in Kano during the first half of the 12/18 century. The chronicler reports that, owing to certain disturbances that took place in the city during Kumbari's reign, 'the foreign merchants left the town and went to Katsina'. It may be concluded from this that Katsina was, at this time, a near equal of Kano in its commercial importance, otherwise there would have been little point in the foreign merchants choosing it as an alternative settlement.

As regards Katsina, Dr Mahdi Adamu states that:

> Though Kano was described by the nineteenth century travellers who saw it as the commercial emporium of Hausaland, it may not have held that position in the eighteenth century. There is evidence to show that it was Katsina town that held the premier position before the outbreak of the Sokoto *Jihād* of 1804.[21]

He goes on to say:

> But how early before the eighteenth century Katsina had held this position of leadership in the economy of Hausaland is not known; it may have been as early as the beginning of the sixteenth century, for during that century Katsina, with Cairo and Fez, were the three largest markets in Africa where goods of all descriptions could be got.[22]

There is no doubt that Katsina was important, even as early as the 10/16 century, but that it was more important than Kano seems unlikely. If it had been, surely the 10/16-century Ragusans would have settled there and not in Kano. Moreover, one of the Ragusans left this comment behind him:

> Cheuno, which others call Cano, is one of three towns of Africa, the others being Fez and Cairo, concerning which the Moors say that there is nothing in the world that one cannot find there.[22]

He added the interesting information that the Portuguese had considered setting up an agency in Kano but had been dissuaded from doing so by the merchants in Cairo. Obviously then, Kano was of considerable commercial importance during the 10/16 century to trading interests in Portugal, in the Italian cities and in the Middle East.

There is little evidence to show what the relative commercial importance of each of the two centres – Kano and Katsina – was during the 11/17 century. Each appears to have defeated the other in war from time to time. However, as was said above, by the middle of the century peace was made between them. This may mean that a long-standing rivalry was satisfactorily resolved and that a commercial, as well as a military balance was established between the two. By the late 12/18 century and on into the early 13/19 century, the reports from consuls and others in North Africa are full of references to Katsina rather than to Kano. On the other hand, in Clapperton's accounts, which relate to the early 13/19 century, Kano certainly does not appear as if it was a new commercial centre. What does seem clear, however, is that Katsina was, at least from the 10/16 century, an important staging point on the caravan route that led into Hausaland; that it was via Katsina that caravans travelled on to Kano. This much is obvious from the account of Anania, who was writing *c.* AD 1570 and who relied on the report of Vincenzo Matteo, who had probably travelled the route in person. For Anania states that Kano 'is one month's distance from Katsina; it is thus that routes are measured in those parts'.[24] In fact, one month seems an inflated estimate of the time required to travel between Kano and Katsina, even for a loaded caravan and this is a little worrying. All the same, the report does establish the relationship of the two cities within the Sudanic communications system. Both were important staging points along the route; whether one or the other was dominant at a particular date may therefore be of secondary importance. No doubt they competed but it is not necessary to assume that one dominated the other for long periods at a time, although of course the fortunes of each are likely to have fluctuated over the short term.

The life of the Hausa people and their social classes from the 8/14 century on

What was the lot of the common people over the course of these centuries after they had emerged from the Bayajidda/Bagauda era? There is little that can be offered by way of certain information before the 13/19 century. Dr Mahdi Adamu has gathered together what is available to build a convincing picture of what the economy of Hausaland may have been like over the long period before adequate sources for economic history came to hand. He suggests that the Hausas were a society based 'on an elaborate system of agriculture and manually operated industrial production geared to both home consumption and export'.[25] That is to say, they were largely peasants who grew crops to feed themselves and to sell to the agents of *fatauci* and the trans-Saharan trade; also craftsmen who manufactured articles for use within Hausaland and for export beyond its borders. It is a picture that fits in well with what is known about the later centuries, when more information is available. If it is a true picture – and I am persuaded that it is – then Hausa society cannot have been unprosperous in the long term. It may have been hard-hit from time to time when afflicted by famine, drought and cattle-plague or when individual communities were scattered 'like a flock of guinea-fowl' by the sudden, brutal onslaught of raiders.

Relying on the account of the 13/19-century traveller Heinrich Barth, Mahdi Adamu proposes that the main crops were guinea-corn, millet, tobacco, groundnuts, coco-yams, sweet potatoes, beans, sesame, as well as the fruits of many useful trees. He believes the major agricultural exports to have been guinea-corn, millet and locust-bean cake (Hausa *daddawa*).[26] He supposes, reasonably, that most of what was true of the 13/19 century was probably true of earlier centuries. Certainly we have good grounds for believing that tobacco was used in Borno early in the 12/18 century. Its use was common in Islamic countries generally by the end of the 10/16 century. It is thus possible that Hausaland was already a producer of this crop by that date. It may, too, have been producing *citta*, the spice known as 'grains of Paradise', in commercial quantities by the middle of that century, for this was one of the commodities that brought foreign merchants to Kano. As for cereals, it has already been pointed out that Hausaland was almost certainly one of the exporters of this foodstuff in the 8/14 century.

These details of crop production give a clear picture of what the staple grain and vegetable constituents in the Hausas' diet must have been. Except during periods of prolonged drought it seems unlikely that any but the very poor went hungry in this fertile and abundant land.

As for meat, domestic meat-producing animals, especially goats and sheep, thrive in the savanna of Hausaland; again, only severe drought is ever likely to have reduced the stock of these hardy creatures. A large lexicon of names of indigenous, not Arabic origin, for meat-based foods in the Hausa language suggests that such foods have always been part of the Hausas' diet; not only for the wealthy but also for the general population, at any rate in the form of soups and stews of which meat forms part. Roast meat on the other hand, particularly the choice cuts such as the greatly relished hump of the local cattle and poultry meat, appear to have been luxury foods enjoyed mainly by the aristocracy and the wealthy. If their literature is a reliable guide, it seems the ordinary Hausas looked forward to such foods only in Paradise, as part of their Divine reward!

This grain, vegetable and meat diet was supplemented by a variety of sweetmeats, many of them of North African or Middle Eastern origin, of which honey, sugar and sometimes rice were the main constituents.

Islamic food prohibitions appear to have been widely known, as far as the record of Hausa literature shows. Forbidden foods were undoubtedly sometimes consumed by backsliders – and the *ᶜulamā'* did not cease to threaten them with Hell Fire for this. On the other hand the domestic pig, the meat of which is strictly forbidden to all Muslims, is at the present time an unknown animal in the Hausa towns and cities and most of the countryside; the consumption of carrion, wild pig, the hedgehog and other doubtful bush meats is constantly condemned in the literature. Even if the Hausas did not always observe the Islamic food prohibitions, they certainly had no excuse for pleading ignorance of them.

Apart from sweetmeats, most Hausa food names are indigenous, not Arabic, and few Middle Eastern dishes seem to have been adopted by the mass of the people. Except in so far as the Islamic prohibitions are concerned, the Hausas' adherence to Islam does not seem to have influenced their food habits to the same extent that it has influenced their dress and other aspects of social behaviour.

There is no direct evidence, as far as I know, for comparing the price of foodstuffs in Hausaland during earlier centuries with those that prevailed during the second half of the 13/19 century, when something is known.[27] At that time, however, it seems that grain was cheap when assessed according to the rate of the cowrie to the gold *mithqāl* (approx. 4.7 grammes), namely 3,500 to 4,000 cowries to the *mithqāl*. Heinrich Barth prices two loads of corn at 24 cowries. By 'load' he probably means the Hausa *dami* or head-load of unthreshed grain on the stalk since a 'mat' of threshed millet or rice, approximately half a hundredweight, cost 1,000 cowries. A live ram cost 4,000 cowries and a live goat 2,500 cowries or about one silver dollar. Since both prices obviously included the animal's skin, which was of some value, the meat hardly seems expensive. Approximately four pounds of honey cost 200 cowries, although it appears that high quality honey was considerably more costly. It is difficult to assess such prices in the absence of information as to the average income among the Hausas at this time. However, it is hard to believe that a few handfuls of grain, some scraps of meat, a few vegetables and a little honey – enough for a daily portion – was beyond the reach of any able-bodied person except perhaps during the 10/16 century, when prices may have been considerably inflated.

Concerning manufactured goods, Dr Mahdi Adamu says, 'One would perhaps not be wrong if one described Hausaland as the workshop of West Africa in the textile and leather industries.'[28] He goes on to suggest that the whole economy, both on its agricultural and manufacturing sides, was largely dependent on slave labour. He also draws an attractive and convincing picture of Hausa society busily revolving, socially and economically, around what is still the main focus of Hausa life today, the *kasuwa*, 'market-place'. The highly developed nature of the Hausa economy becomes clear when Dr Mahdi Adamu points to the level of price and quality control exercised by the Kano chiefs over the markets and export agencies within their jurisdiction and to the important function of *dillalai*, commercial agents, who, apparently, were guarantors of the quality of the goods that passed through their hands.[29] Such a system is unlikely to have developed within recent generations. Folklore and the Hausa language, which is so rich in specialised commercial terms, both suggest that it has been a feature of Hausa society since long ago.

It is unlikely that, throughout this long period of several centuries, there was much social mobility in Hausa society, except perhaps among slaves. Many slaves achieved spectacular material and professional advancement and the possibility of earning manumission always existed. Otherwise, few commoners had much opportunity to escape from the class into which they were born, except perhaps by converting to Islam and acquiring some literate education. This was not easy, for the profession of the *ᶜālim* was usually passed down from father to son and was thus exclusive. However, there must have been some recruitment into it as the generations passed, for it is known that the *ᶜulamā'* class increased considerably, especially during the 10/16 century.

Apart from the *ᶜulamā'* and the wealthy merchants (Hausa *attajirai*) there were four main classes in Hausaland *c.* 1214/1800 and no doubt they had been much the same for several centuries. They were: the *sarakuna*, 'chiefs', and *fadawa*, 'courtiers', who together made up the ruling class; the *'yan birni*, the town and city population, both slave and free; the people of the countryside comprising free peasants and both the slaves of the *rumada* (sing. *runji/rinji*), 'slave-villages', and the agricultural slaves who worked the *gandaye* (sing. *gandu*), 'farms', ranging from large holdings owned by the *sarakuna*, *fadawa* and rich merchants, to the smallholdings of individual freemen and freed slaves. Finally, there were the nomads, the people of the *rugage* (sing. *rugga*), the Fulani cattle-encampments.

The ruling class lived partly by slave-raiding and slave-trading, partly on taxes and customary dues and partly on the income from their *gandaye*, worked for them by the *rinji* slaves. Most of them probably considered themselves to be Muslims but in Haɓe times their observance of Islam seems to have been easy-going. How wealthy the Haɓe aristocrats and merchants were in relation to commoners is not known for certain. However, the schedule of the estate of a Kano nobleman who probably flourished in the middle of the 13/19 century has survived.[30] It is true there had been an Islamic revolution in the meanwhile, but his estate does testify to what wealth consisted of among his class. It is unlikely that the aristocrats of the Haɓe era were more self-denying than this 13/19-century nobleman. He owned 43 male and female slaves, seven horses and numerous saddles and items of saddlery, a large quantity of assorted gowns, many of them of rich fabric and embroidered with gold thread, as well as numerous other items of clothing. He also owned many bales of cloth, sundry perfumes, a large stock of threshed grain and quantities of luxury foodstuffs, a camel and two muskets. His whole estate was valued at 599 mats (Hausa *takrufa*, Arabic *ḥaṣīr*) of cowries and a mat contained approximately 20,000 cowries. If the nobleman died *c.* AD 1850, when the least advantageous rate of exchange was about 4000 cowries to the *mithqāl*, a 'mat' then was worth about 5 *mithqāls* and the value of the whole estate was 2995 such gold pieces. Prices given for individual items in the schedule suggest that this was probably the exchange rate when the estate was valued. In this case, in relation to the cost of living in his society which the schedule helps to establish, and indeed through the world of his day, the nobleman's fortune was a modest, but certainly not an enormous one. If he died later, say about 1890, when the exchange rate was as much as 15,000 cowries or more to the *mithqāl*, then of course the estate had become almost valueless. Be that as it may, praise-songs to Haɓe chiefs and courtiers do at least confirm that slaves, horses, saddlery and gowns were among the main items that made up a nobleman's wealth in Haɓe times, as they were in the 13/19 century.

The *'yan birni*, the townspeople, consisted of craftsmen, shopkeepers, petty traders and members of other service industries, also, no doubt, a substantial number of beggars, unemployed and unemployable, and other categories of the very poor who do not normally appear in the sources. The beggars, however, were by no means necessarily poor. They were the recipients of Muslim charity, virtually institutionalised in Hausa Muslim society. Moreover, they formed a powerful guild and, if the situation at the present day is any guide to the past, some of them became quite wealthy. Many beggars were blind people and it must be concluded that institutionalised begging was the society's way of coping with this common affliction, a form of social welfare. According to Hausa tradition beggars had been a feature of Kano society even before the coming of Islam. Their blindness was God's punishment for their early opposition to the building of mosques. During the Muslim era beggars have customarily been the reciters of the vernacular religious songs mentioned above and a few even mastered certain well-known classical Arabic poems. Some toured certain quarters of the town performing their recitations in return for alms while others stationed themselves outside the mosques for the same purpose.

Several categories of slaves lived in the towns and cities. There were the *cucanawa*, persons born into slavery; they were often slaves of chiefs and kings, who filled positions of considerable responsibility and enjoyed a relatively high social position. They were very vulnerable, however, to the whims of their masters and liable to fall from grace if they incurred the displeasure of those whom they served. Therefore, although they were often powerful, they were also usually very insecure.

There were the eunuchs, Hausa *babanni*, male, castrated slaves who may sometimes have been members of the larger class of *cucanawa*. They too were widely employed in the Haɓe courts. The operation necessary to make eunuchs of them was often carried out when they were very young boys. Although Muslims employed eunuchs, the actual performing of the operation of castration is forbidden in Islam and it might therefore be assumed that it was normally carried out by non-Muslims. Older men were also operated upon and certain methods of operation were less dangerous than others. However, the survival rate, especially among boys, was low. Yet it is known that young men sometimes volunteered for the operation because, if successful, it enhanced their chances of personal advancement. Because of the dangers involved in any form of operation upon them for the purpose of castration, eunuchs were a most expensive class of slave. In well-to-do households there were those slaves known in Hausa as *bayin gida*, 'house slaves', who performed the duties of domestic servants. It is obvious from Hausa literature that these *bayin gida* were often treated very much as members of the family, although it was generally believed that slaves were less reliable in character than free people and not fully trustworthy. It was the custom to give them punning nicknames, to which the slave was supposed to give an appropriate answer when called. Thus one of the Kano nobleman's female slaves was called 'Naroƙa' (I beseech), to which she was supposed to answer '*Allah ya ba ni*' (May God grant me) whenever she was called by name. Another was called 'Nufimmudasu' (Our intention towards them), to which she was supposed to reply, '*Anniya ta gari*' (The intention is good). Among the *bayin gida* were the *ƙwaraƙwarai* (Hausa, sing. *ƙwarƙwara*) or *saɗokoki* (Hausa, sing. *saɗaka*, from the classical Arabic *ṣadaqa*, 'legal alms' or 'dowry'), the concubines. Naturally, they were often treated with great affection and could not be sold after they had born their master a child, but Hausa literature suggests that those who were reluctant to conform to what their masters wished sometimes suffered severe punishments. Islamic law as well as local custom carefully regulated a man's relations with his concubines, in order to try and ensure that they were not favoured above wives. For instance, among the Muslim Hausas a man was only supposed to have intercourse with his concubines during the hours of daylight; the nights belonged to his wives. He was not supposed to give presents to his concubines over and above what he gave to his wives. Hausa literature makes it clear that although this was the law and the custom, it was not always observed.

The price of slaves varied considerably. Young female slaves were more expensive than males. During Haɓe times a slave girl could probably have been purchased for about 30 *mithqāls*. By the middle of the 13/19 century the price had risen to about 40. Slaves were, of course, legally property and were inherited with the rest of a man's estate.

In the countryside, beyond the city and sometimes so far distant from it as to be barely subject to its control except through *hakimai*, 'village headmen', was the third main class, the rural population. This was made up of several different categories, slave and free. First, there were the people of the *gandaye* (Hausa sing. *gandu*), agricultural holdings that varied from small farms to large units that have been called 'plantations', although there are obviously inappropriate associations attaching to the use of this word in a Sudanic context. The size of a *gandu* and the nature of its organisation seem to have varied according to the chiefdom, emirate and so on in which it was located. Polly Hill, perhaps the most informed and certainly the most constructively argumentative of contemporary scholars on this subject, has pointed out that the whole question of agricultural slavery in the west and central Sudan is immensely complex and defies generalisations.[31] The smaller *gandaye*, or smallholdings, were farmed by free peasants with the help of a few slaves – a typical *gandu* workforce might be three or four slaves working side by side with the farmer's two sons. These people lived together on the *gandu* and there was probably little social and economic differentiation in their ways of life and standards of living. The larger *gandaye*, which were often organised specially to produce cereals for the middle-distance *fatauci* trade as well as for the *kasuwa* or local market trade, were usually owned by princes, noblemen and rich merchants. They were often absentee landlords who lived in the towns off the profits of the *gandu* and such large *gandaye* were worked by much larger slave workforces.

Also part of the agricultural complex of the countryside were the people of the *rumada* (sing. *runji/rinji*), the 'slave-villages'. There has been much scholarly debate about *rumada*, where they occurred, who owned them and how they were organised. That they existed in Gobir at the end of the 13/18 century is beyond reasonable doubt, for they are mentioned in the Hausa verse of the Muslim reformers. It seems they also existed in Kano, although Polly Hill believes that 'the great majority of farm-slaves in rural Kano, as elsewhere in the central Hausa emirates, were owned by private farmers!'[32] This would suggest that most of the Kano farm-slaves lived with the farmers' families on the *gandaye*, not in *rumada*. The *rumada* were owned, for the most part, by the larger, absentee slave-owners mentioned above who farmed the large *gandaye*. The status of the inhabitants of the *rumada* has also been the subject of much argument – were they truly slaves or should they be called serfs and so on? It is not appropriate to pursue that discussion here but only to say that they must, necessarily, have enjoyed a large measure of freedom. They had their own plots which they worked, the produce of which was their own, and custom allowed them adequate time for this as well as for the pursuit of crafts for their own profit. The slave-owner was wholly responsible for the upkeep of newly acquired slaves but they became progressively more self-supporting as time went on. By the second generation it seems that many *rumada* slaves became, to all intents and purposes, free peasants.

It seems, too, that this system of the *gandaye/rumada*, upon which agriculture in Hausaland, and indeed much of the west and central Sudan, was based, was a highly efficient one that gives the lie to the widely held but largely unsubstantiated claim that slave labour is necessarily less productive than hired, paid labour. On this point Polly Hill has commented:

> The fact of the matter is that farm-slavery systems were far more profitable . . . than any system that might have involved free labourers – and this quite apart from the fact that the concept of 'wage-labour' existed nowhere in the West African savanna in the nineteenth century.[33]

In so far as Hausa literature has a bearing on this point, it certainly tends to confirm Polly Hill's view. Moreover, there can be little doubt about the general efficiency of the agricultural system based on farm slavery regulated by the comprehensive provisions of Mālikī law, that Heinrich Barth observed in the middle of the 13/19 century. It was also a most efficient system for the propagation of Islam as within a generation almost all the slaves became Muslims.

Some scholars, impressed by the widespread nature of the *gandu/rinji* system, have questioned whether there were any really free peasants in Hausaland during the 12/18 and 13/19 centuries. In fact, there must have been a considerable number. One way in which the peasants showed resentment against excessive taxation or other injustices was by moving out of the territory of an oppressive chief and this can only have been possible for persons who were free. Apart from this, however, the objection overlooks the rather ambiguous status of the *rumada* slaves. It was obviously impossible, as well as undesirable, to keep large numbers of agricultural workers on the end of a ball and chain; there comes a point when it is no longer useful to argue as to whether these people were 'slaves' in any widely accepted meaning of that term, or simply peasants bound to the land by custom and the nature of their way of life.

Some comments on the export slave-trade and the purposes and conditions of slavery

The above discussion relates to domestic and farm-slavery. There is, however, another aspect of the institution – the acquiring of slaves for the purpose of exporting them to markets beyond the Sudan.

The subject is enormous in respect of the volume of material involved and the complexity of it. My intention below is to do no more than draw attention to a few salient points that seem to me to relate particularly to the Muslim states of the west and central Sudan.

It is well known that the 17 and 18 centuries AD marked the height of the Atlantic slave-trade. Certainly the Muslim states of the west and central Sudan were involved in this to some extent. For example, Muslim traders in the Senegambia were exporting slaves to the Caribbean as early as *c.* AD 1615. Non-Muslim states were involved too and the trade was by no means an exclusively Muslim affair as one might suppose from the accounts of certain Christian missionary and humanitarian commentators of the 19 and early 20 centuries AD. On the contrary, it was largely conducted by coastal, non-Muslim Africans and their European partners.

The medieval trade in slaves across the Sahara, on the other hand, was much more characteristically Islamic, if only because most – though still not all – of the states concerned in it were Muslim. The slaves required for the trade were obtained, in part, by raiding the loosely organised family-and-clan-group people on the edges of the great centralised Sudanic empires – the Lamlam of the medieval Arabic writers. They were obtained, too, from war captives, so that enslavement was, in some measure, a by-product of war waged for political purposes and not an end in itself. In addition, some slaves have probably always been acquired by kidnapping, as described in the historical novel, *Shaihu Umar*,[34] which is based on fact, but these must surely have been only a small proportion of the total number enslaved. According to the accounts of the Arabic and Portuguese sources, large numbers of slaves who were exported across the Sahara were exchanged for horses, similarly imported.

To judge from the prestigious *History of West Africa (HWA)*, there is a wide consensus of agreement among scholars that this medieval trans-Saharan export trade in slaves was both considerable and carried on by all the major states of the west and central Sudan, more or less continuously. Some rather sweeping statements have been made about it, as will become apparent below. However, some voices have recently been raised in partial disagreement with this view and have suggested, moreover, that enslavement in general in the Sudanic Muslim states may have been exaggerated in its extent and that its purposes have been misunderstood. The following is an interesting case in point.

The Kano chronicler tells how, during the 8/14 century, slaves were brought to Kano not individually and in small groups, but in large companies of several hundreds and even thousands. This went on until, in the reign of Abdullahi Burja (841/1438–856/1452), he notes that the Galadima of Kano founded twenty-one towns, in each of which he settled a thousand 'slaves', five hundred males and five hundred females. In commenting on this Professor Hunwick, who is primarily concerned with describing Hausaland in the 10/16 century, writes:

> Under Runfa's grandfather, ᶜAbdullāh Burja, enormous numbers of slaves had been obtained from the southlands. These slaves formed the nucleus of a labour force upon which Kano built its prosperity, using them for agriculture and other labour, as porters and guards on the trade routes soon to be opened up with Borno, Gonja and Agades, as soldiers for military campaigns and as barter items for Mediterranean imports, in particular the all-important horses.[35]

In the first place, it is questionable whether even many thousands of 'slaves' deserve to be described as 'enormous numbers' when they were apparently quickly dispersed over the surrounding countryside – 21,000 persons settled in twenty-one towns. Professor Hunwick's robust statement may, therefore, exaggerate the extent of slavery within Birnin Kano, such as that city may have been in the 9/15 century. Apart from that, however, there are grounds for challenging the assumption that it was slaves that were exported from Kano in exchange for Mediterranean goods in the 10/16 century. It would of course be rash to assert that they were never used for this purpose. However, Anania's evidence referred to above, suggests that it may have been other goods, and not slaves, that were used in this exchange, at least at certain times. Even if slaves were exported, there is no reason to suppose that they were drawn from the descendants of those with whom the Galadima populated the twenty-one towns in the previous century. On the contrary, this seems most unlikely.

As one scholar has pointed out, the activities of the Galadima of Kano in Abdullahi Burja's reign ought not to be associated with 'slavery' in the generally accepted meaning of that term. They were more in the nature of enforced population movements and were an aspect of state-building that had no connection with trade, domestic slavery nor even perhaps, with the farm slavery of the *rumada*, described above; although certainly they must have had a wider agricultural purpose.[36] Also, it is interesting to speculate as to whether these so-called slaves can have been subjected to the restrictions on freedom of movement normally imposed on the newly enslaved. How did the Galadima keep 21,000 people confined in twenty-one towns? Certainly, distance from their original homeland, and the perils of lonely travel through the bush, helped to keep them where they had been settled. There must, none the less, have been a considerable element of cooperation on the part of these 21,000 souls if the policy of moving them and re-settling them was to be worth undertaking in the first place. The object of the Galadima's initiative was thus surely to populate empty lands, boost agriculture and strengthen the security of metropolitan Kano, not to provide a reservoir of house slaves and trade slaves upon which Kano could draw for generations to come. It is to be expected that, within two or three generations, the descendants of these 21,000 persons settled around Kano by the Galadima would have become free; that by the 10/16 century they were the rural, tax-paying subjects of the Kano chiefs. To have depopulated the countryside all over again by enslaving them and selling them for export would have been the height of folly. What slaves Kano required must surely have been obtained in the course of her constant wars with her neighbours – in which, it is worth observing, she was as often as not defeated.

The situation in Borno during the 10/16 century was apparently different from that in Kano. There is evidence that slaves were an important item in Borno's trade with North Africa and that they, and not other products, were the particular items exchanged for horses. However, it would be rash to assume that this situation was typical of what always obtained in Borno. It may have been due to special circumstances, namely, the exceptional availability of war captives and the exceptional demand for horses created by the expansion of the Saifawid empire during that century, culminating in the wars of Mai Idrīs Aloma.

Another aspect of slavery about which there has been considerable misunderstanding is that which concerns the degree of liberty normally enjoyed by slaves in Muslim communities. The slave, roped by the neck to a line of other slaves and driven through the bush or exposed for sale in the market, deprived of all physical freedom and stripped of all human dignity, is not a wholly untruthful picture. It is merely an overworked one for it usually applied only for brief periods and in special situations. Generally speaking, it was true of first-generation slaves at the time of, or shortly after capture. Those who were most likely to suffer such treatment for long periods were those unlucky enough to be driven down to the coast or exported across the Sahara. Most slaves destined for the internal markets of the west and central Sudan quickly entered what was, in effect, a servile profession. They became soldiers, civil servants, commercial agents, concubines and, at lower levels, domestic servants, craftsmen and labourers, whose relationship to their owners was one of client to patron and not one of abject, total servitude. The limitation on their freedom of movement was, in most cases, no more than that they could not leave the service of their master without his consent and the payment of what may reasonably be termed a 'transfer fee' by the new owner. In Muslim Hausa society, at any rate, while slave concubines like free women of aristocratic rank were normally confined in purdah, male slaves such as the *cucanawa* had full freedom of movement in the towns and cities. Some, like the palace slave Gumuzu, in the story of *Sheihu Umar*, were sufficiently physically independent to go off on kidnapping expeditions on their own account. It is clear that slaves also enjoyed considerable freedom in 8/14-century Mali as described by Ibn Baṭṭūṭa. Among the Wolofs and Serers of the Senegambia, one may instance the *jambor*, who were roughly equivalent to the *cucanawa* among the Hausas, and the *tyeddo*, the powerful crown slaves upon whom the rulers depended for their fighting forces and who frequently dominated politics. Such persons were essentially professional clients, who enjoyed considerable status in their societies and had numerous opportunities for advancement, limited in their personal freedom more by the ties of self-interest and custom than by restraints imposed by force. Indeed, to understand the true nature of slavery in the Muslim west and central Sudan, it is necessary to appreciate that, while there was a legal distinction between servile and free, there was very little social distinction and virtually no economic distinction. Slaves could own slaves and the slaves of slaves could own slaves, and so on, indefinitely. Slaves could reach the highest levels of the state service; they could become distinguished scholars or military commanders in whose hands the fate of kingdoms rested. They could even aspire to supreme office, for Sakura, an early ruler of Mali, was a freed slave.

None the less, it remains true that most slaves, especially domestic slaves in the lower social orders, laboured under the ultimate restriction upon their freedom, in that they could not run away. This certainly did not mean that they were locked up or went around in chains. They were usually allowed to move freely about the towns and villages in which they lived, to go to market, visit socially and so on, but they were placed on trust not to attempt to escape. If they did so there were, at least in Hausaland, professional slave-catchers whose job was to recover them.

It is also true that, at certain times in the history of Hausaland, for example in the 13/19 century, carefully organised raids which were not part of wider campaigns waged for political and military ends, were carried out against villages specifically for the purpose of obtaining slaves. One such raid is vividly described in the historical novel *Sheihu Umar*, mentioned above, and is no doubt true to life. It cannot be said for certain that such deliberate slave raids, as opposed to more generalised warfare in which prisoners-of-war were incidentally enslaved, were common in earlier centuries. It is at least possible that it was the European demand for slaves on the Coast that caused such raiding to develop and that it was not a feature of Sudanic life before this demand arose.

Slave-owners

Where there were slaves, there were obviously slave-owners. In Hausaland, as in the west and central Sudan generally, they were drawn from all classes, for even slaves could own their own slaves. It is known that the *ᶜulamā'* were major slave-owners during the 12/18 century and it was this that gave them leisure to pursue their scholarly calling.

The *ᶜulamā'* were normally freemen and, being Muslims, could not therefore be enslaved according to Islamic law. Such was the prestige of their calling that this immunity was widely respected. Merchants were also usually immune, probably because they, too, were conspicuously Muslim and claimed free status. Like the *ᶜulamā'* they were commonly major owners of slaves. Other major owners were, of course, the noblemen and office-holders, whether themselves slave or free. In major cities such as Kano, foreign merchants, especially North Africans, probably owned a significant number of the slaves. The wives of wealthy persons also appear to have been able to own slaves, both males and females, in their own right, and young slaves were commonly given to them as gifts. Muslim owners had a strict obligation to educate their slaves in Islam. The evidence of Hausa literature suggests that, among the Muslim Hausas, this obligation was usually, though not always, conscientiously observed. Slaves who had received such an education and who were then given their freedom sometimes became *ᶜulamā'*; their slave origin seems to have been no obstacle to this, at any rate not during the 13/19 century.

The people of the rugage

The fourth main class of the population of Hausaland was that of the people of the *rugage* (sing. *rugga*), 'cattle-encampments' of the nomadic, cattle-raising Fulani. They lived in the bush, far from the towns and cities for most of the year but came into town seasonally, to trade and to buy supplies. The *rugage* of the cattle Fulani shifted as they migrated across their grazing grounds. They were subject to their own *ardo'en* (sing. *ardo*), clan chiefs, and were allowed grazing rights by the Haɓe chiefs in whose territories they roamed. This had been so for many generations and their grazing rights were usually hereditary. It was part of the chief's function to keep the peace between nomads and peasants,

> The last [of the Haɓe] was King Garba,
> who ruled [in Hadejia],
> In his time a Harɗo [Ardo] came with numerous flocks,
> He found the king of the Haɓe, Garba Abubakar,
> He was one who loved men, he did not practise any
> separation [between nomads and peasants].[37]

Such fairness and even-handedness was not always easy, for although there was some cooperation between nomads and peasants in the exchange of produce, there was also frequent tension. The nomads' cattle trampled the peasants' crops and fouled their water sources, the peasants cultivated the land that the nomads required for grazing and from time to time violence broke out between the two sides. Since the chief was a land-owner, his sympathies usually lay with the peasants. Indeed, there is evidence to suggest that, during the 9/15 century, the practice of enclosing large *gandaye* had increased. This must have been at the expense of the nomads' grazing rights. Their resentment at this encroachment may have persisted over the centuries and perhaps accounts for the dissatisfaction that certainly existed among the nomadic Fulani *c.* 1213/1799. Other causes of dissatisfaction among them were that they were subject to punitive raids by certain Haɓe chiefs, perhaps because they failed to pay their taxes or perhaps because the local peasants had complained about the destruction of their crops. As a result of these raids some of them were sometimes enslaved. Also, they were forced to pay *jangali*, the hated cattle-tax. It may have been specifically the nomadic Fulanis' habit of trying to avoid this tax that was the main cause of the raids against them that occurred in Gobir immediately before the outbreak of the *jihād*. At any rate, it is clear that many of the nomadic Fulani in Hausaland, and in Borno, too, were in a rebellious mood when the 12/18 century closed. They were thus very ready to listen to the anti-Haɓe preaching of their Muslim kinsmen.

Other taxes levied by the Haɓe chiefs were *kurɗin gari*, a tax on townspeople; *kurɗin ƙasa*, a land tax on cultivators; *kurɗin salla*, a tax levied at the time of Islamic festivals; *tasuwa*, a tax on meat, and *agama*, a general term that covered a variety of market dues. In addition, the people had to give *gaisuwa*, customary presents, to office-holders. They were also liable to *gargaɗi*, compulsory military service. Some of these taxes were certainly not sanctioned by the Sharīᶜa, and, naturally, the Muslim reformers made much of this in their attacks on the Haɓe. However, although there were many demands made on the peasants and nomads, there is little to suggest that any of them were unduly oppressive.

As was said above, Islam had begun to make headway among the common people as from the middle of the 12/18 century. According to the Shehu Usumanu ɗan Fodio, conversion among the town population, the *rinji* slaves and the *rugga* Fulani was far advanced by the end of that century. He says:

> We know that the true religion
> Has now spread to the towns,
> Everyone knows the Truth,
> In the Fulani cattle-encampment (*rugga*],
> in the slave-hamlet [*rinji*] and even
> in the town quarter.[38]

Indeed, he implies that only the chiefs and courtiers still held out. Unfortunately, there is little evidence as to the state of mind of the city and town population or the cultivators, whether servile or free, at the time when the Shehu made this comment. Subsequent events suggest that at least some of them shared the dissatisfaction of the nomadic Fulani.

Social and economic factors helpful to the spread of Islam

Islam is a moving of the spirit and an ideology accepted in the mind. The reader may therefore enquire what the above discussion of economic and social factors, to say nothing of population explosions in the Mediterranean, has to do with the theme of this book.

To suggest that the circumstances and developments I have described above were the sole factors that brought about the spread of Islam in the west and central Sudan, would be to exaggerate their importance. It is certainly my opinion, which I have stressed in several places in this book, that it is the spiritual longings and the conscious decisions of thinking men and women that are the prime determinants of all history, not blind forces. However, economic and social events were associated with it, if not directly, then in many subtle and roundabout ways. First, it seems clear that the people of Hausaland moved gradually out of an early hunting-gathering and subsistence-farming economy into an export/import economy. Out of this unfolding economic pattern there arose social and material conditions that were favourable, in certain ways, to the spread of Islam. For example, as was pointed out above, merchants and traders, especially those engaged in *fatauci* and the trans-Saharan trade, tended to be Muslims. Thus Islam spread as their activities became more general. So it can be argued that the growth of an export/import economy was, quite by chance, a factor that led to the spread of Islam. Second, increasing wealth helped to promote literacy which was inseparable from Islam before the 20 century AD, when Christian missionaries and the colonial administrations introduced a rival literacy. Moreover, the growth of the slave labour force gave the propertied classes the leisure in which the arts of literacy could be pursued, and in which the educational system of the *Katātīb* and the *madāris* could thrive. Once again, Islam was the beneficiary, this time because of a more deliberate and calculated chain of events – those that add up to Islamic education. The link was perhaps more complex than this, for, as economic activity increased, so the *ᶜulamā'* ensured that Islamic institutions became more and more entwined in it and essential to it. Since this was in any case convenient, it was widely accepted. In consequence, disputes were resolved and contracts sealed in the court of the *alkali*, Muslim magistrate, and the slavery that largely underpinned the economy was itself regulated according to the Sharīᶜa. Even the day-to-day activities of the *kasuwa* were drawn ever more tightly within the net of Islamic regulations. How this may have come about can be seen from the following passage from an Arabic poem composed by the Borno *ᶜālim*, Muḥammad b. al-Ḥājj ᶜAbd al-Raḥmān al-Barnāwī, early in the eighteenth century:

> And the withholding of anything [in order to obtain a higher price] is illegal if it harms the people, according to what has been made known,
> But [the learned] disagree concerning the withholding of food, in so far as this does not harm the people,
> But they permitted it in things other than food, so long as it does no harm.
> But its prohibition in times of distress is well known,
> . . .
> An example is the storing of the grain foodstuffs of a year.
> This is legal according to the Sunna.[39]

Thus the Muslim ᶜ*ulamā'* invoked the Sharīᶜa to control the common practice of raising prices by hoarding. We should not imagine that the market traders were able to read Arabic. But the authority of the Imām al-Barnāwī was such that his ruling was certainly known among them. Later, in the late 12–13/18 century or the early 13/19 century, Shaykh ᶜAbd Allāh b. Muḥammad, the brother of the Shehu Usumanu ɗan Fodio, wrote the following lines in Hausa, which certainly were addressed directly to a Hausa-speaking audience:

> Leave off cheating according to the way of the world,
> Debtors, do not refuse to pay your debts
> While you continue to squander your wealth,
> Ha! You tailor, you corn merchant,
> Do not put yourselves in Hell Fire.
>
> Ha! The weaver and the dyer,
> Ha! The butcher, make sure the animal has been properly bled,
> The seller of salt and soap,
> Those who labour for someone else,
> Refrain from cheating, do you hear?
>
> The itinerant trader (*mai fatauci*) and the market trader (*mai kasuwa*),
> The sellers of *tuwo* and of locust-bean cake,
> You who measure out guinea corn, listen to my warning and give just measure,
> . . .
> Those who buy cheap, measuring it out [in small portions to sell dear],
> . . .
> Your torment is rumbling [like thunder in the Fire of Hell].[40]

And later still, in the 13/19 century Isan Kware, the posthumous son of the Shehu wrote,

> Those who play the market, they eat poison by their swindling, [The world] causes some to rob and some to cheat,
> Against the law of Islam. . .[41]

These quotations show how the ᶜ*ulamā'* sought, over many generations and with considerable success, to influence the bustling life of the *kasuwa* and the ceaseless activity of the *fatake*, the Hausa *fatauci* traders, always reaching farther afield so that these were carried on within the framework of Islamic commercial regulations and social morality. It was not only the conduct of commerce that had to be in accordance with the Sharīᶜa, to satisfy these guardians of the Muslim conscience; the working day of the trader or the craftsman had to be so ordered that he was able to fulfil his obligations as a Muslim,

> Some make their living in the place of pounding mud floors,
> some sing *bori* [spirit possession cult] songs,
> They forget the time of noon prayer,
> All the prayer-times pass without giving thanks to God.[42]

Clearly then, not all the people were scrupulous in observing these obligations; yet the widespread recognition that such duties existed powerfully influenced the pattern of life in the Hausa cities, towns and villages. So too it began to make an impact on those areas beyond Hausaland, where *fatauci* extended. As the social and legal patterns of Islam became more widely adopted, they carried conversion with them, not always from theological conviction, but, as was said above, sometimes from convenience. Nevertheless, before long, it becomes difficult to imagine how the life of the community in the Hausa towns and cities could be conducted at all, outside the framework of Islam and it becomes easy to understand how and why Islam began to spread among the Hausas' neighbours.

NOTES

1 Hiskett, *Hausa Islamic verse*, 1975. pp. 143–5.
2 Hiskett, *BSOAS*, XXVIII, 1, 1965, pp. 113–16.
3 Hodgkin, 1975, pp.74–6.
4 W.K.R. Hallam, *JAH*, VII, 1, 1966.
5 'Towards a less orthodox history of Hausaland', *JAH*, 20, 1979
6 Murray Last, unpublished seminar paper 'Before Zaria: Evidence for Kankuma (Kangoma) and its successor states' (submitted for Essays in honour of Professor Abdullahi Smith, 1980), Institute of Commonwealth Studies, SOAS, London, African History Seminar, 28 January, 1981.
7 *HWA*, I, second ed., pp.277–8.
8 Gibb, p.336.
9 A. Épaulard, 1956, II, pp.472–3.
10 1978, p.105–6.
11 Palmer, 1928, III, p.108.
12 Burdon, 1909, p.94.
13 Palmer, 1928, III, p.116.
14 Fuglestad, *JAH*, XIX, 3, 1978, pp.319–39.
15 Hiskett, Ibadan, 1963, p.87.
16 Dierk Lange and Silvio Berthoud, 'L'interieur de l'Afrique Occidentale d'apres Giovanni Lorenzo Anania (XVI siecle)' *Cahiers d'histoire mondiale*, 14(2), 1972. All further references to the work of Anania in this chapter are based on information given in Lange and Berthoud's article and will not be separately annotated except in the case of direct quotations, or when particular comment is required.
17 Lange and Berthoud, 1972, tentatively identify 'Nin' with Ningi, 'Calon' with Kalam and 'Doma' with present-day Doma. 'Aqua' they leave unidentified. They are clearly puzzled, however, by 'Magredi' and simply comment on the resemblance between this name and the river Magrida near Tunis, which is mentioned by Leo Africanus. This identification seems to me to be most improbable. Anania gives a long account of Kano (Cheunò) and immediately following this he says, '*Indi non molto lontano si scorge Magredi e Nin. . .*', 'Then not very far distant, one comes on Magredi and Nin. . .' This surely suggests that he believed Magredi to be in some way associated with Kano. His picture of Hausaland, like his picture of the area south-east of Lake Chad, is generally very detailed and accurate and there therefore seems to me no reason to look for Magredi in North Africa. A route passing from Kano via either Ningi or Zaria, Akwanga and Doma would naturally terminate at a fording point on the north bank of the Benue. Magidi appears on the 1901 Ordnance Survey map of the Niger Territories, linked to Doma by a track and although it disappears from subsequent maps of Nigeria it continued to be known as a canoe station for many years after 1901. Another possibility, of course, is that Magredi was not Magidi but Makurdi. This town is sometimes said to have arisen as a railway centre after the beginning of the colonial occupation but it seems likely that there was a place of that name on the Benue before the railway was built. However, the name Makurdi comes from the Hausa *makurdī/mukurdī*, 'the narrows of a river' and the place is thus unlikely to have been a crossing-point. On the whole, I am persuaded that Magredi was Magidi. I have discussed this whole question in detail in a seminar paper

'The location of placenames on the 10/16-century map of Hausaland and the search for Prester John of the Niger Delta', History Department Seminar, SOAS, London, 17 June, 1981. Since this book went to press I have come upon evidence that strongly suggests that Anania's Nin is not Ningi, as suggested by Lange and Berthoud, but the Nunkoro, 'Nun of the Koro people', the early importance of which was discovered by Adamu (1978, pp. 45–6). Also, it has been pointed out to me by Hausa colleagues who know the area well that, although Makurdi is indeed the 'Narrows of the River', it is none the less wide enough for canoe-men to cross with ease at the present day and obviously, this may also have been the case in the 10/16 century. Thus, while I still marginally favour Magidi as Anania's Magridi, the case for Makurdi is now somewhat more persuasive. I discuss these matters in greater detail in an article 'Reflections on the location of place names on the 10/16-century map of Hausaland and their relation to *fatauci* routes', *Kano Studies*, forthcoming.

18 Marion Johnson, *JAH*, XI, 3, 1970. II, 1966. p.358.

19 op. cit. i, p.403.

20 ibid, p.410.

21 1978, p.12.

22 ibid, p.13.

23 Lange, 'Anania', p.339.

24 ibid. p.339.

25 1978, p.10.

26 ibid, p.10.

27 Hiskett, 'Cowry Currency', I, gives details of the values, in cowries of a number of items of foodstuff, clothing and so on.

28 Adamu, 1978, p.11.

29 ibid, p.12.

30 Hiskett, 'Cowry Currency', I.

31 Unpublished seminar paper, 'Comparative West African Farm-Slavery Systems (south of the Sahel) with special reference to Muslim Kano Emirate (N. Nigeria)', Princeton, 1977. See also 'From Slavery to Freedom', 1976 and *Population, Prosperity and Poverty*, 1977 by the same author.

32 ibid.

33 ibid.

34 *Shaihu Umar*, by Alhaji Abubakar Tafawa Balewa, translated by Mervyn Hiskett, London, 1967.

35 *HWA*, I, p.278. The new, third edition of *HWA*, I, had not been published at the time this book went to press. However, I understand that in the account of Kano in the 10/16 century that he gives there, Professor Hunwick has revised his comment on slavery. His chapter in *HWA*, I, is of course in general a most valuable and scholarly account of Songhay, Borno and Hausaland and his revised chapter in the new edition is eagerly awaited.

36 John E. Lavers, in correspondence on the question of slavery in the west and central Sudan.

37 Hiskett, *Hausa Islamic verse*, 1975, p.143.

38 Hausa manuscript, *WG*.

39 Bivar and Hiskett, 1962, p.126.

40 Dr Abdulgadir Dangambo, PhD thesis, London 1980, I. p.135ff.

41 ibid, 251 ff.

42 ibid, 251 ff.

CHAPTER SIX

Neighbours of the Hausas

In addition to the 'Hausa Bakwai', the seven Hausa states described in Chapter 5, Hausa tradition distinguishes seven other groups, the 'Banza Bakwai', the 'Bastard Seven'. These are said to be people who, not originally Hausa-speaking, adopted Hausa as a first or second language; and who at the same time adopted certain characteristics of the Hausa way of life.

In fact, most of them are not related to the Hausas either by language or by blood. Geographically, most had their origins south or south-west of Hausaland; some belong to the area of the Niger-Benue Confluence, the point at which the two rivers join, rather than to the sub-Saharan savanna. Most of them were closely connected with the Hausas through trade and therein lies the explanation of how they came to be the 'Bastard Seven'.

Zamfara

The nearest of the Bastard Seven to the Hausas are the Zamfarawa who, during the 12/18 century, lived south of Gobir, with Kebbi to the west and Katsina to the east.

According to Zamfara tradition, Islam was introduced by the Zamfara chief Aliyu (fl. *c.* 1050/1640). However, the names of earlier chiefs, Zaudai, *c.* 1035/1625 and perhaps Daudafanau, suggest traces of Islam at a rather earlier date.

During the first half of the 12/18 century, Zamfara was an important market where much of the *fatauci* trade of Hausaland was centred. It therefore seems likely that it was also a centre for the spread of Islamic ideas at this time, since, as has been pointed out above, trade and the dissemination of Islam normally went together. In 1178/1764 the Gobirawa invaded Zamfara, sacked the capital, Birnin Zamfara, and continued to harass the kingdom for the rest of the century. Zamfara never recovered from this setback and its commercial position declined until the *jihād* of the early 13/19 century intervened. This finally altered the commercial pattern of Hausaland in favour of the new towns and cities established by the jihadists.

Despite the introduction of Islam in the 11/17 century, it appears that the ancestral cult was not completely driven out. According to the Muslim Fulani reformers of the late 12/18 century, traces of such a cult still survived in their day.

Kebbi

Next door to Zamfara, on its western border, lay the kingdom of Kebbi. Kebbi was probably founded in the 9/15 century and emerged as a powerful independent kingdom when it broke away from the Songhay empire in the

10/16 century. Its subsequent turbulent military and imperial history has been told elsewhere and falls outside the scope of this book as it has nothing in particular to do with Islam. Kebbi must have come under Islamic influence during the *askiya* period of the Songhay empire, although it is possible that it was touched by earlier Islamic tendencies from the Sahara. Its ruling family was Muslim by 921/1515.

The capital of Kebbi, Surame, was built by the well-known king, Muḥammad Kanta, early in the 10/16 century. Near to it he constructed a wall, called *siraɗi*, from Arabic *ṣirāṭ*, the narrow bridge that spans the chasm of Hell Fire across which all mankind must pass on the Day of Judgement. Criminals, and others who incurred the king's displeasure, were made to walk along the narrow top of this wall. Beneath them, on either side, were deep trenches lined with stakes and spears, in which fires were lit and few survived this horrible ordeal. The ruins of the wall Siraɗi can still be seen today. There can hardly be more gruesome evidence that Islamic ideas had reached Kebbi by the early 10/16 century!

Why should the Kebbawa be classed among the Banza Bakwai? It is true that the Kanta dynasty claimed to originate from Katsina and this may be part of the reason. However, they must also have been connected with the Hausas through trade almost from the very foundation of the kingdom. It has already been pointed out that Kebbi and Borno competed for dominance over the southern termini of the Saharan trade routes during the 10/16 century, as well as for hegemony over Hausaland and the southern Sahara generally. This interest in trade must have brought them into constant contact with the Hausas as well as with the people of Borno. The acquiring of a little Hausa as a trade language by certain Kebbawa was probably enough to cause the Hausas to award them the doubtful distinction of belonging to the Bastard Seven.

Yauri

South-east of Kebbi lay the kingdom of Yauri. One tradition claims that it began as an offshoot of the Songhay empire. However, Dr Mahdi Adamu considers that Hausa traders from Katsina, who settled in the Niger valley, had established political authority over Yauri during the 8/14 century and suggests that its first kings were Hausas.[1]

Islam is said to have been introduced there by Jerabana II, *c.* 1025/1616 but it was not until *c.* 1112/1700 that Muslim names began to appear regularly in the king-list. All the same, the early 11/17 century seems, on other grounds, a likely date for the coming of Islam. Yauri lay on the route out of Hausaland to the gold-bearing areas of the Volta and by *c.* 856/1452, if not earlier, Hausas and Dyula/Wangarawa were conducting the gold trade. They must surely have spread Islamic ideas along the routes they followed. By 1025/1616 it seems likely that a considerable number of Muslim Hausas were settled in Birnin Yauri, the capital of the kingdom. It is to be expected that the kings of Yauri, profitably situated in control of the Niger fording points used by the trade caravans, would begin to associate themselves openly with Islam by adopting Muslim names, for it was on the goodwill of the Muslims that the smooth running of trade, and thus the prosperity of the kingdom, depended. It must have been as a result of the early settlement of Hausas in Yauri that the Yaurawa qualified for inclusion among the Banza Bakwai.

The Yorubas

The Yoruba people, also included among the Banza Bakwai, are heirs to an ancient non-Islamic culture. It centres on Ile-Ife, the place where the cult hero, Oduduwa, descended from heaven. Out of it grew a highly developed Yoruba civilization and a collection of traditions of origin and history that at no point link to that of the Hausas. However there are several accounts of Yoruba origin. One of them goes as follows: they are descended from Lamurudu, Nimrūd, the same ancestral figure who was mentioned above in connection with the Gobirawa. Lamurudu was a king of Mecca. One of his sons, Oduduwa, was brought up a Muslim, then slipped back into misbelief and carried many of the people with him. With the help of the priest Asara, Oduduwa converted the great mosque of Mecca into a temple for idols. Asara was an idol-carver by trade and when his son, Braima (Yoruba from Arabic Ibrāhīm), grew up, Asara made him sell idols. Braima, who had become a Muslim, hated the work and used to invite custom by crying out 'Who will buy falsehood?' Then, one day, he took an axe and smashed all the idols in the temple except the chief one, around the neck of which he hung the axe. When they discovered this insult to their gods, the people were furious. They thought the culprit was Braima and challenged him with the offence. Braima told them to go and ask the chief idol who had done the deed. The people replied that Braima knew perfectly well that the idol could not speak. 'So,' replied Braima pertly, 'why do you worship that which cannot speak?' So angry were the people at this saucy answer that Lamurudu, their king, ordered Braima to be burned alive and a huge bonfire was built for the purpose. When it was about to be lit, this was the signal for civil war to break out between the Muslims and non-Muslims. Lamurudu was slain and his sons, including Oduduwa, were driven out of Mecca. Oduduwa went east and finally reached Yorubaland. There he set up the Ife worship.[2]

The first thing to be said about this entertaining and colourful story is that it cannot be regarded as an historically accurate account of Yoruba origins. Linguistic evidence alone makes that clear. Yoruba is a West African language, closely related to a number of other languages spoken in the area of the Niger-Benue Confluence. The people who speak it certainly did not originate from ancestors speaking a Middle Eastern tongue. Moreover, archaeological evidence shows that people who were the ancestors of the present Yorubas have populated southern Nigeria since long before the Koran was revealed to the Prophet in Arabia. How then did the story arise and what is its significance?

There are two interesting points about the story. First, apart from the introduction into it of the Yoruba cult hero, Oduduwa, and the civil war between his followers and those of the Muslim hero, Braima, it is identical with the story of Nimrūd and Ibrāhīm (Abraham) in the classical Arabic *Qiṣaṣ al-anbiyā'*,[3] the 'Stories of the Muslim Prophets' of the 5/11-century Arabic author, Aḥmad b. Muḥammad al-Thaᶜlabī. Even the name of the idol-carving priest, Asara, is the same in the Yoruba story and the Arabic *Qiṣaṣ*. Indeed, the total correspondence between the *Qiṣaṣ* version of the story of Ibrāhīm and the Yoruba legend of origin seems too close to be coincidental. It is true that the story occurs in other classical Arabic sources as well as the *Qiṣaṣ* but several stories that are to be found in *Qiṣaṣ* will also be found in various forms in the folklore of the peoples of West Africa. The *Qiṣaṣ* is at the present day a most popular work among the *ᶜulamā'* in West Africa and the Middle East and there is every reason to believe that it has been for several centuries. Thus the *Qiṣaṣ* is the most likely, even if not the certain, source of these stories which probably reached West Africa from Egypt, or perhaps from Mecca and Medina, passed on to West African pilgrims by professional story-tellers among whom they seem to have been popular. They were then gradually spread as tales and legends by these returned pilgrims, and by other Muslim literates who were familiar with them; and it seems that the Muslims often dressed them up in such a way as to make them fit local circumstances and histories in West Africa.

The second point of interest is that the story does not identify the Yorubas with the Muslim party but with the defeated, idol-worshipping son of the tyrant king, Lamurudu, who is so clearly the same individual as the Nimrūd of the *Qiṣaṣ*. Some scholars have concluded that the Yorubas' first contact with Islam was a hostile one and that they deliberately cast their own cult hero, Oduduwa, in an anti-Muslim role in order to express their rejection of Islam. This is very improbable for non-Muslim people are hardly likely to compose their folklore in Islamic terms. No one could have made up this story except a Muslim literate, with the *Qiṣaṣ al-anbiyā'* and similar classical sources at the tip of his tongue. It does not symbolise the Yorubas' deliberate defiance of Islam; it simply reflects a Muslim *ᶜālim*'s strong sense of religious superiority over the misbelievers with whom he came into contact – almost certainly through trade – and his attempt to account for their stubborn refusal to bend their necks to Islam. Religious men, whether Muslims or Christians, have always tended to be both puzzled and frustrated by the spectacle of those who persist in what they hold to be misbelief after the 'truth' has been revealed to them. Such puzzlement and frustration is, of course, a consequence of their own certainties and whatever explanation they adopt must necessarily be consistent with those certainties. In the same way that the early Christian missionaries in Africa and elsewhere had to explain continued rejection of Christianity in terms of stubbornness and blindness, so the Muslim literate framed an explanation that fitted in with his own beliefs and view of history. Later on, the Yorubas themselves, even the official non-Muslim historians of the Yoruba nation, accepted the story. There was no reason for them not to do so; they saw nothing shameful in it and it seemed to explain the difference between themselves and the Muslims who lived among them.

Of course there are other possible explanations for the presence of this obviously Muslim story among the non-Muslim Yorubas. It may have been that they adopted it purely for its entertainment value and that it has no significance beyond that. Perhaps they accepted it simply because it was old and therefore deserved respect, regardless of what source it first came from. However, the explanation given above is the one that seems most probable and most convincing to me. One thing, at least, is certain: the non-Muslim Yorubas did not invent the story.

The Yoruba name for a Muslim is *Imale*. A number of explanations have been offered for the origin of this word. The most convincing, in my opinion, is that it comes from the word Mali. That the Yorubas use a word associated with Mali as a term to describe a Muslim does not necessarily mean that their first contact with Islam was through the Mali empire although it may have been. There is nothing improbable in that; Dyula Muslims from the Mali empire could indeed have reached Old Ọyọ when that empire was at its height, that is during the 8/14 century. On the other hand, family and clan names derived from the word Mali are common throughout West Africa. For instance, one branch of the emiral family of Zaria, in Hausaland, is known as the Mallawa. This indicates merely that the family believes its ancestors to have come originally from Mali. It does not mean that there is any other historical link between the emirate of Zaria and the 8/14-century Mali empire, on the contrary, it is clear that no such link exists. As was pointed out above, when Mali began to decline, Dyula Muslims moved to Songhay and to Borgu and after the collapse of Songhay they moved in increasing numbers to Borgu. No doubt they took their family names with them and Dyula/Wangarawa Muslims bearing names derived from Mali could have reached Yorubaland from several starting-points at any time from the mid-8/14 century on. Such persons might well have claimed Malian origins and this may account for the presence of the term *Imale* in the Yoruba language.

There is one small piece of evidence that supports the view that the Yorubas' first contact with Islam was through Songhay. It is the fact that the Yoruba word for an *ᶜālim* is *alufa*. This seems to be from the Songhay *alfa*. At any rate, it is not from the Hausa *malam*. Thus, despite the known importance of Muslim Hausas in spreading Islam in Yorubaland during the 13/19 century, it can be argued that they were not the first to establish it there. However, too much significance ought not to be attached to arguments that rest on such isolated scraps of evidence. What is known of the development of trade in the west and central Sudan makes it seem likely that both Hausa Muslims and Dyula/Wangarawa Muslims reached Yorubaland during, at the latest, the 9/15 century. They may well have done so in the 8/14 century. That the Yorubas chose *alufa* as their word for *ᶜālim* may indeed indicate that their first contact with Islam was through Songhay-speakers; on the other hand, it is just as likely to have been due to mere chance. The notion that one individual, or group of individuals, suddenly begins to spread a new religion and system of ideas in an area that has been entirely free of them up to that point, may be misleading. It is probably nearer the truth to describe the spread of ideas in any human society as like the spread of water through a porous substance. This happens slowly, at first unnoticed, and by a multitude of different channels of which none can realistically be regarded as first. To the north of the Yorubas lay a wide band of Islamic territory that stretched from west to east and included the empires of Mali, Songhay and Borno as well as the Hausa states. Perhaps the first Islamic ideas drifted across from Mali or down from Songhay, but by *c.* 906/1500 they must surely have been entering Yorubaland from several directions at once: from declining Mali, from rising Songhay and from busy Hausa and Borno traders pushing their donkey and slave caravans farther and farther south. Thus the search for the first Muslim to set foot in Yorubaland is unlikely to yield any certain conclusion.

All the same, Yoruba tradition has preserved the name of one early *ᶜālim* who is believed to have been important in bringing Islam to Old Ọyọ. He is known as Baba-Yigi, who may be the same person as Alfa-Yigi, another name also mentioned in Yoruba tradition. Some say this man was a Muslim of foreign origin who arrived from Nupe in the late 11/16 century, but another opinion has him arriving about a hundred years later, in the 12/17 century.

The presence of such foreign *ᶜulamā'* in Yorubaland must mean that Islamic ideas were present there. It does not of course necessarily mean that native Yorubas converted to Islam in significant numbers. However, there is some evidence to suggest that they did and that a Muslim community large enough to support a group of *ʿulamāʾ* lived there before 1078/1667. The Katsina *ʿālim*, Ɗan Masani, who died in that year, is said to have composed a work answering the questions sent to him by these Yoruba *ʿulamāʾ* concerning a matter of Islamic ritual. The work itself is lost but its title, which contains the words *fuqahāʾ yurubāʾ* 'Yoruba jurists', is preserved in another book by the same author.[4] It should be understood that Ɗan Masani must have meant 'inhabitants of Old Ọyọ' when he used the word *yurubāʾ* for only they were known as Yorubas before the 13/19 century. Sultan Muhammadu Bello quotes a similar title in his *Infāq al-mayṣūr*, which may refer to the same work. There is no way of telling how large this Muslim community in Ọyọ was, or whether it was composed of foreign Muslims resident there, or of native Yorubas. However, the fact that the *ʿulamāʾ* consulted a Hausa *ʿālim* on what was quite a simple matter of Islamic ritual – how to determine the precise moment of sunset – certainly suggests that they were native Yorubas without much previous experience in such matters. Foreign *ʿulamāʾ*, present in Yorubaland as traders or teachers, would surely have had no need to make such enquiries from an *ʿālim* in Hausaland.

From 1214/1799 Islam began to make rapid strides in Yorubaland and from this point on conversion to Islam became frequent. By this time, too, Hausas had begun to make an important contribution to the spread of Islam among the Yorubas. They did so as Muslim slaves working in Yoruba households, as craftsmen, both slave and free, and as teachers and advisers in the courts of the Yoruba chiefs. Moreover, Hausa *ʿulamāʾ*, preaching and teaching in Yorubaland, proved to be among the most effective opponents of the Christian missionaries when these people began to arrive among the Yorubas.

By the early 14/19 century, a movement of Islamic reform had developed in the Ọyọ empire, headed by certain *ʿulamāʾ* resident there. They became involved in political rivalries that arose in Yorubaland at that time. As will be explained in chapter 11, the result of this was in the end, to extend the Fulani *jihād* into Yorubaland and to bring about the setting-up of a Muslim emirate, not in Ọyọ but in Ilorin.

The Nupes

The Nupes, like the Yorubas, have a long, independent tradition and a highly developed non-Islamic religion and culture. Their language, like that of the Yorubas, belongs to the large Kwa group of the Niger-Benue area and it is in no way related to Hausa. Their history has linked them more closely to the Yorubas and the Borgawa (the people of Borgu) than to the Hausa kingdoms. However, from *c.* 824/1421, they were in trading contact with the Hausas and this, no doubt, explains their inclusion among the Banza Bakwai.

Unlike the Yoruba legend, that of the Nupes shows no obvious trace of Islam but Muslim names occur in the Nupe king-list at least as early as 1080–1/1670. According to Nupe tradition, however, it was Etsu Jibirin (1159/1746–1172–3/1759) who first introduced Islam officially into the Nupe court. This suggests that, for two and a half centuries, that is from early in the

9/15 century to the second half of the 11/17 century, Islam slowly increased its hold on that court to the point that the rulers began to adopt Muslim names. Rather less than a century later it had made sufficient progress to embolden the ruler to declare Islam the official religion of his court, in the hope that this would prove generally acceptable. In this case it seems he was mistaken, for he was apparently later deposed by discontented traditionalists, resentful of his innovations.

The Kwararafas

The Kwararafas, who so troubled Hausaland in the 10/16 and 11/17 centuries, are a warlike people who inhabit the Gongola and Benue valleys. Their legend of origin claims that they originally lived in the country of 'Yemil', clearly the Yemen. Under their chief, Agadu, they marched out to make war on the Prophet Muḥammad but abandoned the attempt and returned to Yemil. The Prophet got to hear of this and sent them a letter and some presents, but they, in fear, left their country and migrated westwards until they came to the country west of Lake Chad. Here some of them stopped and settled while others continued on their way until they reached the Benue.

This legend, like that of the Yorubas, bears the obvious imprint of the Muslim *ᶜulamā'*. Indeed, it echoes the account in the *Sīra*, the classical Arabic biography of the Prophet, that tells how he sent letters to neighbouring potentates calling them to Islam. It can only have been adapted to apply to the Kwararafas by Muslim literates. If one seeks for a reason why they should do so, it was surely in order to explain the infidelity of these non-Muslim people among whom they traded. Linguistic and historical evidence together make it impossible to believe that the Kwararafas actually did originate in the Yemen.

The Kwararafas have a long record of war with the Hausas, especially the Kanawa but despite this, they are still numbered among the Banza Bakwai. This almost certainly reflects the fact that they came into contact with the Hausas of Zaria, as tribute payers and thus probably as trading partners too, at some time between 824/1421 and 841/1438. It follows from this that they must have come into contact with Islam by *c.* 905/1500, by which time Zaria had accepted Islam. Between that date and the outbreak of the 13/19-century *jihād* in Hausaland, some Hausa-speaking traders and craftsmen settled among them, although it is not possible to say how early this may have taken place. There is also a tradition among the Kwararafas that Muslim literates were employed at their court. Beyond this they apparently made no attempt to adopt Islam and remained faithful to their ancestral cult. However, recent research has revealed 12–13/18-century reports from North Africa, telling of Christianity among an African people who may have been the Kwararafas.[5] If it was the Kwararafas to whom these reports refer – and this seems very probable – Christianity may have reached them from the Nubian Christian kingdoms described in chapter 1, before they moved from the Chad area to the Benue; or perhaps it came from Benin, after that migration had taken place. However, it must be said that the reports of British colonial officials, who studied the Kwararafas' institutions and religious beliefs early in the present century, reveal no traces of Christianity. On the contrary, they report solid adherence to an advanced form of African polytheism. It is true that the symbol of the cross occurs among them but this very ancient emblem is not necessarily to be associated with Christianity; it appears from time to time in societies that have had no Christian contacts. The most likely explanation for the tale of Christianity among a people who may have been the Kwararafas lies in the habit of Muslim traders of assuming that any people who were neither Muslim nor simple and obvious animists, must be Christians. This notion, in the case of the Kwararafas, may well have been strengthened by their use of the cross symbol. All the same, perhaps the Kwararafas were touched by Christianity at some point in their history, but if so, it seems to have died out among them by the early 20 century AD.

There may be more than this to the tale of the 'Christian' Kwararafas. It was widely believed in Christian Europe during the Middle Ages that there existed somewhere in India or the interior of Africa the kingdom of a great and powerful Christian priest-king called Prester John, whose country was the source of great wealth. This Prester John, one day, would march his armies against Islam in alliance with his fellow Christians from Europe. European Christians had sought the kingdom of Prester John at least since the 6/12 century and they continued to do so until the 11/17 century, after which the legend seems to have faded. As I said above, some believed that Prester John's kingdom was in India, others located it in Ethiopia, yet others looked for it in the interior of West Africa. Vincenzo Matteo, the informant of Giovanni Lorenzo Anania whom I have mentioned several times already in chapter 5, was one of them. Anania tells us that Vincenzo spent seven years searching for the kingdom of Prester John but failed to find it. Of course he failed. Prester John never existed. He was simply an ideological hero-figure in the imaginations of Christians, who symbolised for them their hopes of victory in their long-standing military and commercial rivalry with the Muslims. All the same, there are some elements of reality in the legend, in so far as real monarchs were seen as the Prester and real people were cast in the role of his subjects.

As was pointed out above, there are good grounds for believing that Vincenzo Matteo, among others of his calling, was well informed about the country between Zaria and the Benue river and may even have found his way down to the Niger-Benue Confluence. I suggested above that it was probably the search for ivory that took him there. What of his search for Prester John? Had Vincenzo Matteo perhaps also heard stories of a powerful, warlike people who revered the cross? Did he, in consequence, conclude that he was at last on the trail that led into the kingdom of Prester John, somewhere south of Zaria? There is no proof that this was so, yet the notion is by no means fanciful when one bears the following historical background in mind.

The Portuguese, who established themselves on the Atlantic coast of West Africa during the 9/15 century, believed that there dwelt, somewhere east of the kingdom of Benin, which was situated west of what we now know to be the Niger Delta, a powerful Christian king, known to the people of Benin as Ogané. So powerful was he said to be that on the accession of a new king of Benin, ambassadors were sent to his court; Ogané then sent them back with the gift of a small cross, a token of his friendship and protection. Inevitably, the Portuguese concluded that here, at last, was the real Prester John. This tale was circulating orally among the Portuguese at some time between AD 1482, when their fortress of São Jorge Da Mina (present Elmina) was founded on the Gold Coast and AD 1495, in which year the Portuguese king, João II died. It was confirmed again in AD 1540 by ambassadors from the kingdom of Benin who visited Portugal in that year. It was finally published by João De Barros, as part of his account of Portuguese voyages and discoveries, in AD 1552. This was probably too late for Vincenzo to have read it before he set out on his own travels in the west and central Sudan, but he must surely have heard the tale recounted orally in the merchant circles in which he moved.[6]

Ogané has been identified by some modern scholars with the Yoruba Oni, sometimes referred to as Oghene, of Ile-Ife; a case can certainly be made out for this, except that Ile-Ife is west of Benin, not east. Another possible identification would seem to be with the Ogoni group of Benue-Congo speakers who inhabit the Niger Delta, south-east of Benin, immediately north of Bonny. However, there are some objections to the direct identification of Ogané with the Ogoni, one of which is that it is rather unlikely that the Delta states in the 15 century AD were so powerful that the Oba of Benin, who probably dominated most of the Delta area at that time, would have sent his ambassadors there to receive recognition from a Delta chief. Moreover, the Portuguese account clearly envisages Ogané as lying 250 leagues (a league is usually reckoned as three miles, thus 750 miles) due east of Benin. The Delta states are barely 150 miles south-east of there. The heart of Kwararafa country, on the other hand, is approximately 400 miles north-east of Benin. That is still a good deal short of 750 miles but the medieval league was a somewhat variable measure. However, Kwararafa country extends south as far as the Benue and is separated at its southern extremity from the Ogoni only by the Tivs to the south-west and by the Ekois to the south-east. Moreover, the Kwararafas may well have dominated this area in the 9/15 century. Given the military power of the Kwararafas and the fact that they are known to have used the cross as a ritual symbol, it certainly seems possible that the name Ogané/Oghene/Ogoni may have become associated with them in a mixture of garbled stories that reached the 9/15-century Portuguese at Elmina. It may be that it was really the Kwararafas and not the Yorubas or the Benue-Congo speaking people of the Delta, who gave rise to the notion that Prester John's kingdom lay east of Benin. This possibility is strengthened by the fact that rumours of a Christian kingdom in the interior of West Africa, that almost certainly was associated with the Kwararafas, persisted into the 12–13/18 century (see inset to Map 5).

To return for a moment to Vincenzo Matteo; apart from the possibility that he was seeking the source of the ivory, his search for the Prester certainly gave him a motive for pushing down toward the Benue. Whether it was the Kwararafas, or the Yorubas, or the Ogoni people of the Delta, who really gave rise to the Prester John legend, there is little doubt that a 10/16-century seeker after Prester John, who had penetrated as far as the savanna country around Kano, would then have been drawn on and on toward the Niger-Benue confluence by his search. The reports he must have brought with him from Portuguese sources in Europe, reinforced by rumours in the savanna of a cross-revering people in the riverain country to the south would have ensured that. Such considerations render it more than ever likely that the Magredi of Anania's account, to which I referred in chapter 5 above, and in footnote 1 to that chapter, really was Magidi or Makurdi and not due to some foolish error that he had copied from Leo Africanus.

The Gwaris

The Gwari people, also counted as Banza Bakwai,[7] form a large tribe scattered over southern Zaria, down to the Benue. They were established there before *c.* 1164/1750 but may have come originally from Zamfara. During the second half of the 12/18 century a Hausa family took over the chieftainship of the Gwaris and incoming Hausas intermarried with the original Gwari people. At the beginning of the present century, when their customs and beliefs were recorded by British administrative officers, they still remained attached to their original African religion. Their customary law regarding succession and inheritance and their burial procedures showed no evidence of Islam. They practised a cult similar to the *bori* cult of the non-Muslim Hausas, but some had a god called 'Allah Bango'. It seems likely that this deity was borrowed from the Muslim Hausas. *Bango* is a Hausa word meaning 'wall' and also the 'cover of a book'. It is probably from this latter meaning that the Gwaris took the name. It presumably signifies 'Allah in the Koran' or more exactly, 'Allah of the leather-covered boards' between which the *malams* carry their manuscript Korans. Among other Gwaris the supreme god was known as 'Sheshu' or 'Shekohi', perhaps derived from Hausa 'Shehu'. Among yet others the chief god was 'Mama', which may well be a naturalised Gwari form of Muḥammad. The Gwari women, too, had certain cults known as 'Maleka', a word that resembles the Arabic *malā'ika*, 'angels', and which is also likely to have reached them from the Hausas.

Unfortunately, it is impossible to say whether these traces of Islam – if this is what they are – reached the Gwaris before or after the *jihād* in Hausaland. 'Sheshu' is likely to have been borrowed after the *jihād*, perhaps at the time when the well-known poet and *walī* Muhammadu Na Birnin Gwari (fl. *c.* 1266/1850) carried out missionary work among the Gwaris. Also, since they were subject to the chief of Zazzau (Zaria) before the *jihād*, some Islamic influences may have reached them during the 12/18 century.

NOTES

1 1978, p.33.
2 Hodgkin, 1975, p.79.
3 Arabic edition, Cairo, nd, p.43 ff.
4 Bivar and Hiskett, 1962.
5 Gray, *JAH*, VIII, 3, 1967.
6 An English translation of extracts from Barros will be found in Crone, 1937; the account of Ogané is at p.126 ff.
7 But Sultan Muhammadu Bello places Gwari among the original Hausa Bakwai and substitutes Borgu for Gwari among the Banza Bakwai. Occasionally, too, Bauchi is included among the Banza Bakwai and the Yorubas are omitted.

CHAPTER SEVEN

Islam in the area of the Volta to *c.*1267/1850

The detailed history of Islam in the Volta region seems tangled and difficult to follow, but the broad sweep of it is simple. It came first as a small wave of the tide of Islam that swept the Mali empire. It became firmly established as a result of a second, more powerful wave that came from Hausaland and Borno.

Islam in Gonja

Before the end of the 16 century AD, that is 1008/1599, the area known as Gonja, north of the Black Volta, was dominated by the Mossi kingdom of Dagomba. By this time Muslim traders, probably of Dyula origin, had already settled there. Then, at the end of the century, Mande-speaking cavalry raiders, thought to have come from Mali, conquered the area and set up their own, independent kingdom of Gonja. In this they were helped by Dyula Muslims, the same people who, in Hausa-speaking areas, are referred to as 'Wangarawa'. The Mande-speaking warriors formed an alliance with these Dyula Muslims which probably took place over several generations. It has been condensed and dramatised in Gonja tradition in the story of Jakpa, the conquering warrior-hero, and Muḥammad al-Abyaḍ, 'Muḥammad the White', his Muslim adviser and *imām*. This story tells how, on a Friday, Muḥammad al-Abyaḍ found the Gonja leader fighting against his enemies. In his hand the Imām Muḥammad carried a staff, the head of which was covered with leather. He struck the ground between the two armies with this staff and then planted it there. As soon as they saw this, the enemies of the Gonja people turned and fled. The Gonja people were so impressed by the power of Islam, which the *imām* had just demonstrated, that they decided, there and then, to become Muslims. There is no reason why this story, or something like it, should not be substantially true. In the 10/16 century, one man's confidence in his God-given powers, and his willingness to demonstrate that confidence, fearlessly, in the midst of a battle, could certainly have been enough to decide the issue of that battle. It also illustrates, in a particular instance, the general truth that Islam first impressed non-Muslim Sūdānīs by the power of its ideas and especially, its claim to be helped by the supernatural power of God. Having conquered the land with the Muslims' help, the 'Jakpa' conquerors established their capital at Yagbum and then divided their empire into districts, governed by vassal 'sons'.

Gonja society then developed into the following classes. First, were the *gbanya*, the chiefly class descended from the Jakpa conquerors. They had become Muslim through their association with the Dyula Muslims but their Islam remained imperfect. They still continued to take part in the traditional Earth cult and consulted Earth priests as well as their Muslim advisers. This situation, like that in the Haɓe courts described in the previous chapter, was typically one of contrapuntal paramountcy. The subjects of the *gbanya* were the *nyamase*, the commoners. They remained largely untouched by Islam, except that they took part in certain festivals that mixed Islam with the customs of the Earth cult. In between the ruling *gbanya* and the subject *nyamase* were the Muslims, known collectively as *karamo*. They, in turn, were divided into several groups. First were the *sakpare*, those who claimed descent from Muḥammad al-Abyaḍ and who advised the chiefs as *imāms* and in other literate roles. Second were the *dogtes*. The origin of these people is not entirely certain but they appear to have been descendants of the chiefly families who were displaced by the Jakpa conquerors. They had already become partly Muslim through contact with Muslims settled in Gonja before the conquest took place. After the conquest, they gave up their claim to chiefly rank and took a middle position between the *gbanya* and the *sakpare* Muslims. They, too, sometimes acted as *imāms* and held other offices. Finally, there was a third group of Muslims; the later immigrants who had settled in Gonja after the *sakpare*. Many of them were Hausas but unlike the *sakpare* and the *dogtes*, the later immigrants did not become part of the structure of the Gonja state. However their presence served to strengthen the Islamic influence there.

Islam in Gonja was, and still is, characterised by extensive mixing. A typical example is the *Damba*, a traditional festival that now takes place each year at the time of the *Mawlud*, the Prophet's birthday. So much of the old Earth cult survives in it that it bears little resemblance to the *Mawlud* as this is celebrated in Sunnī Islamic communities. Mixing also shows itself in the use of Islamic objects, especially those bearing Arabic writing, as medicine shrines. Chiefs habitually refer both to shrine priests and Muslim *imāms*, requiring the traditional ritual from the former and Muslim prayers from the latter. These practices have always been regarded with tolerance by the *sakpare* and the *dogtes*. In contrast to the situation in Hausaland, there has never been much zeal for reform among Gonja Muslims. Such an easy-going attitude to mixing is characteristic of Dyula Islam in the Volta region as a whole.

The village of Larabanga, well-known for its fine Dyula-style timbered mosque, is situated centrally in Gonja. Politically it has remained largely independent of the Gonja state and in language and culture it is closer to the neighbouring state of Dagomba. This separateness from Gonja is expressed in the Larabanga legend of origin. The Larabangas claim descent not from Muḥammad al-Abyaḍ but from Abū Ayyūb al-Anṣārī, one of the Prophet Muḥammad's 'Helpers' (Arabic *anṣār*) at the time of his *hijra* (flight) from Mecca to Medina. Once again, linguistic and historical evidence make it difficult to accept such a Middle Eastern origin as historically correct. However the legend does express the Larabangas' belief that their tradition of Islam is separate from, and perhaps older than, that of the Gonja *sakpare*. What evidence there is suggests that the ancestors of the Larabanga people were Muslim traders who came from the direction of Mamprusi, north of Gonja; and then settled in the area of Larabanga before the Jakpa conquest.

Islam in Dagomba, Mamprusi and northern Mossi

Dagomba is the most southerly, Mamprusi the central and Wagadugu the most northerly of the three major Mossi kingdoms that lie in the Volta Basin. The first two, Dagomba and Mamprusi, were the creation of mounted invaders from the north. These invaders set up centralised states where previously there had been family-and-clan-group people whose only authority was that of their Earth priests.

This conquest by mounted invaders may have taken place as early as the 7/13 century, although the kingdom of Dagomba, like the other Mossi kingdoms, seems to have emerged as a distinct entity only in the 9/15 century. Na Gbewa, or Na Bawa, is remembered as the founder of both Dagomba and Mamprusi. Tradition says his sons quarrelled and broke apart, thus creating the two separate kingdoms of Dagomba and Mamprusi.

Islam is traditionally said to have been introduced into Dagomba by the chief Na Zangina, *c.* 1111/1700, although his successor returned to the traditional cult. There may have been Muslims resident in Dagomba during the 11/17 century, or perhaps earlier. Some were probably linked to the Dyula scholarly community in Timbuktu and had arrived at Dagomba as a result of Dyula trading activities. Others may have been *sakpare* from Gonja, or people from the independent Muslim community of Larabanga. The early Dyula Muslim Community in Dagomba was represented by the *yarnas*, a Mande word applied to the leaders of Dyula Muslim communities.

Later, the Islam of the *yarnas* was challenged by that of the Hausa and Borno *imāms*, prayer leaders who also give guidance in the proper observance of Islam. Their presence was due to the expansion of trade with Hausaland and Borno that had begun to develop even before the end of the 10/16 century. They were usually more learned and more strict than the *yarnas*. They represented a new trend in Islam in the Volta region, less tolerant of mixing than that of the Dyulas. This was especially so after the triumphant *jihād* in Hausaland of 1219/1804 to 1227/1812. None the less, mixing continued in Dagomba. Levtzion records at least one instance of a Dagomba Muslim functioning as a shrine priest and as an *imām*.[1] As in Gonja, the chiefs in Dagomba consulted the Earth priests as well as the Dyula *yarnas* and the Hausa or Borno *imāms*. Moreover, Islam was a matter that concerned only chiefs and the Muslim classes; commoners had little or nothing to do with it. They took part in certain Islamic festivals but these were so coloured by pre-Islamic custom that they were hardly Islamic at all. The result was that two levels of Islam emerged, the ancient one of the Dyula *yarnas*, which was at some points barely distinguishable from the native Earth cult, and the new, strictly Sunnī and very literate Islam of the Hausa immigrants. The chiefs held the balance between the two.

Mamprusi was Dagomba's neighbour and shared a common origin with it. Despite this, the development of Islam there was different from that in Dagomba. There is no firm evidence of Muslims in Mamprusi before the first half of the 12/18 century, yet there probably were some. Then, in that century, the chief, Na Atabia (1100/1688–1154/1741–2), appointed a Muslim as 'Mangoshi'. The word comes from Hausa *Mai akushi*, 'Owner of the Bowl'. The Mangoshi's job was to collect payments of duty and similar charges from merchants passing along the trade route from Hausaland, via Fadan Gurma, through Mamprusi, on their way to the Black Volta and Gonja. He also acted as an inn-keeper and supplied them with food. It was for this reason that he was given his title. 'Owner of the Bowl', but he did more than this. As a Muslim literate he also taught the Koran to the chief's children and to others. His Hausa title is evidence of the strength of Hausa influence in Mamprusi at this time. However, the person who held the office may not necessarily always have been a Hausa. It seems it was sometimes held by one of the Dyula Muslims settled in Mamprusi.

The Mangoshis introduced more and more Hausas into Mamprusi. Some of them settled permanently, especially in the capital, Gambaga. One of them, a certain Maḥmūd, was officially appointed *imām* at the court of the ruler of Mamprusi. In due course Gambaga became a local centre of Islamic education, conducted largely by Hausas. It is even said that the king of Mamprusi, although he remained a non-Muslim, nevertheless took part in the Islamic festival of *Laylat al-qadr*, the 'Night of Power'. This was the night upon which the Prophet first began to receive the revelation of the Koran. Muslims in Mamprusi were not so much part of government and society as they were in Dagomba; this was, perhaps, because they were mainly Hausas, not Dyulas. Tension grew between the Muslim *imāms* and the chiefs, as well as the Earth priests. The *imāms* tended to take over control of the towns and to act independently of the chiefs. Na Atabia eventually moved his court from Gambaga to Nalerigu, because he resented the Muslims' constant attempts to persuade him to observe Islam more carefully. Later, things became easier between the chiefs and the *imāms*. They developed what they referred to as a 'husband and wife' relationship. This meant there was to be no political rivalry between them; rivalry comes between fathers and sons, not between husbands and wives. The *imāms* now began to officiate at the installation of the chief. At least one of them, the Imām Adam, was also responsible for setting up good relations with the Ashanti government in Kumasi. All the same, Mamprusi Muslims never became so closely associated with the chiefs as did the Dagomba Muslims.

The situation that developed in both Dagomba and Mamprusi with regard to the formation of these states, and the division of authority within them, conforms, once again, to the contrapuntal theory that has been applied in the case of the Haɓe states and Gonja. However, the degree of influence exercised by the Islamic side or the polytheist side varied considerably in the different instances. In the case of Mamprusi the polytheists remained strong while the Islamic side was relatively weak.

To the north of Mamprusi lie a group of Mossi towns that formed independent kingdoms. The most powerful were Wagadugu and Yatenga, which broke away from Wagadugu, probably in the 10/16 century. Like the southern Mossi of Mamprusi and Dagomba, the northern Mossi also claim descent from the legendary Na Gbewa, but through his daughter, not his sons. From early times the northern Mossi opposed Islam. Unlike their southern neighbours they do not seem to have been affected by early Malian Islam but remained faithful to their ancestral African religion. The decline of the Mali empire tempted them to expand into its territory. *C.* 874/1470 they invaded Masina. About ten years later they advance against Walata but were driven back by Sonni ᶜAlī. This early clash with the Islamic state of Songhay was followed by Askiya Muḥammad's *jihād* against them in 903/1497–8. The northern Mossi now became the unbending enemies of the Songhay state. For them, Islam meant Songhay domination and they wanted nothing to do with it, but it was the Islam of the Songhay imperialists that they rejected. They proved more open to the peaceful entry among them of the Dyula Muslim traders.

These Dyula Muslims, known locally as *yarse*, were present in Wagadugu by *c.* 905/1500. Groups of *yarse* then began to settle in other Mossi towns and villages along the caravan routes. They adopted the Mossi language and customs but remained Muslim. Their presence was slow to spread Islam but during the 12/18 century *yarse* Muslims exercised more influence at the Wagadugu court. A mosque was built there in the second half of the century.

Some of the chiefs of the northern Mossi accepted Islam before the commoners. Whereas in the southern Mossi kingdoms it was expected that chiefs would be Muslims, at least in name, among the northern Mossi this was not so. It was a matter for personal choice and some chiefs remained openly polytheist. Also, in contrast with the southern Mossi, the northern Mossi retained their traditional festivals in their original form; nothing Islamic was introduced into them. The *yarse* Muslims, despite their acceptance at court, remained more distant from the rest of the population than did Dyula Muslims elsewhere in the kingdoms of the Volta Basin. Moreover, there is little evidence that Hausa Muslims had any influence on the northern Mossi. Despite several centuries of contact with Islam, sometimes violent and sometimes peaceful, they remained, for the most part, the champions of traditional African religion that they were in the days of Sonni ᶜAlī.

It will be clear from what has been said above that there are differences between the way in which Islam was received among the northern Mossi and its reception farther south, in Gonja, Dagomba and even Mamprusi. In the case of these southern societies, Islam did become integrated into political and social life, if not sufficiently to take the society over completely, at least to a significant extent. In the case of the northern Mossi, although it certainly established a presence, it remained very much on the surface – something that existed in the society without really becoming part of it.

The reason for this difference probably lies in the political and military history of the different areas. In Gonja there was the early Jakpa conquest, when the conquerers allied themselves with Muslims. Thus these Muslims were, at this time, directly involved in the setting up of the state. Having once got a foothold, their influence continued to expand without the same degree of tension with the ancestral cult that developed elsewhere.

The entry of Islam into Dagomba was made easier by that kingdom's nearness to Gonja. Although Islam was not officially introduced until early in the 12/18 century, there is little doubt that contacts with the *sakpare* Muslims of Gonja smoothed its path. Following the Gonja model, the rulers of Dagomba had no need to regard Islam as a threat; they were able to accept it as an ally without the necessity to abandon their identification with the Earth cult, upon which their authority among the people at large still depended.

Mamprusi may be thought of as being farther removed from these early influences that smoothed the way for Islam; but still near enough to be affected to some extent. Moreover, its position on the trade route made it especially open to slow, peaceful penetration by Muslim traders and this is shown in the institution of the Mangoshi.

Among the northern Mossi, however, the picture was different. There was no smooth and gradual slide into Islamic ways and attitudes but only an early confrontation with a Muslim imperial power, that offered the stark alternatives of conversion or the sword. This set up psychological barriers against acceptance of Islam that even the presence of pacific traders could not wholly overcome. It also confirmed the Mossi in their loyalty to the ancestral cult, with which the chieftaincy was identified. Thus it became much more difficult for the chiefs to compromise with Islam. The consequence has been that, while Islam is present among the Mossi, it has still failed to make itself part of their culture, even to this day.

To the south of the Mossi kingdoms lies the country of certain family-and-clan group people, those who escaped the early conquerors of the Na Gweba era. These people have, for the most part, remained untouched by Islam for three reasons. First, being organised in family-and-clan groups, they had no chiefly class that could act as a channel for Islam to enter their society. Second, they were short-distance traders and their country lay off the main trade routes; thus they had little contact with Muslim traders. Third, they were for long the victims of Muslim raiders and this did not incline them favourably towards Islam. All the same, small communities of Muslims did grow up among these people. They consisted of Dyula Muslim traders who settled among them and were called 'Kantosi'. Some Kantosi eventually abandoned Islam while others remained faithful but made no attempt to spread it. This was the situation over most of the country of the family-and-clan group people until the 13/19 century. However, in one place Islam did take firm root, it was in Wa.

Islam in Wa

In the middle of the 11/17 century, that is *c.* 1060/1650, Dagomba horsemen founded the centralised state of Wa, in the south-western corner of the family-and-clan group peoples' country. Wa was situated on the trade route that ran along the east bank of the Black Volta, into Mossi country. Its founding probably had something to do with the gold trade from Lobi, that passed along the route.

Wa experienced three waves of Islam. First, Mande-speaking Muslims, perhaps related to the Larabanga Muslims, settled in villages around Wa. This may have happened even before the foundation of the Wa state by the Dagomba warriors perhaps even as early as the 9/15 century. No doubt it was the Lobi gold trade that first attracted these Muslims and soon after the founding of the state they moved into Wa itself. They are sometimes known as Yerina, from the title of their headman, the Yeri Na.

The Yerina Muslims were followed by a second wave from the country around Masina. This second wave was led by a certain Ya Musa probably early in the 12/18 century. He is said to have come to join his fellow Muslims, the Yerina. He was more learned than them, however, and so he was appointed the first *imām* of Wa. With him the Dyula Muslim community became firmly established there.

Wa tradition tells that, at about this time, Hausa Muslim traders also arrived. They founded a Hausa *zongo*, a Muslim Hausa traders' quarter, in Wa but their authority remained restricted to the *zongo*. In contrast to what happened in Dagomba and Mamprusi, in Wa the Hausa *imāms* never seriously challenged the Dyula Muslims. It is said that their marriages with local non-Muslim women helped to spread Islam.

In the first half of the 13/19 century, that is between 1214/1800 and 1266/1850, Wa Muslims became disturbed at the low level of learning in their community. They therefore sent their Imām Saᶜīd to Kong, which had become a centre of Islamic learning directed largely by *shaykhs* of the Saghanughu clan. Imām Saᶜīd returned as a *mujaddid*, a 'Renewer', and reinvigorated Islam in Wa.

The chiefs of Wa, as elsewhere in the Volta states, held the balance between Muslims and non-Muslims. During the second half of the 19 century AD (AH 1267–1317), they became strongly subjected to Islamic influences. Despite this, not all of them became Muslims. In Wa, as among the northern Mossi, this seems to have remained matter of personal choice; conversion to Islam was certainly not expected of them.

Borgu and Zabarma

To the east of the Mossi states lies Borgu, the country of the Ibariba people. They are of Mande origin and developed a number of centralised states – Bussa, Illo, Nikki and Wawa – as a result of their involvement in the long-distance trade passing through Borgu into the Volta region. Like the northern Mossi, the Ibaribas were bitter enemies of the Songhay empire. In 963/1555–6 Askiya Dawūd devastated Bussa but the Ibaribas were not converted to Islam. They resisted all subsequent attempts to win them over. The story goes that at one time certain Muslims persuaded the chief to pray three times a year. He later recanted and from then on defied Islam by beating drums. This the Ibaribas continue to do every year at the appearance of the first moon of Ramaḍān, the month of the Islamic fast. Even so, individual Ibaribas did convert under the influence of Muslim traders passing through Borgu. These Borgu Muslims speak the Dendi dialect of Songhay, a fact that suggests they may have been converted in the first instance by Wangarawa from the Songhay empire. Indeed, some are no doubt descended from Wangarawa who settled in Borgu. Because they speak the Dendi dialect, the Hausas call them 'Dendawa' and this seems the most convenient way to refer to them. Communities of these Dendawa Muslims then grew up along the caravan routes leading to Gonja. In due course Borgu society became divided into two classes – Dendawa Muslims and non-Muslim Ibaribas. They remained largely separate and the Ibaribas retained their suspicion of Islam right up to and beyond 1220/1806, when Borgu was attacked by the Fulani jihadists.

Like the Yorubas, the Gobirawa and the Kwararafas, the Ibaribas have had a legend of origin thrust upon them that identifies them not with a Muslim hero, but with a wicked, non-Muslim, arch-enemy of the Prophet. He is Kisra, the emperor of the Zoroastrian Persians, who is said to have led them out of Arabia, across the Niger, to Borgu. This legend, too, has been interpreted as a deliberate expression of Ibariba hostility to, and rejection of, Islam. Like the Lamurudu legend of the Yorubas and Gobirawa and that of the Kwararafas, it certainly came in the first instance from classical Arabic literature, not from the Ibaribas' own folk literature. The most probable source is the *Sīra*, the 'Biography' of the Prophet Muḥammad; it must therefore have been formulated by Muslim literates, probably Dendawa. Their reason must surely have been to account for the infidelity of the Ibaribas among whom they lived. Once the story had taken root, the Ibaribas accepted it, not because it expressed their hostility to Islam, but simply because it was a good story. Then, various versions of the legend emerged, according to which Kisra, or certain members of his family or one or other of his followers, became the founder of towns in

Borgu, such as Bussa, Nikki and so on. It is clear that the purpose of each of these versions was to establish the seniority of the place in question over other Borgu towns and kingdoms. The legend thus became a useful means of expressing political and dynastic rivalries and local patriotism and this probably accounts for its survival.

North-west of Borgu lies the country of the Zabarmawa or Jerma people, also organised in family-and-clan groups not in centralised states under chieftains. They, like the northern Mossi and the Ibaribas, resisted Islam resolutely right up to 1224/1809, when they were attacked by Fulani jihadists. As a result of that *jihād* and their closeness to the Sokoto empire, Islam began to make rapid progress among them. By 1266/1850, the Zabarmawa had become largely Muslim, although their traditional beliefs still survived to some extent. It was, no doubt, their lack of a strong traditional political structure that enabled this swift conversion to take place, once the Zabarmawa had come within the sphere of influence of the powerful and relatively highly organised caliphate in Sokoto.

Sansanne-Mango and Kotokoli

Sansanne-Mango is the centre of a Chikossi kingdom situated in north-western Togoland. It is the last point on the route out of the Volta Basin into Gurma and thus on to Hausaland. It was founded *c.* 1165–6/1751, or perhaps a little later, by Dyula Muslims at a time of increasing trade with Hausaland. Hausa traders began to settle there shortly after its foundation and they set up their own *zongo.* (Hausa *zango*). This may be reflected in the name of the kingdom, for this comes in the first instance from the Hausa word *sansani*, 'camp' and the name probably means 'the camp of the Mango people'.[2] The kingdom acquired a mixed population of Hausas, Gonjas and Larabanga Muslims. It also developed close relations with Kong, a Mande kingdom to the south-west, founded between 1111/1700 and 1158/1745–6, which became an important centre of Dyula Islamic learning. Despite these early Islamic connections, the chiefs of Sansanne-Mango remained only partly Muslim and the commoners, natives of the area, were hardly affected by Islam at all.

South of Gurma lay a country of family-and-clan group people, now northern Togo. Early in the 12/18 century chiefs of Gurma origin founded a confederation of kingdoms there, known as the kingdoms of the Kotokoli. The most important were Bafilo and Sokode. The foundation of these centralised states was probably due to their position on the route from Hausaland to Gonja. By the end of the century, traders from Hausaland, Borno, Gurma and Gonja had settled there, creating a mixed immigrant Muslim population similar to that in Sansanne-Mango. The chiefs however, remained non-Muslim until late in the 19 century AD (13/14 century AH).

Dahomey and Djougou

Immediately to the east of Togoland lay the country of Dahomey which, at the beginning of the 13/18 century was a powerful West African kingdom. Muslims, some of them from North Africa, some from Nupe but most of them Hausas, probably from Zamfara, had settled there by 1112/1700 or shortly after. Early European travellers who first noted their presence, called them 'Malayes', a word that surely comes from 'Mali' and is a form coined by

Europeans from a local West African term widely used to describe Muslims. The European sources confirm that the Malayes were literate in Arabic and indicate that they came to Dahomey as traders and craftsmen, especially as leather-workers. Moreover, the king of Dahomey employed some of them at his court, as military advisers to foretell the future and to pray for his success. These Muslim Malayes intermarried with the local women and in due course a substantial Muslim community was established in Dahomey. It increased, first, by the fact that the king handed over all Muslim captives taken in war to the leaders of the local Muslims, on condition that the captives settled permanently in his kingdom; second, by the fact that numbers of Muslims, travelling the route from Hausaland to Gonja, branched off at Djougou and came south into Dahomey to join the Muslim community there. Although that Muslim community was by no means composed exclusively of Hausas in the first instance, so powerful was the influence of Hausa culture that almost all its members became Hausa speaking. Most of the Muslims were concentrated at Abomey, on the northern edge of the forest belt but a few may have settled as far south as Whydah, on the coast, during the early 12/18 century.

In the north of Dahomey lay the small Islamic kingdom of Zogho, or Djougou, mentioned above. This first began as a toll post, set up to levy dues on caravans passing through the territory and carrying, in the first place, gold from Gyaman and, later, kolas from Salaga. It was originally under the authority of the local Earth priest but gradually a Muslim settlement grew up there, inhabited by Hausa-speaking merchants of Wangara origin and other merchants from Borno. This settlement was first known as 'Wangara'. Then, in the middle of the 12/18 century, an Earth priest converted to Islam, almost certainly under the influence of the Muslims of Wangara. The first settlement of Hausa-speakers and Borno traders was later considerably enlarged by Muslim merchants of Dendi origin, speaking a Songhay dialect and Djougou, or Wangara, developed into what has been described as a small Islamic sultanate lying on the main caravan route between Hausaland and Salaga. In addition to its importance for the gold and kola trade, Djougou functioned as a gateway for the entry of Islam into southern Dahomey.

Salaga and the kola trade

Salaga is a town in Gonja but it has played such an important part in the Islamic history of West Africa that it deserves to be treated apart. It first rose to prominence as a result of the kola trade.

The kola trade from the kola-bearing forests of the West African coast to the west and central Sudan is believed to be of ancient origin; no doubt existing long before Islam was introduced to the Niger Bend and perhaps even extending back into pre-historic times. Certainly, there is no reason to doubt that these bitter, tangy nuts became a trade article almost from the moment that people beyond the forest edge first developed a taste for them – and that must surely have been from the beginning of human settlement there.

As was mentioned in chapter 4, kolas were known in Hausaland early in the 9/15 century, as an export from Nupe. However, it is thought that these were the *cola acuminata*, that grows in the forest below Yorubaland, not the *cola nitida*, produced in the forest farther west, in what is now southern Ghana. It therefore seems that at this time, the 9/15 century, there were at least two major sources of kola. The western one produced *cola nitida*, that was, in later times at any rate, the more favoured produce, and the eastern one produced the *cola acuminata*. Each source was connected to markets that organised the transport, sale and export of the product.

In the west the trade was in the hands of those same Dyulas who managed the gold trade and it has been suggested that the two trades were linked. Perhaps they were, to the extent that the gold traders, who were the capitalists of their day, also financed the kola caravans. However, the kolas must surely have been handled by specialist traders. Their transport is a skilled craft and they quickly deteriorate if not shifted swiftly from the place of production, through the market and on to the place of consumption. For this reason it seems unlikely that the nuts were carried in the same caravans that transported the gold and other less perishable goods. However, that is surmise, I know of no written source that confirms it.

There were several kola routes out of the western forest – for example, an important one ran along the river Milo – but all major routes headed eventually for the Niger Bend. Jenne has been identified as a main centre in the Bend, from where the kolas were distributed onward into the Sahara and the savanna. No doubt Timbuktu also handled its share of the trade in its commercial heyday. Later, the town of Kankan, founded at the beginning of the 11/17 century, largely to take advantage of the kola trade, also became an important distribution centre for it.

On the eastern side the trade in the *cola acuminata* seems to have lain largely in the hands of the Yorubas of Old Ọyọ and perhaps in those of Nupes as well. They collected it from the forest and transported it north to Hausaland, where it was sold in exchange for savanna products. I know of no source that states positively that the *cola nitida* from the west also reached Hausaland before the 12/18 century. However, it is difficult to believe that it was wholly unobtainable there although it may have been a rare and expensive luxury before the direct east/west kola route between the Volta and Hausaland that by-passed the Bend, developed in the 12/18 century.

Another important kola route from the western forest to the Niger Bend was that which passed through the Volta region. This, too, was closely linked to the gold routes; before the second half of the 12/18 century, the main trading centres along it which handled both gold and kola, had been Bonduku, Biupe and Kafaba. However, during this century the Ashantis successfully attempted to take over the kola trade and organise it from Kumasi, virtually as a 'nationalised' industry. They found the village called Salaga, in Gonja, probably settled by Hausa-speaking traders *c.* 1189/1775, more convenient for their purpose than the older centres. The trade was now diverted from these older centres to Salaga, which rapidly developed into the main market for the collection of kola from the south for sale there and for onward distribution northward to the Niger and eastward to the consumer areas of the Hausa savanna and Borno. An easterly network of routes, bypassing the Niger Bend in the south, and already in use for the transport of gold, now became utilised and further extended to serve the kola trade (see Appendix A, Diagrams III and IV).

Clearly, however, the emergence of Salaga was not solely a consequence of Ashanti initiative. It seems that it reflected the needs of a direct east/west link between the eastern savanna areas and the Volta, that had existed since the

9/15 century and had been slowly growing in importance since that time. By *c.* 1202/1788, the small Islamic sultanate of Djougou, north-east of Salaga, had emerged. It lay across the route that ran from Yauri, through Nikki and Bafilo, to Salaga. Thus the growth of Salaga may also have been part of a gradual settlement of traders from the eastern side, in centres at the western end of the route, which reached a peak at this time. As a result, Hausa-speaking traders, and to a lesser extent Borno traders, took over the earlier near-monopoly of the gold and kola trade enjoyed by the Dyulas. The fact that Salaga soon became almost entirely a town of Hausa-speakers makes it clear how strong the Hausa presence there became.

The name 'Gonja', or 'Gwanja' as it is spelt in the *ajami* script, figures constantly in Hausa folklore as the centre of the kola trade. Salaga is in Gonja, it is true, but the name should be treated with caution. The state of Gonja did not emerge until the late 10/16 century when, as was described above, it was founded by the legendary Jakpa and Muḥammad the White. Of course there may have been a place, or even a chieftaincy of that name in existence before the state emerged there. Reference was made in chapter 5, to the probably misleading passage in the Kano Chronicle that seems to suggest a trade in kolas between 'Gonja' and Hausaland more than a hundred years earlier, in the 9/15 century. As was said there, traders from Hausaland who reached the Volta region at that early date, did so primarily in search of gold, not kolas. The occurrence of the word 'Gonja' in the Kano Chronicle in the context of the 9/15 century is to be accounted for by the fact that the Chronicle was written down at a much later date, by which time the word had become the common Hausa term for the whole Volta region. We may be sure that the chronicler, a remarkably careful and accurate man on most occasions, was quite unaware of the confusion his use of the word would subsequently cause.

There is another reason why the folkloric Gonja should not be confused with the real Gonja, which is a state in the bush savanna north of the river Volta. It will become apparent from the first of the stories told below.

The kola trade with Gonja figures in the miracle stories told in Hausaland about the Shehu Usumanu ɗan Fodio. One day he was out walking with his friend, Umaru Alkammu. Umaru put his hand in the pocket of his gown for a kola nut. There were none there. The Shehu told him not to worry, he would get him some. They walked on. Shortly, they came to a narrow stream, across which they jumped. To Umaru's amazement, they then found that they were in the midst of a kola forest. He picked all he could carry and returned home, delighted. Early the next morning he went out again, intending to pick more kolas. He walked on and on until midday. He found no stream, let alone a forest of kola trees. Disappointed tired and thirsty, he returned home. That evening he told the Shehu what had happened; and how puzzled he was that he could find neither the stream nor the kola forest again. The Shehu smiled. Then he said, 'That stream was the Niger, which God enabled me to bring near and make narrow, so that we could jump across it. The kola forest was in Gonja. Shall we go to Gonja again, you and I, and enjoy ourselves there? It's a journey of three months, that's how far it is!'[3]

On another occasion a *madugu*, a Hausa caravan leader, was crossing the Niger in his canoe, loaded with kolas. Suddenly, his boat was caught in a whirlpool. He was about to capsize and drown. Desperately, he called out the

Shehu's name and promised him a gift of ten calabashes of kolas if he would save him. The Shehu was far away at Sokoto preaching a sermon. His congregation was amazed to see him suddenly stop and wring water out of the sleeve of his gown. Then, without a word, he continued his sermon. At the same moment, far away on the Niger, the *madugu* felt a hand grasp his boat and lift it to safety in calm water. Some time later he arrived in Sokoto, thanked the Shehu for his miracle and offered him a gift of three calabashes of kolas. The Shehu looked at him. Gently he said, 'But you haven't fulfilled your promise. You said "ten calabashes". You have brought only three.' In shame the *madugu* handed him the full amount and said no more.[4] These charming stories, part of the rich store of Hausa Muslim folklore, make it clear how important the kola trade along the Yauri Gonja route was for the Hausas in the early years of the 13 century AH, that is about AD 1785–1800. It is also interesting to note the confusion that occurs in the first story. Of course the kola forests were not in the Gonja kingdom. That lies in the dry, scrub savanna, some two hundred miles north of the magnificent green forests of the rainy belt, where the kola trees flourish. The nuts were harvested by the forest people, whose economy must have depended largely upon this crop, and taken to Ashanti. From here, under strict Ashanti control, they were transported to Salaga. This part of the trade was an Ashanti monopoly. Northern traders were not normally allowed to operate south of Salaga, although a few were permitted to reside in Kumasi as agents. In Salaga, the nuts were sold to the Hausa and Borno traders. Then, on donkeys supplied by the Mossi, and carefully packed in *fita* leaves, to keep them cool and moist, they began the long journey to Yauri and the Niger crossing. It was a highly skilled craft to keep the nuts prime and fresh all the way down the route from Salaga to the Yauri crossing and then on to the markets of Hausaland and Borno. If they dried out, they lost their bitter taste and their soft, waxy texture. Knowing how to keep them in good condition was how a man made his profit, but only someone who knew the trade well would be aware of where the nuts originated from. In the minds of ordinary Hausa consumers of kolas, Gonja was where they grew and where one picked them. This is why caution should be exercised in interpreting the word 'Gonja' when it appears in Hausa sources. Before the 20 century AD, it was used not to describe just the historical state of Gonja but, inaccurately, the whole area that became the Ashanti empire.

The Hausa 'occupation' of Salaga had important consequences for the spread of Islam. It meant that an important centre of Hausa, and to some extent also Borno Islam, was established in the midst of an area that had previously been dominated by Dyula Islam. This opened the way for Hausa penetration into the Ashanti empire. However, as long as the power of Ashanti lasted, the Hausas were not allowed to spread south of Kumasi, the capital of that empire. Later on, after the Ashanti defeat at the hands of the British, in 1291/1874, Salaga began to decline and the Hausa trading community there slowly dispersed to the south. They took their proud, bookish and uncompromising version of Islam with them.

The Akan kingdom of Bono

North of the present city of Kumasi, in the area of Takyiman, in the zone where the forest begins to give way to the savanna, lay Bono, the largest of a cluster of

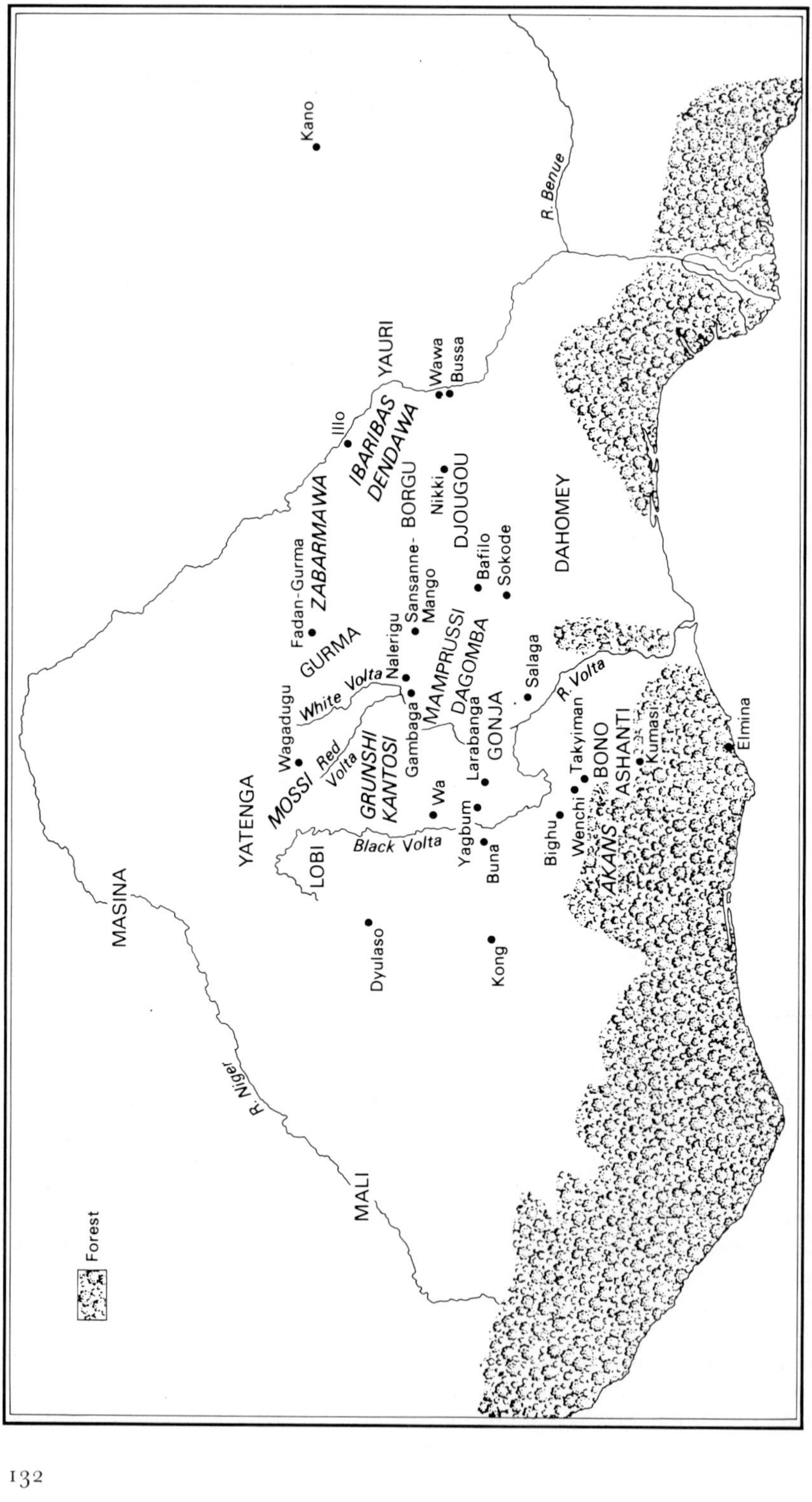

Map 6 The Volta region to c. 1267/1850.

Akan kingdoms. It was probably founded by northern Akans in the late 8/14 or early 9/15 century. Towards the end of the 15 century AD, probably between 879/1475 and 905/1499 gold mining began there. It is said in Bono tradition that the third king of Bono, Obunumankoma, travelled in the western Sudan at about that time, in order to study mining methods. The gold mining quickly attracted Dyula Muslim merchants from the Islamic north, especially from Mali. During the second half of the 16th century AD (AH 956–1008) the royal family adopted Islam, no doubt under the influence of these Dyula merchants. By the late 11/16 century the king, ᶜAlī Kwame, had taken a Muslim name and it is said that he, too, travelled in the western Sudan, to study mining.

In 1135/1722–3, Bono was defeated by the southern Akans of Ashanti and became subject to the Ashanti empire.

The importance of Bono for the spread of Islam lies in the fact that it was a producer and distributor of gold, for gold routes ran from Bono to Jenne, on the Niger Bend. They not only carried the precious metal into the Muslim Sudan; they also carried Islamic ideas back from the Niger Bend to the fringe of the forest. No doubt Dyula Muslims from Bono were among the first to carry Islam into Ashanti. No doubt, too, the more adventurous were among those who moved even farther south to establish relations with the Akan forest-dwellers.

It is, perhaps, with the extension of Bono's influence towards the south that it becomes convenient to think in terms of 'Islam in West Africa' instead of, simply, 'Islam in the west and central Sudan'.

Islam in Ashanti

The Ashanti kingdom was created in the late 17 century AD (11–12 century AH) by southern Akans. By the beginning of the 12/18 century its power was still limited to the areas well south of the savanna. By the middle of that century the savanna kingdom of Gonja lay directly under Ashanti control; Dagomba and Mamprusi were also within its sphere of influence. It had even established diplomatic contact with the Mossi kingdom of Wagadugu by that time, or shortly after. It was this early contact with the Muslim states of the north that formally introduced Islam into the Ashanti empire; Ashanti involvement in the profitable kola trade developed the contact further. Then the Ashanti rulers seem to have become impressed by the roles played by Muslim literates in the northern kingdoms so they began to call on their services for their own purposes.

Between 1177–8/1764–1191/1777, the Asantehene Osei Kwadwo initiated a programme of administrative reforms. This was probably the point at which the Muslim literates began to be officially recruited by the Ashantis, although there is some evidence that Arabic was used for official correspondence as early as 1164/1750. Certainly at least one Muslim *ᶜālim*, Abū Bakr Kyeame, was employed in an official post during this reign and his son, the Imām Saᶜīd Bamba, followed him. Osei Kwame (1191/1777–1212–13/1798) was strongly inclined to Islam and turned increasingly to Muslim advisers. By the end of the 18 century AD (12/13 century AH) a *madrasa* had been established at Buna, west of the Black Volta. It was presided over by a certain ᶜAbd Allāh b. al-Ḥājj Muḥammad al-Watarāwī and gave training to Ashanti civil servants. Buna became an important centre of Islamic scholarship, that attracted scholars not only from Ashanti and the Volta region but also from the Senegambia. Osei Bonsu (1214–15/1800–1238–9/1823) continued to associate with Muslim advisers and set up an office of government records that was probably staffed by men trained at Buna. They were largely responsible for the conduct of Ashanti business with the northern savanna states and also for more extended foreign affairs.

Early in the 13/19 century, Ashanti established friendly relations with Aḥmad b. Muḥammad (Ahmadu Lobbo), the jihadist of Masina. No doubt this was the work of Muslim civil servants in Kumasi and these same civil servants were also responsible for compiling records in Arabic about the history and administration of the Ashanti empire. In this they may have been following a precedent already established in Gonja. Unhappily, these records were destroyed when the British occupied Kumasi. By 1235–6/1820, when the Ashantis were in contact with the British, it was Muslim literates who conducted the negotiations.

Muslims in Ashanti functioned not only as civil servants, some were also physicians, astrologers and, most important of all, manufacturers of charms and amulets. Indeed, it is probable that the appeal of Islamic charms, as protection against witchcraft and weapons, was the greatest single source of Muslim influence and prestige in Ashanti. Equally important, perhaps, was Muslim prayer, which to the Ashantis seemed to be another form of magic; Muslims were constantly called on to pray for victory in war, or to stave off defeat. Muslims also fulfilled another function; they were in Kumasi as commercial agents, looking after the interests of the northern kola traders. Probably, it was as trade representatives that they first settled in Kumasi, even before they began to be recruited as civil servants. They often combined their commercial work with that of political representatives of the northern rulers, from whose kingdoms they came. They also advised the Ashanti authorities on commercial and political conditions in the north.

It was said above that it was from the Muslim states of the north that Islam was formally introduced into the Ashanti empire about the middle of the 12/18 century, that is a little more than half a century after the foundation of the Ashanti kingdom. This is correct in so far as it is the point at which Muslim literates are known to have become active in the empire. However, it must be remembered that Muslims were almost certainly present throughout the whole area of what, in the late 13/17 century became the Ashanti empire, long before that empire developed. There is good reason for believing that Muslim Dyulas were engaged in trade with the Portuguese, in the area of Elmina, before the end of the 9/15 century. They were certainly established in Bono before that largely Islamic state was absorbed into the Ashanti empire. They were also present in the gold distribution town of Bighu, north-west of Bono, before it collapsed early in the 12/18 century. It is therefore misleading to think of the Ashantis as becoming suddenly exposed to Islam as a result of contacts with the Muslim states to their north, in the mid-12/18 century. Some Islamic influences must have been at work among the Akans and throughout the area that became the Ashanti empire, long before it emerged.

Arising from this early settlement of mainly Dyula Muslims in the area between the forest and the northern savanna in pre-Ashanti times, it is reasonable to suppose that the first Muslims to exert an influence on the Ashanti empire must have been Dyulas. However, Dr Mahdi Adamu has suggested that those who first arrived in Kumasi may at least have had Hausas as their leaders.[5] Be that as it may, the presence of Muslims from near at hand soon led to the appearance of others from farther afield.

Among the first of them was a Hausa *malam* from Katsina, who arrived in Ashanti in 1222/1807. Another Hausa was there in 1233–4/1818 and yet another, also from Katsina, in 1235–6/1820. The best-known of these Muslim visitors was no doubt the Sharīf Ibrāhīm, a Borno *ᶜālim* who was resident in Kumasi in 1232–3/1817 as was his companion, another Hausa, called Muḥammad ᶜAbd al-Salām al-Maruwī. The Sharīf Ibrāhīm maintained himself by the profitable business of manufacturing charms and amulets and by offering his prayers in return for presents. However, he was unpopular with the other Muslims in Kumasi who regarded him as a rival.

The Muslims in Kumasi were welcomed by the Asantehenes during the 12/18 and early 13/19 centuries. Then the Muslims' position seems to have worsened until, by about 1266/1850 or perhaps a little later, they were excluded altogether. There were probably several reasons for this exclusion. First, was the Ashanti fear of growing Muslim power in the north, which threatened Ashanti dominance; second, which was perhaps linked to the first reason, was tension created by the successful *jihād* in Hausaland and its aftermath; third may have been the Ashanti decision to establish a much closer control over the kola trade. Finally, it seems that Islamic influences within the Ashanti empire, in particular in Kumasi, had begun to affect Ashanti commoners. This may have brought about a greater political awareness among these people, that was unwelcome to the Ashanti authorities. Ashanti relations with the northern states, and with Muslims in general, now worsened. It recovered somewhat when the Ashantis again called on the Muslims to help them against the invading British. However, Ashanti restrictions on the free movement of Muslims prevented any significant Islamic presence from being established in the southern Gold Coast until the collapse of Ashanti power in 1291/1874.

Despite contact with Muslims and with Islamic ideas for most of its existence, the Ashanti empire never became truly Muslim. Certain aspects of Islam – its literacy, its prayers and its amulets – were welcomed. Few Ashantis, at least among the governing classes, became fully converted. The Ashanti nation was united by its success as an imperial power and by the strength of its ancestral cult. Ashanti civilization sprang from the culture of the forest Akan people. They were too far distant from Mali to have been influenced by the early waves of Dyula Islam that coloured but never fully converted the northern Volta states. Although many Dyula Muslim merchants must have moved among the Akans, they were there to trade, not to win converts and Islam seems to have made very little impact on the southern Akans before the Ashanti empire was founded. As for that empire, having been touched but not converted by the Islam of the northern kingdoms, and of the Muslim traders, it was too far distant from the scene of the Fulani *jihād* in Hausaland to feel the full force of its puritanical, reforming zeal. Until the colonial occupation changed the scene, Ashanti lay at the edge of Islamic penetration; it received what pleased it of Islam but on its own terms and without surrendering its national or cultural identity.

Islam beyond the forest belt and along the Atlantic coast

In the south of Ashanti, extending from the southern edge of the savanna down to the Atlantic coast lies a belt of rain forest. The belt, broken only by a wedge of coastal scrub and grassland at the mouth of the Volta, extends east approximately to present Calabar and west to approximately Freetown, well beyond the limits of the Volta region, which is the subject of this chapter. However, it is convenient to deal with it as a whole here.

It is probable that Hausa traders who reached the Niger-Benue Confluence went on to make contact with the people living on the northern edge of the forest, in their search for forest produce and in the course of general trading. There is no reason to suppose that this may not have happened as early as the 10/16 century, or even the 9/15 century, although this cannot be proved. In the central area, above Elmina, Dyula traders certainly did make contact with the forest people in their quest for gold and kolas; they even settled in considerable numbers along the northern edge of the forest in centres such as Bighu and Bono. This process must have started as soon as these Dyulas began to interest themselves in the produce of the forest. As was said above, the kola trade is surely very ancient, as is the gold trade, and it would therefore be rash to pick on a particular date as the starting point. All the same, it is reasonable to suppose that it may have been under way by the 9/15 century. Some Islamic influences may therefore have touched the most northerly of the forest peoples at that time, although it is clear that they made little permanent impression upon them; the forest marked the limit to further significant Islamic penetration. For example, when the Portuguese began building their fortress of São Jorge Da Mina (Elmina) in AD 1482, it is clear that the king Caramança (Kwamin Ansa?) and his subjects, who inhabited the area, were not Muslims but adherents of a traditional religion that was either animistic or polytheistic. At one point they tried to prevent the Portuguese masons from breaking the rock to prepare the building site, lest the spirit that lived in it should be angered. Thus those few Dyula Muslim merchants who may have made contact with the Portuguese in the same area had clearly not succeeded in converting the local people to Islam. This was not because the forest was an actual physical barrier to all but a few very lucky or very courageous Muslims; only the extreme height of mountain ranges, combined with intense cold and glacial conditions, or very wide and completely waterless deserts, have normally proved to be absolute obstacles to human movements. One should be profoundly doubtful as to the truth of any theory that one group of African people has ever been seriously hindered in making contact with other groups of people in Africa, solely by climatic conditions or the difficulty of crossing particular types of terrain. Isolation has come from cultural barriers and, to a lesser extent, from diseases that kill those who have no immunity to them, not from the physical barriers of nature. As for the forests of Africa, it seems highly probable that they have been criss-crossed by footpaths almost since the dawn of Man. Muslims could have crossed the forests and reached the coast at any time, had they thought it useful to do so and provided they were well enough armed to fight off hostile forest-dwellers. If, as seems likely, Dyula Muslims did make contact with the Portuguese in the area of Elmina during the 9/15 century, they must have crossed the forest, or found a way round it, to get there. It has been suggested that the forest was a tsetse area in which the horses of the Muslims could not survive. This, and the climatic conditions of the forest, may indeed have been sufficient to cause them to dislike travelling in it. It would certainly not have prevented them from doing so, if the jingle of money-bags on the further side had urged them to it and there were, in any case, other forms of transport that could survive in the forest, including slaves.

The reason Muslims did not cross the forest and reach the coast in significant numbers before the colonial era is simply that it was just as profitable, and much less trouble, to settle on the northern edge and let the forest people work the forest for them. Before the heyday of the Atlantic slave-trade – the 11/17 and 12/18 centuries – the only major attraction beyond the forest was the gold trade with the Portuguese, and for this Dyula Muslims probably did penetrate to the coast. However, they were too few in number to make much impression on the coastal people. When the Atlantic slave-trade was at its height it may have attracted rather more Muslim traders to settle on the coast, although the Muslim participation in this trade took place mainly in the northern hinterland. The coastal end of it was handled by coastal Africans and their European partners. It seems that over the course of centuries, individual Muslim traders did set up a scattering of small settlements – Madina, Ni'ima, Darussalam and so on – that were nostalgic reminders of their homeland and their Muslim culture, among the outlandish names and alien landscapes of the fishing villages and hamlets along the Atlantic coast. As was said above, there were a few such Muslims in Whydah early in the 12/18 century and there were others in Lagos. They must have come to trade, whether in slaves or other trade goods. No doubt some of them were petty traders, who sold Islamic charms and medicines to the local people, and hand-manufactured leather goods, as they do today, but they were strangers in a strange land.

The forest people and the coastal people were too remote from the centres of African Islam and too deeply enmeshed in their own ancient, complex, powerful cultures to be swayed by the example of these northern intruders who had the dress and manners of the distant foreign world of the savanna. Conversion to Islam among the forest and coastal peoples did not begin in earnest until the railways and roads of the colonial era abruptly broke down many of the old cultural defences.

NOTES

1 Levtzion, 1968, p.87.

2 But if it were pure Hausa, one would expect *Sansanin-Mangawa*. Perhaps the Hausa *sansani* became adopted in Mande or some other local language as a loan-word, to give 'Sansanne-Mango', in much the same way that the pure Hausa *mai akushi* became 'Mangoshi' among the Dagombas.

3 Alhaji Abubakar Imam, CON, CBE, *Magana jari ce*, Zaria, 1973 edition, Vol. I, pp.112–14.

4 ibid, pp.116–17.

5 *The Hausa factor*, p.81.

CHAPTER EIGHT

Islam in Senegambia from the 8/14 century to the 12/18 century

It will be remembered that when the Mali empire declined, the old state of Takrūr, by then a part of the Mali empire, broke up into kingdoms ruled by Wolof and Denianke kings. In due course three main political groups emerged. First, the Wolof kingdoms in the western half of the area enclosed by the river Senegal and the river Gambia. They were Walo, Cayor, Baol, Sine and Salum, all dominated by the central kingdom of Jolof. Second, north of Jolof, on the south bank of the Senegal, lay the Denianke kingdom of Futa Toro. Finally, in the far south of the area, in the hilly country in which the rivers Gambia and Bafing have their source, was Futa Jalon.

Islam in the successor kingdoms to Takrūr

Islam had been established in most of the northern part of Takrūr by War Jabi (d. 432/1040–1), a generation before the Almoravids. Although some aspects of the old cults survived – the system of land tenure, for instance, and certain other customary practices – Islam became the predominant religion over the generations that followed War Jabi and did much to shape the way of life. *C.* 802/1400, by which time the Wolof kingdoms had emerged, there were no doubt, some communities that still followed the old, pre-Islamic cults. By the middle of the 9/15 century however, both the king and the people of the Wolof kingdom of Cayor were Muslims, according to the reports of Europeans who made contact with the Senegambia along the Atlantic coast. So too were certain rulers and their people along the Gambia river. These local Muslims were served by ᶜ*ulamā*', known to the Europeans as 'Azanaghi', that is Sanhaja, who had come into the Senegambia from neighbouring Shinqīṭ, that is Mauritania. However, despite their presence, the level of Islamic observance was low. The Islamic marriage laws were not observed by the princes and government was conducted according to customary law, not according to the Sharīᶜa. The nobility even drank alcohol openly. What is more, the early Portuguese found some of the rulers very willing to convert to Christianity, apparently because they were attracted by the higher material culture of the Portuguese and by their technology – especially firearms and naval technology. Such easy conversions could certainly not have been obtained in the Islamic heartlands, farther inland, as later missionaries were to discover.

For their part the ᶜ*ulamā*' had built up their position over several centuries of Almoravid and then Malian influence. Islamic literacy among them must have reached a high level of excellence by the 10/16 century. It is known that there were Senegambians (Gialofi in the terminology of the 10/16 century Christian travellers) studying Arabic grammar, Arabic poetry and Islamic astrology in Fez during that century, together with other Sūdānī and North

African students. These ᶜ*ulamā*' became, in due course, a powerful class in the Wolof kingdoms. Many of them had followings of *ṭālibūn* (Ar. sing. *ṭālib*, student/disciple), who were not only religious disciples but also, in a political and sometimes an economic sense, dependent on their masters. The ᶜ*ulamā*' therefore wielded considerable political power and were able, from time to time, to challenge the authority of the Wolof nobility. They regarded the lax Islamic observance of that nobility with contempt. They were literates and felt keenly their superiority over the illiterate. For reasons of genuine religious conviction and, perhaps, to further their material interests as well, they began to advocate Islamic reform in the Wolof kingdoms. However, it is important to bear in mind that, as Professor Lucie Gallistel Colvin has shown,[1] this gathering confrontation was not one between Muslims and non-Muslims. It was between two groups of Muslims, one literate, the other largely illiterate, who interpreted their obligations to Islam at different levels of seriousness.

Futa Toro was ruled by the Denianke, a Fulani dynasty. Islam was present there, too, during the 10/16 century but, as in the neighbouring Wolof kingdoms, there was no attempt to impose an Islamic constitution or to govern by the Sharīᶜa. The kingdom was at the height of its power from the end of the 16 century AD (1008/1599) until *c.* 1081/1670 but from then on began to decline. During the 12/18 century it was greatly harassed by the slave-raiding of the Moors from nearby Mauritania, by highway robbery and by general insecurity. By the middle of the century it was in the grip of civil war.

Futa Jalon, in the south, was ruled by Jalonke kings, of Mande origin. Polytheism there was much stronger than in either Futa Toro or the Wolof kingdoms. Indeed, the mass of the population was still polytheist *c.* 1009/1600. Muslims may have been present here, too, well before that date, though they were certainly not the majority. It seems they were welcomed, none the less, as sellers of Koranic charms and for their literacy. As a result there was little tension between Muslim and non-Muslim. However during the 10/16 and early 11/17 centuries, substantial immigrations of pastoral Fulani took place. They came from the area of Masina, on the right bank of the Niger. Many had been in contact with the Kunta. They were thus at least partially converted to Islam and there may even have been a distinct Qādirī sentiment among them. These people set up settlements known as Fulacundas. Tension between them and the Jalonke rulers grew, for the Fulani were pastoralists and the Jalonke were landlords who favoured the peasants. Moreover, they treated the Fulani as inferiors. During the 11/17 century these Fulani and certain Mande traders associated with them, became increasingly wealthy, owing to a greatly increased demand from European traders for hides and slaves, both of which they supplied. This development had a disturbing effect upon the economic and political balance of power in Futa Jalon. The prosperous Muslims became increasingly reluctant to pay tribute to the Jalonke and more and more restless under their authority. Moreover, a tendency on the part of the Jalonke to disregard traditional Muslim immunity from enslavement further aggravated the tension between them. The result was an alliance between Muslim traders, both Fulani and Mande, against the Jalonke.

The war of Nāṣir al-Dīn

The first major outbreak of revolt on the part of the ᶜ*ulamā*' against the traditional rulers reached the Senegambia as an overflow from southern Mauritania. Here, *c.* 1055/1645, a Muslim of the Banū Daymān, Awbek b. Achfaghu known as the Imām Nāṣir al-Dīn, led a movement of Islamic reform. He was clearly inspired by the teachings of the Mauritanian Zwāya, of whom the Banū Daymān were members. There is evidence that this teaching included Mahdist ideas and the notion of preparing to meet the End of Time and that Nāṣir al-Dīn was influenced by them. Such ideas were widespread in North Africa at this time and it seems likely that it was from there that they reached the Mauritanian Zwāya; although the Zwāya, for their part, may have acquired them on Pilgrimage, in Mecca and Medina. At any rate, they belonged to a wider movement of ideas in the Muslim world at large and were not peculiar to Mauritania. Another idea that seems to have been important in turning Nāṣir al-Dīn into a Muslim reformer and revolutionary was that of the Prophet Muḥammad as al-Insān al-Kāmil, the 'Perfect Man'. This, too, provided a goal of ideological perfection to be realised through Islamic reform and once again, the Mauritanian revolutionary was indebted for his inspiration to ideas that were sweeping across the world of Islam in his day. However, in addition to these religious and ideological motives, it also seems probable that commercial considerations played a part in encouraging him to revolt, especially a desire to control the profitable gum trade of the area.

Nāṣir al-Dīn's aim seems to have been to set up a unified Islamic *jamāᶜa*, community, among the Zwāya, that was free of tribal and blood allegiances and united solely in Islam and in obedience to the divinely appointed *Imām* – in this case Nāṣir al-Dīn himself. To bring this about he tried to set up an administration based on the Sharīᶜa and formed according to the classical Islamic model. His movement soon spread across the Senegal into Futa and the Wolof kingdoms and through his lieutenants he conquered Futa Toro, Jolof, Cayor and Walo. The war became known among the Zwāya as the war of the *Shurbubba*, while European historians are accustomed to describe it as the 'War of the Marabouts'. *Shurbubba* is a word, the exact meaning of which is uncertain; but it is thought to have been a Zwāya war-cry. The war lasted until about 1085/1675, although there is some uncertainty about this date. In the end Nāṣir al-Dīn was killed in battle and his movement was defeated by the Wolof kings, aided by the French from Saint Louis. It failed to bring about a permanent change of government, but it may have served to spread the notion of Islamic revolution in the Senegambia. It also had a number of other important results.

First, as a consequence of Nāṣir al-Dīn's Zwāya influence and teaching, several centres of Islamic learning developed in Senegambia during the early 12/18 century – notably those of Pir and Coki – and links were forged between the *ᶜulamā'* of Futa Toro and the Wolof kingdoms, especially Cayor. The war also brought about an intensified sense of political as well as religious solidarity and self-awareness among the *ᶜulamā'*; it helped to break down the tradition of peaceful scholarship, as opposed to warrior virtues, that had once been characteristic of the Zwāya.

Mālik Sy in Bundu

Bundu is situated south-east of Futa Toro, on the west bank of the Falémé river. There is doubt as to the exact date of the founding of an Islamic imamate there. It was probably at the end of the 17 century AD (1111/1699), when a certain

Tukolor *walī*, Mālik Sy, appeared. He set up a small Islamic state in what was, according to the existing tradition, an area inhabited by polytheists. Here is part of the traditional story that tells how he came:

> When [Mālik Sy] came to Bundu, at that time he found Bundu with the Fadoubé in possession of the land. Their abodes were holes in the ground and they had tails. Now they had a well (*ɓundu*], and this well was dug, but it had not been lined. One of their women whom you know of, called Koumba, was their leader. This well was hers; she was responsible for it. What prevented the well from being completed was that throughout the bush of Bundu at that time, wherever you saw a tree, if you cut it with an axe, a jinn would jump out and strike you and buffet you.
>
> So, when Malik Dauda [Mālik Sy] got here and saw this, he conversed with them and said, 'You there, what prevents you from finishing off your well?' They told him what was stopping them from finishing it. He said, 'Well, now, I'll write an *aaye* for you, to be sprinkled on the trees, and the jinn will run away. Then we will cut the trees down, but when the bush has been cleared and the well has been owned, and received, and contrived, then I, Malik, will own it. I shall own the well.' They said that they agreed, and they told him so. So he wrote an *aaye*, Malik Dauda, and sprinkled it over the trees of Bundu. He cut down all the dead [dry] trees. So they got wood with which they finished the well, which was called Koumba's well. But the one who completed it was Boubou Malik. Hence the name *ɓundu Kumba Bannandu Bumaalik* [lit: Koumba's well completed by Boubou Malik].
>
> Now at this time they used to live in caves. Mālik Sy said to them, 'Your way of life is not right. Come and I will cut off your tails, and [you may] come out of your caves and build huts.' They said, 'How can that be? What if we die?' He said, 'You will not die, I will take care of you.' They looked for the least important of their number and handed him over. Mālik cut off his tail, treated him, and put clothes on him, and he came on out. And then all of them gathered and built huts. He cut off their tails – they were the Fadoubé. Then they said, 'Now that we accept you; you are the owner of the well. But now that you are going to be owner of Bundu, let no descendant of yours do us harm, 'nor will any of our descendants do you or yours any harm.' So began a mutual relationship, the relationship of *jongu*. This relationship has continued at Bundu since 1512 and has still not disappeared in our own day.[2]

The reference to the cutting off of tails has been interpreted to refer to the introduction of the Islamic rite of circumcision. However, it probably indicates no more than the Muslim literates' scorn for the nakedness and polytheist habits of a non-Muslim people and symbolises the abandoning of a primitive life-style, the acceptance of Islam and the wearing of clothes. The reference to the well and to Mālik Sy's 'pouring of an *aaye*' (a verse from the Koran written on a board and then washed off with water) over the trees certainly suggests the superior religious power of the Muslim *walī* over traditional magic. Clearly, the story is a Muslim one. It gives the Muslim viewpoint of this historical incident of Mālik Sy's appearance in Bundu. It does not, of course, describe it through the eyes of the polytheists. Their version, if it could be known, would almost certainly turn out to be rather different. It is, perhaps, the final passage, that tells about the setting up of the relationship of *jongu*, that is the most important part of the story. It is typical of the kind of easy-going arrangements that usually sprang up between Muslim and non-Muslim until Islamic reform and *jihād* intervened to stir up problems again.

The story goes on to tell how Mālik Sy, having established himself as master of Bundu, went on to expand his kingdom at the expense of the ruler of neighbouring Tuabo, ᶜAlī Winji Wanja. He was at first successful in reducing ᶜAlī Winji Wanja and other neighbouring chiefs to submission but was later killed in battle when they turned against him. The final conquest of Bundu was undertaken by Mālik Sy's son, Boubou Mālik.

After Mālik Sy the level of Islamic observance in Bundu declined somewhat and his successors prided themselves more on their talents as warriors than as scholars. However, it was revived again by ᶜAbd al-Qādir's successful *jihād* in Futa Toro in the following century.

It is important to note that Mālik Sy was widely regarded as a miracle-working *walī*, that he underwent a full Koranic education and that he performed Pilgrimage before he embarked on his career as an Islamic preacher and reformer. Thus, although he never declared a *jihād*, he conformed, in these respects, to a pattern that was later to become standard among the great jihadists of the 13/19 century.

It has been suggested that Mālik Sy's initiative was an offshoot of Nāṣir al-Dīn's movement in Mauritania. No doubt this movement had some influence for Mālik Sy can hardly have been unaware of it. There were differences between the two incidents, however; Nāṣir al-Dīn initiated what became a revolt against the well-established political authority of the Wolof and Denianke kings while Mālik Sy took over an area that was apparently in the hands of family-and-clan group polytheists, and then expanded into the surrounding kingdoms. Mālik Sy's movement was, initially, a simple missionary endeavour that turned into a war of conquest, not a reform movement that turned into a revolution.

The *jihād* of Alfa Ba in Futa Jalon

The situation of tension between the Muslim Fulani and the Jalonke of Futa Jalon described above came to a head *c.* 1140/1727–8, when one of the Jalonke kings, Jam Iero, tried to forbid the public performance of Islamic prayers. A certain Ibrāhīm Sori retaliated, so it is said, by entering the royal village and slitting the royal drum. He then fled to his cousin, a Muslim *ᶜālim* known as Karamoko Alfa, or Alfa Ba. Alfa Ba decided that this was a suitable occasion to launch a *jihād*, and did so. The Muslims quickly took over control of Futa Jalon and an Islamic imamate was set up there under Alfa Ba. It continued under his successors until the time of the French occupation in the 13/19 century.

It cannot be definitely stated that Alfa Ba was a Sufi and a Qādirī. However, it is known that he received his education in Kankan, an Islamic centre of learning dominated by the Kuntī *shaykhs* and it is therefore almost certain that he was.

The *jihād* of ᶜAbd al-Qādir in Futa Toro

In Futa Toro the inability of the ruling Denianke to check the deteriorating situation in which the Muslims found themselves, as victims of slave-raiding both by the Brakna Moors from Mauritania and the Denianke themselves, caused great discontent. A Muslim *walī*, Sulaymān Bal, rose at the head of the Muslim Tukolor, against the marauding Moors. He was killed, but another Muslim leader, ᶜAbd al-Qādir, succeeded him as Almamy (*imām*) of the Tukolor, probably in or about 1190/1776. By *c.* 1195/1780 ᶜAbd al-Qādir had overcome the Denianke and, in 1200–1/1786, turned against the Moors on the northern bank of the Senegal. This seems to have been the point at which his movement became truly a *jihād* rather than an internal revolt. The fact that the year 1200/1785–6 marked the turn of the Islamic century may well mean that Mahdist ideology was in the air of the Senegambia at this time and that ᶜAbd al-Qādir took advantage of it. By 1205/1790 he had secured the allegiance of the rulers of the kingdoms of Walo, Jolof and Cayor. However, a new ruler of Cayor subsequently withdrew this allegiance and endeavoured to check the growing power of the reforming *ᶜulamā'* within this kingdom. The result was civil war, in which the Muslim party suffered a number of defeats. The Almamy ᶜAbd al-Qādir now organised an expedition to go to their aid but, in 1211/1796 he was heavily defeated and captured by the Cayor army at the battle of Bunguye. He himself was held as a hostage for some years at the Cayor court but eventually he was released and allowed to return to Futa Toro. His authority had been damaged by his defeat and capture and in 1222/1807 he was murdered. Power then passed to a council of Almamies. ᶜAbd al-Qādir's defeat in 1211/1796 marked a turning point in the history of the reform movements in the Senegambia; from that point on the traditional rulers began to reassert their authority. It was not until the era of the 13/19 century *jihāds* that they were again seriously challenged by the forces of Islamic reform.

ᶜAbd al-Qādir had studied in Mauritania under the Zwāya, Banū Daymān, before he became a jihadist. There is no doubt that he was greatly inspired by the example of Nāṣir al-Dīn, some hundred years earlier. In his case, too, it remains uncertain whether or not he belonged to a Sufi *ṭarīqa*. However, it is known that he was greatly attached to the *Dalā'il al-khayrāt* of al-Jazūlī, a collection of praise names and prayers addressed to the Prophet Muḥammad, and to the *ᶜIshrīniyyāt*, al-Fāzāzī's well-known praise-poem to the Prophet. These two texts are not studied by Sufis alone but they are especially popular among them. This, together with the Futa Toro jihadist's name, suggests that he probably was a Qādirī.

The nature and results of the Islamic movements in the Senegambia from 1055/1645 to 1200–1/1786

There is certainly an ideological connecting link that runs from the Zwāya in Mauritania, through the 11/17 century movement of Nāṣir al-Dīn, down to the 12–13/18 century Islamic revolutions in the Senegambia. Yet these revolutions were small-scale affairs that lacked the over-whelming thrust of the great 13/19 century *jihāds* that were to come. Except in the case of Nāṣir al-Dīn's war, which was preceded by several years of reformist preaching, the ground was not prepared for them by the long, systematic propaganda campaigns, the *jihād al-qawl*, '*jihād* of speech', best rendered into English as 'Preaching *Jihād*', that characterised the 13/19 century *jihāds*. The leaders lacked the support of powerful clan and family networks that were so important in bringing about the success of the 13/19 century movements. No large empires emerged out of them, such as the later jihadists created and indeed, their success was uneven. Nāṣir al-Dīn's initial victories were quickly reversed and ᶜAbd al-Qādir met more than his match in Cayor. Moreover, support for these Senegambian revolutions was largely from town and city-dwellers, they did not attract the mass support of nomads and peasants that, for instance, the Shehu Usumanu ɗan Fodio was later to enjoy in Hausaland. Because they failed to achieve permanent success, thereby destroying the power of the faintly Muslim traditional rulers once and for all, the 12–13/18 century Islamic movements in the Senegambia simply resulted in intensifying the hostility between these rulers and the ᶜ*ulamā*'. To this extent they were divisive, not unifying in their effect. This hostility between the traditional rulers and the Muslim reformers, which characterised the Senegambian scene during the 13/19 century, proved helpful to the French in establishing colonial control over the area. In fact, it was probably the case that the Islamic revolutions drove the traditional rulers further away from Islam than they had ever been in the preceding centuries. Whereas European observers from the 10/16 century on tended to stress that these rulers were Muslims, however imperfect, in the 12–13/18 century there was an increasing tendency to describe them as 'pagans'. Thus the 12–13/18 century Muslim uprisings in the Senegambia may be regarded, at best, as 'unfinished missions' in that they were followed by the later, great *jihād* of al-Ḥājj ᶜUmar al-Fūtī, as well as by several other less effective 13/19 century movements. That these later jihadists were still able to make out convincing cases for Islamic reform in the Senegambia is an indication of how incomplete the 11/17- and 12–13/18-century movements were.

However, these movements did have certain achievements to their credit. Above all, they restored the Muslims' immunity from enslavement that had been so frequently ignored by the Wolof, Jalonke and Denianke kings. They also resulted in an improvement in the quality of Islamic education and in its wider spread. This was especially so in Bundu and Futa Jalon, where statistics of the French colonial administration in the late 19 century AD suggest that the level of literacy in Arabic was remarkably high, perhaps as high as 60 per cent.

In Futa Toro ᶜAbd al-Qādir's *jihād* had the result of improving Futa Toro's position in the river trade and reducing the privileged position that the French had previously enjoyed. By doing so, it may have sparked off French resentment against Islamic states that demanded tolls and trade taxes, and so have helped to provoke the later French wars of colonial conquest.

In Futa Jalon Alfa Ba's *jihād* brought a number of fragmented Jalonke states together into a single Islamic imamate governed, at least in theory, according to the Sharīᶜa. Moreover, Muslims, who had previously been a subject class, now became the possessing class; they turned the old Jalonke hierarchy into a class of civil servants who administered the imamate on their behalf.

Considerable attention has been paid to the changes in land tenure brought about by the Senegambian Muslim revolutions. It is said that a system of land tenure based on the polytheist concept of the spirits as owners of the land was replaced by the system of the Sharīᶜa. In this system the land became the property of the whole *jamāᶜa*, the Muslim community, and was leased out by the *imām* to individuals who farmed it and enjoyed its fruits.[3] Theoretically, this is

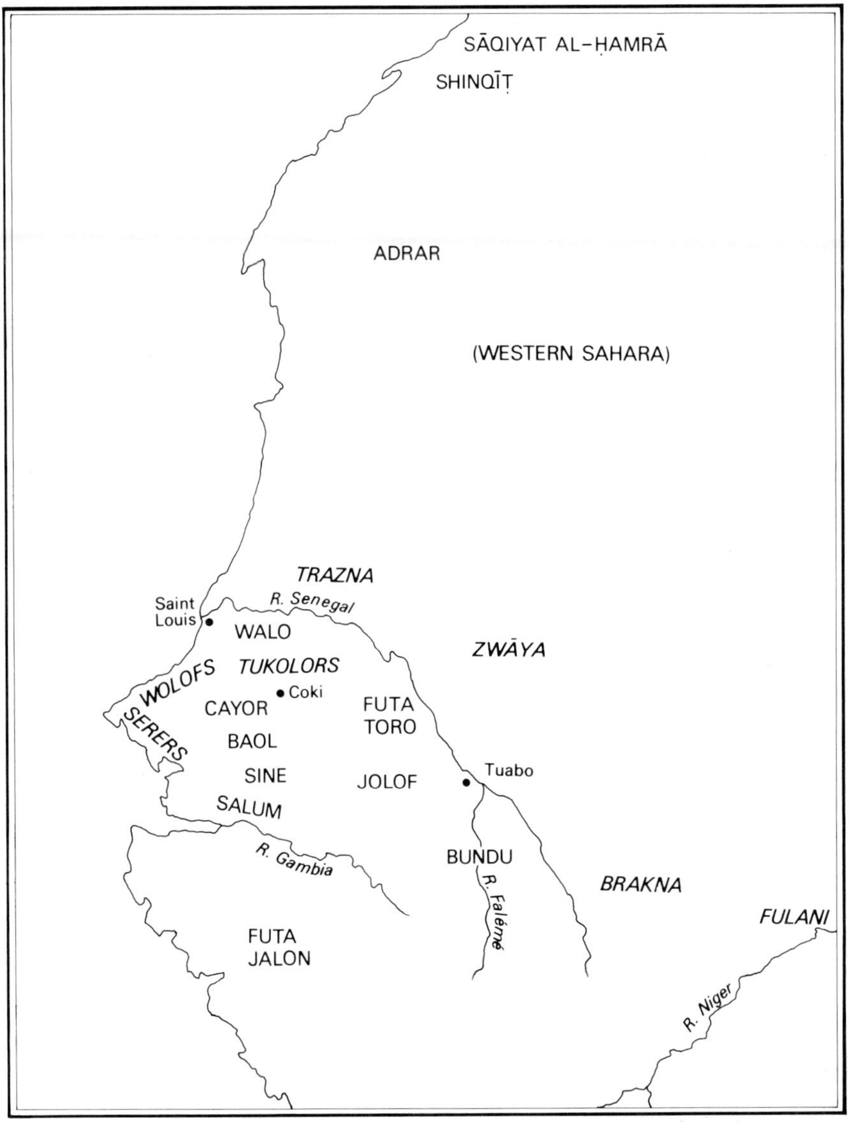

Map 7 The Senegambia in the 11/17 century.

true; one concept of the right by which land was held was discarded and a different one took its place in the minds of the new rulers. That this had any practical consequence seems doubtful. As the story of Mālik Sy makes clear, the price he paid for the cooperation of the traditional landowners in his take-over of Bundu was acceptance of the *jongu* relationship which, according to the chronicler, continued from that time on. Similar agreements were reached in other Senegambian imamates. The traditional owners were left in possession provided they cooperated with the Islamic state. Thus, while it is of intellectual interest, it was at the time of little practical importance whether the farmers continued to believe that the owners of the land were the spirits or whether they adopted the view of the conquerors, that the *imām* was their landlord.

It has been argued that these Senegambian Muslim revolutionaries and jihadists were Torodbe, and should be referred to as such.[4] Some reasons for disagreeing with this point of view were set out in the wider context of chapter 3. In the particular Senegambian context, the term 'Torodbe' is altogether too limited to describe the people who participated in these wars and revolutions. For example, the Fulani of the Fulacundas in Futa Jalon were cattle-nomads and merchants, not Torodbe clerics and the Muslims of Mande origin played an important part in the Futa Jalon movement. It is true that most of the leaders were literate Muslim Fulfulde-speakers who claimed to be Torodbe. Moreover, there is no doubt that their movements were, in large measure, assertions of the right of the literate over the illiterate to political authority – a frequent though not exclusively Torodbe claim. On the other hand, these leaders almost certainly had Wolof, Serer and other Senegambian blood in their veins, thus the best term by which to refer to them remains 'Tukolor'.

The kingdoms discussed above under the general heading of the Senegambia are those which, roughly speaking, became the French colony of Senegal and subsequently the present independent Republic of Senegal, with the British protectorate of the Gambia, present independent Gambia, within it. Immediately to the north of the Senegambia lay a country known to the medieval geographers as Shinqīṭ.

Shinqīṭ

Shinqīṭ is the Saharan Arabs' name for the country that is now, roughly, that of the Islamic Republic of Mauritania. In its far north lay Kākudam, the legendary homeland of the Almoravids. Historically, it belongs rather to North Africa than to the Western Sudan and for this reason it cannot be treated in detail in this book. However, Shinqīṭ has had important influences on the development of Islam in the west and central Sudan. It is therefore appropriate to give a brief account of it here, for although it was not part of the ancient kingdom of Takrūr, it was its northern neighbour.

The name Shinqīṭ was originally that of a small caravan town in the Adrar district of present Mauritania. It was founded *c.* 160–1/777. By the 7/13 century it had become a centre for scholars and pilgrims on their way to and from Pilgrimage. It quickly acquired a reputation as a centre of Islamic scholarship and then the name of the town came to be applied to the country as a whole.

Shinqīṭ was originally populated largely by Berbers and Arabs, but even in early times there were substantial groups of other peoples – Sarakolle, Fulani, Tukolors, Bambaras and so on. The Berbers and Arabs intermarried with these other peoples to produce a population known to Europeans as 'Moors'. However, they themselves do not use this term, they refer to themselves by their tribal or clan names. Of these there are very many; the most important from the point of view of Islamic history in the west and central Sudan is certainly that of the Ḥassāniyya, which describes a people made up of Arabs and Toureg Sanhaja who speak the Ḥassāniyya Arabic dialect. It was from them that the Zwāya class, described in chapter 3, first emerged. Part of the larger group of the Ḥassāniyya are such Zwāya clans as the Banū Daymān, the Idaw al-Ḥajj, the Ahl Bārakallāh and the Awlād Mubārak. As was stated above, it was through the influence of these Mauritanian Zwāya that Nāṣir al-Dīn was first inspired to start his movement of Islamic reform. It was by the Zwāya Banū Daymān that the jihadist ʿAbd al-Qādir was educated. It is thus largely as a channel for the spread of Islamic ideas, especially the reforming ideas of the Zwāya, that Shinqīṭ became important in the history of Islam in the west and central Sudan.

Shinqīṭ has also had considerable military and commercial importance. Two other Moorish tribes, the Trazna in south-west Shinqīṭ, and the Brakna, farther to the east, occupied the north bank of the Senegal river and it was these two who constantly fought for control of the river trade with the Wolofs and Tukolors of the Senegambia. Their history has been intertwined at all points both with that of the Senegambian peoples and with that of the French in Saint Louis. The part they played, on the one hand as teachers and Sufi *walīs*, and on the other hand as brigands and slave-raiders, was important in giving rise to the Islamic revolutions in the Senegambia that have been described above.

The Moors of Shinqīṭ were also among those who adopted the practice of composing Islamic literature in a vernacular language – their Znaga tongue – and of writing these compositions down using the Arabic script. This practice may have helped to encourage the composing of Islamic literature in other West African vernaculars, especially Hausa and Fulfulde. Moreover, stories of miracles performed by the *awliyā'* of Shinqīṭ quickly spread throughout the west and central Sudan. They helped to start up similar miracle traditions that were attributed to Sūdānī holy men.

NOTES

1 *JAH*, XV, 4, 1974, pp.587–606.

2 Skinner and Curtin, *Cahiers d'Études Africaines*, XI, 3, 1971, p.477. The date AD 1512 (AH 917–18) cannot be correct for it conflicts with other, conclusive evidence that Mālik Sy arrived in Bundu at the end of the 11/17 century.

3 See Willis, 'Reflections . . .', in Willis, ed. 1979 for an exposition of this view.

4 Willis, *JAH*, XIX, 2, 1978.

CHAPTER NINE

The aftermath of the fall of Songhay

The Moroccans who occupied Timbuktu after Jawdhar's conquest have usually been portrayed as villains. This is not entirely fair for it seems they were neither vicious nor, at first, inefficient. They were merely faced with what turned out to be an impossible task – to govern Timbuktu as if it were a province of the Sharifian Sa^{c}did empire. Of course they were not always gentle with those who opposed them, but then this is not to be expected of any military conqueror.

The Timbuktu Makhzan

The Moroccans began by establishing a firm control over the Timbuktu ^{c}*ulamā'*. This was not religious persecution for the Moroccans were themselves devout Muslims; it was a political act, understandable in that they feared the ^{c}*ulamā'* might form an opposition to their military government. In fact, not all the ^{c}*ulamā'* opposed the Moroccans. In Timbuktu some regarded their occupation as the judgement of God upon the *askiyas*; what opposition there was, was quickly silenced. However, in the neighbouring city of Jenne there seems to have been more support for the fugitive *askiya* in Dendi.

At first the Moroccans served the Moroccan caliph, Mawlay Aḥmad al-Manṣūr, loyally. The required percentages of gold, and of the gains from other profitable trades, were sent to Morocco regularly and they considerably enriched the Moroccan treasury. The Moroccans realised, sensibly, that if they were to continue to do this, they must not disturb the local structure of government and trade. Thus a system of indirect rule developed in which the Moroccans left the Songhay administration as it was, with a puppet *askiya* nominally at its head, but required it only to work for them. To govern their own Moroccan community that grew up in Timbuktu they set up what they called the Makhzan. This was modelled on the system that Mawlay Aḥmad al-Manṣūr had already set up in Morocco. It had at its head a *pasha*, a military governor, who was responsible to the caliph in Morocco. Next in rank was the *amīn*, also directly responsible to the caliph and in charge of the financial affairs of the province. However, real power lay with the Moroccan commanders of the army divisions and the Moroccan occupation also drew to Timbuktu numbers of *shurafā'*, who became increasingly influential in the city's affairs.

The first generation of Moroccan soldiers quickly married with Songhay women. In due course this produced a community of mixed blood that became known as the 'Ruma' or 'Arma', from an Arabic word meaning 'musketeers'. This community became, increasingly, the Makhzan.

A number of factors contributed to making the Moroccan task difficult. First was the recall to Morocco of the Pasha Jawdhar, who was an able administrator, and his replacement by the Pasha Maḥmūd Zarghūn, who was less loyal to the Moroccan caliph and more tyrannous and less competent than Jawdhar. Then, in 1012/1603, Mawlay Aḥmad al-Manṣūr died and Morocco was plunged into a succession struggle. From *c.* 1021/1612 on the Moroccan rulers lost interest in their Niger province and problems of communication with the disinterested Moroccan authorities became increasingly severe, despite their occasional attempts to re-establish control. The upheavals and disruption that attended the collapse of the Sharifian Saᶜdids and the rise of the ᶜAlawids, who also claimed to be *shurafā'*, enabled the Arma to go their own way with less regard than ever for the metropolitan government. By the time that the ᶜAlawids finally took over from the Sharifian Saᶜdids in 1076/1666, the Makhzan had become for all practical purposes independent. Gradually, too, the Arma abandoned the early, sensible policy of indirect rule and began to interfere increasingly in the Songhay administration. However, they were by no means wholly incompetent. They did make genuine efforts to protect trade by organising military expeditions against brigands and their rule was not deliberately oppressive, only less and less effective. Moreover, as the Makhzan became less subject to control from Morocco, there was an increasing tendency within it for rival parties to plot against each other and to seek the support of mercenaries – Berbers, Fulani, Bambaras and others. These mercenaries often ended by seizing power for themselves. Little by little, central authority crumbled and the Touregs and other local factions took over. By 1163–4/1750, the authority of the Arma was limited to the banks of the Niger and they operated more as rival bands of brigands than as a government. This situation continued until the city was occupied by the French at the beginning of the present century.

The Bambaras and Massassis

The country of the Bambaras, a Mande-speaking people related to their neighbours, the Malinke, lies due north of the Niger source, and straddles the banks of that river. The Bambaras formed part of the Mali empire, and then passed under control of Songhay. With the fall of Songhay they gained their independence. By *c.* 1034/1625, intermarriage between them and Fulani settled in the area of Segu gave rise to the Massassi dynasty, governing a kingdom centred on Segu. The Bambaras were basically polytheist, but among them lived many Mande-speaking Muslims of the Dyula class. Among the Bambaras, however, these Muslims were referred to as 'Marka'. *C.* 1137–8/1725 a certain Mamari Kouloubali, the son of a Bambara peasant and a Muslim Marka woman, succeeded in setting up a strong, centralised Bambara state in Segu. Mamari was certainly influenced by Islam, but he was not a practising Muslim; despite his Marka origin on his mother's side, he fought and defeated the Marka in the course of setting up his kingdom. Shortly after he died his brother, Bakari, who had been fully converted to Islam by the *shaykhs* of the Kunta, reigned briefly during 1170–1/1757. He attempted unwisely, to impose full-scale, puritanical Islam upon his Bambara subjects 'and this policy was angrily rejected by the Bambara clan leaders. Bakari was murdered after he had ruled for only fifteen days and there then followed a period of instability under quarrelling Bambara factions. In the second half of the 18 century AD (AH 1163–1214) the Diara family took power and restored stability. Segu became the centre of a state that controlled a large area to the west of it, including the province of Kaarta, that lay between the river Senegal and the upper Niger.

The Bambaras have often been described in works on West African history as 'pagan'. The word is rather unsatisfactory because it tends to be associated with the early history of Christianity in the Roman empire, not with Islam. It was also widely used by early Christian missionaries in Africa, to contrast what they considered to be 'good' Africans, converts to Christianity, with those 'bad' Africans, who preferred to remain loyal to their traditional religions and of whom the missionaries deeply disapproved. In the case of the Bambaras, its use is especially misleading. The Bambaras, while remaining faithful to their ancestral polytheism, have none the less had a long association with Muslim Markas living among them. Religious and social tensions did occur from time to time between the two groups, but they normally lived peacefully side by side. The result was that the Bambaras came to occupy an intermediate position between Islam and traditional polytheism. In fact, Islam existed in Bambara society at three levels: first, there were the Kunta, Ineslemen and Zwāya who moved to and fro across Bambara country and mixed with the Bambaras; they represented strict Sunnī Islam. Second, attached to these literate Muslims, especially to the Kunta, were certain Marka and Mande-speaking families, who had been converted by them or who studied under them. Third, these Mande-speaking Muslims passed Islam on to the Bambara peasants among whom they lived; but what they passed on was far from pure or complete. To a large extent the Marka Muslims were makers of charms and practitioners of Islamic divination and other forms of the Islamic supernatural. It was, above all, this aspect of Islam – its popular supernatural aspect – that the Bambaras adopted. Thus Islam became for them just an alternative source of magic; it was used alongside their own system, which they still retained. Indeed, many Bambara magicians practised both traditional magic and Islamic divination. However beyond this, the Bambaras did not convert to Islam in any great numbers. They treated Islamic festivals, which were introduced among them by the Markas, much as the Gonjas and the Dagombas did; they combined the Islamic festival with the traditional one. For example, among the Bambaras, the Islamic festivals of ᶜĪd al-fiṭr and ᶜĪd al-aḍḥā were combined with ceremonies renewing the oath to the ancestral god Nyana. As Professor John Willis aptly puts it, 'Allah simply took His place among other supernatural beings in the Bambara pantheon [a head god and lesser gods].[1]

When Mamari Kouloubali set up his centralised state in Segu, certain of his opponents among the Massassi clan were driven out. *C.* 1167/1754 they moved into the province of Kaarta and by the end of the century they had established their own area of control there, which was now populated by the Massassis, Marka Muslims and other Mande-speakers. By the beginning of the 13/19 century Kaarta and Segu shared power in the upper and middle Niger region with the Kunta, the Touregs and the declining Arma of Timbuktu.

Kankan

In the hilly country where the Niger rises lay Kankan. The area was first settled towards the end of the 17 century AD, the turn of the 11 and 12 century AH, by the Kunta and their Mande-speaking associates. In the first instance it was to take advantage of the kola trade from the south, for which Kankan became an important market. Many of the Mande-speakers were Muslim Markas, emigrating out of Segu into the more agreeable Islamic environment of a Kunta sphere of influence. Kankan became a centre for the spread of the Qādiriyya, to the north-west into the Senegambia and east into the Volta region. During the time of Sīdī al-Mukhtār al-Kuntī this Islamic missionary activity became yet more intense and Kankan became a major centre for Islamic, especially Sufi, learning that influenced the whole of the western Sudan.

The Fulani of Masina

Fulani migrating eastwards out of Mauritania during the 8/14 and 9/15 centuries, reached Masina, on the east bank of the upper Niger, north-east of Segu, by the 10/16 century. In this area they settled, under their clan leaders, the *ardo'en*. They formed a society of rigid social classes – serfs, traders and aristocrats. Their economy was based partly on cattle-rearing, partly on agriculture. Originally, they followed their ancestral religion but became influenced by Islam through contact with Mali, and with Muslim Markas and Touregs who also settled alongside them in and around Masina. Sonni ᶜAlī of Songhay was their bitter enemy and attacked them constantly. In the time of

Map 8 The aftermath of the fall of Songhay (12/18 century).

the *askiyas* they became largely independent under their own *ardo'en* but were frequently harrassed by the Songhay armies. When attacked, they simply withdrew into the Sahel, thus the *askiyas* could never win a decisive victory over them. From the Sahel the Fulani constantly preyed on the Songhay caravan routes.

As the influence of the Kunta increased in the Niger country, the Fulani of Masina became increasingly affected by Islam and conversion became frequent among them. However while some individuals became full, Sunnī Muslims, others, including most of the *ardo'en*, remained partial Muslims who continued to devote much of their attention to the rituals of the old, pre-Islamic cult. The Fulani who migrated out of Masina into the Senegambia during the 11/17 century probably did so as a result of Toureg pressure upon them after the fall of Songhay. In the Senegambia they helped to set off the Islamic revolutions described in chapter 8, although it seems that this was for political reasons as well as, in some cases, out of genuine religious conviction. Despite the departure of many Fulani, Masina remained an important Fulani centre. Its people were among those who struggled for power in the Niger region after the fall of the Songhay empire and who made the caravan routes so insecure when the Arma became too weak to protect them.

It was from among the Masina Fulani that one of the great jihadists of the 13/19 century, Aḥmad b. Muḥammad, was destined to arise.

Economic aspects of the fall of Songhay

The Moroccan conquest of Songhay took place at the end of a century of great commercial expansion and consequent prosperity in the western Sudan – even greater, probably, than that which characterised the 8/14 century.

At one time it was though that the destruction of Songhay brought about the abrupt, catastrophic collapse of the Sudanic economy and of that prosperity. It is now clear that this was not so. Songhay's decline did undoubtedly help to speed up the shift in the trans-Saharan trade, from west to east. This however, had for other reasons such as the imperial growth of Borno and the increasing vigour and organisation of the Hausa kingdoms, already been slowly taking place for some time. As was explained in chapter 5, the Moroccan conquest thus led to the accelerated development of the Hausa *fatauci*, the middle-and-long-distance trading system that operated mainly south of the Sahara. The increased use of the direct east/west route from Borno and Hausaland to the Volta, and the rise of small Islamic kingdoms at the western end of that route which reached a peak in the second half of the 12/18 century, is a case in point. What really happened was that one man's misfortune turned out to be another man's opportunity – a frequent occurrence in human history and by no means always a disaster. What the Songhays lost, the Hausas and Bornoese gained and Sudanic trade sustained no setback, only a partial change of management.

At the North African end, certain trading houses may have suffered a temporary inconvenience but they quickly adapted to the new circumstances. They busily set up their agencies in Kano and Borno as those in Timbuktu ceased to be useful. For those beyond the immediate circle of Timbuktu, the conquest was probably of very little consequence, except that it created openings for commercial initiatives that had not existed before. There were plenty of people who were both eager and able to seize them.

Some have argued that the Songhay collapse speeded up the European domination of the West African economy. Certainly, the Europeans did come to dominate that economy but that the Moroccan conquest of Songhay had much to do with it is very doubtful.

European trade with North Africa was already expanding before Mawlay Aḥmad al-Manṣūr ordered his troops to march against Songhay, indeed, he did all he could to encourage it. In turn, this created a demand for European goods in the west and central Sudan, which were paid for by Sudanic products – the gold, ivory and 'grains of Paradise' that the Ragusans were so eager to obtain. Such an exchange was helpful to the trans-Saharan trade when the *askiyas* were at the height of their powers. When Songhay fell the demand for European goods helped to keep the trade going; the Hausas still wanted European cloth and if they could not obtain it through Timbuktu, they soon found a way to bring it direct through Kano. North Africans could still make good profits out of the spices, ivory, hides and other goods from the west and central Sudan, which the Europeans on their shores eagerly demanded. If they could not bring them out of the Sudan via Timbuktu, they quickly made arrangements to do so by other routes. It is true that the Guinea Coast was linked to the Niger Bend, and thus to the interior of the west and central Sudan, by a trade route since *c.* 802/1400. However trade from the Coast did not begin to compete seriously with the Saharan trade until after 1111/1700 and even then, its effect on that trade was marginal. By that time the European demand for goods from the Sudan was so great that there was ample trade for all the routes to carry. The fact is, the Guinea route supplemented the Saharan routes more than it competed with them; it was never a real threat to them. During the second half of the 10/16 century Anania had described Kano as a place 'where there is nothing in the world one cannot find there' and he added 'That city is the most civilized of these [Sudanic] countries and there one lives in great style.'[2] In 1267/1851, when the traveller Heinrich Barth visited Kano, he described Kano market as a bustling centre packed with both European and Middle Eastern goods. It was by the Saharan routes that these goods were still coming in at that time; there is no doubt that trade along these routes was thriving then no less than it was in the days when Giovanni Lorenzo Anania compiled his *La universale fabrica del mondo*. It was the European railways, not the Pasha Jawdhar and his musketeers, that slammed the door on the ancient routes of the Sahara, switched trade down to the coast and thus made the white man the economic master of West Africa.

Where is the link between all this and Islam? In so far as the Moroccan conquest of Songhay broke up the Songhay trade monopoly and caused the trade to flow along several new routes, it probably helped Islam by spreading it more widely than before. Certainly, in so far as it stimulated the *fatauci* of the Hausas, it had this effect. It has already been explained how it was Hausas and Bornoese who carried their own, more strictly Sunnī Islam to the Volta, to the Yorubas, down to the Benue and so on. The Wangarawa, who had moved out of Mali into Songhay, had begun to move from there into Borgu long before the Moroccan conquest of Songhay took place, but that event considerably increased their number in Borgu. Not only their trade but also their Islam moved with them; indeed, this may have been the point when many of those

Malian family names that had long since ceased to have any connection with Mali other than an ancient memory, became scattered among the Yorubas and other late converts to Islam who became hosts to Wangarawa. In these respects, the Moroccan conquest of Songhay can be likened to a stone dropped into a pool of water. The splash spread trade and ideas to areas they might otherwise have reached only slowly, after several more generations had passed.

Political aspects

The failure of the Arma to provide a strong, permanent authority brought about the 'Balkanisation' of the western Sudan. This word, familiar from European history, refers to the process in the 19 century AD by which a number of small Slav nationalist movements broke up the European frontier region of the failing Ottoman empire and turned it into a collection of small, independent states. A similar process took place in the case of Songhay. As the Armas' administration fell apart, the Bambaras of Segu, the Massassis of Kaarta and the Fulani of Masina seized the vacant seats of power. The Kunta and the Touregs, though less inclined to set up states, created their own spheres of influence, in Kankan, Mabrūk and Timbuktu itself. So the fall of Songhay broke the political pattern of great centralised Islamic empires that had been such a feature of the Sahara and the Sahel during the Middle Ages. It was not until the *jihāds* of the 13/19 century had done their work that new centralised empires once again emerged.

At a political level as well as at an economic level, one must be careful not to attribute too much to the single, dramatic event of Songhay's fall; other factors, too, were at work. The pattern might have changed anyway, even if the Pasha Jawdhar and his troops had never left their barracks in Marrākush. A new sense of Islamic unity was growing among the Touregs and perhaps their challenge to the central power of Songhay was inevitable; the weakness of the Arma merely brought it to a head sooner rather than later. The Hausas, too, had been growing in prosperity since at least the 8/14 century. Powerful Haɓe states like Katsina and Kano were rivals to the power of Songhay before the Moroccan musketeers finally turned the balance in their favour. Above all, new ideas were flooding into the west and central Sudan: Sufism, that threw doubt on the value of worldly empires at all; the vision of a Mahdī, who would come to overthrow the oppression of worldly kings, usher in the perfect society and guide it to the End of Time. Moreover, the ancient nomadism of the Sahara and the Sahel was being questioned more and more as a fitting way of life for Muslims. There was among many a longing for the town-dwelling life-style of Islam with its material prosperity and its intellectual satisfactions. With that went the desire to create independent states in which the new life could be realised. The world of the Islamic Sudan was restless *c.* 1009/1600 and apart from the fall of an empire that was already politically weak, there were many other signs that change was on the way. It would be rash to attribute the pattern of the future too exclusively to the failure of the Arma, for they were not the creators of the coming age, they were the victims of the past.

Intellectual aspects

Men of those times, and many after them, have bewailed the fall of Timbuktu as a great intellectual loss. How far was this really so? Certainly, the initial severity of the Moroccans towards the *ᶜulamāʾ* did disorganise the system of higher education. Bandits on the trade routes discouraged scholars and students from venturing along them. Moreover, the Arma do not seem to have been as eager to patronise scholars as many of the *askiyas* were. Thus there was no longer the same incentive for them to settle in Timbuktu. Another factor leading to the intellectual decline of Timbuktu may have been the influx of Moroccan *shurafāʾ*. It seems they eventually replaced the serious, scholarly Islam of the *ᶜulamāʾ* with a more popular version, based on miracles and charms, not learning.

The Moroccans did not make any marked intellectual contribution to Islam in the Sudan. We know of no scholar from among the Arma who pushed the frontiers of Islamic thought even a step further forward. What they did do, however, was to increase the strength of Ottoman cultural influence. The Sharifian Saᶜdids were an independent North African dynasty, they were not subjects of the Ottoman empire. However, Ottoman cultural influence was strong throughout North Africa and the Sharifians had Ottoman administrations for their neighbours in Algeria and Tunisia. The Moroccan Makhzan was copied from an Ottoman model, even to some of the titles of the officials who served in it. Likewise, the Moroccan army, which was the basis of the Makhzan, was organised and equipped along Ottoman lines. There is no doubt that the establishment of this Ottoman institution of the Makhzan in Timbuktu led to the spread of Ottoman forms of Islamic culture in the western Sudan as did the Ottoman way of life of those who served it.

To some extent the seizure of power by faintly Muslim chiefs, as for instance Mamari Kouloubali in Segu, was a setback for Islam. The orthodox, bookish Islam of the Timbuktu *ʿulamāʾ* gave way, in some measure, to the popular Islam mixed with polytheism and with the fortune-telling and charms of the self-styled *shurafāʾ* and *marabouts*. Although this may have made Islam less scholarly, it did nothing to stop it spreading; on the contrary, it probably helped to spread it more widely.

Certainly, the collapse of an ancient intellectual centre was sad, but it did not bring Islamic learning to an end. Other centres of learning soon rose to take the place of Timbuktu – Kankan and Mabrūk in the Niger area, Kong in the Volta region, Agades south of Ahir and Katsina in Hausaland. Thus learning was not destroyed; it was merely dispersed. The fact is, there were advantages and disadvantages for Islam in the fall of Songhay. On the whole, however, this event probably speeded up the spread of Islam in the west and central Sudan by creating new and vigorous centres of Islamic culture and learning.

In conclusion, perhaps the severity of the intellectual blow to Timbuktu, like that of the commercial blow, has been seriously overestimated. As Norris shows, Timbuktu, together with its neighbour, Wādān, was still a highly active and respected centre of learning in the 13/18 century.[3]

NOTES

1 *HWA*, I, p.545.
2 Lange, 'Anania', p.339 and p.341.
3 *BSOAS*, XXX, 3, 1967.

CHAPTER TEN

Jihāds in the pre-colonial period

During the 13/19 century the west and central Sudan was the scene of a number of major Islamic holy wars which were similar in certain religious and political characteristics but different in other respects. One important difference is that some occurred before the colonial era or in its very early days and these are described in this chapter. Others took place after the colonial occupations were well under way and they will be discussed later on. First however, it is necessary to look at the situation in the Islamic world as a whole at this time for it has a bearing on what happened in the Sudan.

The global background

Until *c.* 1008/1600, the Islamic world had good reason to feel secure. The Islamic heartlands of the Middle East were in the hands of powerful Muslim dynasties; whatever their shortcomings and internal quarrels, there was no reason to suppose they would ever give way to the government of infidels. Moreover, Muslim dynasties ruled much of India and the Ottoman Turks were masters of a vast, centralised and very wealthy empire that included Egypt, much of North Africa and part of the Balkans. It is true that by the end of the 9/15 century the Muslims had lost Spain and the vengeful Portuguese and Spanish Christians, eager for booty, were raiding the rich North African sultanates and provinces. In 979/1571, the Turkish fleet suffered a defeat at the hands of the Christians at the battle of Lepanto but the importance of this has often been exaggerated. It was largely offset when, in 986/1578, the great Mawlay Aḥmad al-Manṣūr was credited with his brother's victory over the Portuguese at al-Qaṣr al-Kabīr. Indeed, some now whispered that Mawlay Aḥmad was not only the 'Victor by the help of God' but even, perhaps, the Expected Mahdī himself. Thus Muslims still had no reason to fear that Islam was in mortal danger from these Christians who snapped at its heels but seemed to lack the power to threaten its vital organs. However, from *c.* 1008/1660 on, for reasons that cannot be explained in this book, the power of both the Moroccan Sharifian Saᶜdids and the Ottoman Turks began to ebb while that of the Christian powers of Europe flowed ever more strongly. For the next 200 years this pattern continued and in 1213/1798 the French, under Bonaparte, invaded Egypt and briefly occupied the country. They were only driven out with the help of the British, who promptly replaced them as masters there. In India, the British won the battle of Plassey in 1170/1757 and in 1213/1799 they defeated Sultan Tipu of Mysore; by the end of the 18 century AD they ruled most of Muslim India. Under the protection of the colonial powers Christian missionaries became increasingly daring in their attacks on the Faith, although they had little to show, except in India, for their wordy battles with the ᶜ*ulamā*'.

These misfortunes began to produce a reaction among Muslims. Some accepted them quietly, as the judgement of God while others were provoked to find ways of remedying the evils that beset them. One consequence was the rise of the Wahhābīs. These reformers were Muslim puritans and radicals who sought to return to the simple Islam of the Prophet and his Companions and were especially hostile to the Sufis. They argued that Sufi mysticism, the cult of the *awliyā'*, praying at the tombs of the *awliyā'* and so on, were not sanctioned by the Koran or in the Sunna, the 'Tradition' of the Prophet Muḥammad. Wahhābī ideas were to be found all over the Islamic world and they aroused a sense of urgency and zeal for reform even in those who opposed Wahhābī doctrines. This showed itself in a number of ways.

One of these was a Sufi revival in the Azhar, in Egypt. Hurt by the Wahhābīs' attack, the Egyptian Sufis rallied to the defence of their beliefs and way of life. The Khalwatiyya *ṭarīqa* was at the centre of the movement and the ancient Q̱ādiriyya was given new life by it. In the end, it helped to create a new and powerful *ṭarīqa*, the Tijāniyya. This Sufi revival made itself felt all over the Islamic world, but most especially in the west and central Sudan.

The Muslim reaction to the world situation did not stop with the Sufi revival, however. Many Muslims saw the Christian conquests and occupations as 'Signs of the Hour', signs that the world of time was about to end and that the Day of Judgement was at hand. They knew, too, that before that event took place, God would send His Deliverer, the Mahdī, to preside over the last days. The Mahdī would drive out injustice and misbelief; he would bring true Islam and perfect justice; but before him, once in every century, God would send a *mujaddid*, a 'Renewer', to prepare the way for the Mahdī. The fourth of November AD 1785 marked the beginning of AH 1200, which was also the beginning of a new Islamic century; and so there was every reason to believe a *mujaddid* was near and that the Mahdī himself might not be far away. In the west and central Sudan his arrival was awaited with anxious expectancy and it is against this background that the events there of the 13/19 century should be seen.

The influence of earlier reform movements in West Africa

The history of the Almoravids was discussed above. Did the example of this 5/11 -century *jihād* inspire the 13/19-century jihadists of Hausaland and the Niger Bend? Perhaps, but there is little evidence that this was so. The Sanhaja had long ago put away their swords and taken to preaching – although certainly some of them still preached *jihād*. However, they are certainly not among the heroes whom the 13/19 century reformers looked to in their own writings.

What of the example of the Islamic movements in Senegambia – the War of the Shurbubba and the *jihāds* of Alfa Ba and ᶜAbd al-Q̱ādir? Certainly the later jihadists knew about them but they seldom mention the Senegambian leaders in their writings; and there is no reason to think they looked to them as outstanding examples to be followed. Moreover, the Senegambia was far away from Hausaland and the wars there took place under very different social and political circumstances from those that existed in Hausaland and its neighbours. It would be rash to assume a connection – although some have.

The example of the saintly but prosperous Kuntī *shaykhs* – Sīdī Aḥmad al-Bakkā'ī of pious memory, the miracle-working *shaykhs* of Mabrūk and the divinely favoured Sīdī al-Mukhtār al-Kabīr – no doubt quickened the zeal of many ᶜ*ulamā'* in Hausaland and the Niger Bend for the Qādiriyya. However the Kunta were mystics and traders, not jihadists.

A source of more militant inspiration may have been the Ineslemen Touregs. They led an Islamic revival in the Arawān during the first half of the 11/17 century. In Agades, the Ineslmen leader Ḥadāḥadā led a *jihād* later in the same century. Agades was in close touch with Hausaland and Ḥadāḥadā's movement, together with the example of other militant Touregs like him, may have helped to strengthen the enthusiasm for reform there.

There is room for wide differences of opinion as to which of the events and examples mentioned above had the greatest influence on the thinking and attitudes of the 13/19-century reformers. No doubt they all had some influence, great or small. In my view the truth is to be sought not only in what happened within the west and central Sudan; it has also to do with those powerful, revolutionary ideas – especially Mahdism and Sufism – to which Sūdānī Muslims had by now been exposed for several centuries as a result of their contacts with the Mediterranean world of western Islam. The reasons for this view will become apparent from what is written below. What may be said at this point, however, is that certain scholars have been reluctant to concede the importance of influences from outside the west and central Sudan on what happened within it; and have sought to explain all, or almost all, in terms of local developments in Sūdānī societies. While not wishing to dispute the importance of certain local factors as contributory forces in bringing about Islamic reform and revolution, such an exclusively 'internal' interpretation of the Islamic history of the west and central Sudan seems to me to be unduly narrow and limited.

The Muslim Fulani in Gobir

By 1168/1754–5, the year in which Shaykh ᶜUthmān b. Muḥammad b. ᶜUthmān b. Ṣāliḥ, known among the Hausas as Shehu Usumanu ɗan Fodio, was born, the Muslim Fulani family of the Fodiawa had established themselves in the Haɓe kingdom of Gobir. They were a family of scholars, dedicated to the teaching of Sunnī, Mālikī Islam, and to the pursuit of Islamic studies.

From *c.* 1188/1774 until 1219/1804, Shehu Usumanu, his younger brother ᶜAbd Allāh b. Muḥammad, and a group of his kinsmen from the Toronkawa, conducted a Muslim revivalist campaign in Gobir, Zamfara, Katsina and Kebbi.

C. 1178/1764 Birnin Zamfara, the capital city of the kingdom of Zamfara, had been sacked by the Gobirawa who continued to harass and plunder Zamfara for the rest of the 12/18 century. During the first half of that century, and indeed during the preceding century, Zamfara had been an important trading centre. The depressed conditions brought about by the fall of Birnin Zamfara and the harassment by the Gobirawa must surely have provided the Shehu with fruitful ground for his preaching, especially when it was directed against what he considered to be the godless ways of the Gobir nobility. Kebbi and Katsina had also suffered from the aggression of the Gobirawa; and their people were, no doubt, similarly inclined to listen to the Shehu's preaching. Such campaigns, *jihād al-qawl*, 'Preaching *Jihād*', became the standard practice for later reformers before they embarked on *jihād al-sayf*, 'Jihad of the Sword';

and they were often carried on against a similar background of political, economic and social discontent. The purpose of the Muslim Fulanis' preaching was simply to combat mixed Islam and create an Islamic society nearer in all its aspects to the Sunnī Islamic ideal. However, it is important to realise that this was as much a political endeavour as a moral and religious one. The discontent of the reformers arose not only from the fact that so-called Muslims married more than four wives, or failed to pray correctly, or did not inherit according to the Shariᶜa; it also arose from the fact that the society in which they lived was governed in a manner and through institutions that were not those of Islam. As in the case of the Senegambian reformers, the reformers of Hausaland probably felt in their hearts that they, and not the established rulers, were intended by God to govern. This feeling was probably strengthened by the increasing respect with which the common people treated them during the course of the 12–13/18 century, for it is clear that by this time Islam had begun to take a firm hold on commoners in many different walks of life. Moreover, because the reformers demanded the full observance of Islam from those who called themselves Muslims, the reform movement in Hausaland, like that in Senegambia, was essentially a confrontation between Muslims at different levels of seriousness. It was not one between Believers and infidels, even though the reformers sometimes pretended that it was.

In the course of his preaching the Shehu became increasingly involved in the politics of the Gobir court, as part of his attempt to reform the old chief of Gobir, Bawa Jan Gwarzo, and his obstinate successors. It is unlikely that, initially, the Shehu intended to fight a *jihād*, but the continued failure of the chiefs of Gobir to bend to his wishes convinced him in the end that peaceful persuasion was useless. In or around 1212/1797 he issued a call to his followers to make ready for battle, but it was more by accident than intent that, seven years later in 1219/1804, a series of incidents brought about the first armed encounter in what became a war between the Muslim Fulani and the Haɓe kings. For the Muslims this war was a *jihād*.

What factors contributed to this outcome? One was certainly the Muslim Fulanis' long tradition of Islamic literacy. This created in them a sentiment of Islamic universalism, a feeling that the whole Islamic world was one, and any divergence from the central pattern laid down in the Sunna, the 'Tradition' of the Prophet, was intolerable. Another factor that contributed to this sense of Islamic universalism was Pilgrimage. It was on Pilgrimage that the Muslim saw Islam at its most impressive and felt most strongly his identification with the world-wide Muslim community. Although many of his kinsmen had performed the Pilgrimage, the Shehu Usumanu had not. Once, he had tried but family reasons had prevented him from performing it; he turned instead to classical Arabic literacy sources and to the accounts of those who had performed it, to learn what this great experience was like. From these he gained a vivid and passionate vision that filled his heart and mind in all his waking moments:

> O my friend, I pray that my loneliness may be relieved,
> Within my heart the Prophet springs forth,
> I am longing to see him, the Best of the Prophets,
> Muḥammad, Aḥmad, for he excels all,
>   In my heart I sing his praises.

. . .
Every time that I go out, it is as if I follow
The direction of my eyes, for they desire to be near him,
That they may come to see our Master, the Prophet,
When I go out, in whatever direction, I turn my gaze towards him
  And it is as if I see him, and hear his voice.
. . .
The hearing of my ears, the seeing of my eyes,
And the longing of my heart, let them all increase,
[For] my body has failed me in going there
[on Pilgrimage] that we might be together,
[But] in my heart it is as if I have visited him,
  And Mecca and Medina and the Garden [in which stands his tomb].[1]

For him Pilgrimage was the symbol of the beauty and nobility of true Islam. Mixed Islam was, he felt, an offence against this.

However there was more to his concern than this. The literacy of these Muslim Fulani, and their links with Egypt and Mecca, put them in touch with the new movements of thought that were sweeping the Islamic world of their day. Of course, they were not immediately threatened by the European expansion that influenced the thinking of their co-religionists in India and the Middle East: that did not reach the Sudan until almost a hundred years later. However they were certainly aware of the exciting ideas that were in the air; and somewhat carried away by them. They were also well informed about the European intrusions into *Dār al-islām*, the 'Abode [Territory] of Islam', especially Muslim India.

The Muslim Fulanis' association with the Toureg Ineslemen, especially those of Agades also inclined them strongly towards reform. The historical tradition of reform among these Touregs has already been commented upon. What made it especially powerful as an influence on the Muslim Fulani was the fact that they were closely related to the Touregs, through marriage, and had many interests in common with them. Often they lived in settlements together with the Ineslemen and some of the Fulani spoke the Toureg language. Indeed, they seem to have regarded it with some veneration, as a language of religion. They also took Ineslemen *shaykhs* as teachers and frequently went on minor pilgrimage to the tombs of *awliyā'* buried in and around Agades – almost certainly to that of the great miracle-worker Sīdī Maḥmūd al-Baghdādī.

Shehu Usumanu ɗan Fodio believed that the founder of the Q̄ādiriyya, Shaykh ᶜAbd al-Q̄ādir al-Jaylānī, appeared to him in visions. In one of these visions the Shaykh appointed him as his representative in the Sudan and handed him the 'Sword of Truth', to use against the enemies of God. He appeared to him again on subsequent occasions, to advise him in certain crises that occurred in his relations with the chiefs of Gobir. Such experiences make it clear that it was his mystical link with the founder of the Q̄ādiriyya that helped to turn the Shehu into a reformer and a jihadist.

Like the Ineslemen Touregs, the Muslim Fulani were committed to the idea of the Expected Mahdī and the *mujaddid*, who was to prepare the way for him in every century. Many of his followers insisted that the Shehu Usumanu was himself the Mahdī, but he denied this. However he did claim to be the 'Mujaddid of the Age', and he hinted strongly that he was the last of the *mujaddidūn* and after him the Mahdī himself would at last appear. Certainly, he and his associates firmly believed that the coming of the Mahdī was imminent. The conviction that they had a duty to prepare for this divine event was one of the reasons that caused them to launch their reform movement.

The Fulani reformers were familiar with the teachings of both al-Maghīlī and al-Suyūṭī. Shehu Usumanu quoted from both of them in his own writings and he used al Maghīlī's condemnation of Sonni ᶜAlī's un-Islamic ways to justify his own attacks on the Haɓe. He used al-Suyūṭī's prophecies about the coming of the Mahdī to support his own arguments that this event was near at hand. It cannot be said that either one of these notable scholars influenced the Muslim Fulani more than the other: both were of equal importance.

The Preaching *Jihād*

The Muslim reformers began by challenging the way of life in the Gobir court, and indeed the whole nature of Gobir society. At the beginning of a long, hard-hitting attack on the loose ways of Sarkin Gobir Bawa Jan Gwarzo and his courtiers, ᶜAbd Allāh, b. Muḥammad gives them this blunt warning:

> The Sunna is not something to joke with. Listen,
> Hold to religion with truth,
> Abandon play and laughter,
> Whenever you hear the preaching of the righteous
> and ignore it,
> You cast yourself into Hell Fire![2]

Whereas this warning was addressed to the aristocracy of the Gobir court, the Shehu's preaching in the countryside of Gobir, Zamfara and Kebbi seems to have been directed at Hausa and Fulani commoners. As was suggested above, many members of his congregations were already socially and politically disturbed and this may have had something to do with their enthusiastic response to his message.

He began by calling them to repentance,

> Listen to this song and be afraid,
> Leave off following the many un-Islamic customs,
>
> Let us repent and contain our hearts' desires,
> Let us obey religion and stop putting off our repentance.[3]

Then he reminded them of death, always just around the corner,

> Death does not spare anyone here below,
> It will not fail to come to everyone,
>
> Do not forget, for you know
> That when it comes, one has to go
> . . .
> Whoever delays until he dies,
> Without repenting, know that he has gone to damnation![4]

He frightened them with vivid and horrifying accounts that conjured up the torments of Hell Fire before their very eyes:

> [The sinner] will be taken there to Hell Fire, to burn,
> Behold! There is hunger and no water, for sure,
> Only boiling water will they constantly drink, and they will eat from [the bitter fruit of]
> The Tree of Thorns, they will be screaming out in pain.[5]

Then he soothed them with the promise of Paradise for those who followed the Prophet's Way:

> It is the Way of Muḥammad,
> And his Companions, it is the Way that leads to
> Paradise, the place of rivers of honey
> And of fresh milk, to say nothing of pure water,
> . . .
> They are the dwellings of Muḥammad
> And of his people, for ever, Amen.[6]

Such warnings and appeals moved their hearts and won their minds. Perhaps, above all, it was his constant assurance that the Mahdī was coming and his pointing out the Signs of the approaching End of Time that finally persuaded them,

> Hear, the time when the Mahdī will appear,
> Know that the conditions [of his coming] will be made manifest,
> First of all will be greed among the ᶜ*ulamā*'
> And love of this world, they will not seek after God's mercy,
> Second, legal decisions not based on the Koran,
> Know that in the future there will be no obedience to Islam,
> Third, government will be in the hands of youths,
> Fourth, men will beg from the rich in vain,
> Fifth, it will be the evil ones
> Who will acquire honour and who will increase in boastfulness,
> Sixth, the commoner will become infuriated
> If he lacks what he desires, he will not exercise patience,
> Seventh, neighbourliness will be spoiled,
> Pity will be removed, ill-will will replace it,
> Eighth, the truth will be driven out,
> Lies and hatred will be put in its place,
> Ninth, there will be too much gossip,
> You will abuse your brother without cause,
> Finally, the tenth is that modesty will be removed,
> Men and women will no longer feel shame.
> . . .
> In this situation God will open the way,
> The Mahdī will appear and people will pay allegiance to him.[7]

It was easy for the oppressed, dissatisfied nomads and peasants to whom he was preaching to recognise these signs in the social and political evils of the society in which they themselves lived. It was easy, also, for them to resolve to join the Shehu in preparing for the Mahdī's coming.

As for members of the Haɓe establishment in Gobir, the only effect of such warnings was to convince them that the reform movement was a threat to their own position – and in this they were not wrong. The survival of an ancient dynasty, identified over many generations with the ancestral religion and steeped in the compromises of mixed Islam, was indeed incompatible with the new tide of Islamic universalism and with the fierce determination of Muslim literates to tolerate no further obstacles on their path to full political power.

The Shehu Usumanu was not without influence in the court of Gobir. He had even succeeded in getting Yunfa, the grandson of Bawa Jan Gwarzo, appointed as chief of Gobir. Yunfa was his pupil and he clearly hoped to be able to influence him from behind the throne. However, Yunfa turned on him and deliberately demonstrated his independence in ways that provoked the Muslim reformers; frustration and anger grew on both sides.

In this tense situation events took over. In the month of Dhu'l-Qaᶜda, 1218/February, 1804, a series of confrontations occurred that caused the Shehu and his followers to migrate to Gudu, on the distant border of Gobir and out of reach of the Chief's jurisdiction. This they regarded as their *hijra*, 'Flight', out of *Dār al-kufr*, the 'Territory of Infidelity', into *Dār al-islām*. The parallel with the classical Hijra of the Prophet Muḥammad from Mecca to Medina in 1/622 is obvious. It served to legitimate and sanctify the *jihād* that now followed.

Yunfa, for his part, interpreted the incident as an act of rebellion and he sent a force to punish the rebels who had by now elected the Shehu as their *imām* and leader. The force attacked the Muslims and the Muslims retaliated; the *jihād* in Hausaland had begun.

Jihād of the Sword in Hausaland: 1219/1804 to *c.* 1227/1812

The first stage of the military *jihād* against the state of Gobir was fought in an area bounded in the west and north by the river Rima, in the south by the river Zamfara and in the east by the river Bunsuru. The country was flat scrub savanna, broken by high rocky outcrops. It was excellent country for cavalry, but the only way to make sure of final victory was to capture the walled towns. These could then be used as bases from which to launch expeditions and control the surrounding countryside.

The state of Gobir was a powerful opponent for during the second half of the 12/18 century it had overwhelmed Zamfara and part of Katsina in a series of wars of conquest. However, it seems the Shehu's brother, ᶜAbd Allāh b. Muḥammad, his second son, Muhammadu Bello and Aliyu Jedo, a Fulani clan leader, all of whom commanded Muslim armies at one time or another, understood the art of war better than their Haɓe opponents. This was partly due to their familiarity with classical Arabic military manuals and also, no doubt, to experience of desert raiding with their Toureg associates.

The armies of the Muslim Fulani consisted of their nomadic Fulani kinsmen, those whose discontent against the Haɓe chiefs was described in chapter 4. They were mainly archers, but there were also substantial contingents of Hausa peasants who were foot soldiers armed with swords, clubs and axes. The Hausa presence in the army suggests that the Shehu's preaching must have been well received among them. The cavalry consisted largely of Fulani ᶜ*ulamā*', who formed a mounted elite and who, despite their scholarly calling, were tough, skilled fighters. In addition, there were contingents of Touregs, allied to the Muslim Fulani, who then turned out to be unreliable allies, interested mainly in booty and liable to desert at the end of a successful battle.

As for tactics – the way in which individual commanders handle their units on the battlefield – it has been argued that the Muslim Fulani fought their battles according to the classical order of battle set out in the Arabic military manuals. In this the main mass of infantry advances, screened on each flank by cavalry detachments; and this was indeed the case in certain large, set-piece battles. However, such a picture of parade-ground precision on every occasion fails to do justice to the adaptability of the Muslim Fulani leaders. They proved themselves, over and over again, to be flexible commanders who were masters of tactical improvisation. When the opportunity arose, they disregarded the set-piece pattern and made use of the stealthy dawn attack across an obstacle that the enemy, unwisely, assumed to be unsurmountable. Also, they made use of the ambush; or they used natural features to help them, perhaps a thicket of thorns to trap an unwary enemy pushed back by a frontal attack. Sometimes they combined the various arms of their army – archers, infantry and cavalry – in ways that were unorthodox but excellently adapted to the country and conditions in which they had to fight. They showed an informed cunning, a purposeful ruthlessness and a cool skill in destroying the enemy on every occasion that the terrain and the conjunction of time and circumstances offered; and they gloried in the enemy's unreadiness and in their triumph over him:

> And we came upon them on Thursday,
> At Qurdam before midday, in the high places;
> And they had spitted meats around the fire,
> And gathered ready in tents
> Fine vestments in a chest,
> And all kinds of carpets, with cushions.
> . . .
> They rose up, and made everything ready for war.
> Then they formed up in ranks, according to size.
> Our banner began to draw near to them,
> And it seemed to them like an ogre in striped clothing.
> We fired at them, and they fired naphtha.
> Their fire became like ashes and it was
> As if their arrows had no heads to them;
> And as if their swords were in the hands of inanimate things,
> As if their lances were in the hands of the blind.
> They turned in flight, without provision,
> And their army was scattered, and they were thirsty,
> Confused, like young locusts.
> We slew them, and collected all their wealth
> Which they had left strewn in the valley.[8]

That was a pitched battle, but there were many other actions to probe the enemy and to wear him down without risking everything in a major battle. It is therefore a mistake to imagine that the *jihād* was fought exclusively according to a single tactical pattern.

The strategy, that is the overall military, economic and political planning of the war, of the jihadists was to use the valley of the river Zamfara as their base line and then secure their flanks by capturing Birnin Kebbi in the west and the town of Kanoma in the east. They thus controlled the important grazing grounds of the Zamfara valley that they needed to maintain their cavalry throughout the long campaign. Then they sought to secure the walled towns of the Haɓe, in preference to fighting pitched battles in the open countryside, which were costly and seldom decisive. Finally, they used their links with Fulani communities in other Haɓe kingdoms to stimulate revolt against the Haɓe kings there, and thus deprive the Gobirawa of possible allies.

Despite their tactical skill and the basic soundness of their strategy – they won an important initial victory at Tabkin Kwotto in 1219/1804 – the Muslims suffered some sharp reverses. They were defeated at the battle of Tsuntsuwa also in 1219/1804; and in the initial stages of the battle of Alwasa in 1220/1805; but neither of these defeats proved wholly disastrous, although Tsuntsuwa was a severe blow. Many of the Muslim dead in that battle were *ᶜulamā*ʾ who, had they lived, might have been among the administrators of the Muslim Fulani caliphate. The loss of so many literates from the Muslim ranks is said to have changed, to some extent, the nature of the *jihād*, in that from then on the Shehu had to rely increasingly on the professional warrior element among his supporters, rather than on *ᶜulamā*ʾ. This, it is suggested, may have had something to do with the fact that, in the aftermath of the *jihād*, the Shehu's own high ideals were not always lived up to. By 1223/1808, the Shehu's forces had taken Alkalawa, the capital of Gobir, and the resistance of the Gobirawa was then at an end.

The victory in Gobir did not end the *jihād*, however, for the campaign there had set off Fulani campaigns in other Haɓe kingdoms, Kano, Zaria, Bauchi and elsewhere. Even the Fulani living in the ancient kingdom of Borno rose in revolt against the *mai*. These outlying campaigns, although inspired by the Shehu, were conducted by Fulani clan leaders in these kingdoms. The clan leaders were recognised by the Shehu as his 'flag-bearers'; and when they were successful, they became emirs of the territories they had conquered. These they held as largely independent principalities, but in allegiance, Arabic *bayᶜa*, to the Shehu.

By 1227/1812, a Muslim Fulani empire was in being. It consisted of a south-western half, ruled from Gwandu, by the Shehu's brother ᶜAbd Allāh b. Muḥammad; and a north-eastern half, ruled from Wurno and later Sokoto by the Shehu's second son, Muhammadu Bello. The Shehu himself held the title of Khalīfa, 'Caliph', and in theory presided over both halves of the empire. In fact, it was his two lietuenants who conducted day-to-day affairs, while he devoted most of his time to scholarship and writing.

By 1227/1812 the Fulani caliphate had established firm control over most of Hausaland south of Birni Konni. While it did not directly rule the kingdom of Ahir, to its north, it does appear that for a time at least, the sultan in Agades entered into an alliance with the caliphate; and he may have given some kind of allegiance to the caliph. However, it seems likely that this amounted to little more than an agreement between the two states to protect the trade routes upon which both depended.

The south-eastern border of the caliphate had reached, approximately, the Benue river by this date. The western edge of permanent control settled along the east bank of the Niger, although some shadowy authority may have extended to the west bank. The eastern border of the empire remained in dispute for many years and in 1227/1812 it still ebbed and flowed just east of the emirate of Gombe. The southern border remained open and the *jihād* there continued for many years to come.

Results of the *Jihād* in Hausaland

The *jihād* in Hausaland had a multitude of long-term results, some of which will become apparent as this book proceeds. It also had certain immediate consequences. One was that it changed Islam from a tolerated minority religion to which rulers subscribed when it suited them, into the official state ideology – that is the set of beliefs and attitudes according to which the rulers expected the people to conduct their lives. Another was that it opened the highest political offices in Hausaland to the *ᶜulamāʾ*, whereas previously these had been the preserve of ancient dynastic families. It therefore fulfilled a persistent demand that was heard as far back as the days of the Sanhaja *ᶜulamāʾ* in Timbuktu during the time of Sonni ᶜAlī, and which was repeated in the Senegambia. This was the demand of the literate, that they and not the illiterate, should be, by God's intention, the sole custodians of political power. Yet another consequence was that it replaced the decentralised collection of separate Haɓe kingdoms with a centralised structure of Islamic emirates united by common allegiance to the caliphal centre, in Sokoto. It thus created a large, new area of *Dār al-islām*, in a political as well as in a religious sense; it satisfied the powerful Muslim urge that this was how men ought, by divine command, to arrange their societies; but it also increased the problem of mixed Islam with which the central Muslim authorities now had to deal – for conquest may have replaced polytheist rulers and administrations with Muslim alternatives, but it did little to change the beliefs and way of life of the conquered people until several generations had passed.

Arising out of these political consequences, it has been suggested that the *jihād* also had certain immediate economic consequences in that it altered the pattern of trade within Hausaland. Certain traditional centres of trade, associated with the old Haɓe kingdoms, were destroyed or fell into disuse while new centres, corresponding to the new distribution of political power, were created. Likewise, trade routes changed direction in order to link up with the new towns and cities that quickly grew up in the empire of the successful jihadists.[9]

Another immediate result of the conquest was to prove that *jihād* on a major scale could be startlingly successful. It seemed to Muslim reformers elsewhere in the Sudan that a swift, determined appeal to the sword could achieve more than centuries of preaching; and they proved quick to learn from this lesson.

The *Jihād* in Masina

The first to apply the lesson of the Shehu Usumanu's success was a Fulani *ᶜālim* from Masina, Aḥmad b. Muḥammad b. Abī Bakr b. Saᶜīd, commonly known as Ahmadu Lobbo or Seku Ahmadu. He was one of a number of Muslim reformers who were active in the area of Masina *c.* 1214/1800, but it was he, among them all, who emerged as the victorious military leader.

Aḥmad b. Muḥammad was a disciple of the Shehu Usumanu ɗan Fodio and had studied under him. He was, of course, a strict Mālikī and also a member of the Qādiriyya order of Sufis. Some say he fought in the *jihād* in Hausaland but this is uncertain. After many years of preaching to his nomadic kinsmen, who seem to have accepted his message, and to the Fulani *ardo'en* of the Dikko clan who did not, he finally raised a *jihād* against those *ardo'en*, whom he accused of misbelief. This happened in 1225/1810, or perhaps in 1234/1818, accounts differ.

It is said that he sought and received a flag from the Shehu Usumanu. The Shehu died in 1232/1817, so perhaps 1225/1810 is the most likely date for the beginning of his *jihād*. On the other hand, of course, Aḥmad b. Muḥammad may not have begun to fight until some time after he received the flag and so 1234/1818 is still a possible date. To ask for, and receive, such a flag suggests that he regarded the Shehu as his spiritual master; and perhaps also his temporal overlord. It seems to have been in this last sense that the authorities in Sokoto interpreted it, for friction subsequently arose between Shaykh Aḥmad b. Muḥammad and the Sokoto caliphate over this matter of *bayᶜa*, allegiance, which the Sokoto authorities claimed he owed to them.

While it seems clear that Aḥmad b. Muḥammad's ideological debt to the Fulani reformers in Hausaland was considerable, some scholars have also emphasised the influence upon him of the Kunta of the Azawād.[10] For example, it is known that one of his closest counsellors was a certain Alfa Nūḥ b. Ṭāhir, who was a student of the Kunti *shaykh*, Sīdī Muḥammad b. Sīdī al-Mukhtār al-Kuntī. No doubt Shaykh Aḥmad b. Muḥammad drew inspiration and advice from both sources.

At the time the *jihād* in Masina broke out the Fulani there were tributaries of the Bambaras of Segu. It was not long before Aḥmad b. Muḥammad extended his *jihād* against the Bambaras too. He was soon successful in establishing his authority over them, whereupon he founded the city of Hamdullahi, as the centre of an empire that included the Masina Fulani, the Segu Bambaras and Kaarta. He even claimed authority over Timbuktu. How he administered his empire, and what his relations were with his neighbours, will be described in chapter 11.

It seems clear that the forces behind Shaykh Aḥmad b. Muḥammad's *jihād* were similar to those that inspired that of Shehu Usumanu ɗan Fodio. Aḥmad b. Muḥammad was a devout Qādirī and like the jihadists of Hausaland he was also inspired by fervour for the Mahdī. He did not actually claim to be the Mahdī, but he did claim to be the Mujaddid. He also claimed to be the Prophet's successor and the twelfth *imām* after him. This was almost as pretentious as claiming the mahdiship. It certainly shows that Aḥmad b. Muḥammad, like Shehu Usumanu ɗan Fodio, was influenced by the general climate of mahdist excitement in the Islamic world of the 12/18 and 13/19 centuries.

From a purely political point of view, Aḥmad b. Muḥammad's *jihād* can be seen as a reaction to the decline of the Arma in Timbuktu. He was one of those who took the opportunity that this decline presented, to seize power in what was formerly part of the Songhay empire; but this is, perhaps, rather a narrow way of looking at it.

Results of the *Jihād* in Masina

The immediate consequences of Aḥmad b. Muḥammad's *jihād* were, first, to join together again the broken fragments of that empire – Masina, Segu, Kaarta, Timbuktu – into a single, Islamic, imperial unit. Second, to impose the strict Sunna on those who had previously been no more than faintly Muslim at best. Thus, like the jihadists in Hausaland, Aḥmad b. Muḥammad extended *Dār al-islām* in the western Sudan, but his reforms were slow to take effect among the ordinary people and the problem of mixing remained.

Another consequence of Shaykh Aḥmad's *jihād* was to turn the Masina Fulani, or at any rate those of them who were his supporters, from nomads who lived largely by raiding, into sedentary landlords. Non-Fulani cultivators tended to become their serfs. Indeed, as Professor Marion Johnson has pointed out, this process probably began before the *jihād*; the success of the *jihād* can be accounted for, to some extent, by the fact that it encouraged changes already under way.[11]

As in the case of the *jihād* in Hausaland, Shaykh Aḥmad's *jihād*, too, was a step forward in the victory of the militant Islam of the reformers over the passive Islam of the quietists. It was also another step forward in the process by which Muslim literates were, with increasing daring and success, seizing ultimate political power – a political as well as a cultural triumph for literacy. Yet in the case of Shaykh Aḥmad, this last aspect needs to be qualified. In so far as he confronted the Fulani *ardo'en* and the Bambaras, his *jihād* was indeed a victory of the literate over the illiterate; but in so far as he confronted the *ᶜulamā'* of Timbuktu, this did not apply. Indeed, to some extent, Shaykh Aḥmad's *jihād* was a revolt against a too scholarly and over-literate form of Islam, that neglected active reform in favour of excessive bookishness. For their part the *ᶜulamā'* of Timbuktu considered Shaykh Aḥmad to be no scholar but a mere half-educated upstart.

The *Jihād* of al-Ḥājj Maḥmūd *c.* 1266/1850

The next *jihād* took place farther to the south-east, in the upper bend of the Black Volta, in the country of the family-and-clan group people, *c.* 1266/1850. By this time the French colonial penetration of the west and central Sudan had begun; moreover, the British had started to attack the Ashanti empire. However, this *jihād* seems to have been a clash between reformist Muslims and the polytheist family-and-clan group people. It was not complicated by the French presence nor did the jihadists come into contact with European forces, as far as is known. It therefore seems most convenient to regard it as belonging to the era of the pre-colonial *jihāds*.

The leader of this *jihād* was not a Fulani, let alone a man of the Torodbe. He was a Dyula *ᶜālim* from Dourala, called al-Ḥājj Maḥmūd. He was educated by a *shaykh* of Dyulasso, the Imām Yaḥyā b. ᶜAbd al-Raḥmān, from whom he took the Qādirī *wird* (Sufi litany). He then went on Pilgrimage and returned by way of Syria, where he encountered a certain Shaykh ᶜAbd al-Raḥīm. From him he renewed his Qādirī *wird*. He also promised this *shaykh* that he would return to

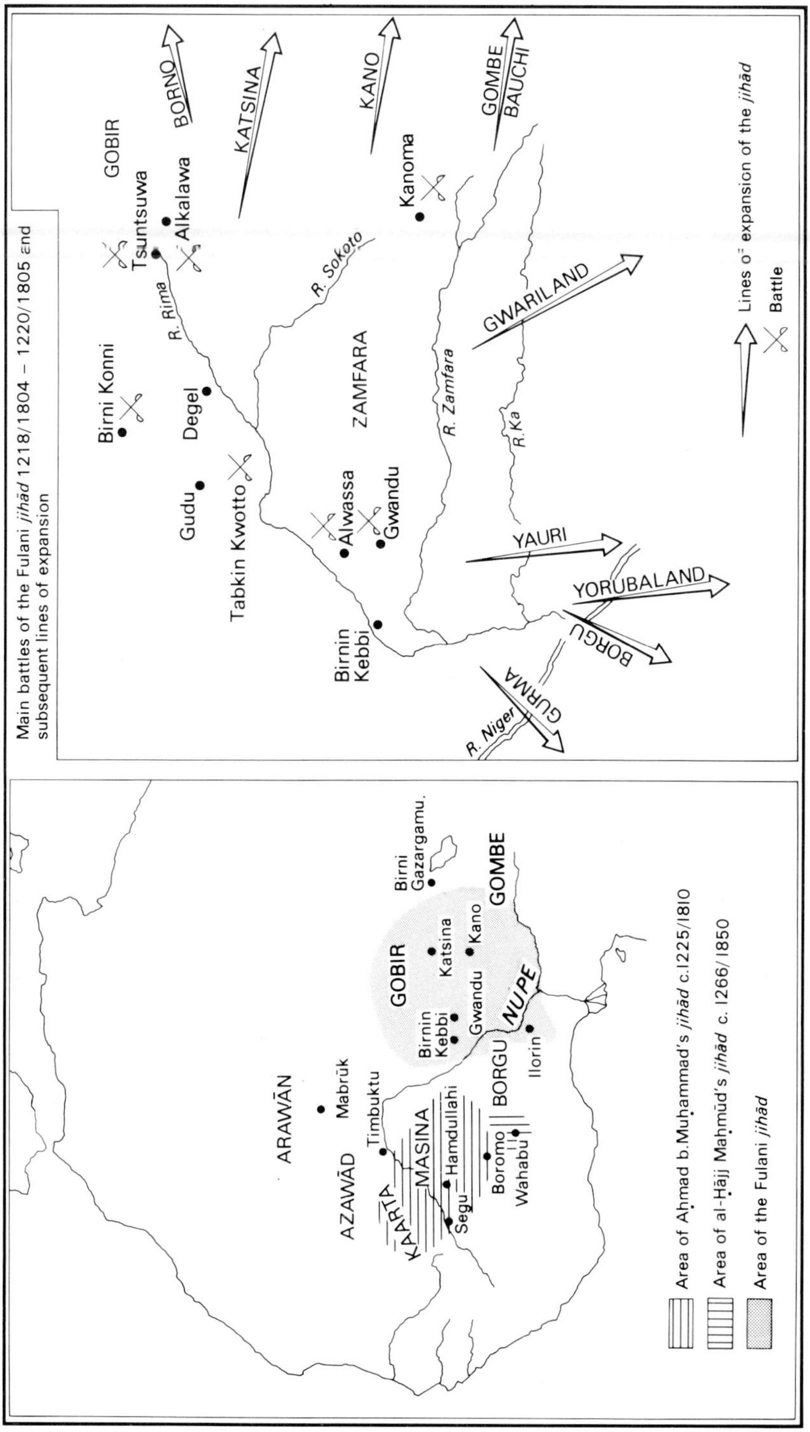
Main battles of the Fulani *jihād* 1218/1804 – 1220/1805 and subsequent lines of expansion
GOBIR
BORNO
KATSINA
KANO
GOMBE
BAUCHI
Tsuntsuwa
Alkalawa
Birni Konni
Degel
Gudu
Tabkin Kwotto
R. Rima
R. Sokoto
Kanoma
ZAMFARA
Alwassa
Gwandu
Birnin Kebbi
R. Zamfara
R. Ka
GWARILAND
YAURI
YORUBALAND
BORGU
GURMA
R. Niger
Lines of expansion of the *jihād*
Battle
ARAWĀN
AZAWĀD
Mabrūk
Timbuktu
KAARTA
MASINA
Hamdullahi
Segu
Boromo
Wahabu
BORGU
Ilorin
NUPE
Birnin Kebbi
Gwandu
GOBIR
Katsina
Kano
GOMBE
Birni Gazargamu.
Area of Aḥmad b.Muḥammad's *jihād* c.1225/1810
Area of al-Ḥājj Maḥmūd's *jihād* c. 1266/1850
Area of the Fulani *jihād*

Map 9 Areas of the pre-colonial jihāds.

his own country, conquer it and build a mosque in every town that he took.[12] It is therefore clear that it was the inspiration of Pilgrimage, together with militant Qādirī ideology acquired not in the western Sudan but in the Middle East, that were the driving forces behind him. After a period of propaganda, by which he sought to gather the local Muslims to his side – his *jihād al-qawl* – he began by attacking the non-Muslim people of Boromo, on the west bank of the Black Volta. He was supported by a number of Kantosi, the Dyula Muslims who had settled in the country of the family-and-clan group people. It appears that these Kantosi, affected by the reforming tendencies of the times, had at last given up their traditionally passive attitude towards the polytheists among whom they lived. They represent the first major response in the Volta region to the reform movement that began farther afield, to the north and east among the Ineslemen of the Sahara/Sahel and the Fulani of Hausaland.

Al-Ḥājj Maḥmūd enjoyed some early success. He was able to set up a small Islamic state centred on Wahabu, the name he gave to the village where he had his headquarters. On his death he was succeeded by his nephew, Karamoko Mukhtār, who joined forces with the Zabarma leader, Babatu. With Babatu's help Mukhtār tried to extend the *jihād*, but other Muslims who opposed it, turned on him. Deserted by Babatu, he was ambushed and defeated by these rebellious Muslims.

It seems clear that, although some Dyula Muslims initially supported this Voltaic *jihād*, others opposed it because it upset their relationship with the local polytheists. This relationship, built up over many generations, had long enabled them to trade peacefully among the non-Muslims. They had no enthusiasm for a war that disturbed these profitable business arrangements. The *jihād* from Wahabu is thus an interesting example of how the force of pan-Islamic revivalism, that had its source far beyond the western Sudan, clashed with the local self-interest of a predominantly trading Muslim community and thus came to nothing. For the new *Dār al-islām* that al-Ḥājj Maḥmūd created soon shrank to little more than a few villages.

Factors common to the pre-colonial *Jihāds*

The three *jihāds* described here have certain features in common. First, they were all the outcome of the revolt of idealistic Muslim literates against mixed Islam, or against the polytheism by which they were surrounded. Second, they enabled Muslim literates to seize supreme political power. Third, in the case of Shehu Usumanu ɗan Fodio and al-Ḥājj Maḥmūd, the Islamic institution of Pilgrimage and the power of Qādirī ideology were crucial factors in driving them to do what they did. In the Shehu's case it was the pilgrim's vision of perfect Islam acquired from literary sources; in al-Ḥājj Maḥmūd's case it was direct, personal experience. It is not known whether Aḥmad b. Muḥammad performed Pilgrimage or not, but there is certainly no doubt about the power Qādirī ideology exercised over him.

These forces of Islamic ideology served to create in these men a sense of Islamic universalism. That is to say, they had a vision of a single, world-wide Islam, in which the way of life, the way of government and the morality and social behaviour of all individuals were regulated strictly according to the Sharīʿa and the Sunna, the Law and the Tradition of the Prophet. They were determined that they would tolerate nothing less than this in their own countries. The *jihāds* were the practical expression of this determination – and perhaps, too, an expression of frustration at their failure to create such an ideal society through *jihād al-qawl*.

In the cases of the Shehu Usumanu ɗan Fodio and Aḥmad b. Muḥammad, Mahdism is also known to have been important as a motivation. It is not known whether al-Ḥājj Maḥmūd awaited the Mahdī, but in view of his education and background, it seems almost certain that he did.

All the *jihāds* extended the area of *Dār al-islām*; and imposed Islamic constitutions where previously there had been non-Islamic forms of government. In the Volta region this was short-lived but in the Niger country and Hausaland it was more lasting.

NOTES

1 Hausa manuscript, *M*.
2 Hausa manuscript, *WW*.
3 Hausa manuscript, *WG*.
4 Hausa manuscript, *WG*.
5 Hausa manuscript, *WG*.
6 Hausa manuscript, *WG*.
7 Hausa manuscript, *ABM*.
8 Hiskett, Ibadan, 1963, pp. 112–13.
9 Adamu, Mahdi, 1975, passim.
10 For example, Stewart, *JAH*, XVII, 4, 1976.
11 *JAH*, XVII, 4, 1976.
12 From a manuscript in IAS, Legon, that appears to be a second, revised copy of IAS ARR66, supplied by al-Ḥājj Muḥammad b. Muḥammad al-Munīr of Bobo Dioulasso.

CHAPTER ELEVEN

The Sokoto caliphate and the Hamdullahi *dina*: 1232/1817 to c.AD 1900

The Shehu Usumanu ɗan Fodio died in 1232/1817. His second son, Shaykh Muhammadu Bello, succeeded him as head of the Muslim Fulani empire. This ushered in a period of just under a hundred years that is usually referred to as that of the 'Sokoto caliphate', following the custom of the Muslim Fulani writers of the period, who use the Arabic term *khilāfa* to describe it. In practice, however, the title *khalīfa*, 'caliph', dropped out of use for everyday purposes and was replaced by the Arabic *Amīr al-mu'minīn*, 'Commander of the Believers' or its Hausa equivalent, *Sarkin Musulmi*, among the officials of the empire and its other subjects. Also, to judge from the accounts of European travellers who visited the caliphate, the Arabic title *sulṭān*, 'sultan', was commonly used there as well.

The terms *Khalīfa/Khilāfa*

Much has been written in discussing the significance of the terms *khalīfa/khilāfa*, caliph/caliphate, in relation to the Sokoto empire in Hausaland. Theoretically, *khalīfa/khilāfa* implies headship not just of a local Muslim community but of the whole Islamic world, while *sulṭān*, *amīr* (emir) and certain other Arabic titles imply subordination to a higher Muslim religious or political authority – for instance the Sharīf of Mecca, or possibly the ruler of the Ottoman empire. Therefore, did the Shehu Usumanu ɗan Fodio and his associates aspire to some wider authority in the Islamic world, beyond just the west and central Sudan when they adopted the terms *khalīfa/khilāfa*? Did Shaykh Muhammadu Bello and his successors later recognise that such pretentions were unrealistic and thus content themselves with the lesser, limited status of a sultan or another less prestigious title?

Such discussions probably overlook two important considerations. First, despite its early universalist implication, the title *khalīfa* became somewhat devalued in the course of the Middle Ages, in that it was used increasingly frequently by local Muslim rulers who had no serious claim to worldwide authority. Thus, by the end of the 10/16 century both Mawlay Aḥmad al-Manṣūr of Morocco and Mai Idrīs Aloma of Borno styled themselves *khalīfa*. Mawlay Aḥmad may indeed have had ambitions beyond his Moroccan domain, although it is unlikely that they extended to the whole of Islam, except perhaps in his diplomatic rhetoric; but it is surely improbable that Mai Idrīs Aloma seriously considered himself to be the head of the Islamic world. This somewhat reduced view of the authority of the *khilāfa* is reflected in the writings of the Fulani reformers themselves. As Dr Muhammad Sani Zahradeen points out in his excellent doctrinal dissertation on ᶜAbd Allāh b. Muḥammad, the Shehu Usumanu explains in his *Najm al-ikhwān*, the 'Star of the Brethren', that the terms *khilāfa*, *imāma* (imamate), *imāra* (emirate), *salṭana* (sultanate) and so on, are all authorised by the Sharīᶜa, thereby apparently implying that he considers them to be equivalents.[1]

But, as Dr Muhammad Sani Zahradeen goes on to make clear, this was not really what concerned the reformers. What was important for them was not whether the title *khalīfa* carried with it greater authority than *sulṭān* or *amīr* but rather than any Muslim title authorised by the Sharīᶜa implied a total breakaway from the evil, pre-Islamic tradition of *mulk*, 'kingship'. ᶜAbd Allāh b. Muḥammad expressed this clearly on the first page of his well-known *Ḍiyā' al-ḥukkām*, the 'Light of the Jurists', which he begins with the words,

> Praise be to God . . . who enacted laws for His servants and turned them away by the carrying out of these laws from tyranny and corruption; and gave them the Islamic Sharīᶜa in place of the profane laws of Chosroes [the Persian emperor, overthrown by the early Muslims].

Thus the true significance of the use of the terms *khilāfa/khalīfa* and *salṭana/sulṭān* lies not in how much authority they may or may not be thought to lay claim to, but rather in the fact that both of them imply absolute rejection of the secular and profane *mulk/malik*, 'kingship/king', – of which the Hausa equivalent is *sarauta/sarki*, 'chieftaincy/chief' – and all that they stand for. Herein, of course, lies part of the evidence for the statement made on several occasions above – that the Fulani *jihād* was as much a movement of political as of religious reform; and that political and religious concepts are inseparable from one another in Islam. Later, the rulers of the Fulani empire were forced by circumstances to compromise and permit the continued use of certain traditional, non-Islamic titles. None the less, this was undoubtedly contrary to the principle they had first endeavoured to establish and, in this book, the political structure they set up is referred to as a 'caliphate', while the ruler in Sokoto is referred to as 'caliph' up to AD 1903. From then on he was generally referred to under the British administration as 'Sultan' or '*Sarkin Musulmi*' (Hausa 'Chief of the Muslims') and 'Caliph' became, for obvious reasons, inappropriate.

The situation *c.* 1232/1817

The setting up of the Sokoto caliphate did not mark the end of the *jihād*; it merely ended one phase of it – that phase that established a hold over the central Haɓe states. The next phase, that continued throughout the rest of the 19 century AD (AH 1232–1317/18) was one of further expansion. It brought into the empire those members of the Banza Bakwai that had not been accounted for before 1227/1812, including Nupe and that part of Yorubaland that became the emirate of Ilorin. Indeed, the southern frontier of the empire remained open and was being continually pushed farther south during the 13–14/19 century. Thus the *jihād* can be seen as an incomplete Islamic revolution that went on right up to the moment of the British conquest of Sokoto in AD 1903.

Although the first phase of the *jihād* had been largely successful the subjugation of Hausaland was by no means complete. For example, there were several large areas where the rule of the Muslim jihadists had never been established. Here, non-Muslim peoples remained independent, and were often thorns in the side of Sokoto. Most important among these independent areas were what is now Ningi, the Bauchi highlands and large areas south of Gwandu inhabited by family-and-clan group people who were not Muslims.

As for the conquered territories on the west of the empire, Kebbi, Gurma and Borgu, these never submitted completely to the central authority. Kebbi liberated itself from Sokoto and waged war against it. In the case of Gurma and Borgu, the control of Sokoto simply lapsed because, 'the caliph's arm was not long enough to stretch that far'.

The Haɓe of Gobir and Katsina were driven out of their kingdoms. However, they never accepted defeat but established their own little states just beyond the northern boundary of the caliphate and from there they stood ready to counter-attack, to regain their heritage. Meanwhile, Borno threatened the caliphate from the east. Thus in the period after the first phase of the *jihād* had been concluded, the caliphate found itself hemmed in on three sides by enemies eager for revenge. However due south it was still possible for the able and ambitious to extend *Dār al-islām* towards the coastal forest; there their most dangerous enemies were not men, but tsetse flies that killed their horses.

The ideology of the *ribāṭ*

From the first, the reformers had tended to explain and justify their own activities in Islamic terms. The Shehu's flight to Gudu was their *hijra*, equivalent to the Prophet's Hijra in AH 1. Their war against the Haɓe was a *jihād*; their enemies were *munāfiqūn*, the 'hypocrites' of the Koran who had plotted against the Prophet; their empire was a *khilāfa*, a 'caliphate' and so on. This practice of setting themselves and their society in a classical Islamic frame of reference continued throughout the caliphate's history. In some respects it was a strength; for the appeal to Islamic ideology was the strongest moral force available to the rulers in Sokoto. In other respects it was a weakness, because it led to a romantic ideal that did not always fit the realities of life in the 13/19 -century west and central Sudan. Following their habit of rationalising in Islamic terms, the Sokoto establishment applied a classical Islamic concept to its military situation. It was that of *Dār al-islām*, the 'Territory of Islam' versus *Dār al-ḥarb*, the 'Territory of War', sometimes *Dār al-kufr*, the 'Territory of Infidelity'. This is how medieval Islam had described the division of the world of the Middle Ages into Islamic and non-Islamic halves. It fitted the Sokoto empire neatly in 1233/1817, for it required the discharge of two obligations: first, to defend the frontiers of *Dār al-islām* against attacks from *Dār al-ḥarb* on its northern, western and eastern borders; second, to extend *Dār al-islām* at the expense of *Dār al-kufr* in the south. Such a policy, expressed in classical Islamic terms, was acceptable to the flag-bearers, the emirs of the provinces; it was also acceptable to the *ᶜulamā'*, whose support the Caliph Muhammadu Bello and his successors needed – thus it helped to bind the empire together.

Islamic history also supplied another useful concept that complemented that of *Dār al-islām* and *Dār al-ḥarb*; it was that of the *ribāṭ* (plur. *rubuṭ*). This notion of the frontier fortress, standing in defence of *Dār al-islām* and confronting the hostile world of *Dār al-ḥarb*, went back into early Islamic history. It was, of course, associated with the Almoravids. However, there is no reason to assume that the Caliph Muhammadu Bello, who took up the idea and applied it to his own circumstances, was copying the particular Almoravid example. The function of *rubuṭ* is fully described in classical Arabic literature relating to the early wars of Islam, especially those against the Byzantines; and what Muhammadu Bello did was to build a ring of walled fortress towns around the threatened western, northern and eastern borders of his empire. These were not a single screen across his front line; they were staggered, that is to say, some were placed well forward, right on the edge of *Dār al-ḥarb*; others stood well back, deep inside *Dār al-islām*. They were so sited as to be able to deal with an invader at any point to which he might penetrate into the caliphate and therefore secured what is known in military science as 'defence in depth'. His understanding of this sensible military principle, and his ability to apply it practically, are further evidence of the Caliph Muhammadu Bello's competence as a military thinker. This military strategy of the *rubuṭ* did much to help him consolidate his empire; the fortress towns served not only for defence but also as centres from which the surrounding countryside could be settled and colonised by the subjects of the caliphate.

However the southern border was not protected by *rubuṭ*; it was defended only by military camps and villages. This was because the war in the south was essentially aggressive, not defensive, and the threat of invasion by the fragmented, family-and-clan group peoples of the orchard bush was slight. Their land was *Dār al-kufr*, the 'Territory of Infidelity', and therefore subject to slave-raiding and conquest not *Dār al-ḥarb*, the 'Territory of War' in the sense that it was a jumping-off point for attacks against the caliphate. *Rubuṭ* were not necessary in a situation where Islam was being constantly pushed forward.

The *rubuṭ* were not only important from a military point of view; they also reinforced the Islamic ideology of the caliphate. They created a mentality that was like an intellectual and spiritual fortress, according to which the Muslim community regarded itself as the guardian of Islamic truths and certainties against the misbelief beyond. Thus *rubuṭ* of the mind and spirit defended its ideological frontiers while walled cities guarded those of its territory; this is made very clear in the literature of the period. The poets of the Sokoto caliphate describe the Muslim community as one set apart by God, having knowledge, and obeying the divinely given laws of Islam while the misbelievers are those who dwell outside the community, cut off from knowledge and the law. Sa'idu ɗan Bello, a member of the Sokoto establishment, made this very clear when he wrote,

> Let us thank God, the Lord of Office, the Unique,
> The king who shows no mercy to the misbeliever,
> . . .
> He gave us the Sunna of Muḥammad, the Prophet,
> He gave us the means of salvation that the misbeliever does not
> possess,
> O community of Muslims, come all, let us entreat Him,
> For with knowledge shall we be ransomed on the Last Day,
> . . .
> Through knowledge a man is taken out of prison,
> Whoever obtains it has more hope of justification than any other,
> A man who has no knowledge, he is a mere creature of the bush,
> He can have no wish to live among men.[2]

Thus *Dār al-islām* is the inner empire, secure behind its physical and moral fortresses. *Dār al-ḥarb* and *Dār al-kufr* are the wilderness beyond.

Also characteristic of this closed Muslim society in its early days was the alliance between the ᶜ*ulamā*' and the political rulers. The ᶜ*ulamā*' were the guardians of social and personal morality and their example and their literature upheld the truths and the values of Islam. They supported the political hierarchy, which claimed to be founded on these truths and values. Sa'idu ɗan Bello expressed this relationship clearly when he wrote:

> Let us concentrate on the roads to religion of the ᶜ*ulamā*',
> Let us not lose our way, let us dwell among men,
> Let us remain among the community, all warning and encouraging [one another],
> So that he who is destined for divine reward may be
> Saved and may abandon intercourse with the misbeliever.[3]

So the rulers and the ᶜ*ulamā*' upheld each other in a relationship that gave considerable strength to the caliphate so long as the conditions it created were acceptable to the ᶜ*ulamā*'. However when the problems of trying to rule a large and complex empire began to multiply, the caliphate's ideological attachment to the past, and the contradictions between the ideal and the reality, proved more and more troublesome. Under these circumstances the alliance between the ᶜ*ulamā*' and the rulers became subject to increasing strains.

Internal dissension and external attack in the Caliph Muhammadu Bello's reign

During the *jihād* the Shehu had appointed his younger brother, Shaykh ᶜAbd Allāh b. Muḥammad, as his *wazīr*, that is his prime minister. On the Shehu's death in 1232/1817 however, the electors in Sokoto had appointed the Shehu's second son, Muhammadu Bello, not Shaykh ᶜAbd Allāh, as caliph. They did this on the reasonable ground that, had they appointed Shaykh ᶜAbd Allāh, his sons and not those of the Shehu, would have had to succeed to the caliphate in the future; this, they feared, would cause disagreement. Although Shaykh ᶜAbd Allāh later accepted the wisdom of this judgement, he did not know of it at the time the appointment was made. He thus felt he had been unjustly passed over and tension arose between him and the Caliph Muhammadu Bello.

Meanwhile, rebellion had broken out against the caliph. A certain ᶜAbd al-Salām was a Hausa follower of the Shehu who had fought with him in the *jihād*. For his services he was given the governorship of Sabiel, in the western half of the empire, ruled by Shaykh ᶜAbd Allāh. He was dissatisfied with this, which he considered too small a reward, so he rebelled against the Caliph Muhammadu Bello and went so far as to proclaim himself caliph. He was supported mainly by rebels from Zamfara. Although he expressed his opposition to the caliph in Islamic terms – he accused him of tyranny in breach of the Sharīᶜa – it seems likely that his rebellion was a show of Hausa resentment against Fulani domination; and even perhaps specifically at the practice of giving high office almost exclusively to Fulani clan leaders and members of the Shehu's family. ᶜAbd al-Salām was eventually defeated by the caliph's forces and killed, but his followers continued to cause trouble in Shaykh ᶜAbd Allāh's half of the empire.

Finally, they established themselves in strength at Kalembina, near Gwandu, where they seriously threatened ᶜAbd Allāh's position.

At first, owing to the tension between them, the Caliph Muhammadu Bello was reluctant to go to his uncle's aid; eventually, however, he was persuaded to do so. The result was the battle of Kalembina, in 1236/1820–1, in which Shaykh ᶜAbd Allāh and the Caliph Muhammadu Bello joined forces to defeat the rebels. After the battle a reconciliation took place between the two men and Shaykh ᶜAbd Allāh gave his allegiance to the Caliph. The reasons why the electors had not appointed him were explained and he accepted that these reasons were just; thus unity was restored within the caliphate. However, the affair of ᶜAbd al-Salām was a warning of the tensions and worldly ambitions destined to darken the Shehu's shining vision of a selfless, other-worldly Muslim community.

The ᶜAbd al-Salām affair was followed by a series of revolts by the conquered peoples of Zamfara and Kebbi. Moreover, from 1240–1/1825 to 1241–2/1826 Borno attacked the caliphate from the east but was driven back by the eastern guardian of the marches, the Emir Yaƙubu of Bauchi.

The high point of Bello's reign, at least in the military sphere, was the battle of Gawakuke, in 1251/1836. Here he defeated a coalition of resurgent Gobirawa, Katsinawa and Touregs. This checked the immediate danger to the caliphate, but it did not remove it entirely. The Gobirawa simply fell back to the north and founded the walled town of Tsibiri, from which they continued to launch attacks on the caliphate for the rest of the century. However, Gawakuke did give Caliph Muhammadu Bello a period of respite, in which he secured his frontiers, incorporated a number of non-Muslim groups into his empire, and subdued internal revolts. It also enabled him to embark on the most important of his social policies – that of settling the nomadic Fulani. This he did on the ground that Islam is better served in a town and village setting than in a nomadic setting. He expressed this view in a letter to the Ineslemen *shaykh*, Muḥammad al-Jaylānī, who was also worried about the contradictions between Islam and the nomadic way of life. The Caliph Muhammadu Bello's argument was summed up in the following passage from that letter:

> The concern of the Sharīᶜa to promote community life is well known. Due to this the jurists have ruled that it is lawful to transfer a foundling from the desert to the village and from the latter to the town but not the opposite. There is no doubt that man is urban by nature. Human perfection is not reached save through urbanisation and civilisation.[4]

The Caliph Muhammadu Bello's preference for the city and town-dwelling way of life is echoed in the poem of Sa'idu ɗan Bello, quoted from above, when he says, 'A man who has no knowledge is a mere creature of the bush. He can have no wish to live among men'. It seems to have been an idea that deeply impressed Muslim intellectuals in the western Sudan since the time of the Toureg revivalist movement in the Azawād during the first half of the 11/17 century; and it may have reflected the dazzling impact made on Sūdānī Pilgrims by Cairo, Mecca and other great cities of the Middle East. It also certainly reflects the influence upon the intellectuals of the ideas of the 8/14 century Arabic historian, Ibn Khaldūn, who argued that man is a city-dweller by nature and therefore best fulfils his destiny in a city environment.

The caliph's policy of settling the Fulani nomads in towns and villages had the result of integrating them with the town Hausas to some extent; it may also have made stricter Muslims of them. It had another, probably unintended result – to extend the range of the Hausa language at the expense of Fulfulde – for the settled Fulani quickly became Hausa-speaking.

The *dina* of Hamdullahi and its relations with Sokoto

The neighbour of the Sokoto caliphate was the powerful empire of Masina, founded by Shaykh Aḥmad b. Muḥammad, with its capital at Hamdullahi. Like the reformers in Sokoto, he, too, tried to model his empire along classical Islamic lines; in this respect he was somewhat more successful than the Sokoto reformers. Whereas they had taken over the ancient and complex structure of the Haɓe states, he had taken over the recently formed kingdom of the non-Muslim, or barely Muslim Bambaras. This was a much simpler political organisation and it was, therefore, much easier for him to form it to his will.

The pattern he adopted was simple too. He called his empire a *dina*, from Arabic *dīn*, 'religion', and then set up a council of forty ᶜ*ulamā*', that supervised the work of the governors appointed to rule the provinces of the *dina*. These governors, in their turn, set up their own councils of ᶜ*ulamā*', who advised them on how to rule their provinces strictly according to the Sharīᶜa. Thus Shaykh Aḥmad b. Muḥammad, even more than the Shehu Usumanu ɗan Fodio, elevated the ᶜ*ulamā*' to positions of political power as well as religious authority.

Not only administratively, but morally too he was strict. He prohibited all music and dancing and forbade the smoking of tobacco; and he even banned the wearing of dyed cloth. He inaugurated a programme of mosque-building but decreed that the mosques should have no towers, for he felt this to be mere 'showing-off'. Like the Caliph Muhammadu Bello, he tried to settle the nomads; in the case of the Fulani he was quite successful, but with the Touregs, less so. They responded by rebelling against him. Shaykh Aḥmad's power was based largely on a conscript army through which he exercised autocratic control to such an extent that the Kunta of Timbuktu, at one point, accused him of creating a *mulk*, a 'kingdom'. In Islamic terms this was much the same as accusing him of setting up a godless dictatorship.

Thanks to the work of Professor Marion Johnson quite a lot is now known about the economy of Shaykh Aḥmad's empire.[5] It depended mainly on pastoral activities, cattle-rearing and so on, and on the cultivation of state lands by slaves. Booty taken in raids against non-Muslims also contributed substantially to the *dina*'s treasury. Nevertheless, as Professor Johnson has pointed out, Masina, unlike Sokoto, was far from rich. It lacked the manufacturing industries, such as leather-working, dyeing, weaving and so on, that sustained the Hausa economy. Professor Johnson argues that this economic weakness may well have contributed to the fall of Masina before its African enemies, whereas the economically stronger Sokoto caliphate survived until the arrival of the British.

It was mentioned in chapter 10 that Shaykh Aḥmad b. Muḥammad at first enjoyed the support of the Kuntī *shaykhs* of the Azawād, but after the successful conclusion of his *jihād*, this changed. It seems the Kunta became concerned about his attempt to control Timbuktu, which he occupied in 1241–2/1826, as well as other economically important areas in the Niger Bend, that they considered to be within their own sphere of interest. Such policies, of course, threatened the Kuntas' commercial supremacy. In particular, it may even be that his prohibition of tobacco-smoking in his empire upset them for they were the main sellers of this commodity in the western Sudan. At any rate, they now changed their attitude towards him and began to support his rivals and those who revolted against him. Later still, however, they seem to have become reconciled with him and even mediated in the differences that arose between him and Sokoto. The result was that the Kunta, the caliphate of Masina and the caliphate of Sokoto came to dominate the commerce of the western Sudan. One scholar has described this commercial cooperation between the three centres of power as giving rise to a 'Sokoto common market'.[6] This expression well describes how the arrangement worked. It also draws attention to the fact, often overlooked by earlier historians of West Africa, that the Sudanic Muslim states did not function in isolation from one another; there was a great deal of diplomatic, commercial and cultural exchange between them and they were in many ways dependent on one another.

As was pointed out in chapter 10, Shaykh Aḥmad's *bayᶜa*, his allegiance, to the Shehu Usumanu ɗan Fodio was interpreted in Sokoto as an acknowledgement of Sokoto overlordship. At first, Shaykh Aḥmad seems to have acquiesced in this, but later he withdrew his *bayᶜa* and even claimed to be a caliph in his own right. This caused tension between the two states, which persisted from *c.* 1232–3/1817 until 1236/1820–1. Shaykh Aḥmad's reason for withdrawing his *bayᶜa* seems to have lain in the disagreement between Shaykh ᶜAbd Allāh b. Muḥammad and the Caliph Muhammadu Bello, described above. Shaykh Aḥmad argued that, when the Shehu died, he genuinely did not know to whom *bayᶜa* rightly belonged, whether to ᶜAbd Allāh b. Muḥammad or to Muhammadu Bello. He was therefore acting in accordance with the Sharīᶜa in withdrawing it altogether. After Kalembina had brought about a reconciliation between Caliph Muhammadu Bello and Shaykh ᶜAbd Allāh, the Caliph Muhammadu Bello accepted Shaykh Aḥmad's reason and good relations were restored between the two empires.

Shaykh Aḥmad b. Muḥammad died *c.* 1260/1844 and was succeeded by his son, Aḥmad b. Aḥmad and then by his grandson, also called Aḥmad. He ruled the empire until the time that it was overthrown by al-Ḥājj ᶜUmar al-Fūṭī in 1278–9/1862.

Intellectual life under the early Sokoto caliphate

The Caliph Muhammadu Bello's reign was a period of considerable intellectual activity. The Fodiawa had already established a tradition of scholarship and authorship in the pre-*jihād* era. This was carried on during the caliphate, through writing in classical Arabic and Hausa. In particular, it became customary among the *wuzarā'* (sing. *wazīr*, chief minister) of Sokoto to compose historical annals and theological works in classical Arabic. The first to establish this tradition was the Wazīr Giɗaɗo ɗan Laima, who held office from 1232/1817 to 1258/1842 and who died in 1267/1851. Outstanding among his works is his *Rawḍ al-jinān*, the 'Meadow of Paradise', in which he lists and describes the miracles attributed to the Shehu Usumanu ɗan Fodio. It was this work that was largely responsible for the growth of the miracle tradition around the memory of the Shehu.

Equally important was the work of Asmā' bint al-Shaykh, popularly known as Nana Asma'u, the Shehu's daughter and the wife of Giɗaɗo ɗan Laima. She was an accomplished authoress, both in Arabic and in Hausa. Her Hausa poem, *Waƙar gewaye*, the 'Song of the Wandering', was a verse account of her father's life. It covered the period of his early preaching in Zamfara and Kebbi, the campaigns of the *jihād* and the events that occurred after it, up to the time of his death. It, too, contributed much to the miracle tradition and to the growth of an heroic legend around the Shehu's memory. So great was this veneration for the Shehu that there soon emerged in Sokoto a sub-order of the Qādiriyya *ṭarīqa*, known as the ᶜUthmāniyya, after the Shehu Usumanu (Arabic ᶜUthmān). It had more than a purely religious significance; through allegiance to it people expressed their loyalty to the Sokoto community and their sense of identification with it. Through devotion to the Shehu's memory they made clear their pride in origin and their feeling that they belonged to a group specially favoured by God. The ᶜUthmāniyya gradually spread beyond Sokoto and gained adherents throughout the caliphate. It seems to have dropped into the background towards the end of the period of the caliphate and during the colonial period, but it was revived again, largely as a symbol of pride in Islam and the Hausa/Fulani contribution to it, during the period immediately preceding northern Nigerian independence.

Certainly the most notable of all the scholars of the early caliphate was the Caliph Muhammadu Bello himself. More than ninety works in classical Arabic are attributed to him, most of them learned treatises on theology. His work was especially important in that it helped to make Mahdism and the doctrines of the End of Time a part of the official ideology of the Sokoto caliphate. That is to say, it was the need to be ready for the coming of the Mahdī, the End of Time and the Day of Judgement that justified the *jihād*, the setting up of the caliphate and its continuance until the Mahdī actually arrived. The caliph's writings were important, too, because they helped to spread certain new and exciting Sufi doctrines in Hausaland.

This, then, was the situation in the Sokoto caliphate during the 'age of the *rubuṭ*'. Militarily, it was under pressure from three fronts but enjoyed freedom of action on the southern front. Morally and intellectually, it was secure, held up by the universalist Islamic concept of *Dār al-islām*, by the holy legend of the Shehu and by the conviction that it was a chosen society whose destiny would be gloriously fulfilled in the coming of the Mahdī and the events of the Last Day.

The crumbling of the ideal

From about 1260/1844 matters developed in such a way that they modified this comfortable situation considerably. From that time on the Haɓe of Gobir and Katsina, as well as the rebels of Kebbi and Zamfara, showed themselves increasingly able to raid into the caliphate. The caliphate proved less and less able to stop them, for it possessed neither the military power nor the administrative machinery to hold back the rising tide of opposition. It therefore had to recognise the impossibility of absolute control over its enemies; *Dār al-islām* was no longer inviolable and *rubuṭ* were not enough; compromise and some trimming of principles were now needed as well, in order to safeguard it. However, the enemies of the caliphate were unable to do more than harass it, for they were themselves too disunited to be fully effective. Moreover, while the provincial emirs – the successors to the Shehu's flag-bearers – were prepared to see the caliph suffer set-backs, they normally came to his aid when his position was seriously threatened. Thus neither the caliphate nor its enemies possessed the decisive power necessary for total victory. A balance of power emerged between them in which the ideal of an unchanging and uncompromising *Dār al-islām*, standing in absolute opposition to its enemies, had to give way to practical politics. This took the form of treaties with the Gobirawa and Katsinawa in the north.

Another problem with which the caliphate had to deal was that of internal dynastic revolts. These were not revolts by conquered peoples seeking to free themselves, they were rebellions against the central caliphate by dissatisfied members of the caliphal establishment. During the Caliph Muhammadu Bello's reign his moral authority and political skill had largely checked such tendencies but under his less able successors they broke out with some force. An example was the revolt of the Emir Buhari of Hadejia.

Emir Buhari was an impatient and wilful chieftain, whose emirate was probably the least closely supervised by the central administration of all those that owed allegiance to Sokoto. However, he earned the wrath of the Caliph Aliyu Babba because of his constant raids after slaves into neighbouring emirates and the caliph ordered him to be deposed. *C.* 1267–8/1851 Buhari rebelled and succeeded in maintaining himself in independence until his death *c.* 1279–80/1863. His revolt was only partly successful, however, for the other emirs rallied to the caliph's support and isolated Buhari. Thus, although he was able to defy the caliph from within Hadejia, he did not become a more serious threat to the caliph's authority, as at one time it seemed he might.

In the same way that the representatives of the caliphate tried to rationalise their activities in Islamic terms, so too did those who rebelled against it. An appeal to Mahdism was one way in which rebels sought to justify themselves and win support. The rebel leader would assert that he and not the caliph in Sokoto was the true representative of the Mahdī; and that those who awaited the Mahdī's coming should support his cause against the caliph. Such appeals were powerful in a society where belief in the Mahdī was strong and political and social discontents frequent and bitter.

The revolt of Hayatu ɗan Sa'idu, the grandson of the Caliph Muhammadu Bello, is a case in point. There are two versions as to why Hayatu was dissatisfied. One is that he was discontented because his father had been excluded from the succession to the caliphate, the other is that he considered himself the rightful heir to that office. Certainly his verse writings, in which he bitterly attacks the Sokoto establishment, give some support to the latter view, but the two versions are not necessarily incompatible with one another. He may well have resented his father's exclusion while at the same time considering that he had inherited his father's claim. Against the will of the reigning caliph, Mu'azu, who regarded his departure as a slight to himself, he left Sokoto *c.* 1291/1873, leaving behind him a bitter taunt against his enemies who, he implied, were no better than the early enemies of Islam, held up to scorn in the Koran,

> Lord protect me from intrigue,
> From the schemers and the mischief-makers,
> From the envious and the hostile,
> The inciters, the treacherous,
> . . .
> For the sake of Muḥammad, O God
> Of the Throne, save me from my enemies.[7]

He made his way to Adamawa, and from there he made contact with Muḥammad Aḥmad, the Mahdī of the Nilotic Sudan (*d.* 1302/1885). He then attempted to persuade the caliph in Sokoto and the provincial emirs that the Nilotic Mahdī's claims were genuine, and at the same time he claimed to be the Mahdī's true representative in the western Sudan. This, of course, also implied a claim to the Sokoto caliphate, for it was part of the ideology of that caliphate that the caliph in Sokoto was the expected Mahdī's representative on earth, whose duty it was to preserve the Islamic community of the Sudan until that Mahdī's coming. However Hayatu had no success in these endeavours and so he set himself up with his people in Adamawa and defied the authority of the emir of the province. Later, he moved north-east and in 1310/1893 he joined Rābiḥ, in Baghirmi. Rābiḥ was a follower of Zubayr Pasha, of the Nilotic Sudan, and a fugitive from the Egyptian administration there, who had become associated with the Nilotic Mahdī and his successor, the Khalīfa, ᶜAbd Allāh b. Muḥammad. One account has it that Hayatu intended to return to Sokoto and enforce his claim to the caliphate with Rābiḥ's help. In pursuit of this joint aim Rābiḥ made preparations to attack Sokoto, but the attack never materialised because Rābiḥ himself came under pressure from the French, at that time advancing towards Borno. A different account denies that Rābiḥ ever made any hostile move against the Sokoto caliphate and maintains that he tried to set up friendly relations with it. Whatever the truth about his intentions, it seems clear that the Sokoto establishment did fear Rābiḥ, at one point, and did genuinely believe that he threatened it. However by 1315/1897 Hayatu and Rābiḥ had quarrelled; fighting broke out between Hayatu's party and Rābiḥ's son, Faḍl Allāh, while Rābiḥ himself was absent observing the progress of the French expedition. Hayatu was killed in battle against Faḍl Allāh in 1315/1898 or early 1316/1898.

Hayatu failed largely because he was unable to persuade the emir of Adamawa and the other emirs to support him in his campaign on behalf of the Mahdī of the Nilotic Sudan, which was, of course, a challenge to the position of the caliph in Sokoto. He also failed because he was unable to construct a lasting alliance with Rābiḥ. However, the threat that he and Rābiḥ posed – or appeared to pose – to the caliphate alarmed the Sokoto establishment and added to its difficulties.

Another Mahdist revolt against the caliphate was that of Liman Yamusa. *C.* 1299/1882 he set out from Dutsin Gadawur to join the Mahdī in the Nilotic Sudan, taking a large following of supporters with him. He was intercepted and stopped by the armies of the emirs of Hadejia and Misau, acting under orders from the caliph.

More serious was the movement of Jibrīl Gaini that was inspired by Hayatu ɗan Bello. This man rose in revolt against the emir of Gombe and established himself in Burmi, claiming to be awaiting the Mahdī's coming. Meanwhile, he ravaged the Gombe emirate and attacked neighbouring emirates. Despite the caliph's efforts to suppress him, he survived until *c.* AD 1902, when he was defeated by the British under Lieutenant-Colonel Morland. It is significant that these Mahdist revolts all occurred from *c.* 1290/1873 to 1300/1882. It was widely believed that the Mahdī would come at the turn of the century, therefore, appeals made in the name of the Mahdī were especially compelling at this time.

Two other incidents tested the nature of the caliph's authority. One was the Talata Mafara affair. In 1308/1891 the chief of Talata Mafara, in Zamfara, refused to pay homage to the caliph or to accept his arbitration in a land dispute. The caliph proclaimed him and his associates rebels and, with the help of other emirates, the revolt was put down. Sarkin Mafara and his allies then submitted to the caliph. In this case, therefore, the caliph's moral authority, backed by the support of his emirs, was fully effective.

In 1311/1893 the death of the reigning emir of Kano brought a longstanding quarrel about the succession to a head. The caliph attempted to appoint a successor unacceptable to the majority of the people and to the Kano Council of Electors. This set off a civil war and a settlement was only reached as a result of the death of one of the two main claimants to the Kano throne. Once again, it was the support of other provincial emirs for the central caliphate that prevented the affair from becoming a more serious danger to the caliph's authority. Each of these incidents can be seen as arising from the breakdown of the ideal solidarity of *Dār al-islām*, brought about by tensions within the caliphate and the caliph's own limited powers. However, they also demonstrate where the caliph's true strength lay, for although the caliph did not have, under his own command, enough military strength to crush major revolts, none the less the provincial emirs – the successors to the Shehu's flagbearers – did rally to the caliph's support sufficiently to limit the dangers. These emirs had an interest in preserving the Islamic caliphate for their own authority rested on the Sharīᶜa. The caliph personified the Sharīᶜa and revolt against him was defiance of the Sharīᶜa. If they permitted that defiance to succeed, they undermined their own positions as well as the caliph's. So, although they might have their private quarrels with the caliph, they could not afford to see the caliphate break up. Therefore, when his authority was seriously threatened, they came to his aid; not to have done so would have been foolish as well as disloyal.

Signs of the End of Time

It was said above that there was an element of weakness in the caliphate's attachment to a romantic Islamic ideal. This romantic ideal was particularly apparent in the structure of the empire's administration, and in the terminology of government. As from the Shehu's day, government had been deliberately fashioned after the pattern of the classical ideal; although more often than not this pattern turned out to be that of the medieval caliphate in Baghdad rather than that of the Prophet in Medina. In theory, everything had to conform to the Sharīᶜa; in practise, much of it did, although certain Haɓe customs and offices undoubtedly survived. As a rule, however, the old Haɓe titles were discarded, and classical Arabic titles replaced them. Thus the chief of police was *Wālī al-shurṭa*, the army commander was *Amīr al-jaysh*, and so on.

Moreover, the ᶜ*ulamā'* were given considerable authority, as *quḍā* (sing. *qāḍī*, Hausa *alƙalai*), 'magistrates', and in other official capacities. Similarly, taxation was modelled according to early Islamic practice. The conquered peoples were referred to as *dhimmis*, the non-Muslim subjects of the 1/7-century Arab empire; and an attempt was made to tax them according to the system evolved at that time. In their personal lives the Sokoto caliphs consciously tried to imitate the life-style of the patriarchal caliphs of the first Islamic century. The *wuzarā'*, the heads of the caliphal civil service, deliberately preserved a tradition of Sufi mysticism passed down by Malama Nana Asma'u, the Shehu's daughter and wife of the first *wazīr* of Sokoto, Giɗaɗo ɗan Laima. Their literature, too, reveals the same pious preoccupations, for they attempted to reproduce the forms and categories of medieval Arabic literature. Thus they wrote frequently in *naẓm*, the 'versification' in which late medieval Arabic poets summarised the earlier prose texts of classical theologians and jurists. The subjects of their verse works were *Wa'azi*, from classical Arabic *wa*ᶜ*z*, 'admonition'; *Madahu*, from classical Arabic *madḥ*, 'praise poetry', especially in praise of the Prophet; *Farilla*, from Arabic *farīḍ*, 'legal versification', and so on. Similarly, in their image of the Prophet Muḥammad, whom they took as their example and whose praise was the purpose of much of their literature, they were more influenced by late Sufi mystical concepts of him as the 'Perfect Man' and the 'Most Excellent of [God's] Creation' than by the bare historical account of his life.

While all of this was a source of moral strength in the days of the Caliph Muhammadu Bello when the community was upheld by the memory of recent triumphs in the *jihād*, it seems to have become increasingly distant from reality as time passed. The veneration for the past made it difficult to come to terms with the present and the classical Islamic administrative model proved impossible to maintain. Traditional, non-Islamic titles crept back into use, largely because the common people insisted on using them in preference to the new, unfamiliar Arabic titles. The ambitions of powerful individuals shattered the ideal of the universal caliphate in which all bowed to the Sharīᶜa and dutifully obeyed its representative, the caliph. The outside world defiantly refused to accept its subordinate place in the neat division of *Dār al-islām* and *Dār al-ḥarb* or *Dār al-kufr*. *Dhimmis* refused to behave like *dhimmis*; even tax-payers protested at the divinely-given order according to which they were ordained to pay taxes to a caliph who was ordained to receive them. As their problems became more difficult, and as life diverged more and more from the ideal model, so both the caliphs and the *wuzarā'*, seem to have taken refuge in mere personal piety and mysticism rather than in reforming policies and positive statecraft. They tended to interpret the problems of their society as the signs of the End of Time and therefore beyond their power to control. This feeling is expressed most clearly in a poem by Buhari, the last of the Sokoto *wuzarā'* before the British occupation. He says,

> If you seek to enquire what troubles me,
> The circumstances of yesterday, today they are different.
> . . .
> I fear, I am confused. . . .
> That which was among us, its power has declined,
> . . .

> Woe to us, O community, let us fly up [to God] like birds,
> This is what the wise men of the past have done,
> . . .
> According as we are able to see, the Hour [the end of the world] is nigh,
> Our rulers, our scholars, they feared God,
> Our righteous men, the martyrs, I have heard tell of them. . . .

And then, as if to say that they have tried their best, he adds,

> In truth, you have not inherited fear from us.[8]

Too much should not be read into such expressions of gloom. Men's moods change from day to day. No doubt members of the Sokoto establishment remained fully able to carry out their daily duties and to cope with the ordinary problems of life. No doubt, too, they lived full and happy lives in the warm companionship of the clan and the Muslim extended family. Their belief that the End of Time was at hand probably did nothing to spoil their enjoyment of the latter days, for their faith was firm and confident. As the *Wazīr* Buhari says, they had not inherited fear. This was true of the spirit as it was also certainly true of the heart; for some years later they faced death in battle fearlessly, against the overwhelmingly superior military technology of the British. However, this poem and others like it, do seem to express a certain disappointment that the expectation of an ideal Islamic society had not been realised; and a conviction that this can only be explained as part of a wider, impending disaster. They also express the quiet conviction of men of principle, that they have done their duty and been true to what they believed in. In this they were surely justified.

The new *Dār al-Islām* in the south

Nupe

In 1220–1/1805, on the death of Etsu Mohammadu, a succession dispute broke out in Nupe between two rival princes, Jimada in the east and Majiya in the west. Malam Dendo, a Muslim teacher and member of the Toronkawa, who lived in Nupe, allied himself with Majiya and helped him to defeat Jimada. Malam Dendo thereupon became influential as Majiya's adviser and Muslim Fulani began to flock into Raba, where Majiya had his headquarters. Soon, however, Majiya became jealous of Malam Dendo's power, quarrelled with him and drove his Fulani supporters out. Malam Dendo now allied himself with Malam Ṣāliḥ of Ilorin, sometimes known as Alimi, and took the side of Idrisu, the son of his former enemy Jimada. Majiya thereupon attacked Malam Dendo but was defeated and driven back to Raba. Malam Dendo then turned to the Shehu Usumanu ɗan Fodio for help. In 1225/1810 the Fulani general Aliyu Jedo led an expedition against the Nupe and helped Malam Dendo to install himself as Sarkin Fulani. Malam Dendo quickly became the real ruler of Nupe under a nominal Nupe Etsu. When he died in 1248–9/1833, he was succeeded by his son Usumanu Zaki, a full Fulani with no Nupe blood in him. He declared himself emir and with this the Fulani emirate of Nupe was officially created. Usumanu Zaki was later replaced as emir by Masaba, who was half Fulani, half Nupe. He became the ally of the Nagwamatse of Kontagora, described below.

Ilorin

The setting-up of a Fulani emirate in Yorubaland took place in much the same way as in Nupe. Dissension among the Yorubas themselves, and the decline of Old Ọyọ, led a Yoruba military commander, Afonja, to ally himself with Malam Ṣāliḥ, alias Malam Alimi, an influential Fulani Muslim teacher in Ilorin. Malam Ṣāliḥ encouraged large numbers of Muslim Hausas and Fulani to come to Ilorin; and Afonja, with the help of Malam Ṣāliḥ and his followers, rebelled against the Alafin in 1232–3/1817. He was victorious but later quarrelled with his Muslim allies. He tried to rid himself of them but was killed in battle against them. Ṣāliḥ died *c.* 1238/1823. He was succeeded as leader of the Muslim *jamāᶜa*, community, by his son, ᶜAbd al-Salām, who finally defeated the Afonja party and made himself master of Ilorin. He was thereupon presented with a flag by the emir of Gwandu; and Ilorin was recognised as an emirate of the Sokoto caliphate *c.* 1246–7/1831.

The result of this series of events was to establish Ilorin as a Muslim stronghold in Yorubaland, but this did not have the immediate result of strengthening Islam there. The effect of Afonja's revolt and his alliance with the Muslims was to turn the non-Muslim Yorubas strongly against Muslims, including the Yoruba Muslims. These Muslims were persecuted and many of them fled to Ilorin or to other Muslim centres. Thus, Islamic influences were for the time being weakened in Yorubaland outside Ilorin; and Muslim Ilorin confronted the rest of the hostile Yoruba nation. By *c.* 1256/1840, the situation had become more settled. Intellectually enriched by the influx of Fulani and Hausa Muslims, Ilorin now began to exert a powerful influence in Yorubaland. In consequence, Islam was regenerated. This process was assisted by the fact that many of those Muslims who had earlier fled from persecution, now became Muslim teachers and missionaries in their new homes. They thus contributed to the spread of Islam generally in the west and central Sudan, as well as among their own fellow-countrymen.

Kontagora

The Nagwamatse were a splinter group of the caliphal family of Sokoto. Under their leader, Umaru Nagwamatse, they became most active in pushing forward expansion in the south – in creating a new *Dār al-islām* there. *C.* 1275–6/1859 Umaru conquered a large part of the territory of the family-and-clan group people, south of Gwandu. He was given a flag by the authorities in Sokoto, who thus officially recognised his activities as a continuation of the *jihād*. He then set up the new emirate of Kontagora. In the process he became so powerful that he was able to defy Sokoto on occasions, without however, resorting to open rebellion. Umaru Nagwamatse and his successors ruled as robber chieftains, nominally in allegiance to Sokoto but able to do as they pleased, and too powerful to be disciplined by the caliph. They and their ally, Masaba, emir of Nupe, ravaged Gwariland and southern Zaria by constant slave-raiding, in the course of which they enslaved Muslims as well as non-Muslims. There is no doubt that the caliphate's inability to control them did much to make its representatives feel that the situation had got wholly out of control; the Nagwamatse represented power without restraint and Sokoto's helplessness was evident for all to see. Increasingly, this situation began to draw adverse comment from the *ᶜulamā'*, particularly from the influential poet

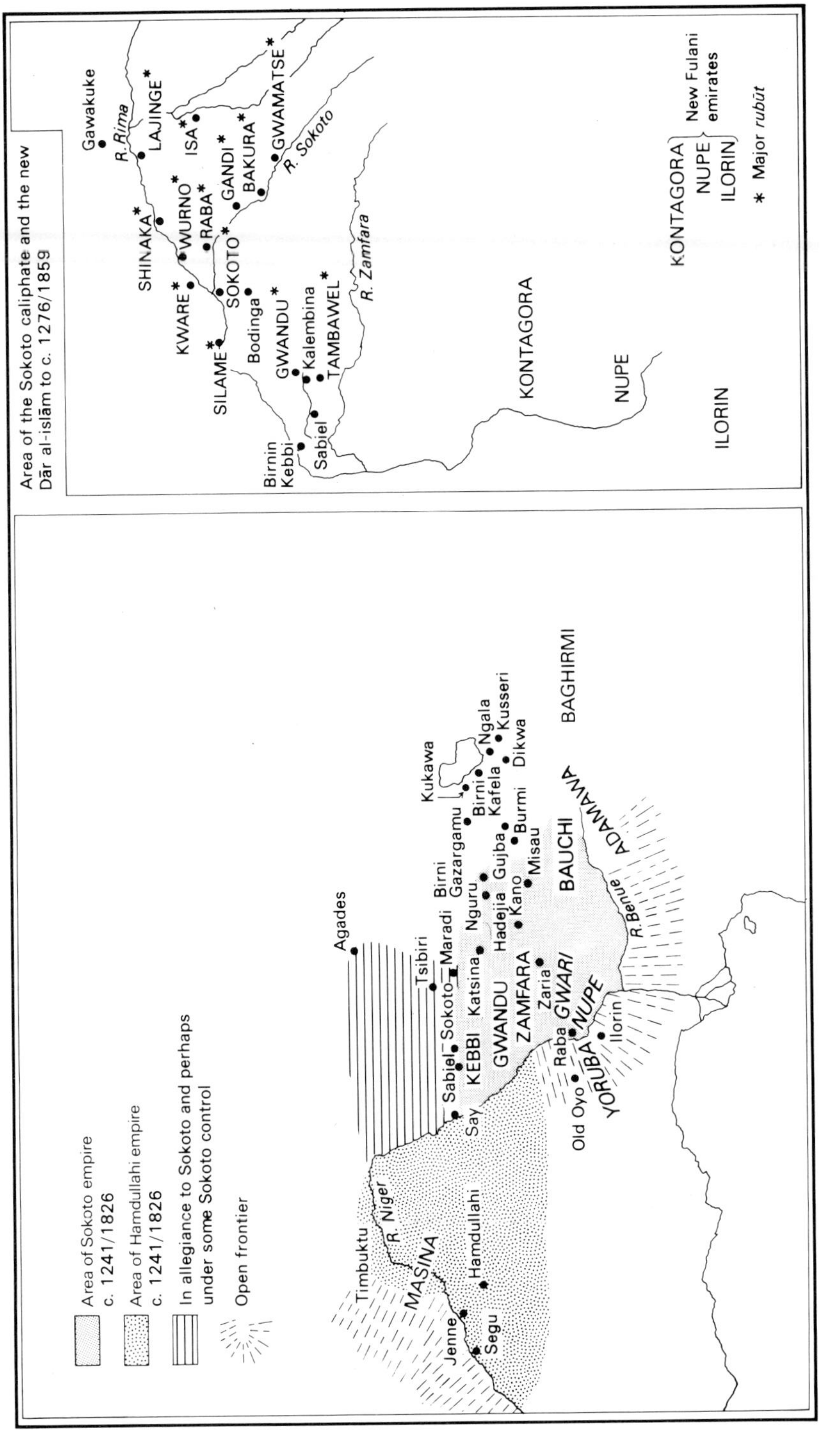
Area of the Sokoto caliphate and the new Dār al-islām to c. 1276/1859
Gawakuke
R. Rima
LAJINGE*
ISA*
GWAMATSE*
R. Sokoto
BAKURA*
GANDI*
RABA*
WURNO*
SHINAKA*
SOKOTO*
KWARE*
Bodinga
GWANDU*
SILAME*
Kalembina
TAMBAWEL*
R. Zamfara
Birnin Kebbi
Sabiel
KONTAGORA
NUPE
ILORIN
KONTAGORA
NUPE
ILORIN
New Fulani emirates
* Major rubūt
Area of Sokoto empire c. 1241/1826
Area of Hamdullahi empire c. 1241/1826
In allegiance to Sokoto and perhaps under some Sokoto control
Open frontier
Timbuktu
R. Niger
MASINA
Hamdullahi
Jenne
Segu
Say
Sabiel
KEBBI
Sokoto
Tsibiri
Agades
Maradi
Katsina
GWANDU
ZAMFARA
Zaria
GWARI
NUPE
Raba
Ilorin
Old Oyo
YORUBA
Birni Gazargamu
Nguru
Hadejia
Kano
Gujba
Misau
Burmi
BAUCHI
Kukawa
Birni Kafela
Ngala
Kusseri
Dikwa
BAGHIRMI
ADAMAWA
R. Benue

Map 10 The Sokoto and Hamdullahi empires c. 1241/1826.

Muhammadu Na Birnin Gwari, who flourished after 1266/1850. In an obvious reference to the way in which the Nagwamatse tyrannised his people, he wrote:

> Do not despise the people of this world,
> People of the bush and of the scattered villages,
> . . .
> Do not practise confiscation as the courtiers do,
> Galloping, galloping upon their ponies,
> They seize by force from the peasants and leave them
> With nothing save the sweat of their brows.[9]

In the end it was the excesses of the Nagwamatse and their allies that helped to give Sir Frederick, later Lord, Lugard the excuse he wanted to intervene militarily in the affairs of the caliphate; and the Nagwamatse contributed, to this extent, to the caliphate's downfall. So it came about that the real challenge to the caliph's power did not come from a second generation of Gobirawa or Kebbi rebels; it came from new, vigorous, ruthless elements within the caliphate itself. These elements saw the opportunities for power that lay beyond the southern frontier and seized them. The new *Dār al-islām* they thus created was in many ways more secure than the old. The southern family-and-clan group people whom they subdued were less well organised and united than the Gobir and Katsina Haɓe; their reaction to conquest was wholly fragmentary. Moreover, Kontagora and Nupe were far enough away from Borno not to be threatened by the rise of Rābiḥ, which had such an unsettling effect on the Sokoto establishment.

Tyrannous as they were, the new emirs in the south acquired great power by their ruthless exploitation of the resources available to them. The extent of this power can be appreciated when, jumping ahead a little, one recalls that they put up an effective fight against the British occupation, whereas Sokoto was overcome with ease. The caliph's resistance did not develop fully until the battle of Burmi, by which time all was lost.

By *c.* 1308/1890 Sokoto exercised little more than moral authority, but that moral authority was not negligible. Even the upstart rulers of Kontagora had an interest in preserving the caliphate. They might defy it at will; it was certainly in their interest that it should be weak; it was not in their interest to see it overthrown. Thus the caliph's position, as guardian of the Sharīᶜa and symbol of the Sunna, was still sufficient to balance the scales against his physical weakness. It was not this weakness that, in the end, was to bring about the downfall of the caliphate; it was the fact that it became caught up in a series of events, originating from outside West Africa and beyond its comprehension let alone its control.

The development of Islam in the Sokoto caliphate and the Hamdullahi *dina*

One of the consequences of Caliph Muhammadu Bello's policy of building *rubuṭ* was to help the spread of Islam. The *rubuṭ* housed not only military garrisons but also the *ᶜulamā'*, who came to them to serve the religious and educational needs of the new Muslim populations. Moreover, the new walled towns soon became centres of attraction for people from the surrounding countryside. They came into the towns to trade and for many social purposes, and in doing so made contact not only with Islamic teachings but also with the Islamic way of life. They saw around them Islamic architecture and Muslim dress; they witnessed Muslims at communal prayer; they watched Muslim burial and marriage, and so on. Thus the new towns became centres from which Islam spread out into the surrounding countryside and there, it quickly took root among the peasant population.

The reformers took up with enthusiasm the composing of religious songs in the vernacular languages, especially Hausa. Although the practice of writing Hausa in the *ajami* script is thought to have begun in the reign of Mohamman Rumfa of Kano (867/1463–904/1499), it seems that few such vernacular songs were written down, though many may have been composed. Paper was expensive and the *ᶜulamā'*, who were the only people who could write, were therefore more concerned to copy out classical Arabic texts. However the vernacular religious compositions of the reformers were special; by memorising them a man could help to ensure his place in Paradise. Moreover, because of their value as propaganda in the cause of Islamic reform, it was worthwhile to copy them and distribute them up and down the country. Thus it became an increasingly common practice to write down these religious songs, using the Arabic script. Then, immediately before and during the Fulani *jihād*, there was a considerable increase in the writing-down of both Fulfulde and Hausa religious verse. During the period of the caliphate the practice was continued even more extensively; Asmā' bint Shehu and her brother, Malam Isa, the posthumous son of the Shehu, were both prolific composers of vernacular verse. Their works, and those of other poets, were copied and the manuscripts were circulated not only in Sokoto but also in the provinces. Thus a considerable written Islamic literature in Fulfulde and Hausa developed which contributed much to the spread of Islamic ideas; and meant that literacy was now increasingly possible through these two vernacular languages as well as through classical Arabic.

As the years passed, the ideas introduced by the early reformers took root under the caliphate. Among the most important were those that concerned life and death; and the nature and purpose of man's earthly life. For instance, some West African ideas about life and death rested on the belief that the spirits of the ancestors survived in the world; they were not visible to the living but they were there all the same and they continued to be interested in the affairs of the community. Some cults taught that the spirits of the dead were born again into future generations. Such ideas as these must have been present among the commoners of Hausaland who were largely drawn, through enslavement, from neighbouring societies where these beliefs were widely held – and indeed still are to the present day. In time, however, such pre-Islamic ideas gave place to Islamic teachings, according to which death is a total separation from the world of men; and the prelude to either divine punishment in Hell or divine reward in Paradise. Certainly the preaching and writing of the *ᶜulamā'* during the period of the caliphate did much to bring this about.

Traditional African views of the cosmos, that is the whole universe and how it is constructed, are many and varied. In West Africa some important cosmological systems rest on the belief that there is a chief god and below him, ranks of lesser gods. These gods inhabit the sky and often use it as a hunting-ground or battle-field. However there are many different, complex systems to explain the relationship between the earth, the sun, the planets and the stars; like ideas on life and death, these must have been represented among the peoples who became subjects of the Sokoto caliphate.

However, Islam, especially Sufi Islam, has its own, luminously beautiful explanation of the universe. It teaches that the whole firmament that lies above the Earth, which includes the Seven Heavens, is constructed in five levels, each level being a nearer approach to knowledge of God and spiritual perfection. These levels were created by God's outpouring of grace, mercy and light upon mankind; but the world of men, in contrast to the worlds above the moon, was created by God as corrupt, impermanent and therefore worthless. Is it not destined to pass away completely when the Mahdī has fulfilled his purpose? Thus the Muslim's duty – and his only hope of salvation – is to strive for the spiritual rewards of the world above; and shun the material rewards of the world below. When Islam became the religion of the state under the caliphate, this Islamic view of the cosmos gradually displaced African views – not completely perhaps, but certainly very widely. It was constantly being impressed upon the imagination of the Hausa people in powerful Hausa verse, that dwelt on the imagery of divine light, transfusing throughout the universe,

> And Jibrīl [Gabriel] ascended, both he and Muḥammad,
> They went up to the First Heaven and Adam they met,
> He rose up and bade Aḥmad [Muḥammad] a joyous welcome,
> They went to the Second Heaven and our Lord ᶜĪsā [Jesus] met them,
> And Yūnus [John] and ᶜĪsā were joyful at meeting Aḥmad,
> . . .
> Then they came to Ibrāhīm [Abraham] there in the Seventh Heaven,
> He rose and bade Muḥammad a joyful welcome,
> . . .
> Then Muḥammad crossed over screens and rivers of light,
> And he came before the King who had created Muḥammad,
> He was crossing the light, he heard someone calling,
> 'Come here, thou favourite of the Palace, the Messenger, Muḥammad'.[10]

Because the Sufi Islamic view of the cosmos was so closely linked to moral attitudes, these cosmological ideas had moral as well as intellectual significance. For the world, *Duniya*, came to be regarded as,

> . . . an old hag, narrow-hipped, in a dyed robe,
> Then she wraps herself in a green cloak, deceiving,
> So that she catches inexperienced men in her snare,[11]

or,

> The like of [the world], you might say, is an old woman who dolls herself up,
> Her body is much shrivelled by disease,
> She decks herself out and smothers her body with make-up,
> . . .

> She minces along, posturing with her hands,
> Men look, hearing the hubbub,
> Lusts of the heart, he who feels them,
> They cover the fool completely, they rise up in their hundreds,
> They overwhelm the great man, making him throw himself into love
> of her,
> . . .[12]

This allegory of the world of men as a worthless harlot was constantly impressed upon the Hausa people in their literature and their folklore. Indeed, it was this way of looking at life as much as the actual problems that beset them, that gave rise to the gloomy outlook of the later Sokoto poets as well as the ruling establishment. In the end, it influenced the outlook of the whole of Hausa Muslim society.

Finally, Sufism and Mahdism were both fundamental to the teaching of the reformers; they became part of the established ideology of the Sokoto caliphate; they were constantly disseminated in vernacular, especially Hausa, verse. Thus they were no longer confined to a small group of Islamic literates familiar with the classical Arabic sources; they now filtered down among the people at large, enriching their folklore and forming their attitudes. The following story, which is said to date back at least to the time of the Shehu, illustrates the way in which the notion of the disasters that will come before the End of the World – a notion that comes in the first instance from written, classical Arabic sources – became changed into a popular, folkloric tale of the kind that the old people tell to children. It concerns ᶜAlī b. Abī Ṭālib (Hausa Aliyu), the Companion and son-in-law of the Prophet Muḥammad and a great hero of Islam. It tells how he set out to try and prevent the disasters that will come before the End of the World and at the same time it illustrates how the Islamic notion of the Seven Heavens found a place in Hausa folklore:

> One day the Prophet Muḥammad said that the only thing he feared was *Jarabar Duniya*, the 'Testing of the World'. When Aliyu heard this, he wondered what *Jarabar Duniya* might be and so he set out to hunt for it and kill it. First, he came upon an old man who had cut too much grass to carry but was still trying to cut more. Aliyu asked him, 'Are you the *Jarabar Duniya* that the son of Amina [the Prophet] fears? If so, I will cut you down with my sword, Bi Sulaymanu'. The old man replied, '*Gaba dai, ba ni ne ba,*' 'Go on your way, it is not I.' Aliyu continued on his journey, seeing many curious things, like a well full of water but its sides were not wet, a donkey with green grass all around him but growing thin from lack of food, and so on. Eventually, he came upon an old woman, with two large ears. And when she lay down, she used one ear as a mat to lie on and the other ear as a quilt, to cover herself. Aliyu asked her the usual question and eventually she admitted that she was *Jarabar Duniya*. He seized her with one hand and hurled her to the ground with such force that she sank in until she reached the Seventh Earth. Then she bounced up again and he seized her again and hurled her up into the sky until she touched the Seventh Heaven. Then she cried out and asked him to forgive her.[13]

There are also many folkloric stories about Dajjāl, Anti-Christ, circulating among the Hausas. Here is one of them:

> When I entered the cave my eyes fell upon a man sitting on a black iron bed, chained with black iron chains on his hands and his feet. When he heard me, he lifted up his head and I realised that he was one-eyed. He said to me, 'Where do you come from?' I said, 'I come from the world of men.' When he heard this he uncovered his face and I saw he was like a djinn. 'Young man,' he said, 'is it now the time of my coming? How have you left the world of men? ' Then I looked about me and to one side I saw two men, being severely tortured. Fire was put in their hands and fire was what they walked on. And they were wailing and roaring, but in vain. When I got back to the world of men, I told the man who had sent me what I had seen and heard. He said, 'Did you see the one-eyed man?' I said, 'Yes'. He said, 'That was Dajjāl. He is the one who is waiting to come at the End of Time. In his time the Prophet's community will be humiliated. People will refuse to give alms. Liars will multiply. Dishonesty and usury will increase. What is illegal will become legal . . . Soil fertility will decrease. Trust will disappear and hearts will dry up. . . . The rulers will oppress the people.[14]

Many such stories – about the End of Time, the Coming of the Mahdī, and Anti-Christ, and other themes and topics from classical Arabic sources – have passed into Hausa folklore. They illustrate the depth and completeness with which Islam has taken over the culture of the Hausa people.

Politically, the caliphate in Sokoto was only partially successful, for the perfect *Dār al-islām* escaped it. Culturally, it achieved much more, for it set up the institutions and promoted the literacy that consolidated the work the reform movement had begun. By *c.* AD 1900 Hausaland was an Islamic country and apart from the Maguzawa, a small group of Hausas who persisted in their non-Muslim practices and beliefs, its population was solidly Muslim. It was firmly identified with the wider culture of the Islamic world. Of course, something of the old, pre-Islamic culture survived as it still does to the present day, but the masses of the people, both urban and rural, had, by AD 1900, come to think of themselves as Muslims and to feel pride in this. For all their heart-searching and their sense of disappointment, the reformers and those who came after them did accomplish a great deal – more indeed than they gave themselves credit for.

The progress of Islam in the *dina* of Hamdullahi differed considerably from that in the empire of Sokoto. First, whereas the *jihād* in Hausaland had taken place against a background of Haɓe mixed Islam, that in Masina was directed on the one hand against the Dikko *ardo'en* and the Bambaras, both of whom were barely Muslim at all. On the other hand, it also involved the two ancient centres of Islamic scholarship, Jenne and Timbuktu. Thus it became, to some extent, a conflict between the party of the long-standing, scholarly and conservative *ᶜulamā'* and the new, upstart and radical party of Shaykh Aḥmad. The *ᶜulamā'* of Jenne and Timbuktu quickly became the opponents of Shaykh Aḥmad's reforms, on the grounds that his version of Islam was shallow and unscholarly. For example, they argued that many of the things that he condemned, such as women attending religious meetings, were in fact permitted by the Sharīᶜa; in condemning them the *shaykh* was, in their view, simply demonstrating his ignorance.

It was, therefore, outside the towns and cities, and among the unschooled nomads, that the *shaykh*'s movement had its greatest influence on Islam. First, his practice of building fortified villages, similar to but smaller and less permanent than the Caliph Muhammadu Bello's *rubuṭ*, created centres of literacy and of strict Sunna in the open countryside. Such centres had some effect in bringing the nomads closer to Sunnī Islam. Similarly, his policy of encouraging the settlement of the Fulani nomads led to a better observance of Islam among them. Even the Touregs, the most rebellious of the *shaykh*'s subjects, were influenced in some measure by his reforming zeal.

Perhaps his greatest achievement was to encourage Islamic literacy among those outside the town and village centres, who had previously had little contact with it. As Professor William Brown has pointed out, Shaykh Aḥmad shifted political legitimacy from birth and tradition – the qualifications of the Dikko *ardo'en* – to Islamic literacy and strict observance of the Sunna;[15] a policy which helped to encourage literacy in his empire.

However, the Islamic achievement of Shaykh Aḥmad, the conqueror of Masina and the founder of Hamdullahi, was less complete and less permanent than that of the Fulani reformers in Hausaland. He largely failed to convert the non-Muslim Bambaras and his attempts to reform the nomads were only partially successful. Professor William Brown has suggested that it was these failures, together with a number of other factors, that caused disappointment and discontent among many of those who had at first supported him.[16] To this was added the fact that his successors, Aḥmad II and Aḥmad III, turned out to be military adventurers rather than religious leaders. They thus further disappointed those earnest and pious Muslims who looked for more from the reform movement in Masina than its leaders were able or ready to give. In the end these discontented pietists turned, instead, to the great Tijānī reformer, al-Ḥājj ᶜUmar al-Fūṭī and the Hamdullahi *dina* was overthrown.

NOTES

1 Muhammad Sani Zahradeen, 1976, pp.187–8.
2 Hiskett, PhD thesis, 1969, I, p.241.
3 ibid, p.243.
4 Norris, 1975, p.150.
5 *JAH*, XVII, 4, 1976.
6 Stewart, *JAH*, XVII, 4, 1976.
7 Hiskett, *Hausa Islamic verse*, 1975, pp.97–8.
8 ibid, pp. 76–7.
9 ibid, p.100.
10 ibid. p.53.
11 Hiskett, Ibadan, 1963, p.103.
12 Hiskett, *Hausa Islamic verse*, 1975, pp.80–1.
13 I am indebted to Malam Abdulgadir Dangambo of Bayero University for this story, which occurs in his PhD thesis, Vol.2, pp.13–14.
14 Malam Abdulgadir Dangambo, PhD thesis, Vol.2, p.15.
15 Brown, PhD thesis, 1969, p.130.
16 ibid, p.149ff.

CHAPTER TWELVE

Borno from *c.*1214–15/1800 to *c.*AD 1900

By 1214–15/1800 Borno was still, by repute, the most powerful state in the west and central Sudan. In fact, its power rested largely on the moral authority and the *baraka* of the *mai*, that is on his religious prestige and his power to confer blessing. In consequence, many of the provinces of the Borno empire were held through the relationship of client to patron and their obedience to the *mai* was voluntary rather than enforced. However, the empire, or caliphate as it was still known, was in difficulties. The Touregs constantly harassed its northern provinces. In the south-east Baghirmi, once tributary to the caliph/*mai*, had become independent in all but name. Only in certain Hausa-speaking provinces to the west was the *mai*'s authority still firm. These provinces were supervised by the Galadima, a Borno territorial grandee who lived in Nguru but he was fated to become the first victim of the Fulani *jihād*, when it erupted in Borno.

The *jihād* in Borno

By 1214–15/1800 there were numerous groups of Fulani in Borno. In that year a certain Bi Abdur, who lived near Hadejia, then tributary to Borno, persuaded the chief of Hadejia to appoint him *ardo* of the Hadejia Fulani. This the chief did, but late in 1219/1804 or 1220/1805, shortly after the *jihād* began in Gobir, Bi Abdur sent his brother, Sambo, there to obtain the Shehu's flag. Together, Bi Abdur and Sambo raised the *jihād* in Hadejia, drove out the chief, Garba Abubakar, and went on to attack Auyo, to the south-west of Hadejia. Other Fulani joined them and, shortly after, the Galadima was driven from his seat at Nguru. At about the same time Fulani from Gujba, south-east of Hadejia, rose in revolt against the reigning *mai*, Mai Aḥmad, under Gwani Mukhtār, the leader of a local community of scholars.

Mai Aḥmad was now faced by a major Fulani uprising similar to that which overtook the Haɓe kings of Hausaland. He reacted by ordering his people to turn on the Fulani and kill them and in consequence more Fulani joined the *jihād* against him. The *mai* now wrote to the Shehu Usumanu ɗan Fodio to enquire the reason for this apparently unprovoked attack upon him. The Shehu attempted to explain the reasons for the *jihād* in Hausaland and then invited the *mai* to join it. He also ordered the Borno Fulani to stop making war on the *mai*, but at the same time he defended their action. The *mai* found the Shehu's reply unsatisfactory and continued his advance against Bi Abdur and his associates in the west; but he was not able to prevent them advancing deep into Borno. In 1223/1808, Bi Abdur died and was replaced by Ibrāhīm Zaki, who at once advanced against Birni Gazargamu but then retreated. Later in the same year Gwani Mukhtār attacked the city, drove the *mai* from it and occupied it. Mai Aḥmad, now old and blind, reacted to this disaster by giving up the throne in favour of his son, who became Mai Dunama. Although this was a wise move, it caused some dissension since it usurped the function of the traditional kingmakers. However, Mai Dunama was able to rally the Borno forces and then he turned for help to a Muslim ʿ*ālim*, al-Ḥājj Muḥammad al-Amīn b. Muḥammad al-Kānamī, at that time living in Ngala, south of Lake Chad.

Muḥammad al-Amīn b. Muḥammad al Kānamī

Muḥammad al-Amīn b. Muḥammad al-Kānamī was a Muslim scholar of the Kanembu people, educated partly in Borno and partly in Murzuk, in the Fazzan. He had performed Pilgrimage *c.* 1204–5/1790 and had lived for several years in the Ḥijāz in Arabia; finally, he had settled in Ngala, in Borno. Here he set up as a religious teacher and soon gained a large following of students. He married the daughter of the local ruler and, when the Fulani attacked the area, assumed leadership of the defence against them. With the help of his Kanembu and Shuwa Arab followers he defeated the Fulani. He thereby established a reputation for saving the day, not only by military means but also by the power of his charms, his visions and his prayers. The latter were addressed especially to Shaykh ʿAbd al-Qādir al-Jaylānī, for, like the Fulani reformers in Hausaland, al-Kānamī, too, was a Qādirī. Impressed by his success and by his reputation, Mai Dunama asked him to assist in the reconquest of Birni Gazargamu, to which he agreed. Helped by al-Kānamī's Kanembu spearmen, who were famous fighters, and by his Shuwa Arab contingent, the *mai* drove the Fulani out of Birni Gazargamu and killed Gwani Mukhtār. This victory greatly increased al-Kānamī's reputation as a military leader and as a *walī*; he returned to Ngala loaded with gifts and favours from the grateful *mai*. However, in 1223/1808 or 1224/1809, Ibrāhīm Zaki renewed the attack and Mai Dunama was forced out of Birni Gazargamu. Once again he sought the help of al-Kānamī who again agreed and Ibrāhīm Zaki retreated before the *shaykh*'s now substantial army of Kanembus and Shuwa Arabs. Further Fulani attacks under Muḥammad Manga, son of Gwani Mukhtār, were defeated by al-Kānamī, who had by now established himself as the one person capable of dealing with the Fulani. Mai Dunama, increasingly ineffective, abandoned Birni Gazargamu and shifted aimlessly from one part of the kingdom to another. He had totally lost control over events and was wholly dependent on al-Kānamī. Al-Kānamī's growing influence and Mai Dunama's own weakness now gave rise to a revolt among his own courtiers; Mai Dunama was ousted and replaced as *mai* by his uncle, Muḥammad Ngileruma. He established a new capital at Birni Kafela but continued to employ al-Kānamī. Al-Kānamī preferred the more easily manageable Dunama and in 1228/1813 he restored him as *mai*. Real authority lay in the hands of al-Kānamī who by this time was the most powerful person in Borno. In 1230/1814 he built his own capital, Kukawa, close by the north-western shore of Lake Chad, and from here, he began to act wholly independently of the *mai*. In particular, he embarked upon a plan to re-establish control over Borno's former tributary, Baghirmi, for the aim of reuniting what had been the provinces of the Borno caliphate at its greatest was always foremost in his mind. To this end he called on the support of friends in the Fazzan and Tripoli. Mai Dunama seized the opportunity, presented by this turn of events, to seek the help of Baghirmi in getting rid of al-Kānamī, but al-Kānamī heard of his plans. In the course of a confused series of events, Mai Dunama was mistakenly killed by his Baghirmi allies. Al-Kānamī was now the effective ruler of Borno. However, he did not declare himself as such but installed Mai Ibrahim as his own man. From 1240/1825 to 1241–2/1826 he waged a campaign in the west against the Sokoto caliphate, the purpose of which was to clear Borno of the rebellious Fulani and recover certain territory that had been lost as a result of their action. However, the result was inconclusive and both sides – al-Kānamī and the Sokoto establishment – seem to have decided at this point to accept the situation as it was. After this, al-Kānamī made no further attempt against the Sokoto caliphate, but concerned himself with eliminating his enemies within Borno. He died in 1253/1837–8.

The correspondence with Sokoto

The correspondence with the jihadists in Hausaland, which began with Mai Aḥmad's letter to the Shehu Usumanu ɗan Fodio, was continued by Shaykh al-Kānamī. He wrote first to Gwani Mukhtār; then to the Shehu Usumanu ɗan Fodio himself. The Caliph Muhammadu Bello answered for the Shehu and the substance of the correspondence was as follows: Al-Kānamī began by reproaching the Fulani as a whole for attacking fellow Muslims without justification in the Law. He then demanded to know why they had done this. The suggestion that they were acting contrary to the Sharīᶜa hurt the Sokoto establishment. A long and often bitter exchange of letters followed. The Caliph Muḥammadu Bello at first argued that the Borno Fulani had risen against the *mai* because he tolerated un-Islamic practices among his subjects. Al-Kānamī admitted that certain non-Islamic customs did survive; but claimed that these went on without the *mai*'s knowledge or his own. He himself, he insisted, had done his best to suppress them, but in any case, such misconduct was no reason in the Sharīᶜa for accusing Muslims of total misbelief; or for making war against them. The Caliph Muhammadu Bello, changing his position somewhat, now replied that this was not the reason that the Fulani had attacked Borno. The real reason, he said, was that the Bornoese had come to the aid of the Haɓe, who were manifestly misbelievers. To aid infidels against Muslims was, so the caliph argued, the equivalent of infidelity; *jihād* against those who acted thus was justified.

The correspondence dragged on without reaching any agreement until 1227/1812. It is said that at one point al-Kānamī suggested putting the dispute to the arbitration of the Ottoman authorities in Tripoli or the *shaykhs* of the Azhar, but Sultan Muhammadu Bello was not in favour of this procedure. The correspondence solved nothing, but it does demonstrate the way in which Islamic concepts were basic, not only to religious life but also to political and inter-state relations in the west and central Sudan. Both sides in this dispute based their arguments squarely on the Sharīᶜa; their interpretations of it differed. However neither questioned that it ought to govern their behaviour. In Sokoto the correspondence caused considerable heart-searching and the Shehu himself was particularly disturbed by al-Kānamī's accusations. He was sensitive to the charge that he had shed Muslim blood wrongfully and the Caliph Muhammadu Bello, too, seems to have taken the matter very seriously.

His arguments against al-Kānamī were somewhat shifting, but it seems he was handicapped by lack of precise knowledge of the circumstances in Borno; also, he probably knew well enough that the case of the Borno Fulani was weak in law. However he was bound by ties of loyalty to his kinfolk; he could not simply accept al-Kānamī's charges against them; he therefore had to put up the best case he could on their behalf.

As for al-Kānamī, the correspondence seems to have increased his prestige; for he thereby proved himself not only the military equal of the Fulani generals but also the intellectual equal of their scholars, whose reputation for learning in the Law was great.

Al-Kānamī's place in the history of Islam

Shaykh al-Kānamī was a devout Muslim disciplinarian, he was not a jihadist. He fought his campaigns to protect the territory of Borno, not to start an Islamic revolution. Certainly, he tried to enforce Islam more strictly and he sometimes did this with considerable severity. However this may have been, to some extent, a reaction to the criticism of laxity levelled against him by his Muslim Fulani critics. On the other hand, in arguing that to continue certain non-Islamic practices did not amount to the abandoning of Islam, he displayed a realism towards mixed Islam that was in contrast to the severity of most – though not all – of the Sokoto ᶜ*ulamā*'. To some extent this may have been due to the fact that he had travelled widely and was experienced in the ways of the world, as well as in books. For example, he knew that unjustifiable practices continued to occur in the Ḥijāz and in Egypt, as they did in Borno and Hausaland, but that it would be absurd, none the less, to suggest that they amounted to total infidelity in these areas. All the same, he shared certain important characteristics and experiences with the Fulani reformers of Hausaland; he was rooted in Islamic literacy; and he had performed Pilgrimage. In Ngala he was the centre of a group of ᶜ*ulamā*' who seem to have been especially dedicated to Islam. Moreover, he was a Sufi who experienced visions and was able to call for aid on the Qādirī founder, Shaykh ᶜAbd al-Qādir al-Jaylānī. Finally, he was widely believed to be a *walī*, whose charms and prayers were highly effective.

Shaykh al-Kānamī's importance lies chiefly in the fact that his career demonstrates how effective ideas were in the struggle between the reforming jihadists and the defenders of the old order of mixed Islam. The Haɓe rulers were well-armed and strong and they fought hard against the jihadists. In the end they were overwhelmed because they lacked the appeal of a powerful ideology to unite their people and fire their hearts. Al-Kānamī, on the other hand, used many of the jihadists' own spiritual weapons against them. This was sufficient to unite the Borno Muslims behind him; and to inspire them with the belief that their cause was that of religion. Al-Kānamī relied not only on Kanembu spears but also on the sword of faith and it was this that made him a match for the Fulani jihadists.

The dynasty of the Shehus

Shaykh al-Kānamī was succeeded by his son, Shaykh or Shehu ᶜUmar. After a series of intrigues, he defeated and killed the last of the *mais*, Mai ᶜAlī, which marked the final destruction of the Saifawid dynasty. Shehu ᶜUmar became the sole ruler of Borno; and with him the dynasty founded by Shaykh al-Kānamī came to be known as that of the Shehus, from the Arabic word *shaykh* that ᶜUmar and his successors adopted as their title.

By all accounts a pleasant, easy-going man, Shehu ᶜUmar lacked his father's character. He was too dependent on his slaves and courtiers and was overshadowed by his more able brother, ᶜAbd al-Raḥmān. In 1270/1853 Shehu ᶜUmar was forced to abdicate in ᶜAbd al-Raḥmān's favour, but ᶜAbd al-Raḥmān's reign was short. The following year he was seized and executed and Shehu ᶜUmar was returned to the throne. However, he remained largely inactive and made no attempt to continue Shaykh al-Kānamī's policy of recovering those former territories now lost to the Borno caliphate. No further major confrontation took place between Borno and Sokoto during his long reign, although he did give some help to Buhari of Hadejia, in his rebellion against the caliph of Sokoto.

Shehu ᶜUmar died in 1298–9/1881 and was succeeded by his son, Shehu Bukar, who was a stronger character than ᶜUmar. However he died prematurely in 1301–2/1884. After a dynastic struggle, he was succeeded by his brother, Ibrāhīm. By this time, however, Borno was in the grip of an economic crisis which was not confined to that state alone, but which was general throughout the west and central Sudan. It was largely the result of a trade depression in the world beyond the Sudan and a particular consequence of this was that Borno's trade with North Africa declined. Shehu Ibrāhīm, too, reigned only for one year and was succeeded by Shehu Hashimi. This Shehu was a devout Muslim, rather more interested in affairs of religion than in affairs of state, and he made a sincere attempt to govern strictly according to the Sharīᶜa. However his reign was troubled by external events over which he had no control that stemmed from the unsettled conditions in the eastern, Nilotic Sudan; and had their origin in the same Mahdism that so harassed the Sokoto caliphate.

Rābiḥ b. Faḍl Allāh

Rābiḥ b. Faḍl Allāh, sometimes known simply as Rābiḥ Zubayr, was one of many young men who joined the eastern Sūdānī ivory and slave-trader, Zubayr Pasha, in opening up the Baḥr al-Ghazāl frontier *c.* 1276/1860. He had previously served in the Egyptian army, from which he had been discharged. In 1291/1874 Zubayr Pasha, who by this time was the representative of the Egyptian government in Baḥr al-Ghazāl, went to Cairo to protest over certain matters relating to the administration of Darfur, which he had attempted to occupy, and was detained there. Zubayr's son, Sulaymān, then took over in Baḥr al-Ghazāl until he was defeated and executed by the Italian adventurer, Gessi Pasha. Rābiḥ succeeded to the leadership of his followers but found himself hard pressed by Egyptian forces. By 1305/1887, two years after the Mahdī, Muḥammad Aḥmad had died, he had associated himself with the Mahdiyya, the movement of the Mahdī of the eastern Sudan. He adopted its outward forms – the patched *jubba* worn by the Mahdī's soldiers, Mahdist prayers and so on – and moved west, building up his army with captured slaves and Mahdist refugees as he marched. From 1309–10/1892 to 1301–11/1893 he attacked Baghirmi and Wadai and defeated both.

There is more than one account of Rābiḥ's relations with Borno. One has it that Rābiḥ now made preparations to attack Borno and that Shehu Hashimi, believing that Rābiḥ's target was the Sokoto caliphate, failed to make adequate preparations to defend his kingdom. It goes on to say that Rābiḥ agreed with Hayatu ɗan Sa'idu that they would join forces, conquer Borno, and then advance on Sokoto. In pursuit of this plan Rābiḥ attacked Borno in 1311/1893 and defeated Shehu Hashimi at the battle of Ngala. Shehu Hashimi fled and Rābiḥ occupied Kukawa and looted it. As a result of this defeat Shehu Hashimi was deposed and Kiyari, a son of the late Shehu Bukar, was appointed in his place. Bravely, Kiyari set out to recapture Kukawa, and although he inflicted an initial reverse on Rābiḥ, he failed to follow it up and was himself captured in a counter-attack. Rābiḥ executed him by having one of his senior officers cut his throat. It seems that this act, and others like it, was carried out in face of the strongest opposition from Malam Hayatu ɗan Sa'idu, an *ᶜālim*, for whom the strict observance of the Sharīᶜa concerning prisoners of war was still important. He and members of his family appear to have been deeply shocked by Rābiḥ's treatment of his prisoners. Many years later, Hayatu's son, Sultan Sa'idu ɓi Hayatu as he became known, recalled Rābiḥ's conduct at this time and denied that Rābiḥ was a true Muslim, adding that at this point in his career he had reverted to the worship of idols.[1] It is true that Hayatu and Rābiḥ had quarrelled and that Sultan Sa'idu ɓi Hayatu may therefore have been prejudiced against Rābiḥ. However, the facts of Rābiḥ's behaviour do seem to lend some justification to Sultan Sa'idu's opinion of him.

There is another version of this train of events that paints a rather different picture.[2] According to this, neither Malam Hayatu nor Rābiḥ wanted war with Borno but planned to attack the kingdom of Mandara. However, they were themselves attacked by the Borno army under Muḥammad Ṭāhir, whom they defeated. Even after this victory Rābiḥ waited at Ngala until he was again attacked by the forces of the Shehu of Borno. His execution of Kiyari, by having his throat cut, is said in this version to have been a mark of respect for his bravery! If this seems rather difficult for present-day readers to believe, the circumstances of the time must, in fairness, be pointed out. At that time in Muslim Africa, the cutting of the throat with a sharp knife, as the sacrificial ram is slaughtered, was regarded by some as a relatively swift and humane way of killing, while shooting was thought to be humiliating and brutal. It is difficult to say, in these days of very different attitudes almost a hundred years later, whether this justification for Rābiḥ's killing of an enemy captured in war ought to be taken seriously or not. I myself find the version given by Sultan Sa'idu ɓi Hayatu, despite its admitted partiality, the more convincing. His account not only condemns Rābiḥ's execution of Kiyari; it also seems to indicate by the words 'Rābiḥ conquered Borno with my father's flag'[3] that Rābiḥ and Hayatu did deliberately set out to conquer Borno before turning on Mandara.

After these events Rābiḥ moved south, to the town of Dikwa, which became his headquarters for the next seven years. However by now, the European powers had begun their occupation of West Africa and Britain, France and Germany had already agreed to divide Borno between them. They now began to move in to occupy their sectors and after a series of clashes between Rābiḥ's forces and the French, Rābiḥ was defeated and killed at the battle of Kusseri, in AD 1900. There now followed a confused period of plotting and rivalry among the European powers; each backed its own candidate as

Shehu in its own sector of Borno. Shehus were made and unmade as the balance of influence swung between the French and British. The British even reached agreement with Rābiḥ's son, Faḍl Allāh, to recognise him as ruler of Borno, but this plan was forestalled when the French defeated and killed him in October, AD 1901. When, in AD 1902, the British finally occupied their sector of Borno, they installed Bukar Garbai, a son of Shehu Ibrāhīm, as ruler. The ancient kingdom of Borno was thus broken apart by the European occupation. However in the British sector, which became part of the larger colonial entity of Northern Nigeria, the line of the Shehus continued to rule under British protection.

Islam in Borno under al-Kānamī and the Shehus

It was pointed out above that al-Kānamī was not primarily a reformer. During his period of effective rule over Borno, periodic attempts were certainly made to enforce Islamic observances more strictly, but his Islamic zeal expressed itself mainly in his conviction that the divine will required him to restore the ancient glory of the Islamic empire of Borno. Thus his energies were taken up in political and military endeavours, not in religious reform. The forceful extension of his power that this involved brought him into conflict with other religious authorities, who resented his pretensions. He clashed with Malam Fannami, a pious leader of the Borno Manga, a clan of the Kanuri. He also clashed with Shehu Abdullahi, the leader of an influential group of Borno *ᶜulamā'*.

The contrast between his practical approach and the Islamic idealism of the Fulani reformers is clearly demonstrated in his attitude to the Borno administration. He introduced considerably greater centralisation than did the Sokoto reformers; for provinces that had previously been largely independent were placed by him under the direct authority of Kukawa. He perhaps gave more power to local *quḍā* (sing. *qāḍī*), Muslim magistrates, than the *mais* had done; and he replaced Saifawid officials with his own people. However he did not make any essential change in the structure of Borno government; he showed none of the tendency of the Sokoto establishment to impose a model of the medieval ᶜAbbasid administration on Borno, nor did he copy their attempt to replace customary titles with classical Arabic ones. Under his rule, *kachellas*, *shettimas* and others retained their traditional titles and functions. In 1287/1870, the practice of dusting, so roundly condemned by Ibn Baṭṭūṭa in 8/14-century Mali, was still openly practised in the Borno court.

In one way Shehu al-Kānamī did increase Islamic influence; his was a period of close association with North Africa, especially Tripoli and the Fazzan, and he encouraged closer trading relations with these areas. He even formed military alliances with them in pursuit of his expansionist policies. The result was an increase in the North African presence in Borno, and of the influence of North African ways of life. Links which he and his successor, Shehu ᶜUmar, formed with Egypt and with Istanboul had the same effect of colouring Borno with Ottoman Islamic culture. Indeed, Shehu ᶜUmar may formally have recognised the authority of the Ottoman sultan, for he referred to himself at least once in a letter written to the Ottoman Pasha of Tripoli as the *Mütevelli*, that is 'deputy governor', of Borno province. This may have been a mere diplomatic courtesy, but nevertheless, by 1308/1891, a British traveller reported that the Ottoman flag was flying over the royal palace at Kukawa.

One significant development during the long reign of Shehu ᶜUmar was the growth of the influence of the *ᶜulamā'* in the Borno court. Shehu ᶜUmar himself was especially open to this influence, and relied largely on the advice of certain scholarly Shuwa Arab companions of his father. They were Malam Ibrāhīm Wadaima, Malam Tirab and Malam Ahmadu Gonimi. Later, al-Ḥājj Bashīr, a son of Malam Tirab, became his close adviser and friend. Another of his favourites was the Chief Qāḍī, Malam Muḥammad Njotkomami. This scholar was renowned throughout North Africa and the Sudan for his learning; and he attracted to himself a large following of students; but he also exercised considerable influence over Shehu ᶜUmar in political matters.

In one field of Islamic scholarship, Borno was especially renowned, namely caligraphy, the art of ornamental writing. This skill was applied especially to the production of handwritten Korans. These were exported and fetched high prices in North Africa and elsewhere in the Islamic world.

One most important aspect of Islamic development in Borno during the second half of the 19 century AD (AH 1266–1317) was the strong influence there of the *shurafā'*. Their presence is remarked on frequently by the German traveller, Nachtigal, who visited the Fazzan, Borno, Baghirmi and Wadai in the course of the years 1285–6/1869 to 1290/1873. It is clear from his reports that *shurafā'* had a strong hold over the populations of these areas; and that they spread popular forms of Islam.[4] Another important Muslim group that Nachtigal commented on frequently was the Sanūsiyya, whose members he describes as 'red-hot Christian-haters'.[5] The reasons for this, and the importance of this order in the west and central Sudan in general, are described in chapter 15.

NOTES

1 Jungraithmayr and Günther, 1977, p.113.
2 I am indebted to Mr John E. Lavers for this second version of the Rābiḥ affair. Mr Lavers was kind enough to set it out for me in private correspondence but informs me that he is preparing an account for publication. This will be awaited with great interest.
3 Jungraithmayr and Günther, 1977, p.113.
4 *Sahara und Sudan*, 2, p.546 and passim.
5 ibid., 1, p.194.

CHAPTER THIRTEEN

The development of European attitudes to Islam in West Africa

A complete account of how Christians and Muslims viewed each other at any given moment in their history would require an enormous number of individual case studies which cannot be undertaken in this book. What can be done is to consider certain views and attitudes that seem to have been widely held; and then draw conclusions.

Romanus Pontifex, Prester John and the Atlantic and Mediterranean axes

In 858/1454, Pope Nicholas V affirmed in his Papal Bull, *Romanus Pontifex*, the right of the Portuguese to the peaceful occupation of all the lands of the misbelievers that might be discovered along the west coast of Africa. This was part of a wider expansive movement on the part of Christian Europe, aimed mainly against Islam. As an apologist for Christian missions has put it,

> It is clear from all the early records that the bold and hardy men who made the great voyages, and the rulers and others who stood behind them, had two great purposes in view; first, to bring the light of the true Gospel to hitherto unknown nations who lived in darkness; and secondly . . . to enter into contact with the Christian Churches which were believed to be in existence in those lands, and so to make a great world alliance of the faithful, through which at last the power of the Muslims would be brought to the ground.[1]

In fact, this movement was not only an ideological attack by Christianity against Islam; it was also an attempt to destroy the Muslim hold over the trade of Asia and Africa; from it resulted the first direct contacts between Christians and Muslims in West Africa.

The earliest European contacts with the west and central Sudan that occurred during the Middle Ages took place by way of the Mediterranean axis, that is through North Africa. However, apart from a single unnamed European traveller who may have reached Ghana at the end of the 7/13 century, they were conducted through Muslim middlemen, or perhaps through Jews living in Islamic territory. Christians were rigorously excluded from entering the West African interior along the northern and eastern approaches, which the Muslims controlled. An Italian, Antoine Malfante, did get as far as Tuwāt in 851/1447. From Tuwāt he gathered a good deal of information, much of it rather fanciful, about the countries farther to the south, but it appears he himself never ventured there. It was, therefore, along the Atlantic axis, which was much less closely guarded by the Muslims, that European Christians, especially the Portuguese, concentrated their efforts.

It is probably the case that the Portuguese had already acquired some knowledge of the west coast of Africa by AD 1346; their main effort, however, began early in the following century. By AD 1448 it seems likely that they had reached as far south as Sierra Leone in the course of their explorations and were beginning to push their caravels, their small, ocean-going sailing ships, farther south. Then, in AD 1455, Alvise Da Ca Da Mosto (Cadamosto), a Venetian in the service of the Portuguese, set out on a voyage that took him along the coast of Senegal. In the following year, he visited the Gambia and sailed as far south as the Rio Grande. By AD 1460 the Portuguese were sufficiently in touch with the Muslims of the Senegambia to trade them swords and other weapons, an enterprise that was strongly condemned by the Portuguese crown; and for which they were punished by death if they were apprehended and captured.

In AD 1482 the Portuguese founded their fortress, São Jorge da Mina, present day Elmina, in Ghana; but it is clear that they were already well established there before the fortress was built. There is good reason to suppose that they had met with a few Dyula Muslim traders by *c.* 875–6/1471, and from the end of the 9/15 century onwards, contacts increased between Portuguese Christians and Muslims on the Senegambia and Guinea coast. In due course European Christians of other nationalities also arrived, to compete with the Portuguese.

These, however, were coastal encounters and before the 13/19 century few Europeans penetrated into the interior. The Portuguese tried to make contact with Timbuktu by way of Wadan, in Mauritania, during the second half of the 15 century AD (AH 854–905) but were apparently unsuccessful. The following century, in 940–1/1534, a Portuguese ambassador, Pere Fernandez, was sent to Mali. At about the same time they attempted to set up a trading station in Kano, which it seems they hoped to approach not from the Atlantic coast but by the eastern route, from Cairo. They failed to do so, because of opposition from the Cairene merchants.

Meanwhile, from the Mediterranean side a Florentine traveller, Benedetto Dei, who was an agent of the Florentine merchant house of Portinari, reached Timbuktu in 874–5/1470. It seems likely that he was only one of a number of Italian-speaking merchants who succeeded in making their way there at about this time. Then, by the middle of the 10/16 century, the Ragusans succeeded in penetrating beyond the Niger Bend, into the southern savanna. That they were able to do so was probably due to the fact that, although they were for the most part Christians, they were also subjects of the Ottoman Turkish empire and therefore enjoyed a special status in Islamic areas. It seems too, that other Christian, Italian-speaking merchants from Mediterranean cities may also have found their way into the savanna with the Ragusans. Perhaps this was because the Mediterranean trading area as a whole, both Christian and Muslim, had by then become so active that it was no longer practical or profitable for the Muslims to exclude them. By the middle of the 10/16 century a substantial community of Ragusans was established in Kano and it seems likely that similar communities existed in other Sudanic cities, although it cannot be proved that this was the case.

In 1099/1100/1688 a Belgian Franciscan friar, Brother Pieter Fardé, starting from North Africa, travelled south from Agades, passing through Gobir, Katsina, Zaria or Zamfara, on route to Kano. Some years later two

Roman Catholic Fathers, also starting from North Africa, penetrated to Katsina, where they died in 1123/1711. Early in the 12/18 century the newly appointed Catholic Prefect of Borno tried to reach his diocese by the eastern Saharan route from Egypt, by way of Sinnar.

These European Christians who succeeded in reaching the west and central Sudan, either along the Atlantic axis or the Mediterranean axis, had various motives. However, there is little doubt that it was primarily trade, rather than missionary ardour, that brought the early Portuguese. All the same, the desire to convert the Muslims of the Senegambia and the Guinea coast was certainly present. For example, Diogo Gomes, who visited the Gambia in AD 1456 or 1457, tells how a local chief, Nomymans, impressed by Diogo's success in theological argument with a local Muslim ᶜ*ālim* of the Azanaghi, the Sanhaja, wished to convert to Christianity and asked Diogo to baptize him. Diogo declined on the ground that he was not an ordained priest but promised to arrange for a priest to come to Nomymans, to instruct him in Christianity and then baptise him. Some two years later a priest was dispatched for this purpose. Ca Da Mosto, too, shows some interest in the conversion of the Muslims of the Atlantic coast; while the purpose of building the fort of São Jorge Da Mina was said to have been in order that it should serve as a bastion of the Catholic Church, and as a base for the conversion of the local people. Much religious ceremony attended the laying of the foundation stone. In fact, the primary purpose of São Jorge Da Mina was surely as a trading post for the trade in gold and as a stronghold from which to extend Portuguese influence inland. However, the religious motivation for building it should not be underestimated.

Along the Mediterranean axis, in contrast to the Atlantic case, there is little evidence, at least in the 9/15 and 10/16 centuries, of religious motivation among the Christians who approached the west and central Sudan from that direction. This was not because these Christians had different religious assumptions from those of their co-religionists on the Atlantic coast; it was simply because circumstances were different. The Ragusans appear to have been concerned essentially with trade, perhaps because their special status as citizens of the Ottoman Turkish empire depended on avoiding religious involvement. It is true that Vincenzo Matteo was searching for Prester John, as well as trading; and no doubt others of his countrymen had similar ambitions. There is no suggestion, however, in Anania's account that the Christian, Italian-speaking traders of the 10/16 century who penetrated into the Sahel and savanna country, combined missionary ardour with commercial zeal. Indeed, it would hardly have been practical for them to have done so. They were relatively few in number compared with their Muslim rivals and, unlike the Portuguese on the Atlantic coast, they were operating in the heartlands of *Dār al-islām*. It was not until the 11–12/17 century, with the arrival of occasional professional missionaries such as Pieter Fardé, that the Christian assault on Sudanic Islam began along the Mediterranean axis. Until the era of the colonial conquests, however, such attempts proved wholly impractical.

Whether these Europeans came to trade or to convert the local people, they all shared a similar attitude toward Islam. They accepted the assumptions of Christians of their day, that the world was divided into Christian believers and the rest who were misbelievers or downright infidels. They were wholly uncritical in their approach to their own beliefs and never doubted for one moment that Christianity was the true faith; believing all other religions, including Islam, to be false. The wrongness of the beliefs of other societies was taken for granted. Scepticism about those of their own society was, apparently, absent from their considerations. One has only to read the accounts of Ca Da Mosto, Diogo Gomes, João de Barros and other travellers to the Atlantic coast in those early times, to become aware of this automatic assumption of moral superiority over both Muslims and adherents of traditional African religions. Indeed, so convinced were the great majority of Christians of those days in what seemed to them the unassailable truths of their own religion, that many of them actually held the wholly incorrect belief that Islam was no more than a particularly wicked form of Christian heresy! However, this did not prevent them from trading with Muslims, or with animists and polytheists for that matter, when it suited them to do so.

The Christian attitude to Islam during the Middle Ages and the Renaissance era cannot be fully understood without some further discussion of the legend of Prester John. As was pointed out in chapter 6, there was up until the 17 century AD, a widespread belief in Christian Europe in the existence of this Christian priest-king (the word 'Prester' is an archaic English word meaning 'priest'). Somewhere in India, Ethiopia or the interior of Africa, this priest-king would one day march his armies to the aid of his fellow Christians of Europe, against the Muslims. The legend was closely associated with the Christians' attempt to extend their trading influence into *Dār al-islām*, an attempt that the Muslims had, understandably, long resisted. Many Christian merchant-adventurers, like Vincenzo Matteo, combined their trading ventures with the search for Prester John, but, as was pointed out in chapter 6, the Prester was no more than a figure of the Christian imagination. He represented Christian frustration in the face of the military and commercial rivalry of the Muslims; and his invincible armies, that were to march against Islam, were simply an expression of Christian wishful thinking.

The legend has a wider significance than that, however. The belief in Prester John points to the fact that, in those times, the Christians of Europe still felt physically threatened by the military power of Islam. Although they felt morally superior, on religious grounds, they had not yet acquired that easy confidence in their own military and technological superiority over non-European peoples that characterised the Europeans of the colonial era. This is, of course, not surprising when one recalls that the Muslim conquest of Spain was still fresh in their memories. It was not until AD 1492 that the Spanish Christians drove 'the Moors' out of the kingdom of Granada and thus virtually completed the Christian reconquest of Spain. Also, despite the spectacular, but in reality not very important, Christian naval victory over the Turks at Lepanto in 979/1571, Christendom still had to suffer the equally spectacular land defeat of the Portuguese at al-Qaṣr al-Kabīr, a few years later. The contest between the two ideologies was fought out on a basis of greater equality in the 10/16 century than it was in the centuries to come; and Christians at that time saw Islam at a physical threat as well as a theological error.

Yet, despite the ideological conflict that undoubtedly existed between Christianity and Islam, the activities of certain Christians and Muslims contributed in some measure to a common end; for, notwithstanding their religious differences, those who inhabited the Mediterranean and Adriatic seaboards shared, to some extent, a common culture. Muslim traders from North Africa and Egypt who pushed down toward the Niger Bend, like the Christian merchants from Ragusa and the merchant cities of the Mediterranean, all carried elements of this culture with them – firearms for example, and the military use of horses. This movement of the Mediterranean toward the Niger Bend reached a violent climax with the Moroccan conquest of Songhay. It may be seen as confirmation of Braudel's thesis of the 'greater Mediterranean' pushing its influence – whether Christian or Muslim – southward, across the Sahara toward the Sahel and the savanna. However, useful as this thesis is in helping to explain how the civilizations of the west and central Sudan developed, it must be remembered that the Mediterranean influence was not the only one at work. As was said above, equally strong pressures were being exerted from the Atlantic side. Here the Portuguese and, subsequently, Europeans of more northerly origins, were all imposing their presence and thus their culture, upon West Africa. There was an important difference, however, for unlike the case of the Mediterranean axis, which was common to Muslims and Christians, the influences that came in along the Atlantic axis were exclusively Christian; Muslims did not penetrate in significant numbers into West Africa by way of the Atlantic, at least not until the 20 century AD. Thus what Islamic influences did reach the Atlantic coast of West Africa, did so along an extension of the Mediterranean axis, down the western side of the Sahara and west from the Niger Bend. Moreover, whereas elsewhere in the west and central Sudan, the confrontation was between Islam and traditional religion, along the Atlantic coast it was, from the 9/15 century on, one not only between Islam and the traditional cults but also one between Islam and Christianity. This is still as true today as it was when Portuguese priests and Azanaghi *ᶜulamā'* competed for the souls and minds of Nomymans and his people; it must be seen as part of the heritage of the early contacts between Africans and Europeans in this area.

Away from the Atlantic coast, however, in the Niger Bend, in Hausaland, and in Borno, Christianity is a much less serious competitor with Islam. What competition there is, is the product of the colonial era because prior to AD 1900, Christianity in these areas was, for all practical purposes, non-existent.

The 'Age of the Enlightenment'

The medieval and Renaissance view of the world which was enshrined in *Romanus Pontifex*, was the Christian counterpart of the Islamic *Dār al-islām* and *Dār al-ḥarb* – a Christian world of true belief and a heathen world of misbelief (the notion of 'unbelief', that is atheism or agnosticism, barely existed in those times). It was challenged by that movement of thought in western Europe known as the 'Enlightenment' or the 'Age of Reason', which began in the 17 century AD and reached its peak at the end of the 18 century AD. What characterised this movement was the ready questioning of traditional assumptions in religion and politics; and an increasing interest in science and the nature of human society. One small consequence was the foundation, in London, in AD 1788, of the 'Society for the Promotion of the Discovery of the Interior of Africa'. This association initiated a series of expeditions to West Africa by British and German explorers whose main objective was usually geographical and botanical discovery. They were Christians in the sense that they had been brought up in a Christian culture and some, like Mungo Park and the Calvinist, Hugh Clapperton, were perhaps more devout than others. No doubt most of them started from the assumption that Christianity was superior to other systems of belief and cultures, but they were certainly not Christian missionaries. They were interested in what they found in West Africa and its societies not in changing these societies to conform to a Christian pattern. Among the best known of those who were English-speaking, or who were sponsored by English organisations, were Mungo Park, Denham, Clapperton, Oudney, Lander and, later, Heinrich Barth.

Among these men, Heinrich Barth was outstanding for his qualities of mind and character, as well as for the amount of information he gives on the history of the Islamic states of West Africa. He was a German, not an Englishman, but he was employed by the British Government; and his account of his travels was published in English as well as in German. His picture of Islam is, in general, sympathetic and kindly. For example:

> . . . about fifty little boys repeating with energy and enthusiasm the verses of the Koran which their master had written for them on their little wooden tablets. . . .[2]

He was also prepared to pray together with Muslims, something that apparently shocked some sections of Christian opinion in his day. Barth was typically a man of the Age of Reason; his tolerant attitudes are in striking contrast to those of most of the Christian missionaries of a later age, who are discussed further on in this chapter. As far as African Muslims were concerned, because of his knowledge of Arabic and his great interest in Islam and Sudanic history, he was recognised as a fellow scholar by the Sūdānī ᶜ*ulamā*'. This was in contrast with most other European travellers, who were regarded not only as non-Muslims but also as ignorant and uncultured.

Some of these early travellers, including Barth, were forced to disguise themselves as Muslim Arabs from time to time, otherwise, as Christians, their lives might have been in danger. This was mainly around Timbuktu, in the country of the Moors, and in the Sahara. They were often inconvenienced but in far less real danger in the Negro Sudan; for the most part they seem to have accepted this danger to which they were sometimes exposed, as just one more hazard of exploration. In their subsequent accounts they do not condemn Islam as a whole because of the excesses of some of its adherents, and all of them record their friendships with individual Muslims. Some of them, especially Barth, made considerable intellectual contacts with Muslim literates.

The message they took back to Europe was that trade with the Islamic Sudan was both possible and desirable, but unfortunately, in the end, they had little influence over the way in which events developed. This was to be shaped by the massive forces of international politics and by sweeping tides of emotion, not reason.

British public opinion and 'Mohammedanism'

Events in British India, especially the Indian Mutiny of 1273/1857 when some Muslim troops, as well as Hindus, turned on their British officers and killed them, deeply shocked British public opinion. These events served to turn public opinion against 'Mohammedanism', as Islam was normally referred to in those days. Thus much, if not all, of that opinion was already hostile to Islam at the time Heinrich Barth was about to publish his account of his travels in West Africa. The further hardening of this hostility was largely the consequence of British imperial policy during the 19 century AD.

The main preoccupation of British imperial policy-makers during this period was to safeguard the Indian empire and it was this that involved Britain in Egypt. Whoever controlled Egypt stood astride the route to India; but no sooner was Britain established in Egypt than she became involved in the affairs of the eastern, Nilotic Sudan. This area was in a greatly disturbed state owing to the activities of Muslim ivory and slave-traders, the Mahdī, Muḥammad Aḥmad and certain European adventurers. In 1302/1885, General Charles Gordon, already the hero of the British public because of his exploits in China, was killed by the Mahdī's men in Khartoum. Gordon was a strange, complex and interesting man who, regarded as a hero by the Victorians, was later denigrated, probably unfairly, in the course of a general reaction against Victorian attitudes and values. He was, first and foremost, a fine soldier and an extremely brave officer, who faced his death at Khartoum with an unflinching courage that won the admiration and respect of his Mahdist enemies. He was also a devout, and some might say a bigoted Christian, who openly supported the Christian missionaries. However, he was by no means unsympathetic to Islam; he insisted that his own Muslim soldiers should regularly attend Friday mosque and he had a number of friends among Muslim literates. He probably understood Islam better than most European Christians in his day. Despite this background, on his death he at once passed into British folklore as the heroic champion of Christian civilization against those whom the British public had now come to regard as 'wicked' Mohammedans. Public pressure to avenge him continued until Kitchener finally defeated the Mahdists at Omdurman in 1316/1896.

In East Africa after about 1298/1880 relations between Muslims, especially Arab Muslims, and Europeans became worse; Arab political ambitions in East Africa began to rise at this time and the Arabs now attempted to drive the Europeans out. This they did, largely, to safeguard their commercial interests, especially the slave trade. The series of incidents that arose as a result of the tension between Muslims and Europeans in East Africa drew the attention of the British public to the activities of certain notorious Muslim slave-traders. The public's attention became fixed on their exploits and these traders' misdeeds tended to condemn the whole of Islam. The anti-slavery propaganda of Christian missionaries and humanitarians simply served to sweep this hostile tide along.

This tide of British public opinion was given added momentum by events outside Africa. For centuries, areas of the Balkans, including the country now known as Bulgaria, had been part of the Ottoman Turkish empire. During the second half of the 19 century AD (AH 1266–1317) a nationalist movement arose there against the Turkish rule. This resulted in the emergence of the independent kingdom of Bulgaria in AD 1908, but before this happened, there was a bloody struggle between the Muslim Turks and the Christian Bulgarian nationalists, during which the Turks executed numbers of Bulgarian Christians. This aroused yet more public anger in Britain and Gladstone, Liberal

Prime Minister several times between AD 1868 and 1894, thundered against the 'unspeakable Turk'. He ignored the fact that the Bulgarian nationalists had provoked Turkish reprisals by their own savage attacks on Turkish Muslims, peasants and townsmen as well as soldiers. Neither he nor the British public were in a mood to see both sides of the question; the affair, known as the 'Bulgarian atrocities', became an ugly, emotive issue that gave another twist to the spiral of one-sided, anti-Mohammedan feeling in Britain, and indeed in much of western Europe.

So throughout the last half of the 19 century AD (AH 1266–1317) a series of events, none of them having any direct link with West Africa, had none the less turned a large section of British opinion against Mohammedanism. In consequence, many people were predisposed to look unfavourably upon it when the question of occupying West African Muslim territories was brought to their attention.

One of those who had most influence in forming British public opinion on this question during the last few years of the 19 century AD and the early 20 century was Flora Shaw, later Lady Lugard. This lady was for many years colonial correspondent of the London *Times*. She also became the wife of Sir Frederick, later Lord Lugard, the first High Commissioner of the Protectorate of Northern Nigeria and later Governor-General of the Colony and Protectorate of Nigeria. In AD 1906 she published a book entitled *A Tropical Dependency*, in which she was seeking to justify the British occupation of Hausaland that Lugard had just completed. The views she sets out in this book are those she had already been advocating for some years through her journalism, coupled with vigorous parliamentary lobbying and a general canvass of public opinion.

She starts from the notion that Islam in the west and central Sudan had once enjoyed a golden age of civilization but had then betrayed its own ideals and given itself over to decadence:

> . . . in the reign of the later Askias the strenuous spirit of heroism, which had marked the rise of that dynasty, was dead, and the aspiration to live on a higher plane of civilization . . . had given place to nothing more noble than a love of luxury.[3]

That there had been a high level of Islamic civilization in the 10/16-century west and central Sudan is by no means wrong. It is merely that the idea, as she presents it, is clouded in language of such sentimentality and prejudice that its true historical significance is lost. Her error was to see a moral issue rather than an objective historical phenomenon; and to see decadence where the historian sees simply change. She goes on, with equal prejudice, to describe the Muslim Fulani as 'a foreign power which fastened itself upon the necks of already existing and well-established native rulers',[4] and elsewhere speaks of 'the degradation of Fulani rule'.[5] In chapter XLIV of her book she gives a long and detailed account of slave-raiding. Finally, she concludes, Islam having failed, Britain can no longer avoid the responsibility to take over:

> Other nations . . . were quicker than Great Britain to perceive that the true solution of the problem of European relations with uncivilized Africa

> lay in accepting, not in abandoning, the responsibilities of civilized administration.[6]

Flora Shaw was typical of many informed and intelligent Europeans of her day in her attitude to Islam. She admired Muslim literacy and Islam's great cultural achievements, but she was unable to concede the Muslim right to a way of life and a system of morality that were, at many points, objectionable to Europeans raised in a Christian culture and ethic.

There were some thoughtful men in Britain, both in the government and among the general public, who questioned such views as Flora Shaw publicly expressed. For example, C.B. Adderley, Under-Secretary for the Colonies from AD 1866–8, spoke out bluntly against the 'wasteful and mischievous' policy of 'sentimental colonisation'.[7] He went on to argue that, in West Africa:

> The future lies between French and Mahometan conquest – and we should not lose time in honourably getting out of the way.[8]

The most outspoken champion of Islam in West Africa was the scholar, traveller, author, and vigorous free-thinker, Sir Richard Burton. Already an accomplished Arabist with much experience in the Arab Middle East, Burton had also travelled widely on the West Coast of Africa, including Yorubaland, Dahomey and the Cameroons. He did not approve of Christian missionaries and made no secret of his admiration for Islam. He refers to it as 'the young and vigorous creed' and describes the cry of the muezzin, whose duty it is to call the faithful to prayer, as 'how much more human and heart-stirring than the clang of the brazen-tongued bell!' In speaking of Yorubaland and the attempts of the Abeokutans to regain the territories taken from them as a result of the Fulani *jihād* he says:

> I doubt the probability of their so doing. The weak outlying states of El Islam, Ilori, for instance – now the last ripple of the mighty wave urged southwards by an irresistible current – though at present unable to sweep away the barriers of Paganism, is strong enough to resist any encroachments. And the day will come when the Law of the Prophet shall rule throughout the lands, when Ethiopia shall stretch forth her hands unto Allah, and shall thus rise to her highest point of civilization. Meanwhile, those who support Abeokuta are but shoring up a falling wall.[9]

Burton's opinions carried some weight, especially among those who disliked the moral judgements of missionaries and humanitarians. However these moral judgements continued to be widely and uncritically accepted by the British public.

Less deliberately provocative in his defence of Islam than Burton, but probably just as effective, was the West Indian-born writer and educationalist, Edward Blyden. He held many offices in Liberia and Sierra Leone and was, perhaps, the first true African nationalist. Blyden regarded Islam as the most effective instrument in moulding African intellectual and social character and as the most effective educational force in Africa. His views were widely known and were certainly familiar to Lugard who used them, when it suited him, to refute the more extreme arguments of the Christian missionaries.

Some French views on Islam in West Africa

In France, as in Britain, views about Islam were largely the outcome of attitudes that sprang from French domestic politics and France's involvement in international affairs. They had little direct connection with Islam as such, let alone Islam in West Africa.

One powerful influence that coloured the French view was the republicanism that was the heritage of the French Revolution and the Napoleonic Wars. From AD 1789 to 1815, the French first toppled their own monarchy replacing it with a Republic, and then went on, forcibly, to do the same in those parts of Europe that fell to their revolutionary armies. Many of the early revolutionaries were atheists and strongly anti-clerical, that is opposed to the power of priests, and rejected both Christianity and the authority of the Roman Catholic Church. Therefore, having no religious beliefs of their own, they did not judge non-Christian religions by comparing them unfavourably with Christianity. Furthermore, during the French occupation of Egypt, Bonaparte had become captivated by Islam; he openly admired Muḥammad above the Christian Jesus and deliberately cultivated the Egyptian *ᶜulamā'*. Indeed, many Muslims believed that he was, or was about to become, a Muslim.

The consequence of all this was that by 1214/1800, many Frenchmen were not only disposed to look favourably on Islam in general, but were also very sympathetic towards Islamic revolutions, especially when these seemed to be aimed against tyrannical 'monarchies'. Such attitudes appear clearly in the account of the young French traveller Gaspard Théodore Mollien, who explored the Senegambia in 1233–4/1818. He seems to have been a Christian, but he certainly displays a very open-minded attitude to Islam that is obviously influenced by republicanism. He comments warmly on the manner in which Islam had inspired the Negroes with a spirit of independence; and goes on to state, with evident approval, that all Islamic states he visited were 'federalist', while the non-Muslims 'groaned beneath the most atrocious tyranny'. The fact that this was, to say the least, a considerable over-simplification, is beside the point; it is his attitude that matters. Elsewhere, speaking of the movement of ᶜAbd al-Qādir in Futa Toro, he says:

> Towards the end of the 18 century, Abdoul [ᶜAbd al-Qādir], a simple mahometan priest, raised the standard of revolt; the enthusiasm for liberty and religious fanaticism made his little band invincible; he gained the victory and made the *amtore* prisoner, exposed him for a whole day to the heat of the sun, then stripped him publicly of all marks of royalty and caused him to return to the condition of a simple subject.[10]

This uncritical approval for revolutionary republicanism – including its brutalities – continues throughout his account and it clearly reflects the attitudes of many Frenchmen in his day.

Mollien was followed by another young French explorer, René Caillié. From 1239–40/1824 to 1243–4/1828, Caillié travelled across the Sudan, from Senegal to Timbuktu, and then on across the Sahara to Morocco. Unlike Mollien, whose background was that of the first Napoleonic empire, Caillié was a monarchist who even named certain islands in the Niger after members of the French royal family. Although, throughout his journey, he deliberately passed himself off as a Muslim, or at least as one who was about to convert to Islam, he was, none the less, a devout Catholic. This, of course, was to be expected in a supporter of the monarchist cause in France, but his preoccupations were with geography and science, not theology. When he mentions Islam, it is usually to comment peevishly on Muslim fanaticism, or scornfully on what he considers to be the laziness and lack of hygiene in the Muslim communities through which he passed. Like Mollien, he seems to have found Moorish and Fulani Muslims much more hostile than black Sūdānī Muslims, and was certainly unfortunate in his choice of guides. Despite the fact that he knew Arabic well and was able to recite the Koran and certain Islamic prayers, he shows none of Mollien's friendliness towards Islam, nor did he ever establish any real intellectual contact with Muslim literates.

In AD 1852 the Second Empire was set up in France under the Emperor Napoleon III. Far from being revolutionary and anti-clerical, his administration was based on the support of the French middle class and on that of the Catholic Church. Indeed, at one time, Napoleon III liked to think of himself as the protector of Catholicism, not only in France but also abroad. Under him, the Second Empire entered the colonial scramble in Africa in the conviction that France had a mission and a duty to spread French Catholic culture and civilization. Typical of this school of French thinking were Frédéric Carrère and Paul Holle, joint authors of *De la Sénégambie française*, published in AD 1855. Carrère was an official of the Imperial Government; Holle, a citizen of Saint Louis of mixed French and African descent was Commandant of the French fort at Médine and was an excellent soldier by all accounts. Their book was intended not only to describe the customs and institutions of the Senegambian people but also to advocate certain views as to how French possessions in Senegambia ought to be governed. They make their position clear in such passages as the following:

> In these parts, as elsewhere, the mission of our country seems higher [than mere commercial profit]; is it not to march at the head of progress in initiating the peoples to civilization? How shall France be the foremost Catholic power if, by all means, preaching, war, commerce, she does not lead the people with whom God has put her into contact, to moral and material betterment?[11]

They go on to say: 'Already the children of France, their weapons in their hands, map out the path of the future'.[12] Their attitude to Islam was wholly hostile. They refer to it in their book as *cette idolâtrie*, 'that idolatry'; and make no secret of their wish to see it replaced by Christianity. For example:

> The Islamic idea is here still in its period of development, and in consequence, of fanaticism, and St Louis has become, as it were, the focus of idolatry, above all in that the mosque, confronting our church, has given an official consecration to Mahometanism.[13]

In reference to the ᶜ*ulamā*',

> . . . preachers of a doctrine of which the effect is to maintain or throw back

> the Blacks into barbarism, by rendering them deaf to the teachings of a divine religion which will infallibly bring about their intellectual and moral transformation?[14]

There is much more of the same viewpoint and with the triumph of the Catholic party under the Second Empire, there is no doubt that such views became influential in French public opinion – especially in the French settlement of Saint Louis.

In 1245–6/1830 the French deposed the Dey of Algiers. This was the beginning of a costly war against the Algerian Muslims that led to the final occupation of the whole country by the French in 1260/1844, but the fighting continued, on and off, until AD 1904. French attitudes to Islam were coloured by it; the fierce hostility of the Algerian Muslim leader, ᶜAbd al-Qādir of Mascara, towards the French intensified anti-Islamic sentiments among them. Moreover, they tended to regard their Muslim enemies as inferiors and extended this attitude to Muslims as a whole. Islamic states in West Africa had, for a long time, imposed certain taxes and levies on the trade between them and the French merchants of Saint Louis. Before about 1245–6/1830, this had been accepted by the French as normal practice, but after the outbreak of the Algerian war they became increasingly reluctant to pay taxes to 'inferior' rulers. They also became more apt to regard Islam as the enemy of the French civilizing mission in West Africa.

The French writer and traveller Henri Duveyrier was typical of this attitude that interpreted Islam not according to its own values and beliefs, but in terms of its effect on the extension of French influence. *C.* 1277/1860, he visited Ghat and was unfavourably impressed by the Sanūsiyya. In AD 1864, he published his book, *Les Toureg du Nord*. He does not condemn Islam in the same wholesale fashion as Carrère and Holle, he maintains that there are tolerant and cooperative Muslims, with whom the French can work. However, there are also 'fanatics', who must be regarded as enemies:

> The organisation of this work imposes on me the obligation to deal first with the Sanūsīs, our enemies, before concerning myself with our friends, the Tijānīs, the Bakkā'īs and the Awlād Sīdī al-Shaykh, in order the better to demonstrate that, if blind fanaticism can create difficulties for us, enlightened reason is powerful enough to assist us to overcome them.[15]

There is nothing surprising about Duveyrier's views, which should be read in the context of the times and the society in which he lived. He was not an unreasonable man and although he was a convinced believer in the French mission, he was certainly a good deal less intolerant than Carrère and Holle. However, his views demonstrate the point that among the men of those days – French, British and Germans alike – there was a widespread tendency to assume that their own, western European, Christian standards and values must be superior to those of peoples of other cultures and religions. They tended to ignore the possibility that Muslims, for example, might have different standards and values by which they preferred to live. This view of Islam, that saw it simply in terms of how it fitted, or failed to fit in with French imperial ambitions, became that of the early French colonial administrations in West Africa.

A most important factor in forming the French outlook on Islam was anti-slavery sentiment, of which the French Roman Catholic churchman, Cardinal Lavigerie, was the leading exponent. Lavigerie shared the views of the British missionary, Livingstone, whom he much admired, and like Livingstone, he headed a major propaganda attack against slavery, especially in Africa. He was successful and his efforts led to the setting-up of an international conference on the subject in Brussels, in AD 1890. This conference resolved that slavery could only be fought by extending European control in the areas where it existed; it thus implied approval for further colonial occupations of Muslim territories. Lavigerie's views had a profound influence on Catholic opinion in France and indeed elsewhere in Europe.

One section, at least, of French opinion was more favourable than the rest towards Islam during the second half of the 19 century AD (AH 1266–1317). It consisted of supporters of that policy with regard to Algeria known as *Royaume arabe*. These were mainly officials and soldiers serving in Algeria who favoured racial integration between French and Arabs; and advocated Algerian Arab independence within the French community. They were, perhaps, the heirs to Bonaparte's sympathetic attitude towards Muslims. At one point members of the *Royaume arabe* school gained considerable influence over the Emperor Napoleon III. However, they were fiercely opposed by the Catholic interest at court but some *Royaume arabe* ideas were carried over into the field of French relations with Islam in the west and central Sudan. General Louis Faidherbe, a highly intelligent and admirable soldier, who was for some years governor of Senegal, was probably influenced by them to some extent.

Some German views

Although Germany was a late-comer to the field of colonialisation in West Africa, her contribution to West African exploration was early and important. In AD 1798 a young German, Frederick Hornemann, set out from Cairo and followed a caravan to Siwa and Murzuk. He is thought finally to have reached Nupeland, where he perished. Heinrich Barth and his companion on part of his journey, Adolf Overweg, were also Germans, but employed by the British government, as was Eduard Vogel. He was a German who travelled in the company of two Englishmen, Church and McGuire, as far as Wadai where he perished. Then came Gerhardt Rohlfs, who travelled from Tripoli to Borno, on through Bauchi to the Benue and then to Lagos, between the years AD 1864 to 1868. At about the same time, the German Dr Gustav Nachtigal, who has been mentioned above, was travelling in the area of Borno and Chad. There were a number of other German explorers who followed them but these were the pioneers.

Among the most important of these German pioneers, from the point of view of the completeness of his account, is Gerhardt Rohlfs. He left behind detailed reflections on what he saw and experienced on his journey, upon which the following assessment of his attitude to Islam is based.

Gerhardt Rohlfs was decidedly pro-Christian and, like Flora Shaw, he adopted a strongly moralistic and rather overbearing attitude towards Islam, holding it to task for its alleged inadequacies. He assumed that there was a clear Christian duty to civilise Islam, that was not open to question. He held the view that, in North Africa and the Sahara, this could best be done by persuading Arab and Berber Muslims to wear European clothes.[16] He also advocated that the European powers should set up consulates in the Fazzan and Ghadames for the purpose of purchasing young slaves; the Christian missions could then convert them and thus establish centres of Christianity in the heart of Islamic territory. He felt this was a better way of achieving the goal of conversion than sending 'costly missions to Mohammedan countries and to inner Africa'.[17] He frequently complained about the Muslim fanaticism that he experienced without, however, displaying much understanding of the factors that caused it – among which may have been his own attitudes. Like Carrère and Hollo, he openly advocated direct military action – in this case the armed occupation of the Jos Plateau in Hausaland – 'so that a strong barrier could be placed against the farther spread of Islam. . .'[18] Rohlfs was greatly concerned about the slave-trade and what he saw of it during his travels shocked him deeply. Perhaps this had something to do with the fiercenesss of his attack on Islam, and his one-sided approval of Christian missions.

From AD 1869 to 1874 (AH 1285–1291), while Rohlfs had still not completed his journey, Gustav Nachtigal travelled through those countries now known as Libya, Chad, Niger, Nigeria, Cameroon and Sudan. His comment on the Sanūsiyya has been noted above but apart from this he gives only incidental information about Islam. As A.G.B. and H.J. Fisher point out:

> While in one way or another the background of Islamic society was evident wherever he went, he apparently did not think of attempting any thorough-going analysis of Islam in the Sudanic countries.[19]

It is interesting, and to his credit, to note that, unlike Caillié and others, Nachtigal never attempted to disguise himself as a Muslim; and made no secret of the fact that he was a Christian. However, he came to no harm, for although certain Sanūsīs plotted to kill him, he was protected by the goodwill of more moderate Muslims.

One of the chief architects of German public opinion concerning Islam was the civil servant and orientalist, C.H. Becker. He wrote a number of studies of Islam in both East and West Africa. As B.G. Martin puts it, his work 'shows many of the views and attitudes of an "establishment" German orientalist towards the "problem of Islam" in what was then a German colony.'[20] The expression 'the problem of Islam' is central. As in the case of the Frenchman Duveyrier, it expressed the attitude that Islam was to be judged not by its own cultural achievements, nor by the intellectual power of its theology, or even its success as a social and political system, but simply in the light of its usefulness or otherwise to German colonial policies. To quote Martin again:

> Becker . . . is none too sympathetic to Africans, thinks that Islam and its spread may be a serious challenge to German colonial rule, and feels that 'stiff punishments' are 'indispensable' to the German authorities in warding off the doings of Muslim 'troublemakers' from outside the colony. Having these views, he is completely a man of his time and class. . . .[21]

Becker was also strongly sympathetic to Christian, especially German, missionary activity; he speaks approvingly of the missionaries' attempts to convert Muslims. Nevertheless, Becker had a profound and scholarly understanding of Islam and its culture. He was no mere propagandist but an orientalist of merit, informed enough to contradict the statements of certain missionaries that Islam in East Africa was in retreat. Despite his advocacy of 'stiff punishments', he also seems to have understood that military repression of Islamic movements simply gave rise to more intense Muslim opposition to the German colonial authorities.

The first German colonial administration in East Africa was established in AD 1885 (AH 1302–3). No sooner was it set up than the Germans found themselves confronted by the opposition of East African Arabs and, later, by such Muslim slavers as the notorious Rumaliza. This resistance was certainly partly in defence of Muslim trading, especially slaving, interests but it was also ideological. It was closely associated with Mahdism and, like the Muslims of West Africa, the East African Muslims saw the Europeans and their armies as the followers of the great tyrant Anti-Christ, (Ar. Dajjāl), who was to come before the End of Time. Like the Sanūsīs of West Africa, they believed it their duty to resist these evil forces, until the Mahdī appeared to drive them back for ever. For the Germans this was all a manifestation of Muslim fanaticism, and as a result, they evolved an official policy that distinguished between 'genuinely pious Muslims' and 'Islamic agitators'. While they attempted to suppress the agitators, they declared that German policy 'does not signify any limitation of Islamic belief'. Again, the distinction they were really making was that which Duveyrier had made in the French case, between Muslims who were prepared to cooperate with the colonial regime and those who were not.

German experience in East Africa, the influence of Lavigerie over German Catholics, and the propaganda of powerful German Protestant mission interests, all combined to turn much German public opinion against Islam. There was increasing pressure from the Reichstag, the German parliament, to cooperate with other European powers to suppress slavery. Inevitably, this meant the use of force against Muslims and the occupation of Muslim territory; as colonial officials constantly pointed out, there was no other way to comply with German popular demand.

Throughout all this, the German Imperial Government found itself at odds, to some extent with public opinion. First, Count Bismarck, the great German imperial Chancellor, was cautious about colonial adventuring. He much disliked the French policy of outright colonising. At most, he favoured setting up 'protected territories', where Germany simply protected her trading interests, without committing herself to more permanent and far-reaching forms of intervention. Moreover, the Franco-Prussian war of AD 1870–1 had caused the Germans to seek the support of the Muslim Turks against the French in North Africa. Thus, in purely political terms, the German Government was inclined to regard the Islamic world, or at least the Ottoman Empire, as a possible friend. Despite friction between German colonial authorities and 'Muslim fanatics', the official German link with Islamic Turkey was preserved through a carefully cultivated friendship between the German Kaiser and the Sultan of Turkey. Indeed, Nachtigal sometimes tried to use this to win the goodwill of Muslims in the Sudan, but it did not always have the desired result. The Sanūsīs, in particular, were often as hostile to the Turks in Istanboul as they were to the Christian imperialists and missionaries.

In general, the German attitude to Islam resembled that of other European nations, in that it was made up of a variety of different sets of moral, religious, and political assumptions and attitudes, few of which had anything directly to do with Islam as a system of belief or a way of life. Broadly speaking, German public opinion outside official circles was disapproving, if not actively hostile, and for the German Government Islam was a 'problem' in the colonial sphere. However against this stood the fact that it was a potential ally in the international sphere.

The Christian missionaries

Efforts by Christian missionaries to convert Muslims to Christianity go back at least to the 7/13 century. The *Summa contra gentiles* of the well-known Christian theologian Thomas Aquinas (*b.* AD 1225 or 1227; *d.* AD 1274) which was written between 657–8/1259 and 659–60/1261, was intended for the use of preachers to the Muslims. Moreover, as from the beginning of that century, both Franciscan and Dominican friars were preaching against Islam in Tunis. They had little success however; and a number of them lost their lives in the attempt. These missions preceded the work of the better-known early 8/14-century missionary to the Muslims, Ramon Lull, who is often thought to have been the first to undertake such preaching.

It has been said that, after Lull, Christian missionary effort among the Muslims lapsed until the colonial conquests of the 19 and 20 centuries AD offered a renewed opportunity to resume them. This is somewhat misleading, however, for the Christian missionary attack upon Islam has never really ceased. It has diminished from time to time but has been intensified again as soon as circumstances permitted. For example, the Portuguese in India continued mission work among Indian Muslims throughout the 10/16 century and beyond and their efforts there were remarkably successful. Along the Atlantic coast of Africa, also, the Portuguese continued to send in priests with their traders. Here, too, they were quite successful in coastal areas, although they never penetrated far inland. Along the Mediterranean axis, however, Christian missionary effort was limited, and was confined to the North African coast until the 11–12/17 century, when individual Catholic missionaries tried to reach the Muslims of the Sahel and savanna. However, this was not because the Christians of the Mediterranean area had voluntarily withdrawn from missionary activity; it was because the Muslims were powerful enough to deny them the opportunity to practise it. By the 19 century AD the situation had changed, for by this time the technological and economic power of western, Christian Europe had reached a peak. Part of its manifestation was the establishment of British rule in India, and this gave an impetus to renewed Christian missionary endeavour in Muslim areas there. W.G. Palgrave, writing in AD 1872, drew attention to the danger that an Islamic revival in India posed for the British Raj and this was a direct encouragement to the missionaries.[22] Works like W.W. Hunter's *Our Indian Mussulmans*[23] served to arouse interest in areas of the Islamic world that had suddenly become open to Christian influence. The missionaries could now go to these areas and work under the protection of the imperial administrations. The importance of India in arousing missionary interest in Islam is well brought out by Canon C.H. Robinson. He pointed out that the Queen of England (Queen Victoria) had, as Empress of India, more Muslim subjects than the Sultan of Turkey, and added, 'This alone is sufficient to justify the most careful attention that can be paid to the present and future prospects of Islam. . . .'[24] Tales of substantial conversions of Indian Muslims to Christianity made the missionaries eager for similar successes elsewhere.

As their ability to penetrate into the Islamic world increased, so the missionaries began to formulate their own ideological attitudes towards Islam. One idea that particularly appealed to them was that of a renewed Crusade, to win back the former Christian lands of the Middle East and North Africa, now held by the Muslims, or 'Mohammedans' as they called them. Thus Eugene Stock, the historian of the Church Missionary Society, writes, 'The false Prophet still holds sway over the sacred lands of the East. . .'[25] and 'The great mosque [of Damascus] was once a Christian church – fit sign of the usurpation of Christ's throne in those lands by the False Prophet. . .'[26] S.W. Zwemer, a missionary who wrote a number of books on Islam, says 'The old churches of the East, by their unfaithfulness, were the occasion of the great apostasy of Islam; their revival is the pledge of its downfall.'[27] Robinson speaks of 'the Church of North-west Africa which, though at one time represented by nearly seven thousand bishops, has been entirely swept out of existence by Mohammedanism'[28]. In the same book he quotes Pope Urban II's call to the Crusades and adds 'if we have but ears to hear, a call, not unsimilar to that which shook all Christendom eight centuries ago, is sounding in our ears today. . . .'[29]

The attitudes of these missionaries towards Islam are shown yet more clearly in the titles of the books they wrote as well as by what they said in them. C.H. Robinson published a work called *Mohammedanism: Has it any future?* In it he argues that:

> As long as the Koran receives the veneration which it now does from Mohammedans – as long, i.e. as the faith of Islam itself continues – development from within will be impossible,

and goes on to quote from Milne's *Palm Leaves*:

> Mohammed's truth lay in a holy book,
> Christ's in a sacred life,
> So while the world rolls on from change to change,
> And realms of thought expand,
> The letter stands without expanse or range,
> Stiff as a dead man's hand.[30]

S.W. Zwemer called one of his books *Mohammed or Christ?* and another, *Islam, a Challenge to the Faith.* Undoubtedly, the missionaries saw Islam not just as a different faith from their own, but as an enemy. Stock wrote that British influence in Turkey provided an 'opportunity . . . for a direct missionary attack upon Mohammedan Turkey'.[31] Elsewhere he describes the well-known missionary Rev. G.C. Pfander (fl. AD 1854) as 'the most distinguished Christian champion in the war with Islam'.[32]

The Keswick Movement and the Cambridge men

Modern evangelical Christianity owes much to the European Pietist Movement, that arose in the 17 century AD. Whereas the traditional Christian Church in the Middle Ages had placed much of its emphasis on ritual and observance of the outward forms of Christianity, at least as far as its everyday congregations were concerned, the Pietists placed their emphasis on individual conversion and witness; and on the acceptance of Jesus Christ as the individual's own, personal saviour. This emphasis on the role of Jesus Christ as a personal redeemer became increasingly central as Pietism and similar movements developed; it became known as 'Evangelism'.

In Britain, one consequence of this evangelical trend in Christian thought was the founding, in the 19 century AD of what was called the 'Keswick Movement', a Protestant and largely Methodist movement. Its doctrine was 'the infinitely important reality of self-surrender to the Lord [Jesus Christ]'[33]; the Pietist influence is thus clear. The Keswick Movement held its annual conferences at Keswick, in the English Lake District but it had considerable influence in Cambridge University, which became the centre of much student evangelical fervour. Many of these students joined the Keswick Movement or the Mildmay Conference, a similar Protestant evangelical organisation. Stock refers to these young Cambridge evangelists as 'the aggressive evangelical set' and he attributes the extension of the Keswick Movement into the missionary field and the founding of the 'Keswick Missionary Movement' to their enthusiasm. At the same time other evangelical Christian missionary movements were founded, for example the 'Student Volunteer Missionary Union'. The nature of their approach to missionary work can be judged from the titles of their publications; one was called 'Make Jesus King'. This contained a series of diagrams illustrating the non-Christian areas of the world that were ripe for missionary intervention. The Student Volunteer Missionary Union now adopted the slogan 'Evangelization of the World in this Generation', which generated considerable enthusiasm among the more fervently inclined. Certain influential churchmen took up the theme and in AD 1894 the Bishop of Exeter gave an address in which, to quote Stock, he 'put the Evangelization of the World in its right place as the Church's primary duty'.[34] S.W. Zwemer was a leading member of the Keswick Missionary Movement and Stock describes him as 'the most prominent leader in Christian effort among the Moslems'. The Movement's objective as regards Islam is well expressed in the Introduction to one of his books, *The Mohammedan World of Today*. He says, 'Mohammedans need what all men need – salvation through Jesus Christ'[35] and goes on '[Muslims] need an apostle from their own ranks; a Mohammedan scholar . . . thoroughly converted to faith in Jesus, the Son of Mary, as the only Redeemer, who will proclaim that . . . they are all called to accept Christ.'[36]

The history of Christian missionary activity among the Muslim Hausas is a big subject. It has been dealt with by Professor J.F. Ade Ajayi in his book *Christian Missions in Nigeria 1841–1891*; and it is neither possible nor necessary to repeat the story here. It is worth noting that J.A. Robinson, C.H. Robinson, Wilmot-Brooke, Walter Miller and Bishop Tugwell, all of them early missionaries who penetrated into the Muslim areas of Nigeria and in some cases deep into Hausaland, were associated with the Keswick Movement; and all were enthused by the same evangelical commitment to Jesus Christ as a personal redeemer, which they itched to impose upon Muslims. Bishop Tugwell, in complaining of what he felt to be the lack of support for missionary work in Nigeria, said, '[The Church's] sons dare not venture for Christ that which every soldier will gladly venture for his Queen and country, viz. his health and his life.'[37] Protesting against the mild but sensible restrictions placed by the early British administration on the activities of his missionaries in northern Nigeria, he said, 'the name of Christ must not be proclaimed lest this blighting system [the government of the Muslim emirs under the supervision of British officials] should be over-turned'.[38] The way in which this notion of personal commitment to Christ obsessed the minds of these evangelicals becomes especially apparent in the writings of Walter Miller. Miller pursued a long personal vendetta against the Emir Aliyu of Zaria; and in the end succeeded in having him deposed and exiled by the British administration. Having destroyed him, Miller then wrote of him that he was 'such a man as one feels Jesus of Nazareth would have loved and called to Himself with the words: "Follow me." And he would have followed.'[39]

Walter Miller lived for many years in Zaria, where he was allowed to carry on with his missionary activities during the British administration. He undoubtedly exerted considerable personal influence over Lugard, particularly in matters pertaining to education. Miller wrote much about Islam in Nigeria but little of it is edifying. The following quotations, taken from *The Mohammedan World of Today*, demonstrate the degree of prejudice and downright spitefulness that he and his kind displayed towards Islam. He wrote:

> This lack of all homelife; the utter prostitution of virtues; the total disregard of morals, all these have brought moral ruin to the people and made West Africa a seething sink of gross iniquity,

and

> Boys and girls grow up in the densest atmosphere of sin, where there is hardly a redeeming feature, and all this under the strictest adherence to the outward laws of Islam.[40]

Apart from their unpleasantness, such statements about Islamic societies, and about Islam as a religion, are objectively absurd.

The controversy over Islam

The evangelicals, like C.H. Robinson, Miller and the rest, did not have it all their own way and one of the most interesting aspects of the missionary preoccupation with Islam was a controversy it provoked within their own ranks. The great majority of the missionaries were hostile to Islam – at least that is the conclusion that must emerge from the study of their writings – but in AD 1874 a certain R. Bosworth Smith published a book called *Mohammed and Mohammedanism*. In it he argued that, while the ultimate victory of Christianity was inevitable and desirable, the best way to achieve this was to cooperate with Islam. He went on to argue that Islam should not be opposed because, although less beneficial than Christianity, it did put an end to drunkenness, human sacrifice, polytheism and so on. The central point of his argument is expressed in the following quotation, '. . . the main part of the continent [of Africa], if it cannot become Christian, will become what is next best to it, Mohammedan.'[41] Some churchmen agreed with him and argued that the missionaries should concentrate on converting 'pagans' and not waste time and money on missions to Muslims. However, Bosworth Smith was bitterly attacked by the fervent evangelicals, especially certain Keswick men like Canon Robinson and Zwemer, who accused him of 'extravagant glorification of Islam'. Nevertheless Bosworth Smith's ideas may have been important in the history of Nigeria, for Lugard, despite his friendship with Miller, quotes him with approval in his *Dual mandate*.[42] Lugard and many of his officers resisted the militant forward policies of Bishop Tugwell of Lagos, and the other evangelicals in Nigeria, with arguments that often seem to echo those of Bosworth Smith.

German and French missions

What has been said above applies to the missionary movement in Britain, but similar Protestant missionary movements arose in Germany, as well as in Denmark and Switzerland. The most important of them was the Basel Mission which also had direct roots in Pietism. It was very much a Christian peasant movement, preaching what has been described as 'Village Christianity'. To the emphasis on personal commitment to Jesus Christ was added a belief in the religious virtue of physical labour, especially work on the land. For this reason the doctrines of the Basel Mission and others like it have been aptly described as 'The Bible and the Plough'. In this respect the Basel Mission differed from the Keswick evangelicals, for the latter were, in the main, not from peasant communities but from the middle class. Apart from their fervour for Jesus Christ, which seems to have been common to most missions of the 19 century AD including Roman Catholic missions, the values and attitudes of the British evangelicals were middle class, not peasant. The Basel Mission was especially active in the German Cameroons and the British Gold Coast, now Ghana.

French missions were mainly Catholic. Their theology therefore differed somewhat from that of the Protestants, especially, of course, in the prominence they gave to the cult of the Virgin Mary. Most of them however, shared the notion of Jesus Christ as redeemer, as well as that of the sanctity of physical labour. Among the more important of the Roman Catholic missions that worked in West Africa were the Fathers of the Holy Spirit, founded in 1848, the Lyons Society of African Missions, founded in 1856, and the White Fathers, founded by Cardinal Lavigerie in 1868. The White Fathers suffered heavy loss of life in their early attempts to convert Saharan Muslims. After this experience they abandoned attempts to win converts from Islam by direct preaching and contented themselves with living in Muslim areas and seeking to influence Muslims by personal example. They made few conversions, but it seems they gained the confidence and respect of the Muslims to a greater extent than did the more aggressive Protestants.

The missionaries' failure

With the possible exception of the White Fathers in their later years, these Christian missionaries, and especially the Protestant evangelicals, did not want simply to communicate with Muslims in order to understand Islam, nor even to have the opportunity of explaining Christianity to the Muslims. They wanted no less than the total destruction of Islam as a living faith; and its replacement by the wholesale conversion of Muslims to Christianity. This conclusion is inescapable from the study of their writings, whatever subsequent excuses have been made for them by Christian apologists. It is true that some courageous but unrealistic individuals, like Wilmot Brooke, believed they could accomplish this by living among Muslims and preaching to them; and they deliberately avoided the protection of the secular colonial authorities. Such persons usually perished – by disease against which they had no immunity, not at the hands of Muslims. However most, like Bishop Tugwell and Walter Miller, were only too anxious to enlist the military might of the colonial regimes to enforce conversion. In fact, in the west and central Sudan, they failed by either means to convert any but a tiny sprinkling of Muslims to Christianity. Why was this so? An immediate reason was that the colonial regimes declined to support the missionaries on anything like the scale that the achievement of their aims required. They knew well that if they had done so, they would have had religious wars on their hands; but there were deeper reasons than that for the missionaries' failure.

First, Islam is more than a religion, it is a way of life. Thus for the Muslim to abandon Islam and come over to Christianity involved not only changing his beliefs but also cutting himself off from his own society. Islam regards apostasy, that is going over to another religion, as the worst of all sins; the Muslim who committed it was at once totally rejected by all his former friends, and even by his family. He was forced to take up a new life in an entirely strange and alien society; those few who did convert to Christianity usually spent the rest of their days cut off from their own people in a mission compound.

The second reason has more to do with a man's inner belief than with his social situation. When Zwemer, Miller, Tugwell and others asserted so arrogantly that Muslims 'need Christ', they were wrong; the Muslims did not for they had Muḥammad. The German orientalist, Becker, understood this well when he wrote:

> The believer has a living relationship to Muḥammad; he is the chief saint of the individual as he is of the community. He is the central point of a cult of personality, which is very close to being an object of worship . . . Allāh is often mentioned, but Muḥammad lives.[43]

Becker was of course referring to the belief in Muḥammad as *al-Insān al-Kāmil*, the 'Perfect Man'. As is pointed out elsewhere in this book, for many Muslims the Prophet Muḥammad is the reason for which God undertook His creation. He is the source through which divine mercy reaches man. He is man's hope for salvation on the Last Day. To see him and be near him is part of the Believer's reward in Paradise. The Muslim's devotion to Muḥammad is equal in passion and conviction to that of the evangelical Christian to Jesus Christ. *C.* 1220/1805, the Shehu Usumanu ɗan Fodio had written, in Fulfulde,

> O my friends, I will praise [the Prophet], that I may comfort my longing,
> In my heart he springs forward,
> I long to see him, the Most Excellent of the prophets,

Muḥammad, Aḥmad, for he is better than all others,
  In my heart I sing his praises

With my body, every day, in truth,
I long to see Aḥmad, more and more,
And my spirit, truly, its food is praising him,
When I drink the water of his praises,
  Then I hear nothing, except the words of loving him.[44]

In 1304/1886 his son, Malam Isa, rendered this poem into Hausa. When, *c.* AD 1900, Robinson, Tugwell, Miller and other Christian missionaries thrust themselves, uninvited, upon the Muslim Hausas, it was the answer to their ignorant challenge that the faith of Islam was, 'stiff as a dead man's hand'. However, the Christian missionaries may have had an effect upon the Muslims which they certainly did not intend. It seems likely that the Christians' attack on Islam made Muslims more aware of the value of their own religion; and more determined to uphold it. Also, probably, it intensified Sufi activity, as part of the Muslim response to the Christian challenge.

The Sūdānī Muslim view of Europeans

Sūdānī Muslims, unlike those of the Middle East and North Africa, had very little experience by which to judge Europeans. First and foremost, they thought of them not as 'Europeans' but as 'Christians'; and they assumed that their attitudes, like their own, were essentially religious. They had little understanding of the spirit of secular enquiry, the gift of the Age of Reason, that drove the early European travellers to undertake their explorations. They were puzzled by what they observed of their activities. Sometimes they thought they were crazy to wander around as they did; and they saw no point in searching for the sources of rivers or collecting inedible plants and insects. Some, especially the Sanūsīs, assumed that they must be spies while others even declared that it was lawful to kill them. Most Muslims, guided by *ᶜulamā'* learned in the Law, firmly rejected such extreme views and held that the lives and property of Christians must be protected so long as there was not a state of war between them and Islam.

Educated Muslims like the Shehu Usumanu ɗan Fodio and the Caliph Muhammadu Bello, had considerable knowledge of what was going on in the world beyond the Sudan, but they interpreted it in their own terms, not those of Europe. Thus the Shehu Usumanu ɗan Fodio knew of the French occupation of Egypt; but he saw the French as the medieval 'Franks', the traditional enemies of Islam from the days of the Crusades, and thus more of a nuisance than a mortal threat. His main fear seems to have been that unveiled Frankish women would have a disturbing influence on Islamic morality and Muslim family life. He appears not to have appreciated the wider threat that European expansion posed.

Likewise, the Caliph Muhammadu Bello knew of the British occupation of Muslim India. He made his resentment of this Christian intrusion into *Dār al-islām* very clear when he spoke to Clapperton about it; but neither he nor those around him seem to have understood the seriousness of this Christian threat; nor the fact that its progress across the world, from India to Africa, was by then probably inevitable. By Nachtigal's day some Muslims, especially the Sanūsīs, had grasped the extent of the danger in which their religion and their culture stood. It is this new understanding that accounts, in part, for the attitude of some of the Sanūsīs towards Christians. However, even at this late hour, most Muslims still had complete confidence in the strength and stability of *Dār al-islām*; it did not occur to them that it could be militarily overthrown.

Sūdānī Muslims knew about the Crimean War of AD 1854 to 1856, in which Muslim Turkey, allied to the Christian powers, France and Britain, fought the Russians. Many of them believed that the British and French were the subjects of the Sultan of Turkey; and that he had commanded them to come to his aid against his rebellious Russian subjects. Indeed, an exaggerated notion of the power of the Ottoman Turkish empire was certainly a factor that helped to lull the Islamic world into a false sense of security; this was especially the case in the Sudan.

Yet not all Sūdānī Muslims regarded the Turks as champions of Islam. Gerhardt Rohlfs met one member of the former ruling family in the Fazzan, at that time subject to the Ottoman empire, who expressed his hatred of the Turks. He even went so far as to hope that the Christian powers would force them to restore the lands they had seized.

Muslims also knew of the death of General Gordon at the hands of the Mahdī, Muḥammad Aḥmad, and his forces, at Khartoum; but for most of them, this was a sign of hope, that the tide of war was at last about to turn against the Christians in favour of Islam.

As for slavery, which figures so prominently in the European catalogue of evils, the Muslim view was based on an entirely different set of assumptions and attitudes. At the head of their thinking on the subject, was the fact that the institution of slavery is permitted by the Koran. Therefore, what God has permitted cannot in itself be held to be wrong; although, certainly, the *ᶜulamā'* agreed that there was a moral and legal obligation to treat slaves humanely according to the Sharīᶜa. The European campaign against slavery was therefore seen by Muslims not as an humanitarian movement but simply as an attack on their religion. It was also seen as implying a threat to their eternal salvation, for the proper practice of Islam was at that time largely dependent on the existence of slavery. For example, if they could not keep slaves, their wives would have to work – to chop wood, draw water, go to market and so on. Under such circumstances they could not keep them veiled and in seclusion; and would thus risk Hell Fire by disobeying the Koran. As for those who actively practised slave-raiding (a tiny minority of the total Muslim population), some argued simply that God intended infidels to be captured and enslaved. Others argued that it was economically necessary. They also pointed out that they had to have muskets for self-defence and that these could only be obtained in exchange for slaves. Furthermore, many argued that any suffering that slaves endured was outweighed by the opportunity enslavement gave them to save their souls by converting to Islam.

While slave-raiding could be a cruel business, whether practised by Muslims or non-Muslims, it is none the less true that Islamic 'domestic slavery', in which slaves were treated as members of the family and given certain rights, was very different from the 'chattel slavery' of the American trade, in which slaves were often treated as if they were not human at all. The European humanitarians and missionaries did not understand this, or were unwilling to recognise it. The Muslims, on the other hand, did, and they constantly pointed out that their Law required them to treat slaves humanely. It should be mentioned here that during the seventeenth and eighteenth centuries in the British West Indies many Christian clergymen were themselves slave-owners and defended the system of chattel slavery. Moreover, in practice these slaves were, for a long time, denied access to Christianity because the slave owners were worried about the consequences as far as maintaining order was concerned.

As for the popular Muslim image of Christians, it was based largely on myth and fantasy, especially folkloric notions of Dajjāl, Anti-Christ, the wars between him and the Mahdī, the awesome spectre of Gog and Magog and their monstrous armies and, over all, the looming vision of the End of Time. As will be seen later on in this book, this view of the Christians as one of the Signs of the Hour came to a head as soon as the military occupations of West Africa began in earnest.

Many West African Muslims also believed that the Christians had no country of their own but lived permanently on ships. How else could one account for their curious interest in the countries of other people? Why should men who had their own country be so intent on examining rocks, rivers and plants? Christians were also widely credited with miraculous powers. For example, it was believed that they acquired their great riches simply by calling out the name of Jesus – perhaps an interpretation of the evangelicals' doctrine of Christ as a personal redeemer that the evangelicals had certainly not intended!

Despite these fears and fantasies, most of the European travellers were received with hospitality by the ordinary people; they suffered many bureaucratic irritations and hindrances from local rulers but their lives and property were usually protected. They were probably in more danger from tropical diseases than from the people through whose contries they passed. The Moors of Senegal, the Fulani of Timbuktu, and the Sanūsīs in Borno and the Chad area, were the groups most hostile to Christians. The Sūdānī Muslims of the savanna were, by and large, much more friendly; they were also quite ready to open up trading relations. These, at least, are the impressions created by the accounts these travellers left behind.

NOTES

1 Steven Neill, 1977, p.140.
2 Minerva edition, I, p.199.
3 Lady Lugard, 1906, reprint 1964, p.283.
4 ibid. p.399.
5 ibid. p.403.
6 ibid. p.365.
7 Quoted in Hargreaves, 1963, p.65.
8 ibid. p.139.
9 1863, I, p.171.
10 Paris, 1967, p.164.
11 Carrère and Holle, p.3.
12 ibid. p.4.
13 ibid. p.14.
14 ibid. p.15.
15 ibid. p.301.

16 Rohlfs, I, pp.86–7.
17 ibid. p.171.
18 ibid, II, pp.163–4.
19 Allan G.B. Fisher and Humphrey J. Fisher, 1974, p.17.
20 Martin, *Tanzania Notes and Records*, 1968, p.31.
21 ibid. p.32.
22 Palgrave, 1872, passim.
23 London, 1871.
24 Robinson, London, 1897, p.50.
25 Stock, ii, p.155.
26 ibid, iii, p.536.
27 Zwemer, *Arabia*, p.395.
28 Robinson, 1897, p.41.
29 ibid. p.80.
30 ibid. p.77.
31 Stock, ii, p.148.
32 ibid, iii, p.114.
33 ibid, iii, p.287.
34 ibid, iii, p.644.
35 p.14.
36 p.16.
37 Stock, iii, p.727.
38 Quoted in Lugard, *Dual mandate*, p.224.
39 Miller, 1936, p.140. Miller justified his action on the ground that the Emir Aliyu had been involved in an assassination. This was, and still is, vigorously denied in Zaria. In any case, no attempt was made formally to try the emir for this alleged offence.
40 S.M. Zwemer, editor, 1906, pp.48–9.
41 p.40.
42 p.78.
43 Martin, *Tanzania Notes*, 1968, p.48.
44 Hausa manuscripts, *M*.

CHAPTER FOURTEEN

Jihāds and revolutions during the early colonial period

The *jihāds* and revolutions described in this chapter differ from those described in chapter 10 in that they took place during the full tide of French colonial penetration into the interior of the western Sudan. This had a number of unsettling consequences that were not necessarily connected with Islam. It thus becomes necessary to distinguish between what was strictly Islamic *jihād*, what was simply secular conflict between Africans, and what was anti-colonial resistance.

The *jihād* of al-Ḥājj ᶜUmar b. Saᶜīd al-Fūtī

Al-Ḥājj ᶜUmar b. Saᶜīd al-Fūtī was born in Futa Toro *c.* 1209/1794. After a conventional Islamic education he went on Pilgrimage, according to tradition, in the year 1241/1825. He had by this time become a member of the new Tijāniyya order of Sufis, founded by Shaykh Aḥmad al-Tijānī *c.* 1195/1781. On his way to Mecca he spent some time in Sokoto and Gwandu, where he preached the new Tijānī doctrines. When he arrived in Mecca, he came under the influence of the Tijānī mystic, Muḥammad al-Ghālī. After a period of training, al-Ghālī appointed him *khalīfa*, caliph, of the Tijāniyya in the countries of the Sudan. This is the key to what happened later; his experience on Pilgrimage, especially the teachings of al-Ghālī, formed in his mind a picture of Islamic perfection only to be realised through the doctrines of his spiritual master, Aḥmad al-Tijānī. He was now al-Tijānī's *khalīfa*, charged with the duty to impose this state of perfection on the imperfect Islam of the Sudan. Perhaps this could be done by *jihād al-qawl*, 'Preaching *Jihād*'; if not, it must be done by *jihād al-sayf*, '*Jihād* of the Sword'. Thus the course of al-Ḥājj ᶜUmar's career was largely determined from that point on, so too were his enemies. They were, first, the imperfect Muslims and misbelieving African polytheists in and around his homeland. Second, those local rulers who appeared to stand in the way of his grand design. Others who became his enemies, for example the French, did so for incidental reasons, not because he set out to make war on them from the start.

Al-Ḥājj ᶜUmar left Mecca to return to the western Sudan sometime in 1246–7/1831. He passed by way of Egypt and Borno, where he founded Tijānī communities. By 1251/1835–6, he was back again in Sokoto, as the guest of the Caliph Muhammadu Bello. From Sokoto he set out on a preaching mission that resulted in the establishment of Tijānī cells among the hitherto solidly Qādirī *ᶜulamā'* of Hausaland. He left Sokoto in 1253/1837 and travelled north-west, passing through Masina and Segu, where he received an unfriendly reception; from there he moved on towards the Senegambia. By 1256/1840, he had gathered a religious community around him in Diaguku, in Futa Jalon. Once again he set out on missionary journeys, this time through the Wolof kingdoms and Futa Toro. The Almamy of Futa Jalon, alarmed at his growing influence, began to obstruct him, but al-Ḥājj ᶜUmar's response was to undertake the classical *hijra*, the emigration out of what had become the territory of infidelity, into *Dār al-Islām*, beyond the power of the infidel ruler. The place he chose was Dinguiray, in the east of Futa Jalon, just out of reach of the Almamy's jurisdiction. This *hijra* took place in 1267/1851. So far, al-Ḥājj ᶜUmar had relied on *jihād al-qawl*, peaceful preaching, but since this was now clearly ineffective, he began to prepare for *jihād* of the sword. His *ṭālibūn*, student/disciples, mainly Tukolors, had followed him to Dinguiray where he set to work to train them as shock troops and reinforced them with numbers of recently converted followers, known as *sofas*, 'grooms'. He even acquired a substantial number of European rifles, mainly from French traders with which he armed his troops.

Al-Ḥājj ᶜUmar now directed his *jihād* to the north-west, into his homeland, Futa Toro, but in his way stood a cluster of French forts around the confluence of the rivers Senegal and Falémé. With French encouragement, these had become rallying-points for al-Ḥājj ᶜUmar's African enemies. He attempted to gain the cooperation, or at least the neutrality, of the French but was unsuccessful. They saw him as a threat and were not prepared to permit the setting-up of a Muslim empire so close to their own sphere of influence. Al-Ḥājj ᶜUmar was thus left with no military alternative but to attack the forts before continuing his advance down the river Senegal. This he tried to do between 1271–2/1855 and 1275–6/1859 and scored some initial successes. In the end, however, superior French fire-power and discipline defeated him. He suffered a heavy defeat at Médine and more defeats followed. By 1276/1859 al-Ḥājj ᶜUmar had decided to abandon his north-westward thrust. Instead, he turned east, against the Bambaras of Segu and their Qādirī protectors in Masina. Here he won spectacular victories, Segu fell in 1277–8/1861 and Masina in the following year. Al-Ḥājj ᶜUmar was now master of a large wedge of territory from Dinguiray in the south, enclosing Kaarta in the west, Segu, Masina, Hamdullahi in the east and Timbuktu in the north-east. His *jihād* seemed blessed with success, but this did not last for long. The non-Tukolor peoples of his empire were restless under Tukolor domination and in 1278–9/1862, they rose against him and eventually succeeded in cutting him off in Hamdullahi. In 1280/1864 he tried to break out of the siege but he failed and died in the attempt. His empire did not perish with him however, it continued under his son, Aḥmad b. ᶜUmar, until the French finally conquered it in 1308/1891. Although Aḥmad b. ᶜUmar inherited his father's territorial empire, many Tijānīs refused to accept him as the spiritual heir and in consequence, the ᶜUmarian headship of the Tijāniyya was to be challenged in the future on more than one occasion.

What was it that enabled al-Ḥājj ᶜUmar to win such success before luck deserted him at Hamdullahi? In part, he profited from the confusion caused by the French intrusion into the Senegambia which caused large numbers of Tukolor Muslims, unwilling to live under French rule, to emigrate out of the area. Al-Ḥājj ᶜUmar's movement offered them an ideological home. Moreover, many of these Tukolors were still filled with enthusiasm for *jihād*, springing from memories of ᶜAbd al-Qādir's movement in Futa Toro from *c.* 1190/1776 to 1211/1796. They were therefore suitable recruits for al-Ḥājj ᶜUmar. Indeed, many of the non-Tukolor peoples whom al-Ḥājj ᶜUmar subdued seem to have regarded his *jihād* not as a religious war but simply as a war of Tukolor imperialism and it was this that provoked their revolt against him.

Another factor that was helpful to al-Ḥājj ᶜUmar seems to have been the resentment of many Sūdānī Muslims at the domination of the Qādiriyya. After the successful *jihāds* of Shehu Usumanu ɗan Fodio in Hausaland and of Aḥmad b. Muḥammad in Masina, together with the wealth and power of the Kunta establishment in Timbuktu, the Qādiriyya had become a ruling aristocracy. This caused resentment among those who felt affronted by Qādirī elitism and al-Ḥājj ᶜUmar's fervent Tijanism offered them a way of expressing their discontent in Islamic terms. Al-Ḥājj ᶜUmar claimed, however, that he was not opposed to the Qādiriyya as such, which was probably true. His early relations with the Kuntī *shaykhs* of Timbuktu were friendly, as were those with Sokoto, or at least with the Caliph Muhammadu Bello. However, after his *jihād* had started he complained that both the Qādirī establishment in Masina and the Kuntī *shaykhs* aided his non-Muslim African enemies; it was for this reason that he made war against them, or so he said.

Another factor that may have helped him was the dissatisfaction of certain pious Muslims with the results of Shaykh Aḥmad b. Muḥammad's *jihād* in Masina, and especially with the performance of his successors. It was widely felt among these Muslims that the *jihād* had not achieved sufficient conversions; and that Shaykh Aḥmad's son and grandson had not lived up to the ideals of Islamic reform upon which the *jihād* had been based. They therefore looked to al-Ḥājj ᶜUmar al-Fūtī to fulfil their disappointed hopes.

His movement appealed, too, to the slave population, especially to slaves of non-Muslim masters. For them, al-Ḥājj ᶜUmar offered freedom and self-respect; and he made a particular effort to recruit slaves fleeing from non-Muslim Bambara masters.

Some have thought to see in al-Ḥājj ᶜUmar's *jihād* a West African

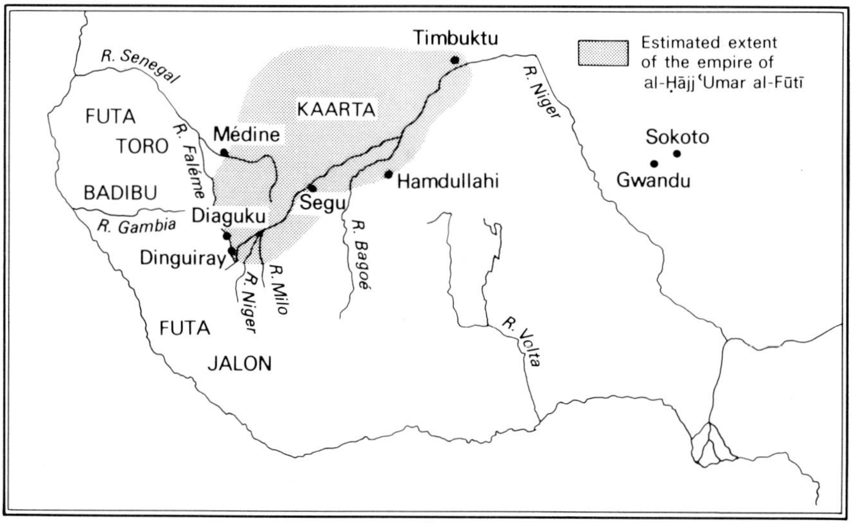

Map 11 The empire of al-Ḥājj ᶜUmar al-Fūtī.

nationalist resistance movement against French imperialism.[1] To what extent is this reasonable? Al-Ḥājj ᶜUmar himself made it clear on several occasions that he had no wish to fight the French. Indeed, he made several attempts to collaborate with them or at least to persuade them to stand aside while he got on with his own business of waging *jihād* against his African enemies. He also indicated that he regarded the French simply as traders, and he was prepared to let them trade in his territories provided they paid the customary dues to him, as the ruler of the territories. It was the fact that the French refused to accept such an arrangement and insisted on supporting his African enemies that, in the end, caused him to attack their forts. It was certainly not any notion of waging some wider war of liberation that would drive them into the sea.

Yet one should not dismiss the notion of his anti-imperialism too lightly. It can be argued that, if he was not a nationalist, he was nearly one – a pan-Islamist. There seems no doubt that he did have a clear intention to create an Islamic state in the western Sudan which would have its allegiance and its ideological roots not solely within African boundaries, but in Mecca. This is not inconsistent with anti-imperialism, provided one bears in mind that the anti-imperialist struggles for the freedom of the multi-national Islamic *jamāᶜa*, not of the nation. Indeed, in the West African interior of the 13–14/19 century (as opposed to the coastal areas, where people had long been in touch with European ideas) nationhood was a concept that had not yet been born. That of the world-wide Islamic *jamāᶜa* was very real indeed, at least to Muslim intellectuals like al-Ḥājj ᶜUmar.

Why did the French reject his attempts to secure their cooperation? First, it seems clear that they had come to feel that the status of tribute-payers to local Muslim rulers was beneath their national dignity. This was one consequence of the mood of Catholic triumphalism mentioned above. Another reason was that they were by this time fully determined to advance from the area of the Senegal to the area of the Niger. Al-Ḥājj ᶜUmar was, at best, a nuisance who got in their way, at worst, he could be a serious threat to their plans. They therefore supported his enemies, blocked his advance down the river Senegal towards Futa Toro and left him no real alternative but to attack their forts.

By 1270–1/1854 the governor of Senegal was Louis Faidherbe. He had served in Algeria before his posting to Senegal and, as was said before, may have been influenced by the ideas of the *Royaume arabe* party. He did not question the correctness of the French policy of penetrating to the Niger, indeed, he was personally committed to it. However he was much more tolerant of Islam than most of his colleagues; he fought Muslims for plain military reasons not because he was affronted by their beliefs. As long as al-Ḥājj ᶜUmar directed his *jihād* up the river Senegal, he opposed him, for whatever al-Ḥājj ᶜUmar's real motives may have been, the French naturally saw his movement as a threat to their presence in Senegal. Once he turned east and established his empire in the interior, Faidherbe began to think in terms of possible cooperation with this powerful Islamic state, at least for as long as that was convenient. He therefore sent an emissary to treat with al-Ḥājj ᶜUmar, but by the time the emissary arrived al-Ḥājj ᶜUmar was dead. The emissary, Captain Mage, negotiated with ᶜUmar's son, Aḥmad, instead. Aḥmad was cautious and suspicious, and, foolishly, turned Mage into a bitter enemy by imprisoning him in Segu for more than two years. Faidherbe's successor, Colonel Pinet-Laprade, did not share Faidherbe's open attitudes for he belonged to the school of Carrère and Holle, who saw Islam only as an enemy. After a period of years, during which rather half-hearted negotiations continued between the French and Sultan Aḥmad, the French decided to attack the Segu empire. In 1307/1890 they took Segu and in 1308/1891 the Tukolor armies were finally defeated in a major battle near Nioro. In 1309/1892, Sultan Aḥmad took refuge as a fugitive in Sokoto and the political and territorial empire founded by al-Ḥājj ᶜUmar was at an end. His spiritual empire however, has remained one of the most powerful influences in forming West African Islam up to the present day.

Al-Ḥājj ᶜUmar's intellectual contribution

At the centre of al-Ḥājj ᶜUmar's thinking lay his attachment to the Tijāniyya. Shaykh Aḥmad al-Tijanī placed great emphasis on the essential role of the *awliyā'*, holy men, in guiding the Believer to knowledge of God and ultimate salvation. This was, above all, the message of al-Ḥājj ᶜUmar too. He taught that true understanding was only to be attained through the mystical intercession of the *awliyā'* with God, not through the legal and intellectual exercises of the *ᶜulamā'*. In his system the *awliyā'* tended to take over the roles and the importance enjoyed by the *ᶜulamā'* – scholars but not necessarily mystics – in other Sudanic Islamic states. It was in part this challenge to the power of the *ᶜulamā'* that turned the more conservative Qādirī establishments against him.

A further challenge to the Qādirī *ᶜulamā'* was his attack on *taqlīd*, the unquestioning obedience to established religious authority; and his advocacy of *ijtihād*, the right to personal interpretation of the Islamic scriptures. This led him to question the universal West African Muslim adherence to the Mālikī *madhhab*; and to support the individual's freedom to follow any of the Sunnī *madhāhib*. He was not alone in this. Shehu Usumanu ɗan Fodio had considered the idea and had not wholly rejected it, but al-Ḥājj ᶜUmar advocated it in a much more positive way.

He also claimed the spiritual gift of *istikhāra*, that is knowledge of a special mystic formula that ensured him divine guidance in times of difficulty. His success in resorting to *istikhāra* probably accounts for his extraordinary hold over his followers.

Like the jihadists before him, al-Ḥājj ᶜUmar, too, held Mahdist beliefs. He did not claim to be the Mahdī, but his followers certainly did make Mahdist claims on his behalf. They believed that he, like Shehu Usumanu ɗan Fodio, was a *majaddid*, but some even went so far as to claim that he was the Mahdī's *wazīr*, his right-hand man.

Perhaps al-Ḥājj ᶜUmar's most important contribution to Islamic thought in the west and central Sudan was the claim he made that the Tijāniyya was superior to all other *ṭuruq*; and that all Tijānīs were superior to other Muslims. This sprang from the Tijānī belief that Shaykh Aḥmad al-Tijānī was the 'Seal of the *awliyā'*', that is the last and the best of the *awliyā'*, in the same way that the Prophet Muḥammad was the 'Seal of the Prophets'. The founder's superiority was thus passed on to his *ṭarīqa* as a whole and to each one of his followers, individually. Such a doctrine gave great self-confidence to the Tijānīs and it had much to do with the rapid spread of the *ṭarīqa* in West Africa.

Despite his undoubted eminence as a Muslim thinker, there were a number of important aspects of Tijānī doctrine that received little or no attention from al-Ḥājj ʿUmar. One was the important idea of the *ḥaḍrāt*, the mystic stages of the universe, another the doctrine of *fayḍa*, 'saving grace'. Certainly he knew of them, but perhaps he did not realise their potential popular appeal for he certainly did not develop them. This was done by his successors. Yet there is no doubt that the establishment of the Tijāniyya as a permanent force in West African Islam must be largely attributed to him.

Maba Diakhou in Gambia

Maba Diakhou was a Muslim Fulani born in 1224/1809, in Badibu, a Soninke state on the north bank of the Gambia river. He underwent the usual Islamic Koranic education in Cayor and in 1266–7/1850 met al-Ḥājj ʿUmar al-Fūtī. He discussed *jihād* with him and probably also joined the Tijāniyya at that time. For the next ten years he followed the now well-established precedent of *jihād al-qawl*, seeking peacefully to extend the Muslim community in Badibu. In 1277–8/1861, when it became clear that these attempts had failed, he declared a *jihād* against the Soninke rulers of that kingdom, quickly drove them out and set himself up as Almamy. Maba now made efforts to gain the support of the British, by this time established in Bathurst, but they regarded his movement as a threat to their trading interests and maintained a suspicious attitude towards him. However, the reluctance of the British Colonial Office in London to be drawn into colonial wars in West Africa prevented the British in West Africa from undertaking anything more than minor military operations against him, usually in cooperation with the French. These imposed some check, but they proved insufficient to prevent his influence from spreading widely throughout the Gambia. His *jihād* now sparked off other Muslim movements along the Gambia and the whole area quickly became the scene of minor conflicts that the British and French described as 'Maraboutic wars'. In fact, they were attempts at Islamic revolution.

Many of the Soninke who had been driven out of Badibu fled to the neighbouring Wolof kingdom of Salum. Soon, Maba became involved in the politics of that kingdom and intervened in a succession struggle there, in favour of his own candidate. This alarmed the French, for they, too, began to fear that his movement might develop into a threat to their interests in Senegal. They therefore intervened against him and defeated him at Kaolak, in 1279/1862. Maba reorganised but was again defeated by the French at Kwinella, in 1279/1863.

These set-backs did not destroy Maba, but they did cause him to turn his attention away from the Gambia, towards the Wolof states of the north. In the course of the year 1280–1/1864, the French, perhaps as a result of Faidherbe's influence, recognised Maba as Almamy of Badibu and entered into an alliance with him. Subsequently, however, his activities alarmed Faidherbe's successor, the strongly anti-Muslim Pinet-Laprade. In 1282/1865, Laprade led an expedition against Maba but suffered a serious set-back. A second expedition, in 1283/1867, was more successful and Maba was killed. This was not the end of the affair, however, and Maba's tomb quickly became a place of pilgrimage. Maraboutic wars, which by now had largely lost their religious character and come to reflect purely worldly conflicts over trade and politics, continued in the Gambia for the next half century. Only the final imposition of colonial rule put a stop to them.

Maba's *jihād* arose from a combination of religious and secular circumstances. By *c.* 1266/1850, the towns along the Gambia river were inhabited largely by Muslims who were economically prosperous as a result of their successful involvement in the new groundnut trade. However they were deeply discontented under the rule of Soninke chiefs who were Muslims only in name. The government of these Soninke was corrupt and ineffective, largely as a result of the decline in the slave trade which had been their main economic support. They, and their provincial governors, tried to recover their fortunes by taxing the Muslims who naturally resented this. A further cause of friction seems to have been the fact that many of the Soninke openly defied Islam by the heavy drinking of alcohol, supplied by European traders. Strict Muslims therefore regarded them as infidels and, more than ever, resented being subject to their government. A situation thus developed in which prosperous and zealous Muslims were subject to the authority of impoverished, weak and oppressive rulers whom they held in contempt. By 1266/1850, the Gambia was ripe for revolt, all that was needed was a leader.

In his social and educational background Maba was typical of the West African Muslim reformers of his day. Literate, ardent and puritanical, his training under al-Ḥājj ᶜUmar enabled him to understand and apply the Islamic revolutionary tactics, so well suited to exploiting the combination of Islamic idealism and economic and secular discontents that characterised the Gambia in his day. First, came the initial ideological preparation – *jihād al-qawl* – which lasted ten years and set up an Islamic shadow state beneath the decaying fabric of Soninke rule. Then came the violent revolution, *jihād al-sayf*, that toppled the old order and made the shadow state a reality.

Some of the most interesting characteristics of Maba's *jihād* were his strongly egalitarian teaching, his equally strong republican attitudes, and his constant attacks on 'kings'. In short, Maba really does seem to have stood for much of what the French explorer, Gaspard Théodore Mollien read into earlier Islamic movements in the Senegambia. The populations of the Gambia and the Wolof kingdoms were, of course, open to influences from the French settlement of Saint Louis. By 1267/1850, these were almost exclusively Catholic or imperialist, but at an earlier period the seductive ideas of the French Revolution – equality, liberty and fraternity – must have been at work there, as in other French-speaking communities. It is certainly possible that Maba's egalitarian and republican version of Islamic *jihād* owed something to such ideas.

Maba's *jihād* had some initial success, but in the end it was defeated by the combined opposition of the British and French to the rise of a unified African Islamic state within their spheres of influence. Yet its achievements were not entirely swept away by defeat. Statistics collected in the middle of the 20 century AD show that by then 80 per cent of the population of the old Soninke states of the Gambia was Muslim. This must be attributed largely to the influence of Maba and the effects of his movement.

The *jihād* of Shaykh Amadu Ba in Jolof

Maba Diakhou's movement was followed shortly by that of Shaykh Amadu (Aḥmad) Ba, sometimes known as Amadou Cheikhou.[2] This *ᶜālim* was born in Futa Toro, where his father, a well-known religious leader, had at one time claimed to be the Mahdī. On his father's death, Shaykh Amadu succeeded to his religious leadership. He was by this time a devout Tijānī, having been initiated into the order by his father. According to some accounts, he was also a follower of al-Ḥājj ᶜUmar al-Fūtī and like these other reformers, he started off with a preaching tour in 1285–6/1869, in which he urged a return to pure Islam and the adoption of the Tijāniyya. It also seems that, amongst other things, he preached against the French being allowed to escape from their traditional status as tribute paying *ahl al-dhimma*, 'people of the compact'. These are non-Muslim followers of a scriptual religion, in this case Christianity, who were recognised by the Muslims as subjects of the Islamic state. Moreover, he preached against the French having taken control of so much of the Senegambia, for which he blamed the rulers of Futa Toro and the Wolof kingdoms. The lax way in which the nobility, as well as commoners, observed Islam angered him in the same way as it had earlier Muslim Tukolor reformers. In fact, it seems clear that his movement was yet another incident in the confrontation between the strict Islam of the ᶜ*ulamā*' and the casual Islam of the rest, that had been characteristic of the Senegambia since the days of Nāṣir al-Dīn. To this was now added the increasing interference of the French in Senegambian affairs, which further angered the ᶜ*ulamā*'.

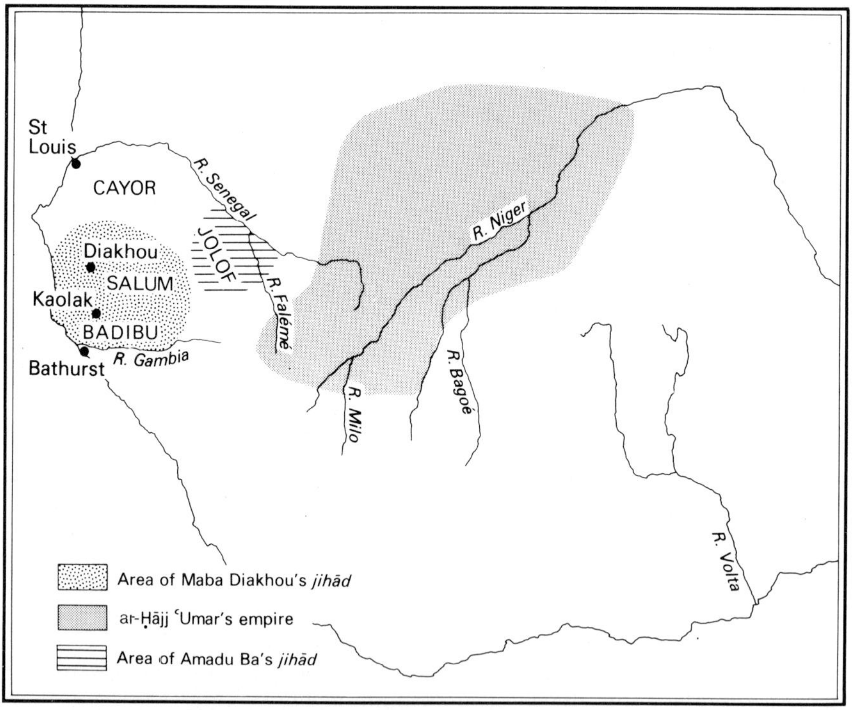

Map 12 The jihād *areas of Maba Diakhou and Amadu Ba.*

Shaykh Amadu Ba launched his *jihād* towards the end of 1286/1869 and began by defeating the chief of Koki, in the Wolof kingdom of Cayor. He then defeated a French force sent against him, but the French attacked again in strength and he was forced back into central Futa. He now turned his attention to the Wolof kingdom of Jolof and besieged its capital compelling the king and his people to submit by cutting off their water supply. He then took political control in Jolof, although the king was retained as his puppet. From Jolof he attempted to extend his *jihād*, but by now not only the French but also the rulers of the other Senegambian kingdoms were alarmed by his success. In 1292/1875, he was attacked by the combined armies of Futa Toro and Cayor, strengthened by a French contingent and was defeated and killed in the battle that followed.

Shaykh Amadu Ba's movement is yet another example of the limited success achieved by Islamic reform movements in the Senegambia. The reasons for this were the lack of wide-ranging unity among the Muslim reform groups, and opposition to reform by traditional rulers and nobility. Though themselves Muslim, these people saw reform as a threat to their own interests, for they realised what was, in fact, the truth – the Muslim activists sought political power as well as moral and religious reform. To this was added the unwillingness of the colonial powers, mainly the French but sometimes the British as well, to see ideologically strong Islamic states replace the often failing kingdoms of the traditional rulers which they were better able to control.

However, popular opinion credits Shaykh Amadu Ba with considerable success in reforming Islam in Jolof. It is said he compelled the king and the nobility to observe Islam properly and that the common people then followed their lead. As for the Tijāniyya, it seems he made no attempt to introduce this among the people of Jolof, perhaps because he was too occupied in ensuring the observance of Islamic fundamentals. The Tijāniyya did not become strong there until the early 20 century AD, when it was introduced by al-Ḥājj Mālik Sy.

The *jihād* of al-Ḥājj Muḥammad al-Amīn

Al-Ḥājj Muḥammad al-Amīn, often known as Mahmadu Lamine, was a Soninke or Sarakoli *shaykh* born *c.* 1251/1835 in Goundiourou, now a well-known centre of Islamic learning south-west of Médine, on the south bank of the Senegal river. Here he pursued Koran studies under his father but while still a youth he was captured, together with his mother, by raiders from Gamon, a village of the non-Muslim Tenda. There he was enslaved and subsequently ransomed, but his mother died of ill-treatment suffered while she was in captivity. This created in him an intense hatred of Gamon and he swore to be revenged.

After his release he continued his studies in Bakel and may even have met al-Ḥājj ʿUmar al-Fūtī there, but this is uncertain. Probably about 1272/1855 – although there is considerable uncertainty about this date – he set out on Pilgrimage to the Ḥijāz. He travelled slowly and may have spent as many as thirty years on the journey to and from Mecca, visiting Egypt and possibly Istanboul on the way. He spent about seven years in Mecca and while there became associated with a Tijānī *zāwiya*. He also sought approval for the *jihād* he now intended to wage against the unbelievers of the Sudan, with no doubt the Tenda of Gamon in mind, and his request was granted.

By 1297/1879 or 1298/1880 he was back in Masina and was well received there by al-Tijānī, the nephew of al-Ḥājj ʿUmar al-Fūtī, who now governed that city. He stayed for a time with al-Tijānī and seems to have set himself up as a Tijānī *shaykh*, initiating people into the *ṭarīqa*. He also put himself forward as the true successor of al-Ḥājj ʿUmar al-Fūtī. He then moved on to Segu, the centre of government of al-Ḥājj ᶜUmar's son, Sultan Aḥmad b. ᶜUmar. Sultan Aḥmad gave him the village of Salām in which to settle but relations between the two men became strained. Tradition says that Aḥmad made several attempts to kill Muḥammad al-Amīn but that on each occasion the Sarakoli *shaykh* miraculously escaped. These miracles added greatly to his reputation and he became widely known as a miracle-working *walī*. The tension between him and Sultan Aḥmad can be accounted for on a number of grounds. First, Aḥmad feared Muḥammad al-Amīn's growing reputation and following, which seemed to pose a political threat to his own position. Second, he resented Muḥammad al-Amīn's claims to be the successor to al-Ḥājj ᶜUmar and felt that Muḥammad al-Amīn treated him with less respect than his position deserved. Third, he probably suspected that the Sarakoli *shaykh* was about to found his own rival branch of the Tijāniyya, for Muḥammad al-Amīn insisted on the adoption of the eleven-bead rosary, whereas al-Ḥājj ᶜUmar had used a twelve-bead rosary. Such apparently minor points of ritual were more important than they seem at first sight, as, traditionally, they indicated that a man was about to make a bid for independence and break away from the main order to try and found one of his own.

Muḥammad al-Amīn appears to have openly criticised the ᶜUmarian empire of Sultan Aḥmad. He complained that under Aḥmad the empire had abandoned the religious ideals of the founder and the Tukolor had become a ruling class, exploiting other groups and tribes. At the root of this attitude there seems to have been resentment on the part of the Sarakoli, at Tukolor supremacy and at the way in which Tukolors assumed themselves to be the masters of other Muslims within the Segu empire. As was customary among Muslims of his day, he expressed his social and political resentments in religious terms and began to formulate the notion of *jihād* against an empire that he now charged with corrupting Islam.

In 1302/1885 Muḥammad al-Amīn left Segu and returned to his birth place, Goundiourou. He was enthusiastically welcomed by the Soninke population, because of his reputation as a great *walī* that had gone before him, and well received by the French who gave him permission to travel freely in their territories. At this point the French seem to have regarded him as a possible ally against Sultan Aḥmad in Segu while he expressed his friendship towards the French, having begun to preach *jihād* against Aḥmad and the Segu Tukolors, hoping for French support. The French, however, were pre-occupied with their struggle against the Almamy Samory (see below, page 239) and were not ready to become involved in war against Segu; they thus made no positive response to Muḥammad al-Amīn's approaches.

When it became clear that the French would not support the wider *jihād* against Segu, Muḥammad al-Amīn turned to preaching *jihād* against Gamon. No doubt this was intended as a revenge for his early sufferings there, but it also seems likely that he needed a successful *jihād* to establish his position. The idea of creating a united Soninke state, based on his own version of what Islam ought to be in opposition to that dominated by Tukolors, had even begun to form in Muḥammed al-Amīn's mind during the time he was in Segu.

Muḥammad al-Amīn now took an extraordinary step. In 1303/1885 he applied to the French for permission to launch *jihād* against Gamon which indicates that he certainly did not regard the French as his enemies. It also suggests that he was sincerely concerned to avoid clashing with them. The French refused his request, but they did so in a manner that left him in some doubt as to their intentions, and he continued to prepare for *jihād*. He now turned towards Bundu, south-west of Goundiourou, and sought permission from its ruler to pass through the kingdom on the way to *jihād*. Again his request was refused and the ruler of Bundu turned to the French for help but this was not immediately forthcoming. In 1303/1886, Muḥammad al-Amīn defeated the Bundu chief and siezed several Bundu towns. He now abandoned his *jihād* against Gamon and settled down to turning Bundu into the centre of a Soninke Islamic state. Soninke poured into Bundu to reinforce his army but even then he continued to offer the French assurances of friendship.

By this time the French were alarmed, for they had come to suspect that Muḥammad al-Amīn was a Sanūsī. This was probably untrue, but by the 1880s the French thought of every Muslim activist as a Sanūsī. They also suspected, again without much evidence, that he was a follower of the Mahdī of the Nilotic Sudan. Moreover, they were naturally reluctant to allow Muḥammad al-Amīn, or anyone else, to make war against African rulers who sought their protection. Above all, however, they were unwilling to see a powerful Islamic state established astride their lines of communication with the Niger region as they were short of troops due to their campaign against Samory. Nevertheless they managed to assemble a force; but Muḥammad al-Amīn anticipated their intentions and reacted by attacking the French fort at Bakel in 1303/1886. He was driven back but continued to make guerilla attacks upon the French for over a year, until he was defeated and killed in 1305/1887.

Muḥammad al-Amīn's career followed the broad pattern of other West African jihadists. First came his Pilgrimage; then the period of ideological preparation, during which he first established himself as a *walī* and then preached *jihād*; finally, he launched a *jihād* that, in his case, was unsuccessful. Yet his movement differed from those of Usumanu ɗan Fodio and al-Ḥājj ᶜUmar al-Fūtī. Its base was narrower, for his motives were limited to ousting the Tukolors and replacing them with his own Soninke. He showed little concept of the universality of the Islamic *jamāᶜa* and had none of Shehu Usumanu ɗan Fodio's breadth of vision or al-Ḥājj ᶜUmar's intellectual power. He wrote nothing and left no new ideas. The single doctrinal point that he adopted, out of al-Ḥājj ᶜUmar's wide-ranging theology, was that of *wilāya*, the power and role of the *walī*. Even his Tijanism seems unconvincing, for despite the fact that he claimed to be the successor of al-Ḥājj ᶜUmar in Masina and Segu, by the time he returned to Goundiourou there was little that was essentially Tijanist in his call to *jihād*. Indeed, many of his supporters were Qādirīs and tradition suggests that in Goundiourou he was no longer insisting on the strict observance of Tijānī ritual.

Like al-Ḥājj ᶜUmar al-Fūtī, al-Ḥājj Muḥammad al-Amīn has sometimes been cast in the role of an anti-imperialist nationalist, whose main concern was to fight the French.[3] This is hard to sustain as his efforts to gain French support were certainly in earnest; had he been offered French help against the Muslims of Segu, there is little doubt that he would have accepted it. It really does not seem that he started out with any ideological hatred for the French, but rather that the French turned on him when he became too successful.

Much nearer the truth is the view that he was the enemy not of French imperialism but of the Tukolor imperialism of Segu; and that he was the champion of the Soninkes attempting to supplant the dominant Tukolors. According to this view, his movement was simply a continuation of the one that led to al-Ḥājj ᶜUmar's death in Hamdullahi in 1280/1864. If the French had been prepared to help Muḥammad al-Amīn, he would surely have overthrown the Tukolor Tijānī state of Segu and replaced it with a Soninke empire of his own. This is hardly consistent with an anti-imperialist ideology.

Samory Ture: 1277/1861–1316/1898

The northern edge of the rain forest that stretches from the Volta across to the Atlantic coast in the south of the Senegambia, was populated, in part, during the 13–14/19 century by Dyula Muslims who had possibly been settled there since the late 8/14 or early 9/15 century. They conducted the trade in forest products in cooperation with the animist forest people who were the producers. For many generations these Dyulas had lived undisturbed among the animists, content with their own prosperous life and making no attempt to convert their animist hosts. During the first half of the 13/19 century this peaceful and profitable situation was unsettled by ripples from the Islamic *jihāds* and revolutions that erupted elsewhere in West Africa. *C.* 1245/1830, a certain Mori Ule Sisi of Kankan proclaimed *jihād* in the area between Toro and Konyan, north of the forest, above what is now Liberia. This resulted in the setting up of the Sisi Islamic kingdom of Moriuledugu. In the following thirty years the Muslim Sisis expanded, threatening the mixed society of Dyula Muslims and animists around them; the social and economic balance between the Dyula Muslims and the animists was thus disturbed. Both sides were forced to adjust to changing circumstances and many of the Dyulas threw in their lot with the Islamic reformers. Others looked for ways to stem the tide of Islamic revolution that proved so damaging to their economic interests. The animists, unable because of the rigid structure of their ancient society and its lack of centralised leadership to take the initiative themselves, awaited a leader from outside.

Samory Ture, a young man of Konyan who had married into the animist Kamara clan, proved equal to the challenge that this situation presented. He had already seen service under the Sisis, *c.* 1269/1853, and had remained with them for about five years, learning the profession of soldiering and picking up some Islamic ideas and attitudes. By 1277/1861, he was back among the Kamaras to whom he now offered his services in their resistance to the Sisis. His offer was accepted and he quickly built up an army that consisted of both animists and Muslims hostile to the Sisis. From then until 1287/1870, he established his control over the area of the Milo river valley and set up his headquarters at Bisandugu, on the east bank of the river Milo, in 1289–90/1873. By now he had become independent of the Kamaras and controlled a large area in his own right and his next move was to ally himself with certain Muslims in Kankan. With their help he defeated the Sisis in 1297/1880 but up to this point his movement had had no apparent religious motivation. His own declared aim was simply to protect the trade routes from the extortions of the local chiefs and open up new routes and he continued to draw his support from Muslims and animists alike. In 1301/1884, however, he changed his title from the traditional *Fama* to the Islamic 'Almamy' (*al-imām*) and at the end of 1304/1886, he proclaimed an Islamic theocracy. He demanded that his subjects convert to Islam and introduced strict regulations to bring this about, setting up a network of *karamogho*, Dyula Muslim *ᶜulamā'*, to supervise the conversions. There seem to have been two reasons for this surprising development: first, the influence of his Muslim allies in Kankan; second, his growing conviction that only through Islam could he unite his empire against the threat from the French and give his government the legitimacy he desired. This policy of forcible conversion quickly gave rise to fierce opposition and Samory soon found himself faced by a revolt.

The Almamy Samory, as he was now styled, had already clashed with the French as early as 1299/1882, but he had no wish to fight them and had subsequently entered into treaty relations with them. However, in 1302–3/1885, apparently disappointed by the lack of any real cooperation from the French, he sent a delegation to seek an alliance with the British in Sierra Leone. This was politely declined, although presents were sent to the Almamy by the British Governor of Sierra Leone, Sir Samuel Rowe. At least one West African newspaper, the *Sierra Leone Weekly News*, criticised the British failure to respond more positively to the Almamy's initiative and spoke approvingly of his programme which it described as 'the opening up to the interior trade routes, and the development of the commercial operations of this Colony with the territories which are under the sway of the Almami.'[4] However later in the same editorial, the writer goes on to deplore the 'melancholy evidence of the ghastly deeds of the sword' which were witnessed in Samory's territories.[5]

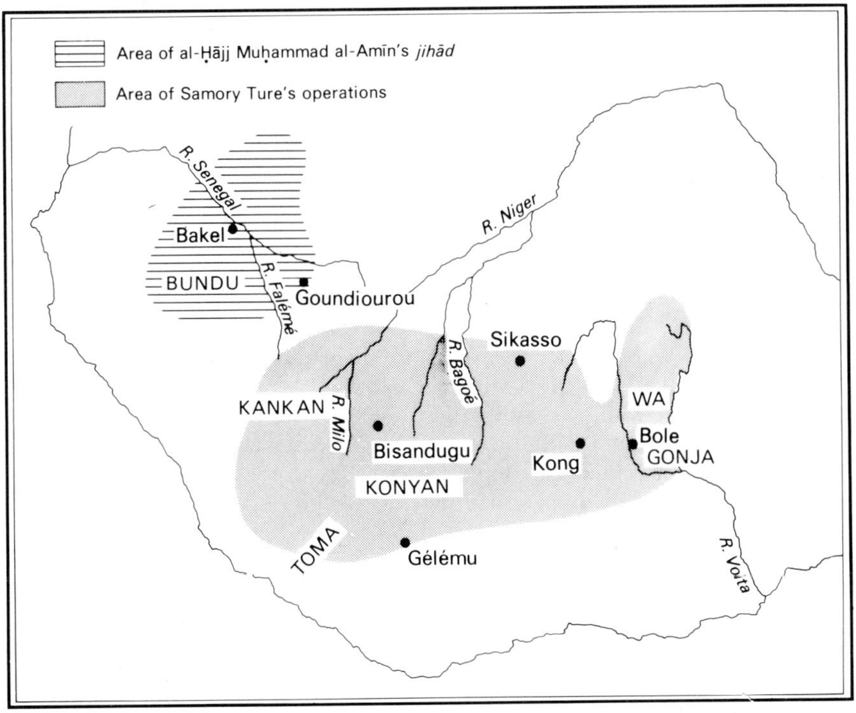

Map 13 The area of Samory Ture's operations (c.1313/1896) and of al-Ḥājj Muḥammad al-Amīn's jihād *(c.1305/1887).*

In 1304/April, 1887, the Almamy decided to attack the town of Sikasso, north-east of Kankan, between the Black Volta and the river Bagoe, which was a centre of the revolt against him. After a prolonged siege that lasted until 1305/August, 1888, he was forced to abandon the attempt and he retired west into his homeland from where he continued trying to crush the revolt. This revolt and his defeat at Sikasso seem to have convinced him that the setting-up of an Islamic theocracy had been a mistake. He now abandoned this policy, although he himself remained devoted to Islam, continued to build mosques in the territories he controlled, and went on persuading – or perhaps compelling – at least some of the conquered people to convert to Islam. Certainly what was said about him in the West African English-language press makes it clear that, even after his defeat at Sikasso, he was still widely regarded as a great Muslim leader and sometimes even compared to the Mahdī of the eastern Sudan.

In 1306/March, 1889 he signed another treaty with the French, but between 1309/1891 and early 1310/1894 more fighting broke out between the two and Samory was pushed south-east, into the Volta region. In 1313/1896 he moved into Gonja and in the following year he attacked and destroyed Kong. Once again he quickly made himself master of a large territory but now he found himself confronting the British, who were moving into the country north of Ashanti. He turned west back into Toma, south of his Konyan homeland, on the edge of the forest and here the French intercepted him at Gélému, in 1316/September, 1898. He was captured and exiled and died in exile in AD 1900.

Despite the widespread idea among other West Africans that he was a great Muslim leader, Samory Ture had little in common with the West African Muslim jihadists. He grew up in an animist background and was illiterate when he began his career, although he later learned to read the Koran. His service with the Muslim Sisis certainly introduced him to Islam but his full conversion does not seem to have taken place until he came into contact with the Muslims of Kankan. His movement did not follow the pattern established by the jihadists for he never performed Pilgrimage, he never preached *jihād*, and he never invoked the principle of *hijra*, although it is possible that admiration for al-Ḥājj ᶜUmar al-Fūtī may have been a factor in firing his ambition. He was essentially an African empire-builder, very like the able but ruthless medieval European 'robber-barons' who carved out kingdoms for themselves by force of arms and their power to hold the loyalty of their followers. In some ways he resembled the Borno conqueror, Rābiḥ b. Faḍl Allāh, for both were concerned essentially with worldly power, not with the Sunna. Both created large but impermanent empires as they swept across huge areas of territory, but neither of them contributed much to civilised and settled life. In this respect, particularly, they differed in their achievements from the jihadists, all of whom left something behind, whether it was an empire, a new idea, or simply the heritage of conversion to Islam. Both profited from the unsettled conditions of their day and both were stopped short by European intervention. Had this not been so, it is certainly possible that either one of them might have created an empire of greater permanence which might have developed into a genuinely Islamic state. Yet perhaps this assessment is, in some respects, not entirely fair to the Almamy Samory, for in the Volta area, especially around Bole, popular memory still attributes the building of several mosques to him and credits him with having converted many of the people to Islam. Moreover, as was said above and whatever later historical judgements may have been made about him, West Africans in his day certainly regarded him not only as a Muslim leader but also, to some extent, as a Muslim reformer.

Samory's movement has been described as a 'Dyula revolution'[6] which seems most inappropriate. He himself was not a Dyula and he began his career as the champion of the animist Kamaras, not the Muslim Dyulas. Some Dyulas certainly supported him, in the hope that by doing so they could protect their profitable trade relationship with the animists and polytheists against interference from Muslim reformers such as the Sisis, but this certainly did not amount to a Dyula revolution. Samory's movement was not exclusively, or even mainly, dependent on Dyula support, the support of non-Muslims was equally important, indeed perhaps more so, as he himself discovered when he rashly tried to force them to accept an Islamic style of government. Moreover, even at the height of his Islamic interlude, there is nothing to suggest that he sought to found a Dyula empire in the way that, for example, al-Ḥājj Muḥammad al-Amīn tried to found a Soninke empire. Samory's movement was a military adventure and his initial intention was to found a great commercial empire, but this goal was not essentially related to Dyula hopes and ambitions. To see it as a Dyula revolution is to misunderstand it; it was rather the product of Samory's own ambition for power and in seeking it he was willing to accept support not only from Dyulas but from any quarter.

As for Samory's relations with the French, he was certainly the most formidable opponent they had to face in the western Sudan. Perhaps he came nearest of all West African leaders of the day to fulfilling the role of an anti-imperialist African nationalist, for he alone united Muslims and animists into a single community regardless of religion or blood line. He certainly did not wish to fight the French, but when he had to do so, the basis of his appeal to his followers was wider than that of the jihadists. Whether it was truly ideological or merely an appeal to their material interests is difficult to say, but clearly it embraced Muslims and non-Muslims alike. Nevertheless, 'nationalist' seems an inappropriate label to attach to him, for it has essentially European intellectual roots that simply did not exist in the West African interior in his day. On the other hand, highly educated coastal West Africans, long exposed to European political and philosophical ideas, do seem to have regarded him, to some extent, as a national leader.

The Almamy Samory was undoubtedly ruthless and sometimes cruel; he was also a brave and able soldier, with outstanding talents as a leader. His slave-raiding and other destructive activities were much emphasised by certain European observers of his time, especially the French, but a study of the West African press shows clearly that, while he was sometimes feared by other West Africans, he was also widely admired. This is as true of West African Christians as it is of Muslims. Moreover, British and American observers of his movement give a rather more sympathetic account of his aims and achievements, as well as of his personal character, than do the French.

Results of the Islamic *jihāds* and revolutions of the 13/19 century

By *c.* AD 1900 the west and central Sudan had experienced a series of *jihāds* and Islamic revolutions that profoundly affected the state of Islam there. Above all, these *jihāds* represented a victory for militant, universalist Islam and a set-back for the easy compromise that usually developed in Sudanic societies when Islam and polytheism/animism were left to work out a way of life without the intervention of armed force. The victory was not absolute and the success of some of the *jihāds* was both short-lived and limited. Mixing continued, indeed, in the areas where conquest had extended Islam into what had been *Dār al-kufr*, the *ᶜulamā'* found themselves faced with the same problems of mixing all over again. However, there was a definite and permanent shift away from local interpretations of the Faith, towards the strict Sunna and universalism – that is a sense of belonging to the wider Islamic world.

The *jihāds* also advanced the cause of Sufism. Shehu Usumanu ɗan Fodio, Shaykh Aḥmad b. Muḥammad and al-Ḥājj Maḥmūd were all devout Qādirīs. In the *jihād* empires of Sokoto and Hamdullahi, Qadirism became the official cult to the extent that not just Islam, but Qādirī Islam was necessary for constitutional legitimacy. In the Niger area al-Ḥājj ᶜUmar al-Fūtī did much the same for the new Tijāniyya, while Maba Diakhou and, to a lesser extent, al-Ḥājj Muḥammad al-Amīn planted the new *ṭarīqa* in Jolof and the Gambia, where it increasingly coloured Muslim life. Thus, as a result of the *jihāds*, a trend that had been going on for several centuries was brought nearer to completion. Sufism now largely took over Islam in the west and central Sudan but its victory was not total, nor was it for ever. It was destined to be challenged soon by the rise of a new group of Muslim radicals known as the Wahhābīs.

Before Islam came to the west and central Sudan no general system of literacy had developed there, as far as is known. Although the use of the *tifinagh* alphabet of the Saharan Berbers extended as far as the Niger Bend, there is as yet no evidence that it was ever used to write any West African language, other than that of the Berbers. However from the moment that Islam made its first appearance, part of its history has been that of an expanding literacy in Arabic that was not limited to one particular tribe or language group but was equally available to all who chose to accept Islam. Moreover, it also brought about the beginning of literacy in certain vernacular West African languages, for instance Fulfulde and Hausa[7].

The *jihāds*, which as has been constantly stressed in this book, were intellectual as well as military movements, took this process several steps further. Not only were they military and political victories for literates over non-literates, to a large extent; they also intensified literate activity in areas where Islam was already established and they introduced it into areas where it had never before existed.

Finally, *jihād* and Islamic revolution accelerated social change; new towns were created, populations were set on the move, old institutions were overthrown and new ones set up in their place. Economic and political patterns were upset and various groups were in consequence forced to seek new combinations and new strategies to preserve their positions and attain their goals. Samory Ture's movement – not in the first instance Islamic but arising out of the consequences of Islamic revolution – is a case in point, for it forced Muslims and non-Muslims to combine to protect their trading interests and, to some extent, to resist the French. What the final result of this process of change might have been, if Africans had been left to work things out for themselves, can only be guessed at; but they were not left to do this. Before the Islamic revolutions were complete, they were overtaken by colonial revolution. At first this was a process of piecemeal interference but from *c.* AD 1900, it gathered speed and became one of outright occupation. This, too, brought with it social, political and economic change that had unimagined consequences for Islam. For the most part these changes were neither intended nor desired by those who were responsible for bringing them about, but that is the subject of another chapter.

NOTES

1 A.S. Kanya-Forstner's essay 'Mali-Tukulor' in Crowder, ed., 1971, is a well-argued exposition of this view. While still maintaining the central theme of 'West African resistance' towards the European conquests, Dr Kanya-Forstner is clearly aware of the contrary arguments, expressed above.

2 The fact that Amadu Ba is sometimes referred to as Amadou Cheikhou, or other variants of this name such as Ahmadu Seku and so on, seems to have given rise to some confusion between him and Shaykh Aḥmad, the son of al-Ḥājj ᶜUmar al-Fūtī, also often known as Ahmadu Seku, etc. This confusion is reflected in the index of *HWA*, II, 1974, *sv* 'A(h)madu (Ahmadu Seku, Shaikh Ahmad)', where the subsequent page numbers indicate that the two persons have become confused. Amadu Ba (also known as Amadou Cheikhou) was killed by the French in AD 1875. Shaykh Aḥmad, the son of al-Ḥājj ᶜUmar al-Fūtī, and ruler of Segu, survived there until 1893, when he was defeated by the French. He died in AD 1897. The career of Amadu Ba is fully and clearly set out in Eunice A. Charles, 'Shaikh Amadu Ba and jihad in Jolof', *IJAHS*, VII, 1975.

3 B. Olatunji Oloruntimẹhin puts the case for this, in his essay 'Senegambia-Mahmadou Lamine' in Crowder, ed. 1971. He, too, seems well aware of the contrary arguments.

4 Georgia McGarry, *Reaction and protest in the West African press*, Leiden and Cambridge, 1978, p.111–12.

5 ibid., p.112.

6 Yves Person, 'Samori and Islam' in Willis, ed. 1979.

7 This statement in no way ignores the interest and importance of West African graphical systems, which are described in 'Methodology and African prehistory' in Ki-Zerbo, J., (ed.), UNESCO *General History of Africa*, Vol. I., 1981, pp.250 ff, as well as elsewhere. But none of these systems came near to attaining the widespread diffusion among many different tribal and language groups in West Africa that was achieved by Arabic script.

CHAPTER FIFTEEN

Sufism in West Africa from the 9/15 century to c.AD 1900

The history of Sufism and the *ṭuruq* in the west and central Sudan is closely associated with that of the teachers and messengers of Islam, discussed in chapter 3, and the jihadists, discussed in chapters 10 and 14. Much of this history has already been discussed and the task of this chapter is to draw together what has already been said and add new information to show how Sufism had spread and developed in the Sudan by *c.* AD 1900.

The Qādiriyya

The Qādiriyya order of Sufis was founded in Baghdad by Shaykh ᶜAbd al-Qādir al-Jaylānī (sometimes Jīlānī, sometimes Kaylānī), during the 6/12 century. It quickly spread to North Africa where it became well established in Morocco by 853/1450. From North Africa it spread to Takedda where it was adopted by the Sanhaja of that city. When, with the decline of Takedda in the 9/15 century, the Sanhaja moved east to Agades and then out into the Sahara, they took the Qādiriyya with them; it spread where they roamed.

The Kel-Es-Suq had also adopted the Qādiriyya from North Africa by the 9/15 century, if not earlier. In that century they dispersed out of Tadmakkat, spreading the *ṭarīqa* in the places where they settled. By *c.* 885/1480 Agallal, in Ahir, had become a Sufi centre largely as a result of their influence, and other Qādirī Kel-Es-Suq became established in the Azawād *c.* 905/1500.

At the same time as the Sanhaja and the Kel-Es-Suq were disseminating the Qādiriyya towards the south-east, the Kunta were at work in the west. As early as 802–3/1400, Sīdī ᶜAlī al-Kuntī was a *quṭb*, a 'pole', of the Qādiriyya. When the Kunta migrated out of Tuwāt, they did so under Sīdī Muḥammad, another Qādirī *quṭb*, who claimed to have taken the *wird*, the formal ritual of the *ṭarīqa* passed down by the 6/12-century Moroccan *shaykh*, Abu 'l-ᶜAbbās b. Jaᶜfar al-Sabatī al-Khazrajī (fl. *c.* 576/1180). Kuntī Qadirism then took another step forward in Walata, in the second half of the 15 century AD (AH 853–905), through the activities there of the well-known *walī*, Sīdī Aḥmad al-Bakkā'ī, whose career was described in chapter 3. The Kuntī custom of *siyāḥa*, the carrying out of preaching tours, which were combined with trading activities, served to spread the Qādiriyya in the western Sahara as well as to the east and the south. Indeed, Kuntī *shaykhs* were visiting Borno even before 843/1439–40.

These early Qādirīs were representatives of the North African tradition of Sufism. Their Qadirism was based on the teachings of ᶜAbd al-Qādir al-Jaylānī together, probably, with influences from the Shādhiliyya order, especially the Jazūliyya branch of the Shādhiliyya. This branch was founded by the 9/15 -century mystic, Abū ᶜAbd Allāh Muḥammad b. Sulaymān al-Jazūlī (*d.*

870/1465) and was influential in the Maghrib during the Marinid period.

The doctrines of the Qādiriyya at this early period were, as far as is known, not very different from those of the non-Sufis. The study of Islamic law was emphasised as was the study of the Koran, but the Qādirī *ᶜulamā'* differed in their approach from the non-Sufi *ᶜulamā'*, in that the Sunnī sources were interpreted in a somewhat more mystical fashion than was the case among the non-Sufis. They also probably taught that through *khalwa*, self-denial, fasting, going out alone into the desert to pray and so on, it was possible for the individual Sufi to achieve *fanā'*, 'absorption' in God; they also believed that certain angels could help them to achieve *fanā'*. During the 9/15 century both the Qādiriyya and the Shādhiliyya began to develop an increasing interest in the idea of the Prophet Muḥammad as *al-Insān al-Kāmil*, the 'Perfect Man' or *Afḍal al-khalq*, the 'Most Excellent of Creation'. Although this idea was common to most Sufis, it was especially popular among North African and Sūdānī Sufis. This popularity was largely due to the influence of both the 7/13-century North African poet, al-Fāzāzī (*d.* 627/1229–30), who wrote a well-known and very popular praise-poem to the Prophet and the work of the 9/15-century al-Jazūlī, mentioned above who was the author of the well-known *Dalā'il al-khayrāt*, the 'Proofs of the Excellences'. The *Dala'il* is a collection of prayers and praise names listing the excellent qualities and characteristics of the Prophet that go to make him the Perfect Man. It was, and still is, widely read and greatly venerated in the west and central Sudan. Added to the influence of these two works was that of the popular *Burda*, the 'Cloak', of the 7/13-century Berber poet, Sharaf al-Dīn Muḥammad al-Buṣīrī (*d. c.* 695–6/1296), also a praise-poem to the Prophet. These and similar works of Arabic literature mark the beginning of a process in which the cult of the Prophet as *al-Insān al-Kāmil* and *Afḍal al-khalq* who, alone, could lead man to God, largely displaced the earlier Sufi idea that it was possible to achieve *fanā'* directly in God or through the Angels. While there are obvious doctrinal and theological differences, this development in Islamic thought has certain similarities with the trend in Christian thought to elevate Jesus Christ to the status of personal redeemer, which was described in chapter 13. In both cases there seems to be the same need for a perfect, but still human, link between man and the remoteness of God. If the Christian missionaries had understood the Sufi doctrine of Muḥammad, they might at least have understood, too, why their own teachings about Christ seemed irrelevant to Muslims.

By *c.* 856/1550 new Sufi ideas began to influence the Qādiriyya in the west and central Sudan. Some came from the east, through Egypt and Turkey, for it was in the second half of the 10/16 century, *c.* 977/1570, that the mystic Sīdī Maḥmūd al-Baghdādī was murdered at Aghalangha, in Ahir, As was explained in chapter 3, he was associated with the Egyptian Khalwatiyya and with the Persian Suhrawardiyya, both strongly mystical orders. On his arrival in Ahir he quickly gained a following among the Sanhaja and Kel-Es-Suq Qādirīs, as well as some Negroes in Agades. Later, he established his own centre for prayer and teaching in Agallal in Ahir. In the end he was assassinated by his enemies, but his tomb became a place of minor pilgrimage. His followers, who referred to themselves as *al-fuqarā'*, the 'Poor Ones', settled in villages in Ahir where they practised agriculture but did not necessarily give up their Qādirī allegiance. Some of them certainly joined a sub-sect which Sīdī Maḥmūd had established and which became known as the Maḥmūdiyya.[1] Most probably they simply adopted his mystical teachings and joined them to their existing beliefs, for these new teachings seem to have been mainly about the power of the *awliyā'* to work miracles; and about how to bring on *wajd*, a state of extreme religious joy. In consequence, the Qādiriyya in and around Agades began to assume a more mystical character. To those Khalwatī and Suhrawardī influences were now added the ideas of the well-known late 9/15-century *shaykh* and author, Aḥmad al-Zarrūq, who also had a strong following in Agades. He, too, was mystical; in particular he taught that it was the duty of the postulant, the Sufi student/disciple, to be absolutely obedient to the miracle-working *shaykh* to whom he chose to attach himself, and to serve only him. The new ideas spread and they can be seen in the teachings of the Kuntī *shaykh*, Sīdī al-Mukhtār al-Kabīr (*d.* 1226/1811), and in those of the Fulani Qādirīs of the reform period in Hausaland. As will be seen, they also helped to prepare the way for the introduction of the new Tijāniyya order.

From Agades the new ideas spread into the Niger region. Also important in spreading Qādirī doctrines in that region were the two Ineslemen Sufis who flourished *c.* 1008/1600, Muḥammad al-Ansārī and Aḥmad al-Sūqī. Then, in 1133/1720/1, the town of Mabrūk, founded by the Kuntī *shaykhs*, became a centre from which the Qādiriyya spread.

In the south-west, where the Niger rises, in the country of the Markas and the Fulani, the Qādiriyya had been introduced into Kankan by the Kunta, even before they founded Mabrūk, farther north, in the Sahara. From Kankan it made its way into the area of the Senegal and then south-east, towards the Volta, but it reached the Volta by another route as well. Qādirī *shaykhs* of the Dyula Saghanughu were at work in Jenne in the late 15 century AD (9/10 century AH) and it is likely to have been through them that the Qādiriyya first spread into the Volta region. That at least is what present-day *salāsil*, Sufi chains of transmission, from the Volta region seem to indicate.

In Hausaland tradition has it that the Qādiriyya was established in Kano by Abdullahi Sikka, an ᶜ*ālim* who flourished *c.* 1019/1610. He had received the *wird* in the Fazzan and is said to have been the pupil of a certain Shaykh Shams al-Dīn al-Najīb b. Muḥammad of Anū-Samman, near Takedda; so this early Kano Sufi must have been influenced by the Ineslemen Qādirī tradition as well as by that from the Fazzan. Kano and Katsina were both visited by Muḥammad b. ᶜAbd al-Karīm al-Maghīlī at the end of the 15 century AD (*c.* AH 905). Al-Maghīlī was a Qādirī who had taught in Ahir and Takedda before coming to Hausaland and so it seems certain that he must have contributed something to Qādirī ideas in these Hausa centres of learning. On the other hand, there is no evidence that Kuntī influences, especially those of the Kuntī *shaykh* Sīdī Aḥmad al-Bakkā'ī, were particularly important in Hausaland at that time, although they certainly were in the Niger Bend and the Sahara. Nevertheless, his reputation, at least, must surely have reached there during his lifetime. Later on, there is no doubt at all that it was the Agades tradition of the Qādiriyya, with its strong Khalwatī and Shādhilī flavour, that made such a great appeal to the Fulani reformers of Hausaland. They were well-informed about Sīdī Maḥmūd al-Baghdādī and his miracles; one story, recorded by Giɗaɗo ɗan Laima about the Shehu Usumanu ɗan Fodio and later put into verse by Malam ᶜĪsā ɗan Usumanu, tells how the Agades saint of the 10/16 century miraculously appeared to greet the Shehu. Because Hausaland was part of *Dār al-kufr* at this time (that is, before the *jihād*), the holy man would not set foot on the ground, he alighted in a tree instead. So the Shehu, also miraculously, rose up into the tree beside him and here they held their conversation until it was time for the holy man to depart:

> Another miracle concerned one of the holy men from far away,
> From Baghdad. They watched out for his light from afar off,
> There in the west, in the direction of Syria,
> . . . . When the holy man came near,
> Upon a *danya* tree he alighted,
> . . .
> The holy man did not alight upon the ground because this Hausa country
> Was a land of unbelief. When the Shehu had spoken,
> Then they greeted each other and Shehu joined him up there in the tree,
> He and Kwairanga, his good friend, who loved him.
> Then they bade the holy man farewell, wishing him a safe journey,
> And as far as Tambagarka they escorted him.[2]

Thus Muslim Fulani of Hausaland frequently went to the Agades region on minor pilgrimage and it was surely his tomb at Aghalangha that they visited. The Caliph Muhammadu Bello refers to him with deep respect and veneration in his well-known *Infāq al-mayṣūr*. The writings of the Fulani *ᶜulamā'* of Sokoto display the influence of his mystical ideas, but important as he was to them, his name does not usually appear in their chains of transmission. These normally pass from Shaykh ᶜAbd al-Qādir al-Jaylānī, through the 7/13-century Aḥmad al-Badawī, the 11/17-century Egyptian *shaykh* Ibrāhīm al-Dassūqī, to the well-known 12/18-century Egyptian *shaykh*, Murtaḍā al-Zabaḍī. After him, it is the Berber *shaykh* from Agades, Jibrīl b. ᶜUmar, one of the teachers of the Shehu Usumanu ɗan Fodio, who is important. The constant recurrence of his name underlines the strength of the Agades connection in the Sufi development of the Muslim Fulani in Hausaland; indeed, it was through Shaykh Jibrīl that the Shehu was linked to the Shādhilī *shaykh*, al-Shaᶜrānī.

As for the Kunta, the Shehu Usumanu mentions Sīdī al-Mukhtār al-Kuntī al-Kabīr in his own *al-Salāsil al-Qādiriyya*, 'Qādirī Mystic Genealogies' and again in his *Bayān wujūb al-hijra*, 'On the Obligation of Emigrating'. Yet despite the *siyāḥa* of the Kunta and their undoubted importance in the Sahara, the Fulani reformers had still not received the Kuntī *wird* at the time when the *jihād* began. They made an attempt to obtain it but were not successful and it was not until later, when he had become caliph, that Muhammadu Bello eventually acquired it. It thus seems clear that the Kuntī *shaykhs* were not among the main cultivators of the Qādiriyya in Hausaland, it was rather the Ineslemen of Ahir and Agades who filled that role.

Certain other great Sufi names were important to the Fulani of Hausaland. The 6/12-century Aḥmad al-rifāᶜī, founder of the Rifāᶜiyya order, is often cited as an authority. The works of the Shādhilī *shaykh*, Aḥmad al-Zarrūq (fl. *c.* 884/1480) were also familiar to them, so too were those of the 5/11-century al-

Ghazzālī and the mystic Muhya al-Dīn b. ᶜArabī, who flourished *c.* 597/1200. He was among the earliest of the Sufis to explain the divine love and its relationship to the mission of the Prophet Muḥammad through the imagery of light. Yet another famous name to which they often refer is that of al-Suyūṭī, who was a Shādhilī with strong Qādirī sympathies.

By 1267/1850, when the Qadirism of the Muslim Fulani had reached its fullest development in the Sokoto caliphate, its doctrines were complex and many-sided, but at the centre of them were two cardinal ideas. The first was the role of Muḥammad as *al-Insān al-Kāmil*, the 'Perfect Man', which, as was pointed out above, began to develop in Sudanic Sufism after 802/1400. Here is an example of how it was expressed in verse which was first composed by the Shehu Usumanu himself in Fulfulde and then rendered into Hausa by his son, Malam ᶜĪsā, during the golden days of the Sokoto caliphate:

> All created beings, Aḥmad [Muḥammad] excels them, in truth,
> The Most Perfect of Mankind, our saviour on the Last Day,
> Truly, you [Muḥammad] have been singled out,
> Among the excellent ones [Muḥammad] has been chosen,
> The Most Perfect of us all – God's Messenger.[3]

The second idea was that of the saving *walī*, who was the intermediary between the Believer and God and who would intercede for those who accepted him on the Last Day. In the following passage, also from the verse of Malam ᶜĪsā, it is the Shehu himself who is that *walī*:

> May God save me from the evil of the djinn,
> And also from the evil of men, for the sake of [the Shehu's] miracles,
> O God, grant me a good death [in the Faith] on the day that
> Death comes as a guest to life and meets with it, . . . for his sake,
> Thus also on the Day of Resurrection,
> Save me on that Day, for his sake,
> On that Day may my good deeds
> Outweigh my evil deeds, I beseech Almighty God, for his sake,
> . . .
> Also, I pray, place me on that Last Day among those
> Saved by the Most Perfect of Mankind [the Prophet],
> I beg, for [the Shehu's] sake.[4]

Another important idea, linked to that of the Prophet as *al-Insān al-Kāmil*, was that of *al-nūr al-muḥammadī*, the 'Muhammadan Light'. According to this idea, the purpose of the Prophet's mission was to spread the divine light of love, mercy and knowledge among mankind; and for many Sufis Muḥammad was himself the personification of that light. The idea was often expressed poetically through the image of the light that, in the well-known legend of infancy, shone at the moment of his birth,

> When dawn breaks I know the good tidings,
> The vision of his light and of his luminance,
> The Yemen was suffused with light, and Syria too, through him alone,

Whenever the dawn breaks, I remember his birth,
For it was the Dawn of his Coming.[5]

As will be seen below, this idea of the divine light and its association with the Prophet Muḥammad helped to prepare the way for the Tijāni doctrine of *al-ḥaqā'iq al-muḥammadiyya*, the 'Muhammadan Truths'.

In neighbouring Borno Sufism almost certainly reached the *ᶜulamā'* in the first instance from North Africa. It is not possible to say how early this may have begun to happen but it is known that a poet from Kanem, Ibrāhīm b. Yaᶜqūb al-Kānamī, visited the court of the Almohad ruler, Yaᶜqūb al-Manṣūr (580/1184–595/1199). It was about this time that Sufi ideas began to become popular in the Maghrib, though as yet no distinct *ṭuruq* had emerged. It is certainly possible that such early contacts between Kanem and the Almohads may have resulted in introducing Sufi ideas into Kanem.

During the 9/15 century, Kuntī *shaykhs* were visiting Borno and they must surely have begun to spread Qādirī ideas there. A certain Shaykh al-Bakrī, of Borno, who flourished towards the end of the 10/16 century, is said to have been trained by Shaykh Shams al-Dīn al-Najīb b. Muḥammad of Anū-Samman, who also taught the Kano Sufi, Malam Abdullahi Sikka.

It is with the rise of the centre of learning at Kalambardo, in the late 11/16 or early 11–12/17 century, that the full extent of Sufi activity in Borno becomes apparent. The scholarly community there was linked to Ahir, which means that it must have been influenced by the mystical ideas associated with the *walī* Sīdī Maḥmūd al-Baghdādī. Indeed, there is evidence that the Toureg *shaykh*, Muḥammad al-Jarmiya al-Tarqī of Kalumbardo, was himself regarded as a miracle-worker. Later, by *c.* 1076/1664, under its leader, Shaykh ᶜAbd Allāh al-Barnāwī, the community was linked not only with Ahir but also with the very active group of Qādirī Sufis of the Nile Valley. Indeed, it seems that at this time, from the 11–12/17 century on, there was a circuit that was regularly followed by wandering Sufi scholars which ran from the Nile Valley to Borno and from Borno on to Ahir, and then from there to Fez thus serving to link all four centres within the Qādirī *ṭarīqa* (see Appendix A, Diagram IV). Indeed, Lavers has pointed to the importance of what he calls the 'frontier activity' of the Sufis of the 11–12/17 century, which he considers supplemented the role of such metropolitan centres as the Azhar and Fez in the task of spreading Sufism, and indeed Islam itself, among Sūdānī animists and polytheists at this time.[6]

It was during the 11–12/17 and 12/18 centuries that the Borno *mais* made frequent Pilgrimages in the course of which they passed through Egypt. Egypt was at this time at the height of that Sufi activity that had earlier produced such noted mystics as Sīdī Maḥmūd al-Baghdādī. During the second half of the 18 century AD (AH 1163–1214) there were at least nineteen distinct Sufi *ṭuruq* active in Egypt. An authority on Islamic intellectual life in Egypt has described the importance of Sufism there during this century as follows:

> The relationship of eighteenth century *taṣawwuf* [Sufism] to religion and to all classes of Moslem society cannot be under-rated. By this time, few seem to have been able to call themselves Moslems without belonging to one or more of the religious orders, and . . . even the orthodox *shaikhs* and *ᶜulamā'* had their own special order; religious life was no longer governed

> by the simple tenets of Islam but rather by the various *ṣufī*-interpretations of religious law and texts. Moral guidance was sought from and given by the *shaikhs* through the channels of this huge superstructure of *sufism* rather than through direct reference to orthodox Islamic principles.[7]

The *mais* and thc Borno ᶜ*ulamā*ʾ who travelled with them cannot have remained uninfluenced by such tendencies. As Borno contacts widened to include other parts of the Ottoman empire, and as Turks became more numerous in Borno itself, so Sufi activity must have increased there.

North Africa and Egypt may not have been the only sources of Sufi influence. There was a strong link between the Fazzan and the Hausa city of Katsina, that developed during the second half of the 16 century AD (AH 955/1008). Al-Maghīlī had already visited that city by that date and the Qādiriyya was also firmly established in Kano. The Fāzzānī link with Katsina seems to have been maintained at least until *c.* 1111/1700 and one of its consequences may have been that Sufi ideas were exchanged between the ᶜ*ulamā*ʾ of Katsina and those of the Fazzan. If so, the consequent intellectual activity is likely to have spread into Borno.

By the late 18 century AD (12–13 century AH) there can be no doubt about the strength of the Qādiriyya in Borno for by that time Shaykh Muḥammad al-Kānamī had set up his school at Ngala. Al-Kānamī was a devout Qādirī and under him and his successors the Qādiriyya became firmly identified with the dynasty he founded. As in Sokoto, so in Kukawa, it was not just Islam, but Qādirī Islam, that was now essential for the legitimacy of the ruler and his government.

In the Volta region the pattern was different. After the North African Qādirī tradition had been introduced by Saghanughu *shaykhs* in the 9/15 century, Kunta influences followed, probably during the 12/18 century. The *salāsil*, the chains of transmission, of Qādirīs in the area were then renewed from time to time by those of Hausas, coming into the areas with their own chains that sprang from several different origins. By 1214/1800 Kong had become a centre of Saghanughu Qādirī *shaykhs* and a Qādirī *shaykh* from Mamprussi was present as far south as Kumasi in 1221–2/1807. However the Volta area lacked the stimulus of Khalwatī ideas that had such a marked influence farther to the east, perhaps because the Volta was too far removed from Egypt, the centre of so much Sufi activity. Thus among Sufis there, there was less evidence of the new Sufi ideas that were described above until the Tijāniyya began to compete with the Qādiriyya towards the end of the 19 century AD (13/14 century AH).

In the Senegambia the Muslim leaders who launched the so-called maraboutic wars against the Wolof, Denianke and Soninke kings, were probably Qādirīs although in view of the lack of first-hand sources giving accounts of their background and education, this is not absolutely certain. Nevertheless, it remains unlikely that the Senegambia was untouched by Sufism before the time of the great Tijānī jihadist, al-Ḥāj ᶜUmar al-Fūtī.

The Tijāniyya

The Tijāniyya was founded in Cairo by Shaykh Aḥmad al-Tijānī (1150/1737–1230/1815), who was originally a member of the Khalwatiyya. From Cairo he returned to North Africa and at ᶜAyn Māḍī, in Fez he set up his *zāwiya*, which became the centre for the new *ṭarīqa*. From here it spread into the western Sudan, Senegal and Mauritania, largely through the efforts of Shaykh Muḥammad al-Ḥāfiẓ b. Mukhtār al-Ḥabīb, an early disciple of Shaykh Aḥmad. Some of its doctrines were surely known to the Shehu Usumanu ɗan Fodio, who appears to have regarded the founder of the *ṭarīqa* with respect but certainly did not adopt it.

The first deliberate attempt to spread the teachings of the order in Hausaland was that of al-Ḥājj ᶜUmar al-Fūtī, who visited Sokoto on his way to Pilgrimage in 1241/1825–6. Shaykh ᶜUmar was already a Tijānī, having taken the *wird* from Shaykh ᶜAbd al-Karīm b. Aḥmad al-Naqīl al-Fūtā Jallūnī. There is evidence that Shaykh ᶜUmar began to expound some of the new teachings to the Sokoto *ᶜulamā'* during the course of this first visit but on his return from Pilgrimage he spent longer there by which time he had undergone further instruction in the doctrines of the *ṭarīqa* from the Meccan *ᶜālim*, Muḥammad al-Ghālī. While in Sokoto he completed his work *Suyūf al-saᶜīd*, the 'Swords of the One Favoured with Good Fortune', and probably started to draft his *Rimāḥ ḥizb al-raḥīm ᶜalā nuḥūr ḥizb al-rajīm*, the 'Spears of the Party of the Compassionate at the Throats of the Party of the Accursed', in which he set down in great detail the doctrines of the Tijāniyya as he understood them. Thus it was during the period of his second visit to Sokoto that the Qādirī establishment there was able to make a further, more detailed assessment of these doctrines. However, apart from the Caliph Muhammadu Bello, it seems they did not much like what they heard and read.

According to oral tradition, al-Ḥājj ᶜUmar al-Fūtī also visited other towns and cities in Hausaland at this time. If so, he no doubt set up small groups of people in these centres who accepted his teachings and began to practise the rituals of the new order.

The elaboration of Tijānī doctrine:
Rafᶜ al-ishtibāḥ of the Caliph Muhammadu Bello[8]

It is clear that al-Ḥājj ᶜUmar did win the respect and friendship of the Caliph Muhammadu Bello. It was probably as a result of the constant queries he received about the ideas of his new friend, that the Caliph now composed his well-known *Rafᶜ al-ishtibāh*, the 'Removal of Uncertainty'. In it he makes clear the extent of his knowledge of al-Ḥājj ᶜUmar's *Suyūf al-saᶜīd* and also of the *Jawāhir al-maᶜānī*, the 'Jewels of Hidden Meanings'. This last work was recorded in writing by Shaykh ᶜAlī Harāzim, from the dictation of Shaykh Aḥmad al-Tijānī himself and was almost certainly introduced into Sokoto by al-Ḥājj ᶜUmar al-Fūtī. It is the source from which Tijānī doctrines subsequently developed. The Caliph Muhammadu Bello quotes extensively from these Tijānī sources, as well as from a number of pre-Tijānī works. His main concern in *Rafᶜ* is with the question of the *wilāya*, the state of being a *walī*, what it means and what the function of a *walī* is. He explains that the Believer needs a link with God, from whom he must never become separated, and that this link can only be achieved through attaching oneself to a *walī*. The *awliyā'* are the deputies of the Prophet Muḥammad and he, in his turn, is the intermediary to God. This, of course, is part of the doctrine of *al-Insān al-Kāmil*, already fully familiar to the Qādirīs.

The Caliph Muhammadu Bello now goes on to discuss the various classes of the *awliyā'*. He says there are certain *awliyā'* who are 'the keys to God's mercy and the mines of wisdom' and that whoever establishes a link with them will be assured of salvation. They are: Aḥmad al-Rifāᶜī, Aḥmad al-Badawī, ᶜAbd al-Qādir al-Jaylānī, Ibrāhīm al-Dassūqī, al-Ḥasan al-Shādhilī and Aḥmad al-Tijānī. He thus clearly recognises Shaykh Aḥmad al-Tijānī as an outstanding *walī* and even records his claim to be the only *walī* able to ensure that his followers enter Paradise without the Judgement and the Punishment that others may have to suffer to cleanse them of minor sins. He also accepts that Shaykh Aḥmad al-Tijānī saw the Prophet Muḥammad in a vision: thus he goes a long way towards accepting the Tijānī claims. This was further than the rest of the Sokoto ᶜ*ulamā'* were apparently prepared to go, as later events were to show, but he stops short of agreeing to the central Tijānī claim – that Aḥmad al-Tijānī was the 'Seal of the *Awliyā'*', the last and greatest of God's *awliyā'* and thus superior to all others who passed before him.

In addition to the Tijānī texts mentioned above, the Caliph Muhammadu Bello quotes extensively from *al-Ibrīz*, the 'Pure Gold', of the North African Sufi Aḥmad b. al-Mubārak. This is a pre-Tijānī work on the *wilāya*, written in 1129/1716. He refers, too, to the ᶜ*Umdat al-murīd*, the 'Support of the Disciple', of the Shādhilī *shaykh*, Aḥmad al-Zarrūq (*d*. 898/1493), as well as to a number of well-known Tijānī authorities. This is important for it clearly shows that there was a tradition of open-mindedness and readiness to accept new ideas among this early generation of Fodiawa in Hausaland, to which Muhammadu Bello remained faithful. Later, the Qādirī establishment in Sokoto became more conservative and rigid.

It is clear from *Raf*ᶜ that the Caliph Muhammadu Bello admired Shaykh Aḥmad al-Tijānī and that he was deeply interested in his teachings. Some of them he obviously accepted, for they were consistent with the developing Sufi ideas of the day with which he was already familiar from other sources. It is also clear, however, from the careful reserve that he maintains on certain crucial issues, that he did not go as far as to desert the Qādiriyya in favour of whole-hearted allegiance to the new *ṭarīqa*. *Raf*ᶜ is a balanced and fair-minded assessment of one aspect of Tijānī teaching – the one that concerns the *wilāya*. It is warm in its regard for the great *shaykh*, Aḥmad al-Tijānī but in no way commits the author to the new *ṭarīqa*.

Despite the evidence of *Raf*ᶜ, a case is often made out that the Caliph Muhammadu Bello did, in the end, abandon the Qādiriyya and go over to the Tijāniyya. This case rests on material in al-Ḥājj ᶜUmar al-Fūtī's *Rimāh*.[9] It is alleged that in this work, al-Ḥājj ᶜUmar implies that his friend Muhammadu Bello did in fact adopt the new *ṭarīqa*. The evidence is too lengthy and complicated to set out here, but in the opinion of the present writer, a careful reading of the *Rimāḥ* shows it to be unsound. What al-Ḥājj ᶜUmar says indicates that the two men were close friends and greatly respected one another, but he nowhere states that Muhammadu Bello joined the Tijāniyya. On the contrary, he records a number of conversations and incidents that imply that the caliph did no such thing. If al-Ḥājj ᶜUmar had wished to give the impression that Muhammadu Bello had become a Tijāni, he certainly would not have included evidence that points in the other direction.

That the Caliph Muhammadu Bello died a Qādirī is finally placed beyond reasonable doubt by the evidence of a certain al-Ḥājj Saᶜīd, tutor to the Caliph

Muhammadu Bello's grandsons and himself a devout Tijānī. He states, on the authority of the caliph's son, Malam Muᶜādh, who was present at his father's bedside just before he died, that his last words were a prayer to Shaykh ᶜAbd al-Qādir al-Jaylānī and to his father, the Qādirī *walī*, Shehu Usumanu ɗan Fodio.[10] Since al-Ḥājj Saᶜīd was a Tijānī himself it is hardly likely that he would have recorded this account unless he knew it to be true.

The Risāla of Muḥammad al-Rājī

The subsequent development of the Tijāniyya and of its doctrines in Hausaland was recorded by a certain Muḥammad al-Rājī, a ᶜ*ālim* of Gwandu. As a young man he had taken the Qādirī *wird* from the Shehu Usumanu ɗan Fodio but subsequently, he transferred to the Tijāniyya after reading al-Ḥājj ᶜUmar's *Suyūf al-saᶜīd*. In 1261/1845 or thereabouts, he composed his *Risāla*, 'Epistle', addressed to the Emir Halilu of Gwandu. In the *Risāla* he explains that he had converted to the Tijāniyya more than ten years earlier, but he concealed the fact because he knew it would greatly offend his Qādirī colleagues. Now, however, membership of the new *ṭarīqa* has become so widespread and its virtues so evident, he feels he can no longer continue this concealment. In his *Risāla* he invites the emir to adopt the new order and come out openly in its support. The centre of his argument in support of the Tijāniyya's superiority is that, whereas founders of earlier *ṭuruq* were all separated from the Prophet Muḥammad by long chains of transmitters, Shaykh Aḥmad al-Tijānī was in direct personal contact with the Prophet through his visions. This nearness to the Prophet is an obvious mark of God's special favour to al-Tijānī and to benefit from this all Muslims now ought to hasten to him. He goes on to say that, in the same way that the Prophet's spirit was the source of power for all the other prophets who came before him, so Shaykh Aḥmad al-Tijānī's spirit is the source of power for all the *awliyā'* who came before him. He also argues that the Caliph Muhammadu Bello did join the Tijāniyya but this fact has been wrongfully concealed by the Qādirīs in Sokoto. From incidental information in the *Risāla* it seems clear that, by Muḥammad al-Rājī's day, widespread conversion to the Tijāniyya had taken place in Hausaland, but the converts were subject to some harassment by the Qādirī authorities and were unwilling or unable to practise the rituals of the order openly and in congregation.

The Emir Halilu did not accept Muḥammad al-Rājī's invitation to support the Tijāniyya. *C.* 1267/1850, Muḥammad al-Rājī left Gwandu with a substantial following, intending to perform Pilgrimage, but he stopped in Adamawa where he settled and spent the rest of his days.

Malam Muḥammad al-Rājī's work gives interesting and important information about the attitude towards the Tijāniyya of the Qādirī establishment in his day; it also sets out the main Tijānī beliefs at that date. However it is clear that, from the time that the Caliph Muhammadu Bello wrote his *Rafᶜ* to the time that Muḥammad al-Rājī published his *Risāla*, little advance had been made in the elaboration of Tijānī teachings. The main concern of both authors is with the *wilāya*; Muḥammad al-Rājī's only addition to the thoughts of Muhammadu Bello is that he attributes a unique status as the ultimate *walī* to Shaykh Aḥmad al-Tijānī, a claim that the Caliph withholds, despite his admiration for the man. Thus Muḥammad al-Rājī simply re-states the Tijānī position as it was put by al-Ḥājj ᶜUmar al-Fūtī and adds nothing to it.

The Kitāb dhikr rijāl al-sanad of Malam ᶜUmar b. Aḥmad al-Wālī[12]

The next major step forward in the doctrinal evolution of Tijanism in Hausaland came from the pen of a Zaria ᶜ*ālim* who flourished *c.* 1303/1885. His name was Malam ᶜUmar b. Aḥmad al-Wālī, usually referred to by the Hausas simply as Malam Umaru Wali. As a boy of fifteen this man took the Tijānī *wird* from Malam Shi'itu, an early Tijānī initiator in Zaria. Many years later he wrote a work entitled *Kitāb dhikr rijāl al-sanad*, 'Book of Mention of the Sufis of the Ascription'. (The Arabic word *rijāl* here bears its specialised Sufi meaning of 'members of the Sufi order', not just 'men' as in everyday Arabic. *Sanad*, here rendered an 'ascription' is close to *silsila* in its meaning and refers to the process by which knowledge, or even an oral commentary on a particular book is passed from teacher to pupil). The *Kitāb dhikr* is certainly the most remarkable of this scholar's several works and in it he expounds Tijānī doctrines as he understands them.

He begins by repeating Muḥammad al-Rājī's complaint that the Tijānīs are forced to worship individually, not in congregation; thus it seems they may still have been subject to harassment. He then goes on to explain several important points of doctrine not touched on by the Caliph Muhammadu Bello or Muḥammad al-Rājī. First, whereas earlier *ṭuruq* tried to teach their members how to achieve *fanā'*, 'absorption', in the divine presence through *khalwa*, religious exercises such as fasting, retreat, prolonged meditation and so on, Tijānīs can arrive at this ultimate spiritual experience simply by creating in their minds the images of their initiating *shaykhs*, through Aḥmad al-Tijānī up to and including the Prophet Muḥammad himself. Then, by holding these images in the mind and concentrating on them, *fanā'* will come about, but he denies that it is possible to achieve *fanā'* in God Himself and argues that the most man can hope for is absorption in the Prophet. The significance of this teaching is, of course, that it makes the ultimate Sufi experience attainable by a much greater number of Sufis; it is no longer confined to those who are willing and able to undergo the rigours of *khalwa*. Spelling out the teaching in this way was an important step towards popularising Sufism among the Muslim Hausas.

Malam Umaru Wali's second major contribution was that he explained the complex mystical doctrine of *al-ḥaqā'iq al-muḥammadiyya*, the 'Muhammadan Truths'. According to this doctrine, the whole universe is divided into five *ḥaḍrāt* (sing. *ḥaḍra*), 'stages' or 'levels', which include the Seven Heavens. The lowest *ḥaḍra* is Nāsūt, the stage of material existence, the highest Hāhūt, the stage of the divine essence. These *ḥaḍrāt* are identified with the attributes of the Prophet Muḥammad, *al-Insān al-Kāmil*. Thus the highest *ḥadra* is that of His secrets; the next one down is that of His spirit; the next, that of His intellect; the next, that of His heart and the lowest one of all, that of His carnal self. These aspects of Muḥammad are the carriers of *al-ḥaqā'iq al-muḥammadiyya*, namely the truths of divine love, mercy and knowledge and all that flows from them. These truths fill the universe in the form of divine light, as they descend down through the *ḥaḍrāt*, to man, but without the intermediacy of the Prophet this could not come about because the divine light is too intense for man to gaze upon directly. Only through the perfection of the Prophet's qualities and attributes can man be made fit to receive it and in this way the Prophet becomes the First Principle of the universe and the intermediary through whom God makes His divine gifts available to man. That these divine gifts are made available in this way is, Malam Umaru explains, the meaning of *fayḍa*, 'saving grace', which passes to the individual Tijānī through his initiating *shaykh*, from the Prophet who in turn receives it from God. Without the Prophet man would be wholly cut off from *fayḍa*, but equally, without his initiating *shaykh*, it is difficult if not impossible for a man to achieve that union with the Prophet that enables him to receive *fayḍa*. Thus the doctrine of the Muhammadan Truths is the fullest expression of the idea of *al-Insān al-Kāmil* which first reached West African Muslims through such early Sufi writers as the 7/13-century North African poet, al-Fāzāzī, and al-Jazūlī, the 9/15-century author of *Dalā'il al-khayrāt*. From this doctrine also, flows the doctrine of the *wilāya*, the role and Powers of the saving *shaykh* or *walī*, and it now becomes clear how the imagery of light in earlier Hausa verse of the Qādirī poets, quoted from above, prepared the way for the more elaborate Tijānī doctrine.

Of course, these ideas were not original to the Tijāniyya, let alone to Malam Umaru Wali in person. They date back at least to the 6–7/12–13 -century Sufi, Muhyi al-Dīn b. ᶜArabī, but the Tijāniyya made them its own by identifying them with the unique spiritual experience of the founding *shaykh*, Aḥmad al-Tijānī. In explaining them in his book, Malam Umaru Wali made a very important contribution to the intellectual and spiritual development of the Muslim Hausas.

The spread of the Tijāniyya in West Africa

A study of Tijānī *salāsil*, chains of transmission, in Hausaland, makes it clear that, while al-Ḥājj ᶜUmar al-Fūtī was certainly the first to introduce the *ṭarīqa* into that area, he did not for long remain the sole transmitter. In the next generation of Tijānīs many trace their initiation into the *ṭarīqa* straight back to the Mauritanian *shaykh*, Mawlūd Fāl and do not mention al-Ḥājj ᶜUmar at all. Others have *salāsil* that go back to transmitters from Fās and even Mecca, none of which mention the Segu *shaykh*, al-Ḥājj ᶜUmar al-Fūtī. Therefore, without diminishing his real importance, it seems probable that, even if he had never visited Hausaland, the Tijāniyya would none the less have reached there during the second half of the 19 century AD (AH 1266–1317).

In the Niger area the same holds good, although in this part of the Sudan there do seem to be rather more *salāsil* that link to al-Ḥājj ᶜUmar al-Fūtī in person.

In Mauritania the Tijāniyya was introduced by Shaykh Muḥammad al-Ḥāfiẓ. It was spread in the Senegambia by the Mauritanian, Shaykh Mawlūd Fāl who passed it on to ᶜAbd al-Karīm b. Aḥmad al-Naqīl al-Fūtā Jallūnī, who first initiated Shaykh ᶜUmar al-Fūtī before his Pilgrimage. It received further impetus in the Senegambia from the preaching tour that al-Ḥājj ᶜUmar al-Fūtī carried out there before 1267/1851, the year in which he moved to Dinguiray. After the death of al-Ḥājj ᶜUmar it was further spread in Senegambia by a number of Mauritanian and Senegalese *shaykhs* amongst whom were the well-known Shaykh ᶜAbd Allāh al-Anyās and Shaykh Mālik Sy. It was promoted, although not very vigorously, among the Soninke, by al-Ḥājj Muḥammad al-Amīn and along the Gambia river by Maba Diakhou.

In the Volta area the Tijāniyya made slow inroads among the conservative Qādirīs there, but Shaykh ᶜUmar al-Fūtī was in touch with certain Saghanughu *shaykhs* in Bobo-Dioulassu before he went on Pilgrimage in 1241/1825 and may have expounded some of the doctrines to them at that time. A Tijānī *shaykh*, al-Ḥājj Isḥāq b. Muḥammad al-Fūtī, was at work in Bonduku before *c.* 1303/1885, when he died. However, the main Tijānī expansion there took place from 1308/1890 onwards, when, after the fall of Sultan Aḥmad's Segu empire, Tijānī leaders dispersed to the east into Hausaland and south-east into the country north of Ashanti. By *c.* 1317/1899 there were at least three lines along which the Tijāniyya was transmitted into the Volta region; one was from Hausaland, especially Kano and Katsina; one was from Jenne via Dyulasso and Kong; and a third was directly from Mecca and Medina, through returning Pilgrims. There may also have been a fourth line directly from Mauritania.

In the southern Gold Coast, present day Ghana, the *ṭarīqa* was brought in at the end of the 19 century AD (13/14 century AH) by Hausa traders, who settled in the Gold Coast *zongos*. Their influence was added to as a result of the policy of the early British administration in the Gold Coast who recruited Hausas as police and troops. A number of these men were Tijānīs who after retiring from the service settled in the *zongos*; thus they further strengthened the Tijānī presence in these Hausa speaking communities.

In Borno the establishment of the Tijāniyya dates from al-Ḥājj ᶜUmar's visit there on his way home from Pilgrimage. The new *ṭarīqa* was particularly well received by supporters of the deposed Saifawid *mais*, for taking the Tijānī *wird* was one way of expressing opposition to the Qādirī dynasty of Shehu al-Kānamī and his successors. For this reason Shehu al-Kānamī opposed the new *ṭarīqa* despite al-Ḥājj ᶜUmar's protests.

By AD 1900 the Tijāniyya had spread a wide network right across the west and central Sudan, from the Senegal to Borno, and had also become the main contender with the Qādiriyya for the allegiance of the Muslim populations of West Africa as a whole. The Qādiriyya and the Tijāniyya were, and still are, the two main *ṭuruq* in West Africa, but two others deserve attention – the Sanūsiyya, that will be discussed below, and the Murīdiyya that will be discussed in chapter 17.

The Sanūsiyya

The Sanūsiyya *ṭarīqa* was founded by Muḥammad ᶜAlī al-Sanūsī (*d.* 1276/1859) and like the Tijāniyya, its emergence was largely the outcome of the Sufi revival in the Azhar at the end of the 18 century AD (12/13 century AH). It was also an attempt to respond to the criticism of the Wahhābīs by reforming Sufism; the Sanūsīs remained Sufis but adopted many Wahhābī ideas and attitudes, which they made their own. Like the Tijānīs, the Sanūsīs disapproved of strict adherence to any one *madhhab*; they advocated *ijtihād*, the freedom of every Muslim to adopt whichever of the four Sunnī schools of law he liked. They objected too, to the doctrine of *taqlīd*, the unquestioning acceptance of tradition and precedent and they questioned the ancient belief of Sufism that it was possible to achieve union with God through spiritual exercises. Instead, they sought union with the Prophet, but their Sufism was expressed as much through active preaching and the conversion of infidels as through the individual mysticism and withdrawal of traditional Sufis. They differed from the earlier Sufi reformers of the western Sudan in that their aims were not limited to the Sudan but extended to North Africa, the Sahara and even the Ottoman empire.

Indeed, it was a central aim of the Sanūsīs to bring about the unification of *Dār al-islām*, but – a point not mentioned by Nachtigal – Muḥammad ᶜAlī al-Sanūsī himself, despite his strong views on the political and religious issues of his day, was a peaceful man who opposed violence. He taught that it was only justifiable to fight if first attacked, although it must be admitted that not all his followers were so pacific.

Muḥammad ᶜAlī al-Sanūsī had intended to base his order in Algeria, but he had been prevented from doing so by the French occupation of that country. The order moved to Cyrenaica, at the eastern end of North Africa where its members set up their base for missionary work in the Sahara. Their method was to found *zawāyā* from which Islam and Sanūsī doctrines were carried far and wide by Sanūsī missionaries. From Cyrenaica the Sanūsiyya spread slowly south, via Zawila, Kawar, Kufra and Borgu until, by Nachtigal's day, it was well established in Kanem, Borno and Wadai from where it spread east and west into the sub-Saharan Sudan. It became established in Kano *c.* 1307–8/1890.

Like the Muslim Fulani reformers, the Sanūsīs were Mahdists. Muḥammad ᶜAlī al-Sanūsī named one of his sons 'Muḥammad al-Mahdī' which was probably a deliberate attempt to draw the widespread Mahdist sympathies of Muslims throughout North Africa, the Sahara and the Ottoman empire to the support of his order. He made Mahdism a central part of his teaching and related it precisely to the political and international circumstances of his day. For example, he accurately prophesied the course of the European conquests and taught that they were to be seen as signs that brought the coming of the Mahdī nearer and nearer. When Muḥammad ᶜAlī al-Sanūsī died attention focused on his son, Muḥammad al-Madhī, as he had intended, and the founder's choice of this name was now seen by many as clear proof that this Muḥammad was indeed the long-awaited Mahdī. It was not seen as a clever political calculation but as supernatural foresight, the excitement this caused being the greater because AD 1882–3 was also AH 1300, the start of a new century of the Hijra. Expectations had been disappointed in 1200/1785 when the Mahdī had not appeared after all, would AH 1300 see the long-awaited realisation of this event?

When attempting to decide whether Nachtigal's description of the Sanūsīs as 'red-hot Christian haters'[13] was justified or not, much depends on whether one regards the teachings of the founder, or the actions and words of his followers, as the deciding factor. In fact, Muḥammad ᶜAlī al-Sanūsī himself was not hostile to Christians as such, but he was hostile to the political and military interference of what he regarded as Christian governments in *Dār al-islām*. He deeply resented the activities of Christian missionaries there. However, there is no denying the physical hostility of certain Sanūsīs toward Nachtigal, indeed, it was only through the intervention of his Muslim friends that his life was saved. Thus the conclusion must be that the Sanūsī rank and file were nearer to Nachtigal's description of them than was their gentle and pacific founder. This is entirely understandable for the Sanūsīs inevitably reflected in their attitudes not only the conflicts and arguments within the Islamic world of the day, but also the mounting tension between the Christian missionaries and imperialists on the one hand and Muslims on the other. The French occupation of Algeria had not only driven the Sanūsīs out of that country; it had also confirmed what many Muslims had long feared – that the Christians were set on a major assault against Islam. This was not only a military assault for, as explained in chapter 13, there was a powerful, well-organised Christian missionary effort starting up, the publicly declared purpose of which was the conversion of the Islamic world to Christianity. This applied even in Arabia, itself the very centre of Islam. As the Reverend George Stone, a missionary who had worked in Arabia, put it,

> I don't know when the explosion is coming but we are putting dynamite under the rock of Islam and some day God will touch it off.[14]

It is necessary to understand that Zwemer quotes this observation to commend it, not to condemn it and this approval must have been shared by a large number of Christians of the day. They put their money in considerable quantities in the missionaries' collecting boxes and it was this money that enabled them to go about their work. So, since the Sanūsīs had ears with which the hear the message of men like Zwemer and Stone, who misused the street corners of the Turkish empire for the purpose of their preaching, it is not surprising if Nachtigal had to fear Sanūsī hostility from time to time.

Sanūsī influence made itself felt even among Muslims who were not necessarily members of the order. A Hausa poet of the early 20 century AD may well have been reflecting Sanūsī attitudes when he wrote:

> It was disobedience to the Word of Muḥammad that brought [the Christians] in the first place,
> And they enslaved everyone,
> May God protect us from servitude to the Christians,
> O our Lord God, protect your servants
> From doing the work of the Christians,
> Be prepared. They will lead you astray. Gird up your loins to follow Muḥammad, that you may escape from the Christians![15]

Aḥmad Bamba, the founder of the Murīds of Senegal (see chapter 17), was more direct in expressing his support for their views. He wrote:

> Presently, people have a tendency to follow the path of the Europeans, accursed be they and may God be without pity for them. . . .
> In the name of the prophet Sanūsī may God be without pity for the infidels, and equally cursed be those who follow them, for they are in the bad path.[16]

The consequences of Sufi development in West Africa

Sufism was present in Sudanic Islam from *c.* 853/1450 while certain of its ideas may well have been circulating at an earlier date. It moved from the 'old' Qādiriyya to the 'new' Qādiriyya under the influences of the new orders that developed in North Africa and Egypt. Its dominant ideas then became that of the Prophet Muḥammad as *al-Insān al-Kāmil* and of the *wilāya*, the role and powers of the *awliyā'*. Out of the intellectual ferment that these ideas created arose the Tijāniyya, which centred these doctrines within itself by associating them with the particular spiritual experience of its founder, Shaykh Aḥmad al-

Tijānī. The Sanūsiyya arose out of the same historical and intellectual process although it was especially conditioned by the influence of Wahhabism and by Christian militancy against Islam.

The rise of the Sufi *ṭuruq* in the west and central Sudan had a number of consequences. First, *ṭarīqa* allegiance was quickly identified with local patriotism and in consequence, charismatic personalities such as Sīdī Aḥmad al-Bakkā'ī, Sīdī al-Mukhtār al-Kabīr, Sīdī Maḥmūd al-Baghdādī and the Shehu Usumanu ɗan Fodio quickly became symbols of self-awareness and solidarity for the Muslim communities among whom they lived. Also, perhaps more importantly, so did their tombs which became places of minor pilgrimage. This helped to give a sense of unity and common identity to Muslim groups, which was an important factor in encouraging the growth of Islamic states.

Alongside this local solidarity, the *ṭuruq* also fostered Islamic universalism, for they encouraged Pilgrimage in the course of which West African pilgrims often visited the great centres of Islamic civilization in North Africa and the Middle East, as well as Mecca and Medina. With Islamic universalism they also acquired ideological notions, some common to Islam as a whole, others peculiar to specific *ṭuruq*. A typical example is that of al-Ḥājj Maḥmūd of Wahabu who, it will be remembered, was inspired by a *shaykh* in Syria to return home and wage *jihād* in the way of God. The experience of al-Ḥājj ᶜUmar al-Fūtī is another, yet more notable example. Certainly this build-up of Islamic ideology was a major factor that helped to drive West African Muslim idealists to *jihād*, but it must also have contributed to the spread of Islam in more peaceful, if less spectacular, ways – by teaching, by personal example and by the daily social intercourse between returned pilgrims and the people among whom they lived.

As the *ṭuruq* became widespread, so they attracted more people into them and thus became the main agents for conversion to Islam. Moreover, as the *ṭuruq* hierarchies developed within West African societies, they became the centres for political as well as religious activity. Thus in Hausaland and in Borno the Qādiriyya became associated with the ruling establishment while the Tijāniyya when it appeared, assumed the role of a political opposition.

Finally, the *ṭuruq* played a big part in promoting literacy, in Arabic through the schools that the *ṭuruq* founded and in vernacular languages especially Fulfulde and Hausa, by encouraging the composition of religious verse in these languages. *Madḥ*, praise-poetry to the Prophet Muḥammad and to the *ṭuruq* founders especially Shaykh ᶜAbd al-Qādir al-Jaylānī and Shaykh Aḥmad al-Tijānī, became widespread among the Sufis.

In all these ways the *ṭuruq* helped to bring people into Islam and coloured the life and culture of the west and central Sudan, and indeed many parts of West Africa beyond the Sudan.

NOTES

1 I am indebted to Dr H.T. Norris for this unpublished information.
2 Hiskett, *ALS*, XII, 1971, p.81.
3 Hausa manuscript, *M*.
4 Hiskett, *ALS*, XII, 1971, p.105.
5 Hausa manuscript, *M*.
6 'Diversions on a journey or the Travels of Shaykh Ahmad al-Yamani (1630–1702) from Arbaji to Fez', unpublished seminar paper presented at Bayero University, Kano, on 29 November, 1977.

7 J. Heyworth-Dunne, 1939, p.10.

8 The information given below is taken from a copy of this unpublished work, given to me by Mr Hassan Cissé.

9 Arabic text in the margin of ᶜAlī Ḥarāzim, *Jawāhir*.

10 Houdas and Benoist, 1966, p.321.

11 Unpublished. My information is taken from a copy given me by Mr Cissé.

12 Unpublished. Again, I am indebted to Mr Cissé.

13 G. Nachtigal, *Sahara and Sudan*, chapter 10, fn.4. There is obviously more than one way of interpreting Nachtigal's well-known comment. His experiences, and those of other travellers such as Duveyrier, leave me with the impression that the Sanūsīs of the Fazzan, Borno and Chad were at that time strongly anti-Christian, a fact which I find understandable. On the other hand, Mr John E. Lavers, with whom I have discussed this subject, and who has a far greater knowledge of conditions in Borno at this time than I, believes that Nachtigal greatly exaggerated both the influence of the Sanūsīs there and the extent of their anti-Christian sentiment. With his characteristic pungency and humour Mr Lavers comments, 'According to Nachtigal, even the mosquitoes were Sanūsīs!'

14 Quoted in Zwemer, *Arabia*, p.388.

15 Hausa *mss*, *KLH*.

16 Creevey (née Behrman), Willis, ed. 1979, p.297, quoting from Sy, 1969.

CHAPTER SIXTEEN

Islam and the European occupations of West Africa

The train of events that led the British, French and Germans to set up their 'spheres of influence', protectorates and finally full-scale colonial administrations in West Africa, is long and complicated and has been recorded in great detail in a number of excellent accounts. It is not the task of this chapter to repeat the story here, except in very brief outline, as a background to the chapter's central theme, which is how West African Muslims reacted to their European conquerors, whom they deemed to be Christians.

The military assault on *Dār al-islām*

The British had been present on the Gold Coast, now Ghana, from *c.* 1030–1/1621. In the course of the 13/19 century they had been in conflict, from time to time, with the powerful Ashanti empire to the north of their coastal settlement; but it was not until 1290/January 1874 that the final phase of colonial conquest there began with General Wolseley's entry into Kumasi in that year. This was followed by the occupation of Ashanti in 1313/1896 and the unsuccessful Ashanti revolt of AD 1900. These were not clashes with an Islamic power, but they did involve Muslims who were subjects of the Ashanti state or advisers to it.

The first major armed clash between the British and a fully Islamic state in West Africa was the Niger Company's expedition of 1314/1897 against Bida, the capital of Nupe and one of the southern emirates of the Sokoto caliphate. This was immediately followed by the capture of Ilorin. In AD 1901 the Islamic emirates of Kontagora and Yola were taken over by British forces. The emirs of Kontagora and Nupe had been largely responsible, by extensive slave-raiding, for providing the British with a reason for war. In AD 1902 the emir of Kontagora was captured and imprisoned and in the same year the emirate of Bauchi submitted to the British, as did Zaria. The emirate of Gombe was occupied and the British column, under Colonel Morland, then went on to Borno where a British nominee to the office of Shehu was installed. In AD 1903 the same British force took the Muslim city of Kano and went on to occupy the capital of Sokoto. As a result, the Caliph Attahiru fled and was pursued by the British who killed him at the battle of Burmi, in the same year. This virtually completed the military occupation of Hausaland apart from the emirate of Hadejia, which was not finally subjugated until AD 1906.

The French penetration into the West African Islamic hinterland began from Senegal, where the French had long had a foothold in their 11/17-century trading-post, Saint Louis. This penetration was further developed from their protectorate of Dahomey, set up in 1310–11/1893. From *c.* 1296/1879 to 1300/1882, they pursued a policy of expansion towards the Upper Niger and in the process they clashed with Sultan Aḥmad of Segu, with al-Ḥājj Muḥammad al-Amīn, with the Muslim ruler of the kingdom of Cayor, with a number of lesser Muslim jihadists and finally with the Almamy Samory. From 1302/1885 French interest in West African conquest lapsed somewhat for reasons that had to do with internal French politics, but from *c.* 1307/1890 on it revived bringing the French into direct confrontation with the British in the Niger region. The result was the incident known as the 'Race for Borgu', in 1311–12/1894, between the French and the British which brought the two powers very close to armed conflict in West Africa. It was avoided however, and they reached an agreement that established their 'spheres of interest'. As a result, vast areas of Islamic West Africa were in the end brought under British and French colonial rule. Both powers together with the Germans then turned their attention to the east, to Borno and Chad.

The Germans, held back by Bismarck's dislike of colonial adventuring did not commit themselves fully to the 'Scramble' for West Africa until 1301–2/1884. In that year, provoked by the imperial forwardness of the French and to a lesser extent the British, and by the consequent threat to their own long-established trading interests in West Africa, they followed suit by declaring a protectorate over the Cameroons and Togoland.

Few Muslims who became caught up in these events had much notion of the complex background of international politics from which they arose, for this had nothing to do with their own experience or their history. Their leaders certainly understood that their attackers were not just Christians – they recognised them as French, British or Germans – and they often played one off against the other with skill. Indeed, such an understanding was essential to their role as middlemen in the West African trade that the Europeans valued. The Almany Samory, for example, had quite an efficient intelligence service and was thus able to exploit the local rivalries of the French and British effectively, but for most Muslim commoners such distinctions seemed unimportant. The identity of Europeans as 'Christians' had already been firmly established through historical contacts between Islam and Christianity and it was also a part of their Muslim folklore and literature. How the Muslims reacted to the Christian intrusion into *Dār al-islām* can best be illustrated by those Muslim authors of the day who recorded what they saw and felt.

The comment of the Imām ᶜUmar b. Abī Bakr of Kete Krachi

The Imām ᶜUmar of Kete Krachi was a Hausa ᶜ*ālim* born in Kano *c.* 127/1854. In his youth he moved to Salaga, *c.* 1293/1876, in time to experience the Salaga Civil War of 1309–10/1892 and then the final, major British assault on Ashanti. He was a prolific author and among his many works are two poems, one in Hausa the other in Arabic, in both of which he comments not only on the British-Ashanti wars but also on the French actions against Sultan Aḥmad of Segu and the Almamy Samory. He also comments on the German campaign in Togoland.

Imām ᶜUmar's account is surprisingly free from resentment and he exhibits little anti-Christian feeling. He is a political realist, who bases his judgements on how events actually affect him and his class, not on abstract ideological principles. He shows himself to have been a humane and kindly man and his poems are of considerable interest in that they reveal certain broad attitudes that were no doubt common to him and his colleagues among the *ᶜulamā'*. However they lack intellectual depth and throw little light on the deeper issues that concerned thoughtful Muslims under the colonial administrations.

Above all, the Imām ᶜUmar Kete-Krachi seems to have been impressed by the overwhelming military power of the Christians, and the futility of opposing them. Expressions of wonder and amazement at the fire-power of their armies occur frequently throughout his Hausa poem[1]. For example:

> The weapons [of the Gobir people] could not reach the Christians,
> But *their* weapons could reach us
> Although they were aiming from afar off.
> . . .
> The Christians had powerful weapons,
> They had a dreadful gun,
> There was the magazine rifle, hear what the Christians had,
> There was a bugler whose call heralds death,
> He is the praise-singer of the Christians!
> . . .
> Quiver, bow, sword and even spears,
> Such weapons are objects of scorn to the Christians!

Sometimes he openly sides with the Christians against Africans of whom he disapproves. For example, he describes the British attack on the Ashanti rebels in 1900 as follows:

> Then it got hot, it became severe,
> In the battle between the Ashantes and the Christians,
> Then Major Murrey [?] arrived with soldiers,
> To reinforce the Governor of the Christians,
> Only with difficulty did he reach
> Kumasi, his eyes red with fury,
> . . .
> Then he attacked in force, causing heavy casualties,
> Only with difficulty did he clear the way for the Christians,
> ,. . .
> Greetings to you, black bull of the Christians!

Of the Almamy Samory, who had ravaged the country around Salaga, he says

> Before [the Christians captured him] he had done great damage, he had waged war,
> Men were being slain and women were weeping,
> They were being slaughtered like hens and guinea fowl,
> Help! Come quickly to our rescue, Christians.

He speaks in similar terms of the eastern conqueror, Rābiḥ, who wrought such havoc in Borno. However towards the defeat of Sultan Aḥmad of Segu his attitude is quite different,

Aḥmad, ruler of Segu, was a great man,
Here in Segu the Christians fell upon him,
It was his younger brother, Aguibou, who desired the chieftaincy,
Who went and called the Christians in,
And Aḥmad, he was expelled from his country,
He went as far as Kebbi, to Dutsin Kura,
It is said he died [there]. May God have mercy on him,
He was a true Believer, a grateful servant of God.

The Imām ᶜUmar's sense of the futility of destroying Sultan Aḥmad has point, for as one historian has put it:

'. . . this attempt . . . to create a new type of African Moslem state – one that would transcend ethnic quarrels, draw through trade on the technology of the European world, and utilise the skills of Africans, whose experience or training might be relevant to this aim was cut short by this French action'.[2]

In the case of the British deposition of Umaru, Emir of Bauchi, in AD 1902, Imām ᶜUmar Kete-Krachi is simply puzzled as to why the Christians behaved so harshly towards him,

There was our Umaru, son of Salmanu of Bauchi,
They seized him while he was at Yarba – the Christians!
As for his offence against them, it is unknown to us, to all of us,
Only God knows it – the Christians!

He describes the German expedition to Sansanne-Mango in 1313–14/1896 with some detachment, in the following lines:

The Dagombas were a brave people, and hot-tempered ones,
They killed a German, a Christian,
Then [the Germans] killed many Dagomba people,
And they passed through, on their way to Yendi – the Christians!
. . .
They were assembling the Dagomba people in the strangers' quarter,
The Yarima of Yendi, they seized him, the Christians,
Previously the Dagombas had made ready to fight each other,
Now they settled their quarrel in order [to fight] the Christians,
And the pagans rose and led the Christians on,
[Among them] was Mister Graf, the tall Christian,
They had but few weapons. [The Christians] bowled them over,
And they broke up saying, 'Woe to us, the Christians!'

On the flight and subsequent death of the Caliph Attahiru at the battle of Burmi, he makes the following, sad comment:

Where is Attahiru, the grandson of Atiku,
The *walī* of God. They drove him out – the Christians!

So he made ready and he left his country,
He was setting out, fearing the Christians,
And the whole country fled with him – city and village,
They were saying, 'We don't want the rule of the Christians',
Then the Commander of the Believers set out with the women and children straggling along behind him,
It was a terrible thing to see – Oh you, Christians!
They pursued him, as if he owed them money,
Or as if he had abused the king of the Christians!
He passed through camping places without stopping overnight until he reached Burmi,
There they deceived him, the army of the Christians!
There they killed him on a Friday,
At the very hour of prayer – the Christians!
There they buried the Commander of the Believers,
Who died as a martyr, fighting against the Christians,
O God, O you who are without end,
Have mercy on Attahiru, the faithful servant.

The Imām ᶜUmar Kete-Krachi's feeling is understandable for, as Professor D.J.M. Muffett has shown, Burmi was a battle that need never have been fought.[3] However, despite his bewilderment at what seems to him to have been the needless killing of the fugitive caliph, Imām ᶜUmar ends his poem with a long passage in which he praises the Christians for introducing law, order and justice. He then describes himself as happy under their rule but, at the same time, appears to distinguish between their 'rule' and their 'dominion',

As for me, I thank God for their time,
For they have treated me kindly – the Christians,
As for me, may their time last for ever,
For I am happy under the rule of the Christians.
All the same, O Cloak of the Believers, O Lord of His servants,
Preserve us from the dominion of the Christians,
For the sake of the rank of Muḥammad, Noah and Moses,
And the Spirit of God, Jesus, Lord of the Christians.

By this distinction he probably implies that, while he is happy under the temporal rule of the Christians, he still feels the need to be protected against their spiritual dominion; that is, he is willing to be governed and administered by Christians but he is not willing that they should force Christianity upon him.

In his Arabic poem, however, which was probably written later in his life, he speaks somewhat more bitterly of the Christian conquerors:

A sun of disaster has risen in the west,
Glaring down on people and populated places,
Poetically speaking, I mean the catastrophe of the Christians.
The Christian calamity has come upon us like a dust-cloud,
At the start of the affair they came peacefully,
With soft sweet talk,

'We've come to trade', they said,
'To reform the beliefs of the people'.
'To halt oppression here below, and theft,'
'To clean up and overthrow corruption.'
Not all of us grasped their motives,
So now we've become their inferiors.
They deluded us with little gifts,
And fed us tasty foods. . . .
But recently they have changed their tune.[4]

One cannot know, of course, whether this change in attitude on the part of the Imām ᶜUmar was simply due to a mood of the moment or to more considered reflection. Whatever the case, he remained a much respected figure to the British administration in the Gold Coast and its officials frequently sought his advice on Islamic affairs. He died in AD 1934.

Imām ᶜUmar Kete-Krachi's reaction to the conquest of his community by the Europeans was in many ways typical of his class – that of the conservative, order-loving and politically realistic *ᶜulamā'* – but in other respects it reflects his particular situation and experience. He was one of a group of Hausa immigrants into Salaga who lived under the dominion of the non-Muslim Ashanti and during the Salaga civil war the Hausas there suffered considerable disruption with many of them forced to move elsewhere. Indeed, it was the civil war that caused the Imām ᶜUmar to leave Salaga and settle in Kete-Krachi. Moreover, long before the civil war broke out, the Hausas had been subject to trade restrictions that the Ashantis had placed on them to protect their own commerce, thus Imām ᶜUmar and his compatriots had no cause to love the Ashantis. The Imām ᶜUmar had also experienced the realities of life under Almamy Samory who terrorised the country north of Ashanti. Thus, in a situation where the non-Muslim Ashanti authorities had proved unsympathetic and even, perhaps, oppressive and so-called Muslims had proved destructive and downright tyrannous, it is not surprising that this pacific and order-loving scholar turned to the Christians for the security he longed for. In this respect his position was different from that of the *ᶜulamā'* of Hausaland for they had, at least, the moral security of living under an Islamic caliphate based solidly on the Sharīᶜa at the time when the Europeans arrived on the scene.

His account is interesting for what it leaves out as well as for what it includes. Unlike many other Sūdānī Muslim writers of the period, he shows no tendency in his poem that describes the coming of the Christians to attribute the whole affair to the impending End of Time. Indeed, there are no traces of Mahdism in it. This is certainly not because he was unaware of such ideas for later on he vigorously opposed a Mahdist pretender who arose in the Gold Coast. His lack of interest in Mahdism and the End of Time as an explanation for the conquests is probably to be explained by his conservatism and concern for order; for while the conservative *ᶜulamā'* were prepared to give intellectual assent to the Mahdist idea, the popular attempt to apply it to the events of the day was often disturbing to them. It seems then, that the Imām ᶜUmar Kete-Krachi was among those who were content to leave the Mahdī to the future and to make the best of the present, which turned out not to be wholly unacceptable to them.

The reaction of the Sokoto establishment

The Sokoto establishment had conducted diplomatic relations with the Christians since the time of Clapperton's visit to Sokoto in 1239–40/1824. The Caliph Muhammadu Bello had then signed an agreement giving British subjects the right to trade in the Sokoto empire and Dr Barth had signed a similar agreement with the Caliph Aliyu ɗan Muhammadu Bello in 1269/1853. The Sokoto caliphate later entered into other treaties with the Royal Niger Company and with the Germans. From the point of view of the Muslim authorities in Sokoto, these treaties were simply *amānāt* (sing. *amān*), unilateral grants from the Islamic government giving the Christians permission to trade in its territories under guarantees of safe-conduct. Such *amānāt* were well-known and recognised diplomatic instruments throughout the Islamic world and the caliph in Sokoto had no reason to believe that they committed him to any obligation beyond those that *amānāt* usually implied. He certainly did not suppose that they obliged him to govern his empire under the supervision of Christian overlords.

Clapperton and Barth undoubtedly understood the nature of *amānāt* and accepted them for what they were, but for the later British and French they became no more than pieces in a game of diplomatic chess, in which each tried to get the better of his rival. The so-called treaties were used, in the course of negotiations, to prove that one power or the other had a prior right to a 'sphere of influence' and then to a 'protectorate' in this or that territory and both the British and the French assumed – or chose to assume – that these 'treaties' gave them the right to a military presence and an overriding authority that were certainly not implicit in the Islamic concept of an *amān*.

The first unmistakable indication that the Christians in their territories were prepared to overstep the terms of the *amānāt* received by the Sokoto authorities was the Niger Company's attacks on Bida and Ilorin in 1314/1897. This was followed by the action against Kontagora in AD 1901. The chain of events that led up to these actions, and the catalogue of rights and wrongs that both sides appealed to, to justify themselves, cannot be told here. It is clear, however, that the central government in Sokoto was not to blame for the behaviour of the southern emirs that provoked these attacks. Indeed, it probably deplored the haste and lack of judgement that brought unsought-for troubles on its own head, but lack of military power and the delicate nature of its relations with its too-mighty subjects prevented the caliphate in Sokoto from taking any effective action.

Some correspondence now took place between Lugard, at that time High Commissioner of the Protectorate declared by the British in 1900 in Northern Nigeria, and the caliph in Sokoto. Lugard's letters informed the caliph that he had taken the law into his own hands and had deposed, or was about to depose, the emirs of Bauchi and Kontagora. The caliph is alleged to have replied,

> From us to you. I do not consent that any one from you should ever dwell with us. I will never agree with you. I will have nothing ever to do with you. Between us and you there are no dealings except as between Muslims and unbelievers, war, as God Almighty has enjoined on us. There is no power or strength save in God Most High. This with salutations.[5]

Lugard chose to interpret this letter, in effect, as a declaration of war. However, as Professor D.J.M. Muffett has shown, it is doubtful whether the caliph did, in fact, write this letter for much confusion surrounds the correspondence that took place between the two sides at this time – that is immediately before the British attack on Sokoto in March, 1903. Professor Muffett concludes that the letter in question may not have been addressed to Lugard at all, but to the Royal Niger Company about a quite different matter, and it was translated incorrectly and in much more aggressive terms than was justified by the original Arabic. Lugard may then have seized upon it and used it as part of his subsequent justification for the attack on Sokoto.

Nevertheless, one letter that the caliph certainly did write referred to Lugard's intervention in the affairs of the emirate of Bauchi. It was as follows,

> To Governor Lugard. Be it known to you that I did not call on you to enter on the pacification of Bauchi or any other place whatever, nor that you should enter on the pacification of towns or territories – I seek help from no one except from God. You have your faith, we have ours – God is our defence and our sure refuge: there is no strength or power except in God on high, the Almighty –
>
> This with salutations.[6]

This was by no means an aggressive or unreasonable letter, but it shows that what was for Lugard merely a problem of law and order was, for the caliph, a fundamental issue of religious belief and of loyalty to fellow Muslims. The British never understood this and in consequence misjudged the caliph's intentions. This led to a military conquest where, with more patience and better understanding, a peaceful agreement might still have been reached.

As is well known, the incident that finally sparked off the British attack on Kano and Sokoto was the killing of a British officer, Captain Moloney, by the Magaji of Keffi. This, most certainly, was not the fault of the caliph, although the Emir of Kano was unwise to give the Magaji refuge because, as a result, the British seized Kano. Then Lieutenant-Colonel Morland who commanded the British force sent a letter to the caliph requiring him to accept a British military presence in Sokoto, to arrest the Magaji who had fled there and assuring him that if these conditions were fulfilled, there would be no war.[7] He also sent a present with the letter, as a peace offering. These terms were severe, yet this letter from the soldier in the field was more courteous and more pacific in tone than those the High Commissioner Lugard tended to write.

The Caliph Attahiru ɗan Ahmadu, who had only just succeeded to the caliphate on the death of ᶜAbd al-Raḥmān, sent the following reply:

> From us to Colonel Morland. All salutations to you. Know that I have seen your messenger with your letter, the purport of which I understand, I have sent to call in my councillors from every district, but now that I see they are taking some time to asemble, I am sending you back your messenger. When we have assembled and have agreed on our decision, I will write to you what is enjoined on me by them for the settlement of this affair. Salutations.[8]

In fact, discussions had already been going on in Sokoto as to what was the proper response to a Christian attack, for this had been anticipated for some time. There were three opinions. Some were for fighting, while others regarded this as futile and counselled submission according to the Islamic doctrine of *taqiyya*, 'dissembling', which allowed the Muslim to submit to an infidel enemy, at the same time preserving his inner loyalty to Islam, in circumstances where physical resistance was hopeless. The third opinion was for *hijra*, emigration out of infidel territory to regain *Dār al-islām* beyond, and, according to the prevailing view that the approaching disaster heralded the End of Time it was held that the emigration should be to Mecca and Medina. It was believed on the authority of *ḥadīth*, the recorded sayings of the Prophet, that Dajjāl, Anti-Christ, cannot enter Mecca or Medina; therefore Muslims might safely await the Mahdī there. No firm decision on the right course to take had been reached by the time the British decided to attack on 15 March, 1903, thus the Sokoto forces had no alternative but to fight. They did so bravely but with no hope of success for they were cut down like corn by the British rifle and machine-gun fire. The battle was quickly over and the Caliph Attahiru, who survived it, had already prepared to emigrate. With a large following he now set out, making ultimately for Mecca, but he was harassed by the pursuing British and took refuge in Burmi, the stronghold of the Mahdist Jibrīl Gaini. Here he was trapped and killed in the ensuing battle, which was not only unnecessary but also the bloodiest encounter of the whole occupation. He left a poem in Hausa, probably composed shortly before the battle of Sokoto and in it describes the situation as he saw it, declaring his intention to emigrate out of reach of the Christians with the reasons for that decision:

In the Name of God, I intend to compose a song,
  About the enemies of Muḥammad, the Christians,
We pray to the King, the Lord of Office,
  That we may escape, that we may leave the company of the Christians,

. . .

O God, if you will it that we should remain [in Hausaland],
  We pray you to foil the intention of the Christians,
But if we find the strength and depart,
  Then bring us to Medina, far away from the Christians!
If, O God, you will it that we depart,
  Then let us abandon this place so that none will remain except the company of the Christians,

. . .

It is a prophecy the Shehu [Usumanu ɗan Fodio] made before he passed on,
  That the country will become the possession of the Christians,

. . .

Even if I have to set out alone, I will not stay,
  For, by God, I will not obey the Christians,
Between the two things one must choose and bear the consequences,
  Either one gets up and goes or one obeys the Christians.
Even the chiefs have left their towns [emigrating],

Therefore how much more incumbent is it upon you commoners,
[otherwise] you will become Christians!

. . .

If you say that it is difficult to get up and leave,
Then I say there is a blemish in all those who obey the Christians,

. . .

They admonish us to stop oppression,
But they are themselves oppressors, these Christians,
They bring evil civil strife and intrigue
That spoil the religion of Islam – the Christians!
The state that we are in today [that is our own failure to observe Islam as we should], it has been made clear
That *it* is the reason God has loosed the Christians upon us,
Stop listening to those who say we should not get up and go,
How can one remain here with the Christians?
Let us face straight ahead to Mecca, let us go to Medina,
Only Medina and Mecca are free from the Christians.
It is the Shehu's prophecy, that will not go away,
It is the Hour of which he spoke, the Hour of the Christians.

. . .

It is obligatory in Islamic law to make ready for such a journey,
Muslims, do not consent to obey the Christians,
Let us constantly chant the Remembrance of God's Name,
Let us also invoke blessing upon the Prophet,
[And let us pray for] justice, that we may overthrow the Christians,
Peasants and rulers, all are one to them,
What you get from the Christians is contempt for a man's rights!
Government is no longer within the power of chiefs,
For what can we do to rid ourselves of the Christians?
If God has mercy upon us,
He will send a Renewer [*mujaddidi*], that we may rid ourselves of the Christians,
The hypocrites among us are many,
Those who cooperate with the Christians,
And those who mix with them on good terms,
There are our hypocrites in respect of the Christians.

. . .

The bodies of the Christians are white,
But within they are jet black – the Christians!

. . .

The Hour of the Resurrection is nigh,
Of its Signs we have seen one, for here are the Christians!
The grip of Gog and Magog, yet to come, has its own evils,
They will fill the world, they are yet more terrible than the Christians,
But we have our remedy, let us stand firm with God,
It is upon Him that we rely to rid ourselves of the Christians.

. . .

Cause us to die in the Faith, O God,
For there is something else to fear, beyond the Christians!
It is the day of death and the Day of Resurrection.
When *this* awaits mortal man, what has he to fear from the Christians?
With praise to God I have finished this poem
With the power of Him who created us and who also created the Christians![9]

The poem points to a much wider range of attitudes and reactions than are apparent in the blander comment of the Imām ᶜUmar Kete-Krachi. There is the fear that the Christians will destroy Islam and that commoners will be converted to Christianity under Christian masters. There is the conviction that emigration out of Christian dominion is a moral obligation as well as a practical necessity and the realisation that only the appearance, not the reality, of government will be left to the Muslims under Christian supervision – which certainly proved to be entirely correct. What had happened is seen as the fulfilment of a prophecy concerning the Signs of the End of Time made by the Shehu Usumanu ɗan Fodio, and which ever since had been part of the ideology of the Sokoto caliphate. The poem asks if an explanation for these disasters is required, then states it has been made clear they are God's punishment for the community's failure to live Islam as it should be lived. The caliph's Sufi background becomes apparent in his plea to the people to recite the *dhikr*, the 'Remembrance' of God's Name. The poem also shows clearly that the intervention of the Christians was felt to have brutally destroyed the ideal of fraternal peace and fellowship in the Muslim community; it points to the distressing division of opinion that certainly occurred in the Sokoto councils on the eve of the occupation. So, too, do the caliph's angry allegations that those who collaborate with the Christians are hypocrites and no better than Christians themselves. Finally, there is what seems to be an answer to Lugard's complaints about the tyranny of Kontagora and Bida. The Christians accuse the Muslims of tyranny, he says, but the Christians are themselves the worst tyrants of all.

It would be superfluous to comment further on the just anger, the dignity of deeply held convictions and the moral courage of this sorely troubled man.

For the caliph, flight from the Christians was no doubt the only course left open to him. Quite apart from his belief that submission to the Christians was morally wrong, such submission would have brought shame upon him. For the rest of the Sokoto community, the choice was more open and after a period of doubt and some confusion, during which he, too, made a half-hearted attempt at flight, Muḥammad al-Bukhārī, the Wazīr of Sokoto, often known by the Hausa form Buhari, decided on the alternative of *taqiyya*. He wrote and advised his colleagues to adopt the same course when he became convinced that the Christians did not, after all, intend to interfere with the practice of Islam nor were they out to make conversions.[10] He argued the case for *taqiyya* on the ground that 'it is permissible to befriend the Christians with the tongue but not with the heart'. His letter demonstrates his great concern that the behaviour of the people and their leaders, at this difficult time, should be fully in accordance with the Sharīᶜa, the civilized law of Islam that governed his community. It should be remembered that when making this recommendation, he was faced by overwhelming military force against which resistance had been shown to be useless.

The Mahdist reaction

As has been explained in earlier chapters, Mahdism existed in the west and central Sudan long before the Christians began to threaten it. The 9/15-century ᶜ*ālim*, Jalāl al-Dīn al-Suyūṭī foretold social upheavals and natural disasters that would precede the End of Time. So too did the Shehu Usumanu ɗan Fodio and many well-known Saharan *shaykhs* of the Ineslemen and Zwāya. Thus the Christian conquests were not the sole cause of the rise of the Mahdist expectancy during the 13–14/19 and early 20 centuries, but they were among the most dramatic signs in a total pattern of prophecy that now seemed about to be fulfilled. In the latter days the Sanūsīs focused particular attention upon these signs and brought excitement to a head.

Several Mahdist movements arose in Hausaland and Borno during the 13–14/19 century, before the European occupations of West Africa were fully under way. The actions of the Mahdist Malam Hayatu and those of the Limam Yamusa and Jibrīl Gaini were directed against the Sokoto caliphate. However, the activities of the French in North Africa and of certain European adventurers in the Nilotic Sudan must surely have contributed to the state of mind of these men and their followers.

Once the Christians arrived in the immediate neighbourhood, it was inevitable that they should be seen by some in the guise of the Mahdī's monstrous enemies – Gog and Magog and the terrible Dajjāl, the Muslim Anti-Christ. An unnamed Hausa poet wrote some verses *c.* AD 1900 and called them *Bakandamiyya*, the 'Hippo-hide Whip'. His purpose was to 'whip' his fellow Muslims for their failure to observe Islam properly thus causing God to loose the Christians upon them. In the course of these verses he tells how he sees the advancing armies of the Christians (in this case the British column advancing on Zaria after the fall of Kontagora in AD 1901):

> Gog and Magog are coming, they approach,
> They are small people, with big ears,
> They are those who cause destruction at the ends of the earth,
> When they approach a town, its crops will not sprout,
> . . .
> The fertility of the world will be taken away,
> The place that once gave seventy bushels will not give seven,
> Anti-Christ is coming,
> He will come and have authority over the world,
> The Mahdī and Jesus, they are coming
> In order to straighten out the tangle [of the world].[11]

In the Gold Coast, *c.* AD 1900, an unknown Muslim, with a very imperfect knowledge of Arabic, wrote down his version of the prophecy. His Arabic is so incorrect that it is difficult to translate precisely what he wanted to say. But it begins like this,

> A certain good man saw the Prophet on a Monday, in front of him. The

> Prophet said, 'Men are divided into three classes. The first class will die of hunger. The second class will fall into the hands of the Christians and chains will be put on their necks. The third class will obtain peace. They are the people of the Mahdī. . .'

He goes on to predict a series of disasters, the final one of which is to be the end of the world and he concludes as follows,

> It has been said, 'The Mahdī is here in this world, and in the world to come, for God has said, "All that is in the world will pass away. But the face of your Lord, the Glorious, the Most Noble, will remain".'[12]

Such prophecies and dramatic accounts of devastating armies and natural disasters spread like a bush fire throughout the west and central Sudan, from the turn of the 19 century AD to the 20 century AD (AH 1317). Some Muslims were prepared to turn their Mahdist beliefs into action. Both al-Ḥājj ᶜUmar al-Fūṭī and al-Ḥājj Muḥammad al-Amīn exploited Mahdist sentiments in their fight against their enemies, including the French. In AD 1902 a certain Malam Maizanna reacted to the British occupation of Bida by claiming to be the Mahdī and inviting people to drive the Christians out. He was quickly arrested and imprisoned.

The Caliph Attahiru, driven into a corner and prevented from fulfilling his intention to travel to Mecca by the British pursuit, took refuge in the Mahdist stronghold of Burmi. By this action he probably indicated that, let down by those who had collaborated with the Christian enemy and now desperate, he finally turned to active Mahdist resistance as the only course left open to him.

In 1312–13/1895 a certain Muḥammad ᶜUthmān, who claimed to be the emissary of the true Mahdī, was operating in Bonduku, in French territory. He was driven out by the French but none the less, seems to have been in the area in AD 1905. In AD 1906 the British Deputy Governor of the Gold Coast reported that he was aware 'that during the past year various emissaries of the class to which Mohammed Ousman belongs have entered Ashanti and the Protectorate of the Northern Territories'[13], but adds that they gained little support. In AD 1905 a Mahdist, Malam Mūsā and three lieutenants appeared in Gonja, where they caused some unrest and in the same year the French arrested a Mahdist called ᶜUmar Farūk who was active in their territories.

Meanwhile, in British Nigeria, emissaries of the Mahdī arose in Jebba and Yelwa in AD 1906. Others appeared in Bauchi, proclaiming that, in accordance with an ancient prophecy, the Mahdī was about to appear on Bima Hill, in Gombe emirate. Indeed, AD 1906 was a year of widespread Mahdist reactions in Hausaland and neighbouring areas while there were similar Mahdist events in German Adamawa.

However the most serious Mahdist rising against the British was certainly that of Malam ᶜĪsā in Satiru, near Sokoto, in AD 1906. This Mahdist leader severely defeated a small British force, killing three officers and twenty-five men. The Sultan of Sokoto (for under the British administration, this became his official title) was called on by the British to help put down the rising. He complied and his troops, under Malam Mai Turare, held back the Mahdists until another British force arrived but it was only with difficulty that this force eventually defeated and routed them. This Satiru rebellion had been preceded by a similar Mahdist uprising in neighbouring French territory, in AD 1905, and was probably an extension of it. It was followed by yet more risings in French-held Zabarma that cost several French lives.

Satiru was the last major Mahdist insurrection against the British but minor Mahdist incidents continued to occur in both British and French territories for many years to come.

As Norman Cohn has pointed out in his fine study of millenial movements in medieval Europe,[14] messianism, at any rate in its active and militant form, appeals mainly to the politically, socially and economically underprivileged and to those who, for one reason or another, feel insecure. This was certainly also true of Mahdism in West Africa. The Mahdī Mūsā of Gonja drew his support not only from Muslims but also from non-Muslim animists who, finding no focus for their discontent at European domination in their own fragmented societies, turned to the Muslim Mahdists for direction and leadership. In the case of the Satiru revolt, this appears to have been not only a direct attack on the British, but also a protest, on the part of many commoner subjects of the former Sokoto caliphate, at its failure to deal with the Christian invaders and at its subsequent submission to them. Moreover, people who had little to lose were easily persuaded by Mahdist preachers that heaven on earth was just around the corner if only they would turn on their masters. Participation in Mahdist activity gave such people a sense of purpose and a sense of importance. These were deep needs in people whose societies had been overthrown and whose self-respect had been shattered by defeat at the hands of alien conquerors. Above all, they felt themselves divinely singled out to share in the extraordinary qualities and achievements of the Mahdist leader. Finally, the perfect society that the Mahdī promised as their reward – in which, needless to say, they were themselves at last to be the masters – seemed infinitely worthwhile.

However not all Muslims felt this way about Mahdism and self-proclaimed Mahdīs. Even before the Christians arrived on the scene, Islamic governments in the west and central Sudan had looked with disfavour on active Mahdist movements for they threatened the established Muslim authorities of the day, just as they did the later colonial administrations. Thus the Sokoto caliphate eventually felt compelled to oppose the Mahdist dissenter Hayatu ɗan Sa'idu and it reached a local agreement with Jibrīl Gaini only because it did not possess the military strength to dispose of him finally. The Sultan of Sokoto, who owed his position to the British, was aware that he might not survive a Mahdist victory and did his best to help the colonial authorities to suppress the Satiru revolt. Not only established Muslim rulers were wary of Mahdism, it was disliked and feared by many of the ᶜ*ulamā'* who also had an interest in preserving the established order and felt threatened by Mahdist revolution. The attitude of the Imām ᶜUmar Kete-Krachi towards the Mahdī Mūsā in Gonja demonstrates this conservative and cautious approach of the ᶜ*ālim* class. The Imām ᶜUmar Kete-Krachi wrote a poem attacking the Gonja Mahdī in which he marshalled weighty evidence to prove that Mūsā was not, and could not be, the Mahdī. On the contrary, said the Imām ᶜUmar, he was nothing but a dishonest imposter and this attitude was widespread among Muslims of Imām ᶜUmar Kete-Krachi's class. Intellectually, they accepted Mahdism and the

End of Time but they pushed it forward to a remote future. They qualified it with so many careful reservations that it became no more than a theoretical possibility that could never be translated into reality in their time and place. An example is that of the Caliph Muhammadu Bello himself. He had once felt it necessary to compose a pamphlet[15] to reassure certain of his excited people that a comet appearing in the skies over Hausaland did not predict the appearance of the Mahdī and the end of the world. In the pamphlet he pointed out that the moon must be eclipsed on the first night of the fasting month of Ramadan before this could happen and the sun must be eclipsed in the middle of that month! Thus the learned and the rulers sought to protect themselves, not so much from the idea of Mahdism and the End of Time which was often useful to them as a convenient explanation for the political and social events of their day, but from its unwelcome and disruptive popular manifestations. This was as true during the colonial period as it was before for once Muslims like the Imām ᶜUmar Kete-Krachi and the Wazīr of Sokoto, Muḥammad al-Bukhārī, were satisfied that the colonial authorities intended no harm to Islam, they had no wish to see their communities thrown into further turmoil by Mahdist upheavals.

NOTES

1 In quoting from al-Ḥājj ᶜUmar Kete-Krachi's Hausa poem, I have used the Hausa text established in Pilaszewicz, Warsaw, 1975, but have adopted my own translation from time to time.

2 Crowder, 1968, quoting from Hargreaves, 1963.

3 Muffett, 1964, chapter 13 and passim.

4 From B. G. Martin's excellent translation and essay in Braimah and Goody, 1976. Both Martin and Pilaszewicz see the Imām ᶜUmar as somewhat more anti-European in his attitudes than I have felt justified in presenting him. The Imām ᶜUmar was certainly somewhat inconsistent in what he wrote. No doubt his mood changed from time to time, but his Hausa *Waƙar Annasara*, 'Song of the Christians', which is a major work, can certainly not be regarded as anti-European. Moreover, he lived on excellent terms with the British administration in the Gold Coast and was one of their most trusted advisers on Muslim affairs. Towards the end of his life, after an operation for gall stones, he wrote a long Arabic poem in which he thanked the British for their kindness towards him and praised them for their medical knowledge and skill (IAS/AR 182).

5 Backwell, 1927, pp.13–14.

6 Muffett, 1964, p.45. Muffett gives the Arabic facsimile of this letter facing p.33. If one compares the accurate translation of it that he gives at p.45 with the rather inaccurate English paraphrase of the same letter that Backwell (op.cit. 1927) gives at p.14, it is easy to believe that mistranslation and thus misunderstandings may have occurred frequently throughout this correspondence.

7 Backwell, 1927, p.14.

8 ibid, p.14.

9 Hausa manuscript *mss*, *WZA*

10 The text of this letter is given in Adeleye, *JHSN*, IV, 2, 1968.

11 Hiskett, *Hausa Islamic verse*, pp.103–04.

12 Translated in the field from an unregistered fragment in IAS. IAS/AR 19 is a longer work, dating from about the same time, listing forty Signs of the Hour.

13 Kumasi Archives, D561.

14 N. Cohn, *The Pursuit of the Millenium*, London, 1970.

15 *Masāʾil jamm al-ghafīr*, unpublished and probably the same as *Masāʾil ᶜan shaʾn najm ṭalaᶜa fī Ṣafar*, listed in Last, 1967, p.246.

CHAPTER SEVENTEEN

Islam in West Africa under the colonial administrations

The colonial period was one in which the attitude of the European rulers towards their Muslim subjects underwent considerable and unforeseen change; while the fears of the Muslims that the colonial occupations would be damaging to Islam were shown, in practice, to have been largely, though not entirely, groundless.

Attitudes to Islam of the colonial administrations:
Of the three colonial powers, France, Britain and Germany, France occupied the largest area of Islamic territory. Her occupation was made possible only by a longer and more thorough military subjugation of Sudanic Islamic states than was the case with her two rivals, Britain and Germany.

There was an influential body of French opinion that was openly hostile to Islam, even before that subjugation was complete. This opinion was represented by Carrère and Holle whose views were shared by certain soldiers who took part in the campaigns against Muslims, notably Archinard, the conqueror of Segu, and Mage who both expressed bitter hostility towards Islam. At first, such views prevailed over the more moderate attitudes of men like Faidherbe and Duveyrier; thus the early administrators of French West African possessions beyond Senegal were inclined to think in terms of the 'Peril of Islam'.[1] They saw Islam as a cultural, political and continuing military threat to their plans for colonial development.

Quite soon, however, the error of this extreme view became obvious and French administrators in the field quickly came to realise that Duveyrier was right. It was possible to work advantageously, if not with Muslims as a whole, at least with large and important groups of them such as the Tijāniyya and the conservative *ᶜulamā*', who were prepared to cooperate. Certain other groups such as the Ḥamāliyya, a reformist group that had broken off from the main Tijāniyya, and the West African Wahhābīs became great problems for the French administration.

But despite the enlightened views of certain individuals the majority of the French in West Africa probably never entirely overcame their feeling that Islam was, in the last resort, the enemy of the French civilizing mission. Indeed, there was good reason for such a view, for the goal of French colonial policy remained the integration of African populations into French culture and a French political union. This policy was at first applied only to quite restricted 'Direct Administration' territories but later, about 1307/1890, it was extended to Protectorate territories as well, and they were largely Muslim. The Muslims' own priority was to maintain and reassert their Islamic cultural and political identity, so, intellectually at any rate, they were opposed to the French civilizing mission or to many aspects of it. Some French administrators in the field recognised this and regarded the policy of assimilation imposed from Paris, as unworkable. They therefore left Muslims to go their own way so long as they made no trouble, but they did little to further Islamic culture. There thus grew up in the Federation of French West Africa created in 1312–13/1895, an assimilated elite, French-speaking and educationally and socially privileged, and an unprivileged and somewhat disadvantaged class that was largely Muslim.

It would be a mistake, none the less, to assume that the French colonial administrations in West Africa were entirely disadvantageous to Islam for in some respects the contrary was true, as will be explained below.

The difference between the early British attitude to Islam and that of the French was for the most part one of emphasis rather than substance. There was an initial hostility to Islam among Lugard and some of his colleagues, who saw the Muslim Fulani as an enemy potentially as dangerous as the Mahdists of the Nilotic Sudan. In this they were greatly mistaken but it none the less coloured the British outlook in the early days. Certain British officers who fought in the Nigerian campaigns expressed attitudes towards Islam that were just as antagonistic as those of Archinard and Mage, but the military weakness of the Sokoto caliphate and the ease with which it fell, made continued exaggerated fears of Islamic militancy pointless. Once the battles were over, the British quickly came to terms with Sokoto. In quite a short time, therefore, the British in Hausaland came to regard the traditional Islamic establishment as an ally; there was not, from that point on, the distance between the British and their Muslim subjects in Northern Nigeria that continued to exist for many years over the border in French territory. The easier relationship between the colonial administration and the traditional Islamic establishment was given expression in the British policy of 'Indirect Rule'. This meant that, after the initial process of conquest, traditional Muslim rulers who cooperated with the British were not only left in their places, but were also actively supported by the colonial administration. Moreover, the day-to-day government of their emirates was left in their hands, subject only to the supervision of British Residents and District Officers. This supervision was exercised in such matters as taxation, in the abolition of slave-raiding and slave-trading and in the administration ofjustice. Moreover, Islamic law was retained intact and even in some cases extended to neighbouring non-Muslim areas. The only restriction upon its operation was the prohibition of what the British administration considered to be inhumane punishments. This removed mutilation as the penalty for theft and gave convicted murderers the doubtful advantage of being hanged instead of beheaded.

In one important respect, however, the British attitude differed from that of the French not only in emphasis but also in its ultimate objective. Whereas the final goal of French policy was assimilation, that of the British was self-government. This certainly involved the adoption of some British political institutions, of British education, of English as a second language and so on, but it did not aim at the total cultural assimilation that was the French goal. Thus the persistence of the Muslim cultural identity – even political identity – did not present the British in northern Nigeria with the same dilemma that it did their French counterparts. The French were emotionally involved with Islam, for whichever way they turned, it remained at odds with the French sense of mission. The British, on the other hand, felt more detached because the concept of full political independence, even within the British Commonwealth, presupposed from the start that the Muslim constituency of Hausaland must eventually become responsible for its own political future.

What has been said above about British attitudes to Islam applies mainly to northern Nigeria, which included Hausaland and British Borno, but the British also occupied the Gold Coast, modern Ghana, and its hinterland, known as the Northern Territories. Both these areas were predominantly polytheist or animist at the time of the occupation, although there were already significant Christian communities on the coast. In the Northern Territories however – in Gonja, Dagomba, Larabanga and elsewhere – there were substantial communities of Muslims while in the area south of Ashanti right down to the coast there were a number of Muslim *zongos*, Muslim settlements consisting of immigrant Dyula Muslims from the Northern Territories and Hausa and Yoruba Muslims who had settled in the southern Gold Coast.

The attitude of British officials in the Gold Coast towards Islam and the Muslims was somewhat different from that of their colleagues in northern Nigeria. The main preoccupation of the paternalistic Gold Coast government was to support the authority of the traditional 'stools', the local non-Muslim rulers of polytheist and animist communities. The Muslims, particularly the immigrant Muslims from Nigeria, they regarded as strangers and a nuisance. This attitude was aggravated by the fact that the immigrant Muslims, especially the Hausas, were imbued with a spirit of moral and intellectual superiority arising from the successful *jihād* in Hausaland and from their long tradition of Islamic literacy. This made them contemptuous of the polytheist Ga, Fante and others by whom they were surrounded, and they did not bother to conceal this contempt. There was often bad feeling between the immigrant Muslims and the local Goldcoasters and the former constantly pressed the British administration to free them from the jurisdiction of non-Muslim chiefs and give them greater control over their own affairs. This the administration firmly refused to do, on the ground that it would weaken the authority of the non-Muslim rulers. This unsympathetic attitude is shown in the comment of a British official, scribbled at the foot of a letter from a Muslim Hausa *zongo* headman. In this letter the headman observes that,

> our laws and customs as of yore are based on the Koran (as the British on the Bible), fundamentally different from these peoples' pagan or fetish rites and ceremonies. . .,[2]

He goes on to plead to be allowed to govern his own Muslim community within the *zongo* without having to be subject to the authority of a non-Muslim Native Authority court. The British official's frosty comment was as follows,

> I see no reason for granting the application. There are courts of arbitration no doubt in the Hausa Community, but for strangers in a strange land to have a recognised Tribunal from whose judgements there must be the right of appeal, I am averse.[3]

There were certain exceptions to this unsympathetic attitude such as Mr Watherston, Chief Commissioner in the Northern Territories from AD 1905 to AD 1909, who was known for his sympathy towards Islam. So too was Mr Duncan-Johnstone, who made a special study of Gold Coast Muslim affairs. However, their views did not carry sufficient weight when put against the more general attitude of sympathy towards the non-Muslim authorities and their subjects.

The attitude of the British Gold Coast administration was understandable but it left the Gold Coast Muslims much disadvantaged as compared with non-Muslims.

German colonial administration in the Cameroons and Togoland was brought to an abrupt end by Germany's defeat in World War I. As long as their rule lasted, German administrators shared some of the attitudes towards Islam of their French and British counterparts. Their experience in East Africa had taught them to make much the same distinction as the French between cooperative Muslims and 'fanatical' Muslims. On the other hand, German links with Turkey and their efforts to gain Muslim support immediately before and during World War I, made them reluctant to take any action that would alienate Muslim world opinion. Moreover, unlike the French, the Germans did not aim at the integration of their West African subjects, whether Muslim or non-Muslim, into German culture. They saw their role simply as administering a *Shutzgebiet*, Bismarck's deliberately limited concept of a protected territory. In consequence many German administrators advocated a policy of 'cultural distance', arguing that this was in the best interest of the African subjects and their German rulers. One result of this was that the Germans encouraged the use of local languages in their territories, as far as this was practical. Thus the mastery of German never became essential for Africans who sought advancement, as the mastery of French did in French territories.

During the short time that they governed Adamawa, the Germans were faced by Mahdist revolts, but, as in neighbouring French and British territories, these proved less dangerous than was at first feared. Like the British, the Germans quickly established good relations with the Muslim Fulani rulers and it is certainly my personal impression that they are generally remembered kindly in the territories they governed. However, the period of their administration was too short to have had any distinctive impact on Islam.

The growth of sympathy towards Islam

Not only were the attitudes towards Islam of all three colonial administrations softened by the fact that their early fears of Islamic militancy proved exaggerated, they were also softened by certain qualities in Muslims and their way of life that favourably impressed the colonial administrators. The first was literacy. As the colonial officials, themselves usually well-educated men if not always particularly intellectual in their interests, became more familiar with Muslims and their institutions, they warmed to the intellectual achievements of Islam – its system of education, its codified law and its respect for learning. They tended to compare Islam favourably with the 'fetishism', illiteracy and nakedness of animists and polytheists. That this was, perhaps, unfair is beside the point, for it happened and in consequence the view developed that, if not the equal of western civilization, Islamic civilization was at least a bridge that could be used to help Africans to advance. There is little doubt that Bosworth Smith's arguments, referred to in chapter 13, were powerful in helping to create such opinions, at least among the British.

Another aspect of Islam that won the sympathy of colonial officials was its respect for law, order and political and social stability. The conservatism of the Sunnī ᶜ*ulamā*' has already been remarked on and men like the Imām ᶜUmar Kete-Krachi quickly became respected figures whom the administrators treated with deference, and whose advice they constantly sought. The Muslims' regard for rank and hierarchy, and their formal code of courtesy, also contributed to good relations and respect between them and the colonial officials. Among the British, at least, the requirement placed on colonial officials to learn the major languages of the areas in which they worked also did much to promote understanding. In consequence, cooperation and considerable good will between the Muslims and the administrators became commonplace.

This growing sympathy for Muslims and their way of life was nowhere more clearly demonstrated than in the policies of the colonial administrations towards what one scholar has called 'impatient mission expansion'[4]. As was shown above, the missionaries were eager to take advantage of the occupations by the colonial powers to extend the range of their activities into the Muslim areas of the west and central Sudan. They based their arguments largely on the principle of 'freedom of conscience' which they interpreted as a licence that ought to give them absolute freedom of action in Muslim as well as non-Muslim areas. The other side of the argument – that Muslims regarded Christian missionary attempts to convert Muslims, and especially their public preaching, as profoundly insulting – was something that the missionaries were either reluctant to admit or dismissed as unimportant. The British and German administrations did consider the Muslim viewpoint important, if not on grounds of moral principle then certainly on grounds of political expediency. Sir Frederic, later Lord, Lugard, was probably less concerned with the philosophical and moral aspects than with the practical political necessity of convincing the Muslim emirs that the British did not intend to suppress Islam. However, Charles Temple, Lieutenant-Governor of the Northern Provinces, was rather more critical of missionaries than his chief, and his attitude was formed on a more intellectual basis. It reflected the mildly liberal, even Fabian notions in which he was interested and carefully ignored the religious arguments which the missionaries used to advocate their case. He insisted on a purely secular, almost anthropological, assessment of the missionaries' impact on African societies and argued that their activities were not only politically undesirable but also culturally inappropriate. He thought these activities would cause the breakdown of traditional tribal life and political structures, and work against the ideas of patriotism, common nationhood among Africans, and development along 'native' lines that he felt the administration ought to encourage. This refusal of Temple and other colonial officials to discuss the issue in terms of their own values of redemption, salvation, surrender to Jesus, and so on, greatly angered the missionaries. However in practice, High Commissioner Lugard gave certain missionaries, especially Walter Miller, a much freer hand than that which would be consistent with his theoretical policy towards the missions. Sir Percy Girouard, who followed him in AD 1907, was much firmer in his attitude towards them as was Chief Commissioner Watherston in the

Northern Territories of the Gold Coast. Watherston considered Islam 'eminently suited to the native'[5] and severely restricted missionary activities. He was even reluctant to allow them to work among animists and polytheists for he felt that these people were more likely to benefit from conversion to Islam than to mission Christianity.

The governor of the German Cameroon, Jesko von Puttkamer, regarded the missionaries' desire to establish stations in the Islamic areas of Adamawa as 'utterly Utopian'[6], that is wholly unrealistic, and refused to allow them to attempt this. Even among the French, where Catholic power had considerable influence over official policy, an anti-clerical feeling developed among many French administrators which caused them to oppose unchecked missionary enthusiasm in Muslim areas.

The spread of Islam during the colonial period

In spite of the inevitable disruption caused by the conquests and the process of occupation, there is little doubt that Islam spread in West Africa more rapidly and more widely during less than a century of colonial occupation than it had done during the preceding nine centuries.

Once the conquests had taken place, the peace that the colonial administrations imposed on their territories was an immediate and powerful aid to the spread of Islam. In the absence of raids and wars between Africans, the movement of people, whether as traders, immigrants or in many other capacities, became easier. Therefore Islam and Islamic ideas were carried to areas where they had not previously been able to penetrate.

The French destruction of the ancient and faintly Muslim ruling dynasties of the Senegambia certainly helped Islam, for it caused the people to turn to the *ᶜulamā'* for leadership. Both the French and the British often used Muslim literates as intermediaries between themselves and non-Muslim rulers which gave these Muslims additional status in the eyes of the non-Muslims. It sometimes even encouraged the non-Muslim ruler to come over to Islam. At first the French made considerable use of Arabic as an administrative language because it was familiar to those of their officials who had served in North Africa and was already the administrative language of many local courts. This helped to uphold the authority of the *ᶜulamā'*, many of whom became, in effect, civil servants of the colonial administration. Later however, the French tended increasingly to insist that local officials and chiefs should learn to use French, and Muslim literates thus lost their advantage. The British made less use of Arabic once their administration in northern Nigeria was established but their practice of learning major African languages, especially Hausa, reduced the need for English among junior African officials. It probably also helped the British officials to understand Islamic ideas and attitudes more readily.

French and British officials sometimes applied Islamic law in non-Muslim territories because it was easier to understand and administer than unwritten customary law. Also, for administrative convenience they sometimes imposed the authority of Muslim emirs upon non-Muslim peoples who might otherwise have resisted such control. So, to some extent, the colonial authorities did the job that Muslim empire-builders might have done had they been free to do it. Indeed, this was one of the grounds on which the missionaries criticised the administrations most severely.

During World War I, both the British and the French colonial administrations sought to counter the German alliance with Muslim Turkey by courting the friendship of leading Muslims in their own colonial territories. In this they were very successful but the result was to build up the authority and prestige of these Muslims.

Another factor that helped the spread of Islam was the colonial policy of building roads and railways which brought about a much wider and more rapid exchange of people between Muslim and non-Muslim areas than had been possible before.

Moreover there was the introduction of modern means of mass communication; printing and newspapers, which increased greatly in number during the colonial period, helped the spread of Islamic ideas. This was not so important in the early days of the occupations but it became increasingly so as time went on. The introduction of radio broadcasting took the process a stage further.

Another powerful aid to the expansion of Islam was the sentiment of Africans towards white colonial rule. Since the conquests, Christianity in particular was seen by many as the White man's religion while Islam did not usually bear such an identity. Therefore Islam seemed a better choice for those African animists and polytheists who became dissatisfied with their old beliefs in the new circumstances that the colonial administrations created.

It has been suggested that local Muslim troops from both the British and French colonial armies were among the most effective agents in spreading Islam in those areas of West Africa where they served. However, their importance in this respect may have been exaggerated. It is true that the British colonial regiments often had Hausa Muslim *imāms* serving with them and that some of the soldiers were Muslim Hausas, but many were neither Muslim nor Hausa. They were non-Muslim Bachamas or other non-Muslims from Bauchi, Adamawa, the Plateau and other areas populated mainly by polytheists and animists. French regiments, too, contained large numbers of non-Muslim soldiers. Certainly the colonial armies helped to spread Islam, especially the local troops and Police introduced by the British into what was then the southern Gold Coast, but they were less important in this respect than has sometimes been supposed.

Some set-backs for Islam

Despite the undoubted advantages that it enjoyed, Islam also suffered certain set-backs under the colonial governments. The first was that the colonial occupations weakened, to some extent, the traditional ties of Muslim society. The division of opinion as to how Muslims should react to the conquests has already been mentioned above but this continued to create difficulties, between those Muslims whom the colonial administrations chose to regard as 'moderates' and those whom they dubbed 'fanatics', throughout the colonial period.

The colonial laws enabling slaves to claim their freedom introduced some indiscipline into Muslim family life, for it created a class of freed slaves who had the right to claim their freedom at will and defy the traditional authority. Even the pro-British Imām ᶜUmar Kete-Krachi complained that freed slaves acted like children, by which he meant irresponsibly and defiantly. The practice of keeping wives in purdah, the seclusion of women, was made more difficult by the limitations placed on slavery: for when slaves freed themselves and no replacements were available, wives had to work fetching water, collecting wood and so on. This loosened the bonds of the Muslim family – or so many Muslims claimed.

The new towns and the expanding old ones proved irresistible to many young men and some young women, as did the European way of life that became increasingly evident in them. Elderly Muslim moralists threatened Hell Fire as the price to be paid in the Hereafter for wearing shirts with buttons or tight trousers, for using hurricane lamps or electric torches, starch, blue-bags, walking sticks and powder puffs as well as for learning English as a second language,[9] but all to no avail. These things caught on and it soon became clear that Islam had not been seriously weakened by them although they did encourage the young to question traditional social conventions more than they had been accustomed to do in the past.

Another disadvantage that Islam suffered was that it was denied any further opportunity for political unification. The Islamic states of the west and central Sudan were certainly not united when the conquests overtook them but it can be argued that they were moving in that direction. Rābiḥ of Borno, the Almamy Samory and Sultan Aḥmad of Segu, even perhaps al-Ḥājj Muḥammad al-Amīn and Maba Diakhou, might all have established permanent Islamic states – or states that would have become fully Islamic – if they had not been interfered with by the Europeans. Once the colonial administrations had been set up there was no further possibility of new Islamic states being formed as long as these administrations lasted.

It has been suggested that both the British and the French tried to discourage cross-border contacts between Muslims, for fear that these would encourage pan-Islamism and forms of disaffection. In consequence, so it is said, participation in the Ḥajj, the Pilgrimage, by West African Muslims, was restricted. Thus these Muslims failed to come into contact with Muslims from other parts of the Islamic world at a time when Middle Eastern Muslim intellectuals were attempting to come to terms with new scientific and technological ideas. This intellectual deprivation is said to have had a depressing effect on the development of Islam in West Africa.

It would be unwise to deny absolutely the possibility that some Sūdānī Muslims were discouraged from going on Pilgrimage by obstacles placed in their way by colonial officials. There certainly were bureaucratic controls on pilgrims, especially in the field of public health, which had not existed in the pre-colonial era but it is difficult to believe that the Pilgrim traffic from West Africa declined, either relatively or absolutely, during the colonial period. Indeed, the evidence surely points to the opposite conclusion although I have to admit that I have only examined the existing records on Pilgrimage in the case of the Gold Coast administration. It is important to remember, however, that the Gold Coast administration was probably the most anti-Muslim of all the British administrations in West Africa and therefore the most likely to obstruct Muslim Pilgrimage, if such obstruction was intended.

The 'Mohammedan Pilgrims' files of the Gold Coast administration, in so far as they are available in the Ghana National Archives, contain innumerable pages of correspondence between the Gold Coast government and other administrations relating to pilgrims who disappeared or got into difficulties in the course of their journey. It is clear from this correspondence that the government accepted that it had a duty to look after the interests of these pilgrims and to assist them as far as possible.

In particular, the Gold Coast government was in frequent correspondence with the Arabian authorities, on behalf of Gold Coast pilgrims. One letter from the Arabian Foreign Ministry, dated 3/11/31, informs the Governor of the Gold Coast that, as to two unfortunate pilgrims, 'It is very likely that they might have been killed by beasts – God forbid! – as they sat at night between mountains full of trees. . .'[8] The Gold Coast authorities clearly did not think much of this explanation.

Another memorable and happier letter is from a party of returned pilgrims, who had left for Mecca twelve years earlier, and who on their return, wrote to thank the British official who gave them a letter at that time to assist them on their way. The letter, they say, was of great help to them throughout their journey. The British official, Major R. Montray-Read, who in the meantime had risen to become Acting Chief Commissioner of the Northern Territories, took the opportunity to reply, through his Provincial Commissioner, as follows:

> Will you also inform them that although it is a source of gratification to me that I was able to help them, it was by no personal powers of my own that the letter was of use to them, but to the far-reaching effect of a letter from an Official of the British Empire, that commands respect all over the world and of which the Gold Coast is as one grain of corn in a Calabash.[9]

Doubtless not all encounters were such models of harmony and concord. Also, it is to be hoped, not all British officials were such masters of ambiguous imagery as Major Montray-Read, whose enthusiasm for the British Empire seems to have been matched by a rather slight opinion of the importance of the Gold Coast! However, this is hardly a letter written by one whose job it was to put obstacles in the way of pilgrims.

The government also went to great trouble to collect statistics from its provincial officials concerning the numbers of persons intending to proceed on Pilgrimage, the purpose of which was to inform the Arabian authorities of the numbers to expect and to facilitate the issue of passports and other travel documents. Of course, the whole wearisome business of travel documentation, inter-state immigration controls and so on was, no doubt, as great a disincentive to travel then (I refer mainly to the period 1890 to 1930, covered by the files), as it is now. The colonial authorities were surely not more blameworthy in this respect than the Ottoman empire and its successor states.

There is certainly no evidence in the surviving records of the Gold Coast government that I have been able to discover that lends any support at all to the notion that it made a deliberate and sustained attempt to discourage Pilgrimage. It seems extremely unlikely that the Nigerian administration, which was most anxious to retain the goodwill of the Muslim establishment, did so either.

Much nearer the truth than the generalised accusation that the colonial administrations obstructed Pilgrimage is the particular one that they discouraged their Muslim subjects from visiting Cairo, whether in the course of Pilgrimage or on any other occasion. Cairo was considered, with some justification, to be a centre of anti-colonial agitation for most of the period from the end of World War I until the colonial era faded into that of approaching independence. However it is, once again, questionable how effective such discouragement was, for it was seldom, if ever, physical. Generally speaking, it took the negative form of not making government scholarship funds so readily available for studies in Cairo as in other, more approved, centres; and the more positive form of encouraging Muslims who wished for an Islamic education outside West Africa, to seek it at centres that were thought to be less politically active than Cairo. The British in northern Nigeria, for example, preferred Muslims to undertake 'Arabic Studies' in British universities, rather than at the Azhar.

However, Islam did suffer some intellectual setback, for other reasons. What these were will be explained when education under the colonial regimes is considered below.

The Sufi *ṭuruq* during the colonial period

The most active agents in spreading Islam during the colonial period were the Sufi *ṭuruq*, especially the Qādiriyya, the Tijāniyya and the Murīds of Senegal.

The Qādiriyya

In northern Nigeria the Qādiriyya was already well established at the time the colonial occupations took place. Many commoners felt themselves to be associated with it, despite the fact that it was identified with the ruling establishment in Sokoto. During the colonial period it greatly widened its appeal and began to recruit more and more Hausas and Yorubas, quickly becoming the *ṭarīqa* of the majority in Hausaland. This was largely due to the stimulus of competition with the populist Tijāniyya that was also developing rapidly, which caused the Qādiriyya to adopt mass participation methods such as recitation of the *wird* in groups and other forms of congregational worship. Moreover, under Malam Nasiru Kabara, who emerged as the leader of the Qādiriyya in Nigeria *c.* AD 1937, the various branches of the order – Kuntiyya, Ahl al-Bayt, ʿUthmāniyya and others – were brought together into a single, united community. This breaking-down of earlier Qādirī elitism and the opening-up of participation in its worship to many more people, did much to encourage conversion to Islam especially in Ilorin and Lagos. However despite the fact that it broadened the basis of its support, the Qādiriyya still remained quite closely identified with the traditional political establishment in northern Nigeria. This was to become apparent during the period of political activity that preceded the granting of independence, for the Qādiriyya then emerged as the chief support for the Northern Peoples' Congress (NPC), the political party founded in 1951 by the late Alhaji Sir Ahmadu Bello, the Sardauna of Sokoto,

> We pray God the Glorious, the King of Truth,
> That NPC may rule Nigeria,
> For the sake of the Lord ʿAbd al-Qādir al-Jaylānī,
> May your rule [O Sardauna] last until the coming of the Mahdī.[10]

In the Gold Coast the ancient Qādiriyya, established mainly in the Northern Territories, was strengthened and extended by the influx of immigrants from Nigeria during the early colonial period. They brought it to the southern Gold Coast and introduced it into the *zongos*. Yorubas, as well as Hausas, played an important part in this and, until he died *c.* 1960, the leader of the Qādiriyya in modern Ghana was a Yoruba *shaykh* called Inda al-Salati.

In French territories there were two main branches of the Qādiriyya, the Kuntiyya, still led by the Kuntī *shaykhs* from Timbuktu and the Shinqīṭiyya in the western Sahara and Mauritania. From the beginning of the present century the Kuntiyya also seems to have been active in the Northern Territories of the Gold Coast, where the repair and renovation of a number of mosques is attributed to a Kuntī *shaykh* from Timbuktu.

The Tijāniyya

The development of the Tijāniyya during the early part of the colonial period was largely in the hands of Shaykh Alfa Hāshim, a nephew of al-Ḥājj ᶜUmar al-Fūtī who became the leader of the *ṭarīqa* throughout West Africa. He did not live in West Africa however, but in Mecca and sometimes Medina where he initiated numbers of West African Muslims, sending them back to their homes as his *muqaddamūn* (sing. *muqaddam*), 'initiators'.

As from AD 1900 the *ṭarīqa* expanded rapidly, particularly in Nigeria where the Emir ᶜAbbās of Kano went over to it shortly after World War I. During the 1920s the leadership of the *ṭarīqa*, not only in Nigeria but also in the neighbouring French territories, was in the hands of the well-known Malam Muhammadu Salga, a Kano *ᶜālim* who had been initiated by the North African *ᶜālim* Muḥammad b. ᶜUthman al-Alawī. Muhammadu Salga died in AD 1938 and his funeral was described in a Hausa poem that is one of the classics of Hausa literature:

> I will put into verse the story of what really happened
> At the time of the funeral of our Malam, worthy to be followed,
> He was Muhammadu Salga, the knight of the *Mukhtaṣar* [a classical Arabic legal text],
> The Shaykh of the *ṭarīqa*, just and trustworthy.[11]

The poet then goes on to tell how huge crowds of people thronged the route of the funeral and struggled to touch the *shaykh*'s bier.

After Muhammadu Salga, the story of the modern Tijāniyya in Nigeria is largely the story of the well-known Senegalese *shaykh*, al-Ḥājj Ibrāhīm b. al-Ḥājj ᶜAbd Allāh al-Anyās, popularly known as Shaykh Ibrāhīm Niass.

In the Gold Coast the Tijāniyya was spread during the 1920s and early 1930s by a number of *muqaddamūn* of Hausa origin. Outstanding among them was Malam ᶜAlī b. Muḥammad al-Salgawī, known as ᶜAlī Barau, who was a pupil of the Imām ᶜUmar Kete-Krachi. He was a Salaga *ᶜālim* who flourished *c.* 1920 and he composed a number of poems, in Arabic, in praise of Shaykh Aḥmad al-Tijānī and another of his teachers, the Tijānī *shaykh*, Maḥmūd b. Saᶜīd Jalyā. Malam ᶜAlī Barau was believed by his followers to be so full of the divine light of *fayḍa* that it was necessary for him to cover his face with the sleeve of his gown after Friday prayer lest the people should be dazzled by the special brightness of the light from him at this moment of particular blessedness. Another well-known Gold Coast Tijānī was al-Ḥājj Ṣaḥīḥ al-Jawānī al-Tijānī who died in Wenchi *c.* AD 1932.

Perhaps the most influential of all the Tijānī *muqaddamūn* in the Gold Coast during the mid-colonial period was the Imām ᶜUmar Kete-Krachi himself. He had been a Qādirī but in late middle-age he went over to the Tijāniyya and then became one of its most influential teachers. After him the leadership of the order passed into the hands of Shaykh Ibrāhīm Niass.

Shaykh Ibrāhīm Niass was born in AD 1900, in the village of Taiba-Niassene, in Senegal. He was educated by his father, al-Ḥājj ᶜAbd Allāh al-Anyās, and soon became associated with the Tijāniyya of which his father was a well-known *muqaddam*. By the time he was thirty he began to experience visions, in one of which he received the divine gift of *fayḍa*. He now became convinced that he was *Ghawth al-zamān*, the 'Succour of the Age' and became widely accepted as such by Tijānīs in West Africa.

In AD 1937 Shaykh Ibrāhīm met the Emir Malam Abdullahi Bayero of Kano while on Pilgrimage, which enabled him to establish his own branch of the Tijāniyya, the *Jamāᶜat al-fayḍa*, the 'Community of Grace', in Nigeria. At about the same time he was recognised as *khalīfa* of the Tijāniyya in West Africa by the leading North African Tijānī of the day, Shaykh Aḥmad Sukayrij, and from this point on *Jamāᶜat al-fayḍa* gained rapidly in popularity in Nigeria, in the Hausa north, and in Yoruba country, especially Lagos and Ibadan.

During the early 1950s Shaykh Ibrāhīm undertook a series of visits to the Gold Coast and other West African countries. These were dramatically successful and adherence to *Jamāᶜat al-fayḍa* spread rapidly. The files of the Provincial Administration in Kumasi for the year AD 1952 contain a number of letters relating to his visit there. One, from leading Muslims in the Northern Territories, begs him to visit Tamale which he did. A British administrative officer wrote a note to the Acting Chief Commissioner of the Northern Territories as follows,

> Sheikh Ibrahim went to Tamale yesterday and received such an ovation at the Airport that he was in danger of injury. 6000 people met him.[12]

Similar scenes occurred throughout West Africa in the towns and cities that he visited, especially in Ivory Coast, Togoland and Mali. Songs in his praise were composed, not only in Hausa and Arabic, but also in French, Ga, Kotokoli and, so it is said, in the Fante language. It is not possible to obtain reliable statistics as to the total number of Muslims belonging to the new Tijānī *Jamāᶜat al-fayḍa* by the end of the colonial period but there is little doubt that it was by then the largest single Muslim organisation in West Africa. It also became an important channel through which not only animists and polytheists but also former Christians converted to Islam. Moreover, it became the main rival not so much of European-style Christianity, which by the end of the colonial period was probably in decline in West Africa anyway, but of the rapidly growing African Christian churches.

Shaykh Ibrāhīm's doctrinal contribution to Islam was two-fold. First, he developed yet further the idea of *fayḍa* as a means of mass salvation. This had first been expounded in Hausaland by Malam Umaru Wali, who had shown how it could be made available to the ordinary *ṭarīqa* followers, as well as to trained Sufis. Shaykh Ibrāhīm Niass now took up this idea and made it the central theme of his teaching; he thus brought to millions of ordinary Believers the possibility of spiritual experiences and development previously restricted to the few who were willing to undergo traditional Sufi disciplines. Moreover, it was widely believed that the Shaykh's power to transmit *fayḍa* to his followers would ensure their salvation on the Last Day,

> On the Last Day they will not be interrogated,
> Or if they are interrogated,
> God Almighty will redeem them
> Their worship will not be questioned,
> Because of your *fayḍa* – Barhāmī [Ibrāhīm][13]

Second, he developed *tarbiyya*, the Sufi initiation, in such a way that it was made readily understandable to simple people who were without any background of Arabic learning. In the past, *tarbiyya* had only been available to the chosen few who had this background, but Shaykh Ibrāhīm now opened it up to anyone who sincerely wished to receive it. He thus took the process of popularising Sufism, already a characteristic of the Tijāniyya, a stage further. Indeed, so important did this new *tarbiyya* become in the view of many West African Muslims that they took to referring to the *Jamāᶜat al-fayḍa* simply as 'Tarbiyya', as if this were the name of the order.

Of course *Jamāᶜat al-fayḍa* had its enemies. It was bitterly opposed by the Wahhābīs, by many Sunnī *ᶜulamā'* who believed that it led to pantheism – the belief that all of nature is not only created by God but is actually part of Him – and by the Ḥamāliyya, the break-away sect of the Tijāniyya that had its own version of Tijānī doctrine. However, there is little doubt that the rise of the Tijānī *Jamāᶜat al-fayḍa* was one of the most important developments in West African Islam during the colonial period and that it contributed greatly to the spread of Islam during that period.

The Tijāniyya in the Gold Coast remained almost entirely non-political until the end of the colonial era, mainly because Muslims as a whole were educationally, economically and politically deprived in that territory. In Nigeria, however, it quickly became identified with opposition to the establishment party, NPC, which was closely linked to the Qādiriyya. But whereas the northern Nigerian Qādiriyya openly supported NPC, the Tijāniyya was less public in its support for the opposition party, NEPU. Nevertheless, the support was real.

In French territory the Tijāniyya generally cooperated with the French colonial authorities. Shaykh Ibrāhīm Niass took the view that his followers should be more concerned with the world to come than with the present world of human politics but he was influential in drawing up the Senegalese constitution immediately before that territory gained its independence from the French.

In Nigeria the Tijāniyya was not directly hostile to the British administration but in so far as the British tended to support the Qādirī-based NPC, Tijānīs of NEPU did find themselves in conflict with the administration from time to time.

The Murīds of Senegal

This *ṭarīqa* was founded *c.* 1303/1886 by Aḥmad Bamba. He was a Senegalese *shaykh* who had been initated into the Qādiriyya by the Mauritanian, Shaykh Sidya who in his turn, was linked to the Kunta of Timbuktu. Aḥmad Bamba's *ṭarīqa* was, initially, a sub-sect of the Qādiriyya but later the Shaykh developed his own *wird* and doctrines which seem to have been influenced by those of the Tijāniyya as well as by those of the parent Qādiriyya. As a result, a new *ṭarīqa* emerged with the followers of Aḥmad Bamba referring to themselves as *murīdūn* (sing. *murīd*), 'initiates'. In consequence the term Murīdiyya has been used to describe the movement but this term is not normally used by the followers themselves and is best avoided.

The most distinctive aspect of Aḥmad Bamba's movement was the emphasis he placed on the duty of the initiate to work for his *shaykh*. To follow one's *shaykh* and work for him was a means of ensuring salvation. Indeed, physical work was regarded as bringing spiritual reward in much the same way as were contemplation and religious exercises in the more traditional *ṭuruq*.

Aḥmad Bamba's movement was essentially Wolof and it arose at a time when Wolof society had been disturbed by the breakdown of its traditional structures such as the old form of kingship and the old economic and trading patterns as well as the French occupation. Aḥmad Bamba thus offered a rallying-point for the discontented and displaced in Wolof society and for those who resented the French and sought a way to protect the Islamic way of life from their influence. He also offered an alternative to reliance upon the traditional rulers who had now shown themselves unable to resist the French.

Unlike the other major *ṭuruq* in West Africa, Aḥmad Bamba's movement drew much of its support from the rural areas rather than from the towns. It also seems to have been more tolerant of the mixing of pre-Islamic with Islamic custom than were the other *ṭuruq* and it lacked their drive towards puritanical Islamic reform.

The Murīds acquired a reputation for being anti-French and at the beginning of his career, Aḥmad Bamba may have had some ambition to overthrow the French and set up his own Islamic state. Later, he recognised that this was unrealistic and reconciled himself to a purely religious life cooperating with the French to a limited extent. However he was never wholeheartedly friendly in his attitude towards the French and they, in turn, distrusted him and kept a close watch on him. Indeed, he was twice exiled from Senegal but each time was allowed to return. Yet despite their distrust the French valued the contribution that the Murīds made to the Senegalese economy. By 1900 relations between the Murīds and the French colonial authorities had settled down to one of limited cooperation although it seems the two sides never really liked or trusted one another. Aḥmad Bamba died in AD 1927.

Although adherence to the Murīds did spread to isolated groups elsewhere in West Africa, the *ṭarīqa* was, and still is, substantially identified with Senegal.

The Wahhābīs in West Africa

Not all Muslims were as ready to come to terms with the Europeans as the Qādiriyya and the Tijāniyya. The Sanūsiyya continued to represent anti-imperialist and, by implication, some degree of anti-Christian sentiment in West Africa. It was soon joined by the Wahhābīs.

The Wahhābī movement, that originated in Arabia *c.* 1137–8/1725 (although it had much older intellectual roots in Islamic theology), was a puritanical movement directed toward Islamic reform. It was strongly opposed to Sufism and particularly to the Sufi cult of the *awliyā'*. The movement was founded by a certain *shaykh* called ᶜAbd al-Wahhāb, thus the name Wahhābiyya which is usually applied to it by European orientalists as well as by many Muslims. Members of the movement do not accept this name, however, they claim that they are simply Sunnī Muslims, *Ahl al-sunna wa'l-kitāb*, 'People of the Sunna and the Book' and not members of a particular sect. For convenience, the terms Wahhābī and Wahhābiyya will be used here to describe those who incline towards the doctrines of ᶜAbd al-Wahhāb and his successors.

In a recent study of the Wahhābiyya in West Africa, Dr Lansiné Kaba has suggested that Wahhābī influences were present in French territory between AD 1920 and AD 1935.[14] He considers that Wahhabism reached West Africa through West African Muslims who had picked up its ideas in the course of Pilgrimage to Saudi Arabia; also as a result of contacts with the Wahhābī-inclined Muslim Brotherhood in Egypt. By AD 1945 the presence of the Wahhābiyya in Mali and the Ivory Coast is beyond doubt and it had almost certainly penetrated into the Gold Coast by that date.

Wahhabism in West Africa was characterised by intense Islamic radicalism and protest, directed partly against what the Wahhābīs considered to be the exploitation of the simple people by the Sufi *awliyā'*; and partly against the readiness of the traditional Islamic hierarchy to compromise with the colonial administrations. The Wahhābīs were also particularly strongly opposed to the Tijānī *Jamāᶜat al-fayḍa* of Shaykh Ibrāhīm Niass and to the Aḥmadiyya (see below).

Sometimes Wahhābī sympathies showed themselves in direct, formal affiliation with the Saudi-Arabian organisations founded to spread Wahhābī ideas but sometimes, the link was with the Egyptian Muslim Brotherhood. More often, probably, these sympathies took the form of a general similarity of aims and outlook with the Wahhābīs but did not necessarily involve formal links with organisations outside West Africa. This tended to be the case in northern Nigeria, where Wahhābī ideas were strong among certain groups of young ᶜ*ulamā'*, but the leadership came from inside the group, not from outside.

In the Ivory Coast and Mali the Wahhābīs adopted the tactic of breaking away from the main Friday mosque and setting up a rival mosque, where they prayed behind their own *imāms*. Sometimes they even 'occupied' the main Friday mosque and prevented the non-Wahhābī *imām* from leading prayers. The Wahhābīs also contested the temporal authority of Muslim rulers recognised by the colonial regimes. Through the Subbanu movement the Wahhābiyya in French territory became strongly political. It became, together with the Ḥamāliyya, the religious wing of the *Rassemblement Démocratique Africain* in French West Africa. The RDA was, of course, the main political organ of African independence in those territories during the colonial period and although it was not exclusively Muslim, Muslims played a large part in it. The French authorities held back, in the main, from direct interference with the Wahhābīs, except when they were obviously the cause of public disorder. However they tried to combat their influence by supporting non-Wahhābī Muslim organisations and interests.

In the Gold Coast the Wahhābīs played a less obvious political role probably because Muslims in that area were, in general, at a considerable educational and economic disadvantage. However, there is evidence that Gold Coast Wahhābīs opposed the British colonial administration as and when they could.

The Aḥmadiyya

The Aḥmadiyya is a modern Muslim organisation that originated in the Indian sub-continent. It takes its name from its founder, Mirza Ghulām Aḥmad (*d.* AD 1908).

The central characteristic of Aḥmadiyya doctrine is the assertion that the founder, Ghulām Aḥmad, is not just a holy man but fully a prophet, in the sense that that term is applied in Islam to the Prophet Muḥammad. This is absolutely contrary to the teaching of Sunnī Islam, according to which Muḥammad was the 'Seal' or last of the prophets. For this reason the great majority of Sunnī Muslims reject Aḥmadī teachings and some go as far as to deny that these people are Muslims at all. So intense is the hostility of the Sunnī majority to the Aḥmadiyya that the Saudi-Arabian Government has recently banned known Aḥmadīs from taking part in the Pilgrimage to the Holy Places. Aḥmadīs vigorously insist that they are Muslims, however; therefore the sect finds a place in this study.

In addition to their eccentric teaching on prophethood, which differs so much from that of Sunnī Muslims, the Aḥmadīs also reject the claim that the Sultan of the old Turkish empire was the caliph of Islam. Moreover, they have their own views about the Mahdī. Unlike most Sunnī Muslims, they deny that the Mahdī will be a warrior. On the contrary, they teach that he will be a man of peace and that his mission will be to bring peace on earth. Since this pacifist doctrine implied cooperation with the colonial authorities it, too, caused the Aḥmadīs to be unpopular with more militant Muslim groups.

Indian Aḥmadī missionaries appeared on the West Coast of Africa *c.* AD 1921. They came first to Lagos and from there moved on into the Gold Coast. In Nigeria they had some success among the new Muslims of the south but they made no progress at all in the north. In the Gold Coast they were much more successful and they won over many Fante animists as well as a number of unsettled Christians who were attracted to Islam but put off it by its domination by Hausas and its background of Arabic literacy. By AD 1921 the Aḥmadīs were well established in Saltpond which became their headquarters. By AD 1928 Aḥmadī missionaries were petitioning the Gold Coast Government for permission to establish a mission in Kumasi but this was vigorously opposed by the Sunnī Muslim community of Kumasi *zongo*. However, by AD 1930 the Aḥmadiyya claimed 5,000 members in the southern Gold Coast.

One of the most dramatic and interesting incidents in the history of the Aḥmadiyya concerns its establishment in Wa, a stronghold of Sunnī Islam in the Northern Territories. A certain Malam Salihu, an Arabic teacher and trader of Wa, visited Saltpond in the early 1930s. Here he became converted to the Aḥmadiyya and then returned to the Northern Territories where he soon gained a considerable following among the Wala and Moshi people. In AD 1933 his followers tried to enter Wa but were roughly handled by some of the local Sunnī Muslims, who regarded them as apostates, people who had abandoned Islam. The Wa Na, Pelpuo III, ordered them to leave but the British District

Commissioner in Wa intervened, saying that Malam Salihu and his people must be allowed to return. They did so against intense opposition from the Sunnī Muslim population in Wa. Throughout AD 1935 Malam Salihu, his family and his followers were subject to considerable persecution and had to be protected by a police guard but eventually the opposition died down. By the time he died in AD 1961, al-Ḥājj Salihu, as he had then become, left a thriving Aḥmadī community behind him in Wa, as well as a fine mosque built entirely by private subscription from Aḥmadī members.

Special reasons account for the success of the Aḥmadīs in Wa, so far away from their usual sphere of operations among the coastal people. The Wala and Mossi people, who formed a large part of the population of Wa, began to be attracted to Islam when their own traditional religion became more and more out of touch with the changing times. Christianity had the disadvantages described (see above) but Islam, as they knew it, was dominated by Hausas and Dyulas. Moreover, it was closely associated with Arabic culture and not all of them were prepared to commit themselves to acquiring this. However, the Aḥmadī missionaries were not associated with the possible domination by people who, historically, had been their rivals or outright enemies; also, the Aḥmadīs' willingness to use translations of the Koran in English or in African languages avoided the problems caused by lack of an Arabic education. Therefore, like the Fantes in the southern Gold Coast, the Wala and the Moshi people in Wa joined the Aḥmadiyya in considerable numbers.

British colonial officials on the Gold Coast were suspicious of the Aḥmadiyya, mainly because its presence aroused such fierce opposition from the Sunnī majority. This attitude is perhaps best expressed in a letter, dated 29 June 1923, from the Acting Governor of the Gold Coast to the Duke of Devonshire, at that time the British Colonial Secretary. He writes:

> My Lord Duke,
>
> I have the honour to acknowledge receipt of Your Grace's Despatches of 19 March and 18 May on the subject of the Ahmadia movement in this Colony.
>
> The centre of the movement is at Ekufaro in the Central Province. The Indian in charge is one E.E. Hakeem, who arrived in 1921 and claims to have now 3,000 adherents. His main mission in the Colony is to the Fanti Pagans and to the unsettled Christians of various sects and he is not on good terms with the Hausa Chiefs who are Mohammedans. He claims that his mission is one of peace and loyalty to the Government of the country and so far there is no evidence that he is exercising any unsettling political influence.
>
> Whether this movement will be of more than passing interest is doubtful. When Nayyar visited the Colony he held meetings at Saltpond but his influence among the Mohammedans there was negligible as the Head of the Mosque is a Malam who has been to Mecca and lived for 10 years in Cairo.
>
> . . .
>
> Adherents of this movement are quite free to pursue their religious observances without molestation but no special recognition can or should be given to it. The Mohammedan religion is recognised to the extent that

there is a Mohammedan Marriage Ordinance but any special recognition of a particular sect would undoubtedly be used to bolster up the claim that Government favoured this in preference to other Mohammedan bodies and as stated above, this movement has so far no adherents among the Mohammedan communities in this Colony.

I have the honour
to be, etc.,
J.C. Maxwell,
Acting Governor.[15]

This cautious view probably represents that of the British administration in southern Nigeria and in the Gold Coast as well as in Sierra Leone, where the movement also established a presence. In northern Nigeria, a solidly Sunnī and Mālikī area, the Aḥmadiyya made no significant progress during the colonial era and therefore warranted little attention from the administration.

Islam and colonial education

The French case

The French education system in their West African territories naturally reflected their overall policy of assimilation, discussed above. How this policy was to be implemented through education is most concisely expressed in an official document of AD 1909 relating to French Guinea. This states that one of the three main aims of French education should be 'to make of the school an instrument for the diffusion of our civilization'.[16] The two other aims were to train local auxiliaries, clerks, telephonists and so on, and to train skilled artisans. In order to achieve these aims the French set up a number of excellent schools but their curriculums were entirely French. In them pupils were given a French literary and scientific education that differed little from that given to children in France, but Arabic and other subjects on the Islamic curriculum were almost entirely neglected. In AD 1909 Monsieur Mariani, the Inspector of Islamic Education in Guinea, proposed that Islamic education should be integrated into the French system but his advice was ignored. However, Islamic education in Guinea survived, although it got little support from the French authorities.

Perhaps the most damaging policy to Islamic education was the French eventual insistence that all African employees of the administration must be graduates of French schools and must speak French. Inevitably, this created a demand for French education that drew at least some young men away from the Islamic system. Similarly, the French insisted that all chiefs must speak French. This too, meant that French, not Arabic education was necessary for chiefly office.

The British system in Nigeria

In northern Nigeria the British educational approach to Islam was somewhat different from that of the French. From the beginning Lugard recommended that existing Koran schools should be integrated into the government system. There were at least two reasons for this. First, the widespread view among the early British administrators that it was desirable in all ways to support and preserve the Islamic system and not alienate Muslim chiefs. Second, economy for money to invest in education was in short supply. The British Colonial Office was not prepared to use British taxpayers' money to support this new exercise in empire-building with which the self-willed Lugard had burdened it, much against its will. Money could be saved, or so it was hoped, by making use of the existing system. There may also have been another reason that was never spelled out officially although it was probably implied in the policy of 'education along native lines'. Many British officials in the Muslim north disliked the southern Nigerian, largely missionary education along strictly European lines that produced African clerks given to wearing European clothes and imitating European life-styles. They felt this to be quite unsuited to the North and paternalistic British officials were much concerned to protect their Muslim charges from it. The British have frequently been blamed for the alleged favouritism and even racialism of this attitude. In so far as it arose from a lack of understanding of, and sympathy for, the natural human aspirations of these southern Nigerians, who had, through no fault of their own, been caught up in an alien system of culture to which they had not at that time become fully adjusted, this was perhaps justified. On the other hand, it can be argued that the British officials' attitudes arose out of a civilised and humane regard for other peoples' cultural identity – that of the northern Muslims – and for the dignity conferred by a great intellectual tradition – that of Islam. This aspect is too often ignored by the critics of the British colonial administration.

At first, the British sought to educate mainly the sons of chiefs in a system that combined a Western, secular and largely literary curriculum with some Arabic and Islamic religious knowledge and which laid careful emphasis on the maintenance of traditional Islamic dress, social custom and so on. Unfortunately however, Arabic and the Islamic Religion were not taught by professional *ᶜulamā'*, who, for the most part refused to serve in 'Christian' schools, but by barely literate persons who were ordered to do the job by the local emirs, under pressure from the administration. In consequence, the standard in these subjects was low and as time went on, the Islamic syllabus was increasingly neglected. Later, the system became open to the sons of commoners as well but whereas chiefs could be persuaded and pushed into sending their sons to school, commoners could not. In fact, they showed themselves reluctant to do so for they naturally feared that government schools might convert their children from Islam to Christianity or, at the very least, introduce them to those European ways against which the Muslim moralists so constantly warned them. Thus, despite the good intentions of the British, the spread of Western secular education in northern Nigeria was slow before World War II.

In spite of some confusion as to what was meant by 'native lines', the British administration did in due course make positive attempts to integrate the Islamic and the Western curriculums. The first attempt began in AD 1927, when courses were run for Koran school teachers. The object was to enable them to teach certain secular subjects – arithmetic, geography and so on – in their Koran schools but the experiment had little success and lapsed after some years.

More successful was the founding of the Kano Law School, in AD 1933. This was staffed largely by teachers from the Anglo-Egyptian Sudan and it taught Islamic law, Arabic and a number of other Islamic subjects as well as English. It acquired a considerable reputation and certainly contributed significantly to maintaining the standards of Islamic education in northern Nigeria before World War II.

One consequence of the war was to create a much wider demand for Western-style education in northern Nigeria than had existed before while at the same time popular demand for better Islamic education became more insistent. Meanwhile, it was realised that one reason for the lack of progress in Islamic education was the gap in educational techniques and attitudes between the traditional *ᶜulamā'* on the one hand, and teachers, whether British or African, trained along Western lines on the other. In consequence, the Kano Law School, while retaining its original legal function, had added to it a teacher training wing and became the Kano School for Arabic Studies. Here teachers of Arabic and Islamic subjects were given modern teacher training and then sent out to teach their subjects in primary and secondary schools. By the late 1950s such teachers were preparing students for the Overseas School Certificate of the Oxford and Cambridge Joint Examination Board in Arabic, Islamic History and Islamic Religious Knowledge. Later still, the School for Arabic Studies began to prepare students for entrance to British and American universities, in the disciplines of Arabic and Islamic Studies. The results of the teacher training programme were only moderately successful however, for, in competition with expatriate teachers of western, secular subjects, who often failed to see the value of Islamic subjects, these graduates of the School for Arabic Studies usually encountered considerable difficulties in promoting Arabic and Islamic subjects in their schools and soon became discouraged. The university entrance programme, on the other hand, was much more successful. It led to the creation of a group of university graduates who were later able to staff university departments in Arabic and Islamic Studies when Nigerian universities were founded.

Overall, the results produced by the British system of education in northern Nigeria were uneven and incomplete. Moreover, the pattern that was eventually evolved was still strongly weighted towards Western, secular concepts of education. Indeed, it could be said that the British system had the disadvantages of the French system and lacked only its advantages! It certainly ignored for far too long the teaching of Islamic literature, both in Arabic and the vernacular languages, as well as the teaching of the history of Islam in Africa. However, in northern Nigeria and to a lesser extent in other Islamic areas of Nigeria, the process of integration between the Islamic system and the Western, secular system has made some progress.

The British system in the Gold Coast

The relationship between the colonial system of education and Islam in the Gold Coast was quite different from that in northern Nigeria because it reflected the attitudes of the British administration there towards Islam, that were described earlier in this chapter.

First, the Gold Coast administration relied heavily on Christian missions to provide education. This was well suited to the needs of the substantial Christian population of the country and it was not seriously objectionable to animists and polytheists, because for them it had long been accepted that literacy, other than Islamic literacy, was inseparable from conversion to Christianity. However for the Muslims it was obviously unacceptable. Even when the Christian mission schools did not actively try to convert Muslim children – and some of them did so quite deliberately and made clear public attempts to justify such a policy – it was almost impossible for a Muslim child to spend several years in a Christian missionary school without being influenced. What government schools there were, were probably more actively Christian and less religiously impartial in their conduct of education than were government schools in northern Nigeria and Gold Coast Muslim parents regarded them with deep suspicion.

The Gold Coast Government gave some limited help to Islamic schools in the Northern Territories but in the Colony, that is the southern Gold Coast, it gave no help at all except to a few Aḥmadī schools. These were in fact excellent educational institutions, academically the equals of most government and mission schools but the price of attending them was indoctrination with Aḥmadī ideas, at least that is what Sunnī parents feared. These parents had three choices open to them: to send their children to mission or government schools and risk losing them to the Christians; to send them to Aḥmadī schools and expose them to what they considered to be heresy; or to send them to the *zongo* Koran schools that attempted to give them a traditional and purely Arabic-based education. It was the third choice that most of them adopted but unfortunately, these *zongo* schools were, with few exceptions, not very efficient. Few of them taught English and those that did, employed untrained teachers whose own standard in that language was often low. There was little attempt also, to teach secular subjects such as geography or science. The consequence has been that, in an area where English is the official language and is also widely spoken socially, Muslims have been at a disadvantage, socially and economically. Following from this, they have suffered considerable political handicaps, especially after the Gold Coast gained its independence.

In this chapter, so far, attention has been directed to the territories known, as a whole, under the heading of 'French West Africa', although of course this unit subsequently became split up into a number of independent states. Attention has also been drawn to the two major British possessions, Nigeria and the Gold Coast, now Ghana, but there were two other British possessions, Sierra Leone and the Gambia, that both contained Muslim populations. In addition, there is the independent West African state of Liberia, which has never been formally under colonial control.

Islam in Sierra Leone

Sierra Leone is a small coastal strip bordered on the north and east by Guinea, and in the south by Liberia and it became a British protectorate in AD 1895. Largely coast and forest, it did not become influenced by Islam until the early 12/18 century when it began to be affected by migrations of Muslim people, reaching it from the Islamic centres of Kankan, in the Niger area, and Kong, north-west of the Black Volta.

Sierra Leone is peculiar among West African states for its small but influential population of Creoles, descendants of freed slaves who speak their own Creole language. Although these people are a numerical minority in the total population, they none the less dominate much of the economic, social and political life of the country. They are also among the most westernised of West African populations and are almost exclusively Christian. When the British administration was set up in Sierra Leone, it attempted, successfully, to govern with the cooperation of the Creoles. Indeed, it has been suggested that British policy was to deliberately divide the Creoles from the Mendes, Vais, Temnes and others, in order to facilitate colonial rule. Whether this is true or not seems to me to be largely a matter of interpretation and emphasis but in my opinion I doubt that it was ever a deliberate and conscious policy. However, the strong bias of the British administration in favour of the Christian Creole minority certainly had the effect of isolating the Muslims, who were largely Mendes, Vais and Temnes, from power and influence. In this situation it is hardly surprising that colonial education developed almost entirely in the interest of the Christian population, of which the Creoles were the most influential members. Moreover, it was largely in the hands of Christian missionary organisations. Thus the Church Missionary Society (CMS) founded a boys' grammar school in Freetown in AD 1845 and a girls' secondary school in 1849. Similar schools were founded by other missionary organisations. The well-known Fourah Bay College was also a CMS foundation. As might be expected, these institutions offered a distinctly Christian education and produced an educated, Christian and largely Creole elite, on which the administration relied for its local administrative personnel. Moreover, the legal profession, medicine, banking and so on, were largely in the hands of Christian Creoles. Muslims, for whom this education was closed except at an unacceptable risk to their religion, consequently remained educationally, and thus economically, disadvantaged.

What education along western lines there was that was available for Muslims, was offered mainly by the Aḥmadiyya, established in Sierra Leone since 1937. Sunnī Islamic education was left to the various Muslim communities to make what arrangements they could. The Muslim population now probably forms at least 50 per cent of the total, in comparison with the Christian element of between four and five per cent. Since World War II there has been a growing tendency in Sierra Leone, as in other West African coastal territories, for former Christians to go over to Islam. This is probably to be attributed to the increasing community of interest between Islam and African nationalism, as well as to reaction against Christianity as the White man's religion.

The Aḥmadiyya has alwás been strong in Sierra Leone but there is also a large Sunnī element, composed largely of immigrant Muslims from Nigeria. The Tijānī *Jamāᶜat al-fayḍa* also claims to have made considerable headway in Sierra Leone and may be largely responsible for the movement of conversion to Islam mentioned above.

Freetown is now the location of several Muslim societies, of which the largest are the Muslim Congress, the Muslim Reformation Society and the Ikhwan al-Muslimin Association. Since *c.* 1961 the Egyptian government has taken considerable interest in the Sierra Leonean Muslim communities and has made important contributions to the development of Arabic and Islamic education there. However, as elsewhere in West Africa, such Arabic education suffers from the disadvantage that it is of limited vocational value in a country that is now, for better or for worse, very largely English-speaking.

Islam in the Gambia

The Gambia is a narrow strip of territory along both sides of the Gambia river, within the present Republic of Senegal. The history of Islam there has already been considered under the heading of the Senegambia, of which, historically, the area formed part. It was colonised by the British as early as the 11/17 century and was fought over, at different times, by the Dutch, British and French until AD 1857, when it finally came under British control and became a British protectorate. Although the territory is tiny, amounting to only 4003 square miles, it extends eastward from the coast into the savanna and in consequence includes a relatively large Muslim population, amounting to approximately 80 per cent at the present time.

The policy of the early British administration towards Islam along the Gambia river was governed by two main considerations: rivalry with the French for control of the area and the interests of British trade there. In particular, the British, like the French, regarded the 'Maraboutic wars' of the area, which were in fact political struggles between Muslim revolutionaries and the traditional Soninke dynasties, with unease because they disrupted trade and because there was a danger they might create strong, centralised Islamic kingdoms that would challenge European control. George D'Arcy, British Governor of the Gambia from AD 1859–67, was certainly anti-Muslim. He was also identified with the interests of the local African Christian traders in Bathurst and wanted to create barriers to the advance of what he thought of as militant Islam. The British Colonial Office, on the other hand, was deeply reluctant to be drawn into what it feared would be religious wars in the Gambia and declined to support D'Arcy's policies. Indeed, C.B. Adderley, Under-Secretary for the Colonies from AD 1866–8, disagreed with D'Arcy's anti-Muslim views; he favoured the Muslim element in the Gambia, on the ground that Muslims would provide strong government and would encourage trade.

Because Muslims represented such an overwhelming majority of the Gambian population, there was not the same tension there between a westernised, Christian educated elite and Muslim traditionalists as arose in those coastal territories where the Muslim element was less numerous. Thus Muslims played a bigger part in the political evolution of the territory, especially through the influential Muslim Congress Party. However, while traditional Islamic education under the control of the local *ᶜulamā'* remained vigorous in the Gambia and received some help from the British administration, secular, western education was, as usual in British West African coastal territories, largely in the hands of Christian missionaries. Moreover, there was no Aḥmadiyya presence in the Gambia and it therefore lacked the Aḥmadī-sponsored education that existed in the Gold Coast and Sierra Leone. The result was that, here as elsewhere, the educated elite was largely Christian.

At the time the British protectorate was set up, the Qādiriyya *ṭarīqa* was strong in the Gambia but, as might be expected, the territory has always been closely influenced by events and developments in neighbouring Senegal. Thus the Tijāniyya also quickly established itself in the Gambia, especially the *Jamāᶜat al-fayḍa* of Shaykh Ibrāhīm Niass. The Gambia is now one of the English-speaking areas of West Africa in which *Jamāᶜat al-fayḍa* is strongest and there are close links between the *Jamāᶜat* in the Gambia and in Ghana.

The Aḥmadiyya attempted to establish a footing in the Gambia *c.* 1956 but was refused permission to set up its organisation there by the British administration. This was not due to British antagonism to the Aḥmadiyya as such, but rather to the representations of the Sunnī *ᶜulamā'* in the Gambia, who were strongly opposed to the Aḥmadiyya. It has, however, recently been allowed to operate there.

Islam is undoubtedly strong in the Gambia at the present time and Bathurst, the capital, is the centre of numerous Muslim societies, several of which have links with parent Muslim organisations in Senegal. There is also a school for the teaching of Arabic in Bathurst, founded by the Gambian Muslim Association.

Islam in Liberia

Liberia has the distinction of not having been formally colonised by any European power, although the area has been visited by Europeans since the 8/14 century. The population, largely coastal and forest-dwelling, did not become influenced by Islam until, probably, the 10/16 century, when migrations of Muslim Mendes, Vais and others carried Islam down from Kankan and the upper Niger region. The present Muslim population is not large when compared with other West African countries but it does amount to 26 per cent of the total, of which a large proportion is Christian.

Although there has been no colonial administration in Liberia, the Christian missionary element there, especially American missions, has been strong ever since *c.* AD 1816, at which date an American society first began to repatriate freed slaves to Liberia. Once again, therefore, western, secular education in Liberia has always had a definite Christian bias and has tended to produce a Christian elite. This has had social and political consequences, for political power has rested almost wholly in the hands of Protestant Christian groups and the Muslims have been almost entirely unrepresented.

The consequences for Islam of the colonial experience

There is room for more than one view as to the overall consequences of the colonial experience for Islam in West Africa. Michael Crowder has written,

> Islam under colonial rule became a force for conservatism rather than social change, as it had been in the nineteenth century.

How far is this true? In the first place, there has always been within Islam, whether in West Africa or elsewhere, a conservative 'right wing' and a radical 'left wing', as there must be in any religion or ideology. From time to time one or the other seems uppermost but both are always present and at work. If one considers the *jihād* movements of the 12/18 and 13/19 centuries in the west and central Sudan, these can certainly be regarded as triumphs for Islamic radicalism. Change – social, political and intellectual – followed from them. If one then goes on to consider, for example, the Sokoto caliphate, it at once becomes clear that a period of considerable Islamic conservatism had set in long before the colonial occupations were planned, let alone carried out. So it seems an over-simplification to attribute Islamic conservatism simply to the influence of the colonial regimes. This conservatism can just as readily be regarded as a period – and a very necessary period – of reaction and consolidation that began after the upheavals and violent changes brought about by *jihād* and which continued into the colonial era. That kindly, empirical and very level-headed observer of his times, the Imām ᶜUmar Kete-Krachi was no radical; his views and attitudes were formed before the occupations took place and he was typical of a large proportion of his colleagues among the ʿ*ulamā*ʾ. There is, therefore, no need to assume a direct connection between so-called Islamic conservatism and the colonial occupations.

In the second place, how deep was this conservatism of the colonial era? Certainly colonial security made it more difficult for movements of dissent such as Mahdism, the Sanūsiyya and the Wahhābiyya to find open expression. Perhaps, too, greater material prosperity under the colonial administrations, particularly among the common people, as well as better law and order, reduced the number of the discontented who might otherwise have supported such movements; although resentment at colonial rule no doubt gained them other adherents. However these movements existed all the same and played their part in preserving and nourishing a spirit of Muslim solidarity and the desire for political independence. The influence of the Tijāniyya, of the Wahhābī-inclined Muslim Brotherhood and a number of other Islamic organisations such as the Ansar-ud-Din, all contributed powerfully to this growing demand for independence from colonial rule. In Nigeria, even the ancient, elitist Qādiriyya turned itself into a populist movement that supported independence through its alliance with the Northern Peoples' Congress. The Aḥmadiyya was disapproved of by the Sunnī majority but it was an influence for progress in West African Islam, all the same. In particular, by its policy of competing with Christian mission schools in the provision of sound secular education, it forced the Sunnīs to think about their own attitudes to that education. In the end, the Sunnī organisations such as the Ansar-ud-Din followed the lead of the Aḥmadīs and began to organise similar education for themselves. So perhaps the conservatism, such as it was, was more apparent than real.

The colonial era was one in which political, social and ideological change was deliberately restricted by the colonial governments. Certainly, there was some change, but it was carefully supervised. In this situation there were Muslim groups that saw their best interests served by a policy of conservatism while there were others that worked for change. It must remain a matter of opinion which 'wing' of Islamic ideology predominated, but to see Islam before the occupations as progressive and as an instrument of change, and after the occupations as conservative, static and opposed to change, is certainly too simplistic. History is seldom so clear-cut.

NOTES

1 *Le Péril de l'Islam* was in fact the title of a book published in 1906, by L.G. Binger.
2 Ghana Archives, Accra, ADM 11/1435.
3 Accra, ADM 11/1435, Ag. CWP to SNA, 8/–/27.
4 A.H.M. Kirk-Greene in his Introduction to Sir George Orr, *The making of northern Nigeria*, second ed., London, 1965, p.xxxiv.
5 Quoted by Crowder, 1968, p.359.
6 Rudin, 1938, p.91.
7 These, and many other aspects of European influence are condemned in a number of Hausa poems composed by *malams*, especially during the period 1920–40.
8 Ghana Archives, Accra, ADM 56/1/101.
9 ibid. ADM 56/1/101.
10 Hausa manuscript, *WY*.
11 Hausa manuscript, *MB*.
12 Ghana Archives, Kumasi, D1989.

13 Hausa manuscript, *KG*.
14 Evenston, 1974 pp.25–7.
15 Ghana Archive Cape Coast, ADM 23/1/353.
16 Brown and Hiskett, eds. 1975, p.214.

CHAPTER EIGHTEEN

Reflections and conclusions

Throughout this book certain main themes have constantly recurred, even though the times and places in question have been as far apart as those of the 5/11-century Ghana and the 13/19-century Volta state of Wahabu. The purpose of this chapter is to reflect again on each of these themes which may indeed represent permanent structures of the society, not now in the light of a particular age and circumstance, but in relation to the total history of Islam in the west and central Sudan, in order to see whether any general conclusions emerge.

Conversion to Islam

The process of conversion to Islam from a traditional African religion – whether animism or polytheism – began as soon as the first Sūdānī started to copy certain of the habits of his Muslim acquaintances, and to interest himself in their ideas. It has continued ever since. Under what circumstances did this process begin? What course did it then take? What were its end results?

It is at once clear that there were at least two ways in which conversion to Islam took place. The first was by military conquest. Perhaps this is what happened in the state of Ghana, when the Almoravids allegedly conquered it and imposed Islam on its people. Conquest was apparently the initial factor in bringing about conversion to Islam when 10/16-century mounted warriors from Mali swept into the Volta region and set up their kingdoms there. Conquest, again, enjoyed a brief success in Wahabu, under the 13/19-century jihadist al-Ḥājj Maḥmūd, and in the territories of the Almamy Samory, during his short career as a fighter in the way of God. In all these instances it seems true to say that Islam was imposed in the first place by conquest, even though there is room for argument as to whether conquest alone was effective or whether other factors played a part as well. Such conversions, by force of arms rather than by the persuasions of argument and example, tended to bring clans and yet larger political and social groups nominally into Islam. This happened all together and all at once because at the stroke of the sword, Islamic institutions and the government of the *Sharīᶜa* were imposed upon them. However, while this may have compelled some of the people to conform to Islamic law and behaviour to some extent, no one can say how many of them really accepted Islam in their hearts.

The second method was persuasion by peaceful Muslims who entered non-Muslim societies within which they then lived and worked. As far as is known, this is what brought about the conversion of Gao, Tadmakkat and the other cities of the western Sudan before the 5/11 century, although there may have been some violent interludes as well. Perhaps it was peaceful persuasion, after all, and not the sword, that led to the conversion of Ghana. It was certainly peaceful penetration that brought Islam to Mali; apart from the initial and partly legendary fight between Sunjata and Sumanguru, there is no evidence that military force had created the largely Muslim society that Ibn Baṭṭūṭa visited in the 8/13 century, but there is ample evidence that trade had. Songhay swords failed to convert the Bambaras and the northern Mossis, yet wandering *shurafā'*, Kuntī *shaykhs* and their Marka followers did much to spread Islamic ideas among them, even though, in most cases, this fell short of final conversion. Later, however, the swords of the 13/19-century jihadists proved somewhat more compelling.

A number of scholars have been inclined to think that this peaceful form of conversion has been much more successful in the west and central Sudan than conversion by the sword. In support of this view they have pointed to the very real successes of such peaceful persuaders as the Dyula/Wangarawa, the Jakhankes, the Kuntī *shaykhs*, *shurafā'*, miracle-working *awliyā'*, Muslim scholars serving in Sudanic courts and so on. There is certainly much truth in this and nothing has been written in this book that disputes the considerable importance of such peaceful teachers and messengers of Islam. However, it is possible to press this view too far, and one should not underestimate the real effectiveness of more violent methods of conversion. Military conquest cannot, of itself, force men to abandon their beliefs and ideas, but conquerors can, and do, set up the political and social institutions that, given time, will persuade them or pressurise them into doing so. Regrettable as it may be, force is a powerful instrument in bringing about ideological change. If Muslim idealists had not been prepared to impose their demands by force, it is probable that Islam would, in the end, have been smothered by the recovery of traditional religions; or that the process of mixing would have gone so far that the end result would not have been recognisable as Sunnī Islam at all.

However this way of presenting the two forms of conversion – by force or in peace – may involve some distortion of the reality, in that it suggests two distinct and separate processes and that there can be a choice between them. In fact, this may not be so, for conversion is better seen as a continuum, a single line, that runs through peace and violence according to the circumstances of place and time. Seen in this way, it becomes clear that peaceful conversion is not really an alternative to forceful conversion; it is merely one phase of the total process by which conversion takes place. Moreover, it has within itself the seeds of violence, for the inevitable inadequacy of peaceful methods which involve acceptance of anything from making use of a few Islamic amulets to the advanced mixing of the type found in the Mali empire, is the very provocation that sets violent reform in motion. Thus to say that conversion has taken place by peaceful means may be no more than to stop short at a given point and ignore the inevitability of violence that must follow.

An aspect of conversion that has interested scholars is that of the role of trade (see Appendix A, Diagrams I-IV). Some have argued that the effectiveness of traders as spreaders of Islam in the west and central Sudan has been over-emphasised. They believe that scribes, astrologers, charm-makers, physicians, theologians and other literate professionals were equally as important, if not more important than traders. There is no need to doubt the contribution of such people for as Ryan has shown, *ᶜulamā'* who had no obvious connection with trade may have been influential in bringing Islam to the Yoruba capital of Old Ọyọ by the 11/16 century.[1] He also points out that Muslim Hausa slaves of non-Muslim Yorubas helped to spread Islam in Yorubaland during the 12–13/18 century.[2] No doubt many other examples could be quoted to demonstrate what is in any case obvious – that a man did not have to be a trader to practise Islam and preach it to others. However, in pursuing this discussion, it is necessary to make a clear distinction between 'trade', which was an institution or permanent structure of Sudanic society and 'traders', who were the people mainly engaged in making use of that structure and whose contributions arose from temporary conjunctions of time and circumstance which they themselves did not determine. Failure to make this distinction has sometimes led to confusion, for not all of those who spread Islam were traders. That it was trade, none the less, that was the most important factor in spreading Islam in the west and central Sudan, seems beyond reasonable doubt.

When one considers how Islam came to centres such as Gao, Ghana and Tadmakkat, it is necessary to ask how and why the Muslim literates who brought it, got to these places in the first instance. They can only have got there along the caravan routes as there was no other way. Some may have followed Muslim traders, to act as *imāms*, teachers and Muslim magistrates to the communities of Muslim merchants that grew up in these centres. Others may have gone as merchants and then discovered that they could make a better living as scribes and so on. Be that as it may, it is reasonable to argue that there was a direct link between trade and Islam, even if certain individual *ᶜulamā'* never bargained over a bale of cloth or argued over the price of a slave throughout the whole of their careers. The reality of this link can be demonstrated by reference to the map. Areas that the trade routes missed, for example the territory of the family-and-clan-group people in the north-west of the Volta Basin, remained almost untouched by Islam except in one locality. That was Wa, which lay on the route to the Lobi goldfields, where Islam took root and thrived because it was nourished by the continual influx of Muslims drawn to the area by the trade. Certainly some of them may have been *imāms*, Sufi *awliyā'* and other literates who did not participate directly in trade, but, none the less, trade was the essential factor that brought Islam to Wa and helped it to develop there.

As time went on, no doubt the link between trade and the presence of Muslim literates in certain areas became less direct. However, it would be misleading to discount the importance of trade as a factor that brought about the spread of Islam in the west and central Sudan. Undoubtedly it began to spread along the trade routes and if, for any reason, trade between the west and central Sudan and the countries on its borders had ever lapsed, these routes would have disappeared beneath Saharan sands. Under such circumstances it is difficult to imagine how Islam could have survived for long. Thus the argument as to whether those who brought Islam were predominantly traders or not has little to do with the essential link between the spread of Islam and the development of trade.

Some have regarded nomads as among the most influential spreaders of Islam in the west and central Sudan. This theory is beset by the difficulty of defining precisely who and what a nomad is. If the nomad also trades, like the

Kunta who were certainly nomadic at times, is the spread of Islam for which he is responsible to be attributed to trade or to nomadism?

There were nomads among the Sanhaja and the Kel-Es-Suq but substantial groups of these people settled in the Saharan caravan cities and became city-dwellers. Later, they were driven out of these cities and became partly nomadic again. If an individual nomad was literate, certainly he must have contributed something to the spread of Islam, but it then becomes difficult to decide whether it was his nomadic habit of roaming or his knowledge of Islamic texts that he owed to his literacy that was the more important factor in enabling him to spread Islam. On the whole, it seems that Islam in the west and central Sudan was spread, in the first instance, by traders and by persons of town or city background rather than by pure nomads. However, those nomads who possessed Islamic literacy – and they can have been no more than a tiny minority of the total nomadic population of the Sahara and the Sahel – no doubt contributed to making Islamic ideas more widely known. In some cases that contribution seems to have taken the form of a criticism of nomadism as a way of life and a call to their fellow nomads to abandon it and adopt a town-dwelling life-style, in which Islam could be more correctly observed.

Humphrey Fisher has tried to bring a welcome order to understanding the stages by which conversion to Islam has taken place in the societies of the west and central Sudan. He proposes the following three: quarantine, mixing and reform.[3]

Quarantine, or isolation, is the period during which foreign Muslims – North Africans, Egyptians, Berbers – enter Sudanic societies but live apart from the local people, in their own quarter, having little, if any, intellectual contact with them. A typical example is that of the Muslims in ancient Ghana who lived in their own town, several miles distant from the royal palace and the town of their non-Muslim hosts.

Mixing is the period when the quarantine of the Muslims begins to break down; local people begin to adopt Islamic ideas and Muslim clothes; the court begins to celebrate Islamic festivals as well as traditional ones and so on. However, Islam is not fully established; the traditional religion retains its hold on the common people and the ruler is compelled to recognise this fact. A typical example is that of Mali in the age of Ibn Baṭṭūṭa.

Reform is the final stage in the conversion process. It usually reaches a violent climax, namely *jihād*, although there can also be degrees of peaceful reform. The object of the reformers is to bring about the abolition of mixing and enforce the full observance of the Sunna.

Dr Fisher's model is a useful one but as he himself points out, it should not be applied too rigidly. Reform, which strives to achieve an ideal, can for this reason never be fully realised in any human society. Thus, in applying the model, it must be understood that the process it involves is never susceptible to completion. Islamic reform in the west and central Sudan ranged from the largely unsuccessful movements in the Senegambia during the 11/17 and 12/18 centuries, to the substantial successes of the 13/19-century jihadists. However, even these were incomplete in that some mixing continued or on other occasions reform never materialised at all, as was the case in Mali. Here, as far as is known, mixing remained a way of life until that empire faded away and was forgotten. Indeed, it can be argued that reform is essentially an attitude of mind rather than a physical state. In a community where Islamic reform has taken hold – whether it leads in the end to successful *jihād* or not – the difference between that community and an unreformed community lies in the fact that in the reformed community there are many more voices calling for strict observance of the Sunna and there is much more evidence of disquiet about mixing. The amount of mixing that takes place in both communities may, none the less, be much the same.

It is even possible, in certain instances, for the process not to advance significantly beyond the stage of quarantine for so long that there seems to be no movement at all. This was the situation among the northern Mossis and the Bambaras. It was also the case in the *zongos* of the southern Gold Coast and perhaps still is in some areas of modern Ghana at the present time. There certain Muslim communities still live almost entirely cut off, culturally and socially, from the surrounding Ghanaian Christians and polytheists.

Such differences in the rate at which Islam has advanced in the west and central Sudan have been the result of many factors: the political and social structures of the communities in which Islam arrived; the historical nature of the first encounter, whether through war or by peaceful contacts; the geographical location of the host society; the strength of the traditional culture in resisting the onslaught of Islam and, perhaps more important than all of these, the characters and convictions of outstanding men who emerged as leaders of thought and action.

What is meant when we say that a society has been converted to Islam? There are probably as many answers to this question as there are scholars who choose to ask it. Is a man a Muslim once the Sharīᶜa has been set up as the legal and political system under which he must live? Is he a Muslim as soon as he abandons his traditional form of dress and adopts Muslim clothes? The German traveller Rohlfs certainly thought that the adopting of European dress was one way of bringing about the conversion of Muslims to Christianity, so perhaps there is more to the clothes a man wears than just personal choice. Is a man a Muslim when he attends Islamic festivals? Or not until he starts to pray? What if he prays incorrectly? If Hausa Islamic verse is to be taken as an authority, this alone is sufficient to invalidate a persons's Islam in the opinion of many Hausa *ᶜulamā'*. We could go on but the answer most frequently given by Muslims is simple. It is, that a man becomes a Muslim as soon as he has recited the Islamic *Shahāda*, the declaration of faith that 'There is no god but Allāh; Muḥammad is the Messenger of Allāh', and accepted it in his heart. However, this passes the decision back to God Himself, for what man can know what another man accepts in his heart? There can be no certain answer to the question but scholars continue to ask it, all the same. So too did certain Muslim reformers such as the Shehu Usumanu ɗan Fodio who made several attempts to define a Muslim in the confusing circumstances of mixing that he found in Hausaland. In the end he seems to have concluded that, while deliberate mixing of non-islamic practices with Islam does constitute infidelity, wrong-doing due to ignorance does not.[4] Moreover, he clearly believed that to aid misbelievers against Muslims in a way that is injurious to Islam is also a form of infidelity.

There is a school of thought that holds that conversion to Islam, or for that matter to Christianity, only takes place when political, economic and and social conditions have created a situation in which change must come anyway. The social anthropologist Robin Horton, writing of both Islam and Christianity in Africa, has put this view as follows:

> Such a conclusion reduces Islam and Christianity to the role of catalysts – i.e. stimulators and accelerators of changes which were 'in the air' anyway; triggers for reactions in which they do not always appear among the end products.[5]

This can be described as a determinist view of conversion; that is one that holds that the act of conversion is determined by social and political forces over which the individual has no control and the operation of which he may not even be aware. Or, put metaphorically, the individual is a leaf blown by the wind of change, even when he may think he has conscious control over his own actions. Such a view of conversion was touched on toward the end of chapter 5 and I indicated there that I find it largely unsatisfactory. The following arguments seem to me to reinforce that point of view.

When applied to conversion to Islam in the west and central Sudan, there are many difficulties attaching to this theory that Islam is no more than a catalyst or trigger. The greatest of them is that of recognising, let alone of defining, what the 'changes in the air' have been at any given time and place. Conversion to Islam has been taking place in West Africa continuously from, probably, the 1/7 century to the present day. How can one know what changes were in the air of Tadmakkat *c.* 184/800? So Horton's theory cannot be shown to be valid in a West African context; it must remain a guess based on an interpretation of societies' behaviour in situations where, in the opinion of social anthropologists, the evidence does support their theory.

Even if one could know much more about the circumstances of 2/9-century Tadmakkat, how could one be sure that when a Berber inhabitant of that city converted to Islam, he did so only because he was reacting to certain social, political and economic ideas that were in the air? Why could it not have been because his own, individual reason led him to believe, first, that there can be only one God; second, that that god must be Allāh; third, that Allāh surely has some means of communicating with men and that therefore Muḥammad was indeed the Messenger of Allāh? Perhaps, having thought along these lines for many years, he then decided to adopt Ibāḍī Islam because Ibāḍī notions of challenging Arab elitism – the 'change in the air' of that day – attracted him. In this case it is surely the change in the air – resentment at Arab elitism – that is the mere trigger, while intellectual conviction leading to the deliberate acceptance of Islam is the deep factor.

A similar argument can be advanced to account for conversion that took place more than ten centuries later. It was pointed out in chapter 17 that some African Christians went over to Islam at the time when dissatisfaction with colonial rule was at its height. Certainly, change was in the air at this time – African nationalism, Pan-Africanism and similar new and exciting ideas – and, of course, these former African Christians may have been influenced in making their decisions by all or some of these. However, is it therefore correct to regard Islam as the catalyst or trigger of change that had to come anyway? Is it not equally possible that some, at least, of these people had thought seriously about such issues as the purpose of human life, the relation of man to his fellow men, the nature of God, the possibility of salvation in a future life and many other fundamental issues that have perplexed thoughtful men and women throughout history and which cannot be regarded as mere changes in the air. Such people might well have arrived at the reasoned and reasonable conclusion that Islam offered a better answer to these problems than Christianity. Then, a wish to show solidarity with other Africans might finally have persuaded them to take a step they had been contemplating for years. In this case, it is surely the change in the air that is the trigger, not Islam.

The fact is, the final proof for or against the determinist theory must always elude us, for no man can ever know what goes on in another man's mind; indeed he cannot always even be sure what goes on in his own mind. The same is also true of the ideational view which says that change is more likely to be the result of deliberate decision on the part of individual men and women, consciously applying ideas in an attempt to influence the societies in which they live. The choice between the two theories is therefore a subjective one, that depends on one's own experience of how one reacts and upon how one interprets other peoples' reactions. Probably the truth lies somewhere between the two and determinist factors interact continuously with conscious deliberation, to influence human behaviour. I can only say that I believe Horton and those who think like him press the determinist view too far.

Those who belong to the determinist school are also inclined to argue that when Africans convert to Islam, or to Christianity, they simply retain their old beliefs and express them in new forms that fit in with an Islamic or Christian pattern. To illustrate this view in the case of Islam they point to such facts as that certain of the pre-Islamic *bori* spirits of the Hausas have passed over into the Islamic era as Muslim djinns, and that they have been given such Muslim names as Alhaji. They also argue, for instance, that the practice of praying at the tombs of the *awliyā'* is merely the old ancestor-worship re-appearing in a new form, so that conversion is only on the surface and nothing has changed beneath.

The end result of such arguments is to throw doubt on whether any man or woman can ever be accurately described as a Muslim at all, for it must always be possible to point to ways in which he or she is still linked to the past. However interesting the theoretical argument may be, in practical terms such a conclusion seems unrealistic.

It is probably not useful to ask whether such uncertain interpretations of what conversion is, or is not, are in any outright sense correct or incorrect. It is more useful to agree that pre-Islamic survivals have been present in West African Islam throughout its history, for this is what is meant by a mixed society. What one may reasonably ask, however, is how much this matters in deciding whether a person or a society is Muslim or not. A comparison with western European society, where Christianity has existed and exerted its influence for many hundreds of years, is one way of throwing light on this question.

It is no doubt well known to most readers of this book that many western European families celebrate the Christian festival of Easter by painting the shells of hens' or gooses' eggs in bright coloured patterns and then eating the eggs for breakfast on Easter morning; or sometimes the family buys chocolate Easter eggs that are given to the children as gifts on Easter morning. In Britain this custom has been practised by many thousands of families over many generations, and is still practised at the present time. There is little doubt that the practice is a survival from the pre-Christian past. The eggs are symbols of fertility; Easter falls in the spring of the year. In pre-Christian times the ancestors of the present-day populations of western European countries no doubt attempted to ensure a good growing season by offering eggs to their gods. The practice continued on into Christian times because the early Christian missionaries could not stop it. They therefore accepted it and associated it with the Christian teaching of the resurrection of Christ. The families that continue this practice of giving eggs at Easter at the the present day may be believing Christians who attend church regularly and strictly observe the rules of Christian morality and behaviour, or they may be people who would describe themselves as secularists and who have no religious beliefs at all. In either case, whether Christian or secularist, it is hardly realistic to argue that nothing has really changed since the days of their pre-Christian ancestors, simply because they eat painted eggs or chocolate eggs on Easter morning.

The point of view of those who make much of a *bori* spirit called Alhaji, or who see ancestor-worship in a woman's visit to the tomb of a *walī*, while at the same time ignoring the fact that she dresses as a Muslim, was married as a Muslim and will be buried as a Muslim, seems to me equally unrealistic. It is not that statements about the survival of pre-Islamic practices in West African Islam are untrue; they are simply inconclusive as evidence in the matter of deciding whether individuals and societies are Muslim or something else. They have to be balanced against such evidence as how people dress, how they marry, how they inherit, how they conduct funerals and so on. They also have to be weighed against the evidence of political institutions, literature, folklore and so on – are these wholly Islamic, or partly Islamic or not Islamic at all? If such evidence points, in the main, towards Islam, then it seems reasonable to argue that for all practical purposes the society is a Muslim one, despite the fact that it retains some of its old beliefs. Even negative evidence can support this conclusion. It is well known that many Hausa villagers do not observe the Islamic laws of inheritance very strictly but continue to apply the old pre-Islamic custom in this matter. When questioned about this, most of them turn out to be rather ashamed of it. They apologise but excuse themselves on the grounds that to apply the Islamic system would cause too many quarrels and disputes and this sense of shame shows clearly that they feel themselves to be Muslims.

In commenting on Horton's views, Humphrey Fisher remarks,

> [Horton] has over-estimated the survival . . . of original African elements of religion; and more important, has under-estimated the willingness and ability of Africans to make even rigorous [very strict] Islam and Christianity their own.[6]

I see no reason to disagree with this assessment when applied, in particular, to conversion to Islam in the west and central Sudan.

The formation of states

The way in which Islam has contributed to the formation of states in the west and central Sudan has been discussed frequently throughout this book. This section is intended to draw the threads of the discussion together, to see what conclusions emerge from it.

Islam is a set of beliefs and ideas and a way of life; it cannot of itself create states or destroy them. However, Muslim people, in pursuit of conquest, trade or other human goals, can. Then, having done so, they generally attempt to impose Islamic institutions and the Islamic life-style on what they have created, so that this becomes what can be described as an 'Islamic state'. It is important to remember that these essential activities – conquest, trade, the arrival of strangers, slave-raiding and slave-trading – which were necessary in the process of forming states, are not in themselves Islamic. Islam can only be said to form states, or to contribute to their development, in so far as Muslim people engage in activities that have this result. It follows that non-Muslims can also create states by engaging in similar activities. Thus states existed in the west and central Sudan long before Islam arrived on the scene. While Muslims have certainly set up states for the first time where none existed before, as in Bundu and Wahabu for example, their more usual role has been to influence the development of existing states in an Islamic direction. The process by which this took place was often closely linked to the stages of conversion described above. Indeed, in so far as a certain pattern of political activity and institutions are part of the Sharīᶜa, the adoption of them is simply one aspect of the total process of conversion to Islam.

A very early example of the formation of a state in which Islam had a hand is that of Gao. Here trade carried Islam to what seems to have been a pre-Islamic kingdom and in due course the rulers of this kingdom converted to Islam, no doubt because they found it advantageous to their trading interests. They then changed from what had probably been a semi-nomadic way of life and settled in the Muslim trading town of Gao, which became the capital of an Islamic kingdom. Thus trade and Islam combined to form a settled state out of what was previously a loose association of nomads and fishermen.

A similar example of how trade carried Islam into an existing state and influenced the way in which it then developed is that of Wa. Here Muslims, in peaceful pursuit of the gold of the Lobi fields, were instrumental in turning the state set up by the original Dagomba horsemen in the direction of Islam. Later waves of Muslims, also peaceful, pushed the society even further towards Islam, but the change was never completed. The traditional Earth Cult remained strong and what resulted was that situation of checks and balance in which incoming Muslim strangers and the non-Muslim natives competed for influence. The sequence of events in this instance can be seen as the opportunity for trade that led to the arrival of Muslim strangers; this in turn brought about a society characterised by that balance of Islam and traditional religion that is called mixed Islam and which, as far as the division of authority within it is concerned, has been so aptly described as contrapuntal paramountcy.

Much the same process, but on a much larger scale and over a longer period, can be seen at work in Kano and Katsina from the 8/14 century on, where the incoming Wangarawa almost certainly came in search of gold. On their arrival they seem to have established some sort of relationship with the local rulers and found themselves, initially, in quite sharp opposition to the supporters of the traditional religion. We can imagine that political ambitions were soon added to their commercial interests and a process of political manoeuvring resulted, in which the rulers were swayed at times by the Muslims and at other times by the traditional priests. The result was a state that displayed many Islamic features without, however, finally adopting the full Islamic constitution of the caliphate; before this could take place, reform was needed, backed by successful *jihād*.

In all of these situations there were clearly three factors, not one, at work. The first was trade, the second incoming strangers and the third Islam. The function of trade is clear for it led to the first contacts that started the process off. The function of Islam is also clear for it provided the ideas and institutions that shaped the end result – mixed Islam. However, what role did the incoming strangers play? Why should the arrival of these strangers have had any constitutional consequences at all? Why did the two sides not remain in perpetual quarantine, cut off from each other except for purposes of exchanging their goods and produce in the course of trade? At least part of the answer seems to lie in the fact that one party, that of the non-Muslim polytheists or animists, had its own customary law which satisfied its needs as long as it remained undisturbed by outsiders while the incoming party, the Muslims, had an entirely different set of laws and customs. The customary law of the non-Muslims did not satisfy the Muslims and when disputes arose there was therefore no final authority to settle them. Thus, in time, the need was felt on both sides for some form of centralised government that could deal with this situation with the result, sometimes, of the emergence of the institution of kingship or chieftainship that could arbitrate between the two parties. According to this theory, it seems it was in such cases the arrival of strangers that was the really important factor in bringing about the centralised state, while the role of Islam was confined to determining certain of the characteristics of that state, once it emerged.

In all the instances described above the Muslims arrived as peaceful newcomers. In other instances, for example that of Gonja, the sequence of events was different, mainly in that there does seem to have been an initial act of conquest, the Jakpa conquest with which Muslims, represented by Muḥammad al-Abyaḍ, were associated. However, once the conquerors had established themselves, the process that followed was similar. The conquerors found it impossible to destroy the old, pre-Islamic culture and the non-Muslim priests remained strong. Later waves of Muslims arrived, attracted by the trade that passed through the Jakpa state, and the interplay between all these interests led to the emergence of a centralised office of kingship. This resembled that of Kano or Katsina in the way in which it held the balance between the needs and ambitions of Muslims and non-Muslims. For reasons that were peculiar to the Volta region, the drive behind the Muslim influence was never as strong in Gonja as it was in the Haɓe kingdoms; thus Islam in the court of the Gonja kings never became as developed as it did in that of, for example, Muhamman Rumfa of Kano, but the same forces were at work, leading ultimately to a similar end.

It is obvious that slavery had been closely involved in the process of building states in the west and central Sudan, but it is important to realise that slavery was, until recently, an almost universal human institution. Muslims owned slaves and engaged in slave-raiding; so did non-Muslims. Thus slavery contributed to the building of non-Muslim states, as in the case of the non-Muslim, slave-owning Bambaras or the early, pre-Islamic state of Ghana. It also contributed to the building of states characterised by mixed Islam, as in the case of Kano during the Haɓe period. Finally, it contributed to the formation of reformed, fully Sunnī states, such as the Sokoto caliphate – especially its southern emirates in the new *Dār al-islām*.

How did the institution of slavery – in which I include slave-owning, slave-raiding and slave-trading – function to this end? First, as was argued in chapter 5, it seems to have been the practice in certain early chiefdoms, specifically Kano, to adopt a policy of enforced migrations of captive populations in order to populate empty lands and create a network of towns around the royal capital. Clearly, this was a form of state-building. Second, it may be that, in some cases, early chiefdoms came to regard certain tracts of land around them as their own private property for the purpose of hunting, including slave-hunting. They then fought to keep intruders from neighbouring chiefdoms out and, in time, these areas became part of the chiefdom which in consequence became a territorial kingdom. However, as was argued in the case of the Banū Dūkū, this practice must, in the end, have given rise to the cessation of slave-hunting there by the original hunters, otherwise the chief would have ruled over nothing but an empty land. Eventually, therefore, some form of ruler/subject relationship must have developed, by which the ruler undertook to protect his subjects in return for their allegiance and their tribute. Perhaps some such process as this accounts for the need to populate the countryside of Kano during the 9/15 century. Perhaps this was, in fact, a repopulation needed to repair the ravages of earlier wars and slave-raiding; but it must be emphasised that there is no firm evidence to show that this was, in fact, the case.

Another way in which slavery influenced the process of building states was through the prestige it gave the ruler. The prosperity of the state and the wealth of its leading citizens depended largely on how successful the ruler was in gathering slaves in the course of his wars against neighbouring states and raids into the country of the surrounding family-and-clan group people. The king who succeeded was secure in his power while the king who did not was liable to be replaced by a more able rival. This function of successful slave-gathering, to support the authority of the ruling establishment, is clearly evident in the *kirari*, the 'praise-epithets', of the Kano court. The chief Kanajeji (792/1390–812/1410) was praised as follows:

> Kanajeji, drinker of the waters of Shika [that is, he conquered and enslaved the people of Shika],
> Preventer of washing in Kubanni [so too in Kubanni],
> Lord, lord of the enemies' town,
> Lord, lord of the enemies' land.[7]

The Galadima Dauda, an official in the Kano court *c.* 854/1450, earned this *kirari*,

> Champion of the axes of the south,
> Champion of the young men of the south,
> Messenger of wealth [because he brought back slaves from his wars]
> Galadima![8]

Even as late as *c.* 1244/1828 the chief of Daura, Nuhu, was hailed as, 'Make ready, Lord of the bush, Conquer infidels!'[9]

Not only did successful slave-gathering help to establish the authority of the chief and his important officials; it also enabled the chief to hold the loyalty of those officials, of his territorial governors, of his head slaves and so on. Slaves and horses, between them, made up the greater part of the gifts that the chiefs distributed to their powerful vassals, and slaves, in turn, formed part of the tribute the chief received from those who owed him allegiance. Thus the institution of slavery contributed to the economic strength of the state; it also cemented the internal loyalties that held the state together.

To what extent the export of slaves to markets beyond the state contributed to the economy of particular states is an open question, to be decided only in the light of relevant evidence. In the case of Borno in the 10/16 century, it seems it did; so, too, in the case of the Senegambian kingdoms of the Atlantic seaboard. Whether it did so in the case of Kano and the other Haɓe kingdoms, either in the 10/16 century or earlier, is more doubtful. On the whole the evidence suggests that it did so only to a limited extent.

There was one other way in which slavery contributed to the development of states. From *c.* 824/1421 on slave-eunuchs began to be employed in the Haɓe courts and in due course they rose to positions of considerable power and influence and came to constitute a professional civil service. The same practice also arose in Borno. There is no doubt that the custom of employing slave-eunuchs as civil servants reached the west and central Sudan from the surrounding Islamic states of Egypt and North Africa, as well as perhaps from Arabia, through the influence of Pilgrimage. It helped to make possible the development of highly centralised states, served by officials trained in the skills of organising taxation, conducting war and diplomacy, keeping records and many other activities of state-craft.

Among the Islamic institutions that made the most important contributions to the development of states already formed is Pilgrimage. The outstanding examples of this are, of course, the empires of Mali and Songhay. In the case of Mali hereditary rulers whose conversion to Islam was superficial, performed Pilgrimage and thus made their governments legitimate in the eyes of the powerful class of the ᶜ*ulamā*'. Moreover, the international recognition that Pilgrimage brought them caused them to become greatly respected even by their non-Muslim subjects. The links they formed with the Islamic world outside the western Sudan led to the further economic and cultural development of the states they ruled. In the case of Songhay, Askiya Muḥammad's Pilgrimage not only conferred these advantages upon him, it also gave legitimacy to one who began by being a usurper.

Finally, the Sharīᶜa itself played an important role in the development of states. Conquest by Muslims could lead to the imposition of the Sharīᶜa in place of whatever system of customary law had existed before. Such forcible imposition was seldom effective when Islam was introduced for the first time and it usually resulted in some compromise such as the *jongu* that emerged in Bundu. It was more effective at the reform stage when imposed by *jihād* on a society that had already been exposed to Islam for a long period of mixing. The Hausa states are a typical example, where the forcible imposition of the Sharīᶜa turned an unreformed society into one much closer to the strict Sunna.

However the Sharīᶜa was more often introduced by the peaceful presence of Muslims, simply as a result of their gaining increasing influence in the affairs of the state. Mali is an obvious example, for there the Sharīᶜa played some part in promoting Islamic institutions in a state that was already socially and politically well on the way to being Islamic, though it still fell short of observing the strict Sunna and failed to adopt a fully Islamic constitution.

A similar situation arose in Songhay. Under Sonniᶜ Alī the Sharīᶜa had little influence, but under the *askiyas*, because of their alliance with the ᶜ*ulamā*', the Sharīᶜa took a large stride forward. It gained almost complete control in the cities of the Songhay empire, especially Timbuktu, turning them into centres of the correct Sunna, but it failed to spread to the countryside.

The Haɓe state of Kano provides a further example. This time it was the incoming Wangarawa who first introduced the Sharīᶜa and its influence was reinforced by later visitors, especially al-Maghīlī and a number of Egyptian ᶜ*ulamā*'. There is no doubt that by Mohamman Rumfa's time it exercised a considerable influence in the ruler's court, yet it did not win complete control, nor did it extend to the countryside, as far as is known. The reform movement of the Muslim Fulani was needed before that further stage of development could begin.

Whether its influence was limited to colouring the law and government of a society, or whether it took over that law and government more comprehensively, the Sharīᶜa was certainly one of those Islamic institutions that contributed most to forming the states and empires of the west and central Sudan in an Islamic pattern. In all of these examples – Mali, Songhay and perhaps Kano – a state of sorts existed before Muslims arrived on the scene. They cannot therefore be credited with founding these states, but they certainly were largely responsible for creating the empires that grew out of the states. The same is true in the case of Kanem and even Takrūr. So it seems there is a distinction to be made between Muslims as creators of states in the first instance – which they were only rarely – and Muslims as builders of empires – which they were quite frequently.

From what has been said above about the role of Islam in building states and empires in the west and central Sudan, two main conclusions emerge. First, Islam was, of itself, never the sole agent in forming these states and empires. Many other factors such as conquest, trade, incoming strangers, slave-raiding and slave-trading, were also involved; what mattered was whether the persons engaged in these activities were Muslims or non-Muslims. If they were Muslims, the political organisations that they created, whether simple states or more complex empires, naturally bore the marks of Islam to a greater or lesser extent. Otherwise, these organisations remained non-Islamic. Second, Muslims seldom founded entirely new states; more frequently, they helped to turn existing states into empires.

Literacy

Literacy has been a constantly recurring theme throughout this book. Clearly, literacy played a most important part in the process by which the Muslim communities moved from quarantine, through mixing, to the final stage of reform that is a deliberate attempt to implement the full Sunna. Indeed, like the adoption of an Islamic constitutional system, the achievement of literacy is also part of the process of conversion to Islam.

A fine study of literacy in the west and central Sudan comes from the pen of the distinguished anthropologist, Professor Jack Goody.[10] It was he who used the expression 'restricted literacy' to describe the situation that arises when literacy first becomes established in a previously non-literate society. Goody points out that the first impact of literacy on a non-literate society that begins to experience the activities of literates within it, is that literacy is seen as magic. This is because it provides a mysterious means of communicating over distance and time. That is to say, the literate can correspond with those who are too far distant for speech communication; he can also, apparently, correspond with the dead. Thus literacy seems miraculous. Literacy is also associated with magic because letters and numbers are capable of being manipulated into shapes and patterns that are thought to be helpful to men. An obvious example of this is the Islamic divinatory technique of *khaṭṭ al-raml*, 'sandwriting' and the use of Koranic squares, arrangements of letters and numbers that represent Koran verses, used in amulets and for astrology.

Very clear examples of how Islamic literacy may be turned to a magical purpose at the stage of restricted literacy are afforded by the 7/13-century *mune* of Kanem, an object of popular worship that seems likely to have been a Koran encased in leather; the 10/16-century *dirki* of Kano, which certainly was a Koran in leather wrapping; and the Koran of the Muslim village of Larabanga, in Gonja. This Koran, which is said to have descended from Heaven, is never read but is treated as a holy object and is only displayed on the Islamic feast-day of 10 Muharram.

Another clear example of the magic of literacy is to be seen in the Ashanti war-coats. These garments are hung with leather amulets, containing either written verses from the Koran or the Koranic squares referred to above. They are believed to protect the wearer from bullets or weapon-cuts in war. In the case of the Ashanti war-coats the manufacturers of the amulets were Muslim literates, but the purchasers and wearers may not have been Muslims, they are more likely to have been non-Muslim Ashanti chieftains. Thus it is clear from this, and many other examples that could be cited, that Islamic literacy is accepted as magical not only by some Muslims but also by non-literate animists and polytheists.

Such magical uses of literacy are powerful agents in bringing about a form of attachment to Islam that some have described as 'adhesion' rather than true conversion. This is a useful notion to describe the position of those who make use of what seems to them to be Islamic magic in addition to their own traditional magic, but who fall short of making the necessary positive declaration of faith that is required to become a Muslim. They thus attach themselves to, or 'adhere' to Islam without really becoming part of it. Examples are the Bambaras and the northern Mossis, many of whom have been inclined to accept the magical advantages of Islamic literacy, in the form of charms, amulets and so on, without making any formal act of conversion to Islam.

The use of the magic of Islamic literacy is also characteristic of societies that have progressed rather further than the 'adhering' Bambaras and Mossis along the way of mixing. This can be seen in the case of Mali and Songhay, where there was a real Islamic identity, even though the determination to observe the Sunna was still incomplete. Yet there is little doubt that restricted literacy, with all its magical exploitations, existed in Mali as Ibn Baṭṭūṭa knew it, and in Songhay as al-Maghīlī knew it. However, whereas among the merely adhering Bambaras and Mossis there were few, if any voices raised against these magical uses of literacy, in more advanced societies where mixing occured, such as Mali, Songhay and the Haɓe kingdoms of the 11/17 century, one would expect to find a strong reaction on the part of the strict Sunnī ᶜ*ulamā*' against these practices. Such a reaction did indeed take place. Al-Maghīlī had this to say about the inadequacy of certain so-called ᶜ*ulamā* in the 9/15-century society of Songhay:

> One of their characteristics is that they are not Arabic-speaking; they understand no Arabic except a little of the speech of the Arabs of their towns, in an incorrect and corrupted fashion, and a great deal of non-Arabic, so that they do not understand the intention of the [truly learned] ᶜ*ulamā*' . . . yet despite that they have books which they study and tales and stories which they utter concerning God's religion, and they maintain that they are the inheritors of the prophets. . . .[11]

He then summed up his view of the activities of these semi-literates as follows:

> It is said by the scriptures and the Sunna and the consensus of the learned that many of the Koran readers of this community are only venal ᶜ*ulamā*', and they are more harmful to the Muslims than all the mischief-makers.[12]

A similar reaction, this time specifically against the magical uses of literacy rather than against the generally harmful effects of inadequate literacy, took place in 11/17-century Katsina, when Malam Muḥammad al-Ṣabbāgh, having allowed himself to be tempted by the profession of fortune-telling, turned against it 'for fear of the wickedness in it'. It also took place again, much more emphatically, *c.* 1119/1707, when the reforming *imām*, Muḥammad b. al-Ḥājj ᶜAbd al-Raḥmān, of Borno origin, wrote in his poem *Shurb al-zulāl*, the 'Draught of Pure Water',

> Leave any craft concerned with writing [in the sand] and astrology, and spells of djinns, and chanting.[13]

From the evidence given above it seems that the exploitation of the non-literate by at least some of the literate, or the semi-literate, is indeed one outcome of the initial impact of Islamic literacy on a non-literate society. It is important to realise that this restricted literacy carries within itself the seeds of a reaction; for not only does it become a source of profit for some who use it, it also becomes a provocation and a challenge to others who see it as an abuse. Indeed, it is possible to argue that the moment they begin to protest against it, this marks the beginning of reform.

However, it would be wrong to imagine that Islamic reform brings about the disappearance of restricted literacy and its magical uses. This is certainly not so, as anyone familiar with the Muslim areas of present-day West Africa must be aware. The use of Islamic charms, amulets, Koranic squares, sand-writing, astrology and so on, flourished in the 13/19 century, despite the attempts of the reformers to establish the strict Sunna in their empires. This is made clear in a Hausa poem dating from *c.* 1267/1850, in which the poet delivers a resounding condemnation of the restricted literacy and magical exploitation that he saw all around him, even in a reformed society where elementary and advanced Islamic education was undoubtedly widespread. He writes:

> . . . the rustic malams of the village
> With their satchels that contain [not manuscripts but] only
> cockroaches,
> . . .
> They practise divination that they may discern the hidden mysteries
> of God
> In their drawing on the ground, because of their apostasy.
> Both the fortune-teller and he who believes him,
> The Angel of Hell Fire will they meet with!
> Stop seeking the counsel of a magician
> And keep away from the [bogus] Malam Gagarau, if you heed my
> advice,
> They entice the ignorant and the blind,
> And lead them into water that engulfs them.[14]

It still flourishes today. Thus restricted literacy is not exclusively the characteristic of the stage of mixing; it continues on into the stage of reform. So it becomes clear, once again, that a reformed society differs from a mixing society not so much in the way that Islam is actually practised but rather in the climate of opinion towards mixing. Under reform, mixing, including the magical exploitation of restricted literacy, is more generally disapproved of but it continues all the same.

Goody proposed the term 'restricted literacy' to describe that stage of literacy that begins as soon as quarantine breaks down and mixing begins. In fact, however, it is not the only form of literacy that can exist at that time. It is possible, at any given moment in a society where literacy has once made an appearance, for different individuals to achieve different levels of literacy. Thus the restricted literacy of the village *malams* and the half-educated *ʿulamāʾ* of al-Maghīlī's day may thrive alongside the full literacy of the highly educated, strictly Sunnī *ʿulamāʾ*. Their more developed stage of literacy I shall call 'ideational literacy'. By this I mean a stage of literacy that does more than put the literate in possession of magical skills; it also puts him in touch with creative ideas. This is not to suggest that non-literate people are shut off from creative ideas completely, but the fully literate clearly have much wider access to such ideas and many more opportunities to apply them to the circumstances of their own environment. In consequence, they tend to become the intellectual and sometimes the political and even military leaders of communities that are still largely composed of non-literates or semi-literates. Al-Maghīlī was such an intellectual leader in that his high level of literacy had, as it were, turned him into a dynamo of ideas that he passed on to those around him – Mahdism, the Mujaddid, the theory of *jihād*, misbelief and its political significance, the role of literacy in a Muslim society, and a host of other intellectual and ideological issues. Thereupon these ideas became the source of action that, in due course, helped to bring about change in the Haɓe states and perhaps in Agades, although they seem to have had little effect in Songhay. The influence of al-Suyūṭī, although he never visited the Sudan, is also an example of literacy functioning creatively at the ideational level. To these examples one could add that of Sīdī Maḥmūd al-Baghdādī, who was probably the first to introduce the ideas of the eastern, illuministic school of Sufism – that is the school that claims special enlightenment and knowledge through divine light – into the western Sudan. One could also add a long list of the names of Toureg *ᶜulamā'*, whose creative, ideational literacy – the literacy that enabled them to acquire, understand, explain, adapt and spread new ideas – brought about the changes in Toureg society described earlier in this book.

Yet another striking example of ideational literacy at work is that of the 11/17-century Senegambian reformer, Nāṣir al-Dīn. As a result of his high level of literate achievement under the guidance of the Mauritanian Zwāya, in other words his high level of education, he was able to apply the ideas of Mahdism and the End of Time to bring about revolution in the Senegambia.

Because more is known about the careers of the 13/19-century jihadists, it is possible to point to a wider range of creative ideas that came to them through their achievement of ideational literacy. In the case of the Shehu Usumanu ɗan Fodio, there were not only the ideas of Mahdism and the End of Time, there were also those powerful ideas springing from a wide background of Sufi mysticism, especially that of the Prophet as *al-Insān al-Kāmil.* A particularly relevant example of creative ideational literacy is his vision of the Pilgrimage, which became for him symbolic of the way of life and the intellectual and spiritual attitudes to be recreated in the west and central Sudan. This ideal reached him not through direct experience but from the mirror of literature.

Yet another example of the power of ideational literacy to promote Islamic reform occurs in the case of al-Ḥājj Maḥmūd of Wahabu. This man received a literate education from his *shaykh* in Dyulasso which enabled him to take the Qādirī *wird*, in itself a highly literate achievement. His education then opened up for him a whole world of ideas, not just in the western Sudan but as far afield as Syria. It was, above all else, the ideas that he acquired there as a result of his advanced literacy that enabled him to take on the role of Muslim reformer and jihadist.

In the case of al-Ḥājj ᶜUmar al-Fūtī the effects of ideational literacy are to be seen at work in an even more intricate fashion. What motivated him was that system of interlocking ideas, of intense intellectuality and mystical complexity, associated with the newly founded *ṭarīqa* of the Tijāniyya. Islam in the west and central Sudan could not have reached its present stage of development had it not been for these creative ideas and the initiative of highly literate men in applying them.

Many attempts have been made to identify a recurring pattern that explains the progress of Islam in the west and central Sudan from its beginnings to the present day. Some have proposed race and colour, that is tension between blacks and whites, while others have looked to the interplay of relations between towns and the countryside, or to peasants versus nomads, commoners versus aristocrats, slaves versus masters, and so on. In most cases there is some evidence to support the view that these factors operated at certain times and in certain circumstances; but when one looks at the whole, immensely involved and constantly changing spectacle of Islam's spread and development in the west and central Sudan, it becomes clear that none of them really do form a consistent pattern that can be discerned throughout this whole long period of almost twelve hundred years. The fact is, there is no pattern; but there is a single, unbroken thread. It is that the history of Islam in the west and central Sudan, from its beginning until now, has been a triumph for the power of literate ideas.

NOTES

1 Ryan, p.129.
2 ibid, p.129.
3 *Africa*, XLIII, 1973, p.31.
4 El-Masri, 1978, pp.7–8.
5 Quoted in Fisher, *Africa*, XLIII, 1973, p.28.
6 ibid. p.27.
7 Translated from an unpublished Arabic manuscript of the 'Kano Chronicle'; Palmer, *Memoirs*, III, p.108, gives a slightly different translation.
8 Palmer, *Memoirs*, III, p.110
9 Hiskett, *Hausa Islamic verse*, p.5.
10 'Restricted Literacy in Northern Ghana', in Goody, ed. 1968.
11 Hiskett, *BSOAS*, XXV, 3, 1962, p.580.
12 ibid, p.581.
13 Bivar and Hiskett, *BSOAS*, XXV, 1, 1962, p.125.
14 Hiskett, *BSOAS*, XXVIII, *T*1, 1965, pp.132–3.

APPENDIX A

Directional lines on the diagrams bear letters alongside them which are intended to refer the reader to corresponding letters in brackets in the explanatory notes.

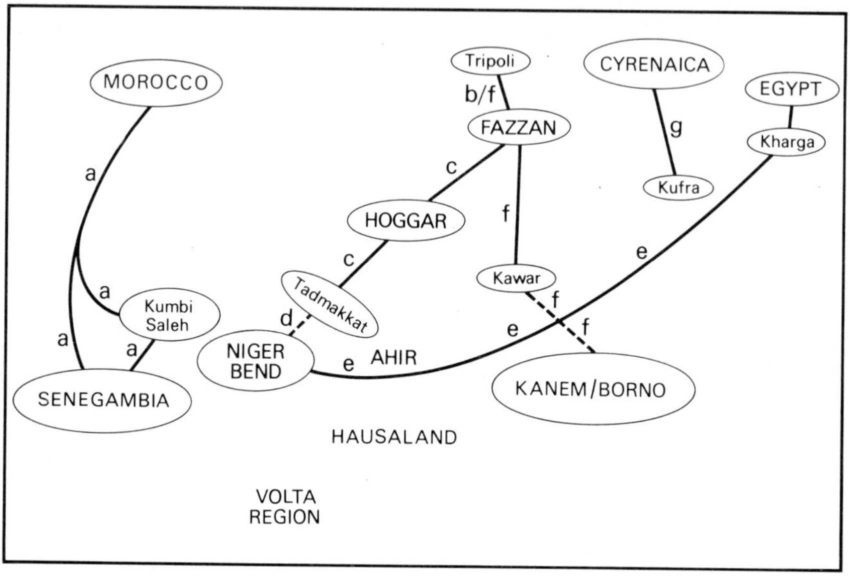

I Probable pattern of main trade links in the Sahara and the west and central Sudan in the pre-Islamic era.

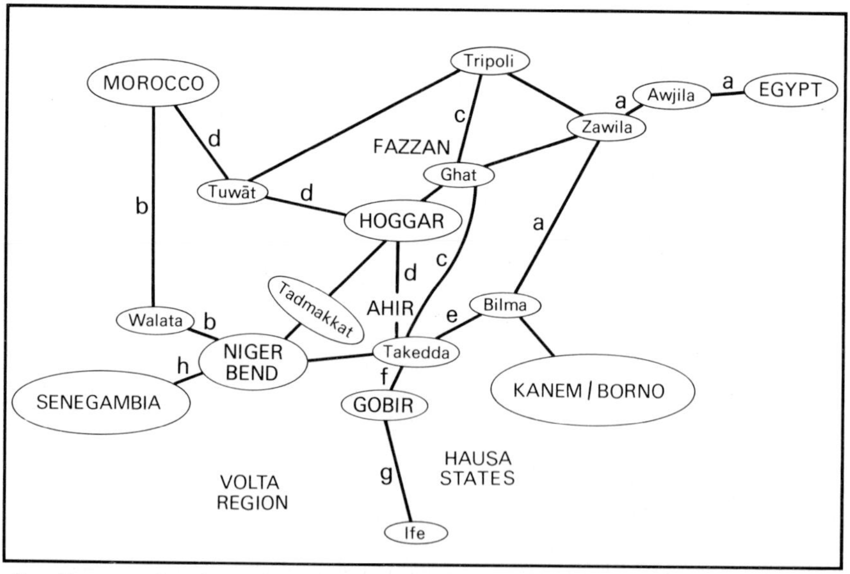

II Pattern of main trade links in the Sahara and the west and central Sudan c. 751/1350.

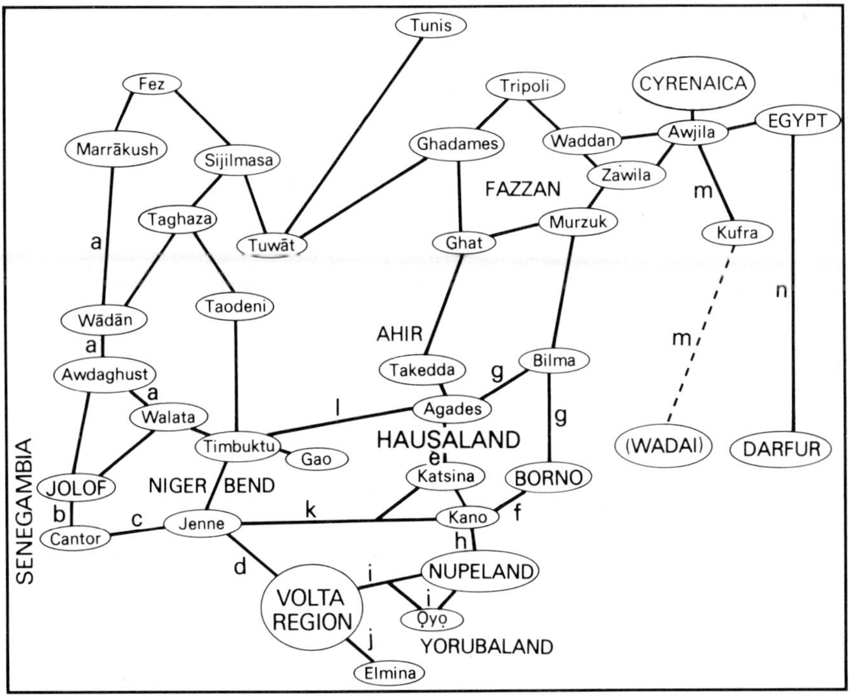

III Pattern of main trade links in the Sahara and the west and central Sudan c. *906/1500.*

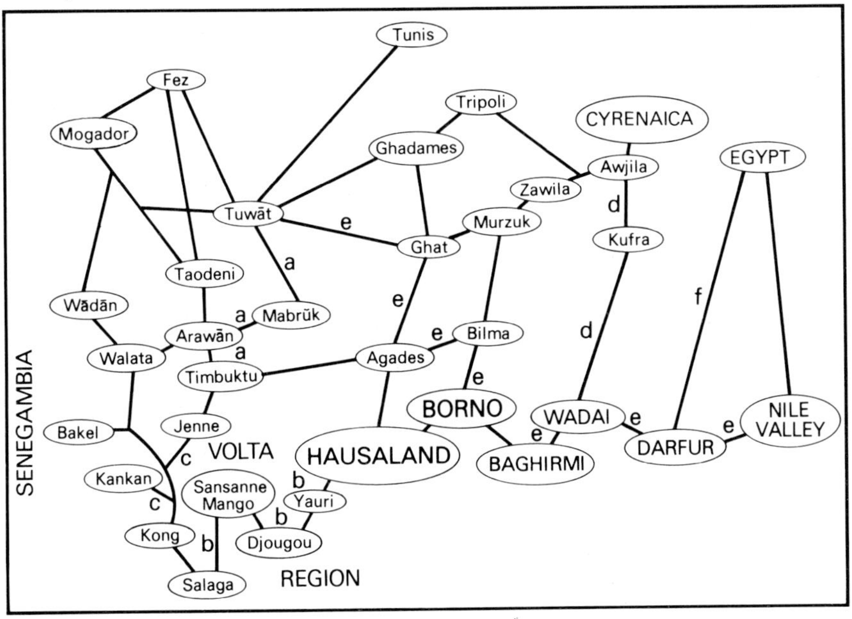

IV Pattern of main trade and caravan links in the Sahara west and central Sudan c. *1215/1800 and after.*

PROBABLE PATTERN OF MAIN TRADE LINKS IN THE SAHARA AND THE WEST AND CENTRAL SUDAN IN THE PRE-ISLAMIC ERA

Diagram I

The points to note in this diagram are the following:

1. It is believed that, as early as 1000BC there was a western route (a) from Morocco that ran down the western side of the Sahara, through present Mauritania, as far as the river Senegal (Boahen, 1964, p. 103). An eastern branch off the main route led to Kumbi Saleh. It may have been this route that was used by the Arab expedition that started from southern Morocco in the 2/8 century, penetrated into the desert and returned with much gold. The route probably continued in use until the 5/11 or 6/12 century, when the goldfields of Bure, in the Niger Bend, began to displace those of Bambuk, on the Senegal, as the primary source of Sudanic gold. The route then became less frequented, although it is unlikely that it ever went out of use altogether. It was revived in the 9/15 century, however, when the Portuguese set up a trading station at Wadan (Diagram III, a); and it remained in use at least until the end of the 10/16 century. Boahen (1964, p. 103) shows it as still a main route during the 13/19 century.
2. Prior to the arrival of Islam in North Africa, and perhaps as early as the Roman period, it seems probable that a route (b) from Tripoli to the Fazzan continued on from the Fazzan south-westwards to Tadmakkat (c). It is even possible that from Tadmakkat it continued as far as the Niger Bend (d). If so, it certainly depended on ox, horse or human transport before the introduction of the camel into the Sahara in the 2 century AD. There is however some doubt as to whether this route did extend so far into the desert. Although some scholars are convinced that it did, others dispute this and I have shown this part of the route by a dotted line.
3. The 'diagonal' Saharan route (e), passing from Gao, south-west of Ahir and on to the Kharga oasis, was almost certainly open before the planting of Islam in North Africa, though for how long is not known. It was abandoned during the 3/9 century owing to its insecurity. However, west/east/west communications between the Niger Bend and Egypt were resumed by the 8/14 century, although it seems that it was now necessary to go north to the Fazzan before joining the routes that led into Egypt. Much later, in the 11/17 century, the so-called 'Sudan Road', from the upper Nile valley, through Funj, Darfur, Wadai and on to Borno, was opened.
4. In the east an ancient route (f) is known to have run from Tripoli to Kanem, via the Fazzan and the Kawar oasis. According to Martin (*JAH*, X, 1, 1969), this route was in use during Carthaginian times, that is in the 3 century BC. It is probable, if not wholly certain, that it was extended to Lake Chad at some time before the 7 century AD. It may have been closed briefly during the Arab invasion of North Africa in the 1/7 century but was quickly opened again and continued in use with only periodic interruptions up to the 20 century AD. Another ancient route (g), probably used in Garamantean times, that is perhaps as early as the first millenium BC, linked Cyrenaica with the oasis of Kufra.
5. There is no firm evidence to suggest that Hausaland was linked to the Saharan caravan routes at this time, although in the light of recent archaeological discoveries in the Sahara and the Niger it would be rash to assume that it was entirely isolated. There is also no evidence to show that the Volta region was linked to the Niger Bend in pre-Islamic times. All the same, since it was a kola-producing area, as well as a gold-producing one, it is reasonable to suppose that it may have been.

PATTERN OF MAIN TRADE LINKS IN THE SAHARA AND THE WEST AND CENTRAL SUDAN *c.* 751/1350

Diagram II

This diagram represents the state of development of the Saharan communication system in Ibn Baṭṭūṭa's day.

1. On the eastern side the interrupted communications between Egypt and the Niger Bend, associated with the closing of the diagonal route (see Diagram I, e) in the 3/9 century were resumed as a result of the opening-up of more northerly routes (a) connecting the area to lower Egypt via the Fazzan.
2. In the west the old western route from Morocco to Ghana had fallen largely out of use. This was partly due to the decline of Ghana and the rise of the empire of Mali, and partly due to the increased importance of Bure, in the Niger Bend, as a gold-producing area, although it was probably not abandoned entirely. The main route (b) on this side now took a more easterly course, running from Morocco to Walata and from Walata to the Bend. Note also that Walata was at this time still the main commercial centre of the Bend. Although Timbuktu had been founded and was mentioned by Ibn Baṭṭūṭa it had still not become the great commercial and intellectual centre into which it later developed.
3. Farther to the east, Ahir was certainly linked to North Africa. There was a route from Ahir to Tripoli (c) and Ibn Baṭṭūṭa took a diagonal route (d) from Ahir, through the Hoggar and Tuwāt to Morocco. Since Takedda exported copper to Borno there must have been a link between Ahir and Borno, probably via Bilma (e). Takedda's links with Egypt were no doubt also via Bilma. Gobir must have been linked to Ahir and Takedda (f) and probably to Ife in the south (g), as a result of its involvement in the copper trade. Moreover, the evidence of Frank Willis suggests that a traffic in glass of European origin (waste from Venice?) passed through Hausaland en route to Ife as early as the 9th century AD.
4. In the Volta region the gold mining industry at Bono did not develop until the second half of the 9/15 century and so it cannot be assumed that a major link existed between the Volta area and the Niger Bend before that date. It is certainly possible however that a link did exist for the transport of kolas and perhaps for gold dust produced by early, primitive washing techniques that may have dated back to the remote past, before systematic mining began.
5. As for the Senegambia, the Ghanaians were obviously in touch with that area and, with the rise of Mali, it may reasonably be assumed that a direct link (h) was maintained by the Malians.

PATTERN OF MAIN TRADE LINKS IN THE SAHARA AND THE WEST AND CENTRAL SUDAN *c.* 906/1500

Diagram III

This diagram represents the situation at a time when the Portuguese were well established in the Senegambia, had built their fortress at Elmina on what became known as the 'Gold Coast' and had even set up a trading station at Wādān, in Mauritania. Meanwhile, from North Africa Italian-speaking merchants from the Mediterranean trading cities, attracted to the Sudan by the trade in gold, ivory and spices, had in the 9/15 century begun to penetrate as far inland as Timbuktu, from where they subsequently spread farther south and south-east, into the savanna.

1. A complex of routes now led from Fez, Tunis and other points on the North

Africa coast, via Sijilmasa, Taghaza, Taodeni, Tuwāt, into the Niger Bend. Tadmakkat, so important in earlier centuries, had declined by the end of the 9/15 century but its role was taken over by new commercial centres, especially Walata, Timbuktu and Agades. The old westerly route marked (a) on Diagram I had regained its importance but now passed through Wādān and on to the Niger Bend (a). It is known to have been used by the Portuguese towards the end of the 9/15 century. It was used again by Jawdhar Pasha at the end of the 10/16 century. Tadmakkat, so important in earlier times, had declined by the end of the 9/15 century but its role was taken over by new commercial centres, especially Walata, Timbuktu and Agades. However, Awdaghust was still sufficiently important to have been mentioned by Anania. As for the area within the Bend, this must have been quite well known to travellers of the day for Anania not only knew the positions of a number of towns and geographical features of the area, but also the locations of such peoples as the Sarakoles and Mandingoes.

2. In the Senegambia, known to European travellers in the 9/15 and 10/16 centuries as Gialofi (Jolof), a link existed with Morocco and was much frequented by scholars as well as merchants. It was probably route (a), described above. The Gambia was also linked to the Niger Bend from the town of Cantor (Crone, 1937, p.93), probably by a direct route to Jenne (c) as well as via the Senegal area (b).

3. In the Volta region the founding of Bono in the second half of the 9/15 century led to opening up of the gold trade with the Niger Bend and an established link (d) between the two areas now existed, for which Jenne was the terminus.

4. Farther to the east the Hausa states were by 906/1500 firmly tied in to the Saharan system of communication via Takedda and later Agades and substantial numbers of travellers, both merchants and *ᶜulamā*', passed up and down the route (e) that led into Hausaland. In fact, there were a number of branch routes leading into different parts of Hausaland although for the purpose of this diagram the link is shown here as a single line. By this time too there was almost certainly a direct east/west/east link between Hausaland and Borno (f), in addition to a more northerly route (e/g) that passed via Bilma. From Hausaland to the south and south-west the Hausa diaspora was well under way and a network of routes led to the river Benue (h) and on into Nupe and Yoruba country. Other sub-Saharan routes linked Kebbi, Hausaland and Borno from east/west/east (see inset to Map 5).

From Yoruba and Nupe country routes turned west to the Volta region (i), serving the gold trade. The Volta in turn was linked to the Portuguese coastal station of Elmina (j). The pattern (h), (i), (d) formed the three sides of a sub-Sahelian triangle of routes that linked Hausaland with the Volta and the Volta with the Niger Bend. The triangle was completed by a direct route from Jenne to Hausaland (k) that avoided the more northerly routes from the Bend to Ahir (l).

5. Yet farther east a network of routes linked Tripoli, Cyrenaica and Egypt to Borno and Lake Chad. Anania mentions Libya, that is Cyrenaica; he also knows Uri, the capital of Western Darfur and is obviously familiar with the country around Baghirmi. Whether Wadai existed under this name at this date is questionable (see chapter 2, f.n. 16). According to Dennis D. Cordell ('Eastern Libya, Wadai and the Sanūsīya: a Tarīqa and a trade route', *JAH, XVIII*, I, 1977), the route from Kufra to Wadai was not opened until a date between AD 1804 and 1813, by Sultan Sābūn of what was by then the Islamic sultanate of Wadai. However, while I accept that this route became much more generally used as from the beginning of the 19 century AD, owing to the patronage of Sultan Sābūn and the protection of the Sanūsiyya, I find it difficult to believe, in view of Anania's extraordinarily detailed knowledge of the area east of Lake Chad, that the country between Kufra and Wadai was continuously closed in earlier centuries, although certainly it may have been so from time to time. I have accordingly marked the route from Kufra to Wadai (m) with a dotted line, to indicate, first, the possibility

that the route was not in existence in the 10/16 century; and, second, that the name Wadai did not exist at that time. All the same, I consider both these possibilities unlikely. What does seem clear, however, is that the direct west/east/west route, the later 'Sudan Road' through Wadai and Darfur was not extensively used in the 10/16 century. But again, having regard to Anania's evidence, it is difficult to believe that some direct communication along a west/east/west axis did not exist, as a westerly extension of the route (n) that ran up the Nile valley.

PATTERN OF MAIN TRADE AND CARAVAN LINKS IN THE SAHARA AND THE WEST AND CENTRAL SUDAN *c.*1215/1800 AND AFTER

Diagram IV

This diagram represents the Saharan communications system immediately before it was thrown into decline by the opening-up of railways from the Atlantic coast to the interior by the colonial powers, early in the 20 century AD. Particular points to note are:

1. The appearance of Mabrūk linking with Tuwāt and the Niger Bend (a). This town, founded by the Kuntī *shaykhs* in the 12/18 century, became an important trading centre competing with the more ancient centres of the western Sudan and contributing to the expansion of trade in the area. Mabrūk was not only commercially important, it was also a centre for the spread of the Qādiriyya in the western Sahara and the western Sudan.

2. The Volta region and Hausaland were by this date linked by the 'kola route' passing from Salaga via Sansanne Mango, Djougou and Yauri, into Hausaland (b). This route grew up after the emergence of Salaga as a centre for the kola trade in the 12/18 century. Kankan, another Kuntī centre, was founded largely for the kola trade at the end of the 11–12/17 century and was linked to Jenne in the Niger Bend (c).

3. On the eastern side the ancient route (d) from Cyrenaica to Kufra was by now certainly extended to Wadai and became very active during the second half of the 13/19 century, probably as a result of the introduction of the Sanūsiyya into Cyrenaica at this time. For the authority of the Sanūsīs established much greater security in the desert south of Cyrenaica and thus promoted trade along the route.

4. The Sudan Road (e), that is the route east/west/east through the savanna country, linking the Sudan directly with the Nile valley was now certainly open. This had been so from the 11/17 century when the emergence of stable kingdoms in Baghirmi, Wadai, and Darfur, farther to the east, had made the country more secure (although, as was suggested in reference to Diagram III, it is difficult to believe that this route had not been used at all in earlier times). This 'Sudan Road', which linked Borno with Ahir and terminated in Morocco, was not only commercially important; it also contributed much to the spread of Sufism, since it facilitated communications between the Sufis of North Africa, the west and central Sudan and those of the Nile valley. The northern end of the route had a number of branch routes that are not shown on this diagram.

5. A route from Cairo, through Dongola, in Nubia, now led into Darfur (f). This is probably the same route as that known to Anania in the 10/16 century (see Diagram III, n).

Glossary

Arabic, Hausa and other non-English terms occurring in the text

Afḍal al-khalq (Arabic) – the 'Most Excellent of the Creation', a title of the Prophet Muḥammad.
ajami (Hausa) – the modified form of the Arabic script in which Hausa is written.
ᶜālim (Arabic) – plur. *ᶜulamā'*, a Muslim literate.
alƙali (Hausa) – from Arabic *al-qāḍī*, qv, Hausa plur. *alƙalai*, a Muslim magistrate.
Alkur'an (Hausa) – from Arabic *al-qur'ān*, qv, the Koran.
amān (Arabic) – plur. *amānāt*, safe conduct; commercial agreement.
amānāt (Arabic) – see *amān*.
amīr (Arabic) – army commander; also used as the title of a local Muslim ruler. Anglicized as 'emir', ruler of an emirate.
aqṭāb (Arabic) – see *quṭb*.
ardo (Fulfulde) – plur. *ardo'en*, Fulani clan leader.
ardo'en (Fulfulde) – see *ardo*.
awliyā' (Arabic) – see *walī*.

Banza Bakwai (Hausa) – the 'Bastard Seven', a term referring to certain neighbours of the Hausa Bakwai, the seven Hausa states.
baraka (Arabic) – 'blessedness' that can be passed on by a *walī* (qv) to his followers.
bayᶜa (Arabic) – allegiance, fealty
bori (Hausa) – the spirit possession cult of the Hausas

Dār al-islām (Arabic) – the 'Territory of Islam'.
Dār al-ḥarb (Arabic) – the 'Territory of War'.
Dār al-kufr (Arabic) – the 'Territory of Infidelity'.
dhikr (Arabic) – A Sufi term meaning 'Remembrance' and indicating the prayerful repetition of the Name of God.
dīn (Arabic) – religion, the Faith, thus Islam.
duᶜā' (Arabic) – supplicatory prayer, prayer on a special occasion or on behalf of someone.

fadawa (Hausa) – courtiers.
fanā' (Arabic) – a state of religious ecstasy in which the mystic becomes absorbed in the divinity. The state produced by *khalwa*, qv.
faqīh (Arabic) – one skilled in Islamic law, a legal theoretician. Plur. *fuqahā'*.
farilla (Hausa) – from Arabic *farīḍ*, 'what is obligatory in Islamic law'
fatauci (Hausa) – long-distance or middle-distance trade; the travelling required to conduct it.
fayḍa (Arabic) – literally 'overflowing', applied to the divine gifts of God to man – forgiveness, knowledge, the Law, salvation, etc. – and approximately equivalent to the Christian notion of 'saving grace'.
fiqh (Arabic) – the written, theoretical corpus of Islamic law.
fuqahā' (Arabic) – see *faqīh*.

gandaye (Hausa) – see *gandu*.
gandu (Hausa) – plur. *gandaye*; farm, plantation.
Ghawth al-zamān (Arabic) – the 'Succour of the Age', a Sufi title.

ḥadīth (Arabic) – the written record of the acts and sayings of the Prophet Muḥammad. Together with the Koran, *ḥadīth* is the basis of the Sunna, qv.

ḥaḍra (Arabic) – (plur.) *ḥaḍrāt*, a stage or level of the mystic cosmos of the Sufis.
ḥaḍrāt (Arabic) – see *ḥaḍra.*
ḥaqā'iq al-muhammadiyya 'al- (Arabic) – the 'Muhammadan Truths', a Sufi term associated with the *ḥaḍrāt*, qv.
Hausa Bakwai (Hausa) – the 'Hausa Seven', the seven Haɓe states.
hijra (Arabic) – 'flight', the 'Hijra', the Flight of the Prophet Muḥammad from Mecca to Medina in 1/622.

ijāza (Arabic) – a licence to teach given to a Muslim who has completed his studies under a recognised teacher. plur. *ijāzāt.*
ijāzāt (Arabic) – see *ijāza.*
ijtihād (Arabic) – individualistic interpretation of the Islamic scriptures, as opposed to *taqlīd*, qv.
ᶜilm (Arabic) – Islamic religious knowledge.
imām (Arabic) – a Muslim prayer-leader; also in certain contexts 'head of the Islamic state', equivalent of *khalīfa*, qv.

jamāᶜa (Arabic) – community, often used to refer to a particular Muslim community to distinguish it from surrounding non-Muslims.
jangali (Hausa) – tax on nomads' cattle.
jihād (Arabic) – Islamic holy war.
jihād al-qawl (Arabic) – 'Preaching *Jihād*', a period of preaching that usually precedes resort to *jihād* by arms.
jihād al-sayf (Arabic) – '*Jihād* of the Sword', armed *jihād.*

kashf (Arabic) – a Sufi term referring to the unveiling of divine mysteries.
katātīb (Arabic) – see *kuttāb.*
khalīfa (Arabic) – caliph, the political and religious head of the world-wide Islamic community, but often adopted from the 9/15 century on by local Muslim rulers.
khalwa (Arabic) – Sufi retreat. See also *fanā'.*
kirari (Hausa) – praise-epithet.
kuttāb (Arabic) – plur. *katātīb*, an Islamic primary school where Koran recitation and the Arabic alphabet are taught.

lithām (Arabic) – a mouth veil worn by certain Saharan people.

madahu (Hausa) – from Arabic *madḥ*, 'praise', 'panegyric', applied to a category of Hausa Islamic verse.
madhāhib (Arabic) – see *madhhab.*
madhhab (Arabic) – plur. *madhāhib*, a legal rite or system of Islam.
madrasa (Arabic) – plur. *madāris*, a school of higher learning.
madugu (Hausa) – caravan leader and organiser.
Mahdī (Arabic) – the Islamic Deliverer who shall come at the End of Time.
Mai (Kanuri) – the title of the ruler of Borno prior to 1263/1846.
makarantan allo (Hausa) – see *kuttāb*, of which it is the Hausa equivalent.
makarantan ilmi (Hausa) – see *madrasa* of which it is the Hausa equivalent.
Makhzan (Arabic) – a form of Islamic military administration.
malam (Hausa) – plur. *malamai*, a Muslim literate, equivalent of *ᶜālim*, qv.
malamai (Hausa) – see *malam.*
mujaddid (Arabic) – the 'Renewer' whom God will send once in every century to prepare the way for the Mahdī, qv.
Mulaththamūn, al- (Arabic) – wearers of the mouth-veil *lithām*, qv.
muqaddam (Arabic) – plur. *muqaddamūn*, 'initiator', one who has the authority to initiate others into a Sufi *ṭarīqa.*
muqaddamūn (Arabic) –see *muqaddam.*
Murābiṭ (Arabic) – plur. *Murābiṭūn, al-*, 'frontier warrior'. See also *Murābiṭūn, al-.*
Murābiṭūn, al- (Arabic) – see *Murābiṭ* above. The plural form is used to describe a sect of Muslim reformers and is latinized as Almoravids.

nūr al-muḥammadī, al- (Arabic) – the 'Muhammadan light', a Sufi term associated with the *ḥaḍrāt*, qv.

qāḍī, al- (Arabic) – plur. *quḍā*, Muslim magistrate.

qur'ān, al- (Arabic) – the Koran.
quṭb (Arabic) – plur. *aqṭāb*, literally 'axis', applied as a title to the founder of a Sufi *ṭarīqa* or sub-*ṭarīqa*.

ribāṭ (Arabic) – plur. *rubuṭ*, or *ribāṭāt* a frontier fortress.
rinji (Hausa) – plur. *rumada*, slave-hamlet.
rubuṭ (Arabic) – see *ribāṭ*.
rugage (Hausa) – see *rugga*.
rugga (Hausa) – plur. *rugage*. A Fulani cattle-encampment.
rumada (Hausa) – see *rinji*.

salāsil (Arabic) – see *silsila*.
ṣalāt (Arabic) – the prescribed prayers of Islam.
salla (Hausa) – see *ṣalāt*, of which this is the Hausa equivalent. It is also used by the Muslim Hausas to refer to the two major festivals of the Islamic year.
sarakuna (Hausa) – see *sarki*.
sarki (Hausa) – plur. *sarakuna*, chief.
Shahāda (Arabic) – the Islamic declaration of faith.
Sharīᶜa (Arabic) – the Islamic canon law.
sharīf (Arabic) plur. *shurafā'*, a member of the tribe of Quraysh; claimant to descent from the Prophet's family.
shaykh (Arabic) – a learned and respected Muslim; sometimes used as a Sufi title applied to a *walī*, qv.
silsila (Arabic) – plur. *salāsil*, a Sufi mystic genealogy.
siradi (Hausa) – from Arabic *ṣirāṭ*, qv.
ṣirāṭ (Arabic) – the Bridge that spans Hell Fire and leads to Paradise.
siyāḥa (Arabic) – 'tour', especially the preaching and trading journeys carried out by Kunti *shaykhs*.
Sunna (Arabic) – the tradition based on the Koran and on the acts and sayings of the Prophet Muḥammad which governs the practice of Sunnī Islam.
Sunnī (Arabic) – pertaining to the *Sunna*, qv.

tafsīr (Arabic) – Koran exegesis, commentary.
tajdīd (Arabic) – peaceful reform, as opposed to *jihād*.
ṭālib (Arabic) – plur. *ṭālibūn*, student.
ṭālibūn (Arabic) – see *ṭālib*.
taqiyya (Arabic) – dissembling.
taqlīd (Arabic) – unquestioning obedience to established religious authority.
ṭarīqa (Arabic) – plur. *ṭuruq*, a Sufi order.
ṭuruq (Arabic) – see *ṭarīqa*.

ᶜulamā' (Arabic) – see *ᶜālim*.

wa'azi (Hausa) – from Arabic *waᶜẓ*, 'warning', 'admonition' applied to a category of Hausa Islamic verse.
walī (Arabic) – a Muslim holy man. plur. *awliyā'*.
wazīr (Arabic) – plur. *wuzarā'*, chief minister of an Islamic government.
wilāya (Arabic) – the state of being a *walī*.
wird (Arabic) – a Sufi litany.
wuzarā' (Arabic) – see *wazīr*.

zango (Hausa) – a settlement of Hausa and Hausa-speaking traders.
zawāya (Arabic) – see *zāwiya*.
zāwiya (Arabic) – plur. *zawāya*, a Sufi hostel and seminary.
zongo (Gold Coast Hausa) – see *zango*, of which this is a Gold Coast form.

Bibliography

Books and theses

ᶜAbdullāh ibn Muḥammad, see Hiskett, M. 1963.
Abubakar Tafawa Balewa, Alhaji Sir, *Shaihu Umar*, edited and translated into English by M. Hiskett, London, 1967.
Adamu, Mahdi, *The Hausa factor in West African history*, Zaria and Ibadan, 1978.
Adeleye, R.A. *Power and diplomacy in northern Nigeria, 1804–1906*, London, 1971.
Ajayi, J.F. Ade, *Christian missions in Nigeria 1841–1891*, 1965
Ajayi, J.F. Ade and Michael Crowder, eds., *History of West Africa*, vol. I, second edition, 1976; vol. II, 1974.
ᶜAlī Harāzim, *Jawāhir al-maᶜānī*, Cairo, nd.
Arnett, E.J. *The rise of the Sokoto Fulani: Being a paraphrase and in some parts a translation of the* 'Infaku'l Maisuri' *of Sultan Mohammed Bello*, Kano, 1922.
Backwell, H.F. *The occupation of Hausaland 1900–1904*, Lagos, 1927 (reprinted London, 1969).
Barth, Heinrich, *Travels*, Minerva edition.
Batran, A.A. 'The Kunta, Sīdī al-Mukhtār al-Kuntī and the Office of Shaykh al-Ṭarīq al-Qādiriyya' in Willis, ed., 1979.
Behrman, Lucy C. *Muslim brotherhoods and politics in Senegal*, Harvard, 1970.
Behrman, Lucy C., see Creevey.
Binger, Louis Gustave, *Le péril de l'Islam*, Paris, 1906.
Bivar, A.D.H. KITĀBĀT, 5. 'In West Africa', *Encyclopaedia of Islam*, new edition.
Boahen, A.Adu, *Britain, the Sahara, and the western Sudan 1788–1861*, Oxford, 1964.
Bosworth Smith, R. *Mohammed and Mohammedanism*, London, 1874.
Braimah, J.A. and J.R. Goody, *Salaga: The struggle for power*, London, 1967.
Braudel, Fernand, *The Mediterranean and the Mediterranean World in the age of Philip II*, vols I and II, English edition, London, 1972.
Brenner, Louis, *The Shehus of Kukawa*, Oxford, 1973.
Brown, Godfrey and Mervyn Hiskett, eds. *Conflict and harmony in education in tropical Africa*, London, 1975.
Brown W.A. 'The caliphate of Hamdullahi *c.* 1818–64: a study in African history and tradition', PhD thesis, Wisconsin, 1969.
Burdon J.A., *Northern Nigeria: Historical notes on certain emirates and tribes*, London, 1909 (reprinted London, 1972)
Burton, Sir Richard Francis, *Abeokuta and the Cameroon Mountain*, vols. I, and II, London, 1863.
Caillié, René, *Travels through central Africa to Timbuktu*, London, 1830.
Carrère, Frédéric and Paul Holle, *De la Senegambia Française*, Paris, 1955.
Cohn, Norman, *The pursuit of the millenium*, London, 1970.
Creevey, Lucy, C., (née Behrman), 'Ahmad Bamba 1850–1927' in Willis, ed. 1979.
Crocker, W.R. *Nigeria: a critique of British colonial administration*, London, 1936.

Crone, G.R. editor and translator, *The voyages of Cadamosto*, The Hakylut Society, 1937.

Crowder, Michael, *West Africa under colonial rule*, London, 1968.

Crowder, Michael, editor, *West African resistance*, London, 1971.

Cuoq, Joseph M. *Les Musulmans en Afrique*, Paris, 1975.

Cuoq, Joseph M, *Recueil des sources arabes concernant l'Afrique occidentale du VIIIe siècle*, Paris, 1975

Duveyrier, Henri, *Les Toureg du Nord*, Paris, 1864.

Épaulard, A., editor and translator *Description de l'Afrique*, Paris, 1956.

Fage, J.D. and Roland Oliver, general editors, *Cambridge history of Africa*, vol. 3, Cambridge, 1977; vol. 5 Cambridge, 1976.

Fisher, H.J., *Ahmadiyya: a study in contemporary Islam on the West African Coast*, Oxford, 1963.

Gbadamosi, T.G.O. *The growth of Islam among the Yoruba 1841–1908*, London, 1978.

Gibb, H.A.R., *Ibn Battuta: Travels in Asia and Africa*, London, 1939 (fifth impression, London, 1963).

Goody, Jack, ed., *Literacy in traditional societies*, Cambridge, 1968.

Goody, J.R., 'Reform, renewal and resistance: a Mahdī in northern Ghana' in *African perspectives*, edited by C.H. Allen and R.W. Johnson, Cambridge, 1970.

Gwarzo, Hassan Ibrahim, 'The life and teachings of al-Maglīlī, with particular reference to the Saharan Jewish Community', PhD thesis, London, 1972.

Hadeja, Mu'azu, *Wak̄okin Mu'azu Hadeja*, Zaria, 1964.

Hargreaves, John D., *Prelude to the partition of West Africa*, London, 1963.

Ḥasan b. Muḥammad, alias Leo Africanus, see Épaulard, A., editor and translator.

Heyworth-Dunne, J., *An introduction to the history of education in modern Egypt*, London, 1939 (reprint, 1968).

Hill, Polly, *Population, prosperity and poverty*, Cambridge, 1977.

Hiskett, M., see Abubakar Tafawa Balewa, Alhaji Sir.

Hiskett, M., editor and translator, *Tazyīn al-waraqāt of ᶜAbdullāh ibn Muḥammad*, Ibadan, 1963.

Hiskett, M., 'Hausa Islamic verse: its sources and development prior to 1920', vols 1, 2 and 3, PhD thesis, London, 1969.

Hiskett, M., *The sword of truth: the life and times of the Shehu Usuman Dan Fodio*, New York, 1973.

Hiskett, M., *A history of Hausa Islamic verse*, London, 1975.

Hodgkin, Thomas, *Nigerian perspectives*, second edition, Oxford, 1975.

Hogben, S.J. and A.H.M. Kirk-Greene, *The emirates of northern Nigeria*, London, 1966.

Holt, P.M., Ann K.S. Lambton and Bernard Lewis, eds. *The Cambridge history of Islam*, Cambridge, 1970, vol. 2A, Part VII.

Houdas, O. and E. Benoist, *Tadzkiret-en-Nisian*, Paris, 1966.

Hunter, W.W., *Our Indian Mussulmans*, London, 1871.

Hunwick, John, 'Notes on a late fifteenth-century document concerning 'al-Takrūr'' in *African perspectives*, editors C.H. Allen and R.W. Johnson, Cambridge, 1970.

Hunwick, John, 'Songhay, Borno and Hausaland in the sixteenth century', in Ajayi and Crowder, eds. vol. I, 1976.

Innes, Gordon, *Sunjata: Three Mandinka versions*, London, 1974.

Johnston, H.A.S., *The Fulani of Sokoto*, London, 1967.

Jungraithmayr, Herrmann, and Wilfried Günther, translators and editors, *Sultan Sa'idu ɓi Hayatu tells the story of his and his father's life*, Abhandlungen der Marburger Gelehrten Gesellschaft, Jahrgang, 1977, Nr. 2.

Kaba, Lansiné, *The Wahhabiyya: Islamic reform and politics in French West Africa*, Evanston, Illinois, 1974.

Kanya-Forstner, A.S., 'Mali-Tukolor' in Crowder, ed., London, 1971.
Klein, Martin, *Islam and imperialism in Senegal*, Edinburgh, 1968.
Last, Murrey, *The Sokoto caliphate*, London, 1967.
Leo Africanus, see Épaulard, A., ed. and translator.
Levtzion, Nehemia, *Muslims and chiefs in West Africa*, Oxford, 1968.
Lewicki, Tadeusz, *Arabic external sources for the history of Africa to the south of the Sahara*, Polska Akademia, Warsaw, 1969.
Low, Victor N., *Three Nigerian Emirates*, Evanston, Illinois, 1972.
Lugard, Lady (née Flora Shaw), *A tropical dependency*, London, 1906 (reprint London, 1964).
Lugard, Lord, *The dual mandate in British tropical Africa*, London, 1922 (fifth edition, London, 1965).
Martin, B.G., 'A short history of the Khalwati order of Dervishes' in *Scholars, saints and Sufis*, ed. Nikki R. Keddie, California, 1972.
Martin, B.G., *Muslim brotherhoods in 19th-century Africa*, Cambridge, 1976.
Masri, El, F.H. editor and translator, *Bayān wujūb al-hijra* ᶜ*ala 'l-*ᶜ*ibad, of* ᶜ*Uthmān b. Fūdī*, Khartoum, 1978.
McGarry, Georgia, *Reaction and protest in the West African press*, Leiden and Cambridge, 1978.
Miller, W.R.S., *Reflections of a pioneer*, London, 1936.
Mollien, Gaspard Théodore, *L'Afrique occidentale en 1818*, Paris, 1967.
Muffett, D.J.M., *Concerning brave captains*, London, 1964.
Muffett, D.J.M., ed. *The Dukkawa of north-western Nigeria*, see Ceslaus Prazan.
Nachtigal, Gustav, *Sahara and Sudan*, Vols 1–3, Berlin/Leipzig, 1879. English edition, London, 1971.
Neill, Stephen, *A history of Christian missions*, 1964 (Penguin reprint, 1977).
Norris, H.T., *Shinqīṭī folk literature and song*, Oxford, 1968.
Norris, H.T., *Saharan myth and saga*, Oxford, 1972.
Norris, H.T., *The Tuaregs: Their Islamic legacy and its diffusion in the Sahel*, Warminster, 1975.
Norris, H.T., 'Muslim Sanhaja scholars of Mauritania' in Willis, 1979.
O'Brien, Donal B. Cruise, *The Mourides of Senegal: the political and economic organisation of an Islamic brotherhood*, Oxford, 1971.
Orr, Sir Charles, *The making of northern Nigeria*, second ed., London, 1965.
Paden, John N., *Religion and Political culture in Kano*, London, 1973.
Palgrave, W.G., *Essays on eastern questions*, London, 1872.
Palmer, H.R., *Sudanese memoirs*, vols I-III, Lagos, 1928 (reprinted London 1967).
Palmer, H.R., *The Bornu, Sahara and Sudan*, London, 1936.
Person, Yves, 'Samori and Islam', in Willis, ed. 1979.
Prazan, Ceslaus, *The Dukkawa of northwestern Nigeria*, edited by D.J.M. Muffett, Pittsburgh, 1977.
Quinn, Charlotte Alison, 'Maba Diakhou and the Gambian *jihād*, 1850–1890', in Willis, ed., 1979.
Robinson, C.H., *Mohammedanism: Has it any future?*, London, 1897.
Robinson, David, *Chiefs and clerics*, London, 1975.
Rohlfs, Gerhardt, *Quer durch Afrika*, vols I and II, Leipzig, 1874.
Rudin, Harry R., *Germans in the Cameroons 1884–1914*, London, 1938.
Ryan, Patrick J., *Imale: Yoruba participation in the Muslim tradition*, Harvard, 1978.
Sanneh, Lamin Ousman, 'The history of the Jakhanke people of Senegambia: a study of the clerical tradition in West African Islam', PhD thesis, London, 1974.
Shaw, Flora, see Lady Lugard.
Stock, Eugene, *History of the Church Missionary Society*, London, 1916.
Sy, Cheikh Tidjane, *La Confrérie Sénégalaise des Mourides*, Paris, Presence Africaine, 1969.

Temple, C.L., *Native races and their rulers*, second edition, London, 1968.
ᶜUmar al-Fūtī, al-Ḥājj, *Rimāḥ ḥizb al-raḥīm*, in margin of ᶜ*Alī* Harāzim, *Jawahir*.
Usumanu ɗan Fodio, see ᶜUthmān b. Fūdī.
ᶜUthmān b. Fūdī, see Masri, El, and also M. Hiskett.
Wilks, Ivor, *The northern factor in Ashanti history*, Lagon, 1961.
Willis, John Ralph, ed., *Studies in West African Islamic history*, vol. 1, 'The cultivators of Islam', London, 1979.
Willis, John Ralph, 'Reflections on the diffusion of Islam in West Africa' in Willis, editor, 1979.
Willis, John Ralph, 'The writings of al-Ḥājj ᶜUmar al-Fūtī and Shaykh Mukhtār b. Wadīᶜ at Allāh: Literary themes, sources and influences', in Willis, ed. 1979.
Works, John A. *Pilgrims in a strange land*, New York, 1976.
Zahradeen, Muhammad Sani, 'ᶜAbd Allāh ibn Fodio's contributions to the Fulani *jihād* in nineteenth-century Hausaland', PhD thesis, McGill University, 1976.
Zwemer, S.M., *Arabia: the cradle of Islam*, New York, 1900.
Zwemer, S.M., editor, *The Mohammedan world of today*, New York, 1906.
Zwemer, S.M., *Mohammed or Christ*, London, 1916.

Articles and seminar papers

Adamu, Mahdi, 'Distribution of trading centres in the central Sudan in the eighteen and nineteenth centuries', paper delivered at the Sokoto Seminar, Sokoto, Nigeria, January 1975.
Adeleye, R.A., 'The dilemma of the Wazir', *JHSN*, IV, 2, 1968.
Batrān, ᶜAbd al-ᶜAzīz ᶜAbd Allāh, 'A contribution to the biography of Shaikh Muḥammad ibn ᶜAbd al-Karīm ibn Muḥammad (ᶜUmar-Aᶜmar) al-Maghīlī', *JAH*, XIV, 3, 1973.
Beckingham, C.F., 'The achievements of Prester John', Inaugural Lecture, 17 May 1966, University of London.
Bivar, A.D.H., and M. Hiskett, 'The Arabic literature of Nigeria to 1804: a provisional account', *BSOAS*, XXV, 1, 1962.
Charles, Eunice A., 'Shaikh Amadu Ba and *jihad* in Jolof', *IJAHS*, VIII, 1975.
Colvin, Lucie Gallistel, 'Islam and the state of Kajoor: a case of successful resistance to *jihād*', *JAH*, XV, 4, 1974.
Curtin, Philip D., '*Jihad* in West Africa: early phases and inter-relations in Mauritania and Senegal', *JAH*, XII, 1, 1971.
Farias, Paulo Fernando de Moraes, 'The Almoravids: some questions concerning the movement during its period of closest contact with the western Sudan', *Bulletin de l'IFAN*, XXIX, 3–4, 1967.
Farias, Paulo Fernando de Moraes, 'Great states revisited', *JAH*, XV, 1974.
Fisher, Allen G.B. and H.J. Fisher, 'Nachtigal's experience in Tibesti, 1869', *Adab*, I, 1972.
Fisher, Allen G.B. and H.J. Fisher, 'A Christian among Muslims: Nachtigal in Muslim black Africa' in 'Gedenkschrift Gustav Nachtigal', *Deutscher Geographische Blatter*, NF, Band I, 1974.
Fisher, H.J., 'The early life and Pilgrimage of al-Ḥājj Muḥammad al-Amīn the Soninke', *JAH*, XI, 1, 1970.
Fisher, H.J., 'Prayer and military activity in the history of Muslim Africa south of the Sahara', JAH, XII, 3, 1971.
Fisher, H.J., 'Conversion reconsidered: some historical aspects of religious conversion in Black Africa', *Africa*, XLIII, 1, 1973.
Fisher, H.J., 'Leo Africanus and the Songhay conquest of Hausaland', *IJAHS*, XI, 1, 1978.
Fọlayan, Kọla, 'Tripoli-Bornu political relations, 1817–1825', *JHSN*, V, 4, 1971.

Fuglestad, Finn, 'A reconsideration of Hausa history before the *jihād*', *JAH*, XIX, 3, 1978.
Goody, J.R. and T.M. Mustapha, 'The caravan trade from Kano to Salaga', *JHSN*, III, 4, 1967.
Goody, J.R., 'The impact of Islamic writing on the oral cultures of West Africa', *Cahiers d'études africaines*, XI, 3e cahier, 1971.
Gray, Richard, 'Christian traces and a Franciscan mission in the Central Sudan, 1700–11,' *JAH* VIII, 3, 1967.
Hajj, Muhammad A. Al-, 'A seventeenth-century chronicle on the origins and missionary activity of the Wangarawa', *Kano Studies*, I, 4, 1968.
Hajj, Muhammad A. Al-, 'The thirteenth century in Muslim eschatology: Mahdist expectations in the Sokoto caliphate', *RBCAD*, 3, 2, 1967.
Hallam, W.K.R., 'The Bayajida legend in Hausa folklore', *JAH*, VII, 1, 1966.
Hill, Polly, 'Comparative West African farm-slavery systems (south of the Sahel) with special reference to Muslim Kano Emirate (N. Nigeria)' unpublished seminar paper, Princeton, 1977.
Hill, Polly, 'From slavery to freedom: The case of farm-slavery in Nigerian Hausaland', *Comparative studies in society and history*, 18, 3, 1976.
Hiskett, M., 'Material relating to the state of learning among the Fulani before their *jihād*,' *BSOAS*, 3, 1967.
Hiskett, M., 'An Islamic tradition of reform in the Western Sudan from the sixteenth to the eighteenth century', *BSOAS*, XIX, 3, 1962.
Hiskett, M., 'The historical background to the naturalisation of Arabic loan-words in Hausa', *ALS*, VI, 1965.
Hiskett, M., 'The "Song of the Shaihu's miracles": a Hausa hagiography from Sokoto', *ALS*, XII, 1971.
Hiskett, M., 'The development of Sa'adu Zungur's political thought. . .' *ALS*, XVI, 1975.
Hiskett, M., 'Commissioner of Police v. Musa Kommanda and aspects of the working of the Gold Coast Marriage of Mohammedans Ordinance', *JAL*, 20, 2, 1976.
Hunwick, J.O. 'Ahmad Baba and the Moroccan invasion of the Sudan', *JHSN*, II, 3, 1962.
Johnson, Marion, 'The economic foundations of an Islamic theocracy – the case of Masina', *JAH* XVII, 4, 1976.
Johnson, Marion, 'The cowrie currencies of West Africa,' *JAH*, XI, 3, 1970, Part II.
Klein, Martin A., 'Social and economic factors in the Muslim revolution in Senegambia,' *JAH*, XIII, 3, 1972.
Lange, Dierk and Silvio Berthoud, 'L'interieur de l'Afrique occidentale d'après Giovanni Lorenzo Anania (XVIe siècle)', *Cahiers d'histoire mondiale*, 14, (2), 1972.
Lange, Dierk, 'Progrès de l'Islam et changement politique au Kānem du XIe au XIIIe siècle: un essai d'interprétation', *JAH*, XIX, 4, 1978.
Last, D.H. and M.A. al-Hajj, 'Attempts at defining a Muslim. . .', *JHSN* III, 2, 1965.
Last, Murray, 'Aspects of the Caliph Bello's social policy', *Kano Studies*, 2, 1966.
Lavers, J.E., 'Jibril Gaini: a preliminary account of the career of a Mahdist leader in north-eastern Nigeria', *RBCAD*, III, 1, 1967.
Lavers, J.E., 'Islam in the Bornu Caliphate: A survey', *Odu*, 1971.
Lavers, J.E., 'Diversions on a journey or the travels of Shaykh Ahmad al-Yamani (1630–1702) from Arbaji to Fez', unpublished seminar paper delivered at Bayero University, Kano, 29 November, 1977.
Lovejoy, Paul E., 'The role of the Wangarawa in the economic transformation of the central Sudan in the fifteenth and sixteenth centuries', *JAH*, XIX, 2, 1978.

Martin, B.G., 'Five letters from the Tripoli archives', *JHSN*, II, 3, 1962.
Martin, B.G., 'A Mahdist document from Futa Jallon', *Bulletin de l'IFAN*, XXV, 1–2, 1963.
Martin, B.G., 'Material for the understanding of Islam in German East Africa', *Tanzania Notes and Records*, No. 68, 1968.
Martin, B.G., 'Kanem, Bornu and the Fezzān; Notes on the political history of a trade route', *JAH*, X, 1, 1969.
Martin, B.G., 'Mai Idrīs of Bornu and the Ottoman Turks 1576–8', *MES*, 3, 1972.
Mason, Michael, 'The *jihād* in the south: an outline of the nineteenth-century Nupe hegemony in north-eastern Yorubaland and Afenmai', *JHSN*, V, 2, 1970.
Masri, El-, F.H. and others, 'Sifofin Shehu', *RBCAD*, 2, 1, 1966.
Norris, H.T., 'Sanhaja scholars of Timbuktou,' *BSOAS*, XXX, 3, 1967.
O'Brien, Donal Cruise, 'Towards an "Islamic policy" in French West Africa,' *JAH*, VIII, 2, 1967.
Pilaszewiez, Stanislaw, 'The arrival of the Christians': a Hausa poem on the colonial conquest of West Africa by al-Ḥājj ᶜUmar', *Africana Bulletin*, No. 22, Warsaw, 1975.
Porter, Andrew, 'The Hausa Association: Sir George Goldie, the Bishop of Dover, and the Niger in the 1880s', *JICH*, VII, 2, 1979.
Robinson, David, 'The Islamic revolution of Futa Toro', *IJAHS*, VIII, 2, 1975.
Rodney, W., '*Jihad* and social revolution in Futa Djalon in the eighteenth century', *JHSN*, IV, 2, 1968.
Sanneh, Lamin Ousman, 'The origins of clericalism in West Africa', *JAH*, XVII, 1, 1976.
Skinner, David E., 'Mande settlement and the development of Islamic institutions in Sierra Leone' (*IJAHS*, XI, I, 1978).
Skinner, Neil and Philip Curtin, with the assistance of Hammady Amadu Sy, 'The story of Malik Sy', *Cahiers d'Études Africaines*, XI, 3, 1971.
Smith, Abdullahil, 'Some considerations relating to the formation of states in Hausaland', *JHSN*, V, 3, 1970.
Stewart, C.C., 'Southern Saharan scholarship and the *Bilad al-sudan*', *JAH*, XVII, 1, 1976.
Stewart, C.C., 'Frontier disputes and problems of legitimation: Sokoto-Masina relations 1817–1837,' *JAH*, XVII, 4, 1976.
Sutton, J.E.G., 'Towards a less orthodox history of Hausaland, *JAH*, XX, 1979.
Webster, J.B., 'The Bible and the plough', *JHSN*, II, 4, 1963.
Wilks, Ivor, 'The growth of Islamic learning in Ghana', *JHSN*, II, 4, 1963.
Wilks, Ivor, 'The Saghanughu and the spread of Mālikī law', *RBCAD*, II, 2, 1966.
Willis, J.R., '*Jihād* Fī Sabīl Allāh . . .', *JAH*, VIII, 3, 1967.
Willis, J.R., 'The Torodbe clerisy: a social view', *JAH*, XIX, 2, 1978.

Index